Study Guide

Psychology
A Journey

FOURTH EDITION

Dennis Coon

John O. Mitterer
Brock University

Prepared by

Danielle Gagne
Alfred University

WADSWORTH
CENGAGE Learning™

Australia • Brazil • Japan • Korea • Mexico • Singapore • Spain • United Kingdom • United States

ISBN-13: 978-0-8400-3222-5
ISBN-10: 0-8400-3222-6

Wadsworth
20 Davis Drive
Belmont, CA 94002-3098
USA

Cengage Learning is a leading provider of customized learning solutions with office locations around the globe, including Singapore, the United Kingdom, Australia, Mexico, Brazil, and Japan. Locate your local office at: **www.cengage.com/global**

Cengage Learning products are represented in Canada by Nelson Education, Ltd.

To learn more about Wadsworth, visit
www.cengage.com/wadsworth

Purchase any of our products at your local college store or at our preferred online store
www.ichapters.com

Printed in the United States of America
2 3 4 5 6 7   13 12 11

Contents

PREFACE

HOW TO USE THIS STUDY GUIDE

This *Study Guide* has been developed to help you master the material in your textbook, *Psychology: A Journey, 4th edition* by Dennis Coon and John Mitterrer. It is designed to help you learn more, study efficiently, and get better grades. The chapters of the *Study Guide* are closely coordinated with the chapters of the text so that you can easily move from one to the other, as necessary.

THE BASIC STRUCTURE OF THE GUIDE

STUDY ASSISTANCE

In particular, the Study Guide has been designed with the **SQ4R** method described in the Introduction of the text. This acronym stands for **s**urvey, **q**uestion, **r**ead, **r**ecite, **r**eflect, and **r**eview. To assist with your use of this method, the first section of each of the Guide's chapters includes the following: a chapter overview, a set of learning objectives, recite-and-review questions, connections problems, check-your-memory questions, final survey-and-review questions, a mastery test, and answers for all of these. Each of these is described in detail in the following Student Integrator section. However, before you read that section, you should read about the SQ4R method in the text to make sure you fully understand it.

LANGUAGE DEVELOPMENT

The second section of each chapter contains a language development guide that focus on many idioms, phrases, proverbs, historical and cultural allusions, and challenging vocabulary that might be unfamiliar to you. Many students, especially those entering college for the first time, find the level of reading required to comprehend Introductory Psychology texts somewhat intimidating. To assist with this adjustment, this guide offers you simple definitions for many words and phrases as they are applied in the text. An index of terms and phrases has been alphabetized for quick and easy access at the end of this book. Next to the terms are page numbers where the terms can be found in the textbook.

USING THE GUIDE

The following study resources can be used in a variety of different ways. Therefore, although effort is made to connect the resources to the SQ4R method and research in learning and cognitive psychology, the following is not a guaranteed recipe for success. Students come in many varieties and what works for you is likely not to work for someone else. So, try out the following suggested uses for the study resources and modify where necessary.

CHAPTER OVERVIEW

The Chapter Overview is a highly focused summary of major ideas in the text. By boiling the text chapters down to their essence, the Chapter Overview will give you a framework to build on as you learn additional ideas, concepts, and facts. In fact, research suggests that starting with such a framework facilitates learning new material. (See Chapter 7 of the text for coverage of the importance of organization and memory.)

Also, the Overview is a very useful tool for the first step in the SQ4R method: Survey. Specifically, it offers the major points provided by the text, assisting you in your survey of the chapter. (It should not be used as a substitute for surveying the chapter; the Guide is not meant to replace your use of the SQ4R method with the text, but serve as an aide to this process.)

Before you work on any other sections of this guide, read the Chapter Overview. In fact, it would be a good idea to re-read the Chapter Overview each time you use the *Study Guide*.

LEARNING OBJECTIVES

The Learning Objectives will show you, in detail, if you have mastered a reading assignment. To use them, you might want to write brief responses for each objective after you finish reading a chapter of the text. As an alternative, you may want to just read the Learning Objectives, pausing after each to see if you can respond in your own words. Then, after you have completed all of the other exercises in the *Study Guide* you can return to the Learning Objectives. At that time, you can either respond verbally or in writing. In either case, give special attention to any objectives you can't complete.

Notice that this process is tied to the question portion of the SQ4R method. The authors of the text suggest that you turn each section heading of the text into a question to help you "read with a purpose." The learning objectives can aid in this process. (Gathering *feedback* about what Objectives you can and cannot complete is important for learning—see Chapter 6.)

It must also be noted that this study guide and the text have the same Survey Questions before major sections of material. These too will help you with purposeful, structured reading.

RECITE AND REVIEW

This section will give you a chance to review major terms and concepts. Recite and Review is organized with the same Survey Questions found in the textbook chapters. This exercise will help you actively process information, so that it becomes more meaningful. Recite and Review also gives you a chance to practice recalling ideas from your reading, after you've closed the book.

As you work through Recite and Review, don't worry if you can't fill in all of the blanks. All of the answers are listed at the end of each *Study Guide* chapter. Filling in missing terms with the help of the answer key will focus your attention on gaps in your knowledge. That way, you can add new information to what you *were* able to remember. Page numbers are provided for each section of Recite and Review so you can return to the text to clarify any points that you missed.

Again, note the connection between this section and the SQ4R method. In particular, this section will help you with the first two Rs of this process, reading and reciting. As the authors suggest, you should divide up the material as much as necessary to keep the material manageable. (According to Chapter 7, we can hold only so much information in our short-term memory at one time. Dividing the material into small, meaningful pieces prevents you from losing information.)

CONNECTIONS

This section contains matching-type items. It will help you build associations between related terms, facts, concepts, and ideas. Where appropriate, art is reproduced from the text so that you can match to images, rather than words. This is a good way to add links to your memory networks. (See Chapter 7 for a discussion about memory networks.) Again, answers are listed at the end of the chapter.

The point of these is to see if you can understand the pieces of material as they relate to one another. For example, if you see a type of depth perception cue, you should be able to classify it as either a monocular or binocular cue. (See Chapter 4 for information about depth perception.)

CHECK YOUR MEMORY

The true-false statements in Check Your Memory highlight facts and details that you may have overlooked when you read the text. It's easy to fool yourself about how much you are remembering as you read. If you answered wrong for any of the items in Check Your Memory, you should return to the textbook to find out why. Page numbers listed for each group of items will make it easy for you to locate the relevant information in the textbook.

In short, one way to think about these is as back-up checks of your reading and recitation of material. That is, they are a useful check on the progress you have made so far.

FINAL SURVEY AND REVIEW

This exercise might seem like a repeat of the Recite and Review section, but it's not. Although some of the items are identical to ones you have seen before, you must often supply a different set of more difficult terms and concepts to complete the review. The Final Survey and Review challenges you to consolidate your earlier learning and to master key concepts from the text. The Final Survey and Review is not a test. Don't be upset if you can't fill in some of the blanks. But do give missing ideas extra practice when you check your answers. Indeed, try to learn more each time you complete a *Study Guide* exercise, check your answers, or return to the text for review and clarification.

These problems encourage the use of the 4th R in the SQ4R method, review. Go over these items more than once to be sure you have a full understanding of the chapter. (Of course, you can use any portion of the *Study Guide* to help you with the review process. But, this section lends itself most readily to this process.)

MASTERY TEST

The multiple-choice items of the Mastery Test are designed to assess the degree to which you understand the material presented in the chapter. In some cases, the questions cover information that was not reviewed in any of the preceding *Study Guide* sections. The Mastery Tests are designed to continue the learning process, as well as to give you feedback about your progress.

Whenever possible, you should apply the third R in the SQ4R method to your studies, reflect. As describe in the text, this involves thinking about the material is a more meaningful way as opposed to simple memorization. In particular, think about how the material applies to your everyday life. As indicated in Chapter 7, linking new information with information already consolidated in long-term memory helps you to retain the new information. This is a form of *elaborative rehearsal*.

(The mastery test should be considered an estimate of how much you know and not a guarantee of how well you will do on a class test. Testing styles vary a great deal from instructor to instructor. Although the mastery test offers a variety of different questions, your instructor may give more weight to some types than others.)

ANSWERS

Answers for all of the preceding exercises are listed at the end of each *Study Guide* chapter. Answers for the Mastery Test include page numbers so you can locate the source of the question in the textbook.

LANGUAGE DEVELOPMENT

It's a good idea to read with a dictionary close at hand. Looking up words you don't know will add to your general vocabulary, as well as your understanding of the textbook. However, it can be difficult to find the meaning of idioms, slang, and references to history, literature, and popular culture. If you come across an unfamiliar word or phrase in the text, you may look for the definition in this language development section of the *Study Guide* chapter. To make it easy to use, this section has been divided into manageable topics as they correspond with the text. In addition, each defined word or phrase is preceded by the page number on which it appears.

The Language Development Guide has three major parts:

- The Word Roots section will provide information about the origin of important words found in the text. You should start with the Word Roots section when you begin a new chapter.
- A list of idioms, words, phrases, or names with further explanations to help you better understand their use in the text. The terms are shown in italics and their meanings follow the colon.
- Next to each idiom, word, phrase, or name, a page number is given to indicating where the idiom, word, phrase, or name can be found in the text.

LANGUAGE DEVELOPMENT INDEX

Since some of the terms and phrases are repeated in later chapters of the text, the terms and phrases of all 14 chapters (and the appendix) have been alphabetized for quick and easy access at the end of the *Study Guide*. Next to the terms and phrases are page numbers where the terms and phrases can be found in the textbook.

A FIVE-DAY STUDY PLAN

As indicated earlier, there is no single "best" way to use this guide. Getting the most out of the *Study Guide* depends greatly on your personal learning style and study habits. Nevertheless, as a starting point, you might want to give the following plan a try.

Days 1 and 2: Read the assigned chapter in the textbook. As you do, be sure to make use of the Learning Checks and all the steps of the SQ4R method described in the textbook.

Day 3: Review the textbook chapter and any notes you made as you read it. Read the Chapter Overview in the *Study Guide* and read the Learning Objectives. Now do the Recite and Review section.

Day 4: Read the margin definitions in the textbook and the Chapter Overview in the *Study Guide*. Do the Connections and Check Your Memory sections of the *Study Guide*. Return to the textbook and make sure you understand why any items you missed were wrong.

Day 5: Review the textbook chapter and any notes you made as you read it. Read the Chapter Overview in the *Study Guide*. Then do the Final Survey and Review section, and check your answers. Return to the textbook and clarify any items you missed. Now take the Mastery Test. If you miss any questions, review appropriate sections of the textbook again. To really consolidate your learning, say or write responses to all of the Learning Objectives.

SUMMARY

The close ties between *Introduction to Psychology* and the *Study Guide* make it possible for the *Study Guide* to be used in a variety of ways. You may prefer to turn to the *Study Guide* for practice and review after you have completed a reading assignment, as suggested in the Five-Day Plan. Or, you might find it more helpful to treat the *Study Guide* as a reading companion. In that case, you would complete appropriate *Study Guide* sections from each type of exercise as you progress through the text. In any event, it is nearly certain that if you use the *Study Guide* conscientiously, you will retain more, learn more efficiently, and perform better on tests. Good luck.

CHAPTER 1

Discovering Psychology and Research Methods

Chapter Overview

Psychology is the scientific study of behavior and mental processes. Psychology's goals are to describe, understand, predict, and control behavior. Psychologists from different research specialties answer questions about behavior by applying the scientific method, gathering empirical evidence, and using critical thinking strategies

A key element of critical thinking is an ability to weigh the evidence bearing on a claim and to evaluate the quality of that evidence through careful comparisons, analyses, critiques, and syntheses. Belief in various pseudopsychologies is based in part on uncritical acceptance, the fallacy of positive instances, and the Barnum effect.

Scientific investigation involves observing behavior, defining a problem, proposing a hypothesis, gathering evidence/testing the hypothesis, publishing results, and forming a theory.

Psychology is a relatively young science. The first psychological laboratory was established by Wilhelm Wundt, who studied conscious experience. The first school of thought in psychology was structuralism, a kind of "mental chemistry" that relied on introspection. Structuralism fell out of favor but was followed by the rise of functionalism, behaviorism, Gestalt psychology, psychoanalytic psychology, and humanistic psychology. Broad views in modern psychology are the biological, psychological, and sociocultural perspectives.

Individuals may pursue training to specialize as psychologists, psychiatrists, psychoanalysts, counselors, and social workers. Not all psychologists offer "therapy" — psychologists also teach, conduct basic and applied research, and act as consultants. Other specialties include industrial-organizational, educational, consumer, school, developmental, engineering, medical, environmental, forensic, and health psychology.

Psychologists use experiments to discover cause-and-effect connections. An experiment shows whether an independent variable has an effect on a dependent variable. Single-blind and double-blind designs, control groups, and random selection allow psychologists to consider researcher and participant bias, as well as placebo effects.

Non-experimental research investigations begin with naturalistic observation, which is informative despite its limitations. In the correlational method, the strength of the relationship between two or more variables is investigated. Correlations allow predictions and a wider range of topics of investigation than experiments, but they do not demonstrate cause-and-effect connections. The clinical method employs detailed case studies of single individuals. In the survey method, people in a representative sample are asked a series of questions. This provides information on the behavior of large groups of people.

Information in the popular media varies greatly in quality and accuracy. It is wise to approach such information with skepticism regarding the source of information, over-simplification, single examples, uncontrolled observation, correlation and causation, inferences, and unrepeatable results.

Learning Objectives

1. Define psychology, list reasons for studying psychology, and explain how psychology can be both a science and a profession.

2. Define the term *behavior* and differentiate overt from covert behavior.

3. Describe what is meant by "empirical evidence" and identify examples of empirical evidence; define the terms *data*, *scientific observation*, and *research method*; explain why the study of some topics in psychology is difficult.

4. Write a brief summary of each of the following areas of specialization in psychology:
    a. personality
    b. developmental
    c. learning
    d. sensation and perception
    e. comparative
    f. cognitive
    g. biopsychology
    h. gender
    i. social
    j. evolutionary
    k. cultural
    l. forensic

5. Explain why animals are used in research and define the term *animal model* in your discussion.

6. Explain the four goals of psychology.

7. For each of these schools of psychology—structuralism, functionalism, behaviorism, Gestalt psychology, psychoanalytic, and humanism—answer each of the following questions:
    a. its founder
    b. reasons it was founded
    c. its goal or main focus
    d. its impact on modern psychology and/or possible use in psychotherapy

8. Define the term *critical thinking* and describe each of the four principles that form the foundation of critical thinking.

9. Briefly describe each of the following pseudopsychologies—palmistry, phrenology, graphology, and astrology—and explain why they continue to thrive even though they have no scientific basis.

10. List and define the six steps of the scientific method; define the terms *hypothesis*, *operational definition*, and *theory* (building).

11. Explain the importance of publishing, and list and describe the parts of a research report.

12. Identify notable events within the history of psychology

13. Describe the contribution of women and minorities to the early history of psychology and their representation in the field then and now.

14. Explain what is meant by the eclectic approach that is used by most psychologists today.

15. Describe the various views within the biological, psychological, and sociocultural perspectives that are used in understanding behavior. Include a brief discussion of positive psychology, cultural relativity, and social norms.

16. Describe the media's portrayal of mental health professionals; characterize the differences in training, emphasis, expertise, and sources of employment among psychologists, psychiatrists, psychoanalysts, counselors, and psychiatric social workers.

17. Identify the types of research conducted by different psychological specialties.

18. Describe the advantages and disadvantages to using an experiment; list and describe the three essential variables of the experimental method; explain the nature and purpose of the control group and the experimental group in an experiment, as well as the purpose of randomly assigning subjects to these two groups.

19. Describe the single-blind and double-blind experimental approaches and how they control for the placebo effect and the experimenter effects, respectively. Include a discussion of what a placebo is and how it works, and the concept of the self-fulfilling prophecy.

20. Describe the technique of naturalistic observation and its advantages and limitations; include the concepts of *observer effect*, *observer bias*, and *anthropomorphic error* in your discussion; define the term *observation record*.

21. Describe a correlational study and identify its advantages and limitations. Explain how a correlation coefficient is expressed and what it means; describe the difference between a positive correlation and a negative correlation; indicate why correlation does NOT demonstrate causation.

22. Briefly describe the clinical method, or case study method, including when it is used and its advantages and limitations.

23. Briefly describe the use of the survey method, including its advantages and limitations and the new use of internet surveys, and define the terms *population*, *representative sample*, *random selection*, *biased sample*, and *courtesy bias*.

24. List suggestions that your author gives to help you become a more critical reader of psychological information in the popular press.

RECITE AND REVIEW

Psychology—Spotlight on Behavior

Survey Questions: What is psychology and what are its goals? Pages 15-18

1. Psychology is both a science and a _____.

2. Psychology is defined as the scientific study of behavior and _____ processes.

3. Psychologists study overt and covert _____.

4. Psychologists seek empirical _____ based on scientific observation.

5. Scientific observation is _____ so that it answers questions about the world.

6. Scientific observations are _____, which means they can be confirmed by more than one observer.

7. Answering psychological questions requires a valid research _____.

8. Developmental psychologists study the course of _____.

9. Learning theorists study how and why _____ occurs.

10. _____ theorists study personality traits and dynamics.

11. Sensation and perception psychologists study the _____ organs and perception.

12. Comparative psychologists study different species, especially _____.

13. Biopsychologists study the connection between _____ and _____.

14. Social psychologists study _____ behavior.

15. Cultural psychologists study the ways that _____ affects _____.

16. Evolutionary psychologists are interested in patterns of behavior that were shaped by _____.

17. _____ psychologists apply psychological principles to legal issues

18. Other species are used as _____ models in psychological research to discover principles that apply to human behavior.

19. Psychology's goals are to describe, _____, predict, and control behavior.

Science and Critical Thinking—Healthy Skepticism

Survey Question: What is critical thinking? Pages 19-20

1. Critical thinking is the ability to reflect on, _____, compare, analyze, critique, and synthesize information.

2. Critical thinking involves a willingness to question _____ and look for alternate conclusions.

3. _____ or _____ does not automatically make an idea true.

4. Being able to judge the _____ of evidence is crucial to critical thinking.

Pseudopsychologies—Palms, Planets, and Personality

Survey Question: How does psychology differ from false explanations of behavior? Pages 20-22

1. Palmistry, phrenology, graphology, and astrology are _____ systems, or pseudopsychologies.

2. Followers of pseudopsychologies seek evidence that _____ their beliefs and _____ contradictory evidence.

3. _____ is a pseudopsychology that claims lines on the hand reveal personality traits and predict the future.

4. Graphologists falsely believe that personality traits can be revealed in an individual's _____.

5. Belief in pseudopsychologies is encouraged by uncritical acceptance, the fallacy of positive instances, and the _____ effect, named after a famous showman who had "something for everyone."

Scientific Research—How to Think Like a Psychologist

Survey Questions: How is the scientific method applied in psychological research? Pages 23-25

1. Scientific investigation in psychology is based on reliable evidence, accurate description and _____, precise definition, controlled observation, and repeatable results.

2. Six elements of a scientific method involve making observations, defining a _____, proposing a hypothesis, gathering evidence/testing the hypothesis, publishing _____, and forming a theory.

3. To be scientifically _____, a hypothesis must be testable.

4. Psychological concepts are given operational _____ so that they can be observed and tested.

5. Covert _____ are operationally defined in terms of overt behavior for the purposes of scientific study.

6. A _____ is a system of ideas that interrelates facts and concepts.

7. Scientific information must be _____ so that other researchers can read about the results.

8. Published research reports usually include the following sections: an _____, an introduction, a methods section, a _____ section, and a final discussion.

A Brief History of Psychology—Psychology's Family Album

Survey Question: How did the field of psychology emerge? Pages 26-29

1. People have been interested in observing and understanding human behavior for thousands of years, long before psychology was a _____.

2. The first psychological laboratory was established in _____ by Wilhelm Wundt.

3. Wundt tried to apply scientific methods to the study of _____ experience by using introspection or "looking inward."

4. The ideas of structuralism were brought to the United States by _____.

5. Structuralism fell out of favor because the structuralists _____ over the results.

6. Functionalism was concerned with how the mind helps us _____ to our environments.

7. Behaviorism was launched by John B. _____.

8. Behaviorists objectively study the relationship between stimuli and _____.

9. The modern behaviorist B. F. Skinner believed that most behavior is controlled by _____ reinforcers.

10. Gestalt psychology emphasizes the study of _____ units, not pieces.

11. According to the Gestalt view, in psychology the whole is often _____ than the sum of its parts.

12. The psychoanalytic approach emphasized the _____ origins of behavior.

13. Psychoanalytic psychology, developed by Austrian physician Sigmund _____, is an early psychodynamic approach.

14. Freud theorized that many unconscious thoughts are held out of awareness, or _____.

15. Humanistic psychology emphasizes free will, subjective experience, human potentials, and personal _____.

16. Psychologically, humanists believe that self-_____ and self-evaluation are important elements of personal adjustment.

17. Humanists also emphasize a capacity for self-actualization—the full development of personal _____.

18. The first woman to be awarded a Ph.D. in psychology was _____.

19. _____ became the first African-American to earn a doctoral degree in psychology.

Psychology Today—Three Complementary Perspectives on Behavior

Survey Question: What are the current perspectives in psychology? Pages 30-33

1. Three views in modern psychology are the sociocultural, the _____, and the psychological perspectives.

2. Much of contemporary psychology is an _____ of the best features of various viewpoints.

3. The _____ perspective seeks to explain all behavior in terms of physical mechanisms.

4. The field of neuroscience includes biopsychologists who study the brain and _____.

5. The _____ psychologists assume that human and animal behavior is the result of evolutionary processes.

6. _____ psychologists study covert mental behaviors, such as memory, language, and problem solving.

7. The study of topics such as love and happiness make up _____ psychology.

8. To fully understand behavior, psychologists must be aware of human _____ as well as human universals.

9. Our behavior is greatly affected by cultural _____ and by _____ (rules that define acceptable behavior).

10. Cultural _____ suggests that behavior should be judged by the values of the culture in which it occurs.

Psychologists—Guaranteed Not to Shrink

Survey Question: What are the major specialties in psychology? Pages 33-35

1. Real psychologists follow an ethical code that stresses respect for people's privacy, dignity, confidentiality, and _____.

2. _____ psychologists tend to treat individuals with "mild" problems, such as troubles at work or school.

3. Psychiatrists typically use both _____ and psychotherapy to treat emotional problems.

4. Both counselors and psychiatric social workers have _____ degrees.

5. Some major _____ in psychology are clinical, counseling, industrial-organizational, educational, consumer, school, developmental, engineering, medical, environmental, forensic, psychometric, and experimental psychology.

6. Scientific research in psychology may be either _____ or applied.

The Psychology Experiment—Where Cause Meets Effect

Survey Question: How is an experiment performed? Pages 36-38

1. In an experiment, conditions that might affect behavior are intentionally _____. Then, changes in behavior are observed and recorded.

2. In an experiment, a variable is any condition that can _____ and that might affect the outcome of the experiment (i.e., the behavior of subjects).

3. Experimental conditions that are intentionally varied are called _____ variables.

4. _____ variables measure the results of the experiment.

5. _____ variables are conditions that a researcher wishes to prevent from affecting the outcome of the experiment.

6. Extraneous variables are controlled by making sure that they are the same for all _____ in an experiment.

7. Subjects exposed to the independent variable are in the _____ group. Those not exposed to the independent variable form the _____ group.

8. Extraneous variables that involve personal characteristics, such as age or intelligence, can be controlled by _____ subjects to the experimental and control groups.

9. If all extraneous variables are _____ for the experimental group and the control group, any differences in behavior must be caused by differences in the independent variable.

10. A control group provides a _____ for comparison of scores.

Double Blind—On Placebos and Self-Fulfilling Prophecies

Survey Question: What is a double blind experiment? Pages 38-40

1. Researchers must minimize research participant bias (the tendency for people to do what is _____ of them).

2. Experiments involving drugs must control for the _____, which is always present when drugs are involved in a study.

3. In many situations, researcher bias leads to self-fulfilling _____.

4. In a _____ study, subjects don't know if they are getting a drug or a placebo. In a _____ study, neither experimenters nor subjects know who is receiving a real drug.

Nonexperimental Research Methods—Different Strokes

Survey Question: What nonexperimental research methods do psychologists use? Pages 41-46

1. Naturalistic observation refers to actively observing behavior in _____ settings.

2. Naturalistic observation only provides _____ of behavior, not explanations of observations.

3. Two problems with naturalistic studies are the effects of the observer on the observed (the observer _____) and _____ bias.

4. The anthropomorphic fallacy is the error of attributing _____ qualities to _____.

5. Problems with naturalistic studies can be minimized by keeping careful observational _____.

6. In the correlational method, the _____ between two traits, responses, or events is measured.

7. Correlation coefficients range from _____ to _____.

8. A correlation of _____ indicates that there is no relationship between two measures.

9. Correlations of +1.00 and −1.00 reveal that _____ relationships exist between two measures.

10. The closer a correlation coefficient is to plus or _____ 1, the stronger the measured relationship is.

11. A positive correlation shows that _____ in one measure correspond to increases in a second measure.

12. In a negative correlation, _____ in one measure correspond to decreases in a second measure.

13. Correlations allow us to make _____, but correlation does not demonstrate causation.

14. _____-and-effect relationships in psychology are best identified by doing a controlled experiment.

15. Clinical psychologists frequently gain information from _____ studies.

16. Case studies may be thought of as _____ clinical tests.

17. In the survey method, information about large populations is gained by asking people in a _____ a series of carefully worded questions.

18. _____ in research can occur when the race, ethnicity, age, sexual orientation, and gender of researchers and participants are not representative.

19. The value of surveys is lowered when the sample is biased and when replies to questions are _____ because of _____ a tendency to give socially desirable answers).

Psychology in Action: Psychology in the Media—Separating Fact from Fiction

Survey Question: How good is psychological information found in the popular media? Pages 46-49

1. _____ and critical thinking are called for when evaluating claims in the popular media.

2. You should be on guard for _____ or biased sources of information in the media.

3. Many claims in the media are based on unscientific observations that lack _____ groups.

4. In the popular media, a failure to distinguish between correlation and _____ is common.

5. Inferences and opinions may be reported as if they were _____ observations.

6. Single cases, unusual _____, and testimonials are frequently reported as if they were valid generalizations.

CONNECTIONS

Psychology—Spotlight on Behavior

Survey Questions: What is psychology and what are its goals? Pages 15-18

1. _____ biopsychology

2. _____ psychology

3. _____ personality theorist

4. _____ covert behavior

5. _____ commonsense beliefs

6. _____ scientific observation

7. _____ understanding

8. _____ EEG

9. _____ empirical evidence

10. _____ comparative psychology

11. _____ description

12. _____ control

A. hidden from view

B. brain waves

C. systematic observation

D. animal behavior and models

E. detailed record

F. human and animal behavior

G. "why" questions

H. brain and behavior

I. direct observation

J. traits, dynamics, individual differences

K. frame of reference

L. proof based on everyday experiences

Science and Critical Thinking—Healthy Skepticism, Pseudopsychologies—Palms, Planets, and Personality, and Psychology in the Media—Separating Fact from Fiction

Survey Questions: What is critical thinking? How does psychology differ from false explanations of behavior? How is the scientific method applied in psychological research? Pages 19-25

1. _____ pseudopsychology

2. _____ phrenology

3. _____ critical thinking

4. _____ anecdotal evidence

5. _____ graphology

6. _____ hypothesis

7. _____ scientific method

8. _____ operational definition

9. _____ commonsense

A. evaluating claims and evidence

B. astrology

C. handwriting analysis

D. analysis of the shape of skulls

E. evidence explaining a claim

F. controlled observation

G. tentative explanation

H. Specific procedures

I. unscientific observations

A Brief History of Psychology—Psychology's Family Album

Survey Question: How did the field of psychology emerge? Pages 26-29

1. _____ Wundt

2. _____ Titchener

3. _____ James

4. _____ Darwin

5. _____ Maslow

6. _____ Pavlov

7. _____ Skinner

8. _____ Wertheimer

9. _____ Freud

A. father of psychology

B. natural selection

C. behaviorism

D. functionalism

E. conditioned responses

F. Gestalt

G. introspection

H. psychoanalysis

I. self-actualization

Psychology Today—Three Complementary Perspectives on Behavior and Psychologists—Guaranteed Not to Shrink

Survey Question: What are the current perspectives in psychology? What are the major specialties in psychology? Pages 30-36

1. _____ social psychologist
2. _____ psychodynamic view
3. _____ behavioristic view
4. _____ humanistic view
5. _____ biopsychology
6. _____ cognitive view
7. _____ counseling psychologist
8. _____ social norms
9. _____ psychologist
10. _____ positive psychology
11. _____ psychiatrist

A. self-image
B. information processing
C. Ph.D., Psy.D., Ed.D.
D. M.D.
E. internal forces
F. physiological processes
G. environmental forces
H. investigates attitudes and persuasion
I. marital consultant
J. optimal behavior
K. guides for behavior

The Psychology Experiment—Where Cause Meets Effect and Double Blind—On Placebos and Self-Fulfilling Prophecies

Survey Question: How is an experiment performed? What is a double blind experiment? Pages 36-40

1. _____ single-blind experiment
2. _____ identify causes of behavior
3. _____ participant bias
4. _____ independent variable
5. _____ dependent variable
6. _____ extraneous variables
7. _____ researcher bias
8. _____ control group
9. _____ random assignment to groups
10. _____ placebos

A. effect on behavior
B. experimental method
C. varied by experimenter
D. excluded by experimenter
E. reference for comparison
F. done by using chance
G. sugar pills
H. control placebo effects
I. unintended influence
J. behavioral change due to expectations

Nonexperimental Research Methods—Different Strokes

Survey Questions: What nonexperimental research methods do psychologists use?

Pages 41-46

1. _____ observer effect
2. _____ case study
3. _____ Anthropomorphic error
4. _____ Jane Goodall
5. _____ observational record
6. _____ correlational study
7. _____ correlation of +3.5
8. _____ survey methods
9. _____ lobotomy
10. _____ case studies
11. _____ gender bias
12. _____ valid sample
13. _____ courtesy bias
14. _____ ethical research

A. formal log
B. related traits, behaviors
C. coefficient error
D. naturalistic observation
E. behavioral change due to awareness
F. giving human feelings to animals
G. in-depth focus
H. Phineas Gage
I. participation is voluntary
J. clinical method
K. representative of population
L. inaccurate answers
M. public polling techniques
N. under-representation of women

CHECK YOUR MEMORY

Psychology—Spotlight on Behavior

Survey Questions: What is psychology and what are its goals? Pages 15-18

1. Psychology can best be described as a profession, not a science.

   TRUE or FALSE

2. Psychology is defined as the scientific study of human behavior.

   TRUE or FALSE

3. Although it is a covert activity, dreaming is a behavior.

   TRUE or FALSE

4. Evolutionary psychology attempts to explain human and animal behavior as the result of socialization.

   TRUE or FALSE

5. A gender psychologist studies the difference between males and females
    TRUE or FALSE

6. The term *empirical evidence* refers to the opinion of an acknowledged authority.
    TRUE or FALSE

7. Animal models are used in psychology to discover principles of behavior that apply to humans
    TRUE or FALSE

8. The term *data* refers to a systematic procedure for answering scientific questions.
    TRUE or FALSE

9. Naming and classifying are the heart of psychology's second goal, understanding behavior.
    TRUE or FALSE

Science and Critical Thinking—Healthy Skepticism and Pseudopsychologies—Palms, Planets, and Personality

Survey Questions: What is critical thinking? How does psychology differ from false explanations of behavior? Pages 19-22

1. Critical thinking utilizes commonsense beliefs as the foundation for evaluating and judging the quality of evidence obtained.
    TRUE or FALSE

2. Critical thinking is the ability to make good use of intuition and mental imagery.
    TRUE or FALSE

3. Critical thinkers actively evaluate claims, ideas, and propositions.
    TRUE or FALSE

4. A key element of critical thinking is evaluating the quality of evidence related to a claim.
    TRUE or FALSE

5. Critical thinkers recognize that the opinions of experts and authorities should be respected without question.
    TRUE or FALSE

6. Pseudoscientists test their concepts by gathering data.
    TRUE or FALSE

7. Phrenologists believe that lines on the hands reveal personality traits.
    TRUE or FALSE

8. Graphology is only valid if a large enough sample of handwriting is analyzed.

TRUE or FALSE

9. Astrological charts consisting of positive traits tend to be perceived as "accurate" or true, even if they are not.

TRUE or FALSE

10. The Barnum effect refers to our tendency to remember things that confirm our expectations.

TRUE or FALSE

Scientific Research—How to Think Like a Psychologist

Survey Questions: Why is the scientific method important to psychologists? How do psychologists collect information? Pages 23-25

1. The scientific method involves testing a proposition by systematic observation.

TRUE or FALSE

2. An operational definition states the exact hypothesis used to represent a concept.

TRUE or FALSE

3. Contemporary researchers agree that covert behaviors cannot be scientifically studied.

TRUE or FALSE

4. Operational definitions link concepts with concrete observations.

TRUE or FALSE

5. Most research reports begin with an abstract.

TRUE or FALSE

A Brief History of Psychology—Psychology's Family Album

Survey Question: How did the field of psychology emerge? Pages 26-29

1. In 1879, Wundt established a lab to study the philosophy of behavior.

TRUE or FALSE

2. Wundt used introspection to study conscious experiences.

TRUE or FALSE

3. Edward Titchener is best known for promoting functionalism in America.

TRUE or FALSE

4. The functionalists were influenced by the ideas of Charles Darwin.

TRUE or FALSE

5. Behaviorists define psychology as the study of conscious experience.

   TRUE or FALSE

6. Watson used Pavlov's concept of conditioned responses to explain most behavior.

   TRUE or FALSE

7. Believing that human behavior is controlled by rewards, B. F. Skinner invented the "Skinner box" to study primarily animals' responses.

   TRUE or FALSE

8. The word Gestalt means "form, pattern, or whole".

   TRUE or FALSE

9. Margaret Washburn was the first woman in America to be awarded a Ph.D. in psychology.

   TRUE or FALSE

10. According to Freud, repressed thoughts are held out of awareness, in the unconscious.

   TRUE or FALSE

11. Humanists generally reject the determinism of the behavioristic and psychodynamic approaches.

   TRUE or FALSE

Psychology Today—Three Complementary Perspectives on Behavior and Psychologists—Guaranteed Not to Shrink

Survey Question: What are the current perspectives in psychology? What are the major specialties in psychology? Pages 30-36

1. The three major perspectives in psychology today are behaviorism, humanism, and functionalism.

   TRUE or FALSE

2. Humanism offers a positive, philosophical view of human nature.

   TRUE or FALSE

3. The cognitive view explains behavior in terms of information processing.

   TRUE or FALSE

4. To understand behavior, psychologists must be aware of the cultural relativity of standards for evaluating behavior.

   TRUE or FALSE

5. Most psychologists work in private practice.

   TRUE or FALSE

6. The differences between clinical and counseling psychology are beginning to fade.

   TRUE or FALSE

7. To enter the profession of psychology today you would need to earn a doctorate degree.

   TRUE or FALSE

8. The Psy.D. degree emphasizes scientific research skills.

   TRUE or FALSE

9. More than half of all psychologists specialize in clinical or counseling psychology.

   TRUE or FALSE

10. Clinical psychologists must be licensed to practice legally.

    TRUE or FALSE

11. Over 40 percent of all psychologists are employed by the military.

    TRUE or FALSE

12. Studying ways to improve the memories of eyewitnesses to crimes would be an example of applied research.

    TRUE or FALSE

The Psychology Experiment—Where Cause Meets Effect and Double Blind—On Placebos and Self-Fulfilling Prophecies

Survey Question: How is an experiment performed? What is a double blind experiment? Pages 36-40

1. Extraneous variables are those that are varied by the experimenter.

   TRUE or FALSE

2. Independent variables are suspected causes for differences in behavior.

   TRUE or FALSE

3. In an experiment to test whether hunger affects memory, hunger is the dependent variable.

   TRUE or FALSE

4. The control group and the experimental group are treated exactly alike in an experiment.

   TRUE or FALSE

5. Independent variables are randomly assigned to the experimental and control groups.

   TRUE or FALSE

6. An experiment allows cause-and-effect connections to be made, but it limited in the scope of behaviors to which it can be applied.

   TRUE or FALSE

7. A person who takes a drug may be influenced by his or her expectations about the drug's effects.

   TRUE or FALSE

8. Placebos appear to reduce pain because they alter our experience regarding pain.

   TRUE or FALSE

9. In a single-blind experiment, the experimenter remains blind as to whether she or he is administering a drug.

   TRUE or FALSE

10. Subjects in psychology experiments can be very sensitive to hints about what is expected of them.

    TRUE or FALSE

11. In a double-blind experiment, only the participants in both the experimental and control groups are blind to their assigned condition.

    TRUE or FALSE

Nonexperimental Research Methods—Different Strokes

Survey Question: What nonexperimental research methods do psychologists use? Pages 41-46

1. Naturalistic observation involves keeping careful records of behavior in controlled conditions.

   TRUE or FALSE

2. A change in behavior caused by the awareness that one is being watched is called the behavior magnification effect.

   TRUE or FALSE

3. Jane Goodall's study of chimpanzees made use of the clinical method.

   TRUE or FALSE

4. Concealing the observer helps reduce the observer effect.

   TRUE or FALSE

5. Anthropomorphic error refers to attributing animals' behaviors, thoughts, emotions, and motives to humans.

   TRUE or FALSE

6. A correlation coefficient of +.100 indicates a perfect positive relationship.

    TRUE or FALSE

7. Strong relationships produce positive correlation coefficients; weak relationships produce negative correlations.

    TRUE or FALSE

8. Perfect correlations demonstrate that a causal relationship exists.

    TRUE or FALSE

9. The best way to identify cause-and-effect relationships is to perform a case study.

    TRUE or FALSE

10. Phineas Gage is remembered as the first psychologist to do a case study.

    TRUE or FALSE

11. Case studies may be inconclusive because they lack formal control groups.

    TRUE or FALSE

12. Representative samples are often obtained by randomly selecting people to study.

    TRUE or FALSE

13. Representative sampling is an advantage of web-based research.

    TRUE or FALSE

14. Psychologists are finding ways to limit the sampling bias often involved in Web-based research.

    TRUE or FALSE

15. A tendency to give socially desirable answers to questions can lower the accuracy of surveys.

    TRUE or FALSE

Psychology in Action: Psychology in the Media—Separating Fact from Fiction

Survey Question: How good is psychological information found in the popular media? Pages 46-49

1. The existence of dermo-optical perception (sixth sense) was confirmed by recent experiments.

    TRUE or FALSE

2. Psychological courses and services offered for profit may be misrepresented, just as some other products are.

    TRUE or FALSE

3. At least some psychic ability is necessary to perform as a stage mentalist.

   TRUE or FALSE

4. Successful firewalking requires neurolinguistic programming.

   TRUE or FALSE

5. Violent crime rises and falls with lunar cycles.

   TRUE or FALSE

6. If you see a person crying, you must infer that he or she is sad.

   TRUE or FALSE

7. Individual cases and specific examples tell us nothing about what is true in general.

   TRUE or FALSE

FINAL SURVEY AND REVIEW

Psychology—Spotlight on Behavior

Survey Questions: What is psychology and what are its goals? Pages 15-18

1. Psychology is both a _____ and a _____.

2. Psychology is defined as the scientific study of _____ and _____.

3. Psychologists study _____ and covert behavior.

4. Psychologists seek _____ evidence based on scientific observation. They settle disputes by collecting _____.

5. _____ is systematic or planned so that it answers questions about the world.

6. Scientific observations are intersubjective, which means they can be _____ by more than one observer.

7. Answering psychological questions requires a _____ research method.

8. _____ psychologists study the course of human development.

9. _____ study how and why learning occurs.

10. Personality theorists study personality _____ and _____.

11. _____ and _____ psychologists study the sense (or sensory) organs and perception.

12. Comparative psychologists study different _____, especially animals.

13. _____ study the connection between biological processes and behavior.

14. _____ psychologists study social behavior.

15. _____ psychologists study the ways that culture affects behavior.

16. _____ psychologists are interested in patterns of behavior that were shaped by evolution.

17. Forensic psychologists apply psychological principles to _____.

18. Other species are used as animal models in psychological research to discover principles that apply to _____.

19. Psychology's goals are to _____, understand, predict, and _____ behavior.

Science and Critical Thinking—Healthy Skepticism

Survey Question: What is critical thinking? Pages 19-20

1. Critical thinking is the ability to reflect on, evaluate, compare, _____, critique, and _____ information.

2. Critical thinking involves a willingness to _____ assumptions and look for alternate conclusions.

3. Authority or claimed expertise does not automatically make an idea _____.

4. Being able to _____ the quality of evidence is crucial to critical thinking.

Pseudopsychologies—Palms, Planets, and Personality

Survey Question: How does psychology differ from false explanations of behavior? Pages 20-22

1. Palmistry, phrenology, graphology, and astrology are false systems, or _____.

2. Followers of pseudopsychologies seek evidence that confirms their beliefs and avoids _____ evidence.

3. Palmistry is a pseudopsychology that claims _____ reveal personality traits and predict the future.

4. _____ falsely believe that personality traits can be revealed in an individual's handwriting.

5. Belief in pseudopsychologies is encouraged by _____, the fallacy of positive instances, and the Barnum effect, named after a famous showman who had "something for everyone."

Scientific Research—How to Think Like a Psychologist

Survey Questions: How is the scientific method applied in psychological research?
Pages 23-25

1. Scientific investigation in psychology is based on _____ evidence, accurate description and measurement, _____, controlled observation, and repeatable results.

2. Six elements of a scientific method involve making _____, defining a problem, proposing a hypothesis, gathering evidence/testing the hypothesis, publishing results, and forming a _____.

3. To be scientifically valid (or useful), a hypothesis must be _____.

4. Psychological concepts are given _____ definitions so that they can be observed and tested.

5. Covert behaviors are operationally defined in terms of _____ for the purposes of scientific study.

6. A theory is a system of ideas that interrelates _____ and _____.

7. Scientific information must be publicly available so that other researchers can read about the _____.

8. Published research reports usually include the following sections: an abstract, an _____, a methods section, a results section, and a final _____.

A Brief History of Psychology—Psychology's Family Album

Survey Question: How did the field of psychology emerge? Pages 26-29

1. People have been interested in observing and understanding human behavior for thousands of years, long before _____ was a science.

2. The first psychological laboratory was established in Germany by _____.

3. Wundt tried to apply scientific methods to the study of conscious experience by using _____ or "looking inward."

4. The ideas of _____ were brought to the United States by Edward Titchener.

5. _____ fell out of favor because the structuralists frequently disagreed over the results.

6. _____ was concerned with how the mind helps us adapt to our environments.

7. _____ was launched by John B. Watson.

8. Behaviorists objectively study the relationship between _____ and responses.

9. The modern behaviorist B. F. Skinner believed that most behavior is controlled by positive _____.

10. _____ psychology emphasizes the study of whole units, not pieces.

11. According to the Gestalt view, in psychology the _____ is often greater than the _____ of its parts.

12. The _____ approach emphasized the _____ origins of behavior.

13. Psychoanalytic psychology, developed by Austrian physician Sigmund Freud, is an early _____ approach.

14. Freud theorized that many unconscious thoughts are held out of _____, or repressed.

15. Humanistic psychology emphasizes _____, subjective experience, human potentials, and personal growth.

16. Psychologically, humanists believe that self-image and _____ are important elements of personal adjustment.

17. Humanists also emphasize a capacity for _____—the full development of personal potentials.

18. The first woman to be awarded a _____ in psychology was Margaret Washburn.

19. Francis Cecil Sumner became the first _____ to earn a doctoral degree in psychology.

Psychology Today—Three Complementary Perspectives on Behavior

Survey Question: What are the current perspectives in psychology? Pages 30-33

1. Three views in modern psychology are the _____, the biological, and the psychological perspectives.

2. Much of contemporary psychology is an eclectic blend of the best features of _____ viewpoints.

3. The biological perspective seeks to explain all behavior in terms of _____.

4. The field of _____ includes biopsychologists who study the brain and nervous system.

5. The evolutionary psychologists assume that human and animal behavior is the result of _____ processes.

6. Cognitive psychologists study covert _____, such as memory, language, and problem solving.

7. The study of topics such as _____ and happiness make up positive psychology.

8. To fully understand behavior, psychologists must be aware of human diversity as well as human _____.

9. Our behavior is greatly affected by _____ values and by social norms (rules that define acceptable behavior).

10. Cultural relativity suggests that behavior should be judged by the _____ of the culture in which it occurs.

Psychologists—Guaranteed Not to Shrink

Survey Question: What are the major specialties in psychology? Pages 33-36

1. Real psychologists follow an ethical code that stresses respect for people's privacy, dignity, _____, and welfare.

2. Counseling psychologists tend to treat individuals with _____ problems, such as troubles at work or school.

3. Psychiatrists typically use both drugs and _____ to treat emotional problems.

4. Both _____ and psychiatric social workers have Master's degrees.

5. Some major specialties in psychology are clinical, counseling, _____, educational, consumer, school, developmental, engineering, medical, environmental, _____, psychometric, and experimental psychology.

6. Scientific research in psychology may be either basic or _____.

The Psychology Experiment—Where Cause Meets Effect

Survey Question: How is an experiment performed? Pages 36-38

1. In an experiment, conditions that might affect behavior are intentionally varied. Then, changes in behavior are _____ and _____.

2. In an experiment, a _____ is any condition that can change and that might affect the outcome of the experiment (i.e., the behavior of subjects).

3. _____ conditions that are intentionally varied are called independent variables.

4. Dependent variables measure the _____ of the experiment.

5. Extraneous variables are conditions that a researcher wishes to _____ from affecting the outcome of the experiment.

6. Extraneous variables are controlled by making sure that they are the _____ for all subjects in an experiment.

7. Subjects _____ to the independent variable are in the experimental group. Those _____ to the independent variable form the control group.

8. Extraneous variables that involve personal characteristics, such as age or intelligence, can be _____ by randomly assigning subjects to the experimental and control groups.

9. If all extraneous variables are identical for the experimental group and the control group, any differences in behavior must be caused by differences in the _____.

10. A _____ provides a point of reference for comparison of scores.

Double Blind—On Placebos and Self-Fulfilling Prophecies
Survey Question: What is a double blind experiment? Pages 38-40

1. Researchers must minimize research _____ (the tendency for people to do what is expected of them).

2. Experiments involving drugs must control for the placebo effect, which is always present when _____ are involved in a study.

3. In many situations, _____ leads to self-fulfilling prophecies.

4. In a single-blind study, subjects don't know if they are getting a _____ or a _____. In a double-blind study, neither experimenters nor subjects know who is receiving a real drug.

Nonexperimental Research Methods—Different Strokes
Survey Question: What nonexperimental research methods do psychologists use? Pages 41-46

1. _____ refers to actively observing behavior in natural settings.

2. Naturalistic observation only provides descriptions of behavior, not _____ of observations.

3. Two problems with naturalistic studies are the effects of the _____ on the _____ (the observer effect) and observer bias.

4. The _____ is the error of attributing human qualities to animals.

5. Problems with naturalistic studies can be _____ by keeping careful observational records.

6. In the _____, the correlation (or relationship) between two traits, responses, or events is measured.

7. Correlation _____ range from +1.00 to –1.00.

8. A correlation of zero indicates that there is _____ between two measures.

9. Correlations of _____ and _____ reveal that perfect relationships exist between two measures.

10. The _____ a correlation coefficient is to plus or minus 1, the stronger the measured relationship is.

11. A _____ correlation shows that increases in one measure correspond to increases in a second measure.

12. In a negative correlation, increases in one measure correspond to _____ in a second measure.

13. Correlations allow us to make predictions, but correlation does not demonstrate _____.

14. Cause-and-effect relationships in psychology are best identified by doing a controlled _____.

15. Clinical psychologists frequently gain information from _____ studies.

16. _____ may be thought of as natural clinical tests.

17. In the survey method, information about large populations is gained by asking people in a representative sample a series of _____ questions.

18. Biases in research can occur when the race, ethnicity, age, sexual orientation, and gender of researchers and participants are _____.

19. The value of surveys is _____ when the sample is _____ and when replies to questions are untruthful (or inaccurate) because of courtesy bias (a tendency to give socially desirable answers).

Psychology in Action: Psychology in the Media—Separating Fact from Fiction

Survey Question: How good is psychological information found in the popular media? Pages 46-49

1. Skepticism and _____ are called for when evaluating claims in the popular media.

2. You should be on guard for unreliable (or inaccurate) or _____ sources of information in the media.

3. Many claims in the media are based on _____ observations that lack control groups.

4. In the popular media, a failure to distinguish between _____ and causation is common.

5. _____ and _____ may be reported as if they were valid (or scientific) observations.

6. Single cases, unusual examples, and testimonials are frequently reported as if they were _____ generalizations.

MASTERY TEST

1. Data in psychology are typically gathered to answer questions about
a. clinical problems.
b. human groups.
c. human cognition.
d. overt or covert behavior.

2. Who among the following would most likely study the behavior of gorillas?
a. developmental psychologist
b. comparative psychologist
c. environmental psychologist
d. forensic psychologist

3. An engineering psychologist helps redesign an airplane to make it safer to fly. The psychologist's work reflects which of psychology's goals?
a. understanding
b. control
c. prediction
d. description

4. When critically evaluating claims about behavior it is important to also evaluate
a. the source of anecdotal evidence.
b. the credentials of an authority.
c. the quality of the evidence.
d. the strength of one's intuition.

5. Which of the following pairs is most different?
a. pseudopsychology—critical thinking
b. graphology—pseudopsychology
c. palmistry—phrenology
d. psychology—empirical evidence

6. The German anatomy teacher Franz Gall popularized
a. palmistry
b. phrenology
c. graphology
d. astrology

7. A tendency to believe flattering descriptions of oneself is called
a. the Barnum effect.
b. the astrologer's dilemma.
c. the fallacy of positive instances.
d. uncritical acceptance.

8. Descriptions of personality that contain both sides of several personal dimensions tend to create
a. an illusion of accuracy.
b. disbelief and rejection.

c. the astrologer's dilemma.

d. a system similar to phrenology.

9. Many products of pseudopsychology are stated in such general terms that they appear to be accurate or "on-target"; this can be attributed to

a. the pseudopsychology paralysis

b. astrologer's dilemma

c. the Barnum effect

d. "everybody wins" fallacy

10. Testing the hypothesis that frustration encourages aggression would require

a. a field study.

b. operational definitions.

c. adult subjects.

d. perfect correlations.

11. The specific procedures used to gather data are described in which section of a research report?

a. introduction

b. abstract

c. method

d. discussion

12. Who among the following placed the greatest emphasis on introspection?

a. Watson

b. Wertheimer

c. Washburn

d. Wundt

13. Which pair of persons had the most similar ideas?

a. Titchener—Skinner

b. James—Darwin

c. Watson—Rogers

d. Wertheimer—Maslow

14. The behaviorist definition of psychology clearly places great emphasis on

a. overt behavior.

b. conscious experience.

c. psychodynamic responses.

d. introspective analysis.

15. The idea that threatening thoughts are sometimes repressed would be of most interest to a

a. structuralist.

b. psychoanalyst.

c. humanist.

d. Gestaltist.

16. "A neutral, reductionistic, mechanistic view of human nature." This best describes which viewpoint?

a. psychodynamic

b. cognitive

c. psychoanalytic
d. biopsychological

17. Which of the following professional titles usually requires a doctorate degree?
a. psychologist
b. psychiatric social worker
c. counselor
d. all of the preceding

18. Who among the following is most likely to treat the physical causes of psychological problems?
a. scientist-practitioner
b. psychoanalyst
c. forensic psychologist
d. psychiatrist

19. More than half of all psychologists specialize in what branches of psychology?
a. counseling and comparative
b. applied and counseling
c. psychodynamic and clinical
d. counseling and clinical

20. If an entire population is surveyed, it becomes unnecessary to obtain a
a. control group.
b. random comparison.
c. random sample.
d. control variable.

21. Control groups are most often used in
a. naturalistic observation.
b. the clinical method.
c. parascience.
d. experiments.

22. Concealing the observer can be used to minimize the
a. observer bias effect.
b. double-blind effect.
c. observer effect.
d. effects of extraneous correlations.

23. A psychologist studying lowland gorillas should be careful to avoid the
a. anthropomorphic error.
b. Gestalt fallacy.
c. psychodynamic fallacy.
d. fallacy of positive instances.

24. In experiments involving drugs, experimenters remain unaware of who received placebos in a _____ arrangement.
a. zero-blind
b. single-blind

   c. double-blind
   d. control-blind

25. In psychology, the _____ variable is a suspected cause of differences in _____.
   a. independent, the control group
   b. dependent, the experimenter effect
   c. independent, behavior
   d. dependent, correlations

26. A person who is observed crying may not be sad. This suggests that it is important to distinguish between
   a. individual cases and generalizations.
   b. correlation and causation.
   c. control groups and experimental groups.
   d. observation and inference.

27. In an experiment on the effects of hunger on the reading scores of elementary school children, reading scores are the
   a. control variable.
   b. independent variable.
   c. dependent variable.
   d. reference variable.

28. Which of the following correlation coefficients indicates a perfect relationship?
   a. 1.00
   b. 100.0
   c. −1
   d. both A and C

29. Jane Goodall's studies of chimpanzees in Tanzania are good examples of
   a. field experiments.
   b. experimental control.
   c. correlational studies.
   d. naturalistic observation.

30. To equalize the intelligence of members of the experimental group and the control group in an experiment, you could use
   a. extraneous control.
   b. random assignment.
   c. independent control.
   d. subject replication.

31. Which method would most likely be used to study the effects of tumors in the frontal lobes of the brain?
   a. sampling method
   b. correlational method
   c. clinical method
   d. experimental method

32. Cause is to effect as _____ variable is to
    _____ variable.
    a. extraneous; dependent
    b. dependent; independent
    c. independent; extraneous
    d. independent; dependent

33. Which of the following correlations demonstrates a cause-effect relationship?
    a. .980
    b. 1.00
    c. .50
    d. none of the preceding

34. Appreciating an orchestra playing Mozart's fifth symphony more than a
    musician playing a solo on a clarinet reflects _____ psychology.
    a. Gestalt
    b. cognitive
    c. behavioral
    d. biopsychology

35. Carlie believes that blind people have unusually sensitive organs of touch.
    She based her beliefs on personal experiences and everyday observation.
    Carlie's sound, practical belief is an example of _____.
    a. commonsense
    b. scientific observation
    c. uncritical acceptance
    d. representative sample

36. To control for placebo effects, a _____ study is used.
    a. correlational
    b. single-blind
    c. clinical case
    d. Web based

37. Which of the following approaches to psychology stresses free will?
    a. Structuralism
    b. Behaviorism
    c. Humanistic psychology
    d. Psychodynamic psychology

38. The evolutionary view of psychology best fits the _____ perspective.
    a. psychological
    b. sociocultural
    c. biological
    d. both a & b

39. John recently took what he thought was a pain reliever and reports less
    shoulder pain. However, the pill he took was only a sugar pill. This best
    illustrates the
    a. experimenter effect.
    b. placebo effect.

c. multiple-personality effect.

d. gender-bias effect.

40. When an experimenter unwittingly influences research participants so that they behave in ways consistent with her hypothesis, it best represents

a. the placebo effect.

b. researcher bias.

c. anthropomorphic error.

d. social desirability.

41. Dr. Harlow's research of Phineas Gage's brain damage best represents

a. a natural clinical test.

b. an experiment.

c. a survey.

d. the Barnum effect.

42. Which of the following is most likely to lead to obtaining a representative sample?

a. a random sample

b. a control group

c. a biased sample

d. the courtesy bias

43. Which of the following is not a goal of psychology?

a. understanding

b. prediction

c. description

d. All of the above are goals of psychology.

LANGUAGE DEVELOPMENT

Introduction to Psychology and Research Methods

Word Roots

Cognitare is the Latin word that means "to think" or "to know." Several words in the field of psychology are derived from this Latin root, and these words all refer in some way to the processes of thinking, reasoning, or knowing. Examples you will find in later chapters include cognitive, cognition, and precognition.

Journey into Psychology (p. 14)

    (14)   *eclectic*: marked by diverse and unusual combinations

(14)   *hippies*: slang term for individuals who rejected established mores of U.S. in 1960s; usually advocated for peace, free love, expanded consciousness; often anti-war.

(14)   *rednecks*: negative slang term for uneducated rural laborers from the southern U.S.; usually pro-firearms

(14)   *odds are*: it is likely

(14)   *panorama*: wide-ranging view

Psychology—Focus on Behavior (pgs. 15-18)

What is psychology and what are its goals?

(15)   *boiling hot*: very hot (*boiling* suggests high heat)

(16)   *conception*: the moment when egg and sperm meet and a new being is created

(16)   *discern*: understand

(16)   *porpoises*: a black, blunt-nosed whale of the North Atlantic and Pacific Ocean

(17)   *humankind*: all human beings considered as a whole

(17)   *"bystander apathy"*: lack of interest or concern among witnesses to an accident or crime

(17)   *diffusion of responsibility*: responsibility for action is spread out and lessened; it is not clear who should act

(17*)   *to pitch in* (...so no one feels required *to pitch in*): to get involved

(17)   *perplexing*: very hard to understand

(18)   *forecast*: to predict

(18)   *stranded*: left without means to depart or leave

(18)   *boil down*: to reduce or narrow

Critical Thinking— Take It With a Grain of Salt (pgs. 19-20)

What is critical thinking?

(19)   *skeptical*: critical, not believing that everything you read is true

(19)   *to "buy" outrageous claims*: to believe claims that are too extraordinary to be true

(19)   *synthesize*: to combine into a single unit

(19)   *transcend*: to rise above or go beyond the limits of

(19)   *guru*: personal religious teacher and spiritual guide

(19)   *open-minded*: able to accept new ideas

(19)   *gullible*: believe everything you hear

(20)   *provisional*: until more information can be found

Pseudopsychologies—Palms, Planets, and Personality (pgs. 20-22)

How does psychology differ from false explanations of behavior?

(21)   *vague*: very general, not specific

(21)   *zodiac*: an imaginary belt in the nighttime sky that contains the apparent paths of the planets

(21)   *ring of truth*: sounds like it could be true

(21)   *nitpicking*: unjustified criticism

(21)   *hemmed in*: held back from doing something
(21)   *extroverted:* outward-looking; generally concerned with other people and the outside world
(21)   *introverted*: inward-looking; generally concerned with one's own thoughts and feelings.
(22)   *nuisance*: something that is annoying or troublesome

Scientific Research—How to Think Like a Psychologist (pgs. 23-25)

How is the scientific method applied in psychological research?

(23)   **every cloud has a silver lining**: The bright side of a negative situation
(23)   ***Where there's smoke, there's fire***: If there is an indication of something bad or negative, then usually that indication is correct.
(23)   *haphazard*: not planned; random
(23)   *hunch*: guess
(23)   *educated guesses*: guesses based on the best information available
(24)   *confirm*: prove or verify
(24)   *disconfirm*: prove not true in all cases
(24)   **Psychologists would drown in a sea of disconnected facts**: they would be very confused
(25)   *journals:* periodicals that present research and reviews in a specific subject area
(25)   *implications*: possible results
(25)   **"You can't teach an old dog new tricks"**: it is difficult for people (as well as dogs) to learn new ways of doing things

A Brief History of Psychology—Psychology's Family Album (pgs. 26-29)

How did the field of psychology emerge?

(26)   *evoke*: to trigger, cause
(26)   *probe*: examine in detail
(26)   *systematic*: in an orderly, structured fashion
(26)   *heft*: to get the feel of, to lift something up
(26)   *Charles Darwin*: the scientist who proposed the theory of evolution
(26)   *deduced*: inferred from reason
(27)   *glandular activity*: activity results from glands that make up the endocrine system
(27)   *radical*: changes of a sweeping or extreme nature
(27)   *"designed culture"*: a culture that is created using positive reinforcements to produce wanted behaviors from individuals
(28)   *Freud believed that mental life is like an iceberg*: the unknown of the unconscious mind is hidden below consciousness like the large part of a submerged iceberg below the surface of the water

(28)   **slips of the tongue**: the tongue speaks before the mind realizes all of the consequences

(28)   **Freudian slips**: while the mind is thinking about the obvious, the tongue speaks about hidden, unrevealed thoughts

(28)   **undercurrent**: an underlying or hidden attitude; a hint

Psychology Today—Three Complementary Perspectives on Behavior (pgs. 30-33)

What are the current perspectives in psychology?

(30)   **clashes:** strong disagreements

(30)   **mechanistic**: can be explained by mechanical laws; no free will

(30)   **reductionistic**: reducing to the simplest terms

(30)   **pessimistic**: exceedingly negative perspective

(30)   **interactionist**: assuming behavior is caused by a combination of environment and internal (personal) factors

Psychologists—Guaranteed not to Shrink (pgs. 33-36)

What are the major specialties in psychology?

(33)   **shrinks**: a slang term for psychiatrists or head doctors

(33)   **postgraduate**: training or education beyond the bachelor's degree

(33)   **buffoons**: people who look foolish; clowns

(33)   **distort**: bend out of shape in odd ways

(35)   **keen**: insightful

(35)   **goatee**: a beard that has been trimmed down to a point on the chin

The Psychology Experiment—Where Cause Meets Effect (pgs. 36-38)

How is an experiment performed?

(37)   **iPod**: a digital music device

(38)   **randomly**: by chance; not according to any set plan

(38)   **Heads, and the subject is in the experimental group, tails, it's in the control group**: the person is placed in one group or the other according to which side of a coin lands facing up (in other words, completely according to chance)

(38)   **dunces**: stupid, ignorant people

(38)   **hung over**: feeling sick (headache, stomachache) because of drinking too much alcohol the day before

Double Blind—On Placebos and Self-Fulfilling Prophecies (pgs. 38-40)

What is a double blind experiment?

(39)   **inert substances**: substances that have no active properties to affect behavior

(40)   **simulated**: copied or of similar condition as the original

(40)   *loophole in the statement*: the statement has a misleading logic
(sound judgment based on inference)
(40)   *coincidence*: two events happened to occur at the same time by
chance

Nonexperimental Research Methods—Different Strokes (pgs. 41-46)

What nonexperimental research methods do psychologists use?
(41)   *tampered with*: affected by
(42)   *a wealth of information*: a large amount of information
(42)   *computer-game-zombie*: playing too many computer games turns
people into passive and uninterested students
(43)   *causation*: the act that produces or causes an effect
What other research methods do psychologists use?
(43)   *rampage*: an uncontrollable aggressive act of violence
(43)   *foul-mouthed*: using obscene, crude, and socially unacceptable
language
(44)   *blue-collar workers*: workers in trades, industrial settings, and
manual labor; refers to the blue work shirts many such workers wear on
the job
(45)   *prejudice*: judgments made before contrary information can be
gathered or learned

Chapter in Review (pgs. 49-51)

(50)   *accentuate*: to highlight or stress
(50)   *employs*: uses

Solutions

Recite and Review

Psychology—Spotlight on Behavior

1. profession
2. mental
3. behavior
4. evidence
5. systematic or planned
6. intersubjective
7. method
8. human development
9. learning
10. Personality
11. sense (or sensory)
12. animals
13. biological processes, behavior
14. social
15. culture, behavior
16. evolution
17. Forensic
18. animal
19. understand

Science and Critical Thinking—Healthy Skepticism

1. evaluate
2. assumptions
3. Authority, claimed expertise
4. quality

Pseudopsychologies—Palms, Planets, and Personality

1. false
2. confirms, avoids
3. Palmistry
4. handwriting
5. Barnum

Scientific Research—How to Think Like a Psychologist

1. measurement
2. problem, results
3. valid (or useful)
4. definitions
5. behaviors
6. theory
7. publicly available
8. abstract, results

A Brief History of Psychology—Psychology's Family Album

1. science
2. Germany
3. conscious
4. Edward Titchener
5. frequently disagreed
6. adapt
7. Watson
8. responses
9. positive
10. whole
11. greater
12. unconscious
13. Freud
14. repressed
15. growth
16. image
17. potentials
18. Margaret Washburn
19. Francis Cecil Sumner

Psychology Today—Three Complementary Perspectives on Behavior

1. biological
2. eclectic blend
3. biological
4. nervous system
5. evolutionary
6. Cognitive
7. positive
8. diversity
9. values; social norms
10. relativity

Psychologists—Guaranteed Not to Shrink
1. welfare
2. Counseling
3. drugs
4. Master's
5. specialties
6. basic

The Psychology Experiment—Where Cause Meets Effect
1. varied
2. change
3. independent
4. Dependent
5. Extraneous
6. subjects
7. experimental, control
8. randomly assigning
9. identical
10. point of reference

Double Blind—On Placebos and Self-Fulfilling Prophecies
1. expected
2. placebo effect
3. prophecies
4. single-blind, double-blind

Nonexperimental Research Methods—Different Strokes
1. natural
2. descriptions
3. effect, observer
4. human, animals
5. records
6. correlation (or relationship)
7. +1.00 , −1.00
8. zero
9. perfect
10. minus
11. increases
12. increases
13. predictions
14. Cause
15. case
16. natural
17. representative sample
18. Biases
19. untruthful (or inaccurate), courtesy bias

Psychology in Action: Psychology in the Media—Separating Fact from Fiction
1. Skepticism
2. unreliable (or inaccurate)
3. control
4. causation
5. valid (or scientific)
6. examples

Connections

Psychology—Spotlight on Behavior
1. H.
2. F.
3. J.
4. A.
5. L.
6. C.
7. G.
8. B.
9. I.
10. D.
11. E.
12. K.

Science and Critical Thinking—Healthy Skepticism, Pseudopsychologies—Palms, Planets, and Personality, and Psychology in the Media—Separating Fact from Fiction
1. B.
2. D.
3. A.
4. E.
5. C.
6. G.
7. F.
8. H.
9. I.

A Brief History of Psychology—Psychology's Family Album

1. A.   4. B.   7. C.
2. G.   5. I.   8. F.
3. D.   6. E.   9. H.

Psychology Today—Three Complementary Perspectives on Behavior and Psychologists—Guaranteed Not to Shrink

1. H.   4. A.   7. I.   10. J.
2. E.   5. F.   8. K.   11. D.
3. G.   6. B.   9. C.

The Psychology Experiment—Where Cause Meets Effect and Double Blind—On Placebos and Self-Fulfilling Prophecies

1. H.   4. C.   7. I.   10. G.
2. B.   5. A.   8. E.
3. J.   6. D.   9. F.

Nonexperimental Research Methods—Different Strokes

1. E.   5. A.   9. H.   13. L.
2. G.   6. B.   10. J.   14. I.
3. F.   7. C.   11. N.
4. D.   8. M.   12. K.

Check Your Memory

Psychology—Spotlight on Behavior

1. F   4. F   7. T
2. F   5. T   8. F
3. T   6. F   9. F

Science and Critical Thinking—Healthy Skepticism and Pseudopsychologies—Palms, Planets, and Personality

1. F   3. T   5. F   7. F
2. F   4. T   6. F

Scientific Research—How to Think Like a Psychologist

1. T   3. F   5. T
2. F   4. T

A Brief History of Psychology—Psychology's Family Album

1. F	4. T	7. T	10. T
2. T	5. F	8. T	11. T
3. F	6. T	9. T	

Psychology Today—Three Complementary Perspectives on Behavior and Psychologists—Guaranteed Not to Shrink

1. F	4. T	7. F	10. T
2. T	5. F	8. F	11. F
3. T	6. T	9. T	12. T

The Psychology Experiment—Where Cause Meets Effect and Double Blind—On Placebos and Self-Fulfilling Prophecies

1. F	4. T	7. T	10. T
2. T	5. F	8. T	11. F
3. F	6. T	9. F	

Nonexperimental Research Methods—Different Strokes

1. F	5. F	9. F	13. F
2. F	6. F	10. F	14. T
3. F	7. F	11. T	15. T
4. T	8. F	12. T	

Psychology in Action: Psychology in the Media—Separating Fact from Fiction

1. F	3. F	5. F	7. T
2. T	4. F	6. F	

Final Survey and Review

Psychology—Spotlight on Behavior

1. science, profession
2. behavior, mental processes
3. overt
4. empirical, data
5. Scientific observation
6. confirmed
7. valid
8. Developmental
9. Learning theorists
10. Traits, dynamics
11. Sensation, perception
12. species
13. Biopsychologists
14. Social
15. Cultural
16. Evolutionary
17. legal issues
18. human behavior
19. describe, control

Science and Critical Thinking—Healthy Skepticism

1. analyze
2. synthesize
3. question
4. true
5. judge

Pseudopsychologies—Palms, Planets, and Personality

1. pseudopsychologies.
2. contradictory
3. lines on the hand
4. Graphologists
5. uncritical acceptance

Scientific Research—How to Think Like a Psychologist

1. reliable, precise definition
2. observations, theory
3. testable
4. operational
5. overt behavior
6. facts, concepts
7. results.
8. introduction, discussion

A Brief History of Psychology—Psychology's Family Album

1. psychology
2. Wilhelm Wundt.
3. introspection
4. structuralism
5. Structuralism
6. Functionalism
7. Behaviorism
8. stimuli
9. reinforcers.
10. Gestalt
11. whole, sum
12. psychoanalytic, unconscious
13. psychodynamic
14. awareness
15. free will
16. self-evaluation
17. self-actualization
18. Ph.D.
19. African-American

Psychology Today—Three Complementary Perspectives on Behavior

1. sociocultural
2. various
3. physical mechanisms
4. neuroscience
5. evolutionary
6. mental behaviors
7. love
8. universals
9. cultural
10. values

Psychologists—Guaranteed Not to Shrink

1. confidentiality
2. "mild"
3. psychotherapy
4. counselors
5. industrial-organizational, forensic
6. applied

The Psychology Experiment—Where Cause Meets Effect

1. observed, recorded
2. variable
3. Experimental
4. results
5. prevent
6. same
7. exposed, not exposed
8. controlled
9. independent variable
10. control group

Double Blind—On Placebos and Self-Fulfilling Prophecies

1. participant bias
2. drugs
3. researcher bias
4. drug, placebo

Nonexperimental Research Methods—Different Strokes

1. Naturalistic observation
2. explanations
3. observer, observed
4. anthropomorphic fallacy
5. minimized
6. correlational method
7. coefficients
8. no relationship
9. +1.00, −1.00
10. closer
11. positive
12. decreases
13. causation
14. experiment.
15. case
16. Case studies
17. carefully worded
18. not representative
19. lowered, biased

Psychology in Action: Psychology in the Media—Separating Fact from Fiction

1. critical thinking
2. biased
3. unscientific
4. correlation
5. Inferences, opinions
6. valid

Mastery Test

1. d, p. 24
2. b, p. 16
3. b, p. 18
4. c, p. 19
5. a, p. 20-22
6. b, p. 20
7. d, p. 21
8. a, p. 21-22
9. c, p. 22
10. b, p. 24
11. c, p. 25
12. d, p. 26
13. b, p. 26
14. a, p. 27
15. b, p. 28
16. d, p. 30-31
17. a, p. 34
18. d, p. 35
19. d, p. 35-36
20. c, p. 38
21. d, p. 36-38
22. c, p. 41
23. a, p. 42
24. c, p. 38-40
25. c, p. 37
26. d, p. 48
27. c, p. 37
28. d, p. 42-43
29. d, p. 41-42
30. b, p. 38
31. c, p. 43-44
32. d, p. 37-38
33. d, p. 42-43
34. a, p. 27
35. a, p. 15
36. b, p. 38-39
37. c, p. 28-29
38. c, p. 30-31
39. b, p. 38-39
40. b, p. 39-40
41. a, p. 43
42. a, p. 38
43. d, p. 17-18

CHAPTER 2

Brain and Behavior

Chapter Overview

The brain and nervous system are made up of networks of neurons. Nerve impulses are basically electrical. Communication between neurons is chemical in that neurons release neurotransmitters, which affect other neurons. Rather than merely carrying messages, neuropeptides regulate the activity of neurons in the brain. Neural networks combine the input from other neurons to produce an outgoing message.

The brain changes because of experience (e.g., learning). In the latter case, new brain cells might appear.

The nervous system includes the central nervous system (CNS), consisting of the brain and spinal cord, and the peripheral nervous system (PNS). The PNS includes the somatic system and the autonomic system, with its sympathetic and parasympathetic branches.

If damaged, certain parts of the brain may be able to repair itself. New treatments, such as movement and drug therapy, may speed this process.

Conventional brain research relies on dissection, staining, ablation, deep lesioning, electrical recording, electrical stimulation, micro-electrode recording, EEG recording, and clinical studies. Newer methods such as PET scans and fMRI scans make use of computer-enhanced images of the brain and its activities.

The cerebral cortex of the brain is divided into two cerebral hemispheres connected by the corpus collosum. Each hemisphere has different specialized abilities and contains four lobes. The basic functions of the lobes are as follows: frontal lobes—motor control, speech, and abstract thought; parietal lobes—bodily sensation; temporal lobes—hearing and language; occipital lobes—vision; association areas of the cortex are related to complex abilities such as language, memory, and problem solving.

The brain is subdivided into the forebrain, midbrain, and hindbrain. The subcortex includes important brain structures at all three levels. These are: the medulla ("vegetative" functions), the pons (a bridge between higher and lower brain areas), the cerebellum (coordination, balance), the reticular formation (sensory and motor messages and arousal), the thalamus (sensory information), and the hypothalamus (basic motives). The thalamus and hypothalamus combine with the amygdala and hippocampus to form the limbic system; this is related to emotion and memory.

The endocrine system is the second type of chemical communication in humans. It is made up of glands that secrete hormones into the bloodstream to regulate internal and external behavior such as growth, sex, anxiety, and sleep.

Hand dominance ranges from strongly left- to strongly right-handed, with mixed handedness and ambidexterity in between. In general, the left-handed are less strongly lateralized in brain function than are right-handed persons.

Learning Objectives

1. List and describe the four parts of a neuron.

2. Explain how a nerve impulse (action potential) occurs and how it is an all-or-nothing event; include the terms *resting potential*, *threshold*, *ion channels*, and *negative after-potential*.

3. Discuss the function of myelin and its role in salutatory conduction. Discuss the importance of this process in everyday activities.

4. Describe how nerve impulses are carried from one neuron to another, , and include an explanation of receptor sites, types of neurotransmitters, neuropeptides, and neural networks.

5. Discuss how the brain is able to change in response to experience (learning).

6. Differentiate a nerve from a neuron and explain the role of the neurilemma.

7. Chart the various subparts of the human nervous system and explain their functions.

8. Describe the spinal cord and explain the mechanism of the reflex arc, including the types of neurons involved.

9. Describe the progress being made in repairing neurons in the central nervous system (CNS) and ways to prevent injury to the CNS. Explain what is meant by neurogenesis.

10. Define biopsychology; describe techniques used to map brain structures and brain functions. Discuss how these techniques have been used to detect and understand brain disorders, brain efficiency, and even behaviors, such as lying.

11. Describe the main differences between the brains of lower and higher animals and include a description of the cerebrum, cerebral cortex, gray matter, and corticalization.

12. Discuss hemispheric specialization, including the work of Roger Sperry, how and why the brain is "split" and the resulting effects, the functions of the right and left hemisphere, the function of the corpus collosum, and how a person would be affected by damage to each hemisphere (such as the condition known as "spatial neglect" and neurological "soft signs").

13. Describe the functions of each of the lobes of the brain and of the association areas, including Broca's and Wernicke's areas; explain the effects of damage to each of these brain regions, including the conditions of aphasia, agnosia, and facial agnosia.

14. Discuss the findings of the studies on the differences in brain structure and brain specialization in women and men.

15. List the three areas of the subcortex and explain the function of each of the following parts of the subcortex:

    a. the midbrain

    b. the hindbrain (brainstem), including:

        i. the medulla

        ii. the pons

        iii. the cerebellum

        iv. the reticular formation

    c. the forebrain, including:

        i. the thalamus

        ii. the hypothalamus

16. List the structures that comprise the limbic system and explain its overall function as well as the specific functions of the amygdala and the hippocampus; describe the significance of "pleasure" and "aversive" areas in the limbic system

17. Summarize the brain's basic functions and the latest brain research to aid paralyzed patients.

18. Explain the purpose of the endocrine system, the action of hormones, and the effects that the following glands have on the body and behavior:

    a. pituitary (include a description of giantism, dwarfism, and acromegaly)

    b. pineal (identify the role of melatonin)

    c. thyroid (include a description of hyperthyroidism and hypothyroidism)

    d. adrenal medulla

    e. adrenal cortex (include a description of virilism, premature puberty, and the problem of anabolic steroids)

19. Discuss brain dominance, lateralization, and handness, including their relationship to language processing

20. Identify how and when the dominant hemisphere is determined;

21. Discuss the incidence, advantages, and disadvantages of being right-or left-handed, or inconsistent in dominance.

RECITE AND REVIEW

Neurons—Building a "Biocomputer"

Survey Question: How do neurons operate and communicate? Pages 53-58

1. The _____ and nervous system are made up of linked nerve cells called _____, which pass information from one to another through synapses.

2. The basic conducting fibers of neurons are _____.

3. Dendrites (a receiving area), the soma (the cell body and also a receiving area), and _____ terminals (the branching ends of a neuron) enable communication between neurons.

4. The firing of an action potential (_____) is basically electrical, whereas communication between neurons is chemical.

5. An action potential occurs when the _____ potential is altered enough to reach the threshold for firing.

6. During an action potential, sodium _____ flow into the axon through _____ channels.

7. After each action potential, potassium ions flow out of the _____, restoring the resting potential.

8. The _____ potential is an all-or-nothing event.

9. A _____ after-potential occurs after each nerve impulse. In this state, the cell dips below its resting potential and is temporarily less able to fire.

10. _____ is a fatty substance that coats neurons.

11. Small gaps in the myelin of a neuron allow an action potential to "leap" from gap to gap in a process called _____ conduction.

12. _____ are chemical messages that alter the activity of neurons.

13. Neurotransmitters cross the synapse to _____ sites on the receiving cell.

14. Some transmitters send _____ signals to other neurons (make firing more likely); other transmitters send _____ signals (make firing less likely).

15. More than 100 _____ chemicals are found in the brain.

16. The transmitter chemical acetylcholine activates _____.

17. Disturbances of any neurotransmitters found in the brain can have serious consequences, such as too _____, which can cause muscle tremors of Parkinson's disease or too _____, which can cause schizophrenic symptoms.

18. Chemicals called neuropeptides do not carry messages directly. Instead, they _____ the activity of other neurons.

19. Opiate-like neural regulators called enkephalins and endorphins are released in the brain to relieve _____ and stress.

20. _____ may help explain how some women who suffer from severe premenstrual pain and distress have unusually low endorphin levels.

21. Neural networks _____ the messages from many neurons.

22. Learning creates _____ in your brain.

23. Because of _____, our brains may form new synapses or synaptic connections and may grow stronger in response to experience.

The Nervous System—Wired for Action

Survey Question: What are the major parts of the nervous system? Pages 58-61

1. The nervous system can be divided into the _____ nervous system (the _____ and spinal cord) and the peripheral nervous system.

2. _____ are tiny cells; _____ are bundles of large axons.

3. Nerves in the peripheral nervous system can often regenerate; damage in the central nervous system is usually _____, unless a repair is attempted by grafting or implanting healthy tissue.

4. _____ wraps around axons, and forms a "tunnel" so damaged fibers can repair themselves.

5. The peripheral nervous system includes the somatic nervous system (_____) and autonomic (_____) nervous system.

6. The autonomic system has two divisions: the sympathetic (_____, _____) branch and the parasympathetic (_____, _____) branch.

7. Thirty-one pairs of spinal _____ leave the spinal cord. Twelve pairs of cranial _____ leave the brain directly. Together, they carry sensory and motor messages between the brain and the body.

8. The simplest behavior is a reflex arc, which _____ arises within the spinal cord, without any help from the brain.

9. Reflexive movements may involve a sensory neuron, a connector neuron, and a _____ neuron.

10. Through _____, the brain grows new neurons to replace lost brain cells.

11. A stroke occurs when _____ to the brain is interrupted, causing brain tissue to die.

12. Some new treatments for brain damage include _____ therapy and drug therapy to speed neurogenesis.

Research Methods—Charting the Brain's Inner Realms

Survey Question: How is the brain studied? Pages 61-65

1. Biopsychology is the study of how _____ processes affect
   _____.

2. Conventional brain research relies on dissection, staining, ablation, deep
   lesioning, electrical recording, _____ stimulation, micro-electrode
   recording, EEG recording, and _____ studies.

3. Localization of function involves linking certain _____ with
   psychological or _____ capacities.

4. Clinical _____ are conducted to examine changes in personality,
   behavior, or sensory capacity following brain damage.

5. During electrical stimulation of the brain, an _____ is placed on the
   surface of the brain, and the patient describes the effects of the stimulation.

6. _____ and deep lesioning involve the _____ or destruction
   of brain tissue.

7. The electroencephalograph (EEG) records brain-wave _____ and
   reveals changes in brain activity during various mental states.

8. Computer-enhanced techniques are providing three-dimensional
   _____ of the living human brain and its _____. Examples of
   such techniques are CT scans, MRI scans, fMRI scans, and PET scans.

9. The _____ scan produces images of the brain by using X-rays, the
   _____ scan produces images of the brain by using a magnetic field,
   and the _____ scan produces images of the brain as well as the
   activities of the brain by detecting positrons emitted by a weak radioactive
   glucose in the brain.

10. Using a PET scan, Haier and colleagues found that intelligence is related to
    _____; a less efficient brain works much harder than a more efficient
    brain.

11. _____ (fMRI) images can be used to tell if someone is lying.

The Cerebral Cortex—My, What a Big Brain You Have!

Survey Question: Why is the human cerebral cortex so important and what are its
parts? Pages 65-73

1. The human _____ is marked by advanced corticalization, or
   enlargement of the cerebral _____, which covers the outside surface
   of the cerebrum.

2. The cortex has two sides, called cerebral hemispheres; these are connected
   by the _____.

3. "Split brains" have been created by _____ the corpus callosum. The split-brain individual shows a remarkable degree of independence between the right and left _____.

4. Roger _____ won a Nobel Prize for his discovery that the left and right cerebral hemispheres have different functions.

5. In _____, damage to the right side of the brain may cause someone to ignore the left side of their visual space.

6. The _____ cerebral hemisphere contains speech or language "centers" in most people. It also specializes in _____, calculating, judging time and rhythm, and ordering complex movements.

7. The _____ hemisphere is largely nonverbal. It excels at spatial and perceptual skills, visualization, and recognition of _____, faces, and melodies.

8. Another way to summarize specialization in the brain is to say that the _____ hemisphere is good at analysis and processing information sequentially; the _____ hemisphere processes information simultaneously and holistically.

9. The most basic functions of the lobes of the cerebral cortex are as follows: occipital lobes—_____; parietal lobes—bodily sensation; temporal lobes— _____ and language; frontal lobes—motor control, speech, and abstract thought.

10. The amount of area a body part has in the primary motor cortex is determined by the _____ of the body part, not its actual size.

11. Association areas on the cortex are neither _____ nor _____ in function. They combine information from the senses and they are related to more _____ skills such as language, memory, recognition, and problem solving.

12. Damage to either Broca's area or Wernicke's area causes _____ and language problems known as aphasias.

13. Touch, temperature, and pressure are registered by the primary _____ cortex.

14. The amount of area a body part has in the primary somatosensory cortex is determined by the _____ of the body part, not its actual size.

15. Damage to Broca's area causes problems with _____ and pronunciation; Damage to Wernicke's area causes problems with the _____ of words.

16. A PET scan of your brain while you listened to your MP3 would result in activity in the primary _____ area.

17. Damage in other association areas may cause agnosia, the inability to _____ objects by sight.

18. Facial Agnosia is the inability to perceive _____ faces.

19. Research has shown brain _____ in males and females particularly involving the concentration of gray and white _____ of the brain.

The Subcortex—At the Core of the (Brain) Matter

Survey Question: What are the major parts of the subcortex? Pages 73-76

1. All of the brain areas below the _____ are called the subcortex.

2. The hindbrain contains the medulla, _____, cerebellum, reticular formation, and reticular _____ system.

3. The medulla contains centers essential for reflex control of _____, breathing, and other "vegetative" functions.

4. The pons connects the medulla with _____ brain areas, and it influences _____ and arousal.

5. The cerebellum maintains _____, posture, and muscle tone.

6. The _____ lies inside the medulla and the brainstem, influences _____, and does not mature until _____.

7. The reticular activating system (RAS), acts as an _____ system for the cerebral cortex.

8. The thalamus carries _____ information to the cortex.

9. The hypothalamus exerts powerful control over eating, drinking, sleep cycles, body temperature, and other basic _____ and behaviors.

10. The limbic system is strongly related to _____ and motivated behavior. It also contains distinct reward and punishment areas.

11. A part of the limbic system called the amygdala is related to _____.

12. An area known as the hippocampus is important for forming lasting _____.

The Endocrine System—My Hormones Made Me Do It

Survey Question: Does the glandular system affect behavior? Pages 76-79

1. The endocrine system provides _____ communication in the body through the release of _____ into the bloodstream. Endocrine glands influence moods, behavior, and even personality.

2. Many of the endocrine glands are influenced by the pituitary (the "_____ gland"), which is in turn influenced by the hypothalamus.

3. The pituitary supplies _____ hormone. Too little GH causes hypopituitary _____; too much causes giantism or acromegaly.

4. Body rhythms and _____ cycles are influenced by melatonin, secreted by the pineal gland.

5. The thyroid gland regulates _____. Hyperthyroidism refers to an overactive thyroid gland; hypothyroidism to an underactive thyroid.

6. The adrenal glands supply _____ and norepinephrine to activate the body.

7. The adrenal cortex produces _____; these hormones regulate salt balance, and responses to stress. They are also a secondary source of _____ hormones.

8. An _____ of adrenal sex hormones cause exaggerated male characteristics, known as virilism.

9. Dangerous increases in hostility and aggression have been linked to _____ use.

10. Most drugs like anabolic steroids are synthetic versions of _____.

Psychology in Action: Are You Sinister or Dexterous?

Survey Question: In what ways do right- and left-handed individuals differ? Page 79-83

1. Hand dominance ranges from strongly left- to strongly right-handed, with _____ handedness and ambidexterity in between.

2. Ninety percent of the population is basically _____, 10 percent _____.

3. The vast majority of people are right-handed and therefore _____ brain dominant for motor skills. Ninety-seven percent of right-handed persons and 68 percent of left-handed persons also produce _____ from the left hemisphere.

4. _____ people in the past were forced to _____ as right-handed people; therefore, there are fewer left-handed older people living than right-handed older people.

5. _____ is often measured by assessing hand, foot, eye, and ear preference.

6. Hand preferences are apparent _____ birth.

7. Lateralization refers to _____ in the abilities of the brain hemispheres.

8. In general, the _____ are less strongly lateralized in brain function than are _____ persons.

CONNECTIONS

Neurons—Building a "Biocomputer"

Survey Question: How do neurons operate and communicate? Pages 53-58

1. _____ soma
2. _____ neurilemma
3. _____ axon collateral
4. _____ myelin
5. _____ dendrites
6. _____ axon terminals
7. _____ axon

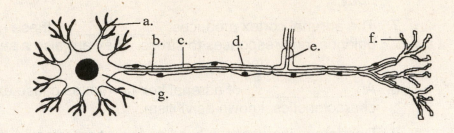

The Nervous System—Wired for Action

Survey Question: What are the major parts of the nervous system? Pages 58-61

1. _____ spinal cord
2. _____ autonomic system
3. _____ parasympathetic branch
4. _____ peripheral nervous system
5. _____ sympathetic branch
6. _____ brain
7. _____ somatic system

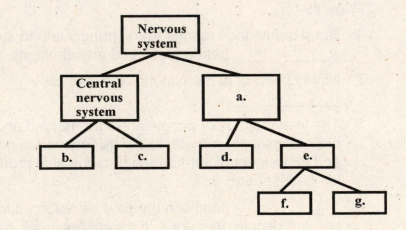

Research Methods—Charting the Brain's Inner Realms

Survey Question: How is the brain studied? Pages 61-65

1. _____ CT scan
2. _____ EEG
3. _____ deep lesioning
4. _____ PET scan
5. _____ ablation

A. brain waves
B. radioactive glucose
C. surgery
D. electrode
E. computerized X-rays

The Cerebral Cortex—My, What a Big Brain You Have!

Survey Question: Why is the human cerebral cortex so important, and what are its parts? Pages 65-73

1. _____ Wernicke's area
2. _____ temporal lobe
3. _____ cerebellum
4. _____ Broca's area
5. _____ parietal lobe
6. _____ frontal lobe
7. _____ occipital lobe

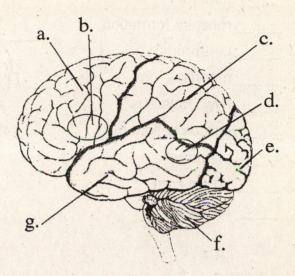

1. _____ Wernicke's Area
2. _____ Left hemisphere
3. _____ Broca's area
4. _____ Corpus collosum
5. _____ facial agnosia
6. _____ aphasia
7. _____ Right hemisphere
8. _____ motor cortex
9. _____ somatosensory area
10. _____ Spatial neglect
11. _____ Corticalization

A. language impairment
B. language production
C. language comprehension
D. receives bodily sensations
E. controls voluntary movements
F. impaired facial recognition
G. increase in size or wrinkling
H. communication between hemispheres
I. inattention to one side
J. overall patterns and general connections
K. Focus on small details

The Subcortex—At the Core of the (Brain) Matter

Survey Question: What are the major parts of the subcortex? Pages 73-76

1. _____ midbrain
2. _____ reticular formation
3. _____ cerebrum
4. _____ medulla
5. _____ hypothalamus
6. _____ corpus callosum
7. _____ pituitary
8. _____ spinal cord
9. _____ thalamus

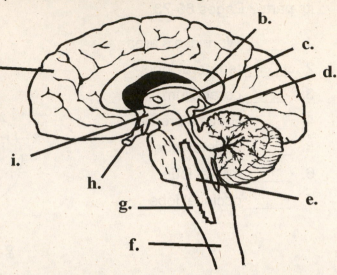

a. _____ Reticular Formation
b. _____ Medulla
c. _____ Limbic System
d. _____ Hypothalamus
e. _____ Amygdala
f. _____ Cerebellum
g. _____ Hippocampus
h. _____ Thalamus
i. _____ Pons

A. "vegetative" functions
B. sensory relay station
C. "crossroads"
D. "bridge" between medulla and other brain areas
E. Regulates muscle tone and coordination
F. Influences attention
G. Primitive "quick pathway" to cortex
H. Lasting memories
I. Pleasure and punishment pathways

The Endocrine System—My Hormones Made Me Do It

Survey Question: Does the glandular system affect behavior? Pages 76-79

1. _____ hypopituitary dwarfism   A. testosterone
2. _____ pituitary   B. metabolism
3. _____ anabolic steroids   C. growth hormone
4. _____ testes   D. epinephrine
5. _____ pineal gland   E. melatonin
6. _____ thyroid gland   F. synthetic of testosterone
7. _____ acromegaly   G. too much growth hormone
8. _____ adrenal glands   H. too little growth hormone

CHECK YOUR MEMORY

Neurons—Building a "Biocomputer"

Survey Question: How do neurons operate and communicate? Pages 53-58

1. The dendrites receive incoming information from the neurilemma.

   TRUE or FALSE

2. Human axons may be up to a meter long.

   TRUE or FALSE

3. Neural activity is instantaneous.

   TRUE or FALSE

4. The resting potential is about plus 70 millivolts.

   TRUE or FALSE

5. The interior of the axon becomes positive during an action potential.

   TRUE or FALSE

6. The action potential is an all-or-nothing event.

   TRUE or FALSE

7. The negative after-potential is due to an inward flow of potassium ions.

   TRUE or FALSE

8. Nerve impulses travel faster in axons surrounded by myelin.

   TRUE or FALSE

9. Small gaps in myelin create "drag" and slow the speed of the neural impulse.

    TRUE or FALSE

10. The resting potential is caused by an inward flow of potassium ions.

    TRUE or FALSE

11. Negative after-potential is a period where the cell is less willing to fire.

    TRUE or FALSE

12. There are approximately 50 different neurotransmitters.

    TRUE or FALSE

13. Neurotransmitters activate other neurons; neuropeptides activate muscles and glands.

    TRUE or FALSE

14. Enkephalins are neuropeptides.

    TRUE or FALSE

15. Neuropeptides regulate the activity of other neurons.

    TRUE or FALSE

16. Many drugs imitate, duplicate, or block neurotransmitters to excite or inhibit an action potential.

    TRUE or FALSE

17. Neural networks react based on the sum of excitatory and inhibitory signals.

    TRUE or FALSE

18. Learning results in the birth of new neurons.

    TRUE or FALSE

The Nervous System—Wired for Action

Survey Question: What are the major parts of the nervous system? Pages 58-61

1. Nerves are large bundles of neuron axons.

    TRUE or FALSE

2. The neurilemma helps damaged nerve cell fibers regenerate after an injury.

    TRUE or FALSE

3. Neurons in the brain and spinal cord must last a lifetime; damage to them is usually permanent.

    TRUE or FALSE

4. The word autonomic means "self-limiting."

    TRUE or FALSE

5. The parasympathetic branch quiets the body and returns it to a lower level of arousal.

    TRUE or FALSE

6. The sympathetic system generally controls voluntary behavior.

    TRUE or FALSE

7. Thirty-one cranial nerves leave the brain directly.

    TRUE or FALSE

8. "Fight-or-flight" emergency reactions are produced by the autonomic nervous system.

    TRUE or FALSE

9. Activity in the parasympathetic system increases heart rate and respiration.

    TRUE or FALSE

10. In a reflex arc, motor neurons carry messages to effector cells.

    TRUE or FALSE

11. A stroke occurs when a neuron in the spinal cord ruptures, interrupting messages to and from the brain.

    TRUE or FALSE

12. Constraint-induced movement therapy has been used to speed neurogenesis.

    TRUE or FALSE

13. Slurred speech is a "soft sign" of possible brain damage.

    TRUE or FALSE

Research Methods—Charting the Brain's Inner Realms

Survey Question: How is the brain studied? Pages 61-65

1. Dissection reveals that the brain is made up of many anatomically distinct parts.

    TRUE or FALSE

2. Ablation and deep lesioning involve the destruction of brain tissue or structures.

    TRUE or FALSE

3. An MRI can form a three-dimensional model of the brain.

    TRUE or FALSE

4. Micro-electrodes are needed in order to record from single neurons.

    TRUE or FALSE

5. CT scans form "maps" of brain activity.

   TRUE or FALSE

6. Electroencephalography records waves of electrical activity produced by the brain.

   TRUE or FALSE

7. Radioactive glucose is used to make PET scans.

   TRUE or FALSE

8. According to computerized scans, people only use 10% of their brain capacity at any one time.

   TRUE or FALSE

9. FMRI can be used to tell if a person is lying.

   TRUE or FALSE

The Cerebral Cortex—My, What a Big Brain You Have!

Survey Question: Why is the human cerebral cortex so important, and what are its parts? Pages 65-73

1. Elephants have brain-body ratios similar to those of humans.

   TRUE or FALSE

2. The fact that humans are more intelligent than other animals is related to lateralization.

   TRUE or FALSE

3. Much of the cerebral cortex is made up of gray matter.

   TRUE or FALSE

4. The corpus callosum connects the right and left brain hemispheres.

   TRUE or FALSE

5. Spatial neglect occurs when a person ignores one side of his or her visual space.

   TRUE or FALSE

6. Damage to the left cerebral hemisphere usually causes spatial neglect.

   TRUE or FALSE

7. In general, smart brains tend to be the hardest working brains.

   TRUE or FALSE

8. The right half of the brain mainly controls left body areas.

   TRUE or FALSE

9. Roger Sperry won a Nobel Prize for his work on corticalization.

TRUE or FALSE

10. According to Richard Haier, a less efficient brain works harder and still accomplishes less than a more efficient brain because a less efficient brain uses less glucose to process information.

TRUE or FALSE

11. Cutting the reticular formation produces a "split brain."

TRUE or FALSE

12. Information from the right side of vision is sent directly to the right cerebral hemisphere.

TRUE or FALSE

13. The right hemisphere tends to be good at speaking, writing, and math.

TRUE or FALSE

14. The left hemisphere is mainly involved with analysis.

TRUE or FALSE

15. The right hemisphere sees overall patterns and general connections. The left brain focuses on small details.

TRUE or FALSE

16. Both brain hemispheres are normally active at all times.

TRUE or FALSE

17. The motor cortex is found on the occipital lobes.

TRUE or FALSE

18. The somatosensory area is located on the parietal lobes.

TRUE or FALSE

19. Electrically stimulating the motor cortex causes movement in various parts of the body.

TRUE or FALSE

20. Large parts of the lobes of the brain are made up of association cortex.

TRUE or FALSE

21. Damage to either brain hemisphere usually causes an aphasia.

TRUE or FALSE

22. People experiencing facial agnosia can recognize a family member's voice.

TRUE or FALSE

23. A person with Broca's aphasia might say "pear" when shown an apple.

    TRUE or FALSE

24. Patients with tumors in the primary visual cortex may experience blind spots in their vision.

    TRUE or FALSE

25. Research has shown women have more white matter and men have more grey matter in their brains.

    TRUE or FALSE

The Subcortex—At the Core of the (Brain) Matter

Survey Question: What are the major parts of the subcortex? Pages 73-76

1. The cerebrum makes up much of the medulla.

    TRUE or FALSE

2. Injury to the medulla may affect breathing.

    TRUE or FALSE

3. Damage to the pons may affect sleep and arousal.

    TRUE or FALSE

4. Injury to the cerebellum affects attention and wakefulness.

    TRUE or FALSE

5. The reticular formation is the switching station for sensory messages and is fully developed at birth.

    TRUE or FALSE

6. Smell is the only major sense that does not pass through the thalamus.

    TRUE or FALSE

7. Stimulating various parts of the limbic system can produce rage, fear, pleasure, or arousal.

    TRUE or FALSE

8. The hippocampus is associated with hunger and eating.

    TRUE or FALSE

The Endocrine System—My Hormones Made Me Do It

Survey Question: Does the glandular system affect behavior? Pages 76-79

1. Androgens ("male" hormones) are related to the sex drive in both men and women.

    TRUE or FALSE

2. "Normal short" children grow faster when given synthetic growth hormone, but their final height is short of average.

    TRUE or FALSE

3. Activity of the pituitary is influenced by the hypothalamus.

    TRUE or FALSE

4. A person who is slow, sleepy, and overweight could be suffering from hypothyroidism.

    TRUE or FALSE

5. Excessively salt cravings may have an imbalance in epinephrine and norepinephrine levels.

    TRUE or FALSE

6. Virilism and premature puberty may be caused by problems with the adrenal glands.

    TRUE or FALSE

7. Steroid drugs may cause sexual impotence and breast enlargement in males.

    TRUE or FALSE

8. There is much evidence to support that steroids do improve performance, which is why all major sports organizations ban the use of steroids.

    TRUE or FALSE

9. Something as simple as watching a movie can alter hormone levels.

    TRUE or FALSE

Psychology in Action: Handedness—Are You Sinister or Dexterous?

Survey Question: In what ways do right- and left-handed individuals differ? Page 79-83

1. Left-handers have an advantage in fencing, boxing, and baseball.

    TRUE or FALSE

2. Most left-handed persons produce speech from their right hemispheres.

    TRUE or FALSE

3. A child's handedness is determined before birth.

   TRUE or FALSE

4. To a degree, left or right handedness is influenced by heredity, especially by a gene on the X chromosome.

   TRUE or FALSE

5. Since most appliances are designed for right-handed people, forcing a left-handed child to use his or her right hand should be encouraged.

   TRUE or FALSE

6. On average, left-handed persons die at younger ages than right-handed persons do.

   TRUE or FALSE

7. Left-handed individuals may recover more easily from a brain injury than right-handed individuals.

   TRUE or FALSE

FINAL SURVEY AND REVIEW

Neurons—Building a "Biocomputer"

Survey Question: How do neurons operate and communicate? Pages 53-58

1. The _____ and _____ are made up of linked nerve cells called neurons, which pass information from one to another through _____.

2. The basic _____ of neurons are axons.

3. _____ (a receiving area), the _____ (the cell body and also a receiving area), and axon terminals (the branching ends of a neuron) enable communication between neurons.

4. The firing of an action potential (nerve impulse) is basically _____, whereas communication between neurons is _____.

5. An action potential occurs when the resting potential is altered enough to reach the _____ for firing.

6. During an action potential, _____ ions flow _____ the axon through ion channels.

7. After each action potential, _____ ions flow _____ of the axon, restoring the resting potential.

8. The action potential is an _____ event.

9. A negative after-potential occurs after each nerve impulse. In this state, the cell dips _____ its resting potential and is temporarily _____ to fire.

10. Myelin is a _____ that coats neurons.

11. Small _____ in the myelin of a neuron allow an action potential to _____ from gap to gap in a process called salutatory conduction.

12. Neurotransmitters are _____ that alter the activity of neurons.

13. Neurotransmitters cross the _____ to receptor sites on the receiving cell.

14. Some transmitters send excitatory signals to other neurons (make firing _____ likely); other transmitters send inhibitory signals (make firing _____ likely).

15. More than _____ transmitter chemicals are found in the brain.

16. The transmitter chemical _____ activates muscles.

17. Disturbances of any neurotransmitters found in the brain can have serious consequences, such as too little dopamine, which can cause muscle tremors of _____ or too much dopamine, which can cause _____ symptoms.

18. Chemicals called _____ do not carry messages directly. Instead, they regulate the activity of other _____.

19. Opiate-like neural regulators called _____ and _____ are released in the brain to relieve pain and stress.

20. Neural regulators may help explain how some women who suffer from severe premenstrual pain and distress have unusually low _____ levels.

21. _____ combine the messages from many neurons.

22. _____ creates changes in your brain.

23. Because of neuroplasticity, our brains may form _____ or synaptic _____ and may grow _____ in response to experience.

The Nervous System—Wired for Action

Survey Question: What are the major parts of the nervous system? Pages 58-61

1. The nervous system can be divided into the _____ nervous system (the brain and spinal cord) and the _____ nervous system.

2. Neurons are tiny _____; nerves are bundles of large _____.

3. Nerves in the _____ nervous system can often _____; damage in the _____ nervous system is usually permanent, unless a repair is attempted by grafting or implanting healthy tissue.

4. Neurilemma wraps around _____, and forms a "tunnel" so damaged fibers can repair themselves.

5. The peripheral nervous system includes the _____ nervous system (voluntary) and _____ (involuntary) nervous system.

6. The autonomic system has two divisions: the _____ (emergency, activating) branch and the _____ (sustaining, conserving) branch.

7. _____ pairs of spinal nerves leave the spinal cord. _____ pairs of cranial nerves leave the brain directly. Together, they carry _____ and _____ messages between the brain and the body.

8. The simplest behavior is a _____, which automatically arises within the spinal cord, without any help from the brain.

9. Reflexive _____ may involve a _____ neuron, a _____ neuron, and a motor neuron.

10. Through neurogenesis, the brain grows _____ neurons to replace _____ brain cells.

11. A stroke occurs when blood flow to the _____ is _____, causing brain tissue to die.

12. Some new treatments for brain damage include constraint-induced movement therapy and drug therapy to speed _____.

Research Methods—Charting the Brain's Inner Realms

Survey Question: How is the brain studied? Pages 61-65

1. _____ is the study of how biological processes affect behavior.

2. Conventional brain research relies on _____, staining, ablation, _____, electrical recording, electrical stimulation, micro-electrode recording, _____ recording, and clinical studies.

3. _____ involves linking certain brain structures with psychological or behavioral capacities.

4. Clinical case studies are conducted to examine changes in _____, _____, or sensory capacity following brain damage.

5. During _____ stimulation of the brain, an electrode is placed on the _____ of the brain, and the patient describes the effects of the stimulation.

6. Ablation and _____ involve the removal or _____ of brain tissue.

7. The _____ records brain-wave patterns and reveals changes in brain activity during various mental states.

8. _____-enhanced techniques are providing _____ images of the living human brain and its activity. Examples of such techniques are CT scans, MRI scans, fMRI scans, and PET scans.

9. The CT scan produces images of the brain by using _____, the MRI scan produces images of the brain by using a _____, and the PET scan produces images of the brain as well as the activities of the brain by detecting _____ emitted by a weak _____ glucose in the brain.

10. Using a PET scan, Haier and colleagues found that intelligence is related to brain efficiency; a _____ efficient brain works much harder than a _____ efficient brain.

11. Functional MRI (fMRI) images can be used to tell if someone is _____.

The Cerebral Cortex—My, What a Big Brain You Have!

Survey Question: Why is the human cerebral cortex so important and what are its parts? Pages 65-73

1. The human brain is marked by advanced _____, or enlargement of the cerebral cortex, which covers the outside surface of the cerebrum.

2. The cortex has two sides, called _____; these are connected by the corpus callosum.

3. _____ have been created by cutting the _____. The split-brain individual shows a remarkable degree of independence between the _____ and _____ hemispheres.

4. Roger Sperry won a _____ for his discovery that the left and right cerebral hemispheres have different _____.

5. In spatial neglect, damage to the _____ side of the brain may cause someone to ignore the _____ side of their visual space.

6. The left cerebral hemisphere contains _____ "centers" in most people. It also specializes in writing, _____, judging _____ and rhythm, and ordering _____ movements.

7. The right hemisphere is largely _____. It excels at _____ and _____ skills, visualization, and recognition of patterns, faces, and _____.

8. Another way to summarize specialization in the brain is to say that the left hemisphere is good at analysis and processing information _____; the right hemisphere processes information _____ and holistically.

9. The most basic functions of the lobes of the cerebral cortex are as follows: _____ lobes—vision; _____ lobes—bodily sensation; _____ lobes— hearing and language; frontal lobes—motor control, speech, and _____ thought.

10. The amount of area a body part has in the _____ cortex is determined by the dexterity of the body part, not its actual size.

11. _____ areas on the cortex are neither sensory nor motor in function. They _____ information from the senses and they are related to more complex skills such as _____, memory, recognition, and _____.

12. Damage to either _____ area or _____ area causes speech and language problems known as aphasias.

13. _____, temperature, and _____ are registered by the primary somatosensory cortex.

14. The amount of area a body part has in the primary _____ cortex is determined by the sensitivity of the body part, not its _____ size.

15. Damage to Broca's area causes problems with _____ and pronunciation; damage to Wernicke's area causes problems with the _____ of words.

16. A PET scan of your brain while you _____ to your _____ would result in activity in the primary auditory area.

17. Damage in other association areas may cause _____, the inability to identify objects by sight.

18. _____ Agnosia is the inability to perceive familiar faces.

19. Research has shown brain specialization in males and females particularly involving the concentration of _____ and _____ matter of the brain.

The Subcortex—At the Core of the (Brain) Matter

Survey Question: What are the major parts of the subcortex? Pages 73-76

1. All of the brain areas below the cortex are called the _____.

2. The _____ contains the medulla, _____, cerebellum, _____, and reticular activating system.

3. The _____ contains centers essential for reflex control of heart rate, breathing, and other "_____" functions.

4. The _____ connects the medulla with higher brain areas, and it influences sleep and _____.

5. The cerebellum maintains coordination, _____, and _____.

6. The reticular formation lies inside the _____ and the _____, influences attention, and does not mature until adolescence.

7. The reticular activating system (RAS), acts as an activating system for the _____ cortex.

8. The _____ carries sensory information to the cortex.

9. The _____ exerts powerful control over eating, drinking, sleep cycles, body temperature, and other basic motives and behaviors.

10. The _____ system is strongly related to emotion and motivated behavior. It also contains distinct _____ and _____ areas.

11. A part of the limbic system called the _____ is related to fear.

12. An area known as the _____ is important for forming lasting memories.

The Endocrine System—Hormones and Behavior

Survey Question: Does the glandular system affect behavior? Pages 76-79

1. The _____ system provides chemical communication in the body through the release of hormones into the bloodstream. Endocrine glands influence _____, behavior, and even _____.

2. Many of the endocrine glands are influenced by the _____ (the "master gland"), which is in turn influenced by the _____.

3. The pituitary supplies growth hormone. _____ GH causes hypopituitary dwarfism; _____ causes giantism or acromegaly.

4. Body rhythms and sleep cycles are influenced by _____, secreted by the _____ gland.

5. The thyroid gland regulates metabolism. _____ refers to an overactive thyroid gland; _____ to an underactive thyroid.

6. The adrenal glands supply epinephrine and _____ to activate the body.

7. The _____ cortex produces corticoids; these hormones regulate _____ balance, and responses to stress. They are also a _____ source of sex hormones.

8. An oversecretion of adrenal sex hormones cause _____ male characteristics, known as virilism.

9. Dangerous _____ in hostility and _____ have been linked to steroid use.

10. Most drugs like anabolic steroids are _____ versions of testosterone.

Psychology in Action: Are You Sinister or Dexterous?

Survey Question: In what ways do right- and left-handed individuals differ? Page 79-83

1. Hand _____ ranges from strongly left- to strongly right-handed, with mixed handedness and _____ in between.

2. _____ of the population is basically right-handed, _____ percent left-handed.

3. The vast majority of people are _____ and therefore left brain dominant for motor skills. Ninety-seven percent of right-handed persons and 68 percent of left-handed persons also produce speech from the _____ hemisphere.

4. Left-handed people in the past were forced to masquerade as _____ people; therefore, there are _____ left-handed older people living than right-handed older people.

5. Sidedness is often measured by assessing hand, foot, eye, and ear _____.

6. Hand _____ are apparent before birth.

7. _____ refers to specialization in the abilities of the brain hemispheres.

8. In general, the left-handed are _____ strongly lateralized in brain function than are right-handed persons.

MASTERY TEST

1. At times of emergency, anger, or fear, what part of the nervous system becomes more active?
a. corpus callosum of the forebrain
b. sympathetic branch of the ANS
c. parasympathetic branch of the PNS
d. Broca's area

2. The highest and largest brain area in humans is the
a. cerebrum.
b. cerebellum.
c. frontal lobes.
d. gray matter of the callosum.

3. A tumor in which brain area would most likely cause blind spots in vision?
a. occipital lobe
b. temporal lobe
c. somatosensory area
d. association cortex

4. Neurotransmitters are found primarily in
a. the spinal cord.
b. neurilemmas.
c. synapses.
d. motor neurons.

5. Enkephalins are an example of
a. acetylcholine blockers.
b. neuropeptides.
c. receptor sites.
d. adrenal hormones.

6. Electrically stimulating a portion of which brain area would produce movements in the body?
a. occipital lobe
b. frontal lobe
c. parietal lobe
d. temporal lobe

7. When a neuron reaches its threshold, a/an _____ occurs.
a. volume potential
b. ion potential
c. action potential
d. dendrite potential

8. A person's ability to work as a commercial artist would be most impaired by damage to the
a. left temporal lobe.
b. right cerebral hemisphere.
c. left cerebral hemisphere.
d. frontal association cortex.

9. Electrically stimulating the brain would most likely produce anger if it activated the
a. association cortex.
b. limbic system.
c. parasympathetic branch.
d. reticular activating system.

10. Information in neurons usually flows in what order?
a. soma, dendrites, axon
b. dendrites, soma, axon
c. dendrites, myelin, axon terminals
d. axon, soma, axon terminals

11. Regulating the activity of other neurons is most characteristic of
a. neuropeptides.
b. acetylcholine.
c. reflex arcs.
d. resting potentials.

12. Nerve impulses occur when _____ rush into the axon.
a. sodium ions
b. potassium ions
c. negative charges
d. neurotransmitters

13. Attempts to repair brain injuries by injecting immature neurons into the
    damaged area make use of the recently discovered existence of
a. myelin.
b. neurogenesis.
c. neuropeptides.
d. corticalization.

14. Negative after-potentials are caused by the outward flow of
    _____ from the axon.
a. negative charges
b. potassium ions
c. neurotransmitters
d. sodium ions

15. A person who says "bife" for bike and "seep" for sleep probably suffers from
a. Broca's aphasia.
b. Wernicke's aphasia.
c. functional agnosia.
d. the condition known as "mindblindness".

16. Damage to which part of the limbic system would most likely impair memory?
a. the thalamus
b. the hypothalamus
c. the amygdala
d. the hippocampus

17. Involuntary changes in heart rate, blood pressure, digestion, and sweating are
    controlled by the
a. thoracic nerves.
b. parietal lobes.
c. somatic system.
d. autonomic system.

18. In which of the following pairs are both structures part of the forebrain?
a. medulla, hypothalamus
b. cerebrum, cerebellum
c. medulla, thalamus
d. cerebrum, thalamus

19. Which of the following is a specialized type of X-ray?
a. PET scan
b. CT scan
c. MRI scan
d. EEG scan

20. Which two problems are associated with the pituitary gland?
a. dwarfism, acromegaly
b. virilism, acromegaly
c. mental retardation, dwarfism
d. giantism, premature puberty

21. The cerebral hemispheres are interconnected by the
a. reticular system.
b. cerebellum.
c. cerebrum.
d. corpus callosum.

22. Damage to which of the following would most likely make it difficult for a person to play catch with a ball?
a. reticular formation
b. limbic system
c. cerebellum
d. association cortex

23. Speech, language, calculation, and analysis are special skills of the
a. right cerebral hemisphere.
b. limbic system.
c. left cerebral hemisphere.
d. right somatosensory area.

24. The usual flow of information in a reflex arc is
a. cranial nerve, connector neuron, spinal nerve
b. sensory neuron, connector neuron, motor neuron
c. effector cell, interneuron, connector neuron
d. sensory neuron, connector neuron, reflex neuron

25. A person will "hear" a series of sounds when which area of the cortex is electrically stimulated?
a. frontal lobe
b. parietal lobe
c. occipital lobe
d. temporal lobe

26. Which of the following pairs contains the "master gland" and its master?
a. pineal—thalamus
b. thyroid—RAS
c. pituitary—hypothalamus
d. adrenal—cortex

27. Many basic motives and emotions are influenced by the
a. thalamus.
b. hypothalamus.
c. corpus callosum.
d. cerebellum.

28. Both surgical ablation and _____ remove brain tissue.
   a. the MEG technique
   b. tomography
   c. micro-electrode sampling
   d. deep lesioning

29. Which of the following techniques requires access to the interior of the brain?
   a. micro-electrode recording
   b. EEG recordings
   c. PET scanning
   d. functional MRI

30. Which of the following statements about handedness is false?
   a. Like eye color, handedness is inherited from one's parents.
   b. A majority of left-handers produce speech from the left hemisphere.
   c. The left-handed are less lateralized than the right-handed.
   d. Left-handedness is an advantage in boxing and fencing.

31. Scott was challenged to catch a dollar bill as fast as he could with his thumb
   and index finger as it fell between them. Scott was successful one time out of
   five trials. Which statement best explains why Scott failed to catch the dollar
   bill?
   a. Scott's injury to the temporal lobe has caused him to not see when the dollar
      bill falls.
   b. This simple yet common test signifies that Scott has serious cognitive deficits
      and must seek a specialist immediately.
   c. From the time Scott processes the information to when his brain tells the
      muscles to grab the dollar bill, the dollar bill has already slipped by.
   d. none of the above

32. People with Parkinson's disease lack or have very little of the
   neurotransmitter _____.
   a. endorphins
   b. epinephrine
   c. serotonin
   d. dopamine

33. Which statement correctly reflects the findings of Haier and his colleagues on
   the relationship between intelligence and brain efficiency?
   a. A less efficient brain works much harder than a more efficient brain.
   b. A more efficient brain works much harder than a less efficient brain.
   c. A less efficient brain uses less glucose when processing information.
   d. A more efficient brain uses more glucose when processing information.

34. Jacob suspects he has had a stroke because he has difficulty controlling his right hand. This behavioral evidence of possible brain damage is called a
a. soft sign.
b. spatial neglect.
c. neurogenesis.
d. virilism.

35. Annette cannot recognize friends by sight, but can tell who they are when they speak to her. This best represents
a. spatial neglect.
b. acromegaly.
c. aphasia.
d. facial agnosia.

36. In the hopes of increasing his athleticism, Jim has begun taking a steroid. This drug may cause
a. shrinking testicles.
b. increased hostility.
c. breast enlargement.
d. all of the above

LANGUAGE DEVELOPMENT

Brain and Behavior

Word Roots

Soma is the Greek word for "body." Several words in the fields of psychology and biology are derived from this Greek word. These words all refer to either the body of a smaller unit like a cell or to the whole physical body in general. Examples: soma, somatic, somesthetic, psychosomatic, somatoform, and somatization. All of these words will appear in the chapters in your textbook.

Journey into Psychology: Finding Music in Walnut-Grapefruit Tofu (p. 52)

(52) *tofu:* soybean curd, often eaten as an alternative to meat
(52) *flamenco*: a vigorous rhythmic dance style characterized by intricate passages and rapid, audible footwork
(52) *in the zone*: peaking in performance in a particular athletic skill
(52) *blob*: a small lump of thick consistency
(52) *exquisite*: beautiful; elaborate
(52) *realm*: area of interest

Neurons—Building a "Biocomputer" (pgs. 53-58)

How do neurons operate and communicate?

(53) *riff*: a repeated phrase of music, usually supporting a solo improvisation

(53) *wired*: refers to how the nervous system is put together and how it works

(53) *sweeps down the axon*: moves very fast down the axon

(55) *zips along*: moves along at a fast speed

(55) *dominoes*: flat, rectangular blocks used as pieces in a game of the same name

(55) *wave of activity*: the advance of a signal

(56) *bullring*: an arena used for fighting bulls

(56) *sensitive*: highly responsive to certain neurotransmitters

(57) *disabling*: to be too painful for functioning

(57) *"runner's high"*: state of intense pleasure often experienced by those who engage in sustained exercise.

(57) *masochism*: the enjoyment of or preference for pain

(57) *acupuncture:* Chinese medical practice in which long needles are inserted into specific sites on the body

(57) *euphoria*: state of intense pleasure or happiness

The Nervous System—Wired for Action (pgs. 58-61)

What are the major parts of the nervous system?

(58) *wired for action*: set up and ready to go

(58) *playing catch with a football:* a game in which a football is thrown back and forth between people

(58) *ablaze with activity*: extremely active

(58) *"wiring diagram"*: diagram illustrating where electrical wires would be placed

(59) *dilate*: to open; widen

(59) *a flash of anger*: a sudden, quick burst of anger

(59) *fight or flight*: a point at which a person or other animal decides to face danger or flee from it

(60) *grandstand catches:* in baseball, to catch the ball so as to impress the fans

(60) *coax*: to persuade gently

(60) *nerve grafts*: to connect or replace nerve tissue

Research Methods—Charting the Brain's Inner Realms (pgs. 61-65)

How is the brain studied?

(62) *euphoria*: a sense of well being; feeling happy and good all over

(62) *sci-fi movies:* science fiction movies

(63) *atlas*: map of the brain

(63) *hypnosis:* an altered state of consciousness in which a person responds easily to suggestions (see Chapter 5)

(64) *until even brighter beacons are flashed into the shadowy inner world of thought:* until newer and better techniques reveal more about the little-understood world of thought

The Cerebral Cortex—My, What a Big Brain You Have! (pgs. 65-73)

Why is the human cerebral cortex so important and what are its parts??

(67) *alien:* foreign; belonging elsewhere

(67) *gallantly:* heroically

(67) *overrides:* takes control over

(67) *right hand not knowing what the left hand is doing*!: a confused state where a person or a group seems to hold two view points at once, and both sides are unaware of the other

(68) *coherent:* the pieces are in an organized and logical manner

(68) *wide-angle view:* an analogy to photography; the big picture; a broad, encompassing view

(68) *zooms in on:* an analogy to photography; gets closer to a small portion of the picture

(69) *twitch:* move with a sudden motion

(69) *labored:* with difficulty

(70) *stuck on mental tasks:* unable to solve problems using thinking

(69) *distorted:* twisted and bent out of its original shape

(71) *MP3 tune:* music in a specific digital format

(70) *your temporal lobes would light up:* your temporal lobes would be activated

(71) *biocomputer:* combination of biology and computing, in this case the brain

The Subcortex—At the Core of the (Brain) Matter (pgs. 73-76)

What are the major parts of the subcortex?

(74) *karate chop:* hitting with the side of the hand

(74) *vigilant:* being alert and on the lookout for trouble

(74) *bombards:* to send without stopping

(74) *switching station:* place where railroad cars are changed from one track to another; in this case, the meaning is that the thalamus is the area of the brain where information from the senses is routed to the correct part of the cortex

(74) *crossroads:* a place where two or more paths come together

(75) *memory-like or dream-like experiences:* experiences that are not real, but seem to be so

(75) *half-truth:* something that appears to be totally true but is not completely so

(75) *virtuoso:* one who is especially skilled, gifted

The Endocrine System—My Hormones Made Me Do It (pgs. 76-79)

Does the glandular system affect behavior?

(76) *jet-lag:* feeling of discomfort and sleepiness following travel across time zones

(77) *The Godfather:* 1972 cult-classic movie featuring the family life of a mafia family; marked by high levels of violence, particularly murder.

(77) *pea-sized*: very small; the size of a pea

(77) *remnant*: left-over; remains

(77) *coming to light:* being discovered

(78) *bark*: outer layer

(78) *anabolic steroids*: any of a group of synthetic steroid hormones; sometimes used by athletes to temporarily increase muscle mass

(78) *ebb and flow:* decreasing and increasing

(78) *ripe old age:* living a long time until you are old

Handedness—Are You Sinister or Dextrous? (pgs. 79-83)

In what ways do right- and left-handed individuals differ?

(79) *sinister:* threatening evil

(79) *dexterous:* having skill; having fine motor ability

(79) *paragon of virtue:* a good person; a person of great worth

(80) *agility:* the ability to move quickly and with coordination

(80) *people with two left feet:* clumsy, uncoordinated people

(81) *leap to any conclusions:* make a decision before looking at all the facts

(81) *foolproof:* absolute; true

(82) *collectivist culture:* culture that puts the needs of the group at a higher priority than the needs of the individual.

(82) *breech birth:* the delivery of a baby rear end first, rather than head first

(82) *masquerading:* wearing a mask to cover and disguise one's face

(83) *lopsided:* not symmetrical or balanced in shape

(83) *ambidextrous:* able to use either the right or left hand equally well

Solutions

Recite and Review

Neurons—Building a "Biocomputer"

1. Brain, neurons
2. axons
3. axon
4. nerve impulse
5. resting
6. ions, ion
7. axon
8. action
9. negative
10. Myelin
11. salutatory
12. Neurotransmitters
13. receptor
14. excitatory, inhibitory
15. transmitter
16. muscles
17. little dopamine, much dopamine
18. regulate
19. pain
20. Neural regulators
21. combine
22. changes
23. neuroplasticity

The Nervous System—Wired for Action

1. Central, brain
2. Neurons, nerves
3. permanent
4. Neurilemma
5. voluntary, involuntary
6. emergency, activating, sustaining, conserving
7. nerves, nerves
8. automatically
9. motor
10. neurogenesis
11. blood flow
12. constraint-induced movement

Research Methods—Charting the Brain's Inner Realms

1. Biological, behavior
2. electrical, clinical
3. brain structures, behavioral
4. case studies
5. electrode
6. Ablation, removal
7. patterns
8. images, activity
9. CT, MRI, PET
10. brain efficiency
11. Functional MRI

The Cerebral Cortex—My, What a Big Brain You Have!

1. Brain, cortex
2. corpus callosum
3. cutting, hemispheres
4. Sperry
5. spatial neglect
6. left, writing
7. right, patterns
8. left, right
9. vision, hearing
10. dexterity
11. sensory, motor, complex
12. speech
13. somatosensory
14. sensitivity
15. grammar, meaning
16. auditory
17. identify
18. familiar
19. specialization, matter

The Subcortex—At the Core of the (Brain) Matter

1. cortex
2. pons, activating
3. heart rate
4. higher, sleep
5. coordination
6. reticular formation, attention, adolescence
7. activating
8. sensory
9. motives
10. emotion
11. fear
12. memories

The Endocrine System—Hormones and Behavior

1. chemical, hormones
2. master
3. growth, dwarfism
4. sleep
5. metabolism
6. epinephrine
7. corticoids, sex
8. oversecretion
9. steroid
10. testosterone

Psychology in Action: Are You Sinister or Dexterous?

1. mixed
2. right-handed, left-handed.
3. left, speech
4. Left-handed, masquerade
5. Sidedness
6. before
7. specialization
8. left-handed, right-handed

CONNECTIONS

Neurons—Building a "Biocomputer"

1. G.
2. B.
3. E.
4. C.
5. A.
6. F.
7. D.

The Nervous System—Wired for Action

1. C or B.
2. E.
3. F. or G.
4. A.
5. F. or G.
6. C. or B.
7. D.

Research Methods—Charting the Brain's Inner Realms

1. E.
2. A.
3. D.
4. B.
5. C.

The Cerebral Cortex—My, What a Big Brain You Have!

1. D.
2. G.
3. F.
4. B.
5. C.
6. A.
7. E.

1. C.
2. K.
3. B.
4. H.
5. F.
6. A.
7. J.
8. E.
9. D.
10. I.
11. G.

The Subcortex—At the Core of the (Brain) Matter

1. D.	4. G.	7. H.
2. E.	5. I.	8. F.
3. A.	6. B.	9. C.

1. F.	4. C.	7. H.
2. A.	5. G.	8. B.
3. I.	6. E.	9. D.

The Endocrine System—Hormones and Behavior

1. H.	3. F.	5. E.	7. G.
2. C.	4. A.	6. B.	8. D.

Check Your Memory

Neurons—Building a "Biocomputer"

1. F	6. T	11. T	16. T
2. T	7. F	12. F	17. T
3. F	8. T	13. F	18. F
4. F	9. F	14. T	
5. T	10. F	15. T	

The Nervous System—Wired for Action

1. T	5. T	9. F	13. T
2. T	6. F	10. T	
3. T	7. F	11. F	
4. F	8. T	12. T	

Research Methods—Charting the Brain's Inner Realms

1. T	4. T	7. T
2. T	5. F	8. T
3. T	6. T	9. T

The Cerebral Cortex—My, What a Big Brain You Have!

1. F	8. T	15. T	22. T
2. F	9. F	16. T	23. F
3. T	10. F	17. F	24. T
4. T	11. F	18. T	25. T
5. T	12. F	19. T	
6. F	13. F	20. T	
7. F	14. T	21. F	

The Subcortex—At the Core of the (Brain) Matter

1. F	3. T	5. F	7. T
2. T	4. F	6. T	8. F

The Endocrine System—Hormones and Behavior

1. T	4. T	7. T
2. T	5. F	8. F
3. T	6. T	9. T

Psychology in Action: Handedness—Are You Sinister or Dexterous?

1. F	3. T	5. F	7. T
2. F	4. T	6. F	

Final Survey and Review

Neurons—Building a "Biocomputer"

1. Brain, nervous system, synapses
2. conducting fibers
3. Dendrites, soma
4. electrical, chemical
5. threshold
6. sodium, into
7. potassium, out
8. all-or-nothing
9. below, less able
10. fatty substance
11. gaps, "leap"
12. chemical messages
13. synapse
14. more, less
15. 100
16. acetylcholine
17. Parkinson's disease, schizophrenic
18. Neuropeptides, neurons.
19. Enkephalins, endorphins
20. endorphin
21. Neural networks
22. Learning
23. new synapses, connections, stronger

The Nervous System—Wired for Action

1. central, peripheral
2. cells, axons.
3. peripheral, regenerate, central
4. axons,
5. somatic, autonomic
6. sympathetic, parasympathetic
7. Thirty-one, Twelve, sensory, motor
8. reflex arc
9. movements, sensory, connector
10. new, lost
11. brain, interrupted
12. neurogenesis.

Research Methods—Charting the Brain's Inner Realms

1. Biopsychology
2. dissection, deep lesioning, EEG
3. Localization of function
4. personality, behavior,
5. electrical, surface
6. deep lesioning, destruction
7. electroencephalog raph (EEG)
8. Computer, three-dimensional
9. X-rays, magnetic field, positrons, radioactive
10. less, more
11. lying

The Cerebral Cortex—My, What a Big Brain You Have!

1. corticalization
2. cerebral hemispheres
3. Split brains, corpus callosum, right, left
4. Nobel Prize, functions
5. right, left
6. speech or language, calculating, time, complex
7. nonverbal, spatial, perceptual, melodies
8. sequentially, simultaneously
9. occipital, parietal, temporal, abstract
10. primary motor
11. Association, combine, language, problem solving
12. Broca's, Wernicke's
13. Touch, pressure
14. Somatosensory, actual
15. Grammar, meaning
16. listened, MP3
17. agnosia
18. Facial
19. gray, white

The Subcortex—At the Core of the (Brain) Matter

1. subcortex
2. hindbrai, pons, reticular formation
3. medulla, vegetative
4. pons, arousal
5. posture, muscle tone
6. medulla, brainstem
7. cerebral
8. thalamus
9. hypothalamus
10. limbic, reward, punishment
11. amygdala
12. hippocampus

The Endocrine System—Hormones and Behavior

1. endocrine, moods, personality
2. pituitary, hypothalamus
3. Too little, too much
4. melatonin, pineal
5. Hyperthyroidism, hypothyroidism
6. norepinephrine
7. adrenal, salt, secondary
8. exaggerated
9. increases, aggression
10. synthetic

Psychology in Action: Are You Sinister or Dexterous?

1. dominance, ambidexterity
2. Ninety percent, ten
3. right-handed, left
4. right-handed, fewer
5. preference
6. preferences
7. Lateralization
8. less

Mastery Test

1. b, p. 59
2. a, p. 66
3. a, p. 71
4. c, p. 56
5. b, p. 57
6. b, p. 69-70
7. c, p. 53-55
8. b, p. 67-68
9. b, p. 74-75
10. b, p. 53
11. a, p. 57
12. a, p. 55
13. b, p. 61
14. b, p. 54-55
15. a, p. 69
16. d, p. 75
17. a, p. 69
18. d, p. 75
19. d, p. 59
20. d, p. 73-75
21. b, p. 61-62
22. a, p. 77
23. d, p. 66
24. c, p. 73-74
25. c, p. 66-69
26. b, p. 60
27. d, p. 71
28. c, p. 77
29. b, p. 74
30. d, p. 63
31. a, p. 62
32. a, p. 79-82
33. c, p. 55
34. a, p. 63
35. d, p. 71
36. d, p. 78

CHAPTER 3

Human Development

Chapter Overview

Heredity affects personal and psychological characteristics and organizes the human growth sequence through the transmission and expression of genes. Environmental influences can have especially lasting effects during sensitive periods in development. Prenatal development is affected by diseases, drugs, radiation, or the mother's diet and health. Early perceptual, intellectual, and emotional deprivation seriously hinders cognitive development and may lead to a risk of mental illness and delinquent behaviors. Deliberate enrichment of the environment has a beneficial effect on early development (e.g., as in cases of poverty).

Most psychologists accept that heredity and environment are inseparable and interacting forces. A child's developmental level reflects heredity, environment, and the effects of the child's own behavior.

Human newborns have adaptive reflexes, are capable of learning, and have visual preferences, especially for familiar faces. Maturation underlies the orderly sequence of motor, cognitive, language, and emotional development, and a minimum maturation level underlies certain developmental milestones (e.g., toilet training).

Emotional attachment of infants to their caregivers is a critical event in social development. Three types of emotional attachments include secure, insecure-avoidant, and insecure-ambivalent. A child may experience separation anxiety disorder when they are reluctant to leave home, go to school, or sleep over at a friend's home. For optimal development, emotional attachment between infants and their caregivers must occur during the infant's first year.

Three major parenting styles are authoritarian, permissive, and authoritative (effective). Mothers and fathers make unique contributions to parenting (maternal and paternal influences, respectively). Effective parental discipline tends to emphasize child management techniques, rather than power assertion or withdrawal of love, resulting in positive traits such as resiliency. Effective parenting depends largely on the culture for which a child is being prepared.

Language development is based on a biological predisposition, which is augmented by learning. Language acquisition begins with prelanguage communication between parent and child and progresses to telegraphic speech. To help children learn language, caregivers tend to use parentese, which is characterized by an inflection of a higher pitched and exaggerated voice and repetition of short and simple sentences.

Jean Piaget theorized that children go through a series of cognitive stages as they develop intellectually. Learning principles provide an alternate explanation, which does not assume that cognitive development occurs in stages. Lev Vygotsky's sociocultural theory says that cognitive gains occur primarily in a child's zone of proximal development. Adults who engage in the scaffolding of a child's intellectual growth also impart cultural values and beliefs to the child.

Adolescence is a period of transition between childhood and adulthood marked by the search for and creation of identity. The length and timing of adolescence varies greatly from culture to culture. Puberty is a biological event that signals sexual and reproductive maturity. Maturing earlier or later than peers can influence self-image, social relations, and sexual activity.

Moral development starts in childhood and continues through adolescence and early adulthood. Lawrence Kohlberg believed that moral development progresses through preconventional, conventional, and postconventional levels.

Development continues over the life span, creating a series of tasks, challenges, milestones, and problems throughout life. According to Erikson, each life stage provokes a different psychosocial dilemma (e.g., integrity vs. despair) that must be resolved for optimal development.

Physical aging presents challenges, but well-being at midlife and in old age is based on many of the same factors as it is in young adulthood. However, ageism can be damaging to older people.

Mutual respect, love, encouragement, clear communication, and constructive and consistent discipline are features of effective parenting. Also, effective discipline involves the use of I-messages and an understanding of both natural and logical consequences.

Learning Objectives

1.   Define *developmental psychology* and explain the roles that heredity and environment play in a person's development.

2.   Explain the basic mechanisms of heredity, include a description of the following terms:
     a. DNA
     b. chromosome
     c. gene
     d. dominant trait (gene)
     e. recessive trait (gene)
     f. polygenic
     g. maturation

3.   Discuss the role of readiness in the human growth sequence

4.   Define the terms *nurture* (environment) and briefly discuss the impact that environment has on development.

5.   Distinguish between congenital and genetic problems

6.   Discuss the effects of environmental influences (including tobacco, alcohol, and other drugs) on an unborn child, including a definition of teratogen and the relationship between the blood supplies of the mother and her developing child. Explain the role of sensitive periods and environmental influences.

7.   Describe the effects of enrichment and deprivation on development.

8.   Define the term *temperament* and describe the characteristics of easy, difficult, and slow-to-warm-up children.

9.   Explain the concepts of reciprocal interactions and developmental level; and list the three factors that combine to determine one's developmental level.

10. Describe the world of the neonate, including their adaptive reflexes and their sensory and intellectual capabilities.

11. Discuss motor development and the concepts of *maturation*, *cephalocaudal pattern*, *proximodistal pattern*.

12. Describe the course of emotional development, according to Bridges and Izard, and explain the importance of the *social smile*.

13. Explain how self-awareness and emotional attachment are related to early social development

14. Define *separation anxiety* and *separation anxiety disorder*

15. Differentiate between the three types of attachment identified by Mary Ainsworth, and describe how these attachments can influence how people relate to others as adults.

16. Explain how parents can promote secure attachments; describe the characteristics of fathers who have securely attached infants; discuss the effects of day care on the quality of attachment (including the criteria for evaluating child care); and explain the importance of attachment in meeting a child's affectional needs.

17. Describe Baumrind's three major styles of parenting, including characteristics of both parents and children in each style; compare maternal and paternal influences on a child; and describe ethnic differences in parenting.

18. Describe the five stages of language acquisition and discuss children's increasing use of language in combination with their growing independence (including the time period known as the "terrible twos").

19. Discuss the roots of language, including Chomsky's theory and the research of other psycholinguists into the role of innate and environmental factors in language acquisition.

20. Explain how parents communicate with infants before the infants can talk, including the concepts of *signals*, *turn-taking*, and *parentese*.

21. With regard to Piaget's theory of cognitive development:
     a. Explain how a child's intelligence and thinking differ from an adult's
     b. Explain the concepts of *assimilation* and *accommodation*.
     c. List (in order) and describe the specific characteristics of each stage.
     d. Explain how parents can best guide their child's intellectual development.
     e. Evaluate the usefulness of Piaget's theory in light of the current research on infant cognition.

22. Briefly discuss Vygotsky's sociocultural theory and define the terms *zone of proximal development* and *scaffolding*.

23. Define adolecence; discuss the role of culture and ethnicity, puberty, and early vs late sexual maturation on adolescent identity formation; describe the new concept of *emerging adulthood*.

24. Discuss the concept of moral development by describing each of Kohlberg's three levels of moral development, the technique he used to study moral development, and the proportion of the population that appears to function at each level.

25. Define the terms *developmental milestones*, *developmental tasks*, and *psychosocial dilemmas*; describe the eight psychosocial dilemmas (life stages) in Erikson's theory and their possible outcomes; give approximate age ranges for each of these eight life stages. and

26. Describe the challenges of mid-life to old age, including Ryff's elements of well-being, Schaie's suggestions for keeping "mentally sharp," ageism, the fluid and crystallized abilities of older workers, and the keys to successful aging.

27. Regarding effective parenting techniques, briefly discuss:
     a. positive parent-child interactions
     b. characteristics of effective discipline
     c. characteristics and effects of the child rearing methods of *power assertion*, *withdrawal of love*, and *management techniques* on children's behavior and their self-esteem
     d. the effects of consistent and inconsistent discipline
     e. the effects of punishment, including spanking, and guidelines for its use
     f. the elements of effective communication, according to Haim Ginott
     g. Thomas Gordon's concepts of I-messages and you-messages
     h. the use of natural and logical consequences

RECITE AND REVIEW

Heredity and Environment—It Takes Two to Tango

Survey Question: How do heredity and environment affect development? Pages 88-93

1. Developmental psychology is the study of progressive changes in _____ and abilities, from _____ to _____.

2. The nature-nurture debate concerns the relative contributions to development of heredity (_____) and environment (_____).

3. Hereditary instructions are carried by _____ (deoxyribonucleic acid) in the form of chromosomes and _____ in each cell of the body.

4. Most characteristics are polygenic (influenced by a combination of _____) and reflect the combined effects of dominant and recessive _____.

5. Heredity influences maturation—the general pattern of _____ and _____.

6. Readiness reflects minimum levels of _____ that must occur before some skills (like toilet-training) can be learned.

7. Environment refers to all _____ conditions that affect development.

8. Compared to an adult brain, newborn babies have neurons with _____ dendrites and _____. These neurons grow rapidly, making millions of connections as the newborns interact with their environment in the first three years.

9. Early learning environments literally shape the developing brain, through "_____ and _____" of synapses.

10. Prenatal development is subject to _____ influences in the form of diseases, drugs, radiation, or the mother's diet and health.

11. Prenatal damage to the fetus may cause congenital problems, or _____. In contrast, genetic problems are inherited from one's parents.

12. Fetal alcohol syndrome (_____) is the result of heavy _____ during pregnancy, which causes the infant to have _____ birth weight, a small head, and _____ malformations.

13. Exposure to any form of _____ such as radiation, lead, and pesticides during pregnancy will likely cause birth defects.

14. A variety of sensitive periods (times of increased _____ to environmental influences) exist in development.

15. Early perceptual, intellectual, and emotional deprivation seriously retards _____.

16. Poverty greatly increases the likelihood that children will experience various forms of _____, which may impede cognitive development and _____ achievement and increase the risk for mental illness and _____ behavior.

17. Deliberate enrichment of the _____ in infancy and early childhood has a beneficial effect on development.

18. Nurture (environment) affects the expression of nature (hereditary tendencies) through ongoing reciprocal _____.

19. Heredity influences differences in temperament (the physical core of _____). Most infants fall into one of three temperament categories: easy children, _____ children, and slow-to-warm-up children.

20. Ultimately, most psychologists accept that _____ and environment are inseparable and interacting forces.

21. A child's developmental level (current state of development) reflects heredity, environment, and the effects of the child's _____.

The Newborn Baby—More Than Meets the Eye

Survey Question: What can newborn babies do? Pages 93-98

1. The human _____ (newborn) has a number of _____ reflexes

2. The _____ reflex aids survival by helping an infant to avoid falling; the rooting reflex is a reflexive head turning to help infants find food; the sucking helps an infant obtain food; the Moro reflex is a _____ motion infants make when startled. .

3. Newborns begin to _____ immediately and they imitate adults.

4. Tests in a looking chamber reveal a number of _____ preferences in the newborn. The neonate is drawn to complex, _____, curved, and brightly-lighted designs.

5. Infants prefer human face patterns, especially _____. In later infancy, interest in the unfamiliar emerges.

6. Maturation of the body and nervous system underlies the orderly _____ of motor, cognitive, language, and emotional development.

7. While the rate of maturation varies from child to child, the _____ is nearly universal.

8. The development of _____ control (motor development) is cephalocaudal (from head to toe) and proximodistal (from the _____ of the body to the extremities).

9. Emotional development begins with a capacity for _____ excitement. After that the first pleasant and unpleasant emotions develop.

10. Some psychologists believe that basic emotional expressions are _____ and that some appear as early as 2.5 months of age.

11. By 8-12 months, babies display a social smile when other _____ are nearby.

12. Babies can communicate their interest in objects through _____.

Social Development—Baby, I'm Stuck on You

Survey Question: Of what significance is a child's emotional bond with adults?
Pages 99-101

1. _____ development refers to the emergence of self-awareness and forming relationships with parents and others.

2. Self-awareness (consciousness of oneself as a person) is an element of early _____ development.

3. For optimal development in human infants, the development of an emotional attachment to their primary _____ is a critical early event that must occur during the _____ (within the first year) of infancy.

4. Infant attachment is reflected by _____ anxiety (distress when infants are away from parents).

5. When experiencing separation anxiety disorder, children cling to their parents and are miserable when _____ from their parents.

6. The quality of attachment can be classified as _____, insecure-avoidant, or insecure-ambivalent.

7. Some psychologists believe that our first _____ continue to affect how we relate to others as adults (e.g., romantic relationships).

8. The relationship between quality of attachment and the type of caregiving that is provided appears to be _____ in all cultures.

9. High-quality day care does not _____ children; high-quality care can, in fact, accelerate some areas of development.

10. Some characteristics of high-quality day care include having a _____ number of children per caregiver, trained caregivers, an overall group size of _____ to _____ children, and minimal staff turnover.

11. A child's _____ development is also affected by playing with other children. For example, cooperative _____ is a major step toward participation in social life outside the family.

12. An infant's affectional _____ are every bit as important as more obvious needs for physical care.

Parental Influences—Life with Mom and Dad

Survey Question: How important are parenting styles? Pages 101-104

1. Parents may exhibit distinct patterns of parental caretaking – _____, overly _____, and authoritative.

2. Authoritarian parents enforce rigid _____ and demand strict obedience to _____.

3. Overly permissive parents give little _____ and don't hold children accountable for their actions.

4. Authoritative (_____) parents supply firm and consistent guidance, combined with love and affection.

5. Authoritative parenting leads to _____ (the ability to bounce back after bad experiences).

6. Caregiving styles among various ethnic groups tend to reflect each culture's _____ and _____. For example, fathers in Arab-American families tend to be strong authority figures, demanding absolute obedience.

7. Paternal influences differ in their impact because _____ tend to function as a playmate for the infant.

8. _____ are most likely to play with their children, whereas _____ are most often responsible for the physical and emotional care of their children.

9. The effectiveness of parenting can only be judged if we know what _____ the child is being prepared to enter.

10. An _____ (effective) style of parenting encourages children to manage their emotions and use _____ coping skills to be _____ (able to bounce back after bad experiences) and competent adults.

Language Development—Who Talks Baby Talk?

Survey Question: How do children acquire language? Pages 104-107

1. Language development proceeds from control of _____, to cooing, then babbling, the use of single words, and then to telegraphic _____.

2. The patterns of early speech suggest a _____ predisposition to acquire language.

3. Psycholinguists (psychologists who study _____) believe that innate language predispositions are augmented by _____.

4. Prelanguage communication between parent and child involves shared rhythms, nonverbal _____, and turn-taking.

5. Parents help children learn language by using distinctive caretaker
_____ or parentese; it helps to get babies' attention, communicate
with them, and teach them the language.

6. Motherese or parentese is characterized by short, simple sentences,
_____ pitch, and frequent repetition and _____.

Cognitive Development—Think Like a Child

Survey Question: How do children learn to think? Pages 108-114

1. The intellects of children are _____ abstract than those of adults.
Children use fewer _____, categories, and principles.

2. Jean Piaget theorized that intellectual growth occurs through a combination of
_____ and accommodation.

3. Piaget also held that children go through a fixed series of cognitive
_____. These are: sensorimotor (0-2), preoperational (2-7),
_____ operational (7-11), and formal _____ (11-adult).

4. Object permanence (the ability to understand that _____ continue to
exist when they are out of sight) emerges during the _____ stage

5. Conservation (the ability to understand that mass, weight, and volume remain
_____ when the shape of objects changes) emerges during the
_____ stage.

6. Children in the preoperational stage of development, tend to exhibit
_____; this is the inability to assume another's perspective or
viewpoint.

7. Children in the formal operational stage of development are less egocentric
and can think _____, hypothetically, and theoretically.

8. Learning theorists dispute the idea that cognitive development occurs in
_____. Recent studies suggest infants are capable of levels of
thinking beyond that observed by Piaget; he may have mistook limited
_____ skills for mental _____.

9. Renee Baillargeon's research on impossible events suggests that
_____ may develop object _____ earlier than suggested by
Piaget's theory.

10. Piaget may have underestimated the impact of _____ on
development.

11. A one-step-ahead strategy that takes into account the child's level of
_____ development helps adapt instruction to a child's needs.

12. Parents should avoid _____ teaching, or "hothousing" as it might
bore and oppress children.

13. According to the sociocultural theory of Russian scholar Lev Vygotsky, a child's interactions with others are most likely to aid _____ development if they take place within the child's _____ of proximal _____.

14. Adults help children learn how to think by scaffolding, or _____, their attempts to solve problems or discover principles.

15. During their collaborations with adults, children learn important cultural _____ and values.

Adolescence and Young Adulthood – The Best of Times, the Worst of Times

Survey Question: Why is the transition from adolescence to adulthood especially challenging? Pages 115-117

1. Adolescence is the culturally defined period between _____ and adulthood

2. Criterion for adult status in North America are: taking responsibility for _____, making _____ decisions, and becoming _____ independent.

3. Adolescence is a social status; puberty is a _____ event

4. During puberty, _____ changes promote rapid _____ growth and sexual maturity

5. Teens who enter puberty earlier than their peers may have more _____ body images, but are also more likely to engage in antisocial behavior.

6. _____ formation is a key task for adolescence; this may be influenced by one's ethnic _____.

7. Twixters are those in their _____ still living at home who are not yet married and with no settled career.

Moral Development—Growing a Conscience

Survey Question: How do we develop morals and values? Pages 117-119

1. Lawrence Kohlberg theorized that _____ development passes through a series of stages revealed by _____ reasoning about _____ dilemmas.

2. Kohlberg identified preconventional, conventional, and postconventional levels of moral _____.

3. At the preconventional level, moral development is guided by consequences of actions, such as _____ and punishments

4. Preconventional morals are typical of _____ children and delinquents; Conventional, _____-oriented morals are typical of older children and _____.

The Story of a Lifetime—Rocky Road or Garden Path?

Survey Question: What are the typical tasks and dilemmas through the life span? Pages 119-121

1. Developmental psychologists are interested in _____ milestones, or prominent landmarks in personal development such as graduation.

2. According to Erik Erikson, each life stage provokes a specific psychosocial _____.

3. During childhood, psychosocial dilemmas include: trust versus mistrust, autonomy versus _____ and doubt, initiative versus _____, and industry versus _____.

4. During the stage of autonomy vs. shame and doubt, children may have "_____" as they try to do things for themselves.

5. In _____, identity versus role confusion is the principal dilemma.

6. In young adulthood we face the dilemma of intimacy versus _____. Later, generativity versus _____ becomes prominent.

7. Old age is a time when the dilemma of integrity versus _____ must be faced.

8. In addition, each life stage requires successful mastery of certain _____ tasks (personal changes required for optimal development).

Middle and Late Adulthood: Will You Still Need Me When I'm 64?

Survey Question: What is involved in well-being during later adulthood? Pages 122-124

1. Well-being at midlife is related to self-acceptance, positive relationships, autonomy, environmental mastery, a _____ in life, and continued personal _____.

2. It is more common to make a "midcourse _____" at _____ than to have a "crisis".

3. A midlife transition may include reworking old _____, achieving goals, finding one's truths, and preparing for old _____.

4. You are most likely to stay mentally fit if you: Stay _____, live in a favorable environment, engage in mentally _____ activities, have a flexible personality, marry a smart spouse, and are _____ with accomplishments at midlife.

5. People entering old age do experience a gradual loss of _____ abilities (those requiring speed or rapid learning); however, these can be offset by _____ abilities (learned knowledge and skills).

6. Ageism refers to prejudice, discrimination, and stereotyping on the basis of _____. It affects people of all ages but is especially damaging to _____ people.

Psychology in Action: Effective Parenting—Raising Healthy Children

Survey Question: How do effective parents discipline and communicate with their children? Pages 124-128

1. Mutual _____, effective discipline, love, encouragement, and clear _____ are features of effective parenting.

2. When disciplining children, consistent discipline (maintaining a stable rule of conduct) fosters security and _____, whereas inconsistent discipline fosters insecurity and _____.

3. Effective child _____ is based on a consistent framework of guidelines for acceptable behavior.

4. Good discipline tends to emphasize child management techniques (especially communication), rather than _____ assertion or withdrawal of _____.

5. _____ techniques tend to produce the highest levels of self-esteem in children. Much misbehavior can be managed by use of I-_____ and by applying _____ and logical consequences to children's behavior.

6. I-messages focus on the _____, and you-messages focus on children's _____.

CONNECTIONS

Heredity and Environment—It Takes Two to Tango

Survey Question: How do heredity and environment affect development? Pages 88-93

1. _____ gene   A. DNA area
2. _____ senescence   B. old age
3. _____ congenital problems   C. nature
4. _____ heredity   D. nurture
5. _____ sensitive period   E. conception to birth
6. _____ Inherited personality   F. prenatal alcohol exposure
7. _____ environment   G. magnified environmental impact
8. _____ enrichment   H. "birth defects"
9. _____ prenatal period   I. stimulating environment
10. _____ FAS   J. temperament

The Newborn Baby—More Than Meets the Eye

Survey Questions: What can newborn babies do? Pages 93-98

1. _____ grasping reflex   A. first emotion
2. _____ rooting reflex   B. palm grip
3. _____ Moro reflex   C. startled embrace
4. _____ neonate   D. food search
5. _____ Excitement   E. control of muscles and movement
6. _____ motor development   F. newborn infant
7. _____ familiar faces   G. physical growth
8. _____ maturation   H. preferred pattern

Social Development—Baby, I'm Stuck on You

Survey Question: Of what significance is a child's emotional bond with adults? Pages 99-101

1. _____ secure attachment
2. _____ insecure-avoidant
3. _____ contact comfort
4. _____ affectional needs
5. _____ separation anxiety
6. _____ resilient
7. _____ self awareness
8. _____ high-quality day care

A. love and attention
B. anxious emotional bond
C. positive emotional bond
D. emotional distress
E. self recognition
F. trained caregivers
G. bouncing back after hardship
H. occurs during bottle or breast-feeding

Parental Influences—Life with Mom and Dad

Survey Question: How important are parenting styles? Pages 101-104

1. _____ Asian-American families
2. _____ paternal influence
3. _____ Hispanic families
4. _____ authoritative style
5. _____ authoritarian style
6. _____ permissive style
7. _____ resilience

A. strict obedience
B. firm and consistent guidance
C. little guidance
D. playmates
E. bounce back from hardship
F. interdependence
G. cooperation vs. competition

Language Development—Who Talks Baby Talk?

Survey Question: How do children acquire language? Pages 104-107

1. _____ biological predisposition
2. _____ cooing
3. _____ Vygotsky
4. _____ babbling
5. _____ telegraphic speech
6. _____ turn-taking
7. _____ Noam Chomsky
8. _____ parentese

A. vowel sounds
B. vowels and consonants
C. caretaker speech
D. "Mama gone"
E. hereditary readiness for language
F. psycholinguists
G. conversational style of communication
H. sociocultural theory

Cognitive Development—Think Like A Child

Survey Questions: How do children learn to think? Pages 108-114

1. _____ assimilation
2. _____ accommodation
3. _____ sensorimotor stage
4. _____ preoperational stage
5. _____ concrete operations
6. _____ formal operations
7. _____ hothousing
8. _____ scaffolding
9. _____ Piaget
10. _____ Baillargon
11. _____ Vygotsky

A. changing existing mental patterns
B. egocentricism
C. impossible events
D. applying mental patterns
E. abstract concept
F. sociocultural factors
G. conservation
H. object permanence
I. skilled support for learning
J. forced teaching
K. stage theory of cognitive development

Adolescence and Young Adulthood – The Best of Times, the Worst of Times and Moral Development

Survey Question: Why is the transition from adolescence to adulthood especially challenging? How do we develop morals and values? Pages 115-119

1. _____ emerging adulthood
2. _____ adolescence
3. _____ preconventional
4. _____ puberty
5. _____ conventional
6. _____ Twixter
7. _____ postconventional
8. _____ "who am I?"
9. _____ Lawrence Kohlberg
10. _____ adult status

A. Between childhood and adulthood
B. Making independent decisions
C. Sexual maturity
D. Identity formation
E. 20s and living at home
F. new social status
G. individual ethical principles
H. moral dilemma of justice
I. good boy or girl/respect for authority
J. avoiding punishment or seeking pleasure

The Story of a Lifetime—Rocky Road or Garden Path? and Middle and Late Adulthood: Will you Still Need Me When I'm 64?

Survey Question: What are the typical tasks and dilemmas through the life span? What is involved in well-being during later adulthood? Pages 119-124

1. _____Erik Erikson

2. _____ageism

3. _____optimal development

4. _____developmental milestones

5. _____generativity versus stagnation

6. _____trust versus mistrust

7. _____midlife transition

8. _____developmental task

9. _____crystallized ability

10. _____autonomy versus shame and doubt

11. _____Integrity versus despair

12. _____initiative versus guilt

13. _____successful aging

14. _____industry versus inferiority

A. received praise versus lacking support

B. self-control versus inadequacy

C. love versus insecurity

D. freedom to choose versus criticism

E. psychosocial dilemmas

F. mastered developmental tasks

G. notable events or marker

H. skills to be attained

J. next generation versus self-interest

K. self-respect versus remorse

L. reworking old identities

M. optimism, gratitude, empathy, connection

N. patronizing language

O. learned knowledge

Psychology in Action: Effective Parenting – Raising Healthy Children

Survey question: How do effective parents discipline and communicate with their children? Pages 124-128

1. _____Logical consequences

2. _____discipline

3. _____power assertion

4. _____Creative communication

5. _____consistency

6. _____I-messages

7. _____management techniques

A. guidance regarding behavior

B. show of force

C. praise, rules, and reasoning

D. stable rules

E. child management

F. effect of behavior on you

G. rational and reasonable effects

CHECK YOUR MEMORY

Heredity and Environment—It Takes Two to Tango

Survey Question: How do heredity and environment affect development? Pages 88-93

1. Developmental psychology is the study of progressive changes in behavior and abilities during childhood.
   TRUE or FALSE

2. Each cell in the human body (except sperm cells and ova) contains 23 chromosomes.
   TRUE or FALSE

3. The order of organic bases in DNA acts as a genetic code.
   TRUE or FALSE

4. Two brown-eyed parents cannot have a blue-eyed child.
   TRUE or FALSE

5. Identical twins have identical genes.
   TRUE or FALSE

6. When a gene is dominant, it must be paired with a second recessive gene before it can be expressed.
   TRUE or FALSE

7. The synapses of the brain are affected by a child's learning environment.
   TRUE or FALSE

8. More children have a slow-to-warm up temperament than a difficult temperament.
   TRUE or FALSE

9. Minimum levels of maturation must occur before some skills (such as toilet training) can occur
   TRUE or FALSE

10. The sensitive period during which German measles can damage the fetus occurs near the end of pregnancy.
    TRUE or FALSE

11. Teratogens are substances capable of causing birth defects.
    TRUE or FALSE

12. An infant damaged by exposure to X-rays during the prenatal period suffers from a genetic problem.
    TRUE or FALSE

13. Many drugs can reach the fetus within the intrauterine environment.
    TRUE or FALSE

14. To prevent FAS, the best advice to pregnant women is to get plenty of rest, vitamins, and good nutrition.
TRUE or FALSE

15. Poverty is associated with retarded emotional and intellectual development.
TRUE or FALSE

16. In animals, enriched environments can actually increase brain size and weight.
TRUE or FALSE

The Newborn Baby—More Than Meets the Eye

Survey Question: What can newborn babies do? Pages 93-98

1. The Moro reflex helps infants hold onto objects placed in their hands.
TRUE or FALSE

2. As early as 9 weeks of age, infants can imitate actions a full day after seeing them.
TRUE or FALSE

3. Babies begin to show a preference for looking at their mother's face over a stranger's face just a few hours after they are born.
TRUE or FALSE

4. Three-day-old infants prefer to look at simple colored backgrounds, rather than more complex patterns.
TRUE or FALSE

5. After age 2, familiar faces begin to hold great interest for infants.
TRUE or FALSE

6. Most infants learn to stand alone before they begin crawling.
TRUE or FALSE

7. Motor development follows a top-down, center-outward pattern.
TRUE or FALSE

8. Toilet training should begin soon after a child is 1 year old.
TRUE or FALSE

9. Anger and fear are the first two emotions to emerge in infancy.
TRUE or FALSE

10. An infant's social smile appears within one month after birth.
TRUE or FALSE

11. Babies can communicate their interest in objects through smiling.
TRUE or FALSE

Social Development—Baby, I'm Stuck on You

Survey Question: Of what significance is a child's emotional bond with adults?
Pages 99-101

1. Most infants have to be 15 weeks old before they can recognize themselves on videotape.
   TRUE or FALSE

2. Securely attached infants turn away from mother when she returns after a period of separation.
   TRUE or FALSE

3. Separation anxiety disorder is the medical term for homesickness.
   TRUE or FALSE

4. Most children with separation anxiety disorder refuse to go to school.
   TRUE or FALSE

5. Affection needs are not as important as food, water, and physical care in infancy.
   TRUE or FALSE

6. Our first emotional attachments appear to affect how we relate to others as adults.
   TRUE or FALSE

7. A small number of children per caregiver is desirable in day care settings.
   TRUE or FALSE

8. The question of when secure attachment occurs is less important than the question of whether it occurs at all.
   TRUE or FALSE

9. Children typically first begin to engage in cooperative play around age 4 or 5.
   TRUE or FALSE

Parental Influences—Life with Mom and Dad

Survey Question: How important are parenting styles? Pages 101-104

1. Fathers typically spend about half their time in caregiving and half playing with the baby.
   TRUE or FALSE

2. Paternal play tends to be more physically arousing for infants than maternal play.
   TRUE or FALSE

3. Since mothers spend more time caring for infants, mothers are more important than fathers.
   TRUE or FALSE

4. Authoritarian parents view children as having adult-like responsibilities.
   TRUE or FALSE

5. Permissive parents basically give their children the message "Do it because I say so."
   TRUE or FALSE

6. The children of authoritarian parents tend to be independent, assertive, and inquiring.
   TRUE or FALSE

7. Resilient children have the ability to recover from bad experiences.
   TRUE or FALSE

8. Culture has little to do with whether certain parenting styles are effective or not.
   TRUE or FALSE

9. Asian cultures tend to be group-oriented and they emphasize interdependence among individuals.
   TRUE or FALSE

10. An authoritarian style of parenting is most effective since it focuses on pampering the child's every need.
    TRUE or FALSE

11. African-American cultures tend to promote self-reliance and resourcefulness in their children
    TRUE or FALSE

Language Development—Who Talks Baby Talk?

Survey Question: How do children acquire language? Pages 104-107

1. The single-word stage begins at about 6 months of age.
   TRUE or FALSE

2. "That red ball mine," is an example of telegraphic speech.
   TRUE or FALSE

3. Infants begin to babble before they begin to coo.
   TRUE or FALSE

4. Noam Chomsky believes that basic language patterns are innate.
   TRUE or FALSE

5. The "terrible twos" refers to the two-word stage of language development.
   TRUE or FALSE

6. The "I'm going to get you" game is an example of prelanguage communication.
   TRUE or FALSE

7. Parentese is spoken in higher pitched tones with a musical inflection.
   TRUE or FALSE

8. Parentese language used by mothers and fathers to talk to their infants does more harm than good to their infants' language development.
   TRUE or FALSE

Cognitive Development—Think Like A Child

Survey Question: How do children learn to think? Pages 108-114

1. Assimilation refers to modifying existing ideas to fit new situations or demands.
   TRUE or FALSE

2. Cognitive development during the sensorimotor stage is mostly nonverbal.
   TRUE or FALSE

3. Reversibility of thoughts and the concept of conservation both appear during the concrete operational stage.
   TRUE or FALSE

4. Three-year-old children are surprisingly good at understanding what other people are thinking.
   TRUE or FALSE

5. An understanding of hypothetical possibilities develops during the preoperational stage.
   TRUE or FALSE

6. Playing peekaboo is a good way to establish the permanence of objects for children in the sensorimotor stage.
   TRUE or FALSE

7. Contrary to what Piaget observed, infants as young as 3 months of age show signs of object permanence.
   TRUE or FALSE

8. Hothousing, or the forced teaching of children to learn reading or math, is encouraged to accelerate their intellectual development and to prevent apathy.
   TRUE or FALSE

9. Forced teaching is an effective means of enhancing a child's intellectual development.
   TRUE or FALSE

10. Vygotsky's key insight was that children's thinking develops through dialogues with more capable persons.
    TRUE or FALSE

11. Learning experiences are most helpful when they take place outside of a child's zone of proximal development.
    TRUE or FALSE

12. Scaffolding is like setting up temporary bridges to help children move into new mental territory.
    TRUE or FALSE

13. Vygotsky emphasized that children use adults to learn about their culture and society.
    TRUE or FALSE

Adolescence and Young Adulthood – The Best of Times, the Worst of Times

Survey Question: Why is the transition from adolescence to adulthood especially challenging? Pages 115-117

1. Adolescence is a biologically determined period between childhood and adulthood.
   TRUE or FALSE

2. Marriage is the primary criterion for adult status in North America.
   TRUE or FALSE

3. During puberty, hormonal changes promote rapid physical growth and sexual maturity.
   TRUE or FALSE

4. In our society, adolescence is a social status with clearly defined roles and expectations.
   TRUE or FALSE

5. Culture and ethnic heritage have little to no influence on an adolescent's search for identity.
   TRUE or FALSE

6. In the United States and Canada, there is a growing trend to encourage young adults to establish an identity and become financially independent in their early twenties.
   TRUE or FALSE

7. Emerging adulthood is most common in affluent cultures, but is less accepted in less affluent countries and poorer areas.
   TRUE or FALSE

8. Making independent decisions and taking responsibility for oneself are widely acceptable criterion for adult status.
   TRUE or FALSE

Moral Development—Growing a Conscience

Survey Question: How do we develop morals and values? Pages 117-119

1. Lawrence Kohlberg used moral dilemmas to assess children's levels of moral development.
   TRUE or FALSE

2. At the preconventional level, moral decisions are guided by the consequences of actions, such as punishment or pleasure.
   TRUE or FALSE

3. The traditional morality of authority defines moral behavior in the preconventional stage.
   TRUE or FALSE

4. Most adults function at the conventional level of moral reasoning.
   TRUE or FALSE

5. All children will achieve Kohlberg's conventional level of moral development, and approximately 80 percent of all adults will achieve the postconventional level of morality.
   TRUE or FALSE

6. Individuals at the preconventional level make decisions based on general and universal principles.
   TRUE or FALSE

The Story of a Lifetime—Rocky Road or Garden Path? and Middle and Late Adulthood: Will You Still Need Me When I'm 64?

Survey Question: What are the typical tasks and dilemmas through the life span? What is involved in well-being during later adulthood? Pages 119-124

1. Learning to read in childhood and establishing a vocation as an adult are typical life stages.
   TRUE or FALSE

2. Adolescence and adulthood can be defined solely in terms of physical maturation.
   TRUE or FALSE

3. Psychosocial dilemmas occur when a person is in conflict with his or her social world.
   TRUE or FALSE

4. Initiative versus guilt is the first psychosocial dilemma a child faces.
   TRUE or FALSE

5. Answering the question "Who am I?" is a primary task during adolescence.
   TRUE or FALSE

6. Generativity is expressed through taking an interest in the next generation.
   TRUE or FALSE

7. Entrance into elementary school provides children with opportunities for success or failure than can affect children's feelings of adequacy.
   TRUE or FALSE

8. Having a sense of purpose in life is one element of well-being during adulthood.
   TRUE or FALSE

9. Ageism refers to prejudice and discrimination toward the elderly.
   TRUE or FALSE

10. Ageism is often expressed via patronizing language.
    TRUE or FALSE

11. The loss of fluid abilities is common among those entering old age.
    TRUE or FALSE

12. Few elderly persons become senile or suffer from mental decay.
    TRUE or FALSE

13. Well-being during adulthood includes self-acceptance, a purpose in life, living independently, and continued personal growth.
    TRUE or FALSE

14. The majority of men and women in their fifties to have a "midlife crisis."
    TRUE or FALSE

15. Reading, travel, and continuing to learn new things can help individuals to stay mentally sharp as they age.
    TRUE or FALSE

16. Workers should be encouraged to retire in their sixties due to age-related losses in intelligence and skill.
    TRUE or FALSE

Psychology in Action: Effective Parenting—Raising Healthy Children

Survey Question: How do effective parents discipline and communicate with their children? Pages 124-128

1. Consistency of child discipline is more important than whether limits on children's behavior are strict or lenient.
   TRUE or FALSE

2. Encouragement means giving recognition for effort and improvement.
   TRUE or FALSE

3. Logical consequences should be stated as you-messages.
   TRUE or FALSE

4. As a means of child discipline, power assertion refers to rejecting a child.
   TRUE or FALSE

5. As a discipline technique, withdrawal of love produces children with a good conscience.
   TRUE or FALSE

6. Management techniques are the most effective form of discipline after the age of 10.
   TRUE or FALSE

7. Natural consequences, such as waking up hungry after refusing dinner the night before, are ineffective when trying to discourage misbehavior.
   TRUE or FALSE

FINAL SURVEY AND REVIEW

Heredity and Environment—It Takes Two to Tango

Survey Question: How do heredity and environment affect development? Pages 88-93

1. _____ psychology is the study of _____ changes in behavior and abilities, from birth to death.

2. The nature-nurture _____ concerns the relative contributions to development of _____ (nature) and _____ (nurture).

3. Hereditary _____ are carried by DNA (deoxyribonucleic acid) in the form of chromosomes and genes in each cell of the body.

4. Most characteristics are _____ (influenced by a combination of genes) and reflect the combined effects of _____ and _____ genes.

5. Heredity influences _____—the general pattern of _____ growth and _____.

6. _____ reflects _____ levels of maturation that must occur before some skills (like toilet-training) can be learned.

7. Environment refers to all _____ conditions that affect development.

8. Compared to an adult brain, newborn babies have neurons with _____dendrites and _____. These neurons grow rapidly, making millions of connections as the newborns interact with their environment in the first three years.

9. Early _____ environments literally _____ the developing brain, through "blooming and pruning" of synapses.

10. Prenatal development is subject to environmental influences in the form of _____, drugs, radiation, or the mother's _____ and health.

11. Prenatal damage to the fetus may cause _____ problems, or birth defects. In contrast, genetic problems are _____ from one's parents.

12. _____ (FAS) is the result of heavy drinking during pregnancy, which causes the infant to have low birth _____, a small head, and facial _____.

13. Exposure to any form of teratogens such as _____, lead, and _____ during pregnancy will likely cause birth defects.

14. A variety of _____ periods (times of increased sensitivity to environmental influences) exist in development.

15. Early perceptual, intellectual, and emotional _____ seriously retards development.

16. Poverty greatly increases the likelihood that children will experience various forms of deprivation, which may impede _____ development and educational achievement and _____ the risk for mental _____ and delinquent behavior.

17. Deliberate enrichment of the environment in infancy and early childhood has a _____ effect on development.

18. Nurture (environment) affects the expression of nature (hereditary tendencies) through ongoing _____ influences.

19. Heredity influences differences in _____ (the physical core of personality). Most infants fall into one of three temperament categories: _____ children, difficult children, and _____ children.

20. Ultimately, most psychologists accept that heredity and _____ are inseparable and _____ forces.

21. A child's developmental _____ (current state of development) reflects heredity, _____, and the effects of the child's own behavior.

The Newborn Baby—More Than Meets the Eye

Survey Question: What can newborn babies do? Pages 93-98

1. The human neonate (_____) has a number of adaptive _____.

2. The grasping reflex aids survival by helping an infant to _____; the _____ reflex is a reflexive head turning to help infants find food; the sucking helps an infant obtain food; the _____ reflex is a hugging motion infants make when startled.

3. _____ begin to learn immediately and they imitate adults.

4. Tests in a looking chamber reveal a number of visual _____ in the newborn. The neonate is drawn to _____, circular, curved, and _____-lighted designs.

5. Infants prefer _____ face patterns, especially familiar faces. In later infancy, interest in the _____ emerges.

6. Maturation of the body and nervous system underlies the _____ sequence of motor, cognitive, language, and _____ development.

7. While the rate of maturation _____ from child to child, the order is nearly _____.

8. The development of muscular control (_____) is _____ (from head to toe) and proximodistal (from the center of the body to the _____).

9. Emotional development begins with a capacity for general excitement. After that the first _____ and _____ emotions develop.

10. Some psychologists believe that basic emotional expressions are innate and that some appear as early as _____ months of age.

11. By 8-12 months, babies display a _____ when other people are nearby.

12. Babies can communicate their _____ in objects through smiling.

Social Development—Baby, I'm Stuck on You

Survey Question: Of what significance is a child's emotional bond with adults? Pages 99-101

1. Social development refers to the emergence of _____ and forming relationships with _____ and others.

2. Self-awareness (_____ of oneself as a person) is an element of early social development.

3. For _____ development in human infants, the development of an emotional attachment to their primary caregivers is a _____ early event that must occur during the sensitive period (within the _____ year) of infancy.

4. Infant _____ is reflected by separation _____ (distress when infants are away from parents).

5. When experiencing separation anxiety _____, children cling to their parents and are _____ when separated from their them.

6. The quality of attachment can be classified as secure, insecure-avoidant, or insecure-_____.

7. Some psychologists believe that our first attachments continue to affect how we relate to others as _____ (e.g., romantic relationships).

8. The relationship between quality of attachment and the type of _____ that is provided appears to be universal in all cultures.

9. High-quality day care does not harm children; _____-quality care can, in fact, _____ some areas of development.

10. Some characteristics of high-quality day care include having a small number of children per caregiver, _____ caregivers, an overall group size of 12 to 15 children, and _____ staff turnover.

11. A child's social development is also affected by _____ with other children. For example, cooperative play is a major step toward participation in _____ life outside the family.

12. An infant's _____ needs are every bit as important as more obvious needs for _____ care.

Parental Influences—Life with Mom and Dad

Survey Question: How important are parenting styles? Pages 101-104

1. Parents may exhibit distinct patterns of parental caretaking – _____, overly permissive, and _____.

2. _____ parents enforce rigid rules and demand _____ obedience to authority.

3. Overly _____ parents give _____ guidance and don't hold children accountable for their actions.

4. _____ (effective) parents supply firm and _____ guidance, combined with love and affection.

5. Authoritative parenting leads to resilience (the ability to _____ back after _____ experiences).

6. Caregiving styles among various ethnic groups tend to reflect each culture's _____ and beliefs. For example, _____ in Arab-American families tend to be strong authority figures, demanding absolute _____.

7. _____ influences differ in their impact because fathers tend to function as a _____ for the infant.

8. Fathers are most likely to _____ with their children, whereas mothers are most often responsible for the physical and _____ care of their children.

9. The _____ of parenting can only be judged if we know what culture the child is being prepared to _____.

10. An authoritative (effective) style of parenting encourages children to manage their emotions and use _____ coping skills to be resilient (able to bounce back after bad experiences) and _____ adults.

Language Development—Who Talks Baby Talk?

Survey Question: How do children acquire language? Pages 104-107

1. Language development proceeds from control of crying, to _____, then babbling, the use of _____ words, and then to telegraphic speech.

2. The patterns of early speech suggest a biological _____ to acquire language.

3. _____ (psychologists who study language) believe that _____ language predispositions are augmented by learning.

4. Prelanguage communication between parent and child involves shared _____, nonverbal signals, and turn-taking.

5. Parents help children learn language by using distinctive _____ speech or parentese; it helps to get babies' _____, communicate with them, and teach them the _____.

6. Mothererse or _____ is characterized by short, _____ sentences, higher pitch, and frequent repetition and gestures.

Cognitive Development—Think Like a Child

Survey Question: How do children learn to think? Pages 108-114

1. The intellects of children are less _____ than those of adults. Children use _____ generalizations, categories, and principles.

2. Jean _____ theorized that intellectual growth occurs through a combination of assimilation and _____.

3. Piaget also held that children go through a fixed series of _____ stages. These are: _____ (0-2), preoperational (2-7), concrete operational (7-11), and _____ operations (11-adult).

4. Object _____ (the ability to understand that objects continue to _____ when they are out of sight) emerges during the sensorimotor stage.

5. _____ (the ability to understand that mass, weight, and volume remain unchanged when the _____ of objects changes) emerges during the concrete operational stage.

6. Children in the _____ stage of development, tend to exhibit egocentrism; this is the inability to assume another's _____ or viewpoint.

7. Children in the _____ operational stage of development are less egocentric and can think abstractly, hypothetically, and _____.

8. Learning theorists dispute the idea that cognitive development occurs in stages. Recent studies suggest infants are capable of levels of thinking beyond that observed by Piaget; he may have _____ limited physical skills for _____ incompetence.

9. Renee Baillargeon's research on _____ events suggests that infants may develop object permanence _____ than suggested by Piaget's theory.

10. Piaget may have _____ the impact of culture on development.

11. A _____ strategy that takes into account the child's level of cognitive development helps adapt instruction to a child's needs.

12. Parents should avoid forced teaching, or "_____" as it might _____ and oppress children.

13. According to the _____ theory of Russian scholar Lev Vygotsky, a child's interactions with others are most likely to aid cognitive development if they take place within the child's zone of _____ development.

14. Adults help children learn how to think by _____, or supporting, their attempts to _____ problems or discover principles.

15. During their _____ with adults, children learn important cultural beliefs and _____.

Adolescence and Young Adulthood – The Best of Times, the Worst of Times

Survey Question: Why is the transition from adolescence to adulthood especially challenging? Pages 115-117

1. Adolescence is the _____ defined period between childhood and _____.

2. Criterion for adult status in North America are: taking _____ for oneself, making independent _____, and becoming financially _____.

3. Adolescence is a _____ status; _____ is a biological event.

4. During puberty, hormonal changes promote rapid _____ growth and _____ maturity.

5. Teens who enter puberty _____ than their peers may have more positive body images, but are also more likely to engage in _____ behavior.

6. Identity formation is a key task for _____; this may be influenced by one's _____ heritage.

7. _____ are those in their twenties still living at home who are not yet married and with no settled _____.

Moral Development—Growing a Conscience

Survey Question: How do we develop morals and values? Pages 117-119

1. Lawrence _____ theorized that moral development passes through a series of stages revealed by moral _____ about moral _____.

2. Kohlberg identified _____, conventional, and postconventional levels of moral reasoning.

3. At the _____ level, moral development is guided by consequences of actions, such as rewards and _____.

4. Preconventional _____ are typical of young children and _____; Conventional, group-oriented morals are typical of _____ children and adults.

The Story of a Lifetime—Rocky Road or Garden Path?

Survey Question: What are the typical tasks and dilemmas through the life span? Pages 119-121

1. Developmental psychologists are interested in developmental _____, or prominent landmarks in personal development such as graduation.

2. According to Erik _____, each life stage provokes a specific _____ dilemma.

3. During childhood, psychosocial dilemmas include: _____ versus mistrust, autonomy versus shame and doubt, _____ versus guilt, and industry versus inferiority.

4. During the stage of _____ vs. shame and doubt, children may have "accidents" as they try to do things for _____.

5. In adolescence, _____ versus role confusion is the principal dilemma.

6. In young adulthood we face the dilemma of _____ versus isolation. Later, _____ versus stagnation becomes prominent.

7. _____ age is a time when the dilemma of integrity versus despair must be faced.

8. In addition, each life stage requires successful _____ of certain developmental tasks (personal changes required for optimal development).

Middle and Late Adulthood: Will You Still Need Me When I'm 64?

Survey Question: What is involved in well-being during later adulthood? Pages 122-124

1. Well-being at _____ is related to self-acceptance, positive _____, autonomy, environmental _____, a purpose in life, and continued personal growth.

2. It is more common to make a "_____ correction" at midlife than to have a "_____."

3. A midlife transition may include _____ old identities, achieving _____, finding one's truths, and preparing for _____ age.

4. You are most likely to stay mentally fit if you: Stay healthy, live in a _____ environment, engage in _____ stimulating activities, have a _____ personality, marry a smart spouse, and are satisfied with accomplishments at midlife.

5. People entering old age do experience a gradual loss of fluid abilities (those requiring _____ or _____ learning); however, these can be offset by crystallized abilities (learned _____ and skills).

6. Ageism refers to _____, discrimination, and _____ on the basis of age. It affects people of all _____ but is especially damaging to older people.

Psychology in Action: Effective Parenting—Raising Healthy Children

Survey Question: How do effective parents discipline and communicate with their children? Pages 124-128

1. Mutual respect, effective _____, love, _____, and clear communication are features of effective parenting.

2. When disciplining children, _____ discipline (maintaining a stable rule of conduct) fosters security and stability, whereas _____ discipline fosters insecurity and unpredictability.

3. Effective child discipline is based on a consistent framework of _____ for _____ behavior.

4. Good discipline tends to emphasize child _____ techniques (especially communication), rather than power assertion or _____ of love.

5. _____ techniques tend to produce the highest levels of self-esteem in children.

6. Much misbehavior can be managed by use of _____-messages and by applying natural and _____ consequences to children's behavior.

7. I-messages focus on the behavior, and _____-messages focus on children's characteristics.

MASTERY TEST

1. The universal patterns of the human growth sequence can be attributed to
a. recessive genes.
b. environment.
c. polygenic imprinting.
d. heredity.

2. Exaggerated or musical voice inflections are characteristic of
a. prelanguage turn-taking.
b. parentese.
c. telegraphic speech.
d. prompting and expansion.

3. The emotion most clearly expressed by newborn infants is
a. joy.
b. fear.
c. anger.
d. excitement.

4. Explaining things abstractly or symbolically to a child becomes most effective during which stage of cognitive development?
a. postconventional
b. formal operations
c. preoperational
d. post-intuitive

5. An infant startled by a loud noise will typically display
a. a Moro reflex.
b. a rooting reflex.
c. a Meltzoff reflex.
d. an imprinting reflex.

6. If one identical twin has a Y chromosome, the other must have a
a. recessive chromosome.
b. sex-linked trait.
c. dominant chromosome.
d. Y chromosome.

7. Ideas about Piaget's stages and the cognitive abilities of infants are challenged by infants' reactions to
a. hypothetical possibilities.
b. impossible events.
c. turn-taking.
d. separation anxiety.

8. The largest percentage of children display what type of temperament?
a. easy
b. difficult
c. slow-to-warm-up
d. generic

9. Which of the following is a congenital problem?
a. FAS
b. sickle-cell anemia
c. hemophilia
d. muscular dystrophy

10. A child might begin to question the idea that Santa Claus' sack could carry millions of toys when the child has grasped the concept of
a. assimilation.
b. geocentricism.
c. conservation.
d. reversibility of permanence.

11. In most areas of development, heredity and environment are
a. independent.
b. interacting.
c. conflicting.
d. responsible for temperament.

12. According to Erikson, developing a sense of integrity is a special challenge in
a. adolescence.
b. young adulthood.
c. middle adulthood.
d. late adulthood.

13. Children who grow up in poverty run a high risk of
a. insecure scaffolding.
b. hospitalism.
c. deprivation.
d. colostrums.

14. According to Erikson, the first dilemma a newborn infant must resolve is
a. independence versus dependence.
b. initiative versus guilt.
c. trust versus mistrust.
d. attachment versus confusion.

15. By definition, a trait that is controlled by a dominant gene cannot be
a. eugenic.
b. hereditary.
c. carried by DNA.
d. polygenic.

16. _____ development proceeds head-down and center-outward.
a. Cognitive
b. Motor
c. Prelanguage
d. Preoperational

17. You could test for _____ by videotaping a child and then letting the child see the video on television.
a. social referencing
b. self-awareness
c. the quality of attachment
d. the degree of readiness

18. Although older individuals may experience some decrements related to speedy decision making, they can often retrieve a great deal of stored facts from long-term memory. This ability to retrieve stored facts exemplifies:
a. crystallized abilities.
b. scaffolding.
c. fluid abilities.
d. intuition.

19. After age 2, infants become much more interested in
a. bonding.
b. nonverbal communication.
c. familiar voices.
d. unfamiliar faces.

20. According to Piaget, one of the major developments during the sensorimotor stage is emergence of the concept of
a. assimilation.
b. accommodation.
c. object permanence.
d. transformation.

21. One of the key tasks of adolescence is _____, which may be influenced by the extent to which a person embraces his or her _____.
a. Identity formation; financial status
b. Identify formation; ethnic heritage
c. Puberty; intimacy potential
d. Assimilation; ethnic heritage

22. Poverty is to deprivation as early childhood stimulation is to
a. imprinting.
b. enrichment.
c. responsiveness.
d. assimilation.

23. Which principle is most relevant to the timing of toilet training?
a. readiness
b. sensitive periods
c. nonverbal signals
d. assimilation

24. High self-esteem is most often a product of what style of child discipline?
a. power assertion
b. child management
c. withdrawal of love
d. the natural consequences method

25. Consonants first enter a child's language when the child begins
a. babbling.
b. cooing.
c. the single word stage.
d. turn-taking.

26. Physically arousing play is typically an element of
a. mother's caregiving style.
b. paternal influences.
c. proactive maternal involvement.
d. secure attachment.

27. Insecure attachment is revealed by
a. separation anxiety.
b. seeking to be near the mother after separation.
c. turning away from the mother after separation.
d. social referencing.

28. Demarco has grown several inches within the past year, and has begun to develop facial hair and chest hair. Demarco is probably experiencing the developmental stage of
a. senescence
b. puberty
c. generativity
d. conservation

29. A healthy balance between the rights of parents and their children is characteristic of
a. authoritarian parenting.
b. permissive parenting.
c. authoritative parenting.
d. consistent parenting.

30. Studies of infant imitation
a. are conducted in a looking chamber.
b. confirm that infants mimic adult facial gestures.
c. show that self-awareness precedes imitation.
d. are used to assess the quality of infant attachment.

31. Threatening, accusing, bossing, and lecturing children is most characteristic of
a. PET.
b. you-messages.
c. applying natural consequences.
d. management techniques.

32. According to Vygotsky, children learn important cultural beliefs and values when adults provide _____ to help them gain new ideas and skills.
a. scaffolding
b. proactive nurturance
c. imprinting stimuli
d. parentese

33. One thing that all forms of effective child discipline have in common is that they
a. are consistent.
b. make use of punishment.
c. involve temporary withdrawal of love.
d. emphasize you-messages.

34. Which of the following is a common myth about old age?
a. Most elderly persons are isolated and neglected.
b. A large percentage of the elderly suffer from senility.
c. A majority of the elderly are dissatisfied with their lives.
d. All of the preceding are myths.

35. Jayla graduated from college a year ago. Although she recently got a job in a customer service department, she has decided to live with her parents so she can save enough money to buy a new car. Jayla would probably be referred to as a(n)
a. adolescent
b. twixter
c. post-pubescent
d. Interlopster

36. Moral thinking is guided by the consequences of actions, such as punishment, reward, or an exchange of favors, in which level of moral development?
a. preconventional
b. postconventional
c. conventional
d. relational exchange

37. Jimmy clings to his mother and refuses to go to school. He is most likely suffering from
a. a secure attachment.
b. parentese.
c. separation anxiety disorder.
d. assimilation.

38. Which one of the following is NOT a widely accepted element for adult status in North America?
a. Taking responsibility for oneself
b. Becoming financially independent
c. Getting married
d. Making independent decisions

39. Julie often expresses concern that her boyfriend does not love her as much as she loves him. This concern best reflects a(n)
a. secure attachment.
b. an anxious/ambivalent attachment.
c. avoidant attachment.
d. none of the above

40. Jack is in his mid twenties and single. He has not yet decided what he wants to do for a career and is still living at home. According to the text, Jim is likely
a. a twixter.
b. egocentric.
c. establishing trust.
d. both b & c

41. Beth, a 75-year-old grandmother, is treated kindly by her family. However, her grandchildren often speak to her like she is a child and speak to her in simple sentences. Such behavior best reflects
a. egocentrism.
b. role confusion.
c. ageism.
d. scaffolding.

42. Parents who use a(an) _____ form of parenting tend to teach their children to manage and control their emotions and to use positive coping skills.
a. authoritative
b. authoritarian
c. overly permissive
d. power assertion

43. Seeking approval and upholding law, order, and authority are characteristics of what stage of moral development?
a. preconventional
b. conventional
c. postconventional
d. postformal

44. According to Erikson, a dilemma concerning _____ usually follows one that focuses on identity.
a. trust
b. industry
c. initiative
d. intimacy

45. Kohlberg believed that moral development typically begins _____ and continues into adulthood with ___ percent of adults achieving postconventional morality.
a. at the onset of puberty, 50
b. in childhood, 20
c. in early adolescence, 40
d. in late adolescence, 80

LANGUAGE DEVELOPMENT
Human Development

Word Roots

Ego is the Latin pronoun that means "I." When combined with other word roots, it refers to the self. Freud used this Latin word to refer to one of the three parts of the personality, which he named id, ego, and superego. Other examples of the use of this root word include egocentric and ego ideal; these uses will be found in later chapters.

Journey into Psychology: It's a Girl! (p. 87)
   (87)   *pudgy*: short and plump
   (87)   *stubby*: short, blunt, and thick like a stub

Nature and Nurture – It Takes Two to Tango (p. 88-93)
   How do heredity and environment affect development?
   (88)   *progressive*: furthering; often implying continuing growth or improvement
   (88)   *the womb to the tomb*: from birth to death
   (88)   *governed*: controlled; guided
   (88)   *civil rights lawyer:* one who advocates for equal rights for all individuals, regardless of race, ethnicity, class, religion, or sexual orientation.
   (88)   *interplay*: the action of affecting one another
   (88)   *nucleus*: the center, in this case of a cell
   (88)   *room left over to spare:* extra capacity
   (88)   *milestone*: a significant point; this might refer to history or development
   (89)   *expressed*: shown
   (89)   *susceptibility*: inability to resist
   (90)   *wet look*: reference to a style in which the hair appears to be damp; Coon is using the phrase humorously
   (90)   *blooming and pruning*: changing the structure of the neural network
   (91)   *cave dwellers*: people who live in caves

(91)   *gangsta rapper*: someone who performs the type of music known as "gangsta rap"

(91)   *Upper Paleolithic*: late Stone Age (30,000 years ago), characterized by use of rough stone tools

(91)   *measles*: a contagious viral disease characterized by red circular spots on the skin

(91)   *syphilis*: a contagious disease transmitted by sexual intercourse or other intimate contact

(91)   *HIV*: human immunodeficiency virus; precursor to AIDS

(91)   *hemophilia*: a condition that characterizes excessive bleeding due to inadequate coagulation of the blood

(91)   *albinism*: hereditary condition that causes a lack of pigment (color) in skin, hair, and eyes (eyes are pink)

(91)   *PCBs*: polychlorinated biphenyls, often found in soil; suspected cancer-causing agents

(91)   *miscarrying*: losing a baby before its birth

(91-92) *caregiver*: a parent or significant other person who cares for a child

(92)   *optimal*: the best

(92)   *impoverished:* poor

(92)   *"child-proof":* to identify and remove items that pose potential health hazards

(93)   *distractibility*: ability to have one's attention drawn in different directions

(93)   *restrained*: held back from responding

(93)   *elicit*: to trigger, cause

The Newborn Baby—More Than Meets the Eye (pgs. 93-98)

What can newborn babies do?

(93)   *inert*: does not have the ability to respond

(94)   *unfolds*: develops

(94)   *acute*: sensitive

(94)   *trapeze artist*: a performer on the "trapeze," a bar suspended in the air by two ropes

(94)   *mimics*: people who copy the actions of others

(94)   *soak up*: gather in information, similar to how a sponge gathers in water

(96)   *universal*: found everywhere, among all cultures (97) *wobbly crawl*: unsteady movement on hands and knees

(97)   *tune*: adjust behavior according to each learned skill

(97)   *hard-wired*: coded into our genes

(97)   *haphazard*: random; without order

(97)   *baby buggy*: baby carriage

(97)   *dazzling speed*: great speed

Social Development—Baby, I'm Stuck on You (pgs. 99-101)

Of what significance is a child's emotional bond with adults?

(99) **Baby I'm Stuck on You**: a song title used by Coon to indicate extreme fondness

(99) **home base**: a baseball reference and a place of safety and refuge

(100) **plight of children**: the crisis condition of children

(100) **Romanian orphanages**: desperately understaffed orphanages in the country of Romania where the children suffer from too little care and attention

(101) **menagerie**: collection of wild animals kept for exhibition

(101) **stockade**: a place where prisoners are kept

(101) **spoiling**: implying that babies will turn out "bad" because of too much attention; being overly indulged

Parental Influences—Life with Mom and Dad (pgs. 101-104)

How important are parenting styles?

(101) **run amok**: behave in a totally wild or undisciplined manner

(102) **conventional**: to be normal, common

(102) **peekaboo**: (peek-a-boo) a game to amuse a baby in which the caregiver repeatedly hides his or her face then reveals it again to the baby

(102) **risk-taking**: behaviors that have a potential for harm

(103) **adversity:** unfortunate conditions or circumstances

(103) **urban areas**: the core or central areas of large cities

(103) **interdependence**: when people view themselves as members of a group from which they receive their status and self-worth

(103) **child-rearing**: raising of children

(104) **prospective**: future; potential

Language Development—Who Talks Baby Talk? (pgs. 104-107)

How do children acquire language?

(105) **and the like**: other similar things

(105) **"This, too, shall pass"**: A Biblical reference meaning "Do not worry, soon this trouble will be over also"

(105) **phenomenal**: to be great, impressive

(105) **What dis?**: What is this?

(106) **getcha**: get you

(106) **gotcha**: got you

(107) **Nein! Nein! Basta! Basta! Not! Dude!**: ways of saying "no" in different languages; the word "dude" is an American slang expression young people, mostly males, use with each other as a form of greeting or as a reference to each other

(107) **OOOh pobrecito**: Spanish for "Oh, poor baby"

(107) **birdie**: variation of the word bird, often used when talking to children

(107) **full flowering of**: full development of

(107) **richer language**: a complex language by which to communicate

Cognitive Development—Think Like A Child (pgs. 108-114)

How do children learn to think?

(108) *illustrious*: well known for extraordinary achievement in academia

(108) *mind's eye:* hypothetical area of visualization or visual memory

(109) *exasperatingly selfish*: to be overly selfish

(110) *panty-girdle*: a woman's elasticized underwear

(110) *Santa Clause*: a mythical figure who delivers toys and other presents to children at Christmastime

(110) *inductive reasoning*: to reason from the specific to the general

(110) *deductive reasoning*: to reason from the general to the specific

(111) *novel*: to be new, different

(111) *hothousing*: a botanical term meaning to force plants into early blooming, and used here to mean to push children too fast, too early

(111) *Monopoly*: a popular board game in which players attempt to buy and control property and industries

(111) *road map*: a guide for getting from place to place

(113) *tutors*: people who serve as one-to-one instructors or guides to others

(114) *tailored*: carefully chosen and fit to certain information

(114) *mental territory*: ways of thinking, reasoning, and problem-solving

(114) *baseball cards*: cards that show famous baseball players that many children use to trade for the cards they want

(114) *grown-ups*: adults

(114) *decipher*: to translate or break down

Adolescence and Young Adulthood – The Best of Times, the Worst of Times (pgs. 115 – 117)

Why is the transition from adolescence to adulthood especially challenging?

(115) *The Best of Times, the Worst of Times:* Coon makes a reference to the novel, "A Tale of Two Cities," which discusses the politics and intrigue leading to the French Revolution (a time of upheaval and turmoil); here used to refer to changes taking place during adolescence.

(115) *transitional*: movement or passage from one state to another

(116) *autonomous*: self-sufficient

(117) *maturity gap:* time period between adolescence and true adulthood. in this case, young adults avoiding or putting off the responsibilities of adulthood

(117) *affluent:* having an abundance of wealth or resources; rich

(117) *turbulent*: state of agitation, disturbance, or disorder

Moral Development—Growing a Conscience (pgs. 117-119)

How do we develop morals and values?

(118) *intermediate*: in the middle, halfway

(118) *"moral compass"*: a sense of right and wrong

The Story of a Lifetime—Rocky Road or Garden Path? (pgs. 119-121)

What are the typical tasks and dilemmas through the life span?
(120) *ridiculed:* made fun of
(120) *dizzying speed*: a very fast pace

Middle and Late Adulthood: Will You Still Need Me When I'm 64? (pgs. 122-124)

What is involved in well-being during later adulthood?
(122) *"Will You Still Need Me When I'm 64?":* a song title Coon uses to indicate worry or anxiety regarding aging
(122) *gauntlet:* a challenge
(122) *taking stock*: gathering an inventory of one's available items or resources
(122) *wake-up calls:* something that alerts an individual to a danger or pressing need
(122) *infirm*: sickly; of poor health or condition
(122) *senile*: showing loss of mental abilities or memory
(122) *Gerontologist*: one who studies aging or the aged
(123) *patronizing language*: language that puts another down; demeaning (and often subtle) language
(123) *perpetuate*: to cause to last indefinitely

Psychology in Action: Effective Parenting—Raising Healthy Children (pgs. 124-128)

How do effective parents discipline their children?
(124) *antisocial*: contrary or hostile to the well-being of society
(125) *"model"*: in this context, the best example of
(125) *empower:* to give power or authority to someone
(125) *entitlement:* belief that one deserves certain powers or priviledges
(125) *self-indulgent*: selfish; taking care of one's own wants and desires
(126) *Brussels sprouts*: one of the small edible heads on the stalks of plants closely related to the cabbage; kids typically dislike them

Chapter in Review

(129) *augmented*: improved; given greater support

Solutions

Recite and Review

Heredity and Environment—It Takes Two to Tango
1. behavior, birth, death
2. nature, nurture
3. DNA, genes
4. genes, genes
5. physical growth, development.
6. maturation
7. external
8. fewer, synapses
9. blooming, pruning
10. environmental
11. birth defects.
12. FAS, drinking, low, facial
13. teratogens
14. sensitivity
15. development.
16. deprivation, educational, delinquent
17. environment
18. influences
19. personality, difficult
20. heredity
21. own behavior

The Newborn Baby—More Than Meets the Eye
1. neonate, adaptive
2. grasping, hugging
3. learn
4. visua, circular
5. familiar faces
6. sequence
7. order
8. muscular, center
9. general
10. innate
11. people
12. smiling

Social Development—Baby, I'm Stuck on You
1. Social
2. social
3. caregivers
4. sensitive period
5. separation
6. separated
7. secure
8. attachments
9. universal
10. harm
11. small, 12, 15
12. social, play
13. needs

Parental Influences—Life with Mom and Dad
1. authoritarian, permissive
2. rules, authority
3. guidance
4. effective
5. resilience
6. customs, beliefs
7. fathers
8. Fathers, mothers
9. culture
10. authoritative, positive, resilient

Language Development—Who Talks Baby Talk?
1. crying, speech
2. biological
3. language, learning.
4. signals
5. speech
6. higher, gestures

Cognitive Development—Think Like a Child

1. less, generalizations
2. assimilation
3. stages, concrete, operations
4. objects, sensorimotor
5. unchanged, concrete operational
6. egocentrism
7. abstractly
8. stages, physical, incompetence
9. infants, permanence
10. culture
11. cognitive
12. forced
13. cognitive, zone, development
14. supporting
15. beliefs

Adolescence and Young Adulthood – The Best of Times, the Worst of Times

1. childhood
2. oneself, independent, financially
3. biological
4. hormonal, physical
5. positive
6. Identity, heritage
7. twenties

Moral Development—Growing a Conscience

1. moral, moral, moral
2. reasoning
3. rewards
4. young, group, adults

The Story of a Lifetime—Rocky Road or Garden Path?

1. developmental
2. dilemma
3. shame, guilt, inferiority
4. accidents
5. adolescence
6. isolation, stagnation
7. despair
8. developmental

Middle and Late Adulthood: Will You Still Need Me When I'm 64?

1. purpose, growth
2. correction, midlife
3. identities, age
4. healthy, stimulating, satisfied
5. fluid, crystallized
6. age, older

Psychology in Action: Effective Parenting—Raising Healthy Children

1. respect, communication
2. stability, unpredictability
3. discipline
4. power, love
5. Management, messages, natural
6. behavior, characteristics

CONNECTIONS

Heredity and Environment—It Takes Two to Tango

1. A.	4. C.	7. D.	10. F.
2. B.	5. G.	8. I.	
3. H.	6. J.	9. E.	

The Newborn Baby—More Than Meets the Eye

1. B.	3. C.	5. A.	7. H.
2. D.	4. F.	6. E.	8. G.

Social Development—Baby, I'm Stuck on You

1. C.	3. H.	5. D.	7. E.
2. B.	4. A.	6. G.	8. F.

Parental Influences—Life with Mom and Dad

1. F.	3. G.	5. A.	7. E.
2. D.	4. B.	6. C.	

Language Development—Who Talks Baby Talk?

1. E.	3. H.	5. D.	7. F.
2. A.	4. B.	6. G.	8. C.

Cognitive Development—Think Like A Child

1. D.	4. B.	7. J.	10. F.
2. A.	5. G.	8. I.	11. C.
3. H.	6. E.	9. K.	

Adolescence and Young Adulthood – The Best of Times, the Worst of Times and Moral Development

1. F.	4. C.	7. G.	10. B.
2. A.	5. I.	8. D.	
3. J.	6. E.	9. H.	

The Story of a Lifetime—Rocky Road or Garden Path? and Middle and Late Adulthood: Will you Still Need Me When I'm 64?

1. E.	5. J.	9. O.	13. M.
2. N.	6. C.	10. B.	14. A.
3. F.	7. L.	11. K.	
4. G.	8. H.	12. D.	

Psychology in Action: Effective Parenting – Raising Healthy Children

1. G.	3. B.	5. D.	7. C.
2. A.	4. E.	6. F.	

Check Your Memory

Heredity and Environment—It Takes Two to Tango

1. F	5. T	9. T	13. T
2. F	6. F	10. F	14. F
3. T	7. T	11. T	15. T
4. F	8. T	12. F	16. T

The Newborn Baby—More Than Meets the Eye

1. F	4. F	7. T	10. F
2. F	5. F	8. F	11. T
3. T	6. F	9. F	

Social Development—Baby, I'm Stuck on You

1. F	4. T	7. T
2. F	5. F	8. T
3. F	6. T	9. T

Parental Influences—Life with Mom and Dad

1. F	4. T	7. T	10. F
2. T	5. F	8. F	11. T
3. F	6. F	9. T	

Language Development—Who Talks Baby Talk?

1. F	3. F	5. F	7. T
2. F	4. T	6. T	8. F

Cognitive Development—Think Like A Child

1. F	5. F	9. F	13. T
2. T	6. T	10. T	
3. T	7. T	11. F	
4. F	8. F	12. T	

Adolescence and Young Adulthood – The Best of Times, the Worst of Times

1. F	3. T	5. F	7. T
2. F	4. F	6. F	8. T

Moral Development—Growing a Conscience

1. T	3. F	5. F
2. T	4. T	6. F

The Story of a Lifetime—Rocky Road or Garden Path? and Middle and Late Adulthood: Will You Still Need Me When I'm 64?

1. F	5. T	9. F	13. F
2. F	6. T	10. T	14. F
3. T	7. T	11. T	15. T
4. F	8. T	12. T	16. F

Psychology in Action: Effective Parenting—Raising Healthy Children

1. T	3. F	5. T	7. F
2. T	4. F	6. F	

Final Survey and Review

Heredity and Environment—It Takes Two to Tango

1. Developmental, progressive
2. debate, heredity, environment
3. instructions
4. polygenic, dominant, recessive
5. maturation, physical, development.
6. Readiness, minimum
7. external
8. fewer, synapses
9. learning, shape
10. diseases, diet
11. congenital, inherited
12. Fetal alcohol syndrome, weight, malformations
13. radiation, pesticides
14. sensitive
15. deprivation
16. cognitive, increase, illness
17. beneficial
18. reciprocal
19. temperament, easy, slow-to-warm-up
20. environment, interacting
21. level, environment

The Newborn Baby—More Than Meets the Eye

1. newborn, reflexes
2. avoid falling, rooting, Moro
3. Newborns
4. preferences, complex, brightly
5. human, unfamiliar
6. orderly, emotional
7. varies, universal
8. motor development, cephalocaudal, extremities
9. pleasant, unpleasant
10. 2 ½
11. social smile
12. interest

Social Development—Baby, I'm Stuck on You

1. self-awareness, parents
2. consciousness
3. optimal, critical, first
4. attachment, anxiety
5. disorder, miserable
6. ambivalent.
7. adults
8. caregiving
9. high, accelerate
10. trained, minimal
11. playing, social
12. affectional, physical

Parental Influences—Life with Mom and Dad

1. authoritarian, authoritative
2. Authoritarian, strict
3. permissive, little
4. Authoritative, consistent
5. bounce, bad
6. customs, fathers, obedience
7. Paternal, playmate
8. play, emotional
9. effectiveness, enter
10. positive, competent

Language Development—Who Talks Baby Talk?

1. cooing, single
2. predisposition
3. Psycholinguists, innate
4. rhythms
5. caretaker, attention, language
6. Parentese, simple

Cognitive Development—Think Like a Child

1. abstract, fewer
2. Piaget, accommodation
3. cognitive, sensorimotor, formal
4. permanence, exist
5. Conservation, shape
6. preoperational, perspective
7. formal, theoretically
8. mistook, mental
9. impossible, earlier
10. underestimated
11. one-step-ahead
12. hothousing, bore
13. sociocultural, proximal
14. scaffolding, solve
15. collaborations, values

Adolescence and Young Adulthood – The Best of Times, the Worst of Times

1. culturally, adulthood
2. responsibility, decisions, independent
3. social, puberty
4. physical, sexual
5. earlier, antisocial
6. adolescence, ethnic
7. Twixters, career

Moral Development—Growing a Conscience

1. Kohlberg, reasoning, dilemmas.
2. preconventional
3. preconventional, punishments
4. morals, delinquents, older

The Story of a Lifetime—Rocky Road or Garden Path?

1. milestones
2. Erikson, psychosocial
3. trust, initiative
4. autonomy, themselves
5. identity
6. intimacy, generativity
7. Old
8. mastery

Middle and Late Adulthood: Will You Still Need Me When I'm 64?

1. midlife, relationships, mastery
2. midcourse, crisis
3. reworking, goals, old
4. favorable, mentally, flexible
5. speed, rapid, knowledge
6. prejudice, stereotyping, ages

Psychology in Action: Effective Parenting—Raising Healthy Children

1. discipline, encouragement
2. consistent, inconsistent
3. guidelines, acceptable
4. management, withdrawal
5. Management
6. I, logical
7. you

Mastery Test

1. a, p. 88
2. b, p. 107
3. d, p. 97
4. b, p. 110
5. a, p. 94
6. d, p. 88
7. b, p. 112-113
8. a, p. 93
9. a, p. 91-92
10. c, p. 110
11. b, p. 92-93
12. d, p. 121
13. c, p. 92
14. c, p. 120
15. d, p. 89
16. b, p. 96-97
17. b, p. 99
18. a, p. 123
19. d, p. 95
20. c, p. 108
21. b, p. 116
22. b, p. 92
23. a, p. 89-90
24. b, p. 125
25. a, p. 104-105
26. b, p. 102
27. c, p. 99-100
28. b, p. 115
29. c, p. 101-102
30. b, p. 94
31. b, p. 127
32. a, p. 114
33. a, p. 125-126
34. d, p. 122-123
35. b, p.117
36. a, p. 118
37. c, p. 99
38. c, p. 115
39. b, p. 100
40. a, p. 117
41. c, p. 123
42. a, p. 101-102
43. b, p. 118
44. d, p. 121
45. b, p. 117-118

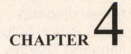

CHAPTER 4

Sensation and Perception

Chapter Overview

Sensations are collected and selected from the environment and transduced into neural energy and sent to the brain; perceptions arise when the brain analyzes, organizes, and codes these stimuli into meaningful patterns.

The visual system transduces electromagnetic radiation and analyzes this light stimuli to identify patterns and basic visual features. The structures of the eye work to focus and resolve incoming images. Common vision defects are myopia, hyperopia, presbyopia, and astigmatism. Color sensations are explained by the trichromatic theory (in the retina) and the opponent-process theory (for the rest of the visual system). Disturbances in these systems may cause color blindness or color weakness.

In the auditory system, the inner ear is a sensory mechanism for transducing sound waves in the air into nerve impulses. The frequency and place theories of hearing explain how sound information is coded.

There are two types of hearing loss: conductive and sensorineural. The latter includes noise-induced hearing loss (e.g., hunter's notch). In many cases, cochlear implants allow people with sensorineural hearing loss to hear human voices again.

Olfaction is based on receptors that respond to gaseous molecules in the air. The lock-and-key theory and the locations of olfactory receptors activated by different scents explain how various odors are coded. Taste is another chemical sense. A lock-and-key match between dissolved molecules and taste receptors also explains many taste sensations.

The somesthetic, or bodily, senses include the skin senses (touch, pressure, pain, temperature), the kinesthetic senses, and the vestibular senses. Sensory conflict theory explains motion sickness.

Our awareness of sensory information is altered by sensory adaptation, selective attention, and sensory gating.

Perception involves organizing sensations into meaningful patterns, although illusions and hallucinations can cause errors in perceptual construction. The most basic perceptual pattern (in vision) is figure-ground organization. Sensations tend to be organized on the basis of nearness, similarity, continuity, closure, contiguity, and common region. Visual perceptions are also stabilized by size, shape, and brightness constancies.

Depth perception depends on binocular cues such as convergence and retinal disparity, and monocular cues, including accommodation and pictorial cues. Pictorial cues include linear perspective, relative size, height in the picture, light and shadow, overlap, texture gradients, aerial perspective, and relative motion. The apparent-distance hypothesis is used to explain common errors in depth perception.

Perceptions are also greatly affected byexpectations (perceptual sets), motives, values, and emotions. Learning, in the form of perceptual habits, also influences perceptions. Parapsychology is the study of purported psi phenomena, including clairvoyance, telepathy, precognition, and psychokinesis. The bulk of the evidence to date is against the existence of extrasensory perception (ESP). Stage ESP is based on deception and tricks.

Because perceptions are reconstructions of events, eyewitness testimony can be unreliable. Perceptual accuracy can be improved by reality testing, dishabituation, actively paying attention, breaking perceptual habits, using broad frames of reference, and being aware of perceptual sets.

Learning Objectives

1. Compare and contrast sensation and perception
2. Describe how our senses act as a data reduction system and biological transducers.
3. Explain the concepts of *perceptual features, feature detectors, sensory analysis, sensory coding,* and *sensory localization*.
4. Describe the visible spectrum and define the concepts of hue, saturation, and brightness
5. Describe the functions of the lens, photoreceptors, and the retina; explain how the eye focuses and the process of accommodation; describe the four vision problems of hyperopia, myopia, astigmatism, and presbyopia.
6. Describe the functions of the rods and cones; explain how the brain compensates for the blind spot; describe the relationship between the fovea and visual acuity and the structures responsible for peripheral vision; discuss night vision and how it can be improved.
7. Compare and contrast the trichromatic and opponent-process theories of color vision, including a description of afterimages, color blindness, color weakness, and the IshiharaTest.
8. Describe the process of dark adaptation.
9. Explain the stimulus for hearing using the terms *compression*, *rarefaction*, *frequency*, and *amplitude,* and describe the location and function(s) of the following parts of the ear:
   a. pinna
   b. eardrum (tympanic membrane)
   c. auditory ossicles
   d. oval window
   e. cochlea
   f. hair cells

      g. stereocilia

      h. organ of Corti

10. Describe the frequency theory and the place theory of hearing.

11. Describe the three general types of deafness, the decibel levels of sounds that can cause temporary and permanent hearing loss, and the methods of artificial hearing.

12. Describe the sense of smell, including the condition dysomia and the lock and key theory

13. Describe the sense of taste, including the five taste sensations, the sensitivity of humans to these tastes, the location and functions of the taste buds, and how taste is affected by smell, texture, temperature, and pain.

14. List the three somesthetic senses and describe the function of each.

15. List the five sensations produced by the skin receptors and explain why certain areas of the body are more sensitive to touch.

16. Differentiate between the warning and reminding systems regarding pain messages; discuss factors that influence pain and three ways to reduce pain.

17. Describe the vestibular system, including the parts of the inner ear involved and how the sensory conflict theory explains motion sickness.

18. Describe how sensory adaptation, sensory gating, and selective attention prevent many sensory events from ever reaching conscious awareness, and include in your discussion the concepts of counterirritation, acupuncture, phantom limb pain, the neuromatrix, and inattentional blindness.

19. Define the term perceptual constructions and discuss how perceptual misconstructions are related to illusions, hallucinations, reality testing, and the Charles Bonnet Syndrome; discuss how bottom-up and top-down processes influence perceptual construction.

20. Define and give examples of the Gestalt organizing principles of figure-ground (include the concept of reversible figures and camouflage). nearness, similarity, continuity, closure, contiguity, and common region;

21. Explain the concepts of perceptual hypothesis, ambiguous stimuli, and impossible figures.

22. Describe the perceptual constancies of size, shape, and brightness.

23. Describe depth perception; discuss the research regarding this perceptual ability; and describe the following depth cues and indicate whether each cue is monocular or binocular:

      a. retinal disparity (include the term stereoscopic vision)

      b. convergence

      c. accommodation

24. Describe and give examples of the following monocular, pictorial depth cues:

      a. linear perspective

      b. relative size

      c. height in the picture plane

      d. light and shadow
      e. overlap
      f. texture gradients
      g. aerial perspective
      h. relative motion or motion parallax (include a discussion of the moon illusion and the apparent-distance hypothesis).

25. Describe the following concepts that influence a person's view of the world: perceptual expectancy (set), motives, emotions, "other-race effect," perceptual learning, perceptual habits, the Ames room illusion, and the Müller-Lyer illusion.

26. Define the terms *extrasensory perception*, *parapsychology*, and *psi phenomenon*; describe the purported psychic abilities of clairvoyance, telepathy, precognition, and psychokinesis, including the research with Zener cards.

27. Explain what most psychologists believe regarding psi abilities and stage ESP.

28. Explain why most eyewitness testimony is inaccurate, and describe how a person can more accurately perceive the world and become a better eyewitness to life.

RECITE AND REVIEW

Sensory Systems—the First Step

Survey Question: In general, how do sensory systems function? Pages 133-134

1. Sensory organs transduce physical energies into _____ impulses.

2. _____ refers to the information brought in by the senses, and _____ refers to the process by which the brain organizes and interprets the information into meaningful patterns.

3. The senses act as _____ reduction systems that select, _____, and filter sensory information.

4. Our sensory receptors cannot _____ all of the energies that they encounter in the environment.

5. A good example of sensory analysis is the identification of basic _____ features in a stimulus pattern.

6. In fact, many sensory systems act as feature _____.

7. Visual _____-out is an example of feature detection in action.

8. Sensory _____ results when we see phosphenes (visual sensations caused by mechanical excitation) when we press slightly on our _____.

9. Sensory response can be partially understood in terms of _____ localization in the brain. That is, the area of the brain _____ ultimately determines which type of sensory experience we have.

Vision—Catching Some Rays

Survey Question: How does the visual system function? Pages 135-141

1. Your eyes transduce only a small part of the entire range of electromagnetic energies; these are called the _____.

2. The electromagnetic spectrum ranges from violet, with a _____ of 400 nanometers, to red, with a _____ of 700 nanometers.

3. Hue refers to a color's name, which corresponds to its _____.

4. Saturated or "pure" colors come from a _____ band of wavelengths.

5. _____ corresponds to the amplitude, or height, of light waves.

6. The eye is in some ways like a camera. At its back lies an array of photoreceptors, called _____ and _____, that make up a light-sensitive layer called the retina.

7. Vision is focused by the _____ of the cornea and lens and by changes in the _____ of the lens, called accommodation.

8. Four common visual defects, correctable with glasses, are myopia (_____), hyperopia (farsightedness), presbyopia (loss of _____), and astigmatism (in which portions of vision are out of focus).

9. In the retina, the _____ specialize in night vision, black-and-white reception, and motion detection.

10. The _____, found exclusively in the fovea and otherwise toward the middle of the eye, specialize in _____ vision, acuity (perception of fine detail), and daylight vision.

11. A "blind spot" occurs in each eye because there are no receptors on the part of the retina where the optic nerve _____ the eye and blood vessels _____.

12. Normal _____ is defined as 20/20 vision.

13. The _____ supply much of our peripheral vision. Loss of peripheral vision is called tunnel vision.

14. In the _____, color vision is explained by the trichromatic theory. The theory says that three types of _____ exist, each most sensitive to red, green, or blue light.

15. Three types of light-sensitive visual pigments are found in the _____, each pigment most sensitive to red, green, or blue light.

16. _____ theory was unable to explain why people experience _____, or visual sensations that persist after a color stimulus is removed.

17. Beyond the retina, the visual system analyzes colors into _____ messages. According to the opponent-process theory, color information can be coded as red or green, yellow or blue, and _____ messages.

18. _____ color blindness is rare, but 8 percent of males and 1 percent of females are red-green color blind or color weak.

19. The Ishihara test is used to detect _____.

20. Dark adaptation, an _____ in sensitivity to light, is caused by increased concentrations of visual pigments in the _____ and the _____.

Hearing—Good Vibrations

Survey Question: What are the mechanisms of hearing? Pages 142-145

1. Sound waves are the stimulus for hearing. Sound travels as waves of compression (_____) and rarefaction (_____) in the air.

2. The _____ of a sound corresponds to the frequency of sound waves. Loudness corresponds to the amplitude (_____) of sound waves.

3. The pinna, or _____ part of the ear, acts like a funnel to concentrate sounds.

4. Sound waves are transduced by the _____, auditory ossicles, oval window, cochlea, and ultimately, the _____ cells in the organ of Corti.

5. The frequency theory says that the _____ of nerve impulses in the auditory nerves matches the _____ of incoming sounds (up to 4,000 hertz).

6. Place theory says that _____ tones register near the base of the cochlea and _____ tones near its tip.

7. Two basic types of deafness are _____ hearing loss and conductive hearing loss.

8. Conduction hearing loss can often be overcome with a hearing aid. _____ hearing loss can sometimes be alleviated by cochlear implants.

9. "Hunter's Notch" occurs when _____ cells in the cochlea are damaged in the area affected by the pitch of gunfire.

10. Too much loud music can create a form of sensorineural hearing loss called _____-induced hearing loss.

11. Noise-induced hearing loss can be prevented by avoiding excessive exposure to _____ sounds. Sounds above 120 decibels pose an immediate danger to hearing.

12. Hair cells in the cochlea are fragile; they can _____ be replaced.

Smell and Taste—The Nose Knows When the Tongue Can't Tell

Survey Question: How do the chemical senses operate? Pages 145-147

1. Olfaction (_____) and gustation (_____) are chemical senses responsive to airborne or liquefied molecules.

2. The lock-and-key theory partially explains smell. In addition, the _____ of the olfactory receptors in the nose helps identify various scents.

3. About 1,000 types of smell _____ are believed to exist; humans can detect _____ different odors.

4. Dysosmia (defective _____) may result from infections, _____, blows to the head, and exposure to certain chemicals.

5. The top outside edges of the tongue are responsive to sweet, salty, sour, and _____ tastes. It is suspected that a fifth taste quality called umami also exists.

6. Taste appears to be based in part on lock-and-key _____ of molecule shapes.

7. Chemical senses of _____ and _____ operate together to allow us to experience the flavor of food.

The Somesthetic Senses—Flying by the Seat of Your Pants

Survey Question: What are the somesthetic senses? Pages 148-150

1. The somesthetic senses include the _____ senses, vestibular senses, and kinesthetic senses (receptors that detect muscle and joint positioning).

2. The skin senses include touch, _____, pain, cold, and warmth. Sensitivity to each is related to the _____ of receptors found in an area of skin.

3. Distinctions can be made between warning system pain and _____ system pain.

4. Individuals born with congenital _____ insensitivity are immune to warning _____ pain.

5. Pain can be reduced by _____ anxiety and redirecting attention to stimuli other than the pain stimulus.

6. Feeling that you have control over a stimulus tends to _____ the amount of pain you experience.

7. Various forms of motion sickness are related to messages received from the vestibular system, which senses gravity and _____ movement.

8. The otolith organs detect the pull of _____ and rapid head movements.

9. The movement of _____ within the semicircular canals, and the movement of the crista, detects head movement and positioning.

10. According to sensory conflict theory, motion sickness is caused by a _____ of visual, kinesthetic, and vestibular sensations. Motion sickness can be avoided by minimizing sensory conflict.

Adaptation, Attention, and Gating —Tuning In and Tuning Out

Survey Question: Why are we more aware of some sensations than others? Pages 150-153

1. Incoming sensations are affected by sensory adaptation (a _____ in the number of nerve impulses sent).

2. Selective attention (selection and diversion of messages in the brain) and sensory _____ (blocking or alteration of messages flowing toward the brain) also alter sensations.

3. We may not see something that is plainly before our eyes when our _____ is narrowly focused, an effect known as inattentional blindness.

4. Creating competing pain sensations and focusing on them is a pain control technique called _____.

5. Selective gating of pain messages takes place in the _____. Gate control theory proposes an explanation for many pain phenomena.

6. _____ is used by pain clinics to reduce people's experiences of pain by introducing an additional, less intense pain signal such as a mild electrical current to the brain through the fast nerve fiber.

7. Phantom limbs are the result of the body relying on a _____, a map or internal model of the body.

Perception—The Second Step

Survey Question: In general, how do we construct our perceptions? Pages 154-160

1. Perception is the process of assembling sensations into _____ that provide a usable mental _____ of the world.

2. Illusions arise from perceptual misconstructions of stimuli that actually _____; hallucinations are perceptual constructions of objects or events that have no _____ existence.

3. People who have lost touch with reality may experience _____ that involve auditory, visual, touch, smell, or taste sensations created by the brain without environmental input.

4. "_____ hallucinations" are created by the brain to interpret sensory input received by partially _____ individuals who "see" objects appearing and disappearing in front of their eyes.

5. Bottom-up processing begins with small sensory units and build _____ to a complete perception; Top-down processing involved using _____ knowledge to organize features into a whole.

6. Perceptions may be based on _____ or bottom-up processing of information.

7. The most basic organization of sensations is a division into figure and ground (_____ and _____). Reversible figures, however, allow figure-ground organization to be reversed.

8. A number of factors, identified by the Gestalt psychologists, contribute to the _____ of sensations. These are nearness, _____, continuity, closure, contiguity, _____ region, and combinations of the preceding.

9. Stimuli near one another tend to be perceptually _____ together. So, too, do stimuli that are similar in _____. Continuity refers to the fact that perceptions tend to be organized as simple, uninterrupted patterns.

10. Closure is the tendency to _____ a broken or incomplete pattern. Contiguity refers to nearness in _____ and space. Stimuli that fall in a defined area, or common region, also tend to be grouped together.

11. A perceptual organization may be thought of as a _____ held until evidence contradicts it. Camouflage patterns disrupt perceptual _____, especially figure-ground perceptions.

12. Perceptual organization shifts for ambiguous _____, which may have more than one interpretation. An example is Necker's _____. Impossible figures resist stable organization altogether.

13. In vision, the retinal _____ changes from moment to moment, but the external world appears stable and undistorted because of _____ constancies.

14. In size and shape _____, the perceived sizes and shapes of objects remain the same even though their retinal images change size and shape.

15. The apparent brightness of objects remains stable (a property called brightness constancy) because each object reflects a _____ proportion of light.

16. Perceptual constancies are partly native (_____) and partly empirical (_____).

Depth Perception—What If the World Were Flat?

Survey Question: How is it possible to see depth and judge distance? Pages 160-167.

1. _____ perception is the ability to perceive three-dimensional space and judge distances.

2. Studies done with the _____ suggest that depth is perception partly learned and partly innate.

3. _____ (one eye) and _____ (two eyes) cues are depth cues in the environment that help us perceive and judge distance and depth.

4. Depth perception depends on the muscular cues of accommodation (bending of the _____) and convergence (inward movement of the _____).

5. A number of pictorial _____, which will work in _____ paintings, drawings, and photographs, also underlie normal depth perception.

6. Some pictorial cues include linear perspective (the apparent convergence of _____), relative size (more distant objects appear _____), height in the _____ plane, light and shadow (shadings of light), and overlap or interposition (one object overlaps another).

7. Additional pictorial cues include texture gradients (textures become _____ in the distance), aerial haze (loss of color and detail at great distances), and relative _____ or _____ parallax (differences in the apparent movement of objects when a viewer is moving).

8. All the pictorial cues are monocular depth cues (only _____ is needed to make use of them).

9. The moon illusion refers to the fact that the moon appears _____ near the horizon than it does when overhead.

10. The moon illusion appears to be explained by the apparent _____ hypothesis, which emphasizes the greater number of depth cues present when the moon is on the _____.

11. Stereoscopic vision (_____ sight) relies on retinal disparity to determine the depth of objects that are within 50 feet of us.

12. Linear perspective, _____ invariance relationships, and mislocating the endpoints of the _____ also contribute to the Müller-Lyer illusion.

Perceptual Learning – Perception from the Top Down

Survey Question: How is perception altered by expectations, motives, emotions, and learning? Pages 168-171

1. Attention, prior experience, suggestion, and motives combine in various ways to create perceptual sets, or _____. A perceptual set is a readiness to perceive in a particular way, induced by strong expectations.

2. Organizing and interpreting sensations is greatly influenced by learned perceptual _____. An example is the Ames room, which looks rectangular but is actually distorted so that objects in the room appear to change _____.

3. Sensitivity to perceptual _____ is also partly learned. Studies of inverted vision show that even the most basic organization is subject to a degree of change.

4. Illusions are often related to perceptual _____. One of the most familiar of all illusions, the Müller-Lyer illusion, seems to be related to perceptual learning based on experience with box-shaped _____ and rooms.

5. Personal motives and _____ often alter perceptions by changing the evaluation of what is seen or by altering attention to specific details.

Extrasensory Perception—Do You Believe in Magic?

Survey Question: Is extrasensory perception possible? Pages 171-175

1. Parapsychology is the study of purported _____ phenomena, including clairvoyance (perceiving events at a distance), _____ ("mind reading"), precognition (perceiving future events), and psychokinesis (mentally influencing inanimate objects).

2. Clairvoyance, telepathy, and precognition are purported types of extrasensory _____.

3. Research in parapsychology remains controversial owing to a variety of problems. _____ and after-the-fact reinterpretation are problems with "natural" ESP episodes.

4. With no evidence supporting the existence of ESP, psychologists strongly suggest that people be _____ of those who claim to have _____ abilities. For example, the owner of the "Miss Cleo" TV-psychic operation made $1 billion from people who believed "Miss Cleo" was a psychic.

5. Many studies of ESP overlook the impact of statistically unusual outcomes that are no more than runs of _____.

6. The bulk of the evidence to date is _____ the existence of ESP. Very few positive results in ESP research have been replicated (_____) by independent scientists.

7. Stage ESP is based on _____ and tricks.

Psychology in Action: Becoming a Better Eyewitness to Life

Survey Question: How can I learn to perceive events more accurately? Page 175-178

1. Perceptions are a reconstruction of events. This is one reason why eyewitness testimony is surprisingly _____.

2. In many crimes, eyewitness accuracy is further damaged by weapon _____.

3. Similar factors, such as observer stress, brief exposure times, cross-racial inaccuracies, and the wording of questions, can _____ eyewitness accuracy.

4. Perceptual accuracy is enhanced by reality _____, dishabituation, and conscious efforts to pay _____.

5. It is also valuable to break perceptual habits, to _____ frames of reference, to beware of perceptual sets, and to be aware of the ways in which motives and emotions influence perceptions, check the accuracy of your perceptions (when possible) and pay attention.

CONNECTIONS

Sensory Systems—The First Step and Vision—Catching Some Rays

Survey Questions: In general, how do sensory systems function? How does the visual system function? Pages 133-141

1. _____ ciliary muscle
2. _____ iris
3. _____ cornea
4. _____ blind spot
5. _____ lens
6. _____ fovea
7. _____ retinal veins
8. _____ optic nerve
9. _____ aqueous humor
10. _____ pupil
11. _____ retina

1. _____ transducer
2. _____ myopia
3. _____ cones
4. _____ rods
5. _____ afterimages
6. _____ sensation
7. _____ trichromatic theory
8. _____ hue
9. _____ opponent process theory
10. _____ accommodation
11. _____ hyperopia
12. _____ perception

A. sensory impression
B. analyze colors in either-or messages
C. convert energy into neural impulse
D. lens modification
E. receptors for dim light
F. receptors for colors
G. three types of cones
H. interpreting sensory input
I. seeing images after stimuli are gone
J. color
K. nearsightedness
L. farsightedness

Hearing—Good Vibrations, and Smell and Taste—The Nose Knows When the Tongue Can't Tell

Survey Questions: What are the mechanisms of hearing? How do the chemical senses operate? Pages 142-147

1. _____ vestibular system
2. _____ cochlea
3. _____ round window
4. _____ auditory canal
5. _____ stapes
6. _____ auditory nerve
7. _____ incus
8. _____ oval window
9. _____ malleus
10. _____ tympanic membrane

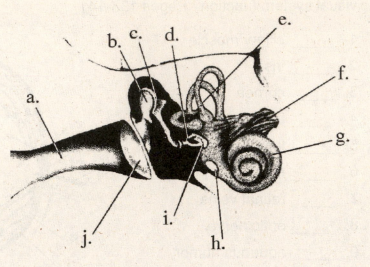

1. _____ frequency theory
2. _____ place theory
3. _____ taste buds
4. _____ auditory ossicles
5. _____ umami
6. _____ dysosmia
7. _____ organ of Corti
8. _____ gustatory
9. _____ olfactory

A. "brothy"
B. matching the speed of incoming frequency
C. contains hair cells
D. malleus, incus, and stapes
E. sense of smell
F. sense of taste
G. taste receptors
H. location of sound processing
I. smell blindness

The Somesthetic Senses—Flying by the Seat of Your Pants, and Adaptation, Gating, and Attention—Tuning In and Tuning Out

Survey Questions: What are the somesthetic senses? Why are we more aware of some sensations than others? Pages 148-153

1. _____ counterirritation
2. _____ kinesthetic
3. _____ neuromatrix
4. _____ semicircular canals
5. _____ sensory adaptation
6. _____ selective attention
7. _____ reminding system pain
8. _____ vestibular
9. _____ inattention blindness
10. _____ gate control theory
11. _____ warning system pain
12. _____ sensory conflict theory

A. body movement
B. sense of balance
C. organs of balance
D. explains motion sickness
E. pain processing
F. applying ice packs to skin
G. bottle neck filtration
H. sharp, bright, fast, specific
I. nagging, aching, slow, widespread
J. reduced responding
K. narrow focus
L. internal model

Perception—The Second Step

Survey Question: In general, how do we construct our perceptions?
Pages 154-160

1. _____ continuity
2. _____ common region
3. _____ closure
4. _____ nearness
5. _____ reversible figure
6. _____ similarity

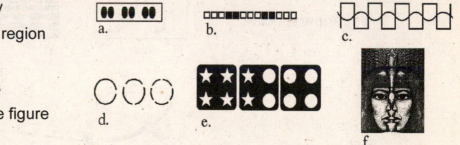

1. _____ Perceptual constructions
2. _____ Reality testing
3. _____ Perceptual hypothesis
4. _____ bottom-up
5. _____ illusions
6. _____ hallucination
7. _____ top-down
8. _____ Reversible figures
9. _____ sane hallucination

A. Mental models of external events
B. misleading perception of real sensations
C. imaginary sensation
D. perception check
E. perceptual expectancy
F. partially blinded perception of images
G. low-level features
H. figure-ground switch
I. initial plan to organize sensation

Depth Perception—What If the World Were Flat?

Survey Question: How is it possible to see depth and judge distance? Pages 160-167

1. _____ texture gradients
2. _____ stereoscopic vision
3. _____ convergence
4. _____ light and shadow
5. _____ relative size
6. _____ overlap
7. _____ retinal disparity
8. _____ linear perspective

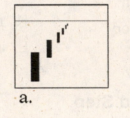

a.

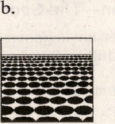

b.

c.

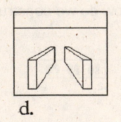

d.

e.

f.

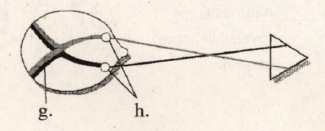

g.   h.

1. _____ binocular depth cue
2. _____ monocular depth cue
3. _____ Zulu
4. _____ Mismatch fusion
5. _____ visual cliff
6. _____ apparent distance

A. infant depth perception
B. convergence
C. stereoscopic vision
D. moon illusion
E. accommodation
F. diminished Müller-Lyer illusion

Perceptual Learning – Perception From the Top Down

Survey Question: How is perception altered by expectations, motives, emotions, and learning? Pages 168-171

1. _____ Perceptual expectancy
2. _____ Other-race effect
3. _____ Americans
4. _____ Perceptual habits
5. _____ Perceptual learning
6. _____ Japanese
7. _____ Negative emotions

A. suggestion
B. face recognition
C. change in constructing information
D. ingrained patterns
E. narrow perceptual focus
F. background alterations
G. figure alterations

Extrasensory Perception—Do You Believe in Magic?

Survey Question: Is extrasensory perception possible? Pages 171-175

1. _____ Zener cards
2. _____ telepathy
3. _____ parapsychology
4. _____ psychokinesis
5. _____ Psi phenomena
6. _____ psychic fraud
7. _____ decline effect

A. run of luck
B. study of ESP
C. mind reader
D. clairvoyance test
E. "Miss Cleo"
F. ability to move objects
G. defy scientific laws

Psychology in Action: Becoming a Better Eyewitness to Life

Survey Question: How can I learn to perceive events more accurately? Pages 175-178

1. _____ Dishabituation	A. inattention to details
2. _____ Weapon focus	B. "surrender" to experience
3. _____ Habituation	C. cease paying attention
4. _____ Perceptual awareness	D. increase in attention

CHECK YOUR MEMORY

Sensory Systems—The First Step

Survey Question: In general, how do sensory systems function? Pages 133-134

1. Sensations arise from stimuli arriving at the sense organs; perceptions arise from the sense organs converting that stimuli into neural activity

   TRUE or FALSE

2. Data reduction systems analyze information and then code and send only the most important data to the brain.

   TRUE or FALSE

3. Data analysis involves dividing the world into perceptual features.

   TRUE or FALSE

4. Sensory localization is important in producing phosphorescence.

   TRUE or FALSE

5. Cats that grow up surrounded by horizontal stripes are unusually sensitive to vertical stripes when they reach maturity.

   TRUE or FALSE

6. Each sensory organ is sensitive to a select range of physical energies.

   TRUE or FALSE

7. The artificial vision system described in the text is based on electrodes implanted in the retina.

   TRUE or FALSE

8. The retina responds to pressure as well as light.

   TRUE or FALSE

Vision—Catching Some Rays

Survey Question: How does the visual system function? Pages 135-141

1. The electromagnetic spectrum includes ultraviolet light and radio waves.

   TRUE or FALSE

2. A nanometer is one-millionth of a meter.

   TRUE or FALSE

3. The lens of the eye is about the size and thickness of a postage stamp.

   TRUE or FALSE

4. Farsightedness is corrected with a convex lens.

   TRUE or FALSE

5. The myopic eye is longer than normal.

   TRUE or FALSE

6. There are more rods than cones in the eyes.

   TRUE or FALSE

7. The blind spot is the point where the optic nerve leaves the eye.

   TRUE or FALSE

8. Vision rated at 20/200 is better than average.

   TRUE or FALSE

9. If your vision is 20/12 like Gordon Cooper, an American astronaut, you would be able to see eight feet farther than someone who has 20/20 vision.

   TRUE or FALSE

10. Blue emergency lights and taxiway lights are used because at night they are more visible to the cones.

    TRUE or FALSE

11. The trichromatic theory of color vision says that black and white are produced by the rods.

    TRUE or FALSE

12. According to the opponent-process theory it is impossible to have a reddish green or yellowish blue.

    TRUE or FALSE

13. Yellow-blue color weakness is very rare.

    TRUE or FALSE

14. In the United States and Canada, stoplights are always on the bottom of traffic signals.

    TRUE or FALSE

15. Complete dark adaptation takes about 12 minutes.

    TRUE or FALSE

Hearing—Good Vibrations

Survey Question: What are the mechanisms of hearing? Pages 142-145

1. Sound cannot travel in a vacuum.

    TRUE or FALSE

2. The visible, external portion of the ear is the malleus.

    TRUE or FALSE

3. The hair cells are part of the organ of Corti.

    TRUE or FALSE

4. Hunter's notch occurs when the auditory ossicles are damaged by the sound of gunfire.

    TRUE or FALSE

5. Place theory suggests that nerve impulses of a corresponding frequency are fed into the auditory nerve.

    TRUE or FALSE

6. Cochlear implants stimulate the auditory nerve directly.

    TRUE or FALSE

7. Hearing aids may help individuals with conductive hearing loss.

    TRUE or FALSE

8. Deaf children can learn spoken language close to a normal rate if they have cochlear implants before the age of two.

    TRUE or FALSE

9. A 40-decibel sound could be described as quiet.

    TRUE or FALSE

10. A 100-decibel sound can damage hearing in less than eight hours.

    TRUE or FALSE

11. Every 20 decibels increases sound energy by a factor of 10.

    TRUE or FALSE

Smell and Taste—The Nose Knows When the Tongue Can't Tell

Survey Question: How do the chemical senses operate? Pages 145-147

1. At least 300 different types of olfactory receptors exist.

    TRUE or FALSE

2. Humans can detect at least 100,000 different odors.

    TRUE or FALSE

3. Etherish odors smell like garlic.

    TRUE or FALSE

4. Infections, allergies, injuries, and exposure to chemicals may cause dysthymia, or "smell blindness."

    TRUE or FALSE

5. Four basic taste sensations include sweet, sour, salty, and buttery.

    TRUE or FALSE

6. Flavors are greatly influenced by odor as well as taste.

    TRUE or FALSE

7. Taste buds are found throughout the mouth, not just on the tongue.

    TRUE or FALSE

8. Umami is a pleasant "brothy" taste.

    TRUE or FALSE

The Somesthetic Senses—Flying by the Seat of Your Pants

Survey Question: What are the somesthetic senses? Pages 148-150

1. Vibration is one of the five basic skin sensations.

    TRUE or FALSE

2. Areas of the skin that have high concentrations of pain receptors are no more sensitive to pain than other areas of the body.

    TRUE or FALSE

3. Small nerve fibers generally carry warning-system pain messages.

    TRUE or FALSE

4. High levels of anxiety tend to amplify the amount of pain a person experiences.

    TRUE or FALSE

5. The level of pain people experience is related to their emotions: Unpleasant emotions increase pain while pleasant emotions decrease pain.

  TRUE or FALSE

6. As a means of reducing pain, acupuncture is an example of counterirritation.

  TRUE or FALSE

7. The semicircular canals are especially sensitive to the pull of gravity.

  TRUE or FALSE

8. Motion sickness is believed to be related to the body's reactions to being poisoned.

  TRUE or FALSE

Adaptation, Gating, and Attention—Tuning In and Tuning Out

Survey Question: Why are we more aware of some sensations than others? Pages 150-153

1. If you wear a ring, you are rarely aware of it because of sensory gating.

  TRUE or FALSE

2. The "seat-of-your-pants" phenomenon is related to selective attention.

  TRUE or FALSE

3. People exhibit inattention blindness when their attention is broadly focused.

  TRUE or FALSE

4. Attention is related to contrast or changes in stimulation.

  TRUE or FALSE

5. Using a cell phone while driving may cause inattention blindness.

  TRUE or FALSE

6. The method of adding a painful stimulus to one already being experienced invariably increases the sense of pain.

  TRUE or FALSE

7. Mild electrical stimulation of the skin can block reminding system pain.

  TRUE or FALSE

8. Phantom Limb pain arises when the neuromatrix fails to adjust to accommodate changes in the physical body.

  TRUE or FALSE

9. Mild electrical stimulation of the skin causes a release of endorphins in free nerve endings.

  TRUE or FALSE

Perception—The Second Step

Survey Question: In general, how do we construct our perceptions? Pages 154-160

1. Perception involves selecting, organizing, and integrating sensory information.

   TRUE or FALSE

2. Some perceptual abilities must be learned after sight is restored to the previously blind.

   TRUE or FALSE

3. The Ames room is primarily used to test the effects of inverted vision.

   TRUE or FALSE

4. Hearing voices when no one is speaking is an example of a perceptual illusion.

   TRUE or FALSE

5. Seeing images appearing and disappearing because one is partially blind can be described as "sane hallucination."

   TRUE or FALSE

6. The fact that people who are partially blind sometimes have "sane hallucinations" shows that the brain seeks meaningful patterns in sensory input.

   TRUE or FALSE

7. Analyzing information into small features and then building a recognizable pattern is called top-up processing.

   TRUE or FALSE

8. Basic figure-ground organization is learned at about age two.

   TRUE or FALSE

9. Contiguity refers to our tendency to see lines as continuous.

   TRUE or FALSE

10. Common region refers to the tendency to see stimuli that are close together as one unit.

    TRUE or FALSE

11. Necker's cube and the "three-pronged widget" are impossible figures.

    TRUE or FALSE

12. A perceptual hypothesis is a plan or guess about how to organize sensations.

    TRUE or FALSE

13. Newborn babies show some evidence of size constancy.

   TRUE or FALSE

14. Houses and cars look like toys from a low-flying airplane because of shape constancy.

   TRUE or FALSE

15. Brightness constancy does not apply to objects illuminated by different amounts of light.

   TRUE or FALSE

Depth Perception—What If the World Were Flat?

Survey Question: How is it possible to see depth and judge distance? Pages 160-167

1. Depth perception is partly learned and partly innate.

   TRUE or FALSE

2. Human depth perception typically emerges at about four months of age.

   TRUE or FALSE

3. Most crawling infants, when coaxed by their mothers, will crawl across the visual cliff.

   TRUE or FALSE

4. Accommodation and convergence are muscular depth cues.

   TRUE or FALSE

5. Accommodation acts as a depth cue primarily for distances greater than four feet from the eyes.

   TRUE or FALSE

6. Convergence acts as a depth cue primarily for distances less than four feet from the eyes.

   TRUE or FALSE

7. With one eye closed, the pictorial depth cues no longer provide information about depth and distance.

   TRUE or FALSE

8. Changing the image size of an object implies that its distance from the viewer has changed too.

   TRUE or FALSE

9. In a drawing, the closer an object is to the horizon line, the nearer it appears to be to the viewer.

   TRUE or FALSE

10. Aerial perspective is most powerful when the air is exceptionally clear.

    TRUE or FALSE

11. When an observer is moving forward, objects beyond the observer's point of fixation appear to move forward too.

    TRUE or FALSE

12. The moon's image is magnified by the dense atmosphere near the horizon.

    TRUE or FALSE

13. More depth cues are present when the moon is viewed near the horizon.

    TRUE or FALSE

14. According to Richard Gregory, the arrowhead-tipped line in the Müller-Lyer illusion looks like the outside corner of a building.

    TRUE or FALSE

15. Zulus rarely see round shapes and therefore fail to experience the Müller-Lyer illusion.

    TRUE or FALSE

Perceptual Learning – Perception from the Top Down

Survey Question: How is perception altered by expectations, motives, emotions, and learning? Pages 168-171

1. Perceptual sets are frequently created by suggestion.

   TRUE or FALSE

2. Positive emotions serve to narrow the scope of attention.

   TRUE or FALSE

3. In tests of facial recognition, people are much better at identifying faces of their own race than of others.

   TRUE or FALSE

4. A novice chef who discovers how to tell the difference between various spices is engaging in perceptual learning.

   TRUE or FALSE

5. Many times we see what we expect to see due to perceptual habits.

   TRUE or FALSE

6. Failing to see a pedestrian crossing a street because one is busy using a cell phone while driving is referred to as attentional blindness.

   TRUE or FALSE

7. Labels and categories have been shown to have little real effect on perceptions.

    TRUE or FALSE

Extrasensory Perception—Do You Believe in Magic?

Survey Question: Is extrasensory perception possible? Pages 171-175

1. James Randi was one of the first researchers in parapsychology to use the Zener cards.

    TRUE or FALSE

2. Psychokinesis is classified as a psi event but not a form of ESP.

    TRUE or FALSE

3. Prophetic dreams are regarded as a form of precognition.

    TRUE or FALSE

4. Strange coincidences are strong evidence for the existence of ESP.

    TRUE or FALSE

5. The Zener cards eliminated the possibility of fraud and "leakage" of information in ESP experiments.

    TRUE or FALSE

6. "Miss Cleo" is one of the few people who truly have psychic abilities.

    TRUE or FALSE

7. "Psi missing" is perhaps the best current evidence for ESP.

    TRUE or FALSE

8. Stage ESP relies on deception, sleight of hand, and patented gadgets to entertain the audience.

    TRUE or FALSE

9. Belief in psi events has declined among parapsychologists in recent years.

    TRUE or FALSE

10. A skeptic of psi means that a person is unconvinced and is against the idea that psi exists.

    TRUE or FALSE

Psychology in Action: Becoming a Better Eyewitness to Life

Survey Question: How can I learn to perceive events more accurately? Page 175-178

1. In many ways we see what we believe as well as believe what we see.

   TRUE or FALSE

2. The more confident an eyewitness is about the accuracy of his or her testimony, the more likely it is to be accurate.

   TRUE or FALSE

3. The testimony of crime victims is generally more accurate than the testimony of bystanders.

   TRUE or FALSE

4. Police officers and other trained observers are more accurate eyewitnesses than the average person.

   TRUE or FALSE

5. Victims tend to not notice detailed information such as the appearance of their attacker because they fall prey to weapon focus.

   TRUE or FALSE

6. Reality testing is the process Abraham Maslow described as a "surrender" to experience.

   TRUE or FALSE

7. Perceptually, Zen masters have been shown to habituate more rapidly than the average person.

   TRUE or FALSE

8. Much like sensory adaptation, habituation involves a failure to pay attention to certain stimuli.

   TRUE or FALSE

9. One way to become a better "eyewitness" to life is to seek out and get used to ordinary experiences.

   TRUE or FALSE

FINAL SURVEY AND REVIEW

Sensory Systems—The First Step

Survey Question: In general, how do sensory systems function? Pages 133-134

1. Sensory organs _____ physical energies into nerve impulses.

2. Sensation refers to the information brought in by the senses, and perception refers to the process by which the brain _____ and _____ the information into meaningful patterns.

3. The senses act as data _____ systems that select, analyze, and _____sensory information.

4. Our sensory _____ cannot transduce all of the energies that they encounter in the environment.

5. A good example of sensory _____ is the identification of basic perceptual features in a stimulus pattern.

6. In fact, many sensory systems act as _____ detectors.

7. Visual pop-out is an example of feature _____ in action.

8. Sensory coding results when we see _____ (visual sensations caused by _____ excitation) when we press slightly on our eyelids.

9. Sensory _____ can be partially understood in terms of sensory localization in the brain. That is, the area of the brain activated ultimately determines which type of sensory _____ we have.

Vision—Catching Some Rays

Survey Question: How does the visual system function? Pages 135-141

1. Your eyes _____ only a small part of the entire range of _____energies; these are called the visible spectrum.

2. The electromagnetic spectrum ranges from _____, with a wavelength of 400 nanometers, to _____, with a wavelength of 700 nanometers.

3. _____ refers to a color's name, which corresponds to its wavelength.

4. Saturated or "_____" colors come from a narrow band of wavelengths.

5. Brightness corresponds to the _____, or height, of light waves.

6. The eye is in some ways like a camera. At its back lies an array of _____, called rods and cones, that make up a light-sensitive layer called the _____.

7. Vision is focused by the shape of the _____ and _____ and by changes in the shape of the lens, called accommodation.

8. Four common visual defects, correctable with glasses, are _____ (nearsightedness), hyperopia (farsightedness), _____ (loss of accommodation), and astigmatism (in which portions of vision are out of focus).

9. In the retina, the rods specialize in _____ vision, black-and-white reception, and _____ detection.

10. The cones, found exclusively in the _____ and otherwise toward the middle of the eye, specialize in color vision, acuity (perception of fine detail), and _____ vision.

11. A "_____" occurs in each eye because there are no receptors on the part of the retina where the _____ nerve exits the eye and blood vessels enter.

12. Normal acuity is defined as _____ vision.

13. The rods supply much of our _____ vision. Loss of peripheral vision is called _____ vision.

14. n the retina, color vision is explained by the _____ theory. The theory says that three types of cones exist, each most sensitive to red, _____, or blue light.

15. Three types of light-sensitive visual _____ are found in the cones, each pigment most sensitive to _____, green, or blue light.

16. Trichromatic theory was _____ to explain why people experience afterimages, or visual sensations that persist after a color stimulus is _____.

17. Beyond the retina, the visual system analyzes colors into either-or _____. According to the opponent-process theory, color information can be coded as red or green, _____ or _____, and black or white messages.

18. Total color _____ is rare, but 8 percent of _____ and 1 percent of females are red-green color blind or color weak.

19. The _____ test is used to detect color blindness.

20. Dark _____, an increase in sensitivity to light, is caused by _____ concentrations of visual pigments in the rods and the cones.

Hearing—Good Vibrations

Survey Question: What are the mechanisms of hearing? Pages 142-145

1. Sound waves are the stimulus for _____. Sound travels as waves of compression (peaks) and _____ (valleys) in the air.

2. The pitch of a sound corresponds to the _____ of sound waves. Loudness corresponds to the _____ (height) of sound waves.

3. The _____, or external part of the ear, acts like a funnel to _____ sounds.

4. Sound waves are _____ by the eardrum, auditory ossicles, oval window, _____, and ultimately, the hair cells in the organ of Corti.

5. The _____ theory says that the frequency of nerve impulses in the auditory nerves matches the frequency of incoming sounds (up to _____ hertz).

6. _____ theory says that high tones register near the _____ of the cochlea and low tones near its tip.

7. Two basic types of _____ are sensorineural hearing loss and _____ hearing loss.

8. Conduction hearing loss can often be overcome with a hearing _____.

9. Sensorineural hearing loss can sometimes be alleviated by cochlear _____.

10. "Hunter's Notch" occurs when hair cells in the _____ are damaged in the area affected by the pitch of _____.

11. Too much loud music can create a form of _____ hearing loss called noise-induced hearing loss.

12. Noise-induced hearing loss can be prevented by avoiding excessive exposure to loud sounds. Sounds above _____ decibels pose an immediate danger to hearing.

13. _____ cells in the cochlea are fragile; they can never be replaced.

Smell and Taste—The Nose Knows When the Tongue Can't Tell

Survey Question: How do the chemical senses operate? Pages 145-147

1. _____ (smell) and _____ (taste) are chemical senses responsive to airborne or liquefied molecules.

2. The _____ theory partially explains smell. In addition, the location of the olfactory receptors in the nose helps identify various scents.

3. About _____ types of smell receptors are believed to exist; humans can detect 10,000 different odors.

4. _____ (defective smell) may result from _____, allergies, blows to the head, and exposure to certain chemicals.

5. The top outside edges of the tongue are responsive to _____, salty, sour, and bitter tastes. It is suspected that a fifth taste quality called _____ also exists.

6. Taste appears to be based in part on lock-and-key coding of molecule _____.

7. Chemical senses of smell and taste operate together to allow us to experience the _____ of food.

The Somesthetic Senses—Flying by the Seat of Your Pants

Survey Question: What are the somesthetic senses? Pages 148-150

1. The _____ senses include the skin senses, vestibular senses, and kinesthetic senses (receptors that detect muscle and _____ positioning).

2. The _____ senses include touch, pressure, pain, cold, and warmth. Sensitivity to each is related to the _____ of receptors found in an area of skin.

3. Distinctions can be made between _____ system pain and reminding system _____.

4. Individuals born with _____ pain insensitivity are immune to warning system pain.

5. Pain can be reduced by lowering _____ and redirecting _____ to stimuli other than the pain stimulus.

6. Feeling that you have _____ over a stimulus tends to reduce the amount of pain you experience.

7. Various forms of motion _____ are related to messages received from the vestibular system, which senses _____ and head movement.

8. The _____ organs detect the pull of gravity and rapid head movements.

9. The movement of fluid within the _____ canals, and the movement of the crista, detects head _____ and positioning.

10. According to sensory _____ theory, motion sickness is caused by a mismatch of visual, kinesthetic, and vestibular sensations. Motion sickness can be avoided by _____ sensory conflict.

Adaptation, Attention, and Gating —Tuning In and Tuning Out

Survey Question: Why are we more aware of some sensations than others? Pages 150-153

1. Incoming _____ are affected by sensory adaptation (a reduction or decrease in the number of nerve _____ sent).

2. _____ attention (selection and diversion of messages in the brain) and sensory gating (blocking or alteration of messages flowing toward the _____) also alter sensations.

3. We may not see something that is plainly before our eyes when our attention is narrowly focused, an effect known as _____ blindness.

4. Creating _____ pain sensations and focusing on them is a _____ control technique called gating.

5. Selective _____ of pain messages takes place in the spinal cord. Gate control theory proposes an explanation for many pain phenomena.

6. Counterirritation is used by pain clinics to reduce people's experiences of pain by introducing an additional, less _____ pain signal such as a mild electrical current to the brain through the fast nerve fiber.

7. _____ limbs are the result of the body relying on a neuromatrix, a map or internal model of the body.

Perception—The Second Step

Survey Question: In general, how do we construct our perceptions? Pages 154-160

1. _____ is the process of assembling sensations into patterns that provide a usable _____ model of the world.

2. _____ arise from perceptual _____ of stimuli that actually exist; hallucinations are perceptual constructions of objects or events that have _____ external existence.

3. People who have _____ touch with reality may experience hallucinations that involve auditory, visual, touch, smell, or taste sensations created by the brain without _____ input.

4. "Sane hallucinations" are created by the brain to interpret sensory input received by partially blind individuals who "see" objects _____ and disappearing in front of their eyes.

5. _____ processing begins with small sensory units and build upward to a _____ perception; Top-down processing involved using pre-existing knowledge to _____ features into a whole.

6. _____ may be based on top-down or bottom-up processing of information.

7. The most basic organization of _____ is a division into _____ and ground (object and background). _____ figures, however, allow figure-ground organization to be reversed.

8. A number of factors, identified by the _____ psychologists, contribute to the organization of sensations. These are _____, similarity, continuity, closure, contiguity, common region, and combinations of the preceding.

9. Stimuli near one another tend to be perceptually grouped together. So, too, do stimuli that are _____ in appearance. _____ refers to the fact that perceptions tend to be organized as simple, uninterrupted patterns.

10. _____ is the tendency to complete a broken or incomplete pattern. Contiguity refers to nearness in time and space. Stimuli that fall in a defined area, or common region, also tend to be _____ together.

11. A perceptual _____ may be thought of as a hypothesis held until evidence contradicts it. Camouflage patterns _____ perceptual organization, especially figure-ground perceptions.

12. Perceptual organization shifts for _____ stimuli, which may have more than one interpretation. An example is Necker's cube. _____ figures resist stable organization altogether.

13. In vision, the _____ image changes from moment to moment, but the external world appears stable and _____ because of perceptual constancies.

14. In size and _____ constancy, the perceived sizes and shapes of objects remain the same even though their retinal images change size and shape.

15. The _____ brightness of objects remains stable (a property called brightness constancy) because each object reflects a constant _____ of light.

16. Perceptual constancies are partly _____ (inborn) and partly _____ (learned).

Depth Perception—What If the World Were Flat?

Survey Question: How is it possible to see depth and judge distance? Pages 160-167

1. Depth perception is the ability to perceive _____-dimensional space and judge distances.

2. Studies done with the visual cliff suggest that depth is perception partly _____ and partly _____.

3. Monocular (_____ eye) and binocular (_____ eyes) cues are depth cues in the environment that help us perceive and judge distance and depth.

4. Depth perception depends on the muscular cues of _____ (bending of the lens) and convergence (_____ movement of the eyes).

5. A number of _____ cues, which will work in flat paintings, _____, and photographs, also underlie normal depth perception.

6. Some pictorial cues include _____ perspective (the apparent convergence of parallel lines), relative size (more distant objects appear smaller), height in the picture plane, light and _____ (shadings of light), and overlap or interposition (one object overlaps another).

7. Additional pictorial cues include _____ gradients (textures become finer in the distance), aerial haze (loss of color and detail at great distances), and relative motion or motion _____ (differences in the apparent movement of objects when a viewer is moving).

8. All the pictorial cues are _____ depth cues (only one eye is needed to make use of them).

9. The _____ illusion refers to the fact that the moon appears larger near the horizon than it does when overhead.

10. The moon illusion appears to be explained by the _____ distance hypothesis, which emphasizes the greater number of _____ cues present when the moon is on the horizon.

11. _____ vision (three-dimensional sight) relies on retinal disparity to determine the depth of objects that are within _____ feet of us.

12. _____ perspective, size-distance invariance relationships, and _____ the endpoints of the lines also contribute to the Müller-Lyer illusion.

Perceptual Learning – Perception from the Top Down

Survey Question: How is perception altered by expectations, motives, emotions, and learning? Pages 168-171

1. Attention, _____ experience, _____, and motives combine in various ways to create perceptual sets, or expectancies.

2. A perceptual _____ is a readiness to perceive in a particular way, induced by strong expectations.

3. Organizing and _____ sensations is greatly influenced by learned perceptual habits. An example is the Ames room, which looks rectangular but is actually distorted so that objects in the room appear to _____ size.

4. Sensitivity to _____ features is also partly learned. Studies of _____ vision show that even the most basic organization is subject to a degree of change.

5. _____ are often related to perceptual habits. One of the most familiar of all illusions, the Müller-Lyer illusion, seems to be related to perceptual learning based on experience with _____-shaped buildings and rooms.

6. Personal _____ and values often alter perceptions by changing the evaluation of what is seen or by altering attention to specific details.

Extrasensory Perception—Do You Believe in Magic?

Survey Question: Is extrasensory perception possible? Pages 171-175

1. _____ is the study of purported psi phenomena, including clairvoyance (perceiving events at a distance), telepathy ("mind reading"), _____ (perceiving future events), and psychokinesis (mentally influencing inanimate objects).

2. Clairvoyance, _____, and precognition are purported types of extrasensory perception.

3. Research in parapsychology remains _____ owing to a variety of problems. _____ and after-the-fact reinterpretation are problems with "natural" ESP episodes.

4. With no evidence supporting the _____ of ESP, psychologists strongly suggest that people be skeptical of those who claim to have psychic abilities. For example, the owner of the "Miss Cleo" TV-psychic operation made $1 billion from people who believed "Miss Cleo" was a psychic.

5. Many studies of ESP overlook the impact of _____ unusual outcomes that are no more than runs of luck.

6. The bulk of the evidence to date is against the existence of ESP. Very few positive results in ESP research have been _____ (repeated) by _____ scientists.

7. Stage ESP is based on deception and _____.

Psychology in Action: Becoming a Better Eyewitness to Life

Survey Question: How can I learn to perceive events more accurately? Page 175-178

1. Perceptions are a _____ of events. This is one reason why _____ testimony is surprisingly inaccurate.

2. In many crimes, eyewitness accuracy is further damaged by _____ focus.

3. Similar factors, such as observer stress, _____ exposure times, cross-racial inaccuracies, and the _____ of questions, can lower eyewitness accuracy.

4. Perceptual accuracy is enhanced by reality testing, _____, and conscious efforts to pay attention.

5. It is also valuable to break _____ habits, to broaden frames of reference, to beware of perceptual sets, and to be aware of the ways in which motives and emotions influence perceptions, check the accuracy of your perceptions (when possible) and pay attention.

MASTERY TEST

1. Sensory conflict theory attributes motion sickness to mismatches between what three systems?
   a. olfaction, kinesthesis, and audition
   b. vision, kinesthesis, and the vestibular system
   c. kinesthesis, audition, and the somesthetic system
   d. vision, gustation, and the skin senses

2. Which of the following types of color blindness is most common?
   a. yellow-blue, male
   b. yellow-blue, female
   c. red-green, female
   d. red-green, male

3. Which of the following does not belong with the others?
   a. Pacinian corpuscle
   b. Merkle's disk
   c. organ of Corti
   d. free nerve endings

4. Which theory of color vision best explains the fact that we do not see yellowish blue?
   a. trichromatic
   b. chromatic gating
   c. Ishihara hypothesis
   d. opponent process

5. Dark adaptation occurs as a result of
   a. low concentration of visual pigments in the aqueous humor.
   b. high concentration of photoreceptor cells in the cones.
   c. the bleaching of visual pigments in the rods.
   d. the bleaching of phosphenes in the optic nerve.

6. Sensory analysis tends to extract perceptual _____ from stimulus patterns.
   a. features
   b. thresholds
   c. transducers
   d. amplitudes

7. Which pair of terms is most closely related?
   a. hyperopia—color blindness
   b. astigmatism—presbyopia
   c. myopia—astigmatism
   d. hyperopia—presbyopia

8. The painkilling effects of acupuncture are partly explained by the
   _____ theory.
   a. lock-and-key
   b. gate control
   c. opponent-process
   d. frequency

9. According to the _____ theory of hearing, low tones cause the
   greatest movement near the _____ of the cochlea.
   a. place, outer tip
   b. frequency, outer tip
   c. place, base
   d. frequency, base

10. Which of the following best represents the concept of a transducer?
   a. translating English into Spanish
   b. copying a computer file from one floppy disk to another
   c. speaking into a telephone receiver
   d. turning water into ice

11. Rods and cones are to vision as _____ are to hearing.
   a. auditory ossicles
   b. vibrations
   c. pinnas
   d. hair cells

12. You lose the ability to smell floral odors. This is called _____ and it is
   compatible with the _____ theory of olfaction.
   a. anhedonia, place
   b. anosmia, lock-and-key
   c. tinnitus, gate-control
   d. sensory adaptation, molecular

13. Which two dimensions of color are related to the wavelength of
   electromagnetic energy?
   a. hue and saturation
   b. saturation and brightness
   c. brightness and hue
   d. brightness and amplitude

14. The existence of the blind spot is explained by a lack of
   a. nerve cells.
   b. peripheral vision.
   c. photoreceptors.
   d. activity in the fovea.

15. In vision, a loss of accommodation is most associated with aging of the
a. iris.
b. fovea.
c. lens.
d. cornea.

16. Visual acuity and color vision are provided by the _____, found in large numbers in the _____ of the eye.
a. cones, fovea
b. cones, periphery
c. rods, fovea
d. rods, periphery

17. The Ames room creates a conflict between
a. horizontal features and vertical features.
b. attention and habituation.
c. top-down and bottom-up processing.
d. shape constancy and size constancy.

18. Weapon focus tends to lower eyewitness accuracy because it affects
a. selective attention.
b. the adaptation level.
c. perceptions of contiguity.
d. dishabituation.

19. Size constancy
a. emerges at about four months of age.
b. is affected by experience with seeing objects of various sizes.
c. requires that objects be illuminated by light of the same intensity.
d. all of the preceding

20. Which of the following cues would be of greatest help to a person trying to thread a needle?
a. light and shadow
b. texture gradients
c. linear perspective
d. overlap

21. Size-distance invariance contributes to which of the following?
a. Müller-Lyer illusion
b. the stroboscopic illusion
c. perceptual hallucinations
d. changes in perceptual sets

22. The visual cliff is used primarily to test infant
a. size constancy.
b. figure-ground perception.
c. depth perception.
d. adaptation to spatial distortions.

23. Which of the following organizational principles is based on nearness in time and space?
a. continuity
b. closure
c. contiguity
d. size constancy

24. Which of the following is both a muscular and a monocular depth cue?
a. convergence
b. relative motion
c. aerial perspective
d. accommodation

25. A previously blind person has just had her sight restored. Which of the following perceptual experiences is she most likely to have?
a. perceptual set
b. size constancy
c. linear perspective
d. figure-ground

26. An artist manages to portray a face with just a few unconnected lines. Apparently the artist has capitalized on
a. closure.
b. contiguity.
c. the reversible figure effect.
d. the principle of camouflage.

27. The most basic source of stereoscopic vision is
a. accommodation.
b. retinal disparity.
c. convergence.
d. stroboscopic motion.

28. Necker's cube is a good example of
a. an ambiguous stimulus.
b. an impossible figure.
c. camouflage.
d. a binocular depth cue.

29. Skeptics regard the decline effect as evidence that _____ occurred in an ESP test.
a. replication
b. cheating
c. a run of luck
d. leakage

30. Which of the following is a binocular depth cue?
a. accommodation
b. convergence
c. linear perspective
d. motion parallax

31. Ambiguous stimuli allow us to hold more than one perceptual
a. gradient.
b. parallax.
c. constancy.
d. hypothesis.

32. Increased perceptual awareness is especially associated with
a. dishabituation.
b. unconscious transference.
c. high levels of stress.
d. stimulus repetition without variation.

33. Joan, failing to see a pedestrian crossing the street because she is too busy using a cell phone, is an example of
a. inattentional blindness.
b. attentional blindness.
c. perceptual habits.
d. apparent-distance hypothesis.

34. Standing eight feet farther away than Jacob who has 20/20 vision, Paul is able to identity the furry animal as a mouse. An optometrist might conclude that Paul has a better-than-average acuity and he has _____ vision.
a. 20/8
b. 20/18
c. 20/12
d. 20/80

35. Children who are born deaf have a good chance at learning spoken language at an almost normal rate if they receive cochlear implants before they reach the age of
a. 2.
b. 9.
c. 12.
d. 16.

36. Chloe screams out loud saying "insects are crawling everywhere!" when none are present, and Hilda, who is partially blind, claims that people are disappearing and appearing in front of her eyes. Chloe is experiencing _____ because she is seeing objects that are not present in her environment, and Hilda is experiencing _____ since her brain in trying to seek meaningful patterns from her sensory input.
   a. hallucinations, "sane hallucinations"
   b. hallucinations, inattentional blindness
   c. illusions, extrasensory perception (ESP)
   d. none of these

37. The fact that American tourists in London tend to look in the wrong direction before stepping into crosswalks is based on
   a. sensory localization.
   b. perceptual habits.
   c. sensory gating.
   d. unconscious transference.

LANGUAGE DEVELOPMENT
Sensation and Perception

Word Roots

Photos is the Greek word that means "light." Combining this Greek root with another term forms several words. These words all refer in some way to the action of light. Examples you will find in this or later chapters in the text include photoreceptors and photographic memory.

The Greek word *stereos* means hard, firm, and solid. Since solids are three-dimensional, the term has come to suggest three-dimensionality in combination with other word roots, the word "stereoscopic," for example. Other words have developed in the English language that make use of the idea of hardness or firmness. For example, the term *stereotype* refers to hard or firmly fixed ideas.

Journey into Psychology: Dancing the Two-Step (p. 130)
   (132) *kaleidoscope*: a constantly changing pattern or scene
   (132) *void*: empty space
   (132) *drink in*: experience
   (132) *passed out*: became unconscious

Sensory Systems—The First Step (pgs. 133-134)
   In general, how do sensory systems function?
   (133) *dewdrop*: a very small drop (amount) of moisture found in the early morning resulting from overnight condensation of moisture in the air
   (133) *stimulus*: something that causes an activity or response

(133) *attuned*: responsive to
(133) *eye catching*: being very noticeable
(133) *"tuned"*: set to pick up specific information
(134) *checkerboard*: a board used for playing the popular games of checkers, chess, and backgammon
(134) *crude*: not sophisticated; simple

Vision—Catching Some Rays (pgs. 135-141)

How is vision accomplished?

(135) *catching some rays*: slang for sun-tanning; Coon is making a joke because in vision the eye actually does "catch" light rays
(135) *drab*: dull
(136) *sharp*: in focus
(136) *misshapen*: deformed; not in the normal shape
(139) *hoots of laughter*: loud laughter
(139) *clashing*: not matching
(139) *sheepishly*: in an embarrassed or timid manner
(140) *embedded*: enclosed in
(141) *zenon (or xenon)*: a gas used for lighting; it is found in some automobile headlights

Hearing—Good Vibrations (pgs. 142-145)

What are the mechanisms of hearing?

(142) *good vibrations*: the title of a well-known pop music song; implies feeling good
(142) *tuning fork*: a metal device that gives a fixed musical tone when it is struck with or against another object
(142) *vacuum*: empty space
(142) *alien*: foreign; belonging elsewhere (in this case, outer space)
(142) *collide*: to hit against something
(142) *"bristles"*: very fine fibers at the top of hair cells
(143) *cobweb*: spider web
(144) *"boom box"*: large and loud radio; often carried
(144) *spurred*: to have increased motivation and interest to start something
(144) *"a radio that isn't quite tuned in"*: a radio that is not receiving a station clearly

Smell and Taste—The Nose Knows When the Tongue Can't Tell (pgs. 145-147)

How do the chemical senses operate?

(145) *wine taster*: a person whose job it is to sample wines in order to judge their quality
(145) *gourmet*: a person very knowledgeable about good food and drink
(145) *camphoric*: having an odor like camphor, a crystalline substance with a strong odor, generally derived from the wood of the camphor tree (similar to Vicks© vapor rub)
(145) *musky*: having an odor like musk, a substance with a penetrating, long lasting odor obtained from the male musk deer and used in perfume
(145) *etherish*: having an odor like ether, a colorless, highly flammable liquid with an aromatic odor

(146) *allergies*: reactions such as sneezing, coughing, and itching caused by sensitivity to substances in the environment such as pollen or dust

(146) *foraged*: searched for

(146) *inedible*: unfit to be eaten; something disgusting

(146) *kelp*: type of seaweed used in cooking

(147) *intricately shaped*: complex and elaborately designed

The Somesthetic Senses—Flying by the Seat of Your Pants (pgs. 148-150)

What are the somesthetic senses and why are they important?

(148) *flying by the seat of your pants*: operating an airplane without the use of instruments; in general, doing a task without really knowing what one is doing

(148) *sobriety test*: a test (such as making a person walk a straight line) to determine if someone has been excessively drinking alcohol

(149) *tattooing*: making designs on the body by inserting color under the skin

(149) *MP3*: a digital music file

(149) *gelatin-like*: soft and very pliable substance

(149) *tug of gravity*: gravity pulling one down

(150) *motion sickness*: nausea, and sometimes vomiting, caused by the motion of a car, boat, or airplane

(150) *kinesthesis*: sensory information given by organs located in the muscles, tendons, and joints and stimulated by bodily movement

(150) *heaving* (two meanings): moving rapidly up and down; vomiting

(150) *expel*: to eject; to get rid of

(150) *"green" and miserable with motion sickness*: feeling nauseated; sick to the stomach

Adaptation, Attention, and Gating—Tuning In and Tuning Out (p. 150-153)

Why are we more aware of some sensations than others?

(150) *tuning in and tuning out*: slang for paying attention (*tuning in*) and not paying attention (*tuning out*)

(150) *sauerkraut*: a salted, fermented cabbage dish from Germany

(150) *head cheese*: sausage made from the head, feet, and sometimes tongue and heart of a pig

(150) *pass out at the door* (you would probably *pass out at the door*): you would faint because of the overpowering bad smell

(151) *"tune in on"*: focus on

(151) *bottleneck*: the relatively narrow area of a bottle; used here to indicate a slowdown in information

(152) *take the edge off*: decrease the pain

(152) *jumbled*: mixed up; not organized

(153) *queasy*: feeling ill or sick to one's stomach

Perception— The Second Step (pgs. 154-160)

In general, how do we construct our perceptions?

(154) *cataract*: clouding of the lens of the eye

(154) *lopsided*: not symmetrical or balanced in shape

(154) *jumble*: a mess; a collection of unorganized materials

(154) *Marilyn Monroe*: famous blonde movie actress (1926-1962)

(154)   *Madonna*: famous blonde popular singer, considered by some people to resemble Marilyn Monroe

(156)   *"Birds of a feather flock together"*: just as birds of one type tend to stay together, so do people or things with similar characteristics group together

(157)   *camouflaged*: disguised, hidden

(158)   *widget*: gadget, unnamed item considered as an example

(158)   *hurdles*: difficulties, problems, barriers

(159)   *innate*: inborn; a biologically inherited ability

(159)   *neon lamps*: type of electric lighting characterized by bright colors that glow

Depth Perception—What If the World Were Flat? (pgs. 160-167)

How is it possible to see depth and judge distance?

(160)   *3-D*: short for three dimensional

(160)   *shoot baskets*: play basketball

(160)   *thread a needle*: putting thread through the very small opening in a needle; the first step in sewing

(160)   *innate*: inborn; a biologically inherited ability

(160)   *"skydiving"*: the sport of jumping out of an airplane with a parachute; here referring to the baby jumping off the table

(161)   *"crash landings"*: landing of an aircraft under emergency conditions, usually with damage to the craft. Here, refers to unexpected falls children take as they learn to crawl and walk (and the bumps and bruises that come with it!)

(161)   *discrepancy*: a difference

(162)   *simulate*: copy or imitate

(162)   *impart*: to show

(163)   *illusions*: misleading images

(163)   *receding*: moving back, retreating

(164)   *gradients*: gradual changes or variations

(164)   *cobblestone street*: a street paved with round, flat stones

(164)   *smog*: a combination of smoke and fog

(165)   *deceptively*: misleading

(166)   *compensate*: neutralize the effect of; counterbalance

(167)   softball: ball used in a game of softball; about 10-12 inches in circumference.

Perceptual Learning – Perception from the Top Down (pgs. 168-171)

How is perception altered by expectations, motives, emotions, and learning?

(168)   *starting blocks*: fixtures on the track where a runner places his or her feet prior to starting a race

(168)   *backfires*: a loud banging noise made by a vehicle due to improper combustion

(168)   *jump the gun*: start the race before the starting gun fires

(168)   *"queer"*: a derogatory term for a homosexual

(168)   *"bitch"*: a derogatory term for a woman

(169)   *are pushed* (other articles *are pushed* in ads): try very hard to sell

(170)   *icons*: small images on a computer screen used to represent functions or programs

(170)   *linebacker*: in football, a defensive player positioned behind the linemen

(170)   *ingrained*: innate, firmly fixed

(170)   *grotesque*: bizarre; differing very much from what is normal
(170)   *doctored*: altered, changed

Extrasensory Perception—Do You Believe in Magic? (pgs. 171-175)

Is extrasensory perception possible?
(171)   *purported*: supposed; claimed
(171)   *paranormal:* supernatural; not scientifically explainable
(171)   *astound*: overwhelm with amazement
(171)   *prophetic*: predictive of the future
(172)   *"hits"*: correct answers
(172)   *plague*: to trouble
(172)   *Jamaican-accented*: a language accent that sounds like the person is from Jamaica
(172)   *faked*: made it all up
(173)   *psychics*: people who claim to be sensitive to nonphysical or supernatural forces and influences
(173)   *meticulous*: very careful and precise; detail oriented
(173)   *premonition*: advance warning
(173)   *hunch*: guess
(174)   *Zero. Zip. Nada:* words meaning "no outcome"
(174)   *Clearly, state lottery organizers have nothing to fear!:* if a person really had ESP, he or she could gamble and be sure of winning lots of money

Psychology In Action: Becoming a Better Eyewitness to Life (pgs. 175-178)

How can I learn to perceive events more accurately?
(175)   *infallible*: without mistakes
(175)   *over-optimism*: too much optimism
(175)   *to put it bluntly*: to say plainly
(176)   *exonerated*: to be cleared of blame
(176)   *culprit*: that which is causing something
(176)   *surrender to experience*: have overconfidence in one's own experience
(177)   MP3: a digital music file
(177)   *if you've seen one tree, you've seen them all*: the tendency to use a single example to generalize to all objects in a category
(177)   *maxims*: sayings; proverbs
(177)   "If the doors of perception were cleansed, man would see everything as it is, infinite.": to see without judgment leads to an accurate view of the surrounding world
(178)   *swayed*: influenced

Solutions

Recite and Review

Sensory Systems—the First Step

1. nerve
2. Sensation, perception
3. data, analyze
4. transduce
5. perceptual
6. detectors
7. pop
8. coding, eyelids
9. sensory, activated

Vision—Catching Some Rays

1. visible spectrum
2. wavelength, wavelength
3. wavelength
4. narrow
5. Brightness
6. rods, cones
7. shape, shape
8. nearsightedness, accommodation
9. rods
10. cones, color
11. exits, enter
12. acuity
13. rods
14. retina, cones
15. cones
16. Trichromatic, afterimages
17. either-or
18. black or white
19. Total
20. color blindness
21. increase, rods, cones

Hearing—Good Vibrations

1. peaks, valleys
2. pitch, height
3. external
4. eardrum, hair
5. frequency, frequency
6. high, low
7. sensorineural
8. Sensorineural
9. hair
10. noise
11. loud
12. never

Smell and Taste—The Nose Knows When the Tongue Can't Tell

1. smell, taste
2. location
3. receptors, 10,000
4. smell, allergies
5. bitter
6. coding
7. smell, taste

The Somesthetic Senses—Flying by the Seat of Your Pants

1. skin
2. pressure, number
3. reminding
4. pain, system
5. lowering
6. reduce
7. head
8. gravity
9. fluid
10. mismatch

Adaptation, Attention, and Gating —Tuning In and Tuning Out

1. reduction or decrease
2. gating
3. attention
4. gating
5. spinal cord
6. Counterirritation, pain
7. neuromatrix

Perception—The Second Step

1. patterns
2. model
3. exist, external
4. hallucinations
5. Sane, blind
6. upward, pre-existing
7. top-down
8. object, background
9. organization, similarity, common
10. grouped, appearance
11. complete, time
12. hypothesis, organization
13. stimuli, cube
14. image, perceptual
15. constancy
16. constant
17. inborn, learned

Depth Perception—What If the World Were Flat?

1. Depth
2. visual cliff
3. Monocular, binocular
4. lens, eyes
5. cues, flat
6. parallel lines, smaller, picture
7. finer, motion, motion
8. one eye
9. larger
10. distance, horizon
11. three-dimensional
12. size-distance, lines

Perceptual Learning – Perception from the Top Down

1. expectancies
2. habits, size
3. features
4. habits, buildings
5. values

Extrasensory Perception—Do You Believe in Magic?

1. psi, telepathy
2. perception.
3. Coincidence
4. skeptical, psychic
5. luck
6. against, repeated
7. deception

Psychology in Action: Becoming a Better Eyewitness to Life

1. inaccurate
2. focus
3. lower
4. testing, attention
5. broaden

CONNECTIONS

Sensory Systems—The First Step and Vision—Catching Some Rays

1. D.
2. F.
3. H.
4. B.
5. I.
6. C.
7. K.
8. A.
9. E.
10. G.
11. J.

1. C.
2. K.
3. F.
4. E.
5. I.
6. A.
7. G.
8. J.
9. B.
10. D.
11. L.
12. H.

Hearing—Good Vibrations, and Smell and Taste—The Nose Knows When the Tongue Can't Tell

1. E.	4. A.	7. C.	10. J.
2. G.	5. D.	8. I.	
3. H.	6. F.	9. B.	

1. B.	4. D.	7. C.
2. H.	5. A.	8. F.
3. G.	6. I.	9. E.

The Somesthetic Senses—Flying by the Seat of Your Pants, and Adaptation, Gating, and Attention—Tuning In and Tuning Out

1. F.	4. C.	7. I.	10. E.
2. A.	5. J.	8. B.	11. H.
3. L.	6. G.	9. K.	12. D.

Perception—The second Step

1. C.	3. D.	5. F.
2. E.	4. A.	6. B.

1. A.	4. G.	7. E.
2. D.	5. B.	8. H.
3. I.	6. C.	9. F.

Depth Perception—What If the World Were Flat?

1. E.	3. F.	5. A.	7. H.
2. G.	4. C.	6. B.	8. D.

1. B.	3. F.	5. A.
2. E.	4. C.	6. D.

Perceptual Learning – Perception From the Top Down

1. A.	3. G.	5. C.	7. E.
2. B.	4. D.	6. F.	

Extrasensory Perception—Do You Believe in Magic?

1. D.	3. B.	5. G.	7. A.
2. C.	4. F.	6. E.	

Psychology in Action: Becoming a Better Eyewitness to Life

1. D.	2. A.	3. C.	4. B.

Check Your Memory

Sensory Systems—The First Step

1. F	3. F	5. F	7. F
2. T	4. F	6. T	8. T

Vision—Catching Some Rays

1. T	5. T	9. T	13. T
2. F	6. T	10. F	14. F
3. F	7. T	11. T	15. F
4. T	8. F	12. T	

Hearing—Good Vibrations

1. T	4. F	7. T	10. T
2. F	5. F	8. T	11. T
3. T	6. T	9. T	

Smell and Taste—The Nose Knows When the Tongue Can't Tell

1. T	3. F	5. F	7. T
2. F	4. F	6. T	8. T

The Somesthetic Senses—Flying by the Seat of Your Pants

1. F	3. F	5. T	7. F
2. F	4. T	6. T	8. T

Adaptation, Gating, and Attention—Tuning In and Tuning Out

1. F	4. T	7. T
2. T	5. T	8. T
3. F	6. F	9. F

Perception—The Second Step

1. T	5. T	9. F	13. T
2. T	6. T	10. T	14. F
3. F	7. F	11. F	15. T
4. F	8. F	12. T	

Depth Perception—What If the World Were Flat?

1. T	7. F	13. T	19. T
2. F	8. T	14. T	20. T
3. F	9. F	15. F	21. F
4. T	10. F	16. T	22. F
5. F	11. T	17. F	
6. F	12. F	18. T	

Extrasensory Perception—Do You Believe in Magic?

1. F	4. F	7. F	10. F
2. T	5. F	8. T	
3. T	6. F	9. T	

Psychology in Action: Becoming a Better Eyewitness to Life

1. T	4. F	7. F
2. F	5. T	8. T
3. F	6. F	9. F

Final Survey and Review

Sensory Systems—The First Step

1. transduce
2. organizes, interprets
3. reduction, filter
4. receptors
5. analysis
6. feature
7. detection
8. phosphenes, mechanical
9. response, experience

Vision—Catching Some Rays

1. transducer, electromagnetic
2. violet, red
3. Hue
4. pure
5. amplitude
6. photoreceptors, retina.
7. cornea, lens
8. myopia, presbyopia
9. night, motion
10. fovea, daylight
11. blind spot, optic
12. 20/20
13. peripheral, tunnel
14. trichromatic, green
15. pigments, red
16. unable, removed
17. messages, yellow, blue
18. blindness, males
19. Ishihara
20. adaptation, increased

Hearing—Good Vibrations

1. hearing, rarefaction
2. frequency, amplitude
3. pinna, concentrate
4. transduced, cochlea
5. frequency, 4,000
6. Place, base
7. deafness, conductive
8. aid
9. implants
10. cochlea, gunfire
11. sensorineural
12. 120
13. Hair

Smell and Taste—The Nose Knows When the Tongue Can't Tell

1. Olfaction, gustation
2. lock-and-key
3. 1,000
4. Dysosmia, infections
5. sweet, umami
6. shapes
7. flavor

The Somesthetic Senses—Flying by the Seat of Your Pants

1. somesthetic, joint
2. skin, number
3. warning, pain
4. congenital
5. anxiety, attention
6. control
7. sickness, gravity
8. otolith
9. semicircular, movement
10. conflict, minimizing

Adaptation, Attention, and Gating —Tuning In and Tuning Out

1. sensations, impulses
2. Selective, brain
3. inattentional
4. competing, pain
5. gating
6. intense
7. Phantom

Perception—The Second Step

1. Perception, mental
2. Illusions, misconstructions, no
3. lost, environmental
4. appearing
5. Bottom-up, complete, organize
6. Perceptions
7. sensations, figure, Reversible
8. Gestalt, nearness
9. similar, Continuity
10. Closure, grouped
11. organization, disrupt
12. ambiguous, Impossible
13. retinal, undistorted
14. shape
15. apparent, proportion
16. native, empirical

Depth Perception—What If the World Were Flat?

1. three
2. learned, innate
3. one, two
4. accommodation, inward
5. pictorial, drawings
6. linear, shadow
7. texture, parallax
8. monocular
9. moon
10. apparent, depth
11. Stereoscopic, 50
12. Linear, mislocating

Perceptual Learning – Perception from the Top Down

1. prior, suggestion
2. set
3. interpreting
4. change
5. perceptual, inverted
6. Illusions, box
7. motives

Extrasensory Perception—Do You Believe in Magic?

1. Parapsychology, precognition
2. telepathy
3. controversial, Coincidence
4. existence
5. statistically
6. replicated, independent
7. tricks

Psychology in Action: Becoming a Better Eyewitness to Life

1. reconstruction, eyewitness
2. weapon
3. brief, wording
4. dishabituation
5. perceptual

Mastery Test

1. b, p. 150
2. d, p. 139
3. c, p. 148
4. d, p. 138-139
5. c, p. 141
6. a, p. 133-134
7. d, p. 136
8. b, p. 152
9. a, p. 142
10. c, p. 133
11. d, p. 142
12. b, p. 145-146
13. a, p. 135
14. c, p. 136
15. c, p. 136
16. a, p. 136-138
17. d, p. 154-155
18. a, p. 175-176
19. b, p. 158
20. d, p. 163
21. a, p. 166
22. c, p. 161
23. c, p. 156-157
24. d. p. 162
25. d, p. 156
26. a, p. 156-157
27. b, p. 161-162
28. a, p. 158
29. c, p. 174
30. b, p. 161-162
31. d, p. 158
32. a, p. 177
33. a, p. 151
34. c, p. 138
35. a, p. 144
36. a, p. 156
37. b, p. 169

CHAPTER 5

States of Consciousness

Chapter Overview

Consciousness consists of everything you are aware of at a given instant. Altered states of consciousness (ASCs) differ significantly from normal waking consciousness. Many conditions produce ASCs, which frequently have culturally defined meanings.

Sleep is an innate biological rhythm characterized by changes in consciousness and brain activity. People who deprive themselves of sleep (particularly adolescents) may experience impairments to physical and cognitive functioning. Brain-wave patterns and sleep behaviors define four stages of sleep. The two most basic forms of sleep are non-rapid eye movement (NREM) sleep and rapid eye movement (REM) sleep. NREM sleep is thought to "calm" the brain while REM sleep "sharpens" memories. During REM sleep, the body's major muscles tend to be paralyzed, but the brain is very active. Sleep disturbances such as insomnia, but generally treatable. Sleepwalking, sleeptalking, sleepsex, and night terrors are NREM events. Nightmares occur primarily in REM sleep. REM rebound occurs when one is deprived of REM sleep the night before. Dreaming appears to be emotionally restorative and it may help form adaptive memories. The psychodynamic view portrays dreams as a form of wish fulfillment; the activation-synthesis hypothesis says that dreaming is a physiological process with little meaning. Neurocognitive dream theory suggests that dreams reflect ordinary, day-to-day thoughts, emotions, and content. Each dream theory has its own strengths and weaknesses.

Hypnosis is a state of altered consciousness characterized by narrowed attention and increased openness to suggestion. People vary in hypnotic susceptibility. Most hypnotic phenomena are related to the basic suggestion effect. Hypnosis can relieve pain, and it has other useful effects, but it is not magic. Stage hypnotists simulate hypnosis in order to entertain. Some believe hypnosis occurs largely through autosuggestion, or hypnotizing oneself.

Meditation is a mental exercise that can be used to alter consciousness, promote relaxation, reduce stress, and reduce the likelihood of various disorders. Sensory deprivation refers to any major reduction in external stimulation. Sensory deprivation also produces deep relaxation and a variety of perceptual effects. It can be used to help people enhance creative thinking and to change bad habits. Meditation can help to increase mindfulness, a condition marked by open awareness and being fully present in each moment.

Psychoactive drugs are substances that alter consciousness by changing the activity of brain cells, mostly in the reward and pleasure systems. Most drugs can be placed on a scale ranging from stimulation to depression, although some drugs are better classified as hallucinogens. Drugs use has both short-term and long-term risks for impairment to physical, cognitive, and behavioral functioning. The potential for abuse is high for drugs that lead to physical dependence, but psychological dependence can also be a serious problem. Polydrug abuse can lead to fatal interactions. Drug abuse is often a symptom, rather than a cause, of personal maladjustment. It is supported by the immediate pleasure (and delayed consequences) associated with many psychoactive drugs, and by cultural values that encourage drug abuse.

Various strategies, ranging from literal to highly symbolic, can be used to reveal the meanings of dreams. Dreaming—especially lucid dreaming—can be a source of creativity and it may be used for problem solving and personal growth.

Learning Objectives

1. Define *consciousness*, *waking consciousness,* the *first- and third-person experience,* and *altered state of consciousness (ASC),* and list causes of an ASC.

2. Describe the basic characteristics of sleep and what skills can be performed when asleep

3. Discuss sleep as a biological rhythm; the concept of *microsleep*; the symptoms of sleep deprivation and temporary sleep deprivation psychosis; hypersomnia in teenagers; the sleep patterns of short and long sleepers; and the relationship between age and sleep needs.

4. Explain what physiologically controls sleep; describe the characteristics of the four stages of sleep, including the different brain wave patterns in each.

5. Differentiate between the two basic states of sleep (REM and NREM).

6. Describe the symptoms of REM behavior disorder and hypnopompic hallucinations.

7. List factors that contribute to sleep problems in American society and describe the following sleep disturbances (Table 5.1):
    a. hypersomnia
    b. narcolepsy
    c. periodic limb movement syndrome
    d. restless legs syndrome
    e. sleep drunkenness
    f. sleep terror disorder
    g. sleep-wake schedule disorder

8. Describe the three types of insomnia, what causes each type, the effectiveness of prescription and nonprescription sleeping pills, and the six behavioral remedies used to treat chronic insomnia.

9. Describe sleepsex, sleepwalking, and sleeptalking; differentiate between nightmares vs. night terrors; state three steps that can be used to eliminate nightmares.

10. Discuss sleep apnea, its causes, its treatments, and its connection to SIDS, including the risk factors and preventative measures for SIDS.

11. Discuss REM sleep and dreaming, including when REM sleep was discovered, the average length and spacing of dreams per night, the research of William Dement, the causes and symptoms of REM rebound, and the functions of REM sleep.

12. Explain Freud's psychodynamic dream theory, the activation-synthesis hypothesis, and the neurocognitive dream theory, and the current research on dream content.

13. Define *hypnosis* and describe its history from Mesmer through its use today; discuss the state and the nonstate theories of hypnosis and the view of hypnosis as autosuggestion.

14. Discuss how "true" hypnosis is conducted, including the basic suggestion effect, hypnotic susceptibility, and what can and cannot be achieved with hypnosis, and escribe how stage hypnotists perform their "acts."

15. Describe the two major forms of meditation and their benefits, including the relaxation response and mindfulness.

16. Discuss sensory deprivation and the beneficial uses of sensory restriction (REST).

17. Define the term *psychoactive drug*; describe how various drugs affect the nervous system.

18. Explain why drug abuse is so common, including effects of reward and punishment systems and predictors of adolescent drug use and abuse; differentiate physical dependence from psychological dependence and explain the concepts of withdrawal and tolerance; discuss patterns of abuse and polydrug abuse.

19. Discuss the medical uses (if any), symptoms of abuse, organic damage potential, withdrawal symptoms, and treatment options for:
    a. amphetamines
    b. cocaine
    c. MDMA (ecstasy)
    d. caffeine
    e. nicotine
    f. barbiturates
    g. GHB
    h. tranquilizers (include the concept of drug interaction)
    i. alcohol
    j. hallucinogens (including marijuana) and explain why drug abuse is such a common problem

20. Explain the procedure for "catching a dream"; how Freud, Hall, Cartwright, and Perls analyzed dreams, including Freud's four dream processes; how dreams can be used to improve creativity; and lucid dreaming.

RECITE AND REVIEW

States of Consciousness—The Many Faces of Awareness

Survey Question: What is consciousness? Page 183

1. States of _____ that differ from normal, alert, and _____ consciousness are called altered states of consciousness (ASCs).

2. In defining consciousness, one needs to distinguish between _____, first-person experiences and objective, _____-person points of view.

3. ASCs involve distinct shifts in the quality and _____ of mental activity.

4. Altered states are especially associated with _____ and _____, hypnosis, meditation, _____ deprivation, and psychoactive drugs.

5. Cultural conditioning greatly affects what altered states a person recognizes, seeks, considers _____, and attains.

Sleep—Catching a Few ZZZ's

Survey Question: What are the effects of sleep loss or changes in sleep patterns? Pages 183-186

1. Sleep is an innate biological _____ essential for _____.

2. Moderate sleep loss mainly affects alertness and self-motivated performance on _____ or boring tasks.

3. Hypersomnia is marked by excessive _____ sleepiness, and can occur after a _____ hours of sleep loss.

4. Higher animals and people deprived of sleep experience _____ microsleeps.

5. _____ change during puberty increases adolescents' need for _____, which many lack since they tend to stay up late and get up early for school. This decreases the quality and quantity of sleep during the teen years.

6. The "storm and stress" that adolescents experience may, in part, be caused by _____ of sleep.

7. Extended sleep _____ can (somewhat rarely) produce a _____ sleep-deprivation psychosis, marked by confusion, delusions, and possibly hallucinations.

8. Biological _____ within the body are closely tied to sleep, activity levels, and energy cycles.

9. The unscheduled human sleep-waking cycle averages _____ hours and _____ minutes, but cycles of _____ and _____ tailor it to 24-hour days.

10. Sleep patterns show some flexibility; _____-sleepers average 5 hours or less per night; long sleepers sleep _____ or more hours on average, but 7 to 8 hours remains average.

11. Adapting to _____ or _____ sleep cycles is difficult and inefficient for most people.

12. The amount of daily sleep _____ steadily from birth to old age and switches from multiple sleep-wake cycles to once-a-day sleep periods.

13. Midafternoon sleepiness is a _____ part of the sleep cycle.

Stages of Sleep—The Nightly Roller-Coaster

Survey Question: Why do we sleep? Pages 186-190

1. Sleepiness is associated with the accumulation of a sleep hormone in the _____ and spinal cord.

2. Sleep depends on which of _____ opposed sleep and waking systems in the _____ is dominant at any given moment.

3. Sleep occurs in _____ stages, defined by changes in behavior and brain _____ recorded with an electroencephalograph (EEG).

4. Stage 1, _____ sleep, has small irregular brain waves. In stage 2, _____ spindles appear. _____ waves appear in stage 3. Stage 4, or deep sleep, is marked by almost pure delta waves.

5. Sleepers _____ between stages 1 and 4 (passing through stages 2 and 3) several times each night.

6. There are two basic sleep states, rapid eye _____ (REM) sleep and non-REM (NREM) sleep.

7. REM sleep is much more strongly associated with _____ than is non-REM sleep.

8. The _____ process hypothesis of sleep suggests that NREM sleep "calms" the brain; REM sleep appears to "sharpen" our _____.

9. A day of _____ exertion generally leads to an increase in NREM sleep, which allows our body to recover from bodily fatigue. A day of _____ would lead to an increase in REM sleep.

10. Dreams during _____ sleep tend to be longer, clearer, more detailed, more bizarre, and more "dream-like" than thoughts and _____ that occur in NREM sleep.

11. Dreaming is accompanied by sexual and _____ arousal but relaxation of the skeletal _____. People who move about violently while asleep may suffer from _____ behavior disorder.

12. _____ _____ occur when one is beginning to wake up, but is still experiencing sleep paralysis.

Sleep Disturbances—Showing Nightly: Sleep Wars!

Survey Question: What are some sleep disorders and unusual sleep events?
Pages 190-194

1. Insomnia, which is difficulty in getting to sleep or staying asleep, may be _____ or chronic.

2. When insomnia is treated with drugs, sleep quality is often _____ and drug-dependency _____ may develop.

3. Sudden cessation from sleeping _____ may result in terrible nightmares or "rebound insomnia".

4. The amino acid tryptophan, found in bread, pasta, and other foods, helps promote _____.

5. Behavioral approaches to managing insomnia, such as relaxation, sleep restriction, _____ control, and paradoxical _____ are quite effective.

6. _____ (somnambulism) and sleeptalking occur during NREM sleep in stages 3 and 4.

7. Night terrors occur in _____ sleep, whereas nightmares occur in _____ sleep.

8. Nightmares can be eliminated by the method called imagery _____.

9. During sleep apnea, people repeatedly stop _____. Apnea is suspected as one cause of _____ infant death syndrome (SIDS).

10. One effective treatment for _____ _____ is the use of a continuous positive airway pressure (CPAP) mask to aid breathing during sleep.

11. The first _____ months are critical for babies who are at risk for SIDS. Other factors include the baby being a _____, breathing through an open _____, having a mother who is a _____, and having a crib that contains soft objects such as a pillow and quilts.

12. The phrase "_____ to sleep" refers to the safest position for most babies: their _____.

Dreams—A Separate Reality?

Survey Question: Do dreams have meaning? Pages 194-196

1. The first dream of the night is typically short (approximately 10 minutes); dreams become _____ over the course of the sleep cycle.

2. People will experience REM _____ if they are deprived of REM sleep the night before.

3. People deprived of REM sleep showed an urgent need to _____ and mental disturbances the next day. However, total sleep loss seems to be more important than loss of a single sleep _____.

4. One of the more important functions of REM sleep appears to be the processing of adaptive _____.

5. The Freudian, or psychodynamic, view is that dreams express unconscious _____, frequently hidden by dream symbols.

6. Freud distinguished between the _____, visible meaning of dreams (manifest content) and the hidden, _____ meaning (latent content).

7. Allan Hobson and Robert McCarley's _____-synthesis model portrays dreaming as a physiological process. The brain, they say, creates dreams to explain _____ and motor messages that occur during REM sleep.

8. Domhoff's neurocognitive dream theory suggests the dreams reflect _____ concerns from daily experiences.

9. Most dream content is about _____ settings, people, and actions. Dreams more often involve negative _____ than positive _____.

Hypnosis—Look into My Eyes

Survey Questions: What is hypnosis? Pages 197-200

1. Hypnosis is an altered state characterized by narrowed attention and _____ suggestibility.

2. In the 1700s, Franz Mesmer (whose name is the basis for the term *mesmerize*) practiced "_____ magnetism," which was actually a demonstration of the power of _____.

3. The term _____ was first used by James Braid, an English doctor.

4. Ernest Hilgard described hypnosis as causing a _____ _____ or "split" in awareness.

5. It is believed that one part of a hypnotized person does not feel or react to _____; the _____ observer is aware of the pain but silently remains in the background.

6. The core of hypnosis is the _____ suggestion effect—a tendency to carry out suggested actions as if they were involuntary. However, a hypnotized person will not perform behaviors that he or she deems to be _____ or repulsive.

7. Many theorists believe that hypnosis is simply a form of self-hypnosis, or _____, where one influences one's own behavior.

8. Hypnosis appears capable of producing relaxation, controlling _____, and altering perceptions.

9. Hypnosis does not produce _____ strength or age regression.

10. People vary in hypnotic susceptibility; _____ out of 10 can be hypnotized, as revealed by scores on the Stanford Hypnotic Susceptibility _____.

11. Stage hypnotism takes advantage of typical stage behavior, _____ suggestibility, responsive subjects, disinhibition, and _____ to simulate hypnosis.

Meditation and Sensory Deprivation—Chilling, the Healthy Way

Survey Questions: Do meditation and sensory deprivation have any benefits? Pages 200-203

1. Meditation refers to mental exercises that are used to alter _____.

2. In mindfulness meditation, attention is _____ to include an awareness of one's entire moment-by-moment experience, which is more _____ to achieve than the concentrative meditation where attention is focused on a _____ object or thought.

3. Two major benefits of meditation are its ability to interrupt anxious thoughts and its ability to elicit the relaxation response (the pattern of changes that occur in the body at times of deep _____).

4. Sensory deprivation takes place when there is a major reduction in the amount or variety of sensory _____ available to a person.

5. Prolonged sensory deprivation is stressful and disruptive, leading to _____ distortions.

6. Brief or mild sensory deprivation can enhance sensory sensitivity and induce deep _____.

7. Research suggests that _____ _____ lessens the symptoms of a variety of psychological disorders; it also reduces aggression and the illegal use of psychoactive drugs.

8. Sensory deprivation also appears to aid the breaking of long-standing _____ and promotes creative thinking. This effect is the basis for Restricted Environmental Stimulation Therapy (REST).

9. Mindfulness involves open, _____ awareness of current experience that is attuned to one's immediate reality.

Drug-Altered Consciousness—The High and Low of It

Survey Question: What are the effects of the more commonly used psychoactive drugs? Pages 203-206

1. A psychoactive drug is a substance that affects the brain in ways that _____ (_____ or _____) consciousness.

2. Drugs alter the activities in the brain by _____ and blocking neurotransmitters (_____ that carry messages between neurons) to produce feelings of pleasure.

3. Most psychoactive drugs can be placed on a scale ranging from stimulation to _____. Some, however, are best described as hallucinogens (drugs that alter _____ impressions).

4. Drugs may cause a physical dependence (_____) or a psychological dependence, or both.

5. Nearly all addictive drugs stimulate the nucleus accumbens to _____ dopamine, which intensifies feelings of _____.

6. Drugs that ease pain, induce sleep, or end _____ have a high potential for abuse.

7. Prolonged use of a drug can lead to drug tolerance (a _____ response to a drug) whereby the abuser must _____ the amount of a drug to receive the same desired effect.

8. Drug use can be classified as experimental, recreational, situational, intensive, and _____. Drug abuse is most often associated with the last three.

9. Drug abuse is related to personal and social maladjustment, attempts to cope, and the _____ reinforcing qualities of psychoactive drugs.

10. Among adolescents, the best _____ of drug use and abuse were: drug use by peers, parental drug use, delinquency, parental maladjustment, _____ self-esteem, social nonconformity, and stressful life changes.

11. When mixed, the _____ of different drugs are multiplied by drug interactions, resulting in _____ drug overdoses.

12. The physically addicting drugs are alcohol, amphetamines, barbiturates, cocaine, codeine, GHB, heroin, methadone, morphine, tobacco, and tranquilizers. All psychoactive drugs can lead to _____ dependence.

Uppers—Amphetamines, Cocaine, MDMA, Caffeine, Nicotine

Pages 206-211

1. Stimulant drugs are readily abused because of the period of _____ that often follows stimulation. The greatest risks are associated with amphetamines, cocaine, MDMA, and nicotine, but even _____ can be a problem.

2. Amphetamines were once widely used for weight loss and to treat _____; now they are used to _____ childhood hyperactivity and depressant overdose.

3. Amphetamines, known as "speed," "bennies," "dexies," "go," and "_____," are synthetic stimulants that produce a rapid drug _____. Abusers typically go on binges that last for several days until they "_____," suffering from _____, confusion, depression, uncontrolled irritability, and aggression.

4. Methamphetamine, known as "_____," "glass," "meth," or "crystal," is cheaply produced in labs and can be snorted or _____.

5. Repeated use of amphetamine can cause brain damage and amphetamine _____. Amphetamine psychosis can cause the abuser to act on their delusions and risk _____-injury or injury to _____.

6. Signs of cocaine abuse are: compulsive use, loss of _____, and a disregard for _____.

7. Cocaine users may experience anhedonia (an inability to feel _____) following a "high."

8. MDMA or "_____," which is similar to amphetamine, has been linked with numerous deaths and with mental impairment.

9. Users of MDMA are likely to risk an _____ in body temperature, liver damage, and unsafe sex.

10. Although MDMA (Ecstasy) users believe the drug _____ sexual pleasure, it can _____ erections in men and retard orgasms in both men and women.

11. Caffeine is the most widely used _____ drug in North America.

12. Caffeine can be found in coffee, _____, soft drinks, and chocolate. It stimulates the brain by _____ chemicals that inhibit nerve activities.

13. Caffeinism can result in _____, irritability, loss of appetite, _____, racing heart, and elevated body temperature.

14. _____ (or _____) includes the added risk of lung cancer, heart disease, and other health problems.

15. The smoking of cigarettes releases carcinogens (_____-causing substances) in the air, which expose people to _____-_____ smoke and place them at risk for developing lung cancer.

16. A 30-minute exposure to a _____ of smokeless tobacco is equivalent to _____ three or four cigarettes.

17. The best method for quitting smoking is scheduled gradual reduction; this may involve delaying the first _____ of the day in greater increments every day, reducing the _____ number of cigarettes smoked each day, and repeatedly quitting for one _____ at a time.

Downers—Sedatives, Tranquilizers, and Alcohol

Pages 211-215

1. Barbiturates are _____ drugs whose overdose level is close to the intoxication dosage, making them dangerous drugs. Common street names for barbiturates are "downers," "_____ heavens," "_____ jackets," "goofballs," "_____ ladies," and "rainbows."

2. The depressant drug _____ (gamma-hydroxybuyrate) can cause coma, breathing failure, and death in relatively low doses. GHB is commonly called "goop," "scoop," "max," or "_____ Home Boy."

3. Benzodiazepine tranquilizers, such as _____, are used to lower anxiety. When abused, they have a strong _____ potential.

4. _____, a tranquilizer, also known as "roofies" and the "_____-rape drug," is odorless and tasteless and is sometimes used to spike drinks and induced short-term amnesia and sleep.

5. Mixing barbiturates and alcohol may result in a fatal _____ interaction (in which the joint effect of two drugs exceeds the effects of adding one drug's effects to the other's).

6. Binge drinking is defined as consuming _____ or more drinks in a short time for men, _____ or more for women.

7. The brain continues to develop into the early 20s; binge drinking may cause teens and young adults to lose as much as ten percent of their _____ capacity (especially _____).

8. Paced drinking may include: thinking about drinking management beforehand, drinking slowly on a _____ stomach, making every other drink _____, limiting drinking to the first hour of a social party, practicing politely _____ drinks, and learning to not rely on alcohol.

9. People who undergo detoxification (the _____ of poison) often experience unpleasant symptoms of drug _____.

Hallucinogens—Tripping the Light Fantastic

Pages 215-218

1. LSD (lysergic acid diethylamide) or "_____" can produce _____ and psychotic-like disturbances in thinking and perception.

2. Three common hallucinogens are _____ (peyote), psilocybin ("magic mushrooms", and PCP (phencyclidine, or "_____ _____")

3. Marijuana ("pot," "grass," and "_____") is a hallucinogen subject to an _____ pattern similar to alcohol. Studies have linked chronic marijuana use with memory impairment, lung cancer, reproductive problems, immune system disorders, and other health problems.

4. _____, the main active chemical in marijuana, accumulates in the cerebral cortex and reproductive organs.

5. Potential problems caused by frequent marijuana use are short-term _____ loss and a decline in learning, _____, and thinking abilities. In addition, people who smoke _____ or more joints a week tend to score four points lower on IQ tests.

Psychology in Action: Exploring and Using Dreams

Survey Question: How can dreams be used to promote personal understanding?
Pages 218-221

1. Freud held that the meaning of dreams is _____ by four dream _____ he called condensation, displacement, symbolization, and secondary elaboration.

2. Calvin Hall emphasizes the setting, cast, _____, and emotions of a dream.

3. Rosalind Cartwright's view of dreams as feeling statements and Fritz Perls' technique of _____ for dream elements are also helpful.

4. Dreams may be used for _____ problem solving, especially when dream control is achieved through lucid dreaming (a dream in which the dreamer feels capable of normal thought and action).

CONNECTIONS

States of Consciousness—The Many Faces of Awareness, and Sleep—Catching a few ZZZs

Survey Questions: What is consciousness? What are the effects of sleep loss or changes in sleep patterns? Pages 183-186

1. _____ hypersomnia
2. _____ Randy Gardner
3. _____ Altered State of Consciousness
4. _____ microsleep
5. _____ Sleep-wake cycle
6. _____ short sleep cycles
7. _____ long sleepers
8. _____ sleep pattern
9. _____ biological rhythms
10. _____ consciousness

A. over nine hours
B. few seconds of repeated sleep
C. biological clocks
D. sleep deprivation
E. 2 to 1 ratio of awake versus sleep
F. excessive sleepiness
G. mental awareness
H. daydreaming
I. infancy
J. 24 hours

Stages of Sleep—The Nightly Roller-Coaster

Survey Question: Why do we sleep? Pages 186-190

1. _____ alpha waves
2. _____ beta waves
3. _____ delta waves
4. _____ REM
5. _____ hypnic jerk
6. _____ REM and NREM
7. _____ hypnopompic hallucinations
8. _____ REM behavior disorder
9. _____ sleep spindles
10. _____ NREM sleep
11. _____ REM
12. _____ REM sleep

A. reflex muscle contraction
B. images created upon awakening
C. relaxed
D. sexual arousal
E. stage 2 of sleep
F. stage 4 of sleep
G. awake, alert
H. produces sleep stages 1–4
I. dual process hypothesis
J. "sharpens" memories
K. "calms" the brain
L. violent actions

Sleep Disturbances—Showing Nightly: Sleep Wars!

Survey Question: What are some sleep disorders and unusual sleep events?
Pages 190-194

1. _____ sleep drunkenness	A. fatal to infants
2. _____ hypersomnia	B. remedy for insomnia
3. _____ Sleep apnea	C. slow awakening
4. _____ stimulus control	D. stages 3 and 4 of NREM
5. _____ nightmares	E. sudden daytime REM sleep
6. _____ narcolepsy	F. during REM sleep
7. _____ withdrawal	G. sleep-inducing foods
8. _____ SIDS	H. excessive sleepiness
9. _____ tryptophan	I. sleep loss caused by *Nytol*
10. _____ drug-dependency insomnia	J. rebound insomnia
11. _____ sleepwalking	K. interrupted breathing

Dreams—A Separate Reality?

Survey Question: Do dreams have meaning? Pages 194-196

1. _____ integrate memories	A. unconscious meanings
2. _____ Latent content	B. wish fulfillment
3. _____ dream symbols	C. extra dream time
4. _____ REM rebound	D. reflect daily events
5. _____ Manifest content	E. function of REM sleep
6. _____ activation-synthesis hypothesis	F. neural firing triggering memories
7. _____ Sigmund Freud	G. obvious and visible
8. _____ Calvin Hall	H. Hidden and symbolic
9. _____ William Domhoff	I. ordinary waking concerns

Hypnosis—Look into My Eyes, and Meditation and Sensory Deprivation—Chilling, the Healthy Way

Survey Questions: What is hypnosis? Do meditation and sensory deprivation have any benefits? Pages 197-203

1. _____ mesmerize		A.	flotation tank
2. _____ use tricks		B.	hypnotize
3. _____ Concentrative meditation		C.	self-hypnosis
4. _____ pain relief		D.	hypnosis effect
5. _____ mindfulness meditation		E.	sensory deprivation visions
6. _____ REST		F.	stage hypnosis
7. _____ suggestion		G.	Franz Mesmer
8. _____ autosuggestion		H.	James Braid
9. _____ hypnagogic images		I.	"open"
10. _____ Hypnosis		J.	focal point

Drug-Altered Consciousness—The High and Low of It; Uppers—Amphetamines, Cocaine, MDMA, Caffeine, Nicotine; Downers—Sedatives, Tranquilizers, and Alcohol; and Hallucinogens—Tripping the Light Fantastic

Survey Question: What are the effects of the more commonly used psychoactive drugs? Pages 203-218

1. _____ drug tolerance		A.	cocaine rush
2. _____ amphetamine		B.	cancer agent
3. _____ Rohypnol		C.	addiction
4. _____ dopamine		D.	sedative
5. _____ nicotine		E.	hallucinogen
6. _____ carcinogen		F.	detoxification
7. _____ GBH		G.	loss of pleasure
8. _____ barbiturate		H.	stimulant
9. _____ MDMA/Ecstasy		I.	self-help group
10. _____ AA		J.	insecticide
11. _____ alcohol treatment		K.	pleasure center
12. _____ nucleus accumbens		L.	extra serotonin
13. _____ LSD		M.	drain cleaner
14. _____ anhedonia		N.	date rape

Psychology in Action: Exploring and Using Dreams

Survey Question: How can dreams be used to promote personal understanding?
Pages 218-221

1. _____ displacement

2. _____ symbolization

3. _____ Rosalind Cartwright

4. _____ secondary elaboration

5. _____ lucid dream

6. _____ Sigmund Freud

7. _____ condensation

8. _____ Fritz Perls

A. redirect actions toward safer images

B. combining events into one image

C. nonliteral forms of dream content

D. feels awake while dreaming

E. add details to make dreams logical

F. dreams as hidden messages

G. dreams as "feeling statements"

H. dreams as gap-filling

CHECK YOUR MEMORY

States of Consciousness—The Many Faces of Awareness

Survey Question: What is consciousness? Page 183

1. The quality and pattern of mental activity changes during an altered state of consciousness.

TRUE or FALSE

2. All people experience at least some altered states of consciousness (ASCs).

TRUE or FALSE

3. Both sensory overload and monotonous stimulation can produce altered states of consciousness (ASCs).

TRUE or FALSE

4. Almost every known religion has accepted some altered states of consciousness (ASCs) as desirable.

TRUE or FALSE

5. Studying consciousness from the third-person perspective is the subjective observation of private phenomenon.

TRUE or FALSE

Sleep—Catching a Few ZZZs

Survey Question: What are the effects of sleep loss or changes in sleep patterns? Pages 183-186

1. Through sleep learning it is possible to master a foreign language.

TRUE or FALSE

2. A total inability to sleep results in death.

TRUE or FALSE

3. Even after extended sleep loss, most symptoms are removed by a single night's sleep.

TRUE or FALSE

4. Hallucinations and delusions are the most common reaction to extended sleep deprivation.

TRUE or FALSE

5. Physical changes during puberty increase adolescents' need for sleep.

TRUE or FALSE

6. Starting high school later to allow students to get more sleep has resulted in better learning and reduced behavioral problems.

TRUE or FALSE

7. Excessive daytime sleepiness (hypersomnia) occurs after extended sleep loss over many nights.

TRUE or FALSE

8. The average human sleep-wake cycle lasts 23 hours and 10 minutes.

TRUE or FALSE

9. Short sleepers are defined as those who average less than 5 hours of sleep per night.

TRUE or FALSE

10. Shortened sleep cycles, such as three hours of sleep to six hours awake, are more efficient than sleeping once a day.

TRUE or FALSE

11. Midafternoon sleepiness is not normal; it is generally a sign of significant sleep deprivation.

TRUE or FALSE

Stages of Sleep—The Nightly Roller-Coaster

Survey Question: Why do we sleep? Pages 186-190

1. Sleep is promoted by a chemical that accumulates in the bloodstream.

TRUE or FALSE

2. Body temperature drops as a person falls asleep.

TRUE or FALSE

3. A hypnic jerk is a sign of serious problems.

TRUE or FALSE

4. Delta waves typically first appear in stage 2 sleep.

TRUE or FALSE

5. About 45 percent of awakenings during REM periods produce reports of dreams.

TRUE or FALSE

6. REM sleep occurs mainly in stages 3 and 4.

TRUE or FALSE

7. REM sleep increases when a person is subjected to daytime stress.

TRUE or FALSE

8. The average dream only lasts three to four minutes.

TRUE or FALSE

9. Most people change positions in bed during REM sleep.

TRUE or FALSE

10. REM behavior disorder causes people to briefly fall asleep and become paralyzed during the day.

TRUE or FALSE

11. According to the dual process hypothesis, there are two types of sleep: REM (dreaming) and deep sleep.

TRUE or FALSE

12. Hypnopompic hallucinations occur just as someone is waking up, and is associated with the sleep paralysis that normally accompanies REM sleep.

TRUE or FALSE

Sleep Disturbances—Showing Nightly: Sleep Wars!

Survey Question: What are some sleep disorders and unusual sleep events?
Pages 190-194

1. Bread, pasta, pretzels, cookies, and cereals all contain melatonin.

TRUE or FALSE

2. Caffeine, alcohol, and tobacco can all contribute to insomnia.

TRUE or FALSE

3. The two most effective behavioral treatments for insomnia are sleep restriction and stimulus control.

TRUE or FALSE

4. Sleepwalking occurs during NREM periods, sleeptalking during REM periods.

TRUE or FALSE

5. You should never wake a sleepwalker

TRUE or FALSE

6. People who have NREM night terrors usually can remember very little afterward.

TRUE or FALSE

7. Imagery rehearsal is an effective way to treat recurrent nightmares.

TRUE or FALSE

8. REM sleep appears to help the brain process memories formed during the day.

TRUE or FALSE

9. People who take barbiturate sleeping pills may develop drug-dependency insomnia.

TRUE or FALSE

10. Newborn babies spend eight or nine hours a day in REM sleep.

TRUE or FALSE

11. Sleep apnea does not increase the risk of having a heart attack. This is only a myth.

TRUE or FALSE

12. Some babies have a weak reticulus ventilation reflex, which puts them at a higher risk for Sudden Infant Death Syndrome (SIDS) than other infants.

TRUE or FALSE

13. Babies at risk or SIDS are often premature, have a shrill high pitched cry, engage in "snoring," breath mainly through an open mouth, awaken frequently at night, and remain passive when their faces roll into a pillow or blanket.

TRUE or FALSE

14. The safest position for infants to sleep is on their backs.

TRUE or FALSE

Dreams—A Separate Reality?

Survey Question: Do dreams have meaning? Pages 194-196

1. REM rebound refers to people having more REM sleep when they do not get enough REM sleep the night before.

TRUE or FALSE

2. The favorite dream setting is outdoors.

TRUE or FALSE

3. People report feeling more negative emotions when they are awakened during REM sleep.

TRUE or FALSE

4. Pleasant emotions are more common in dreams than unpleasant emotions.

TRUE or FALSE

5. According to Freud, dreams represent thoughts and wishes expressed as images.

TRUE or FALSE

6. The activation-synthesis hypothesis emphasizes the unconscious meanings of dream symbols.

TRUE or FALSE

7. The activation-synthesis hypothesis does believe that dreams are created from memories or past experiences.

TRUE or FALSE

8. According to neurocognitive dream theory, dreams are products of a "bored brain," which lacks input during the relative quiet of sleeping.

TRUE or FALSE

Hypnosis—Look into My Eyes

Survey Questions: What is hypnosis? Pages 197-200

1. The Greek word *hypnos* means "magnetism."

TRUE or FALSE

2. State theories of hypnosis describe it as a distinct state of conscious.

TRUE or FALSE

3. The "hidden observer" refers to the detached part of a hypnotized person's awareness that silently observes events.

TRUE or FALSE

4. Only about four people out of ten can be hypnotized.

TRUE or FALSE

5. The "finger-lock" is an example of animal magnetism.

TRUE or FALSE

6. Physical strength cannot be increased with hypnosis.

TRUE or FALSE

7. Hypnosis is better at changing subjective experiences than behaviors.

TRUE or FALSE

8. Stage hypnotists look for responsive volunteers who will cooperate and not spoil the show.

TRUE or FALSE

9. A good hypnotist can hypnotize anyone, even if that person does not want to be hypnotized

TRUE or FALSE

10. Autosuggestion is used by people who believe they have psychic abilities.

TRUE or FALSE

11. Hypnosis is not a valuable tool since its main purpose is entertainment.

TRUE or FALSE

Meditation and Sensory Deprivation—Chilling, the Healthy Way

Survey Questions: Do meditation and sensory deprivation have any benefits?
Pages 200-203

1. Mindfulness meditation is typically harder to do than concentrative meditation.

TRUE or FALSE

2. A mantra is used as a focus for attention during receptive meditation.

TRUE or FALSE

3. Herbert Benson states that the physical benefits of meditation are based on evoking the body's relaxation response.

TRUE or FALSE

4. The harder you try to meditate, the more likely you are to succeed.

TRUE or FALSE

5. Similar to hypnosis, mindfulness meditation does not have any health benefits.

TRUE or FALSE

6. Sensory deprivation is almost always unpleasant, and it usually causes distorted perceptions.

TRUE or FALSE

7. Prolonged sensory deprivation produces deep relaxation.

TRUE or FALSE

8. Sensory sensitivity temporarily increases after a period of sensory deprivation.

TRUE or FALSE

9. REST is a form of brainwashing used during the Vietnam War.

TRUE or FALSE

10. Mindfulness involves being fully present in one's immediate reality.

TRUE or FALSE

Drug-Altered Consciousness—The High and Low of It

Survey Question: What are the effects of the more commonly used psychoactive drugs? Pages 203-206

1. Abuse of any psychoactive drug can produce physical dependence.

TRUE or FALSE

2. People who believe they have used too many drugs and feel they need to reduce their drug use are in need of professional help.

TRUE or FALSE

3. Drug abuse is frequently part of general pattern of personal maladjustment.

TRUE or FALSE

4. The negative consequences of drug use typically follow long after the drug has been taken.

TRUE or FALSE

5. Nearly all drugs stimulate the brain's reward circuits by influencing the action of neurotransmitters

TRUE or FALSE

6. Addiction is marked by an increased response to a drug over time.

TRUE or FALSE

7. Psychological dependence is not as strong physical dependence, and is much easier to overcome with proper psychotherapy or social support (like AA).

TRUE or FALSE

8. Drug interactions occur when the effect of one drug modifies or enhances the effect of another drug that is taken simultaneously.

TRUE or FALSE

9. Drug interactions are responsible for millions of fatal drug overdoses each year.

TRUE or FALSE

Uppers—Amphetamines, Cocaine, MDMA, Caffeine, Nicotine

Pages 206-211

1. Amphetamines are used to treat hyperactivity.

TRUE or FALSE

2. Amphetamine is more rapidly metabolized by the body than cocaine.

TRUE or FALSE

3. MDMA is chemically similar to amphetamine.

TRUE or FALSE

4. Disregarding consequences is a sign of cocaine abuse.

TRUE or FALSE

5. Cocaine influences dopamine and serotonin, both of which are involved in the activation of the brain's reward circuits.

TRUE or FALSE

6. Caffeine can increase the risk of miscarriage during pregnancy.

TRUE or FALSE

7. Unlike other drugs, caffeine does not cause dependency or side effects.

TRUE or FALSE

8. Twenty-five cigarettes could be fatal for a nonsmoker.

TRUE or FALSE

9. Regular use of nicotine leads to drug tolerance, and often to physical addiction.

TRUE or FALSE

10. Every cigarette reduces a smoker's life expectancy by seven minutes.

TRUE or FALSE

11. Secondary smoke only causes harm to the person who smokes, not those around them.

TRUE or FALSE

12. In order to stop smoking, tapering off is generally more successful than quitting abruptly.

TRUE or FALSE

13. One of the most effective ways to stop smoking is to schedule the number of cigarettes smoked each day.

TRUE or FALSE

Downers—Sedatives, Tranquilizers, and Alcohol

Pages 211-215

1. There have been no known deaths caused by barbiturate overdoses.

TRUE or FALSE

2. The amount of GBH typically taken by users is only three times less than that needed for an overdose, making overdoses frequent.

TRUE or FALSE

3. GBH inhibits the gag reflex, so some users choke to death on their own vomit.

TRUE or FALSE

4. Its ability to produce euphoria and relaxation make Rohypnol a high addictive drug, despite its bitter taste.

TRUE or FALSE

5. To pace alcohol intake, you should limit drinking primarily to the first hour of a social event or party.

TRUE or FALSE

6. Research suggests that students underestimate how much their peers drink.

TRUE or FALSE

7. Alcoholics Anonymous (AA) and Secular Organizations for Sobriety are organizations that seek to make money from drug abusers.

TRUE or FALSE

Hallucinogens—Tripping the Light Fantastic

Pages 215-218

1. Hallucinogens generally affect brain transmitter systems.

TRUE or FALSE

2. GHB, a hallucinogen, can be easily purchased over the Internet.

TRUE or FALSE

3. THC receptors are found in large numbers in the cerebellum of the brain.

TRUE or FALSE

4. Marijuana is the most popular illicit drug in America.

TRUE or FALSE

5. People who smoke marijuana on a regular basis report that they are satisfied with their lives, earn more money, and are healthier than nonusers at the age of 29.

TRUE or FALSE

6. Pregnant mothers who use marijuana may increase the risk that their babies will have trouble succeeding in goal-oriented tasks.

TRUE or FALSE

Psychology in Action: Exploring and Using Dreams

Survey Question: How can dreams be used to promote personal understanding?
Pages 218-221

1. Displacement refers to representing two or more people with a single dream image.

TRUE or FALSE

2. Secondary elaboration is the tendency to make a dream more logical when remembering it.

TRUE or FALSE

3. According to Calvin Hall, the overall emotional tone of a dream is the key to its meaning.

TRUE or FALSE

4. Alcohol decreases REM sleep.

TRUE or FALSE

5. It is basically impossible to solve daytime problems in dreams.

TRUE or FALSE

6. Lucid dreams either occur or they don't; there is no way to increase their frequency.

TRUE or FALSE

7. The Gestaltist Fritz Perls believed that dreams were a way of filling in gaps in personal experiences,

TRUE or FALSE

FINAL SURVEY AND REVIEW

States of Consciousness—The Many Faces of Awareness

Survey Question: What is consciousness? Page 183

1. States of awareness that differ from _____, alert, and waking _____ are called altered states of consciousness (ASCs).

2. In defining _____, one needs to distinguish between subjective, _____-person experiences and _____, third-person points of view.

3. ASCs involve distinct shifts in the _____ and pattern of mental activity.

4. Altered states are especially associated with sleep and dreaming, _____, meditation, sensory deprivation, and _____ drugs.

5. Cultural _____ greatly affects what altered states a person _____, seeks, considers normal, and _____.

Sleep—Catching a Few ZZZ's

Survey Question: What are the effects of sleep loss or changes in sleep patterns? Pages 183-186

1. Sleep is an _____ biological rhythm essential for survival.

2. _____ sleep loss mainly affects _____ and self-motivated performance on routine or _____ tasks.

3. Hypersomnia is marked by _____ daytime sleepiness, and can occur after a few hours of sleep loss.

4. Higher animals and people deprived of sleep experience involuntary _____.

5. Physical change during _____ increases adolescents' need for sleep, which many lack since they tend to stay up late and get up early for school. This decreases the _____ and quantity of sleep during the teen years.

6. The "storm and _____" that adolescents experience may, in part, be caused by lack of sleep.

7. Extended sleep loss can (somewhat rarely) produce a temporary sleep-deprivation _____, marked by confusion, _____, and possibly hallucinations.

8. Biological rhythms within the body are closely tied to sleep, _____ levels, and energy _____.

9. The _____ human sleep-waking cycle averages 24 hours and 10 minutes, but cycles of light and dark tailor it to 24-hour days.

10. Sleep patterns show some flexibility; short-sleepers average _____ hours or less per night; long sleepers sleep 9 or more hours on average, but _____ to _____ hours remains average.

11. Adapting to shorter or longer sleep cycles is difficult and _____ for most people.

12. The amount of daily sleep decreases steadily from _____ to old age and switches from multiple sleep-wake cycles to _____-a-day sleep periods.

13. Midafternoon _____ is a natural part of the sleep cycle.

Stages of Sleep—The Nightly Roller-Coaster

Survey Question: Why do we sleep? Pages 186-190

1. Sleepiness is associated with the accumulation of a sleep _____ in the brain and _____ cord.

2. Sleep depends on which of two opposed sleep and _____ systems in the brain is _____ at any given moment.

3. Sleep occurs in four stages, defined by changes in behavior and _____ waves recorded with an _____ (EEG).

4. Stage _____, light sleep, has small irregular brain waves. In stage 2, sleep _____ appear. Delta waves appear in stage _____. Stage 4, or deep sleep, is marked by almost pure _____ waves.

5. Sleepers alternate between stages _____ and 4 (passing through stages 2 and 3) _____ times each night.

6. There are two basic sleep states, _____ eye movement (REM) sleep and non-_____ (NREM) sleep.

7. REM sleep is much more strongly associated with dreaming than is _____ sleep.

8. The dual process hypothesis of sleep suggests that NREM sleep "_____" the brain; REM sleep appears to "_____" our memories.

9. A day of physical exertion generally leads to an increase in _____ sleep, which allows our body to recover from _____ fatigue. A day of stress would lead to an _____ in REM sleep.

10. Dreams during REM sleep tend to be _____, clearer, more detailed, more bizarre, and more "_____-like" than thoughts and images that occur in NREM sleep.

11. Dreaming is accompanied by _____ and emotional arousal but relaxation of the skeletal muscles. People who move about violently while asleep may suffer from REM behavior _____.

12. Hypnopompic hallucinations occur when one is beginning to _____ up, but is still experiencing sleep _____.

Sleep Disturbances—Showing Nightly: Sleep Wars!

Survey Question: What are some sleep disorders and unusual sleep events?
Pages 190-194

1. Insomnia, which is difficulty in _____ to sleep or _____ asleep, may be temporary or chronic.

2. When insomnia is treated with drugs, sleep _____ is often lowered and _____-dependency insomnia may develop.

3. Sudden _____ from sleeping pills may result in terrible _____ or "rebound insomnia".

4. The amino acid _____, found in bread, pasta, and other foods, helps _____ sleep.

5. Behavioral approaches to managing _____, such as relaxation, sleep restriction, stimulus control, and _____ intention are quite effective.

6. Sleepwalking (_____) and sleeptalking occur during NREM sleep in stages _____ and _____.

7. Night _____ occur in NREM sleep, whereas _____ occur in REM sleep.

8. Nightmares can be _____ by the method called imagery rehearsal.

9. During sleep _____, people repeatedly stop breathing. Apnea is suspected as one cause of sudden infant _____ syndrome (SIDS).

10. One effective treatment for sleep apnea is the use of a _____ positive airway pressure (CPAP) mask to aid _____ during sleep.

11. The first six _____ are critical for babies who are at risk for SIDS. Other factors include the baby being a preemie, breathing through an open mouth, having a mother who is a teenager, and having a crib that contains _____ objects such as a pillow and _____.

12. The phrase "*back* to sleep" refers to the _____ position for most babies: their backs.

Dreams—A Separate Reality?

Survey Question: Do dreams have meaning? Pages 194-196

1. The first dream of the night is typically _____ (approximately _____ minutes); dreams become longer over the course of the sleep cycle.

2. People will experience _____ rebound if they are deprived of REM sleep the night before.

3. People deprived of REM sleep showed an urgent need to dream and mental _____ the next day. However, total sleep loss seems to be more important than loss of a single sleep stage.

4. One of the more important functions of REM sleep appears to be the processing of _____ memories.

5. The _____, or psychodynamic, view is that dreams express _____ wishes, frequently hidden by dream symbols.

6. Freud distinguished between the obvious, _____ meaning of dreams (manifest content) and the _____, symbolic meaning (latent content).

7. Allan _____ and Robert McCarley's activation-synthesis model portrays dreaming as a _____ process. The brain, they say, creates dreams to explain sensory and motor messages that occur during REM sleep.

8. Domhoff's _____ dream theory suggests the dreams reflect ordinary concerns from _____ experiences.

9. Most dream content is about familiar _____, people, and actions. Dreams more often involve _____ emotions than _____ emotions.

Hypnosis—Look into My Eyes

Survey Questions: What is hypnosis? Pages 197-200

1. Hypnosis is an _____ state characterized by _____ attention and increased suggestibility.

2. In the 1700s, Franz _____ (whose name is the basis for the term *mesmerize*) practiced "animal _____," which was actually a demonstration of the power of suggestion.

3. The term hypnosis was first used by James _____, an English doctor.

4. Ernest Hilgard described hypnosis as causing a dissociative state or "_____" in awareness.

5. It is believed that one part of a hypnotized person does not feel or react to pain; the hidden _____ is aware of the pain but _____ remains in the background.

6. The core of hypnosis is the basic _____ effect—a tendency to carry out suggested actions as if they were involuntary. However, a hypnotized person will not perform behaviors that he or she deems to be immoral or _____.

7. Many theorists believe that hypnosis is simply a form of _____, or autosuggestion, where one influences one's own behavior.

8. Hypnosis appears capable of producing _____, controlling pain, and altering _____.

9. Hypnosis does not produce superhuman _____ or age _____.

10. People vary in hypnotic _____; eight out of 10 can be hypnotized, as revealed by scores on the Stanford Hypnotic Susceptibility Scale.

11. Stage hypnotism takes advantage of typical stage behavior, waking suggestibility, _____ subjects, _____, and deception to simulate hypnosis.

Meditation and Sensory Deprivation—Chilling, the Healthy Way

Survey Questions: Do meditation and sensory deprivation have any benefits?
Pages 203-206

1. Meditation refers to mental _____ that are used to alter consciousness.

2. In _____ meditation, attention is widened to include an awareness of one's entire moment-by-_____ experience, which is more difficult to achieve than the concentrative meditation where attention is _____ on a single object or thought.

3. Two major benefits of meditation are its ability to interrupt _____ thoughts and its ability to elicit the _____ response (the pattern of changes that occur in the body at times of deep relaxation).

4. Sensory deprivation takes place when there is a major _____ in the amount or variety of sensory stimulation available to a person.

5. Prolonged sensory deprivation is _____ and disruptive, leading to perceptual _____.

6. Brief or _____ sensory deprivation can enhance sensory _____ and induce deep relaxation.

7. Research suggests that sensory deprivation _____ the symptoms of a variety of psychological disorders; it also reduces _____ and the illegal use of psychoactive drugs.

8. Sensory deprivation also appears to aid the breaking of _____-standing habits and promotes _____ thinking. This effect is the basis for Restricted Environmental _____ Therapy (REST).

9. Mindfulness involves _____, nonjudgmental awareness of current experience that is attuned to one's immediate _____.

Drug-Altered Consciousness—The High and Low of It

Survey Question: What are the effects of the more commonly used psychoactive drugs? Pages 203-206

1. A psychoactive drug is a substance that _____ the brain in ways that alter (affect or change) _____.

2. Drugs alter the activities in the brain by mimicking and _____ neurotransmitters (chemicals that carry messages between _____) to produce feelings of pleasure.

3. Most _____ drugs can be placed on a scale ranging from _____ to depression. Some, however, are best described as _____ (drugs that alter sensory impressions).

4. Drugs may cause a physical _____ (addiction) or a psychological _____, or both.

5. Nearly all _____ drugs stimulate the nucleus _____ to release dopamine, which intensifies feelings of pleasure.

6. Drugs that ease pain, _____ sleep, or end depression have a high potential for _____.

7. _____ use of a drug can lead to drug _____ (a reduced response to a drug) whereby the abuser must increase the amount of a drug to receive the same desired effect.

8. Drug use can be classified as _____, recreational, _____, intensive, and compulsive. Drug abuse is most often associated with the last three.

9. Drug abuse is related to personal and social _____, attempts to _____, and the immediate reinforcing qualities of psychoactive drugs.

10. Among _____, the best predictors of drug use and abuse were: drug use by peers, _____ drug use, delinquency, parental maladjustment, _____ self-esteem, social nonconformity, and stressful life changes.

11. When _____, the effects of different drugs are multiplied by drug interactions, resulting in fatal drug _____.

12. The physically addicting drugs are _____, amphetamines, barbiturates, cocaine, codeine, GHB, heroin, methadone, morphine, _____, and tranquilizers. All psychoactive drugs can lead to psychological dependence.

Uppers—Amphetamines, Cocaine, MDMA, Caffeine, Nicotine

Pages 206-211

1. Stimulant drugs are readily abused because of the period of depression that often follows _____. The greatest risks are associated with _____, cocaine, MDMA, and _____, but even caffeine can be a problem.

2. Amphetamines were once widely used for _____ loss and to treat depression; now they are used to treat childhood hyperactivity and _____ overdose.

3. Amphetamines, known as "_____," "bennies," "dexies," "go," and "uppers," are synthetic stimulants that produce a _____ drug tolerance. Abusers typically go on binges that last for several days until they "crash," suffering from fatigue, _____, depression, uncontrolled irritability, and _____.

4. Methamphetamine, known as "Bergs," "glass," "_____," or "crystal," is cheaply produced in _____ and can be snorted or injected.

5. Repeated use of amphetamine can cause brain _____ and amphetamine psychosis. Amphetamine psychosis can cause the abuser to act on their _____ and risk self-injury or injury to others.

6. Signs of cocaine abuse are: _____ use, loss of control, and a _____ for consequences.

7. Cocaine users may experience _____ (an inability to feel pleasure) following a "high."

8. _____ or "Ecstasy," which is similar to amphetamine, has been linked with numerous _____ and with mental impairment.

9. Users of MDMA are likely to risk an increase in body _____, _____ damage, and unsafe sex.

10. Although MDMA (Ecstasy) users believe the drug increases _____ pleasure, it can impair erections in men and retard _____ in both men and women.

11. _____ is the most widely used psychoactive drug in _____ America.

12. Caffeine can be found in _____, tea, soft drinks, and _____. It stimulates the brain by blocking chemicals that _____ nerve activities.

13. Caffeinism can result in insomnia, _____, loss of appetite, chills, racing heart, and _____ body temperature.

14. Nicotine (or smoking) includes the added risk of _____ cancer, heart disease, and other health problems.

15. The smoking of cigarettes releases _____ (cancer-causing substances) in the air, which expose people to second-hand smoke and place them at risk for developing lung _____.

16. A _____ exposure to a pinch of smokeless tobacco is equivalent to smoking three or _____ cigarettes.

17. The best method for quitting smoking is _____ gradual reduction; this may involve delaying the first cigarette of the day in greater _____ every day, reducing the total number of cigarettes smoked each day, and _____ quitting for one week at a time.

Downers—Sedatives, Tranquilizers, and Alcohol

Pages 211-215

1. Barbiturates are depressant drugs whose overdose level is close to the _____ dosage, making them dangerous drugs. Common street names for barbiturates are "downers," "blue heavens," "yellow jackets," "_____," "pink ladies," and "_____."

2. The depressant drug GHB (gamma-hydroxybuyrate) can cause _____, breathing failure, and death in relatively low doses. GHB is commonly called "_____," "scoop," "max," or "Georgia Home Boy."

3. Benzodiazepine tranquilizers, such as Valium, are used to _____ anxiety. When abused, they have a _____ addictive potential.

4. Rohypnol, a tranquilizer, also known as "_____" and the "date-_____ drug," is odorless and _____ and is sometimes used to spike drinks and induced short-term amnesia and sleep.

5. Mixing barbiturates and _____ may result in a fatal drug interaction (in which the joint effect of two drugs _____ the effects of adding one drug's effects to the other's).

6. Binge drinking is defined as consuming five or more drinks in a short time for _____, four or more for _____.

7. The brain continues to _____ into the early 20s; binge drinking may cause teens and young adults to lose as much as _____ percent of their brain capacity (especially memory).

8. _____ drinking may include; thinking about drinking management beforehand, drinking _____ on a full stomach, making every other drink non-alcoholic, limit drinking to the first hour of a social party, practice politely refusing drinks, and learn to not _____ on alcohol.

9. People who undergo _____ (the removal of poison) often experience unpleasant symptoms of drug withdrawal.

Hallucinogens—Tripping the Light Fantastic

Pages 215-218

1. LSD (lysergic acid diethylamide) or "_____" can produce hallucinations and psychotic-like _____ in thinking and perception.

2. Three common hallucinogens are _____ (peyote), psilocybin ("magic _____", and PCP (phencyclidine, or "angel dust")

3. Marijuana ("pot," "grass," and "weed") is a hallucinogen subject to an abuse pattern similar to _____. Studies have linked chronic marijuana use with memory impairment, lung cancer, _____ problems, immune system disorders, and other health problems.

4. THC, the main active chemical in _____, accumulates in the cerebral cortex and reproductive _____.

5. Potential problems caused by frequent marijuana use are _____-term memory loss and a _____ in learning, attention, and thinking abilities. In addition, people who smoke five or more joints a week tend to score four points lower on IQ tests.

Psychology in Action: Exploring and Using Dreams

Survey Question: How can dreams be used to promote personal understanding? Pages 218-221

1. Freud held that the meaning of dreams is hidden by _____ dream processes he called _____, displacement, symbolization, and secondary elaboration.

2. Calvin Hall emphasizes the _____, cast, plot, and _____ of a dream.

3. Rosalind Cartwright's view of dreams as _____ statements and Fritz Perls' technique of speaking for dream _____ are also helpful.

4. Dreams may be used for creative problem _____, especially when dream control is achieved through lucid dreaming (a dream in which the dreamer feels capable of _____ thought and action).

MASTERY TEST

1. Delirium, ecstasy, and daydreaming all have in common the fact that they are
a. forms of normal waking consciousness.
b. caused by sensory deprivation.
c. perceived as subjectively real.
d. Altered States of Consciousness.

2. The street drug GHB is
a. chemically similar to morphine.
b. a depressant.
c. capable of raising body temperature to dangerous levels.
d. a common cause of sleep-deprivation psychosis.

3. Which of the following does not belong with the others?
a. nicotine
b. caffeine
c. cocaine
d. codeine

4. Sleep spindles usually first appear in stage _____, whereas delta waves first appear in stage _____.
a. 1; 2
b. 2; 3
c. 3; 4
d. 1; 4

5. Which of the following is NOT one of the dream processes described by Freud?
a. condensation
b. illumination
c. displacement
d. symbolization

6. Which of the following most clearly occurs under hypnosis?
a. unusual strength
b. memory enhancement
c. pain relief
d. age regression

7. Alcohol, amphetamines, cocaine, and marijuana have in common the fact that they are all
a. physically addicting.
b. psychoactive.
c. stimulants.
d. hallucinogens.

8. Emotional arousal, blood pressure changes, and sexual arousal all primarily occur during
a. REM sleep.
b. NREM sleep.
c. Delta sleep.
d. stage 4 sleep.

9. The REST technique makes use of
a. sensory deprivation.
b. hypodynamic imagery.
c. hallucinogens.
d. a CPAP mask.

10. Mesmerism, hypnosis, hypnotic susceptibility scales, and stage hypnotism all rely in part on
    a. disinhibition.
    b. rapid eye movements.
    c. suggestibility.
    d. imagery rehearsal.

11. Shortened sleep-waking cycles overlook the fact that sleep
    a. must match a 3 to 1 ratio of time awake and time asleep.
    b. is an innate biological rhythm.
    c. is caused by a sleep-promoting substance in the blood.
    d. cycles cannot be altered by external factors.

12. Which of the following statements about sleep is true?
    a. Learning math or a foreign language can be accomplished during sleep.
    b. Some people can learn to do without sleep.
    c. Calvin Hall had hallucinations during a sleep deprivation experiment.
    d. Randy Gardner slept for 14 hours after ending his sleep deprivation.

13. Amphetamine is very similar in effects to
    a. narcotics and tranquilizers.
    b. methaqualone.
    c. codeine.
    d. cocaine.

14. Microsleeps would most likely occur
    a. in stage 4 sleep.
    b. in a 3 to 1 ratio to microawakenings.
    c. in conjunction with delusions and hallucinations.
    d. during sleep deprivation.

15. Adolescents who abuse drugs tend to be
    a. suffering from brain dysfunctions.
    b. high in self-esteem but unrealistic about consequences.
    c. maladjusted and impulsive.
    d. similar in most respects to nonabusers.

16. Sleepwalking, sleeptalking, and severe nightmares all have in common the fact that they
    a. are REM events.
    b. are NREM events.
    c. are sleep disorders.
    d. can be controlled with imagery rehearsal.

17. The basic suggestion effect is closely related to
    a. hypnosis.
    b. sensory enhancement after sensory deprivation.
    c. hypersomnia.
    d. the frequency of dreaming during REM sleep.

18. Which of the following is a hallucinogen?
a. LSD
b. THC
c. hashish
d. all of these

19. The two most basic states of sleep are
a. stage 1 sleep and stage 4 sleep.
b. REM sleep and NREM sleep.
c. alpha sleep and delta sleep.
d. alpha sleep and hypnic sleep.

20. A mantra would most commonly be used in
a. Perls' method of dream interpretation.
b. sensory deprivation research.
c. inducing hypnosis.
d. concentrative meditation.

21. Learning to use a computer would most likely be slowed if you were
_____ each night.
a. deprived of a half hour of NREM sleep
b. allowed to engage in extra REM sleep
c. prevented from dreaming
d. awakened three times at random

22. A particularly dangerous drug interaction occurs when _____ and
_____ are combined.
a. alcohol ; amphetamine
b. barbiturates ; nicotine
c. alcohol; barbiturates
d. amphetamine; codeine

23. Narcolepsy is an example of
a. a night terror.
b. a sleep disorder.
c. a tranquilizer.
d. an addictive drug.

24. Sleep restriction and stimulus control techniques would most likely be used to
treat
a. insomnia.
b. narcolepsy.
c. sleepwalking.
d. REM behavior disorder.

25. In addition to the nicotine they contain, cigarettes release
a. dopamine.
b. tryptophan.
c. noradrenaline.
d. carcinogens.

26. Disguised dream symbols are to psychodynamic dream theory as sensory and motor messages are to
   a. the Freudian theory of dreams.
   b. the activation-synthesis hypothesis.
   c. Fritz Perls' methods of dream interpretation.
   d. paradoxical intention.

27. Which is the most frequently used drug in North America?
   a. caffeine
   b. nicotine
   c. marijuana
   d. cocaine

28. Joan is 14 years old and is experiencing _____ throughout the day because she tends to stay up late and gets up early.
   a. insomnia
   b. narcolepsy
   c. hypersomnia
   d. hypnopompic

29. Gene was awakened throughout the night for a sleep study and did not receive enough REM sleep. The next night, he was allowed to sleep without interruption. Gene would be likely to experience
   a. insomnia.
   b. REM rebound.
   c. sleepwaking disorder.
   d. REM behavior disorder.

30. To impress his friends of his ability, Eric holds a string with a ring attached and mentally made the ring swing back and forth. Eric used _____, which means that as he thought about moving the ring, he made micromuscular movements with his fingers to move the string.
   a. autosuggestion
   b. telekinesis
   c. hypnotic susceptibility
   d. stimulus control

31. Nicotine and opiates stimulate the brain by _____ neurotransmitters.
   a. eliminating
   b. blocking
   c. suppressing
   d. mimicking

32. Upon awakening from sleep, Zack cannot move and as he struggles, he feels evil presences standing over him whispering to each other. Suddenly he hears screams coming from somewhere in his bedroom. Within moments, the evil presences disappear, Zack is able to move again, and realizes the screaming was from the radio. Zack just experienced
   a. a nightmare.
   b. paradoxical hallucinations.
   c. hypnopompic hallucinations.
   d. lucid dreaming.

33. Although James is asleep and dreaming, he feels as though he is awake and able to engage in normal action. He is most likely experiencing
   a. lucid dreaming.
   b. the basic suggestion effect.
   c. REM rebound.
   d. deep relaxation.

34. Sara just spent an hour in a flotation tank where stimuli were restricted. As a result, she is most likely experiencing
   a. REM symbolizations.
   b. deep relaxation.
   c. imagery rehearsal.
   d. tryptophanic images.

LANGUAGE DEVELOPMENT
States of Consciousness

Word Roots

Conscius is a Latin term meaning "knowing with others" (from *con*, a word meaning "with" or "together," and *scire*, a verb meaning "to know"). Several terms in the field of psychology use the English word "conscious" as a base for other words. Examples you will find in the text include consciousness, unconscious, and preconscious.

Journey into Psychology: Bending Your Mind (p. 182)
   (182) **stage fright**: fear of appearing before crowds to perform, give a speech, etc.
   (182) **Navajo:** a member of an American Indian people of northern New Mexico and Arizona
   (182) **peyote**: a primitive drug derived from an American cactus
   (182) **sacrament**: a symbol of grace; usually associated with religious rites
   (182) **Aborigines**: original inhabitants of a region

(182)   *flotation chamber*: an enclosed box where a person can be isolated from most sensory inputs; the person literally "floats" in saline-saturated water and is cut off from sounds, smells, and other sensations as much as possible

(182)   *joint*: slang; a marijuana cigarette

(182)   *spare change*: money that bystanders will give to street performers or beggars

(182)   *cappuccino:* espresso coffee mixed with steamed milk; often flavored with cinnamon and topped with whipped cream.

States of Consciousness—The Many Faces of Awareness (p. 180)

What is consciousness?

(183)   *delirium*: a state of mental confusion accompanied by delusions, hallucinations, and illusions

(183)   *euphoria*: a sense of well being; feeling happy and good all over

(183)   *rave*: all night dance parties for young people

(183)   *Mardi Gras*: a very large, crowded street party celebrated in New Orleans 40 days before Easter

(183)   *mosh pit:* slang term for an area at a music concert where audience members dance aggressively, often slamming themselves into one another

(183)   *monotonous*: unchanging

(183)   *"highway hypnotism"*: refers to the fact that drivers on long distance trips sometimes lose concentration due to the sameness of the road and scenery

(183)   *hyperventilation*: excessive rate of respiration (breathing)

(183)   *dehydration*: abnormal loss of body fluids

(184)   *Whirling Dervish:* individual of a religious order who whirls during certain ceremonies.

(184)   *revelation*: enlightenment; discovery of personal truth

(184)   *"madness"*: archaic term for severe mental illness

(184)   *"possession by spirits"*: the belief that an evil spirit (such as the devil) or the spirit of a dead person can inhabit the body of a living being

Sleep—Catching a Few ZZZs (pgs. 183-186)

What are the effects of sleep loss or changes in sleep patterns?

(184)   *"The lion and the lamb shall lie down together"*: according to the Bible, at the end of the world enemies will become friends, even in the animal world

(184)   *stupor*: a state of limited consciousness

(184)   *The Guinness Book of Records*: Book containing world-records.

(185)   *macro*: large

(185)   *spell disaster*: lead to a disaster

(185)   *hallucinations*: imaginary perceptions of objects that do not exist in reality

(185)   *"siesta"*: nap
(185)   *interns*: recent graduates of medical school (in this case) doing their first year of supervised practice; they tend to work long hours in hospital

Stages of Sleep—The Nightly Roller-Coaster (pgs. 186-190)

Why Do We Sleep?

(186)   *the nightly roller coaster ride*: a roller coaster is an amusement park ride that causes the rider to go up and then quickly down steep inclines; here referring to the fact that sleep is characterized by stages, from the lightest (stage one) to the deepest (stage four)
(186)   *conjoined (twins)*: twins who share one or more body part(s); often bodily fluids are also shared.
(186)   *seesaw back and forth*: going back and forth
(186)   *"shut down"*: turn off; become inactive
(188)   *"sweat the small stuff"*: to be overly anxious or worried about trivial things; spending time and resources on things that don't matter.
(189)   *sinister*: evil
(189)   *iguana*: large tropical American lizard
(189)   *streaming in*: flowing into, often rapidly
(189)   *"off-line"*: not of primary or conscious processing
(189)   *hilarious*: very amusing or funny
(189)   *escapades*: adventures
(189)   *thrash*: to move or toss about
(190)   *retard*: to slow down something

Sleep Disturbances—Showing Nightly: Sleep Wars (pgs. 190-194)

What are the causes of sleep disorders and unusual sleep events?

(190)   *Sleep Wars*: Coon is making reference to the popular science-fiction movie "Star Wars"; the conflict between the "light" and "dark" side was central to the plot; here, refers to the conflict between day (wakefulness) and night (sleep)
(190)   *frenetic*: hectic; very busy
(191)   *irony*: a result that is different, or the opposite, from what is expected
(191)   *sedatives*: drugs that calm nervousness or excitement
(191)   *"sleeping-pill junkies"*: people who are addicted to sleeping pills
(191)   *painstakingly*: thoroughly, often in a step-by-step, slow process
(191)   *weaned*: slowly removed from
(191)   *"rebound insomnia"*: inability to sleep after one has stopped taking sleeping pills
(192)   *paradoxical*: something that seems contradictory yet may still be true
(192)   *progressive*: increasing
(192)   *blotting out*: to get rid of

(192)   *strenuous*: vigorously active
(192)   *starchy foods*: foods high in carbohydrates
(192)   *drop the bomb*: to give bad news
(192)   *eerie*: weird; strange
(192)   *shuffling*: to move something (usually feet) by sliding along in small movements without lifting off the floor
(192)   *brandishing*: to present in a showy manner
(192)   *immobilized*: incapable of movement
(193)   *plague*: bother greatly
(193)   *banish:* send away
(193)   *sage*: wise person
(193)   *"wood-sawing"*: snoring
(193)   *diaphragm*: thin tissue between lungs and central body cavity; involved in breathing.

Dreams—A Separate Reality? (pgs. 194-196)
Do dreams have meaning?

(194)   *"Golden Era"*: period of great happiness, prosperity, and achievement
(194)   *age-old questions*: questions that have been asked for a long time without clear answers
(194)   *memory lapses*: to fall back to a previous level; in this case, lost memories
(195)   *trivial*: of very little importance
(196)   *veteran*: person with long experience

Hypnosis—Look Into My Eyes (pgs. 197-200)
What is hypnosis?

(197)   *"animal magnetism"*: a mysterious force that Mesmer claimed enabled him to hypnotize patients
(197)   *coined*: created
(197)   *detached*: separated, apart from the whole
(197)   *role-playing*: taking on a part, as in a play; pretending to be someone else
(197)   *anesthesia*: loss of feeling
(198)   *Ouija boards*: a game that involves one asking questions and with one's hands on a marker, moving around a board of letters to spell out answers
(198)   *lethargic*: excessively slow and sleepy; drowsy; lacking energy
(198)   *susceptibility*: inability to resist
(199)   *ammonia*: strong, foul-smelling chemical substance
(199)   *intones*: chants, says
(200)   *disinhibits*: takes away inhibitions or restraints on behavior
(200)   *"ham"* (brings out the *"ham"* in many people): actor; a person who overacts

Meditation and Sensory Deprivation— Chilling, the Healthy Way (pgs. 200-203)

Do meditation and sensory deprivation have any benefits?

(200)   *sensory deprivation*: being cut off from information normally received through the five senses

(200)   *chilling*: to become cooler; in this context, to become more relaxed

(202)   *solitary confinement*: kept alone in a prison cell

(202)   *monotonous:* boring, usually from something being repeated over and over again

(202)   *lapses*: interruptions

(202)   marksmanship: extreme accuracy with a firearm (or less commonly, bow and arrow).

(202)   *"space out":* have a period of inattention, the activities during such time may or may not be remembered.

Drug-Altered Consciousness—The High and Low of It (pgs. 203-206)

What are the effects of the more commonly used psychoactive drugs?

(204)   *Ecstasy*: relatively new, chemically-synthesized stimulant drug

(204)   *It's the hook that eventually snares the addict*: the drug produces good feelings that the person wants to repeat, taking it again and again; the repeated behavior causes the person to become an addict

(204)   *compulsion*: desire; urge

(205)   *compulsively*: uncontrollably

(205)   *intravenously*: into one's veins, usually through a needle

(206)   *anticonvulsant:* something that prevents or inhibits convulsions

(206)   *adulterated*: mixed with other (often unknown) substances; made impure

(207)   *convulsion:* spasm; seizure

(207)   *arrhythmias:* irregular heart beats

Uppers—Amphetamines, Cocaine, MDMA, Caffeine, Nicotine (pgs. 206-211)

(206)   *uppers*: stimulant drugs

(206)   *illicit*: illegal

(208)   *speed freak*: a person addicted to stimulant drugs

(208)   *binges*: unrestrained use of drugs

(208)   *crash* (after which they "*crash*"): hit a very low point

(208)   *pose*: present; bring about

(208)   *paranoid delusions*: irrational beliefs that one is being persecuted; distrustfulness

(208)   *boundless*: to be without end; limitless

(208)   *jarring*: harsh

(209)   *Seattle*: the capital city of the state of Washington; well-known for high consumption of coffee

(209) *tremors*: uncontrollable shaking

(210) *cysts*: closed sacs developing abnormally in a structure of the body

(210) *miscarriage*: failure to continue a pregnancy (loss of the fetus)

(210) *cold sweats*: chills caused by sweating due to anxiety, nervousness, or fear

(210) *cardiovascular*: of the heart and blood

(211) *urban cowboy:* individuals who regularly use chewing tobacco; stereotypes of cowboys often showed them spitting tobacco.

(211) *Skol bandit:* individual who regularly uses Skol chewing tobacco.

(211) *quit cold turkey*: stop smoking completely and suddenly instead of gradually

(211) *taper off*: to slowly reduce

Downers—Sedatives, Tranquilizers, and Alcohol (pgs. 211-215)

(212) *degrease your brain*: to slow down your brain's activity; to make it sluggish or slow moving

(212) *spike*: adding a mind-altering substance to someone's drink without his or her knowledge

(213) *aphrodisiac*: a substance that increases sexual performance or desire

(214) *completed wasted:* slang; to become excessively intoxicated to the point where one loses bodily control.

(214) *wit* (as one *wit* once observed): an intelligent and funny person

(215) *"dried out"*: stopped drinking

(215) *dry*: to remain off of alcohol

(215) *premise*: something assumed or taken for granted

(215) *"hit rock bottom"*: reached the lowest point personally and emotionally

Hallucinogens—Tripping the Light Fantastic? (pgs. 215-218)

(216) *potent*: powerful

(216) *"pot"* (What's in the *pot*?): marijuana

(216) *resinous*: of leftover material

(216) *paranoia*: belief that one is being watched, pursued, or persecuted

(217) *chronic*: constant

(217) *ebb and flow*: the coming and going

(218) *subsidize*: to support financially; to fund

Psychology in Action: Exploring and Using Dreams (p. 218-221)

How can dreams be used to promote personal understanding?

(219) *insights*: self-knowledge

(219) *literal*: actual, obvious; exact meaning

(219) *exhibitionist:* a person who displays himself or herself indecently in public

(219) *playwright*: one who writes plays

(219) *puns*: the humorous use of words in such a way as to suggest two or more meanings

(219) *"twisting your arm"*: making you do something that you would rather not do

(220) *paradoxes*: contradictions

(220) *intuitions*: something known or sensed without evident rational thought

(220) *steep yourself*: immerse yourself; concentrate very hard

(220) *lucid*: having a clear understanding and awareness

(221) *clench*: close tightly

(221) *engulfed*: overwhelmed; surrounded

Solutions

Recite and Review

States of Consciousness—The Many Faces of Awareness

1. awareness, waking
2. subjective, third
3. pattern
4. sleep, dreaming, sensory
5. normal

Sleep—Catching a Few ZZZ's

1. rhythm, survival
2. routine
3. daytime, few
4. involuntary
5. Physical, sleep
6. lack
7. loss, temporary
8. rhythms
9. 24, 10, light, dark
10. short, 9
11. shorter, longer
12. decreases
13. natural

Stages of Sleep—The Nightly Roller-Coaster

1. brain
2. two, brain
3. four, waves
4. light, sleep, Delta
5. alternate
6. movement
7. dreaming
8. dual, memories
9. physical, stress
10. REM, images
11. emotional, muscles, REM
12. Hypnopompic, hallucinations

Sleep Disturbances—Showing Nightly: Sleep Wars!

1. temporary
2. lowered, insomnia
3. pills
4. sleep
5. stimulus, intention
6. Sleepwalking
7. NREM, REM
8. rehearsal
9. breathing, sudden
10. sleep, apnea
11. six, preemie, mouth, teenager
12. *back*, backs

Dreams—A Separate Reality?

1. longer
2. rebound
3. dream
4. stage
5. memories
6. wishes
7. obvious, symbolic
8. activation, sensory
9. ordinary
10. familiar, emotions, emotions

Hypnosis—Look into My Eyes

1. increased
2. animal, suggestion
3. hypnosis
4. dissociative, state
5. pain, hidden
6. basic, immoral
7. autosuggestion
8. pain
9. superhuman
10. eight, Scale
11. waking, deception

Meditation and Sensory Deprivation—Chilling, the Healthy Way
1. consciousness
2. widened; difficult; single
3. relaxation
4. stimulation
5. perceptual
6. relaxation
7. sensory, deprivation
8. habits
9. nonjudgmental

Drug-Altered Consciousness—The High and Low of It
1. alter, affect, change
2. mimicking, chemicals
3. depression, sensory
4. addiction
5. release, pleasure
6. depression
7. reduced, increase
8. compulsive
9. immediate
10. predictors, poor
11. effects, fatal
12. psychological

Uppers—Amphetamines, Cocaine, MDMA, Caffeine, Nicotine
1. depression, caffeine
2. depression, treat
3. uppers, tolerance, crash, fatigue
4. Bergs, injected
5. psychosis, self, others
6. control, consequences
7. pleasure
8. Ecstasy
9. increase
10. increases, impair
11. psychoactive
12. tea, blocking
13. insomnia, chills
14. Nicotine, smoking
15. cancer, second, hand
16. pinch, smoking
17. cigarette, total, week

Downers—Sedatives, Tranquilizers, and Alcohol
1. depressant, blue, yellow, pink
2. GHB, Georgia
3. Valium, addictive
4. Rohypnol, date
5. drug
6. five, four
7. brain, memory
8. full, non-alcoholic, refusing
9. removal, withdrawal

Hallucinogens—Tripping the Light Fantastic
1. acid, hallucinations
2. mescaline, angel, dust
3. weed, abuse
4. THC
5. memory, attention, five

Psychology in Action: Exploring and Using Dreams
1. hidden, processes
2. plot
3. speaking
4. creative

CONNECTIONS

States of Consciousness—The Many Faces of Awareness, and Sleep—Catching a few ZZZs

1. F.	4. B.	7. A.	10. G.
2. D.	5. J.	8. E.	
3. H.	6. I.	9. C.	

Stages of Sleep—The Nightly Roller-Coaster

1. C.	4. J.	7. B.	10. H.
2. G.	5. A.	8. L.	11. K.
3. F.	6. I.	9. E.	12. D.

Sleep Disturbances—Showing Nightly: Sleep Wars!

1. C.	4. B.	7. J.	10. I.
2. H.	5. F.	8. A.	11. D.
3. K.	6. E.	9. G.	

Dreams—A Separate Reality?

1. E.	4. C.	7. B.	
2. H.	5. G.	8. D.	
3. A.	6. F.	9. I.	

Hypnosis—Look into My Eyes, and Meditation and Sensory Deprivation—Chilling, the Healthy Way

1. G	4. D.	7. B.	10. H.
2. F.	5. I.	8. C.	
3. J.	6. A.	9. E.	

Drug-Altered Consciousness—The High and Low of It; Uppers—Amphetamines, Cocaine, MDMA, Caffeine, Nicotine; Downers—Sedatives, Tranquilizers, and Alcohol; and Hallucinogens—Tripping the Light Fantastic

1. C.	5. J.	9. L.	13. E.
2. H.	6. B.	10. I.	14. G.
3. N.	7. M.	11. F.	
4. A.	8. D.	12. K.	

Psychology in Action: Exploring and Using Dreams

1. A.	3. G.	5. D.	7. B.
2. C.	4. E.	6. F.	8. H.

Check Your Memory

States of Consciousness—The Many Faces of Awareness

1. T	3. T	5. F
2. T	4. T	

Sleep—Catching a Few ZZZs

1. F	4. F	7. F	10. F
2. T	5. T	8. F	11. F
3. T	6. T	9. T	

Stages of Sleep—The Nightly Roller-Coaster

1. F	4. F	7. T	10. F
2. T	5. F	8. F	11. F
3. F	6. F	9. F	12. T

Sleep Disturbances—Showing Nightly: Sleep Wars!

1. F	5. F	9. T	13. T
2. T	6. T	10. T	14. T
3. T	7. T	11. F	
4. F	8. T	12. F	

Dreams—A Separate Reality?

1. T	3. F	5. T	7. T
2. F	4. F	6. F	8. F

Hypnosis—Look into My Eyes

1. F	4. F	7. T	10. F
2. T	5. F	8. F	
3. T	6. T	9. F	

Meditation and Sensory Deprivation—Chilling, the Healthy Way

1. T	4. F	7. F	10. T
2. F	5. F	8. T	
3. T	6. F	9. F	

Drug-Altered Consciousness—The High and Low of It

1. F	4. T	7. F
2. T	5. T	8. T
3. T	6. F	9. F

Uppers—Amphetamines, Cocaine, MDMA, Caffeine, Nicotine

1. T	5. F	9. T	13. T
2. F	6. T	10. T	
3. T	7. F	11. F	
4. T	8. T	12. T	

Downers—Sedatives, Tranquilizers, and Alcohol

1. F	3. T	5. T	7. F
2. T	4. F	6. F	

Hallucinogens—Tripping the Light Fantastic

1. T	3. F	5. F
2. F	4. T	6. T

Psychology in Action: Exploring and Using Dreams

1. F	3. F	5. F	7. T
2. T	4. T	6. F	

Final Survey and Review

States of Consciousness—The Many Faces of Awareness

1. normal, consciousness
2. consciousness, first, objective
3. quality
4. hypnosis, psychoactive
5. conditioning, recognizes, attains

Sleep—Catching a Few ZZZ's

1. innate
2. Moderate, alertness, boring
3. excessive
4. microsleeps
5. puberty, quality
6. stress
7. psychosis, delusions
8. activity, cycles
9. unscheduled
10. 5, 7, 8
11. inefficient
12. birth, once
13. sleepiness

Stages of Sleep—The Nightly Roller-Coaster

1. hormone, spinal
2. waking, dominant
3. brain, electroencephalograph
4. 1, spindles, 3, delta
5. 1, several
6. rapid, REM
7. non-REM
8. calms, sharpen
9. NREM, bodily, increase
10. longer, dream
11. sexual, disorder
12. wake, paralysis

Sleep Disturbances—Showing Nightly: Sleep Wars!

1. getting, staying
2. quality, drug
3. cessation, nightmares
4. tryptophan, promote
5. insomnia, paradoxical
6. somnambulism, 3, 4
7. terrors, nightmares
8. eliminated
9. apnea, death
10. continuous, breathing
11. months, soft, quilts
12. safest

Dreams—A Separate Reality?

1. short, 10
2. REM
3. disturbances
4. adaptive
5. Freudian, unconscious
6. visible, hidden
7. Hobson, physiological
8. neurocognitive, daily
9. settings, negative, positive

Hypnosis—Look into My Eyes

1. altered, narrowed
2. Mesmer, magnetism
3. Braid
4. split
5. observer, silently
6. suggestion, repulsive
7. self-hypnosis
8. relaxation, perceptions
9. strength, regression
10. susceptibility
11. responsive, disinhibition

Meditation and Sensory Deprivation—Chilling, the Healthy Way

1. exercises
2. mindfulness, moment, focused
3. anxious, relaxation
4. reduction
5. stressful, distortions
6. mild, sensitivity
7. lessens, aggression
8. long, creative, Stimulation
9. open, reality

Drug-Altered Consciousness—The High and Low of It

1. affects, consciousness
2. blocking, neurons
3. psychoactive, stimulation, hallucinogens
4. dependence, dependence
5. addictive, accumbens
6. induce, abuse
7. Prolonged, tolerance
8. experimental, situational
9. maladjustment, cope
10. adolescents, parental, poor
11. mixed, overdoses
12. alcohol, tobacco

Uppers—Amphetamines, Cocaine, MDMA, Caffeine, Nicotine

1. stimulation, amphetamines, nicotine
2. weight, depressant
3. speed, rapid, confusion, aggression
4. meth, labs
5. damage, delusions
6. compulsive, disregard
7. anhedonia
8. MDMA, deaths
9. temperature, liver
10. sexual, orgasms
11. Caffeine, North
12. coffee, chocolate, inhibit
13. irritability, elevated
14. lung
15. carcinogens, cancer
16. 30-minute, four
17. scheduled, increments, repeatedly

Downers—Sedatives, Tranquilizers, and Alcohol

1. intoxication, goofballs, rainbows
2. coma, goop
3. lower, strong
4. roofies, rape, tasteless
5. alcohol, exceeds
6. men, women
7. develop, ten
8. Paced, slowly, rely
9. detoxification

Hallucinogens—Tripping the Light Fantastic

1. acid, disturbances
2. mescaline, mushrooms
3. alcohol, reproductive
4. marijuana, organs
5. short, decline

Psychology in Action: Exploring and Using Dreams

1. four, condensation
2. setting, emotions
3. feeling, elements
4. solving, normal

Mastery Test

1. d, p. 183
2. b, p. 206, 212
3. d, p. 206-207
4. b, p. 186-187
5. b, p. 219
6. c, p. 199
7. b, p. 203-204
8. a, p. 188
9. a, p. 202
10. c, p. 197-200
11. b, p. 185
12. d, p. 184
13. d, p. 207
14. d, p. 185
15. c, p. 204
16. c, p. 192-193
17. a, p. 197
18. d, p. 206, 215-217
19. b, p. 187
20. d, p. 201
21. c, p. 188
22. c, p. 213
23. b, p. 191
24. a, p. 192
25. d, p. 210-211
26. b, p. 195
27. a, p. 209
28. c, p. 184-185
29. b, p. 194
30. a, p. 198
31. d, p. 203-204
32. c, p. 189
33. a, p. 220-221
34. b, p. 202

CHAPTER 6

Conditioning and Learning

Chapter Overview

Learning is a relatively permanent change in behavior due to experience. Two basic forms of learning are associative learning, which comprises classical and operant conditioning, and cognitive learning. Classical conditioning is also called respondent or Pavlovian conditioning. Classical conditioning occurs when a neutral stimulus is associated with an unconditioned stimulus, which reliably elicits an unconditioned response. After many pairings of the neutral stimulus (NS) and the unconditioned stimulus (US), the NS becomes a conditioned stimulus (CS) that elicits a conditioned response (CR). Learning is strengthened during acquisition of a response. Extinction occurs when the US stops following the CS,although some spontaneous recovery of conditioning may occur. It is apparent that stimulus generalization has occurred when a stimulus similar to the conditioned stimulus (CS) also elicits a learned response. In stimulus discrimination, people or animals learn to respond differently to two similar stimuli. Conditioning often involves simple reflex responses, but emotional conditioning is also possible. Vicarious classical conditioning occurs when we respond to a stimulus by watching someone else's reactions.

In operant conditioning (or instrumental learning), the consequences that follow a response alter the probability that it will be made again. Positive and negative reinforcers increase responding; punishment suppresses responding; nonreinforcement leads to extinction. Shaping involves reinforcing successive approximations to a desired behavior. Various types of reinforcers and different patterns of giving reinforcers greatly affect operant learning. Primary reinforcers provide comfort or fulfill a physical need; secondary reinforcers are learned. Four types of schedules of partial reinforcements are fixed ratio, variable ratio, fixed interval, and variable interval. Fixed ratio produces a high response rate, while variable interval produces a slow and steady response rate; it has a strong resistance to extinction.

Informational feedback (knowledge of results) also facilitates learning and performance. Antecedent stimuli (those that precede a response) influence operant learning through stimulus generalization, discrimination, and stimulus control.

Learning, even simple conditioning, is based on acquiring information (such as feedback). Higher level cognitive learning involves memory, thinking, problem solving, and language. At a simpler level, cognitive maps, latent learning, and discovery learning show that learning is based on acquiring information. Learning also occurs through observation and imitating models. Observational learning imparts large amounts of information that would be hard to acquire in other ways.

Operant principles can be applied to manage one's own behavior and to break bad habits. A mixture of operant principles and cognitive learning underlies self-regulated learning—a collection of techniques to improve learning in school.

Learning Objectives

1. Define *learning* and distinguish between *associate learning* and *cognitive learning.*

2. Define *response, reinforcement, antecedents,* and *consequences* and explain how these terms are related to classical and operant conditioning.

3. Briefly describe the history of classical conditioning and give examples of how classical conditioning takes place, utilizing the following terms:
    a. neutral stimulus (NS)
    b. conditioned stimulus (CS)
    c. unconditioned stimulus (UCS)
    d. unconditioned response (UCR)
    e. conditioned response (CR)

4. Explain how reinforcement occurs during the acquisition of a classically conditioned response; describe higher-order conditioning; and discuss the informational view of classical conditioning.

5. Describe and give examples of the following concepts as they relate to classical conditioning:
    a. extinction
    b. spontaneous recovery
    c. stimulus generalization
    d. stimulus discrimination

6. Describe the relationship between classical conditioning and reflex responses.

7. Define the term conditioned emotional response (CER) and explain how it is it is acquired; and discuss the therapy techniques of desensitization and virtual reality exposure, and the concept of vicarious classical conditioning.

8. Compare and contrast classical conditioning versus operant conditioning.

9. Briefly describe the history of operant conditioning, including Thorndike's law of effect and the work of B.F. Skinner; and differentiate between the terms *reward* and *reinforcement*.

10. Explain operant conditioning in terms of the informational view; define response-contingent reinforcement; describe the deterimental effect of delaying reinforcement and how response chaining can counteract this effect.

11. Explain why superstitious behavior develops and why it persists.

12. Describe the process of shaping.

13. Explain how extinction and spontanous recovery occur in operant conditioning, and how reinforcement and extinction are involved in negative attention-seeking behavior.

14. Compare and contrast positive reinforcement, negative reinforcement, and the two types of punishment and give examples of each.

15. Define and give examples of primary reinforcers, secondary reinforcers, tokens, social reinforcers, and feedback (knowledge of results); and explain how conditioning techniques can be applied to energy conservation and learning aids, such as programmed instruction, computer-assisted instruction, and interactive simulations.

16. Compare and contrast the effects of continuous and partial reinforcement and describe, give an example of, and explain the effects of the following schedules of partial reinforcement:
    a. fixed ratio (FR)
    b. variable ratio (VR)
    c. fixed interval (FI)
    d. variable interval (VI)

17. Explain the concept of stimulus control and describe the processes of generalization and discrimination as they relate to operant conditioning.

18. Explain how punishers can be defined by their effects on behavior; discuss the three factors that influence the effectiveness of punishment; differentiate the effects of severe punishment from mild punishment.

19. Describe three problems associated with punishment and the effects of punishment on the behavior of children when it is used frequently; explain the three basic tools available to control simple learning (reinforcement, nonreinforcement, and punishment); discuss seven guidelines for using punishment; explain why using punishment can become "habit-forming."

20. Define cognitive learning; describe the concepts of a cognitive map and latent learning

21. Explain the difference between discovery learning and rote learning.

22. Discuss the factors that determine whether observational learning (modeling) will occur; describe Bandura's Bo-Bo doll; explain why what a parent does may be more important than what a parent says.

23. Briefly describe the general conclusions that can be drawn from studies on the effects of media violence on children and adults.

RECITE AND REVIEW

What Is Learning—Does Practice Make Perfect?

Survey Question: What is learning? Pages 226-227

1. Learning is a relatively permanent change in _____ due to experience. To understand learning we must study antecedents (events that _____ responses) and consequences (events that _____ responses).

2. Associative learning occurs whenever a simple _____ forms among various stimuli and/or responses; cognitive learning refers to understanding, _____, anticipating, and other higher mental processes.

3. Classical, or respondent _____, and instrumental, or operant _____, are two basic types of learning.

4. In classical conditioning, a previously neutral _____ is associated with a stimulus that elicits a response. In operant conditioning, the pattern of voluntary _____ is altered by consequences.

5. Both types of conditioning depend on reinforcement. In classical conditioning, learning is _____ when a US follows the NS or CS. _____ reinforcement is based on the consequences that follow a response.

Classical Conditioning—Does the Name Pavlov Ring a Bell? and Principles of Classical Conditioning – Here's Johnny

Survey Question: How does classical conditioning occur? Pages 227-231

1. Classical conditioning, studied by Ivan Pavlov, occurs when a _____ stimulus (NS) is associated with an unconditioned stimulus (US). The US triggers a reflex called the unconditioned _____ (UR).

2. If the NS is consistently paired with the US, it becomes a conditioned _____ (CS), capable of producing a response by itself. This response is a conditioned (_____) response (CR).

3. During acquisition of classical conditioning, the conditioned stimulus must be consistently followed by the unconditioned _____.

4. Higher-order conditioning occurs when a well-learned conditioned stimulus is used as if it were an unconditioned _____, bringing about further learning.

5. According to the informational view, we look for _____ among events, which brings about thoughts about how events are _____, or mental expectancies.

6. When the CS is repeatedly presented alone, extinction takes place. That is, _____ is weakened or inhibited.

7. After extinction seems to be complete, a rest period may lead to the temporary reappearance of a conditioned _____. This is called spontaneous recovery.

8. Through stimulus generalization, stimuli _____ to the conditioned stimulus will also produce a response.

9. Generalization gives way to _____ discrimination when an organism learns to respond to one stimulus, but not to similar stimuli.

10. From an informational view, conditioning creates expectancies (or expectations about events), which alter _____ patterns.

11. In classical conditioning, the CS creates the expectancy that the US will _____ it.

Classical Conditioning in Humans—An Emotional Topic

Survey Question: Does conditioning affect emotions? Pages 231-233

1. Conditioning applies to visceral or emotional responses as well as simple _____. As a result, _____ emotional responses (CERs) also occur.

2. Irrational fears called phobias may be CERs that are extended to a variety of situations by _____ generalization.

3. The conditioning of emotional responses can occur vicariously (_____) as well as directly. Vicarious classical conditioning occurs when we _____ another person's emotional responses to a stimulus.

4. Desensitization involves _____ exposing a person with a phobia to _____ stimuli while he or she remains calm and relaxed.

5. Vicarious classical conditioning can explain the development of _____ towards foods, political parties, and ethnic groups.

Operant Conditioning—Can Pigeons Play Ping-Pong?

Survey Question: How does operant conditioning occur? Pages 234-239

1. Operant conditioning (or instrumental _____) occurs when a voluntary action is followed by a reinforcer.

2. Reinforcement in operant conditioning _____ the frequency or probability of a response. This result is based on what Edward L. Thorndike called the law of _____.

3. An operant reinforcer is any event that follows a _____ and _____ its probability.

4. Learning in operant conditioning is based on the expectation that a response will have a specific _____.

5. To be effective, operant _____ must be _____ contingent.

6. Delay of reinforcement reduces its effectiveness, but long _____ of responses may be built up so that a _____ reinforcer maintains many responses.

7. Superstitious behaviors (unnecessary responses) often become part of _____ chains because they appear to be associated with reinforcement.

8. In a process called shaping, complex _____ responses can be taught by reinforcing successive approximations (ever closer matches) to a final desired response.

9. If an operant response is not reinforced, it may extinguish (disappear). But after extinction seems complete, it may temporarily reappear (spontaneous _____).

10. In positive reinforcement, _____ or a pleasant event follows a response. In negative reinforcement, a response that _____ discomfort becomes more likely to occur again.

11. Punishment _____ responding. Punishment occurs when a response is followed by the onset of an aversive event or by the removal of a positive event (response _____).

Operant Reinforcers—What's Your Pleasure?

Survey Question: Are there different kinds of operant reinforcement? Pages 239-243

1. Primary reinforcers are "natural," physiologically-based rewards in that they may produce _____, end discomfort, or fill an immediate _____ need.

2. Intra-cranial stimulation of "_____ centers" in the _____ can also serve as a primary reinforcer.

3. Secondary reinforcers are _____. They typically gain their reinforcing value by association with primary reinforcers or because they can be _____ for primary reinforcers.

4. Token reinforcers are _____ reinforcers that can be _____ with primary reinforcers.

5. A major advantage of token reinforcers is that they do not lose their _____ as quickly as do _____ reinforcers.

6. Human behavior is often influenced by social _____, which are based on _____ desires for attention and approval from others.

7. When learning something new, reinforcement comes from _____ that indicates whether you achieved a desired result.

8. Programmed instruction breaks learning into a series of small steps and provides immediate _____.

9. Computer-assisted _____ (CAI) does the same, but has the added advantage of providing alternate exercises and information when needed.

10. Some CAI programs, called _____ _____, make use of instructional games in which stories, competition, and game-like graphics increase interest and motivation.

Partial Reinforcement—Las Vegas, a Human Skinner Box?

Survey Question: How are we influenced by patterns of reward? Pages 243-246

1. Reward or reinforcement may be given continuously (after every _____), or on a schedule of _____ reinforcement. The study of schedules of reinforcement was begun by B. F. Skinner.

2. Partial reinforcement produces greater resistance to extinction. This is the partial reinforcement _____.

3. The four most basic schedules of reinforcement are _____ ratio (FR), variable ratio (VR), _____ interval (FI), and variable interval (VI).

4. In a fixed ratio (FR) schedule, the _____ of reinforcers to responses is fixed, so that a certain number of correct _____ must be made to obtain the reinforcer.

5. In Variable Ratio (VR) and Variable Interval (VI) schedules, correct responses are _____ on the average.

6. FR and VR schedules produce _____ rates of responding. An FI schedule produces moderate rates of responding with alternating periods of activity and inactivity. VI schedules produce _____, steady rates of responding and strong resistance to extinction.

Stimulus Control—Red Light, Green Light

Pages 246-247

1. Stimuli that _____ a reinforced response tend to control the response on future occasions (stimulus control).

2. Two aspects of stimulus control are generalization and _____.

3. In generalization, an operant response tends to occur when stimuli _____ to those preceding reinforcement are present.

4. In discrimination, responses are given in the presence of discriminative stimuli associated with reinforcement (_____) and withheld in the presence of stimuli associated with nonreinforcement (_____).

5. A simplified summary of stimulus control can be described as noticing a stimulus, _____ a behavior, and getting a reward.

Punishment—Putting the Brakes on Behavior

Survey Question: What does punishment do to behavior? Pages 248-251

1. A punisher is any consequence that _____ the frequency of a target behavior.

2. Punishment can involve the onset of an _____ event or the removal of something _____ (i.e., response cost).

3. Punishment is most effective when it is _____, consistent, and intense.

4. Mild punishment tends only to temporarily _____ responses that are also reinforced or were acquired by reinforcement.

5. The undesirable side effects of punishment include the conditioning of fear, the learning of _____ and avoidance responses, and the encouragement of aggression.

6. Escape learning involves making a response to _____ an unpleasant stimulus or situation; avoidance learning involves making a _____ to postpone or prevent an unpleasant stimulus or situation.

7. Reinforcement and nonreinforcement are better ways to change behavior than punishment. When punishment is used, it should be _____ and combined with reinforcement of alternate _____.

Cognitive Learning—Beyond Conditioning

Survey Question: What is cognitive learning? Pages 252-254

1. Cognitive learning involves higher mental processes, such as understanding, _____, or anticipating.

2. Evidence of cognitive learning is provided by cognitive _____ (internal representations of spatial relationships) and latent (hidden) _____.

3. Discovery learning emphasizes insight and _____, in contrast to rote learning. The best teaching strategies are based on _____ discovery.

Modeling—Do as I Do, Not as I Say

Survey Question: Does learning occur by imitation? Pages 254-257

1. Much human learning is achieved through _____, or modeling.

2. Observational learning is influenced by the personal characteristics of the _____ and the success or failure of the _____ behavior.

3. Observational learning involves attention, remembering, _____, and outcome of reproduction.

4. Television characters can act as powerful _____ for observational learning. Televised violence increases the likelihood of aggression by viewers.

5. People who play violent video games such as Mortal Kombat are prone to act _____ toward others.

Psychology in Action: Behavioral Self-Management—A Rewarding Project

Survey Question: How does conditioning apply to everyday problems? Pages 258-260

1. _____ principles can be readily applied to manage behavior in everyday settings.

2. Self-management of behavior is based on self-reinforcement, self-recording, _____, and behavioral contracting.

3. Prepotent, or frequent, high-probability _____, can be used to reinforce low-frequency responses. This is known as the Premack _____.

4. Attempts to break bad habits are aided by reinforcing alternate _____, by extinction, breaking _____ chains, and _____ cues or antecedents.

5. A behavioral contract states a specific problem _____ to control, rewards to be received, privileges forfeited, and punishments.

6. In school, self-regulated _____ typically involves all of the following: setting learning _____, planning learning strategies, using self-instruction, monitoring progress, evaluating oneself, reinforcing _____, and taking corrective action when required.

CONNECTIONS

What Is Learning—Does Practice Make Perfect?; Classical Conditioning—Does the Name Pavlov Ring a Bell?; Principles of Classical Conditioning – Here's Johnny; and Classical Conditioning in Humans—An Emotional Topic.

Survey Questions: What is learning? How does classical conditioning occur? Does conditioning affect emotions? Pages 226-233

1. _____ respondent conditioning
2. _____ antecedents
3. _____ meat powder
4. _____ Cognitive learning
5. _____ spontaneous recovery
6. _____ bell
7. _____ salivation
8. _____ associative learning
9. _____ consequences
10. _____ desensitization
11. _____ expectancies
12. _____ CS used as US
13. _____ Phobia
14. _____ extinction
15. _____ acquisition
16. _____ discrimination

A. before responses
B. Pavlov's CS
C. after responses
D. higher-order conditioning
E. Pavlovian conditioning
F. US missing
G. training period
H. Pavlov's UR
I. Pavlov's US
J. informational view
K. incomplete extinction
L. simple associations
M. anticipating
N. response to specific stimuli
O. CER
P. extinction of fear

Operant Conditioning—Can Pigeons Play Ping-Pong? and Operant Reinforcers—What's Your Pleasure?

Survey Questions: How does operant conditioning occur? Are there different kinds of operant reinforcement? Pages 234-243

1. _____ primary reinforcer
2. _____ secondary reinforcer
3. _____ tokens
4. _____ approval
5. _____ KR
6. _____ CAI
7. _____ response cost
8. _____ shaping
9. _____ negative reinforcement
10. _____ extinction
11. _____ law of effect
12. _____ increases response
13. _____ instrumental learning
14. _____ punishment
15. _____ response chain

A. operant conditioning
B. linked actions
C. losing privileges
D. learned reinforcer
E. increased responding
F. approximations
G. decreased responding
H. Edward Thorndike
I. non-reinforcement
J. nonlearned reinforcer
K. social reinforcer
L. Chimp-O-Mat
M. educational simulations
N. informational feedback
O. success

Partial Reinforcement—Las Vegas, a Human Skinner Box? and Stimulus Control—Red Light, Green Light

Survey Question: How are we influenced by patterns of reward? Pages 243-247

1. _____ stimulus control
2. _____ continuous reinforcement
3. _____ Generalization
4. _____ partial reinforcement
5. _____ fixed ratio
6. _____ variable ratio
7. _____ variable interval
8. _____ discrimination
9. _____ fixed interval
10. _____ discriminative stimuli

A. resistance to extinction
B. reinforcement schedules
C. paper due every two weeks
D. S+ and S-
E. high response rate
F. antecedent stimuli
G. slow, steady response rate
H. reinforce all correct responses
I. similar stimuli
J. "sniffer" dogs

Punishment—Putting the Brakes on Behavior

Survey Question: What does punishment do to behavior? Pages 248-251

1. _____ punishment
2. _____ avoidance learning
3. _____ severe punishment
4. _____ escape learning
5. _____ mild punishment
6. _____ fear and aggression

A. lying to prevent discomfort
B. side effects of punishment
C. suppresses a response
D. running away
E. weak effect
F. can stop a behavior permanently

Cognitive Learning—Beyond Conditioning; Modeling—Do as I Do, Not as I Say; and Psychology in Action: Behavioral Self-Management—Wouldn't You Like to Reward Yourself?

Survey Questions: What is cognitive learning? Does learning occur by imitation? How does conditioning apply to everyday problems? Pages 252-260

1. _____ cognitive map
2. _____ Premack principle
3. _____ observational learning
4. _____ modeling
5. _____ self-recording
6. _____ rote learning
7. _____ televised violence
8. _____ discovery learning
9. _____ latent learning

A. insight
B. imitation
C. mental image of campus
D. learning through repetition
E. Albert Bandura
F. hidden learning
G. can produce aggression
H. self-management program
I. use repeated behavior as reinforcer

CHECK YOUR MEMORY

What Is Learning—Does Practice Make Perfect?

Survey Question: What is learning? Pages 226-227

1. Learning to press the buttons on a vending machine is based on operant conditioning.

TRUE or FALSE

2. In classical conditioning, the consequences that follow responses become associated with one another.

TRUE or FALSE

3. Getting compliments from friends could serve as reinforcement for operant learning.

TRUE or FALSE

4. Learning is defined as a relatively permanent change in behavior due to experience, motivation, fatigue, maturation, and/or drugs.

TRUE or FALSE

5. Cognitive learning occurs whenever a person or animal forms a simple association between various stimuli and/or responses

TRUE or FALSE

Classical Conditioning—Does the Name Pavlov Ring a Bell? and Principles of Classical Conditioning – Here's Johnny

Survey Question: How does classical conditioning occur? Pages 227-231

1. Ivan Pavlov studied digestion and operant conditioning in dogs.

TRUE or FALSE

2. Mental expectancies are thoughts about how events are connected.

TRUE or FALSE

3. Pavlov used meat powder to reinforce conditioned salivation to the sound of a bell.

TRUE or FALSE

4. Conditioned nausea can be prevented in chemotherapy patients by flavoring their favorite foods with an unusual taste.

TRUE or FALSE

5. Responding to a stimulus that is distinctly different from the conditioned stimulus is called stimulus generalization

TRUE or FALSE

6. During successful conditioning, the NS becomes a CS.

TRUE or FALSE

7. During acquisition, the CS is presented repeatedly without the US.

TRUE or FALSE

8. In stimulus discrimination, responding increases as a neutral stimulus becomes more similar to the conditioned stimulus

TRUE or FALSE

9. The optimal delay between the CS and the US is 5 to 15 seconds.

TRUE or FALSE

10. In higher-order conditioning, a well-learned CS (like a bell) can be used to reinforce further learning (like a light)

TRUE or FALSE

11. Spontaneous recovery occurs when a CS becomes strong enough to be used like a US.

TRUE or FALSE

12. According to the informational view, humans look for associations among events

TRUE or FALSE

13. Discriminations are learned when generalized responses to stimuli similar to the CS are extinguished.

TRUE or FALSE

Classical Conditioning in Humans—An Emotional Topic

Survey Question: Does conditioning affect emotions? Pages 231-233

1. Narrowing of the pupils in response to bright lights is learned in early infancy.

TRUE or FALSE

2. Emotional conditioning involves autonomic nervous system responses.

TRUE or FALSE

3. Stimulus generalization helps convert some CERs into phobias.

TRUE or FALSE

4. Pleasant music can be used as a UR to create a CER.

TRUE or FALSE

5. To learn a CER vicariously, you would observe the actions of another person and try to imitate them.

TRUE or FALSE

6. Desensitization therapy has been used to extinguish CERs

TRUE or FALSE

Operant Conditioning—Can Pigeons Play Ping-Pong?

Survey Question: How does operant conditioning occur? Pages 234-239

1. In operant conditioning, learners actively emit responses.

TRUE or FALSE

2. Rewards are the same as reinforcers.

TRUE or FALSE

3. The Skinner box is primarily used to study classical conditioning.

TRUE or FALSE

4. Reinforcement in operant conditioning alters how frequently involuntary responses are elicited.

TRUE or FALSE

5. Operant reinforcers are most effective when they are response-contingent.

TRUE or FALSE

6. Operant learning is most effective if you wait a minute or two after the response is over before reinforcing it.

TRUE or FALSE

7. Response chains allow delayed reinforcers to support learning.

TRUE or FALSE

8. Superstitious responses appear to be associated with reinforcement, but they are not.

TRUE or FALSE

9. Teaching a pigeon to play Ping-Pong would most likely make use of the principle of response cost.

TRUE or FALSE

10. Children who misbehave may be reinforced by attention from parents.

TRUE or FALSE

11. Negative reinforcement is a type of punishment that is used to strengthen learning.

TRUE or FALSE

12. Putting a pair of gloves on to stop the pain caused by the cold outside air is an example of negative reinforcement.

TRUE or FALSE

13. You have stopped offering advice to a friend because she turned distant every time you gave her advice; this is an example of punishment.

TRUE or FALSE

14. Both response cost and negative reinforcement decrease responding.

TRUE or FALSE

Operant Reinforcers—What's Your Pleasure?

Survey Question: Are there different kinds of operant reinforcement? Pages 239-243

1. Food, water, grades, and sex are primary reinforcers.

TRUE or FALSE

2. Intracranial self-stimulation (ICS) is a good example of a secondary reinforcer.

TRUE or FALSE

3. Social reinforcers are secondary reinforcers.

TRUE or FALSE

4. Attention and approval can be used to shape another person's behavior.

TRUE or FALSE

5. The effects of primary reinforcers may quickly decline as the person becomes satiated.

TRUE or FALSE

6. The Chimp-O-Mat accepted primary reinforcers and dispensed secondary reinforcers.

TRUE or FALSE

7. People are more likely to recycle used materials if they receive weekly feedback about how much they have recycled.

TRUE or FALSE

8. Computer assisted Instruction (CAI) involves informational feedback.

TRUE or FALSE

9. In sports, feedback is most effective when a skilled coach directs attention to important details.

TRUE or FALSE

10. The final level of skill and knowledge is almost always higher following computer assisted instruction (CAI) than it is with conventional methods.

TRUE or FALSE

Partial Reinforcement—Las Vegas, a Human Skinner Box?

Survey Question: How are we influenced by patterns of reward? Pages 243-246

1. Continuous reinforcement means that reinforcers are given continuously, regardless of whether or not responses are made.

TRUE or FALSE

2. Variable Interval (VI) schedules provide reinforcement after a particular number of responses has been made.

TRUE or FALSE

3. A partial reinforcement schedule means that reinforcement does not follow every response

TRUE or FALSE

4. A Fixed-Ratio (3) (FR-3) schedule means that each correct response produces three reinforcers.

TRUE or FALSE

5. The time interval in Fixed Interval schedules is measured from the last reinforced response.

TRUE or FALSE

6. Partial reinforcement schedules produce high rates of responding because it is difficult to distinguish between reinforcement and extinction periods.

TRUE or FALSE

7. Continuous schedules of reinforcement are more resistance to extinction than partial reinforcement schedules.

TRUE or FALSE

8. Fixed Ratio (FR) schedules tend to produce slow, steady rates of responding

TRUE or FALSE

9. In business, commissions and profit sharing are examples of Fixed Interval reinforcement.

TRUE or FALSE

Stimulus Control—Red Light, Green Light

Pages 246-247

1. Antecedent stimuli tend to control when and where previously rewarded responses will occur.

TRUE or FALSE

2. Stimulus control refers to noticing an event occurring, performing a behavior, then getting a reward for the behavior.

TRUE or FALSE

3. Stimulus generalization is the primary method used to train dogs to detect contraband.

TRUE or FALSE

4. S+ represents a discriminative stimulus that precedes a nonreinforced response.

TRUE or FALSE

Punishment—Putting the Brakes on Behavior

Survey Question: What does punishment do to behavior? Pages 248-251

1. Like reinforcement, punishment should be response-contingent.

TRUE or FALSE

2. Punishment is most effective if it is unpredictable.

TRUE or FALSE

3. It is much more effective to strengthen desirable behaviors than punish undesirable behaviors.

TRUE or FALSE

4. Speeding tickets are an example of response cost.

TRUE or FALSE

5. Mild punishment causes reinforced responses to extinguish more rapidly.

TRUE or FALSE

6. Generally, punishment should be the last resort for altering behavior.

TRUE or FALSE

7. An apparatus known as a shuttle box is used to study escape and avoidance learning.

TRUE or FALSE

8. Punishment does not have to be consistent to extinguish a behavior quickly as long as positive behaviors are reinforced.

TRUE or FALSE

9. Punishment works best when it occurs as the response is being made, but is still as effective when delivered within six hours of a behavior.

TRUE or FALSE

10. Children may learn to fear their caregivers if punished severely.

TRUE or FALSE

11. For humans, avoidance learning is reinforced by a sense of relief.

TRUE or FALSE

12. Punishment frequently leads to increases in aggression by the person who is punished.

TRUE or FALSE

13. Two-thirds of child abuse cases begin as attempts at physical punishment

TRUE or FALSE

Cognitive Learning—Beyond Conditioning

Survey Question: What is cognitive learning? Pages 252-254

1. Cognitive learning involves thinking, memory, and problem solving.

TRUE or FALSE

2. A cognitive map is an external drawing or representation of an area, such as a maze, city, or campus.

TRUE or FALSE

3. Animals learning their way through a maze memorize the correct order of right and left turns to make.

TRUE or FALSE

4. Typically, reinforcement must be provided in order to make latent learning visible.

TRUE or FALSE

5. In many situations, discovery learning produces better understanding of problems.

TRUE or FALSE

6. Rote learning produces skills through insight and understanding.

TRUE or FALSE

Modeling—Do as I Do, Not as I Say

Survey Question: Does learning occur by imitation? Pages 254-257

1. Modeling is another term for discovery learning.

TRUE or FALSE

2. After a new response is acquired through modeling, normal reinforcement determines if it will be repeated.

TRUE or FALSE

3. Successful observational learning requires two steps: observing and reproducing the behavior.

TRUE or FALSE

4. Individuals are more likely to imitate a behavior ifa chosen model was successful at a task or rewarded for a response.

TRUE or FALSE

5. Children imitate aggressive acts performed by other people, but they are not likely to imitate cartoon characters.

TRUE or FALSE

6. Today's 8–18 year-olds spend only 12 hours a week engaged with various media (e.g., TV, video games, the Internet, etc.).

TRUE or FALSE

7. Violence on television causes children to be more violent.

TRUE or FALSE

8. Playing violent video games tends to increase aggressive behavior in children and young adults.

TRUE or FALSE

9. Children tend to imitate only what they see on TV, not video games.

TRUE or FALSE

Psychology in Action: Behavioral Self-Management—Wouldn't You Like to Reward Yourself?

Survey Question: How does conditioning apply to practical problems? Pages 258-260

1. Choosing reinforcers is the first step in behavioral self-management.

TRUE or FALSE

2. Self-recording can be an effective way to change behavior, even without using specific reinforcers.

TRUE or FALSE

3. According to the Premack principle, you should reward yourself on a continuous reinforcement schedule.

TRUE or FALSE

4. A prepotent response is one that occurs frequently.

TRUE or FALSE

5. To use extinction to break a bad habit, you should remove, avoid, or delay the reinforcement that is supporting the habit.

TRUE or FALSE

6. In a behavioral contract, you spell out what response chains you are going to extinguish.

TRUE or FALSE

7. Self-regulated learners actively seek feedback in both formal and informal ways.

TRUE or FALSE

FINAL SURVEY AND REVIEW

What Is Learning—Does Practice Make Perfect?

Survey Question: What is learning? Pages 226-227

1. Learning is a relatively _____ change in behavior due to _____. To understand learning we must study _____ (events that precede responses) and _____ (events that follow responses).

2. Associative _____ occurs whenever a simple association forms among various stimuli and/or responses; _____ learning refers to understanding, knowing, anticipating, and other higher _____ processes.

3. Classical, or _____ conditioning, and instrumental, or _____ conditioning, are two basic types of learning.

4. In classical conditioning, a previously _____ stimulus is associated with a stimulus that elicits a response. In operant conditioning, the pattern of voluntary responses is altered by _____.

5. Both types of conditioning depend on reinforcement. In classical conditioning, learning is reinforced when a _____ follows the NS or CS. Operant reinforcement is based on the _____ that follow a response.

Classical Conditioning—Does the Name Pavlov Ring a Bell? and Principles of Classical Conditioning – Here's Johnny

Survey Question: How does classical conditioning occur? Pages 227-231

1. Classical conditioning, studied by Ivan _____, occurs when a neutral stimulus (NS) is associated with an _____ stimulus (US). The US triggers a _____ called the unconditioned response (UR).

2. If the _____ is consistently paired with the US, it becomes a _____ stimulus (CS), capable of producing a response by itself. This response is a conditioned (learned) response (CR).

3. During _____ of classical conditioning, the conditioned stimulus must be consistently followed by the _____ stimulus.

4. Higher-order _____ occurs when a well-learned _____ stimulus is used as if it were an unconditioned stimulus, bringing about further learning.

5. According to the _____ view, we look for associations among events, which brings about thoughts about how events are interconnected, or _____ expectancies.

6. When the CS is repeatedly presented alone, _____ takes place. That is, conditioning is _____ or inhibited.

7. After extinction seems to be complete, a rest period may lead to the temporary _____ of a conditioned response. This is called spontaneous _____.

8. Through _____ generalization, stimuli similar to the _____ stimulus will also produce a response.

9. Generalization gives way to stimulus _____ when an organism learns to respond to one stimulus, but not to _____ stimuli.

10. From an informational view, conditioning creates _____ (or expectations about events), which alter response patterns.

11. In classical conditioning, the _____ creates the expectancy that the _____ will follow it.

Classical Conditioning in Humans—An Emotional Topic

Survey Question: Does conditioning affect emotions? Pages 231-233

1. Conditioning applies to visceral or _____ responses as well as simple reflexes. As a result, conditioned emotional responses (_____) also occur.

2. Irrational fears called _____ may be CERs that are extended to a variety of situations by stimulus _____.

CONDITIONING AND LEARNING

3. The conditioning of _____ responses can occur _____ (secondhand) as well as directly. Vicarious classical conditioning occurs when we observe another person's emotional responses to a stimulus.

4. Desensitization involves gradually exposing a person with a _____ to feared stimuli while he or she remains _____ and relaxed.

5. Vicarious _____ conditioning can explain the development of attitudes towards foods, political parties, and ethnic groups.

Operant Conditioning—Can Pigeons Play Ping-Pong?

Survey Question: How does operant conditioning occur? Pages 234–239

1. Operant conditioning (or _____ learning) occurs when a voluntary action is followed by a _____.

2. Reinforcement in _____ conditioning increases the frequency or probability of a response. This result is based on what Edward L. _____ called the law of effect.

3. An operant _____ is any event that _____ a response and increases its probability.

4. Learning in operant conditioning is based on the _____ that a response will have a specific effect.

5. To be effective, operant reinforcement must be response _____.

6. Delay of reinforcement _____ its effectiveness, but long chains of responses may be built up so that a single _____ maintains many responses.

7. Superstitious behaviors (_____ responses) often become part of response chains because they appear to be _____ with reinforcement.

8. In a process called _____, complex operant responses can be taught by reinforcing successive approximations (ever closer matches) to a final desired response.

9. If an operant response is not reinforced, it may _____ (disappear). But after extinction seems complete, it may _____ reappear (spontaneous recovery).

10. In _____ reinforcement, reward or a pleasant event follows a response. In _____ reinforcement, a response that ends discomfort becomes more likely to occur again.

11. Punishment decreases responding. Punishment occurs when a response is followed by the onset of an _____ event or by the removal of a positive event (_____ cost).

© 2011 Cengage Learning. All Rights Reserved. May not be scanned, copied or duplicated, or posted to a publicly accessible website, in whole or in part

Operant Reinforcers—What's Your Pleasure?

Survey Question: Are there different kinds of operant reinforcement? Pages 239-243

1. Primary reinforcers are "_____," physiologically-based rewards in that they may produce comfort, end _____, or fill an immediate physical need.

2. Intra-cranial _____ of "pleasure centers" in the brain can also serve as a primary reinforcer.

3. Secondary _____ are learned. They typically gain their reinforcing value by association with primary reinforcers or because they can be exchanged for primary reinforcers.

4. Token reinforcers are secondary reinforcers that can be exchanged with _____ reinforcers.

5. A major advantage of _____ reinforcers is that they do not lose their value as quickly as do primary _____.

6. Human behavior is often influenced by _____ reinforcers, which are based on learned desires for attention and _____ from others.

7. When learning something _____, reinforcement comes from feedback that indicates whether you achieved a _____ result.

8. Programmed _____ breaks learning into a series of small _____ and provides immediate feedback.

9. Computer-assisted instruction (CAI) does the same, but has the added advantage of providing alternate _____ and information when needed.

10. Some CAI programs, called serious games, make use of instructional games in which stories, _____, and game-like graphics increase interest and _____.

Partial Reinforcement—Las Vegas, a Human Skinner Box?

Survey Question: How are we influenced by patterns of reward? Pages 243-246

1. Reward or reinforcement may be given _____ (after every response), or on a schedule of partial reinforcement. The study of schedules of reinforcement was begun by B. F. _____.

2. Partial reinforcement produces _____ resistance to extinction. This is the partial reinforcement effect.

3. The four most basic schedules of reinforcement are fixed _____ (FR), variable _____ (VR), fixed interval (FI), and variable interval (VI).

4. In a fixed ratio (FR) schedule, the ratio of reinforcers to responses is fixed, so that a certain number of _____ responses must be made to obtain the reinforcer.

5. In Variable Ratio (VR) and Variable Interval (VI) schedules, correct responses are reinforced on the _____.

6. FR and VR schedules produce _____ rates of responding. An FI schedule produces moderate rates of responding with _____ periods of activity and inactivity. VI schedules produce slow, steady rates of responding and strong resistance to extinction.

Stimulus Control—Red Light, Green Light

Pages 246-247

1. Stimuli that precede a reinforced response tend to control the response on future occasions (_____ control).

2. Two aspects of stimulus control are _____ and discrimination.

3. In generalization, an _____ response tends to occur when stimuli similar to those _____ reinforcement are present.

4. In _____, responses are given in the presence of discriminative stimuli associated with reinforcement (S_____) and withheld in the presence of stimuli associated with nonreinforcement (S_____).

5. A simplified summary of stimulus control can be described as _____ a stimulus, performing a behavior, and getting a _____.

Punishment—Putting the Brakes on Behavior

Survey Question: What does punishment do to behavior? Pages 248-251

1. A _____ is any consequence that decreases the frequency of a target behavior.

2. Punishment can involve the _____ of an unpleasant event or the _____ of something pleasant (i.e., response cost).

3. Punishment is most effective when it is immediate, _____, and intense.

4. Mild punishment tends only to _____ suppress responses that are also reinforced or were acquired by reinforcement.

5. The undesirable side effects of punishment include the conditioning of _____, the learning of escape and avoidance responses, and the encouragement of _____.

6. Escape learning involves making a response to end an _____ stimulus or situation; _____ learning involves making a response to postpone or prevent an unpleasant stimulus or situation.

7. Reinforcement and nonreinforcement are better ways to change behavior than _____. When punishment is used, it should be mild and combined with reinforcement of _____ responses.

Cognitive Learning—Beyond Conditioning

Survey Question: What is cognitive learning? Pages 252-254

1. Cognitive learning involves higher _____ processes, such as understanding, knowing, or anticipating.

2. Evidence of cognitive learning is provided by cognitive maps (_____ representations of spatial relationships) and latent (_____) learning.

3. Discovery learning emphasizes _____ and understanding, in contrast to rote learning. The best teaching _____ are based on guided discovery.

Modeling—Do as I Do, Not as I Say

Survey Question: Does learning occur by imitation? Pages 254-257

1. Much human learning is achieved through imitation, or _____.

2. Observational learning is influenced by the personal characteristics of the model and the _____ or _____ of the model's behavior.

3. Observational learning involves _____, remembering, reproduction, and _____ of reproduction.

4. Television characters can act as powerful models for observational learning. Televised violence _____ the likelihood of aggression by viewers.

5. People who play _____ video games such as Mortal Kombat are prone to act aggressively toward others.

Psychology in Action: Behavioral Self-Management—A Rewarding Project

Survey Question: How does conditioning apply to everyday problems? Pages 258-260

1. Operant principles can be readily applied to manage behavior in _____ settings.

2. Self-management of behavior is based on self-_____, self-recording, feedback, and behavioral _____.

3. Prepotent, or frequent, _____ responses, can be used to reinforce low-frequency responses. This is known as the _____ principle.

4. Attempts to break bad habits are aided by reinforcing alternate responses, by _____, _____ response chains, and removing cues or antecedents.

5. A behavioral _____ states a specific problem behavior to control, rewards to be received, privileges _____, and punishments.

6. In school, self-regulated learning typically involves all of the following: setting learning goals, planning learning _____, using self-instruction, monitoring _____, evaluating oneself, reinforcing successes, and taking _____ action when required.

MASTERY TEST

1. The principle of feedback is of particular importance to
a. Conditioned Emotional Responses (CERs).
b. Intracranial Self- Stimulation (ICS).
c. Computer Assisted Instruction (CAI).
d. higher-order conditioning.

2. As a coffee lover, you have become very efficient at carrying out the steps necessary to make a cup of espresso. Your learning is an example of
a. response chaining.
b. spontaneous recovery.
c. vicarious reinforcement.
d. secondary reinforcement.

3. To test for the presence of classical conditioning you would omit the
a. CS.
b. US.
c. CR.
d. S+.

4. Which of the following does not belong with the others?
a. Thorndike
b. Skinner
c. Pavlov
d. instrumental learning

5. To teach a child to say "please" when she asks for things, you should make getting the requested item
a. the CS.
b. a token.
c. a negative reinforcer.
d. response-contingent.

6. Money is to secondary reinforcer as food is to
a. ICS.
b. prepotent responses.
c. primary reinforcer.
d. negative reinforcer.

7. Whether a model is reinforced has a great impact on
a. discovery learning.
b. latent learning.
c. observational learning.
d. self-regulated learning.

8. One thing that classical and operant conditioning have in common is that both
a. were discovered by Pavlov.
b. depend on reinforcement.
c. are affected by the consequences of making a response.
d. permanently change behavior.

9. To shape the behavior of a teacher in one of your classes you would probably have to rely on
a. tokens.
b. primary reinforcers.
c. negative attention seeking.
d. social reinforcers.

10. The concept that best explains persistence at gambling is
a. partial reinforcement.
b. continuous reinforcement.
c. fixed interval reinforcement.
d. fixed ratio reinforcement.

11. Which of the following is NOT a common side effect of mild punishment?
a. escape learning
b. avoidance learning
c. aggression
d. accelerated extinction

12. With respect to televised violence, it can be said that TV violence
a. causes viewers to be more aggressive.
b. is positively related to aggression.
c. has no effect on the majority of viewers.
d. vicariously lowers aggressive urges.

13. Which of the following types of learning is most related to the consequences of making a response?
a. Pavlovian conditioning
b. classical conditioning
c. operant conditioning
d. respondent conditioning

14. Which combination would most likely make a CER into a phobia?
a. CER-discrimination
b. CER-desensitization
c. CER-response cost
d. CER-generalization

15. A loud, unexpected sound causes a startle reflex; thus, a loud sound could be used as a _____ in conditioning.
a. NS
b. CR
c. UR
d. US

16. Antecedents are to _____ as consequences are to
_____.
a. discriminative stimuli; reinforcers
b. shaping; response chaining
c. conditioned stimuli; cognitive maps
d. punishment; negative reinforcement

17. The use of self-recording to change personal behavior is closely related to the principle of
a. response chaining.
b. feedback.
c. two-factor reinforcement.
d. stimulus control.

18. _____ typically only temporarily suppresses reinforced responses.
a. Negative reinforcement
b. Extinction
c. Mild punishment
d. Stimulus generalization

19. In general, the highest rates of responding are associated with
a. delayed reinforcement.
b. variable reinforcement.
c. interval reinforcement.
d. fixed ratio reinforcement.

20. A child who has learned, through classical conditioning, to fear sitting in a dentist's chair becomes frightened when he is placed in a barber's chair. This illustrates the concept of
a. stimulus generalization.
b. spontaneous recovery.
c. higher-order discrimination.
d. vicarious conditioning.

21. The informational view of learning places emphasis on the creation of mental
a. expectancies.
b. reinforcement schedules.
c. contracts.
d. antecedents.

22. For some adults, blushing when embarrassed or ashamed is probably a
    _____ first formed in childhood.
    a. conditioned stimulus
    b. Computer Assisted Instruction
    c. discriminative stimulus
    d. Conditioned Emotional Response

23. Learning to obey traffic signals is related to the phenomenon called
    a. stimulus control.
    b. spontaneous recovery.
    c. avoidance learning.
    d. modeling.

24. To be most effective, punishment should be combined with
    a. response costs.
    b. mild stimuli.
    c. delayed feedback.
    d. reinforcement.

25. Involuntary responses are to _____ conditioning as voluntary
    responses are to _____ conditioning.
    a. classical; respondent
    b. classical; operant
    c. operant; classical
    d. operant; instrumental

26. Which consequence increases the probability that a response will be
    repeated?
    a. punishment
    b. response cost
    c. nonreinforcement
    d. negative reinforcement

27. Helen is trying to teach her dog to use a newly installed dog door. She will be
    most effective if she uses
    a. punishment.
    b. shaping.
    c. delayed reinforcement.
    d. modeling.

28. Whenever a student has perfect attendance for a week, she receives a token
    that can be turned in for candy. In this case, the tokens serve as
    a. secondary reinforcers.
    b. the effects of ICS on behavior.
    c. non-contingent reinforcers.
    d. generalized reinforcers.

29. Jimmy tends to behave badly when he and his parents go to the store. Although this usually results in his being punished, the negative attention likely serves as a
a. negative reinforcer.
b. social reinforcer.
c. discriminative stimulus.
d. conditioned emotional response (CER).

30. Putting on a pair of gloves to stop your hands from hurting while working in the cold weather demonstrates
a. positive reinforcement.
b. negative reinforcement.
c. punishment.
d. response cost.

31. By introducing an energy tax to reduce people's tendency to waste energy or pollute the environment, Congress utilizes _____, a form of operant conditioning.
a. positive reinforcement
b. negative reinforcement
c. punishment
d. response cost

32. _____ gives students enough freedom and guidance to actively think and gain knowledge.
a. Guided discovery
b. Latent discovery
c. Observational learning
d. Classical learning

33. Which of the following is the correct sequence when using observational learning?
a. attention, rewards, reproduction, and remembering
b. attention, remembering, reproduction, and rewards
c. rewards, remembering, attention, and reproduction
d. remembering, rewards, attention, and reproduction

34. Increased aggression and violence among children and adolescents has been attributed to
a. watching violent TV programs.
b. playing violent video games.
c. imitating others' aggressive behaviors.
d. all the preceding.

35. Before going in for his first chemotherapy, Blake had a bread bowl broccoli cheese soup from his favorite soup and sandwich shop. After his session, he got nauseous and vomits as a result of the chemotherapy. Since then, Blake cannot eat broccoli cheese soup as it makes him nauseous. In this example, the unconditioned stimulus is _____ and the conditioned stimulus is _____.

a. broccoli cheese soup; nausea
b. soup and sandwich shop; broccoli cheese soup
c. chemotherapy; broccoli cheese soup
d. chemotherapy; nausea

LANGUAGE DEVELOPMENT
Conditioning and Learning

Word Roots

The word "operant" comes directly from Latin. It is the present participle of the Latin verb *operari*, which means "to work." The word root is used in the type of learning called operant learning. Operant learning refers to spontaneous behavior, as opposed to behavior triggered by a specific stimulus (as in classical conditioning). In this and later chapters you will find words such as operant conditioning, operant response, and operant extinction. The term *operational definition* that we saw in an earlier chapter also derives from this root.

Journey into Psychology: Rats (p. 225)
(225)   *scamper:* to run nimbly and playfully
(225)   *shrieking:* loud shrill yelling
(225)   *ribbed:* teased
(225)   *chastened:* corrected, usually with some sort of punishment
(225)   *Einstein:* reference to Albert Einstein, a 20th century inventor and genius. Used here, it suggests that rats may be smarter than we give them credit for being.

What Is Learning—Does Practice Make Perfect? (pgs. 226-227)
What Is Learning?
(226)   *bassoon:* a musical instrument
(226)   *incapacitated:* incapable of functioning normally
(227)   *snicker:* laugh in an unkind way

Classical Conditioning—Does the Name Pavlov Ring a Bell? (pgs. 227-229)

How does classical conditioning occur?

(227) *ring a bell* (Does the Name Pavlov *Ring a Bell*?): play on words, meaning "Is it familiar to you?" and reference to Pavlov's experiment

(227) *drooled*: salivated

(227) *tidbit*: a small amount of something

(229) *chemotherapy (chemo)*: a treatment given to those with cancer

Principles of Classical Conditioning—Here's Johnny (pgs. 229-231)

(229) *optimal*: maximum

(230) *real hit*: very popular

(230) *get a shot*: get an injection

(230) *hypodermic (needle):* tool for injecting substances beneath the skin

(230) *a catch in your breathing*: a short pause in breathing

(231) *knockoffs*: imitations of famous-brand products

(231) *hide in the closet*: avoid being found

(231) *PlayStation controller*: hand-held video game

Classical Conditioning in Humans—An Emotional Topic (pgs. 231-233)

Does conditioning affect emotions?

(232) *gut responses*: emotional responses, made without thinking

(233) *escalators:* electrical stairs that transport individuals between floors of a building

Operant Conditioning—Can Pigeons Play Ping-Pong? (pgs. 234-239)

How does operant conditioning occur?

(234) *ping-pong*: table tennis; game in which a small white ball is passed between players over a net, usually with paddles.

(234) *state of affairs*: condition; how things are

(234) *obnoxious*: very offensive or objectionable

(234) *elicited*: caused to happen; triggered

(234) *rule of thumb*: guideline; practical method

(234) *grooms*: cleans, licks itself

(235) *contingency*: a connection, relationship

(235) *"treat"*: something good to eat, like candy

(236) *superstitions*: beliefs or practices resulting from trust in magic or chance

(236) *walk under a ladder*: considered by some people to bring bad luck

(237) *shapes up*: improves

(237)   ***throw tantrums***: yell, scream, or throw things in order to get what one wants
(237)   ***show off***: try to attract attention by one's behavior
(237)   ***scolding***: expressing disapproval
(238)   ***turns cold and distant***: one ignores and does not talk to another person

Operant Reinforcers—What's Your Pleasure? (pgs. 239-)
Are there different kinds of operant reinforcement?
(239)   ***tickling your own fancy***: refers to making yourself happy, pleased
(239)   ***iPod-style controller***: a device that is activated much like a popular music-playing device
(239)   ***double latte***: refers to a latte—a drink made with espresso and steamed milk— made with two shots of espresso instead of one
(240)   ***tokens***: something that can be exchanged for desired goods or services
(240)   ***tangible***: something that can be touched
(240)   ***poker chips***: tokens used in a card game to take the place of money
(240)   ***"grab bag"***: a bag that is filled with various small prizes into which a child may reach in and pick a prize that he/she wants as a reward for being good
(240)   ***amenities***: things that provide material comfort
(240)   ***weekend passes***: permission to leave (in this case) the hospital for the weekend
(241)   ***check out their split ends***: examine the ends of one's hair (especially women); a sign of boredom
(241)   ***toying with***: playing with; fingering aimlessly
(241)   ***furiously***: wildly
(241)   Wii – video game console with a wireless remote that detects movement in three dimensions; i.e., physical and bodily movements
(242)   ***"vaporize" an attacker***: make the attacker disappear; destroy the attacker

Partial Reinforcement—Las Vegas, a Human Skinner Box? (pgs. 243-246)
How are we influenced by patterns of reward?
(243)   ***lore***: traditional knowledge; history
(243)   ***slot machines***: a device in a gambling casino into which a patron puts money and hopes to win a larger amount of money
(243)   ***payoff***: money won
(244)   ***"get hooked"***: become compelled to play repeatedly
(244)   ***Bingo!***: "I won!"; Bingo is a board game where the winner yells "Bingo!"
(244)   ***"cleaned out"***: lost all of one's money
(244)   ***piecework***: paid per job completed
(244)   ***keen:*** sharp; accurate

(244)   *spurt*: brief periods of time

(246)   *doggedly*: in a determined or persistent manner

(246)   *bulldog tenacity*: bulldogs were bred to hold on to a bull's nose and not let go; therefore this means extreme stubbornness, refusal to give up

(246)   *anglers*: men or women who fish

Stimulus Control—Red Light, Green Light (pgs. 246-247)

(247)   *"sniffer" dogs*: dogs specially trained to detect certain substances and ignore others.

(247)   *contraband*: illegal items

(247)   *baited*: substances planted to see if the dogs can detect them

(247)   *tailgating*: very closely following a car

(247)   *persistently*: stubborn; determined

Punishment—Putting the Brakes on Behavior (pgs. 248-251)

What does punishment do to behavior?

(248)   Putting the Brakes on Behavior: stopping behavior

(248)   *reprimands*: scolding; expressions of disapproval

(248)   *starved for attention*: badly needing and looking for attention

(248)   *haphazardly*: marked by lack of plan, order, or direction

(248)   *brute*: mean, insensitive person

(249)   *dodge*: avoid

(249)   *sidestep*: to avoid

(249)   *quell*: to end or put a stop to

(250)   *liberal*: generous; free

(250)   *drawbacks*: undesirable effects

(250)   *sparing the rod*: a Biblical phrase meaning to not punish

(250)   *incompatible*: not in accord with each other; not suitable for use together

(250)   *rebuke*: yelling at a person because one disapproves of her/his actions

(250)   *silence may be "golden"*: the common saying "silence is golden" means that quiet moments are rare and should be enjoyed

Cognitive Learning—Beyond Conditioning (pgs. 252-254)

What is cognitive learning?

(252)   *navigate around the town*: move from place to place in your town

(252)   *lowly*: quiet, unassuming

(252)   *mental giant*: extremely intelligent

(253)   *parallelogram*: geometric shape with four straight sides; two sides are one length and the other two sides are of another length.

Modeling—Do as I Do, Not as I Say (pgs. 254-257)

Does learning occur by imitation?

(254)   *tedious:* boring

(254)   *tune-up*: general adjustment of a car to improve performance

(254)   *a large blowup "Bo-Bo the Clown" doll*: an inflatable life-sized plastic doll for children to play with

(255)   *"so why does everybody love Raymond, anyway?"*: reference to the popular TV show, "Everybody Loves Raymond".

(255)   *G-rated*: General audience; something anyone can watch

(256)   *ominously*: threateningly

(256)   *writhe*: to twist in pain

(256)   *desensitizes*: makes less sensitive to something

(257)   *permissible*: allowable; acceptable

Behavioral Self-Management— Wouldn't You Like to Reward Yourself? (pgs. 258-260)

How does conditioning apply to practical problems?

(258)   Guitar Hero: popular video game in which players use a controller to mimic notes and chords played during popular songs.

(258)   *fall short*: fail to reach your goal

(259)   *sharp-edged humor*: harsh, often sarcastic

(259)   *scramble*: mix up; put out of order

(259)   *junk food*: food with little nutritional value

(260)   *forfeit*: give up, lose

(260)   *Ku Klux Klan*: a racist secret society in the U.S.; its members are opposed to minorities

(260)   *American Nazi Party*: racist political group opposed to minorities, especially Jews

Solutions

Recite and Review

What Is Learning—Does Practice Make Perfect?

1. behavior, precede, follow
2. association, knowing
3. conditioning, conditioning
4. stimulus, responses
5. reinforced, Operant

Classical Conditioning—Does the Name Pavlov Ring a Bell? and Principles of Classical Conditioning – Here's Johnny

1. neutral, response
2. stimulus, learned
3. stimulus
4. stimulus
5. associations, interconnected
6. conditioning
7. response
8. similar
9. stimulus
10. response
11. follow

Classical Conditioning in Humans—An Emotional Topic

1. reflexes, conditioned
2. stimulus
3. secondhand, observe
4. gradually, feared
5. attitudes

Operant Conditioning—Can Pigeons Play Ping-Pong?

1. learning
2. increases, effect
3. response, increases
4. effect
5. reinforcement, response
6. chains, single
7. response
8. operant
9. recovery
10. reward, ends
11. decreases, cost

Operant Reinforcers—What's Your Pleasure?

1. comfort, physical
2. pleasure, brain
3. learned, exchanged
4. secondary, exchanged
5. value, primary
6. reinforcers, learned
7. feedback
8. feedback
9. instruction
10. serious, games

Partial Reinforcement—Las Vegas, a Human Skinner Box?

1. response, partial
2. effect
3. fixed, fixed
4. ratio, responses
5. reinforced
6. high, slow

Stimulus Control—Red Light, Green Light

1. precede
2. discrimination
3. similar
4. S+
5. S–
6. performing

Punishment—Putting the Brakes on Behavior

1. decreases
2. unpleasant, pleasant
3. immediate
4. suppress
5. escape
6. end, response
7. mild, responses

Cognitive Learning—Beyond Conditioning

1. knowing
2. maps, learning
3. understanding, guided

Modeling—Do as I Do, Not as I Say

1. imitation
2. model, model's
3. reproduction
4. models
5. aggressively

Psychology in Action: Behavioral Self-Management—A Rewarding Project

1. Operant
2. feedback
3. responses, principle
4. responses, response, removing
5. behavior
6. learning, goals, successes

CONNECTIONS

What Is Learning—Does Practice Make Perfect?; Classical Conditioning—Does the Name Pavlov Ring a Bell?; Principles of Classical Conditioning – Here's Johnny; and Classical Conditioning in Humans—An Emotional Topic.

1. E.
2. A.
3. I.
4. M.
5. K.
6. B.
7. H.
8. L.
9. C.
10. P.
11. J.
12. D.
13. O.
14. F.
15. G.
16. N.

Operant Conditioning—Can Pigeons Play Ping-Pong? and Operant Reinforcers—What's Your Pleasure?

1. J.
2. O.
3. L.
4. K.
5. N.
6. M.
7. C.
8. F.
9. E.
10. I.
11. H.
12. D.
13. A.
14. G.
15. B.

Partial Reinforcement—Las Vegas, a Human Skinner Box? and Stimulus Control—Red Light, Green Light

1. F.
2. H.
3. I.
4. B.
5. E.
6. A.
7. G.
8. K.
9. C.
10. D.

Punishment—Putting the Brakes on Behavior

1. C.	3. F.	5. E.
2. A.	4. D.	6. B.

Cognitive Learning—Beyond Conditioning; Modeling—Do as I Do, Not as I Say; and Psychology in Action: Behavioral Self-Management—Wouldn't You Like to Reward Yourself?

1. C.	4. B.	7. G.
2. I.	5. H.	8. A.
3. E.	6. D.	9. F.

Check Your Memory

What Is Learning—Does Practice Make Perfect?

1. T	3. T	5. F
2. F	4. F	

Classical Conditioning—Does the Name Pavlov Ring a Bell? and Principles of Classical Conditioning – Here's Johnny

1. F	5. F	9. F	13. T
2. T	6. T	10. T	
3. T	7. F	11. F	
4. T	8. F	12. T	

Classical Conditioning in Humans—An Emotional Topic

1. F	3. T	5. F
2. T	4. F	6. T

Operant Conditioning—Can Pigeons Play Ping-Pong?

1. T	5. T	9. F	13. T
2. F	6. F	10. T	14. F
3. F	7. T	11. F	
4. F	8. T	12. T	

Operant Reinforcers—What's Your Pleasure?

1. F	4. T	7. T	10. F
2. F	5. T	8. F	
3. T	6. F	9. T	

Partial Reinforcement—Las Vegas, a Human Skinner Box?

1. F	4. F	7. F
2. F	5. T	8. F
3. T	6. T	9. F

Stimulus Control—Red Light, Green Light

1. T   2. T   3. F   4. F

Punishment—Putting the Brakes on Behavior

1. T	5. F	9. F	13. T
2. F	6. T	10. T	
3. T	7. T	11. T	
4. T	8. F	12. T	

Cognitive Learning—Beyond Conditioning

1. T	3. F	5. T
2. F	4. T	6. F

Modeling—Do as I Do, Not as I Say

1. F	4. T	7. F
2. T	5. F	8. T
3. F	6. F	9. F

Psychology in Action: Behavioral Self-Management—Wouldn't You Like to Reward Yourself?

1. F	3. F	5. T	7. T
2. T	4. T	6. F	

Final Survey and Review

What Is Learning—Does Practice Make Perfect?

1. permanent, experience, antecedents, consequences
2. learning, cognitive, mental
3. respondent, operant
4. neutral, consequences
5. US, consequences

Classical Conditioning—Does the Name Pavlov Ring a Bell? and Principles of Classical Conditioning – Here's Johnny

1. Pavlov, unconditioned, reflex
2. NS, conditioned
3. acquisition, unconditioned
4. conditioning, conditioned
5. informational, mental
6. extinction, weakened
7. reappearance, recovery
8. stimulus, conditioned
9. discrimination, similar
10. expectancies
11. CS, US

Classical Conditioning in Humans—An Emotional Topic
1. emotional, CERs
2. phobias, generalization
3. emotional, vicariously
4. phobia, calm
5. classical

Operant Conditioning—Can Pigeons Play Ping-Pong?
1. instrumental, reinforcer.
2. operant, Thorndike
3. reinforcer, follows
4. expectation
5. contingent
6. reduces, reinforcer
7. unnecessary, associated
8. shaping
9. extinguish, temporarily
10. positive, negative
11. aversive, response

Operant Reinforcers—What's Your Pleasure?
1. natural, discomfort
2. stimulation
3. reinforcers
4. primary
5. token, reinforcers
6. social, approval
7. new, desired
8. instruction, steps
9. exercises
10. competition, motivation

Partial Reinforcement—Las Vegas, a Human Skinner Box?
1. continuously, Skinner
2. greater
3. ratio, ratio
4. correct
5. average
6. high, alternating

Stimulus Control—Red Light, Green Light
1. stimulus
2. generalization
3. operant, preceding
4. discrimination, +, −
5. noticing, reward

Punishment—Putting the Brakes on Behavior
1. punisher
2. onset, removal
3. consistent
4. temporarily
5. fear, aggression
6. unpleasant, avoidance
7. punishment, alternate

Cognitive Learning—Beyond Conditioning
1. mental
2. internal, hidden
3. insight, strategies

Modeling—Do as I Do, Not as I Say
1. modeling
2. success, failure
3. attention, outcome
4. increases
5. violent

Psychology in Action: Behavioral Self-Management—A Rewarding Project

1. everyday
2. reinforcement, contracting
3. high-probability, Premack
4. extinction, breaking
5. contract, forfeited
6. strategies, progress, corrective

Mastery Test

1. c, p. 242
2. a, p. 236
3. b, p. 228
4. c, p. 234
5. d, p. 235
6. c, p.239
7. c, p. 254-255
8. b, p. 226
9. d, p. 240-241
10. a, p. 243-244
11. d, p. 248-249
12. b, p. 255-256
13. c, p. 227
14. d. p. 232
15. d, p. 228-229
16. a, p. 227
17. b, p. 259
18. c, p. 248
19. d, p. 244
20. a, p. 230-231
21. a, p. 230
22. d, p. 232
23. a, p. 246
24. d, p. 248
25. b, p. 234
26. d, p. 238
27. b, p. 237
28. a, p. 240
29. b, 240-241
30. b, p. 238
31. d, p. 238
32. a, p. 252-254
33. b, p. 254
34. d, p. 255-258
35. c, p. 229

CHAPTER 7

Memory

Chapter Overview

Memory systems encode and store information for later retrieval. A popular model divides memory into three systems: sensory memory, short-term memory (STM), and long-term memory (LTM). Sensory memory stores exact copies of sensory information for very brief periods. STM is limited to about seven bits of information, but chunking and recoding allow more information to be stored. Short-term memories last only a limited time and are very sensitive to interference; however, they can be extended through maintenance rehearsal. Elaborative encoding ensures information moves from STM to LTM. LTM has nearly unlimited storage and is relatively permanent. It undergoes updating, revision, constructive processing, and forgetting. Broadly, LTM is thought to be organized as a network of linked ideas.

Long-term memories can be further divided into declarative memories, which may be semantic or episodic, and procedural memories. Explicit memories are revealed by recall, recognition, and relearning tasks. Implicit memories are revealed by priming. Forgetting is most rapid immediately after learning. Some "forgetting" is based on a failure to encode information. Short-term forgetting is partly explained by the decay (weakening) of memory traces. Some long-term forgetting may also occur this way. Some forgetting is related to a lack of memory cues. Much forgetting is related to interference among memories. Clinical psychologists believe that memories are sometimes repressed (unconsciously held out of awareness). Some also believe that repressed childhood memories of abuse can be "recovered." However, there is often no way to separate true memories from fantasies.

The hippocampus is a structure involved in memory consolidation. Information appears to be stored in the brain through changes in nerve cells. Electrical stimulation to certain parts of the brain (e.g., hippocampus) can interfere with the consolidation of recent memories, whereas strong emotions tend to intensify consolidation. Flashbulb memories are particularly vivid memories (usually of especially emotional events).

Eidetic imagery (photographic memory) is fairly common in children but rare among adults. Many people have internal memory images, and some have exceptional memory based on internal imagery. Exceptional memory capacity is based on both learned strategies and natural abilities.

Memory can be improved by the use of mnemonic systems (e.g., the use of mental pictures) and by attention to factors that affect memory, such as rehearsal, serial position, organization, and the like.

Learning Objectives

1. Define *memory;* explain the three processes of memory—encoding, storage, and retrieval.

2. List the three stages of memory—sensory, short-term, and long-term.

3. Describe sensory memory, including icons and echoes, and how information is transferred from sensory memory to short-term memory.

4. Describe short-term memory, including its capacity, how information is encoded, the permanence of short-term memory and its susceptibility to interference, and the concept of working memory.

5. Describe long-term memory in terms of permanence, capacity, and the basis on which information is stored.

6. Define dual memory, and explain how one's culture affects memory.

7. Explain the "magic number" seven, describe chunking, and explain how the two types of rehearsal affect memory.

8. Discuss the permanence of memory, including the work of Penfield and the Loftuses; explain constructive processing and pseudo-memories; describe the effects of hypnosis on memory and how a cognitive interview can improve eyewitness memories.

9. Briefly describe how long-term memories are organized, including the network model and redintegrative memories.

10. Differentiate procedural (skill) memory from declarative (fact) memory, and define and give examples of the two kinds of declarative memory (semantic and episodic).

11. Explain the tip-of-the tongue state and the feeling of knowing, and describe and give examples of each of the following ways of measuring memory:
    a. recall, including the serial position effect
    b. recognition, including a comparison with recall, and the concept of distractors
    c. relearning, including the concept of savings score

12. Distinguish between explicit and implicit memories and describe priming.

13. Differentiate the concepts of internal mental images and eidetic imagery, and explain how these abilities are different from having an exceptional memory.

14. Explain Ebbinghaus' curve of forgetting.

15. Discuss the following explanations of forgetting:
    a. encoding failure
    b. decay of memory traces
    c. disuse, including why this explanation is questioned

      d. cue-dependent forgetting

      e. state-dependent learning

      f. retroactive and proactive interference

      g. repression, including the recovered memory/false memory debate and how repression differs from suppression

16. Describe flashbulb memories and the role of emotion in memory.

17. Define retrograde and anterograde amnesia, and discuss the role of consolidation in memory, including the effects of Electro-Convulsive Shock.

18. Name the structure in the brain that is responsible for switching information from STM to LTM, and discuss the research on where in the brain different types of memories are stored and the relationship between learning and transmitter chemicals.

19. Describe each of the following in terms of how it can improve memory:

      a. knowledge of results

      b. recitation

      c. rehearsal

      d. selection

      e. organization

      f. whole versus part learning

      g. serial position effect

      h. cues

      i. spaced practice

      j. sleep

      k. hunger

      l. extension of memory intervals

      m. review

      n. strategies to aid recall, including the cognitive interview

20. Define mnemonic, explain the four basic principles of using mnemonics, and describe three techniques for using mnemonics to remember things in order.

RECITE AND REVIEW

Stages of Memory—Do You Have a Mind Like Sieve?

Survey Question: How does memory work? Pages 265-267

1. Memory is an active _____.

2. _____ is first encoded (changed into the form in which it will be retained). Next it is _____ in memory. Later it must be retrieved to be put to use.

3. Humans appear to have _____ interrelated memory systems. These are sensory memory, _____ memory (STM), and _____ memory (LTM).

4. Sensory memory holds an _____ copy of what is seen or heard in the form of an icon (_____) or echo (sound sensation).

5. Iconic memories persist for about one _____-second; echoic memories typically last two seconds.

6. Selective attention controls what information is registered in _____ memory and then transferred to short-term memory.

7. Short-term memories tend to be stored as _____. Long-term memories are stored on the basis of _____, or importance.

8. Short-term memories are brief and very sensitive to _____, or interference; however, they can be prolonged by maintenance rehearsal (silent _____).

9. STM acts as a _____ storehouse for small amounts of information. It provides a working memory where thinking, mental arithmetic, and the like take place. LTM acts as a _____ storehouse for meaningful information.

Short-Term Memory—Do You Know the Magic Number?

Survey Question: What are the features of short-term memory? Pages 268-269

1. The digit-span test reveals that STM has an average upper limit of about seven _____ of information. However, this can be extended by chunking, or recoding, information into _____ units or groups.

2. The "_____ number" seven (plus or minus two) refers to the limitation of _____ memory discovered by George Miller. Nelson Cowan believes that the limitation of short-term memory is _____ than seven.

3. Unless they are actively rehearsed, short-term memories last approximately _____ to eighteen seconds.

4. Elaborative encoding, which emphasizes meaning, helps transfer information from _____ to LTM. Elaborative encoding links new information with existing _____.

Long-Term Memory—A Blast from the Past

Survey Question: What are the features of long-term memory? Pages 269- 274

1. LTM seems to have an almost unlimited storage capacity. However, LTM is subject to constructive processing, or ongoing revision and _____.

2. Because memory is so constructive, advertisers "jam" your memory with positive instances of a product, which may create _____ "memories" of their product.

3. Thoughts, inferences, and _____ associations may be mistaken for actual memories. As a result, people often have pseudo-memories (_____ memories) that they believe are true.

4. When using a cognitive interview, the eyewitness is encouraged to revisit the crime scene, so that potentially useful _____ _____ are provided.

5. LTM is highly _____ to allow retrieval of needed information. The pattern, or structure, of memory networks is the subject of current memory research. Network _____ portray LTM as a system of linked ideas.

6. Redintegrative memories unfold as each added memory provides a cue for retrieving the next _____. Seemingly forgotten memories may be reconstructed in this way.

7. Within long-term memory, declarative memories for _____ seem to differ from procedural memories for _____.

8. Long-term procedural memories are likely stored in the _____.

9. _____ memories may be further categorized as semantic memories or episodic memories.

10. Semantic memories consist of basic factual knowledge that is almost immune to _____.

11. Episodic memories record _____ experiences that are associated with specific times and places.

Measuring Memory—The Answer Is on the Tip of My Tongue

Survey Question: How is memory measured? Pages 275-278

1. The tip-of-the-tongue _____ shows that memory is not an all-or-nothing event.

2. People often experience a feeling of _____, during which people can tell beforehand if they are likely to remember something.

3. Memories may be revealed by _____, recognition, or relearning.

4. In recall, memory proceeds without specific cues, as in an _____ exam.

5. Recall of listed information often reveals a serial position effect. Items at the beginning and _____ of the list are remembered better than those in the _____, which are the items on the list that are most subject to errors.

6. A common test of _____ is the multiple-choice question.

7. _____ is very accurate for pictures and photographs, but it is sensitive to the kinds of distractors (wrong choices) used.

8. _____ is often superior to recall.

9. In relearning, "forgotten" material is learned again, and memory is indicated by a _____ score.

10. Recall, recognition, and relearning mainly measure explicit _____ that we are aware of having. Other techniques, such as priming, are necessary to reveal implicit _____, which are unconscious.

11. Priming is used to activate _____ memories

Forgetting—Why We, Uh, Let's See; Why We, Uh . . . Forget!

Survey Question: Why do we forget? Pages 278-284

1. Forgetting and memory were extensively studied by Herman Ebbinghaus, whose _____ of forgetting shows that forgetting is typically most rapid immediately _____ learning.

2. Ebbinghaus used nonsense syllables to study memory. The forgetting of _____ material is much _____ than shown by his curve of forgetting.

3. Failure to encode _____ is a common cause of "forgetting."

4. Forgetting in sensory memory and STM probably reflects decay of memory _____ in the nervous system.

5. Decay or _____ of memories may also account for some LTM loss, but most forgetting cannot be explained this way.

6. Often, forgetting is cue dependent. The power of cues to trigger memories is revealed by state-dependent _____, in which bodily _____ at the time of learning and of retrieval affect memory.

7. Much _____ in both STM and LTM can be attributed to interference of memories with one another.

8. When recent learning _____ with retrieval of prior learning, retroactive interference has occurred. If old memories _____ with new memories, proactive interference has occurred.

9. Repression is the _____ of painful, embarrassing, or traumatic memories.

10. Repression is thought to be unconscious, in contrast to suppression, which is a _____ attempt to avoid thinking about something.

11. Experts are currently debating the validity of childhood memories of _____ that reappear after apparently being repressed for decades.

12. Independent evidence has verified that some recovered memories are _____. However, others have been shown to be _____.

13. In the absence of confirming or disconfirming _____, there is currently no way to separate true memories from fantasies. Caution is

advised for all concerned with attempts to retrieve supposedly hidden memories.

Memory and the Brain—Some "Shocking" Findings

Survey Question: How does the brain form and store memories? Pages 284-287

1. Retrograde amnesia involves forgetting events that occurred _____ an injury or trauma; anterograde amnesia involves forgetting events that _____ an injury or trauma.

2. Retrograde _____ and the effects of electroconvulsive _____ (ECS) may be explained by the concept of consolidation.

3. Until they are consolidated, _____ memories are easily destroyed by amnesia or interference.

4. The hippocampus is a _____ structure associated with the consolidation of memories.

5. Recent memories are more easily disrupted than _____ memories.

6. Flashbulb memories, which seem especially vivid, are created at emotionally significant times. While such memories may not be accurate, we tend to place great _____ in them.

7. Long-term memories tend to be stored in the _____ of the brain, with episodic memories in the front and semantic memories in the back.

Exceptional Memory—Wizards of Recall

Survey Question: What are "photographic" memories? Pages 287-290

1. Eidetic imagery (photographic memory) occurs when a person is able to project an _____ onto an external surface. Such images allow brief, nearly complete recall by some children.

2. Eidetic imagery is rarely found in _____. However, many adults have internal images, which can be very vivid and a basis for remembering.

3. Exceptional memory can be learned by finding ways to directly store information in _____. These include using memory strategies and techniques, have specialized interests and _____, and have naturally superior memory skills.

4. Exceptional memorizers do _____ necessarily have superior intellectual abilities or _____ brains.

Improving Memory—Keys to the Memory Bank

Survey Question: How can I improve my memory? Pages 290-294

1. Memory can be improved by using a combination of _____ and retrieval strategies.

2. Fully encoding information, engaging in _____ rehearsal, selecting and organizing information, using the progressive _____ method, spaced practice, overlearning, and paying attention to _____ are all encoding strategies to improve memory.

3. Retrieval strategies can improve memory, such as _____ and recitation.

4. The _____ interview and planned search of memory help to recapture partial memories.

5. The effects of serial _____, sleep, and hunger should also be kept in mind when studying or memorizing.

Psychology in Action: Mnemonics—Memory Magic

Survey Question: Are there any tricks to help me with my memory? Pages 294-297

1. Mnemonic techniques avoid rote learning and work best during the _____ stages of learning.

2. Mnemonic systems, such as the _____ method, use mental images and unusual associations to link new information with familiar memories already stored in _____. Such strategies give information personal meaning and make it easier to recall.

3. Visual pictures are easier to remember than words, especially if the images form _____, unusual, or exaggerated _____ associations.

CONNECTIONS

Stages of Memory—Do You Have a Mind Like a Sieve?

Survey Question: How does memory work? Pages 265-267

1. _____ storage   A. hard drive

2. _____ encoding   B. STM

3. _____ sensory memory   C. lasts for two to three seconds

4. _____ Long-term memory   D. keyboard

5. _____ echoes and icons   E. sensory memory

6. _____ working memory   F. meaning

1. _____ selective attention
2. _____ long-term memory
3. _____ incoming information
4. _____ encoding for LTM
5. _____ sensory memory
6. _____ short-term memory
7. _____ rehearsal buffer

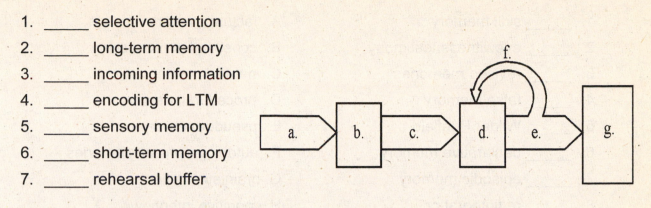

Short-Term Memory—Do You Know the Magic Number?

Survey Question: What are the features of short-term memory? Pages 268-269

1. _____ five to nine information bits   A. magic number
2. _____ maintenance rehearsal   B. recoding
3. _____ elaborative encoding   C. linking new to old memories
4. _____ chunking   D. repetition

Long-Term Memory—A Blast from the Past

Survey Question: What are the features of long-term memory? Pages 269-274

1. _____ semantic memory
2. _____ long-term memory
3. _____ procedural memory
4. _____ sensory memory
5. _____ episodic memory
6. _____ short-term memory
7. _____ declarative memory

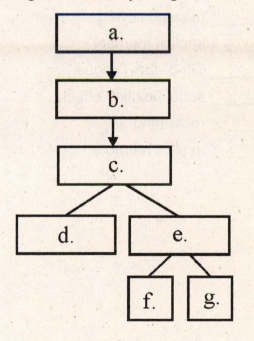

1. _____ skill memory   A. factual memory

2. _____ eyewitness testimony   B. constructive processing

3. _____ revised memories   C. network model

4. _____ false memory   D. procedural memory

5. _____ Wilder Penfield   E. pseudo-memory

6. _____ declarative memory   F. autobiographical memories

7. _____ episodic memory   G. brain stimulation

8. _____ redintegration   H. cognitive interview

Measuring Memory—The Answer Is on the Tip of My Tongue.

Survey Questions: How is memory measured? Pages 275-278

1. _____ relearning   A. retrieval of facts

2. _____ recall   B. middle items are least recalled

3. _____ Feeling of knowing   C. multiple-choice questions

4. _____ recognition memory   D. available but not retrievable

5. _____ Priming   E. conscious memories

6. _____ false positive   F. memories outside of awareness

7. _____ implicit memory   G. memory test

8. _____ Tip-of-the-Tongue   H. mistaken recognition

9. _____ serial position effect   I. likely to remember

10. _____ relearning   J. activating hidden memories

11. _____ explicit memory   K. savings score

Forgetting—Why We, Uh, Let's See; Why We, Uh . . . Forget!

Survey Question: Why do We Forget? Pages 278-284

1. _____ state dependent
2. _____ suppression
3. _____ Disuse
4. _____ nonsense syllable
5. _____ False positive
6. _____ repression
7. _____ Encoding failure
8. _____ cue-dependent memory
9. _____ interference
10. _____ Proactive interference
11. _____ Ebbinghaus

A. WOL
B. forgetting curve
C. in same frame of mind
D. stimulus linked to a memory
E. motivated forgetting
F. conscious forgetting
G. prevent retrieval of information
H. memory never formed
I. infrequent retrieval
J. new learning inhibits old learning
K. mistaken recognition

Memory and the Brain—Some "Shocking" Findings

Survey Question: How does the brain form and store memories? How can I improve my memory? Pages 284-287

1. _____ flashbulb memory
2. _____ cerebellum
3. _____ amnesia
4. _____ hippocampus
5. _____ episodic memory
6. _____ consolidation
7. _____ erases memory
8. _____ semantic memory

A. form lasting memory
B. Electro Convulsive Shock
C. vivid emotional event
D. memory loss
E. frontal cortex
F. back cortex
G. skill memories
H. consolidation of memories

Exceptional Memory – Wizards of Recall and Improving Memory – Keys to the Memory Bank

Survey Question: What are "photographic" memories? How can I improve my memory? Pages 287-294

1. _____ selection
2. _____ Recitation
3. _____ mental images
4. _____ Spaced practice
5. _____ order of events
6. _____ Cues
7. _____ Learned extension of normal
8. _____ Rehearsal
9. _____ eidetic imagery

A. mental pictures
B. photographic memory
C. exceptional memory
D. summarize ideas
E. form a story
F. mental review
G. summarize out loud
I. study in short periods
J. aid retrieval

CHECK YOUR MEMORY

Stages of Memory—Do You Have a Mind Like a Sieve?

Survey Question: How does memory work? Pages 265-267

1. Incoming information must be encoded before it is stored in memory.

   TRUE or FALSE

2. Sensory memories last for a few minutes or less.

   TRUE or FALSE

3. A memory that cannot be retrieved has little value.

   TRUE or FALSE

4. Selective attention influences what information enters STM.

   TRUE or FALSE

5. Working memory is another name for sensory memory.

   TRUE or FALSE

6. Errors in long-term memory tend to focus on the sounds of words.

   TRUE or FALSE

7. Generally, the more you know, the more new information you can store in long-term memory.

TRUE or FALSE

8. The three basic memory systems are short-term memory, long-term memory, and personal memory

TRUE or FALSE

9. Three basic memory processes are encoding, storage, and retrieval

TRUE or FALSE

10. An echoic memory is a brief memory for images

TRUE or FALSE

11. Memories in short-term memory are fragile, and easily disrupted by interference or interruption

TRUE or FALSE

Short-Term Memory—Do You Know the Magic Number?

Survey Question: What are the features of short-term memory? Pages 268-269

1. For many kinds of information, STM can store an average of ten bits of information.

TRUE or FALSE

2. Nelson Cowan coined the term "magic number."

TRUE or FALSE

3. Chunking recodes information into smaller units that are easier to fit into STM.

TRUE or FALSE

4. The more times a short-term memory is rehearsed, the better its chance of being stored in LTM.

TRUE or FALSE

5. On average, short-term memories last only about 18 minutes, unless they are rehearsed.

TRUE or FALSE

6. Maintenance rehearsal keeps memories active in sensory memory.

TRUE or FALSE

7. Elaborative encoding is the best way to move information from short-term memory to long-term memory

TRUE or FALSE

Long-Term Memory—A Blast from the Past

Survey Question: What are the features of long-term memory? Pages 269-274

1. The surface of the brain records the past like a movie, complete with sound track.

TRUE or FALSE

2. Long-term memory is *relatively* permanent as we tend to update, change, lose, or revise our old memories.

TRUE or FALSE

3. Being confident about a memory tells little about the true accuracy of the memory.

TRUE or FALSE

4. Long-term memories appear to be organized alphabetically for speedy access.

TRUE or FALSE

5. False memory refers to having memories that never happened.

TRUE or FALSE

6. It is difficult to implant false memories.

TRUE or FALSE

7. Hypnosis increases false memories more than it does true ones.

TRUE or FALSE

8. Recalling events from different viewpoints is part of doing a cognitive interview.

TRUE or FALSE

9. Cognitive interview and standard questioning produce the same percentage of correct recall given by eyewitnesses.

TRUE or FALSE

10. Knowing how to swing a golf club is a type of declarative memory.

TRUE or FALSE

11. A person lacking declarative memory might still remember how to solve a mechanical puzzle.

TRUE or FALSE

12. Semantic memories are almost immune to forgetting.

TRUE or FALSE

13. Semantic memories are a type of declarative memory.

TRUE or FALSE

14. Episodic memories have no connection to particular times and places.

TRUE or FALSE

15. Redintegration explains how one memory serves as a cue to trigger another

TRUE or FALSE

Measuring Memory—The Answer Is on the Tip of My Tongue

Survey Question: How is memory measured? Pages 275-278

1. Remembering the first sound of a name you are trying to recall is an example of the tip-of-the-tongue state.

TRUE or FALSE

2. Tests of recognition require verbatim memory.

TRUE or FALSE

3. The serial position effect measures the strength of the feeling of knowing.

TRUE or FALSE

4. Recognition tends to be a more sensitive test of memory than recall.

TRUE or FALSE

5. False positives and distractors greatly affect the accuracy of relearning tests.

TRUE or FALSE

6. Recall, recognition, and relearning are used to measure explicit memories.

TRUE or FALSE

7. Priming is used to activate explicit (hidden) memories.

TRUE or FALSE

8. A false sense of recognition may lead to the conviction of an innocent individual.

TRUE or FALSE

9. Relearning is often reported as a learning score.

TRUE or FALSE

Forgetting—Why We, Uh, Let's See; Why We, Uh . . . Forget!

Survey Question: Why Do We Forget? Pages 278-284

1. Ebbinghaus chose to learn nonsense syllables so that they would all be the same length.

TRUE or FALSE

2. Ebbinghaus' curve of forgetting levels off after two days, showing little further memory loss after that.

TRUE or FALSE

3. Ebbinghaus' curve of forgetting only applies to memories of nonsense syllables.

TRUE or FALSE

4. The magic card trick demonstrates our ability to focus and pay attention.

TRUE or FALSE

5. Eyewitnesses are better at identifying members of other ethnic groups since they "look" different.
Choice T: True

6. Things that we considered "forgotten" may have actually never been encoded in the first place.

TRUE or FALSE

7. Decay of memory traces clearly applies to information in STM.

TRUE or FALSE

8. Disuse theories of forgetting answer the question: Have I been storing the information in the first place?

TRUE or FALSE

9. The presence of memory cues almost always improves memory.

TRUE or FALSE

10. Information learned under the influence of a drug may be best remembered when the drugged state occurs again.

TRUE or FALSE

11. If you are in a bad mood, you are more likely to remember unpleasant events.

TRUE or FALSE

12. Categorizing a person as a member of a group tends to limit the accuracy of memories about the person's appearance.

TRUE or FALSE

13. Proactive interference occurs when something that was previously learned interferes with later learning.

TRUE or FALSE

14. Sleeping tends to interfere with retaining new memories.

TRUE or FALSE

15. You learn information A and then information B. If your memory of B is lowered by having first learned A, you have experienced retroactive interference.

TRUE or FALSE

16. Interference only applies to the initial stage of learning. Learned information is permanent and can be easily retrieved.

TRUE or FALSE

17. Unconsciously forgetting painful memories is called negative transfer.

TRUE or FALSE

18. A conscious attempt to put a memory out of mind is called repression.

TRUE or FALSE

19. Elizabeth Loftus demonstrated the ease of implanting false memories by simply suggesting to Alan Alda that he does not like hard-boiled eggs, which he later avoided eating at a picnic.

TRUE or FALSE

20. Suggestion and fantasy are elements of many techniques used in attempts to recover repressed memories.

TRUE or FALSE

21. Unless a memory can be independently confirmed, there is no way to tell if it is real or not.

TRUE or FALSE

Memory and the Brain—Some "Shocking" Findings

Survey Question: How does the brain form and store memories? Pages 284-287

1. Consolidation refers to the process of erasing memories prior to head injury or trauma

TRUE or FALSE

2. After an injury, older memories are more easily disrupted than newer memories, as they are often decayed from disuse

TRUE or FALSE

3. Retrograde amnesia is a gap in memories of events preceding a head injury.

TRUE or FALSE

4. People with damage to the hippocampus typically cannot remember events that occurred before the damage.

TRUE or FALSE

5. Storing memories alters the activity, structure, and chemistry of the brain.

TRUE or FALSE

6. Flashbulb memories tend to be formed when an event is surprising or emotional.

TRUE or FALSE

7. The confidence we have in flashbulb memories is well placed—they are much more accurate than most other memories.

TRUE or FALSE

8. Once formed, declarative memories tend to be stored in the cerebellum of the brain

TRUE or FALSE

Exceptional Memory—Wizards of Recall; Improving Memory— Keys to the Memory Bank, and Psychology in Action: Mnemonics—Memory Magic

Survey Questions: What are "photographic" memories? How can I improve my memory? Are there any tricks to help me with my memory? Pages 287-297

1. Eidetic images last for 30 seconds or more.

TRUE or FALSE

2. About 8 percent of all children have eidetic images.

TRUE or FALSE

3. Eidetic imagery becomes rare by adulthood.

TRUE or FALSE

4. Mr. S. (the mnemonist) had virtually unlimited eidetic imagery.

TRUE or FALSE

5. Practice in remembering one type of information increases the capacity of STM to store other types of information, too.

TRUE or FALSE

6. All contestants in the World Memory Championship performed poorly on tasks that prevented the use of learned strategies.

TRUE or FALSE

7. Exceptional memorizers often possess superior memory abilities and intellectual ability.

TRUE or FALSE

8. Recitation is a good way to generate feedback while studying.

TRUE or FALSE

9. Elaborative encoding involving "why" questions improve memory.

TRUE or FALSE

10. Overlearning is inefficient; you should stop studying at the point of initial mastery of new information.

TRUE or FALSE

11. Massed practice is almost always superior to spaced practice.

TRUE or FALSE

12. When learning, it helps to gradually extend how long you remember new information before reviewing it again.

TRUE or FALSE

13. Roy G. Biv is a mnemonic for the notes on a musical staff.

TRUE or FALSE

14. Many mnemonics make use of mental images or pictures.

TRUE or FALSE

15. Mnemonics often link new information to familiar memories.

TRUE or FALSE

16. The keyword method is superior to rote learning for memorizing vocabulary words in another language.

TRUE or FALSE

17. Memory cues are largely irrelevant and should be ignored while studying to avoid contamination effects.

TRUE or FALSE

18. A good night's rest and a good breakfast are important components for optimal memory performance.

TRUE or FALSE

FINAL SURVEY AND REVIEW

Stages of Memory—Do You Have a Mind Like Sieve?

Survey Question: How does memory work? Pages 265-267

1. Memory is an _____ system.

2. Information is first _____ (changed into the form in which it will be retained). Next it is stored in memory. Later it must be _____ to be put to use.

3. Humans appear to have three interrelated memory systems. These are _____ memory, short-term memory (STM), and long-term memory (LTM).

4. Sensory memory holds an exact _____ of what is seen or heard in the form of an _____ (image) or _____ (sound sensation).

5. Iconic memories persist for about one half-second; _____ memories typically last two seconds.

6. Selective _____ controls what information is registered in sensory memory and then _____ to short-term memory.

7. _____ memories tend to be stored as sounds. _____ memories are stored on the basis of meaning, or importance.

8. Short-term memories are brief and very sensitive to interruption, or _____; however, they can be prolonged by _____ rehearsal (silent repetition).

9. STM acts as a temporary storehouse for small amounts of information. It provides a _____ memory where thinking, mental arithmetic, and the like take place. LTM acts as a permanent storehouse for _____ information.

Short-Term Memory—Do You Know the Magic Number?

Survey Question: What are the features of short-term memory? Pages 268-269

1. The digit-span test reveals that STM has an average upper limit of about _____ bits of information. However, this can be extended by _____, or recoding, information into larger units or groups.

2. The "magic number" seven (plus or minus two) refers to the _____ of short-term memory discovered by George _____. Nelson _____ believes that the limitation of short-term memory is lower than seven.

3. Unless they are actively rehearsed, short-term memories last approximately twelve to _____ seconds.

4. Elaborative encoding, which emphasizes _____, helps transfer information from STM to LTM. Elaborative encoding links new _____ with existing memories.

Long-Term Memory—A Blast from the Past

Survey Question: What are the features of long-term memory? Pages 269- 274

1. LTM seems to have an almost _____ storage capacity. However, LTM is subject to constructive processing, or ongoing _____ and updating.

2. Because memory is so _____, advertisers "jam" your memory with _____ instances of a product, which may create false "memories" of their product.

3. Thoughts, _____, and mental associations may be mistaken for actual memories. As a result, people often have _____-memories (false memories) that they believe are true.

4. When using a _____ interview, the eyewitness is encouraged to revisit the crime scene, so that potentially useful retrieval cues are provided.

5. LTM is highly organized to allow retrieval of needed information. The pattern, or structure, of memory _____ is the subject of current memory research. Network models portray LTM as a system of _____ ideas.

6. Redintegrative memories unfold as each added memory provides a _____ for retrieving the next memory. Seemingly _____ memories may be reconstructed in this way.

7. Within long-term memory, _____ memories for facts seem to differ from _____ memories for skills.

8. Long-term _____ memories are likely stored in the cerebellum.

9. Declarative memories may be further categorized as _____ memories or _____ memories.

10. Semantic memories consist of basic _____ knowledge that is almost immune to forgetting.

11. _____ memories record personal experiences that are associated with specific times and places.

Measuring Memory—The Answer Is on the Tip of My Tongue

Survey Question: How is memory measured? Pages 275-278

1. The _____-of-the-tongue state shows that memory is not an _____ event.

2. People often experience a _____ of knowing, during which people can tell beforehand if they are _____ to remember something.

3. Memories may be revealed by recall, _____, or relearning.

4. In recall, memory proceeds without specific _____, as in an essay exam.

5. Recall of listed information often reveals a _____ position effect. Items at the _____ and end of the list are remembered better than those in the middle, which are the items on the list that are most subject to errors.

6. A common test of recognition is the _____-choice question.

7. Recognition is very accurate for _____ and photographs, but it is sensitive to the kinds of _____ (wrong choices) used.

8. Recognition is often _____ to recall

9. In _____, "forgotten" material is learned again, and memory is indicated by a savings _____.

10. Recall, recognition, and _____ mainly measure explicit memories that we are aware of having. Other techniques, such as _____, are necessary to reveal implicit memories, which are unconscious.

11. _____ is used to activate hidden memories

Forgetting—Why We, Uh, Let's See; Why We, Uh . . . Forget!

Survey Question: Why do we forget? Pages 278-284

1. Forgetting and memory were extensively studied by Herman _____, whose curve of forgetting shows that forgetting is typically most rapid immediately after _____.

2. Ebbinghaus used _____ syllables to study memory. The forgetting of meaningful material is much slower than shown by his curve of _____.

3. Failure to _____ information is a common cause of "forgetting."

4. Forgetting in _____ memory and STM probably reflects decay of memory traces in the nervous system.

5. Decay or disuse of memories may also account for some _____ loss, but most forgetting cannot be explained this way.

6. Often, forgetting is _____ dependent. The power of cues to trigger memories is revealed by _____-dependent learning, in which bodily states at the time of learning and of retrieval affect memory.

7. Much forgetting in both STM and LTM can be attributed to _____ of memories with one another.

8. When recent learning interferes with retrieval of prior learning, _____ interference has occurred. If old memories interfere with _____ memories, proactive interference has occurred.

9. Repression is the forgetting of painful, embarrassing, or _____ memories.

10. Repression is thought to be _____, in contrast to _____, which is a conscious attempt to avoid thinking about something.

11. Experts are currently debating the validity of childhood memories of abuse that reappear after apparently being _____ for decades.

12. Independent evidence has verified that some _____ memories are true. However, others have been shown to be false.

13. In the absence of confirming or disconfirming evidence, there is currently no way to separate true memories from _____. Caution is advised for all concerned with attempts to retrieve supposedly hidden memories.

Memory and the Brain—Some "Shocking" Findings

Survey Question: How does the brain form and store memories? Pages 284-287

1. _____ amnesia involves forgetting events that occurred before an injury or trauma; _____ amnesia involves forgetting events that follow an injury or trauma.

2. Retrograde amnesia and the effects of _____ shock (ECS) may be explained by the concept of consolidation.

3. Until they are _____, long-term memories are easily destroyed by amnesia or interference.

4. The _____ is a brain structure associated with the consolidation of memories.

5. Recent memories are more easily disrupted than _____ memories.

6. Flashbulb memories, which seem especially _____, are created at emotionally significant times. While such memories may not be _____, we tend to place great confidence in them.

7. Long-term memories tend to be stored in the cortex of the brain, with _____ memories in the front and _____ memories in the back.

Exceptional Memory—Wizards of Recall

Survey Question: What are "photographic" memories? Pages 287-290

1. Eidetic imagery (_____ memory) occurs when a person is able to project an image onto an _____ surface. Such images allow brief, nearly complete recall by some children.

2. Eidetic imagery is _____ found in adults. However, many adults have internal images, which can be very _____ and a basis for remembering.

3. Exceptional memory can be learned by finding ways to directly store information in LTM. These include using memory _____ and techniques, have specialized interests and knowledge, and have naturally _____ memory skills.

4. Exceptional memorizers do not necessarily have _____ intellectual abilities or different brains.

Improving Memory—Keys to the Memory Bank

Survey Question: How can I improve my memory? Pages 290-294

1. Memory can be improved by using a combination of encoding and _____ strategies.

2. Fully encoding information, engaging in elaborative encoding, _____ and organizing information, using the progressive part method, _____ practice, overlearning, and paying attention to cues are all encoding strategies to _____ memory.

3. Retrieval strategies can improve memory, such as feedback and _____.

4. The cognitive interview and _____ search of memory help to recapture partial memories.

5. The effects of serial position, _____, and hunger should also be kept in mind when studying or memorizing.

Psychology in Action: Mnemonics—Memory Magic

Survey Question: Are there any tricks to help me with my memory? Pages 294-297

1. Mnemonic techniques avoid _____ learning and work best during the initial stages of learning.

2. Mnemonic systems, such as the keyword method, use mental _____ and _____ associations to link new information with familiar memories already stored in LTM. Such strategies give information personal meaning and make it easier to recall.

3. Visual pictures are easier to remember than words, especially if the images form bizarre, _____, or _____ mental associations.

MASTERY TEST

1. The meaning and importance of information has a strong impact on
a. sensory memory.
b. eidetic memory.
c. long-term memory.
d. procedural memory.

2. Pseudomemories are closely related to the effects of
a. repression.
b. suppression.
c. semantic forgetting.
d. constructive processing.

3. The occurrence of _____ implies that consolidation has been prevented.
a. retrograde amnesia
b. hippocampal transfer
c. suppression
d. changes in the activities of individual nerve cells

4. Most of the techniques used to recover supposedly repressed memories involve
a. redintegration and hypnosis.
b. suggestion and fantasy.
c. reconstruction and priming.
d. coercion and fabrication.

5. Most daily memory chores are handled by
a. sensory memory and LTM.
b. STM and working memory.
c. STM and LTM.
d. STM and declarative memory.

6. Three key processes in memory systems are
a. storage, organization, recovery.
b. encoding, attention, reprocessing.
c. storage, retrieval, encoding.
d. retrieval, reprocessing, reorganization.

7. An ability to answer questions about distances on a map you have seen only once implies that some memories are based on
a. constructive processing.
b. redintegration.
c. mental images.
d. episodic processing.

8. The first potential cause of forgetting that may occur is
a. engram decay.
b. disuse.
c. cue-dependent forgetting.
d. encoding failure.

9. The persistence of icons and echoes is the basis for
a. sensory memory.
b. short-term memory.
c. long-term memory.
d. working memory.

10. Priming is most often used to reveal
a. semantic memories.
b. episodic memories.
c. implicit memories.
d. eidetic memories.

11. "Projection" onto an external surface is most characteristic of
a. sensory memories.
b. eidetic images.
c. flashbulb memories.
d. mnemonic images.

12. Chunking especially helps to extend the capacity of
a. sensory memory.
b. STM.
c. LTM.
d. declarative memory.

13. There is presently no way to tell if a "recovered" memory is true or false unless independent _____ exists.
a. evidence
b. amnesia
c. elaboration
d. consolidation

14. Taking an essay test inevitably requires a person to use
a. recall.
b. recognition.
c. relearning.
d. priming.

15. A savings score is used in what memory task?
a. recall
b. recognition
c. relearning
d. priming

16. _____ encoding helps link new information to existing memories by concentrating on meaning.
a. Redintegrative
b. Constructive
c. Maintenance
d. Elaborative

17. Middle items are neither held in STM nor moved to LTM. This statement explains the
a. feeling of knowing.
b. serial position effect.
c. tip-of-the-tongue state.
d. semantic forgetting curve.

18. According to the curve of forgetting, the greatest decline in the amount recalled occurs during the _____ after learning.
a. first hour
b. second day
c. third to sixth days
d. retroactive period

19. Work with brain stimulation, truth serums, and hypnosis suggests that long-term memories are
a. stored in the hippocampus.
b. relatively permanent.
c. unaffected by later input.
d. always redintegrative.

20. Which of the following is most likely to improve the accuracy of memory?
a. hypnosis
b. constructive processing
c. the serial position effect
d. memory cues

21. To qualify as repression, forgetting must be
a. retroactive.
b. proactive.
c. unconscious.
d. explicit.

22. Which of the following typically is NOT a good way to improve memory?
a. massed practice
b. overlearning
c. rehearsal
d. recall strategies

23. A witness to a crime is questioned in ways that recreate the context of the crime and that provide many memory cues. It appears that she is undergoing
    a. retroactive priming.
    b. the progressive part method.
    c. retroactive consolidation.
    d. a cognitive interview.

24. One thing that is clearly true about flashbulb memories is that
    a. they are unusually accurate.
    b. we place great confidence in them.
    c. they apply primarily to public tragedies.
    d. they are recovered by using visualization and hypnosis.

25. One common mnemonic strategy is the
    a. serial position technique.
    b. feeling of knowing tactic.
    c. network procedure.
    d. keyword method.

26. A perspective that helps explain redintegrative memories is
    a. the feeling of knowing model.
    b. recoding and chunking.
    c. the network model.
    d. mnemonic models.

27. Which of the following is NOT considered a part of long-term memory?
    a. echoic memory
    b. semantic memory
    c. episodic memory
    d. declarative memory

28. You are very thirsty. Suddenly you remember a time years ago when you became very thirsty while hiking. This suggests that your memory is
    a. proactive.
    b. state dependent.
    c. still not consolidated.
    d. eidetic.

29. After memorizing five lists of words you recall less of the last list than a person who only memorized list number five. This observation is explained by
    a. reactive processing.
    b. reconstructive processing.
    c. proactive interference.
    d. retroactive interference.

30. New memories are consolidated by the
    a. cerebellum.
    b. hypothalamus.
    c. cortex.
    d. hippocampus.

31. The fact that James can drive a stick shift without consciously recalling the necessary memories suggests that he is accessing
a. procedural memories.
b. short-term memories.
c. declarative memories.
d. eidetic memories.

32. On a TV game show, you are asked which way Lincoln's head faces on a penny. You are unable to answer correctly and you lose a large prize. Your memory failure is most likely a result of
a. the serial position effect.
b. repression.
c. encoding failure.
d. priming.

33. Semantic memories are stored in the _____ of the cerebral cortex; episodic memories are stored in the _____
a. front; front
b. front; back
c. back; front
d. back; back

34. To reduce false identification from eyewitnesses, police should
a. have witnesses view all the pictures of people at one time.
b. have witnesses view pictures of people one at a time.
c. use hypnosis since it has proven to be a reliable source of data gathering.
d. not use eyewitness testimonies since they are not reliable.

35. A card dealer asks you to silently pick out a card from the six cards laid out in front of you and to memorize it. Without knowing the card you picked, he takes your card away and presents to you the other five cards. To perform this trick properly, the dealer hopes that
a. you failed to encode the other five cards as you memorize the card you picked.
b. you do have eidetic memory.
c. you believe that he can read your mind.
d. the serial position effect does influence your memory.

LANGUAGE DEVELOPMENT
Memory

Word Roots

In Latin, *retro* refers to "backward" or "behind" and is a root word in two terms in this chapter, *retroactive interference* and *retrograde amnesia*. In Latin, *pro* means "for," and as a word root, it often suggests going forward. It is also part of two terms in this chapter, *proactive interference* and *procedural memory*, and it is also found as part of several other psychological terms in later chapters. In upcoming chapters, watch for programmed instruction, projective tests, projection, and prosocial behavior.

Journey into Psychology: Fuhgeddaboudit (p. 264)
(264)   ***Fuhgeddaboudit:*** parody of New York City slang for "forget about it"
(264)   ***mnemonist:*** a person who uses special techniques (mnemonics) to improve the memory

Stages of Memory—Do You Have a Mind Like a Sieve? (pgs. 265-267)
How does memory work?
(265)   ***a mind like a sieve:*** a very poor memory; a sieve is used to drain foods, like pasta
(265)   ***a dusty storehouse:*** a storage area that is not often used
(266)   ***fleeting:*** passing quickly; not lasting
(266)   ***flurry:*** a quick movement
(266)   ***dumped:*** removed
(266)   ***"mental scratch pad":*** an area of the brain for writing and reading notes; it doesn't exist in a literal form, but is used here to represent working memory
(266)   ***aardvark:*** a South African mammal that eats ants and termites
(266)   **Desperate Housewives:** a currently popular TV show
(267)   ***hocked gem:*** a gem that has been pawned or traded in
(267)   ***scornful:*** showing dislike or disrespect
(267)   ***forging along:*** moving along steadily
(267)   ***Columbus:*** explorer credited with discovering America in 1492

Short-Term Memory—Do You Know the Magic Number? (pgs. 268-269)
What are the features of short-term memory?
(268)   ***quirks:*** traits someone has that set him/her apart from other people; peculiar trait
(268)   ***IBM:*** International Business Machines, a very large U.S.-based computer company
(268)   ***USN:*** United States Navy

(268) **YMCA**: Young Men's Christian Association, an international organization that promotes the spiritual, social, and physical welfare of young men (originally)

Long-Term Memory—A Blast From the Past (pgs. 269-274)

What are the features of long-term memory?

(269) *electrode*: a conductor used to establish electrical contact with a nonmetallic part of a circuit; medically, a small circular conductor with adhesive on one side (to attach to the body) and a metal piece on the other side on which a monitoring device is attached,

(270) *Disney:* Film producer and creator of Disney characters, including Mickey Mouse.

(270) *Warner Brothers:* large producer of movies and entertainment. Informal rival of Disney.

(270) *Bugs Bunny:* one of the most well-known Warner Brothers characters.

(270) *Disneyland*: vacation resort in Florida dedicated entirely to the world and characters created by Walt Disney.

(271) *hot girl:* very attractive female

(271) *forensic*: pertaining to the law and/or legal system

(271) *voila*!: French – there it is!

(272) *abducted*: kidnapped; taken against one's will

(272) *break the case*: solve the crime; find the criminals

(272) *to weave*: to form and connect by moving side to side; in this case it refers to inserting false information into memories

(272) *corroborating*: confirming or supporting

(272) *jogging*: to encourage remembering

(272) *unleashed a flood of*: having allowed an abundance of information to be released or come out all at once

(273) *hypothetical*: assumed as an example

(273) *touched off by*: is reached and recalled

(273) *encyclopedia*: a work in several volumes that contains information on all branches of knowledge

(274) *autobiographical*: historical events and records of one's own life

Measuring Memory—The Answer Is on the Tip of My Tongue (pgs. 275-278)

How is memory measured?

(275) *"drew a blank"*: could not remember

(275) *World Series*: a series of baseball games played each fall to decide the professional championship of the U.S.

(275) **Hamlet**: a play written by William Shakespeare

(276) *police lineups*: a line of people arranged for inspection by the victim or witness of a crime to help identify the criminal

(276) *"It's all Greek to me!":* As many people do not read Greek, this expression is meant to indicate confusion over written text.

(277)   *Kanye West:* well-known and popular hip hop music artist
(277)   *"prime":* activate; stimulate

Forgetting—Why We, Uh, Let's See; Why We, Uh . . . Forget! (pgs. 278-284)

Why do we Forget?

(279)   *cramming:* studying a large amount of information in a short amount of time just before an examination
(281)   *senile:* showing a loss of mental abilities as a result of old age
(281)   *trivial:* of very little importance
(281)   *scrapbook:* a blank book in which items such as newspaper articles or pictures are collected and kept
(281)   *Vietnam Veterans Memorial:* a memorial in Washington, D.C. that consists of a black marble wall containing the names of all Americans who died in the Vietnam War
(281)   *unleashes:* releases
(281)   *farfetched:* unbelievable
(282)   *rehashing old arguments:* going over the same points again and again
(283)   *procrastinate:* put off; do later rather than immediately
(284)   *deaden public sensitivity:* to reduce the public's concern

Memory and the Brain—Some "Shocking" Findings (pgs. 284-287)

What happens in the brain when memories are formed?

(285)   *"switching station":* refers to the station at a railroad where trains are switched from one track to another, as memory switches from long term to short term
(285)   *traumatic:* very disturbing or upsetting
(285)   *John F. Kennedy:* President of the U.S. in the early '60s
(285)   *Martin Luther King Jr.:* an African-American political figure who advocated peace and racial equality
(285)   *the Challenger space shuttle disaster:* the spaceship that exploded shortly after take-off, killing everyone on board (January, 1986)
(285)   *the Columbia space shuttle disaster:* the spaceship that disintegrated while reentering the earth's atmosphere, killing everyone on board (February, 2003)
(286)   *crystallized:* formed and hardened
(286)   *flashbacks:* recurrent and abnormally vivid recollection of a traumatic experience, as a battle, sometimes accompanied by hallucinations.
(287)   *marine snail:* sea snail, as opposed to a land snail
(287)   *circuit:* a path

Exceptional Memory—Wizards of Recall (pgs. 287-290)

What are "photographic" memories?

(289)   *avid:* passionate and enthusiastic

(289) *phenomenal*: outstanding
(289) *diligent*: hardworking; careful
(289) *diabolical*: extremely difficult or fiendish

Improving Memory—Keys to the Memory Bank (pgs. 290-294)

How can I improve my memory?
(290) *augment*: to expand
(290) *boil down*: summarize
(291) *daunting*: overwhelming
(291) *jog*: trigger or revive
(292) *scarecrow:* "person" stuffed with straw meant to scare away crows; used on farms (particularly cornfields)
(292) *icing on your study cake*: being easy to review
(292) *eluded*: escaped from
(292) *recapturing*: bringing back

Psychology in Action: Mnemonics—Memory Magic (pgs. 294-297)

Are there any tricks to help me with my memory?
(294) *budding*: inexperienced; just starting out
(294) *port*: left side of a ship, boat, airplane, or space shuttle as one faces forward
(294) *starboard*: right side of a ship, boat, airplane, or space shuttle as one faces forward
(295) *conventional*: normal; traditional
(296) *Van Gogh*: Vincent Van Gogh (1853-1890), a well-known Dutch painter
(296) *orators*: those distinguished for their skill as public speakers
(297) *skeptical*: critical, not believing that everything you read is true

Solutions

Recite and Review

Stages of Memory—Do You Have a Mind Like Sieve?
1. system
2. Information, stored
3. three, short-term, long-term
4. exact, image
5. half
6. sensory
7. sounds, meaning
8. interruption, repetition
9. temporary, permanent

Short-Term Memory—Do You Know the Magic Number?
1. bits, larger
2. magic, short-term, lower
3. twelve
4. STM, memories

Long-Term Memory—A Blast from the Past
1. updating
2. false
3. mental, false
4. retrieval, cues
5. organized, models
6. memory
7. facts, skills
8. cerebellum
9. Declarative
10. forgetting
11. personal

Measuring Memory—The Answer Is on the Tip of My Tongue
1. state
2. knowing
3. recall
4. essay
5. end, middle
6. recognition
7. Recognition
8. Recognition
9. savings
10. memories, memories
11. hidden

Forgetting—Why We, Uh, Let's See; Why We, Uh . . . Forget!
1. curve, after
2. meaningful, slower
3. information
4. traces
5. disuse
6. learning, states
7. forgetting
8. interferes, interfere
9. forgetting
10. conscious
11. abuse
12. true, false
13. evidence

Memory and the Brain—Some "Shocking" Findings
1. before, follow
2. amnesia, shock
3. long-term
4. brain
5. older
6. confidence
7. cortex

Exceptional Memory—Wizards of Recall
1. image
2. adults
3. LTM, knowledge
4. not, different

Improving Memory—Keys to the Memory Bank

1. encoding
2. elaborative, part, cues
3. feedback
4. cognitive
5. position

Psychology in Action: Mnemonics—Memory Magic

1. initial
2. keyword, LTM
3. bizarre, mental

CONNECTIONS

Stages of Memory—Do You Have a Mind Like a Sieve?

1. A.
2. D.
3. C.
4. F.
5. E.
6. B

1. C.
2. G.
3. A.
4. E.
5. B.
6. D.
7. F.

Short-Term Memory—Do You Know the Magic Number?

1. A.
2. D.
3. C.
4. B.

Long-Term Memory—A Blast from the Past

1. F. or G.
2. C.
3. D.
4. A.
5. F. or G.
6. B.
7. E.

1. D.
2. H.
3. B.
4. E.
5. G.
6. A.
7. F.
8. C.

Measuring Memory—The Answer Is on the Tip of My Tongue

1. G.
2. A.
3. I.
4. C.
5. J.
6. H.
7. F.
8. D.
9. B.
10. K.
11. E.

Forgetting—Why We, Uh, Let's See; Why We, Uh . . . Forget!

1. C.
2. F.
3. I.
4. A.
5. K.
6. E.
7. H.
8. D.
9. G.
10. J.
11. B.

Memory and the Brain—Some "Shocking" Findings

1. C.
2. G.
3. D.
4. H.
5. E.
6. A.
7. B.
8. F.

Exceptional Memory – Wizards of Recall and Improving Memory – Keys to the Memory Bank

1. D.	4. I.	7. C.
2. G.	5. E.	8. E.
3. A.	6. J.	9. B

Check Your Memory

Stages of Memory—Do You Have a Mind Like a Sieve?

1. T	4. T	7. T	10. F
2. F	5. F	8. F	11. T
3. T	6. F	9. T	

Short-Term Memory—Do You Know the Magic Number?

1. F	3. F	5. F	7. T
2. F	4. T	6. F	

Long-Term Memory—A Blast from the Past

1. F	5. T	9. F	13. T
2. T	6. F	10. F	14. F
3. T	7. T	11. T	15. T
4. F	8. T	12. T	

Measuring Memory—The Answer Is on the Tip of My Tongue

1. T	4. T	7. F
2. F	5. F	8. T
3. F	6. T	9. F

Forgetting—Why We, Uh, Let's See; Why We, Uh . . . Forget!

1. F	7. T	13. T	19. T
2. T	8. F	14. F	20. T
3. F	9. T	15. F	21. T
4. F	10. T	16. F	
5. F	11. T	17. F	
6. T	12. W	18. F	

Memory and the Brain—Some "Shocking" Findings

1. F	3. T	5. T	7. F
2. F	4. F	6. T	8. F

Exceptional Memory—Wizards of Recall; Improving Memory— Keys to the Memory Bank, and Psychology in Action: Mnemonics—Memory Magic

1. T	6. F	11. F	16. T
2. T	7. F	12. T	17. F
3. T	8. T	13. F	18. T
4. F	9. T	14. T	
5. F	10. F	15. T	

Final Survey and Review

Stages of Memory—Do You Have a Mind Like Sieve?

1. active
2. encoded, retrieved
3. sensory
4. copy, icon, echo
5. echoic
6. attention, transferred
7. Short-term, Long-term
8. interference, maintenance
9. working, meaningful

Short-Term Memory—Do You Know the Magic Number?

1. seven, chunking
2. limitation, Miller, Cowan
3. eighteen
4. meaning, information

Long-Term Memory—A Blast from the Past

1. unlimited, revision
2. constructive, positive
3. inferences, pseudo
4. cognitive
5. networks, linked
6. cue, forgotten
7. declarative, procedural
8. procedural
9. semantic, episodic
10. factual
11. Episodic

Measuring Memory—The Answer Is on the Tip of My Tongue

1. tip, all-or-nothing
2. feeling, likely
3. recognition
4. cues
5. serial, beginnin
6. g
7. multiple
8. pictures, distractors
9. superior
10. relearning, score
11. relearning, priming
12. Priming

Forgetting—Why We, Uh, Let's See; Why We, Uh . . . Forget!

1. Ebbinghaus, learning
2. nonsense, forgetting
3. encode
4. sensory
5. LTM
6. cue, state
7. interference
8. retroactive, new
9. traumatic
10. unconscious, suppression
11. repressed
12. recovered
13. fantasies

Memory and the Brain—Some "Shocking" Findings

1. Retrograde, anterograde
2. electroconvulsive
3. consolidated
4. hippocampus
5. older
6. vivid, accurate
7. episodic, semantic

Exceptional Memory—Wizards of Recall

1. photographic, external
2. rarely, vivid
3. strategies, superior
4. superior

Improving Memory—Keys to the Memory Bank

1. retrieval
2. selecting, spaced, improve
3. recitation
4. planned
5. sleep

Psychology in Action: Mnemonics—Memory Magic

1. rote
2. images, unusual
3. unusual, exaggerated

Mastery Test

1. c, p. 267
2. d, p. 271
3. a, p. 284-285
4. b, p. 284
5. c, p. 266
6. c, p. 265
7. c, p. 288
8. d, p. 279
9. a, p. 265-266
10. c, p. 277
11. b, p. 287-288
12. b, p. 268
13. a, p. 284
14. a, p. 275
15. c, p. 276
16. d, p. 269
17. b, p. 275
18. a, p. 278-279
19. b, p. 269-270
20. d, p. 272, 281, & 291
21. c, p. 283-284
22. a, p. 291-292
23. d, 272 & 292
24. b, p. 285-286
25. d, p. 295
26. c, p. 272-273
27. a, p. 265, 273-274
28. b, p. 281-282
29. c, p.283
30. d, p. 285
31. a, p. 273
32. c, p. 279-281
33. b, p. 287
34. b, p. 275
35. a, p. 280
36. c, p. 279-281

CHAPTER 8

Intelligence, Cognition, Language, and Creativity

Chapter Overview

Intelligence refers to a general capacity to act purposefully, think rationally, and deal effectively with the environment. In practice, intelligence is operationally defined by creating tests. The first practical individual intelligence test was assembled by Alfred Binet; it was used with children and adolescents. A modern version is the Stanford-Binet Intelligence Scale. A second major intelligence test is the Wechsler Adult Intelligence Scale (WAIS) and is used primarily with adults. Intelligence is expressed as an intelligence quotient (IQ) or as a deviation IQ. The distribution of IQ scores approximates a normal curve.

The Stanford-Binet and WAIS are individual tests; group tests, such as the SAT, can be administered to many people at one time. Artificial intelligence in computes is being developed, but is very limited at this point. Computer simulations and expert systems are being used to model how humans think.

People with IQs in the gifted or "genius" range tend to be superior in many respects. In addition, many children are gifted or talented in other ways. The terms *intellectually disabled* and *developmentally disabled* apply to persons who have an IQ below 70 or who lack various adaptive behaviors. About 50 percent of the cases of intellectual disability are organic; the remaining cases are of undetermined cause (many are thought to be familial). Some individuals, called savants, have exceptional abilities in certain domains (e.g., math or music), but have limited intelligence.

Some psychologists believe that there are many types of intelligence, as opposed to a single measure of general mental abilities (g-factor). Culture fairness is an important issue facing intelligence testing, as some cultures place greater value on some aspects of intelligence over others. Intelligence reflects the combined effects of heredity and environment.

Thinking is the mental manipulation of images, concepts, and language (or symbols). Most people use internal images (including kinesthetic images) for thinking, problem solving, improving a skill and/or aiding memory. A concept is a generalized idea of a class of objects or events. We learn concepts from positive and negative instances and from rules. Concepts can be conjunctive, disjunctive, or relational. Prototypes are often used to identify concepts. Faulty concepts can lead to social stereotyping. Language translates events into symbols, which are combined using the rules of grammar and syntax. True languages are productive. Studies suggest that, with training, primates are capable of some language use. Bilingualism is the ability to speak two languages. Being bilingual has cognitive benefits, but can cause children to struggle academically when they are forced to "sink or swim" in educational settings.

The solution to a problem may be arrived at mechanically (by trial and error or by rote). Solutions by understanding usually begin with discovering the general properties of an answer. Next, functional solutions are proposed. Problem solving is frequently aided by heuristics, which narrow the search for solutions. When understanding leads to a rapid solution, insight has occurred. Insight can be blocked by fixations. Work on artificial intelligence has focused on computer simulations and expert systems. Human expertise is based on organized knowledge and acquired strategies.

Creative solutions are practical, sensible, and original. Creative thinking requires divergent thinking and involves fluency, flexibility, and originality. Tests of creativity measure these qualities. Five stages often seen in creative problem solving are orientation, preparation, incubation, illumination, and verification. There is only a small positive correlation between IQ and creativity.

Intuitive thinking often leads to errors. Wrong conclusions may be drawn when an answer seems highly representative of what we already believe is true. A second problem is ignoring the base rate of an event. Clear thinking is usually aided by stating or framing a problem in broad terms. Wise people often have an open and tolerant approach to life.

Some suggestions for enhancing creativity include: breaking mental sets and challenging assumptions, defining problems broadly, restating problems in different ways, allowing time for incubation, seeking varied input, looking for analogies, and delaying evaluation.

Learning Objectives

1. Describe what it means to be a savant.
2. Give a general definition of intelligence; explain the g-factor, what an operational definition of intelligence is, and how other cultures view intelligence.
3. Describe Binet's role in intelligence testing, the development of the original Stanford-Binet, and the five cognitive factors measured by the Stanford-Binet Intelligence Scales, Fifth Edition (SB5).
4. Distinguish the Wechsler tests from the Stanford-Binet tests and between group and individual tests, and describe the distribution of IQ scores observed in the general population.
5. Define mental age and chronological age; use examples to show how they are used to compute an intelligence quotient (IQ); differentiate between this IQ (MA/CA x 100) and deviation IQs; and explain how percentiles are interpreted.

6. Define the term *artificial intelligence* (AI); explain what AI is based on; list its advantages and limitations; and describe how computer simulations and expert systems are being used.

7. Differentiate between the terms *gifted* and *genius*; describe Terman's study of his gifted subjects, including how the successful ones differed from the less successful ones as adults; and explain how gifted children are identified.

8. Define intellectual disability and state the dividing line between normal intelligence and intellectual disability; describe the degrees of intellectual disability, and differentiate between familial and organic intellectual disability.

9. Explain why psychologists are developing broader definitions of intelligence; and describe Howard Gardner's theory of multiple intelligences.

10. Describe the studies that provide evidence for the hereditary view and for the environmental view of intelligence, including the twin studies, the adoption studies, Skeels' study, IQ gains in Westernized nations, and the effects of video games, the Internet, and television.

11. Describe how IQ tests may be unfair to certain groups and what a culture-fair test is; explain how group differences in IQ scores are related to cultural and environmental differences rather than race; and list the advantages and disadvantages of using standardized testing in schools.

12. Define cognition and list the three basic units of thought.

13. Describe the uses and properties of mental images; explain how stored and created images are used and how the size of a mental image may be important; and describe how kinesthetic imagery aids thinking.

14. Define the terms *concept*, *concept formation*, *conceptual rule*, and *prototype*.

15. Explain how children and adults learn concepts; differentiate among the three types of concepts (conjunctive, relational, and disjunctive).

16. Explain the difference between the denotative and the connotative meanings of a word; describe how the connotative meaning is measured; discuss problems associated with faulty concepts (social stereotypes and all-or-nothing thinking).

17. Explain how language aids thought; define semantics.

18. Discuss bilingual education, including the concepts of additive and subtractive bilingualism and two-way bilingual education.

19. Briefly explain the following three requirements of a language and their related concepts:
    a. symbols (phonemes and morphemes)
    b. grammar (syntax and transformation rules)
    c. productivity; describe the characteristics of gestural languages;
    d. Discuss the extent to which primates have been taught to use language, including criticisms

20. Define and explain how each of the following terms are related to problem-solving:
    a. *mechanical solutions*, including trial-and-error and rote
    b. *algorithms*
    c. *solutions by understanding*, including a general solution and functional solutions

d. a *random search strategy*
e. *heuristics*, including the differences in experts and novices
f. *insight*, including selective encoding, selective selective combination, and selective comparison
21. Explain and give examples of how fixation and functional fixedness block problem-solving.
22. Describe the four common barriers to creative thinking.
23. Describe and give examples of the four kinds of thought (inductive, deductive, logical, and illogical).
24. Define the creative processes of fluency, flexibility, and originality; differentiate between convergent and divergent thinking; explain how creativity can be measured and why creativity is more than divergent thinking.
25. Discuss the five stages of creative problem-solving and the typical characteristics of creative persons; list Csikszentmihalyi's recommendations for developing one's creativity.
26. Describe the process of "thin-slicing" and indentify two implications of such thinking.
27. Define intuition; explain the following three common intuitive thinking errors:
a. representativeness (include representativeness heuristic)
b. underlying odds (base rate)
c. framing
d. What is wisdom?

RECITE AND REVIEW

Human Intelligence—The IQ and You

Survey Question: How is human intelligence defined and measured? Pages 302-306

1. The first practical _____ _____ was assembled in 1904, in Paris, by Alfred Binet.

2. Intelligence refers to one's general capacity to act purposefully, think _____, and deal effectively with the _____.

3. In practice, writing an intelligence test provides an operational _____ of intelligence.

4. The core of _____ consists of general mental abilities (the g-factor).

5. A modern version of Binet's test is the Stanford-Binet _____ _____, 5th Edition. It is composed of age-ranked _____, which get progressively more difficult.

6. The Stanford-Binet measures _____ reasoning, quantitative reasoning, visual-spatial processing, working _____, and knowledge.

7. In the _____ reasoning factor of the Stanford-Binet Intelligence Scale, individuals are asked to fill in the missing shape in a group; the _____ reasoning scale measures a person's ability to solve problems involving numbers.

8. A second major intelligence test is the Wechsler _____ Intelligence Scale, 3rd Edition (WAIS-III). The WAIS-III measures both verbal and performance (_____) intelligence.

9. The original Standford-Binet was better suited for _____ and adolescents; the Wechsler Adult Intelligence Scale was better suited for _____.

10. Intelligence is expressed in terms of an intelligence _____ (IQ). IQ is defined as mental age (MA) divided by chronological age (CA) and then multiplied by _____.

11. Modern IQ tests no longer calculate _____ directly. Instead, the final score reported by the test is a deviation IQ, which gives a person's _____ intellectual standing in his or her age group. An average IQ score of 100 would place a person at the _____ percentile.

12. An "average" IQ of _____ occurs when mental age _____ chronological age.

13. Intelligence tests have also been produced for use with _____ of people. The Scholastic Assessment Test (SAT) measures a variety of _____ aptitudes, and it can be used to estimate intelligence.

14. Artificial intelligence refers to _____ programs capable of doing things that require intelligence when performed by humans.

15. Humans are flexible and can mentally "shift gears," whereas computers are constrained by an underlying set of pre-programmed _____.

16. Computer simulations are programs that attempt to duplicate _____ behavior; expert systems respond like a human _____ would respond.

17. Expert human problem solving is based on organized _____ and acquired strategies rather than some general improvement in thinking ability.

Variations in Intelligence—Curved Like a Bell

Survey Question: How much does intelligence vary from person to person?
Pages 306-309

1. When graphed, the distribution (percentage of people receiving each score) of IQ scores approximates a normal (_____-shaped) _____.

2. People with IQs above 140 are considered to be in the _____ or "genius" range.

3. Studies done by Lewis Terman showed that the gifted tend to be
   _____: They earned advanced degrees, held professional positions,
   and had written books.

4. IQ reveals _____; it does not guarantee success.

5. The most successful gifted persons tend to be those who are persistent and
   _____ to learn and succeed. By criteria other than _____, a
   large proportion of children might be considered gifted or talented in one way
   or another.

6. Giftedness may reveal itself in children in the following: tendency to seek out
   _____ children and adults, early fascination with explanations and
   problem solving, talking in complete sentences around _____ years,
   good memory, early interest in books, showing of kindness, understanding,
   and cooperation with others.

7. The terms intellectually _____ and developmentally disabled are
   applied to those whose IQ falls below _____ or who lack various
   adaptive behaviors.

8. Further classifications of intellectual disability are: _____ (50-55 to
   70), moderate (35-40 to 50-55), _____ (20-25 to 35-40), and
   profound (below 20-25).

9. About _____ percent of the cases of intellectual disability are
   organic, being caused by _____ injuries and fetal damage, metabolic
   disorders, or genetic abnormalities. The remaining cases are of
   undetermined cause.

10. Many cases of subnormal intelligence are thought to be the result of familial
    intellectual disability (a low level of _____ stimulation in the home,
    poverty, and poor nutrition).

Questioning Intelligence—How Intelligent is the Idea of Intelligence?

Survey Question: What are some controversies in the study of intelligence?
Pages 309-314

1. One limitation of traditional intelligence testing is its _____ to other
   cultural groups. Because children from various cultures are taught different
   skills, _____ intelligence tests have been implemented to accurately
   assess individuals' intellectual abilities and to reduce biases.

2. Culture-fair tests attempt to measure intelligence without the influence of
   verbal skills, cultural background, and _____ level.

3. The Wechsler and Binet scales are designed to measure the IQ of people from middle-class _____ cultures. To reduce the influence of verbal skills, cultural background, and _____ level when measuring the IQ of people from another culture (e.g., China) or from a different background (e.g., poor community), culture-_____ tests have been implemented.

4. Traditional IQ tests often suffer from a degree of cultural _____ that makes them easier for some groups and harder for others.

5. Culture-fair tests try to measure intelligence in ways that are not strongly affected by _____ background, but no test is entirely _____-free.

6. Differences in the average IQ scores for various racial groups are based on environmental differences, not _____ (or _____).

7. _____ is merely an index of intelligence-based tests that offer a narrow definition of intelligence.

8. Howard Gardner believes that _____ IQ tests define intelligence too narrowly.

9. According to Gardner, intelligence consists of abilities in language, logic and _____, _____ and spatial thinking, music, bodily-kinesthetic skills, intrapersonal skills, interpersonal skills, and naturalist skills.

10. Studies of family relationships in humans, especially comparisons between fraternal twins and identical twins (who have identical _____), also suggest that intelligence is partly _____.

11. Environment is also important, as revealed by changes in tested intelligence induced by _____ environments and improved education.

12. _____ therefore reflects the combined effects of heredity and environment.

13. _____ in education, nutrition, and complex technology have most likely contributed to the increase in average IQ over the past _____ years.

14. _____ intelligence ("street smarts") may be more highly valued in some minority cultures than _____ intelligence ("book smarts").

What Is Thinking?—Brains over Brawn

Survey Question: What is the nature of thought? Pages 314-315

1. Cognition is the _____ processing of information involving daydreaming, _____ solving, and reasoning.

2. Thinking is the manipulation of _____ representations of external problems or situations.

3. Three basic units of thought are images, concepts, and _____ or symbols.

Mental Imagery—Does a Frog Have Lips?

Survey Question: In what ways are images related to thinking? Pages 315-317

1. Many of the systems in the brain that are involved in processing _____ images work in reverse to create mental images.

2. Most people have mental images of one kind or another. Images may be based on information stored in memory or they may be _____.

3. Mental _____ may be used to make a decision, solve a _____, change feelings, improve a skill, and/or aid memory.

4. The size of images used in problem solving may _____. Images may be three-dimensional and they may be rotated in _____ to answer questions.

5. Kinesthetic images are created from produced, remembered, or imagined _____ sensations. _____ sensations and micromovements seem to help structure thinking for many people.

Concepts—I'm Positive, It's a Whatchamacallit

Survey Question: What are concepts? Pages 317-319

1. A concept is a generalized idea of a _____ of objects or events and helps us to identify important features of the world.

2. Forming concepts may be based on experiences with _____ and negative instances.

3. Concepts may also be acquired by learning rules that define the _____.

4. Concepts may be classified as conjunctive ("_____" concepts), disjunctive ("_____-_____" concepts), or relational concepts.

5. In practice, we frequently use prototypes (general _____ of the concept class) to identify concepts.

6. Faulty concepts lead to social _____ and all-or-nothing thinking.

7. The denotative meaning of a word or concept is its exact _____. Connotative meaning is _____ or emotional.

8. Connotative meaning can be measured with the semantic differential. Most connotative meaning involves the dimensions _____-_____, strong-weak, and active-passive.

Language—Don't Leave Home Without It

Survey Question: What is the role of language in thinking? Pages 319-324

1. Thinking in language is influenced by meaning. The study of _____ is called semantics.

2. The Stroop task demonstrates the effectiveness of _____ influencing our thinking. The meaning of the word interferes with our ability to name the color of the word.

3. _____ is the ability to speak two languages.

4. Language allows events to be encoded into _____ for easy mental manipulation.

5. In added bilingualism, learning a _____ language adds to a child's overall competence. In subtractive bilingualism, children ultimately may _____ native language skills and struggle in both languages.

6. Language is built out of phonemes (basic speech _____) and morphemes (speech sounds collected into _____ units).

7. Language carries meaning by combining a set of symbols or signs according to a set of _____ (grammar), which includes rules about word _____ (syntax).

8. Various sentences are created by applying transformation _____ to simple statements.

9. A true language is _____ and can be used to generate new ideas or possibilities. American Sign Language (ASL) and other _____ languages used by the deaf are true languages.

10. Animal communication is relatively limited because it lacks symbols that can be rearranged easily. As a result, it does not have the productive quality of _____ language.

11. Studies that make use of lexigrams (_____ word-symbols) provide the best evidence yet of animal language use.

Problem Solving—Getting an Answer in Sight

Survey Question: What do we know about problem solving? Pages 324-329

1. The solution to a problem may be found mechanically (by trial-and-error or by _____ application of rules). However, trial-and-error solutions are frequently inefficient or ineffective, except where aided by _____.

2. Often a _____ solution is achieved through an algorithm, a _____ set of rules that always leads to a correct solution.

3. Solutions by understanding usually begin with discovery of the _____ properties of an answer. Next, a number of functional _____ are proposed.

4. Random search strategies, like _____-and-_____, may work id the number of alternatives is small, but are generally ineffective.

5. Problem solving is frequently aided by heuristics. These are strategies that typically _____ the search for solutions.

6. When understanding leads to a rapid _____, insight has occurred. Three elements of insight are _____ encoding, selective combination, and selective comparison.

7. The ability to apply _____ comparison (comparing old solutions to new problems) effectively can be influenced by our culture.

8. Insights and other problem-solving attempts can be blocked by fixation (a tendency to repeat _____ solutions).

9. Functional fixedness is a common_____, but emotional blocks, cultural values, learned conventions, and perceptual _____ are also problems.

Creative Thinking—Down Roads Less Traveled

Survey Question: What is creative thinking? Pages 329-332

1. _____ may be deductive or inductive, logical or illogical.

2. Inductive thinking involves going from _____ facts to general principles; deductive thinking goes from _____ principles to specific situations.

3. Creative thinking requires divergent thought, characterized by fluency, flexibility, and _____.

4. Tests of _____, such as the Unusual Uses Test, the Consequences Test, and the Anagrams Test, measure the capacity for divergent thinking.

5. To be creative, a solution must be _____ and sensible as well as original.

6. Five stages often seen in creative problem solving are orientation, _____, incubation, illumination, and verification.

7. Studies suggest that creative persons share a combination of thinking _____, personality characteristics, and a _____ social environment. There is only a small correlation between IQ and creativity.

Intuitive Thought—Mental Shortcut? Or Dangerous Detour?

Survey Question: How accurate is intuition? Pages 332-335

1. Intuitive thinking is quick and impulsive, and often leads to _____. Wrong conclusions may be drawn when an answer seems highly representative of what we already believe is _____, that is, when people apply the representativeness heuristic.

2. A second problem is allowing emotions such as _____, hope, _____, or disgust to guide _____ in decision making.

3. The third problem is ignoring the base rate (or underlying _____) of an event.

4. Clear thinking is usually aided by stating or framing a problem in _____ terms.

5. Wisdom represents a mixture of _____ thinking, intelligence, reason, creativity, and originality. Wise people approach life with _____ and tolerance.

6. Quickly making sense of thin slivers of experiences is called "_____-_____."

Psychology in Action: Enhancing Creativity - Brainstorms

Survey Question: What can be done to improve thinking and promote creativity?
Pages 336-339

1. Some suggestions for enhancing creativity include: breaking mental sets and challenging _____, defining problems broadly, restating problems in different ways, allowing time for incubation, seeking _____ input, looking for analogies, and delaying evaluation.

2. Individuals can become "set" in one way of thinking; this mental set blinds them to possible _____.

3. One way to _____ a problem is to imagine how another person would view it.

4. You are less likely to think creatively if you feel pressed for _____.

5. Worrying about _____ inhibits creativity. Therefore, it is important to delay evaluation

6. To live more _____, try to find something that surprises you every day.

CONNECTIONS

Human Intelligence—The IQ and You; Variations in Intelligence—Curved Like a Bell; and Questioning Intelligence—How Intelligent Is the idea of intelligence?

Survey Question: How is human intelligence defined and measured? How much does intelligence vary from person to person? What are some controversies in the study of intelligence? Pages 302-314

1. _____ Binet

2. _____ Giftedness

3. _____ average intelligence

4. _____ Intelligence Quotient (IQ)

5. _____ Identical twins

6. _____ deviation IQ

7. _____ expert system

8. _____ IQ of 115

9. _____ Fluid reasoning

10. _____ gifted people

11. _____ Artificial intelligence

12. _____ intellectually disabled

13. _____ general mental abilities

14. _____ group test

15. _____ WAIS

16. _____ AI

17. _____ normal curve

18. _____ multiple intelligence

A. relative standing

B. IQ of 140

C. Wechsler test

D. first intelligence test

E. SAT

F. bell shape

G. 84th percentile

H. MA/CA x 100

I. IQ below 70

J. IQ of 100

K. G-Factor

L. Series of pictures

M. computer program

N. special talents

O. knowledge plus rules

P. Deep Blue

Q. "people smart" and "nature smart"

R. same genes

What is Thinking?—Brains over Brawn; Mental Imagery—Does a Frog Have Lips?; and Concepts—I'm Positive, It's a Whatchamacallit

Survey Questions: What is the nature of thought? In what ways are images related to thinking? What are concepts? Pages 314-319

1. _____ cognition
2. _____ Denotative meaning
3. _____ social stereotypes
4. _____ mental rotation
5. _____ Disjunctive concept
6. _____ reverse vision
7. _____ stored images
8. _____ kinesthetic imagery
9. _____ concept
10. _____ prototype
11. _____ Concept formation
12. _____ connotative meaning

A. three-dimensional images
B. remembered perceptions
C. images created by the brain
D. mental class
E. implicit actions
F. thinking
G. ideal or model
H. semantic differential
I. faulty, oversimplified concepts
J. classifying information
K. at least one
L. exact definition

Language—Don't Leave Home Without It

Survey Question: What is the role of language in thinking? Pages 319-324

1. _____ word meanings
2. _____ subtractive bilingualism
3. _____ morpheme
4. _____ phoneme
5. _____ Language
6. _____ "hidden" grammar
7. _____ Washoe
8. _____ bilingual
9. _____ if-then statement
10. _____ Kanzi

A. meaningful unit
B. American Sign Language (ASL)
C. semantics
D. lexigrams
E. language sound
F. conditional relationship
G. transformation rules
H. symbols and rules
I. two languages
J. sink or swim

Problem Solving—Getting an Answer in Sight

Survey Question: What do we know about problem solving? Pages 324-329

1. _____ expert versus novice   A. mechanical solution
2. _____ insight   B. thinking strategy
3. _____ trial-and-error   C. element of insight
4. _____ random search strategy   D. a clear, sudden solution
5. _____ Perceptual barriers   E. trial-and-error
6. _____ heuristic   F. acquired strategies
7. _____ algorithm   G. blind to alternatives
8. _____ understanding   H. deep comprehension
9. _____ selective comparison   I. rote rules
10. _____ fixation   J. taboos

Creative Thinking—Down Roads Less Traveled; Intuitive Thought—Mental Shortcut? Or Dangerous Detour?; and Psychology in Action: Enhancing Creativity

Survey Questions: What is creative thinking? How accurate is intuition? What can be done to improve thinking and promote creativity? Pages 329-339

1. _____ fluency   A. preconceived concept
2. _____ flexibility   B. many types of solutions
3. _____ Thin-slicing   C. one correct answer
4. _____ originality   D. follow explicit rule
5. _____ logical   E. moment of insight
6. _____ convergent thinking   F. underlying odds
7. _____ Hot cognition   G. quick and impulsive thought
8. _____ Anagrams Test   H. many solutions
9. _____ mental set   I. measures divergent thinking
10. _____ orientation   J. novelty of solutions
11. _____ illumination   K. identify problem
12. _____ Live creatively   L. intuitive reaction
13. _____ base rate   M. hope, fear, and anxiety
14. _____ wisdom   N. openness and tolerance
15. _____ intuition   O. find everyday surprises

CHECK YOUR MEMORY

Human Intelligence—The IQ and You

Survey Question: How is human intelligence defined and measured? Pages 302-306

1. How intelligence is understood depends on one's culture.

TRUE or FALSE

2. Alfred Binet's first test was designed to measure mechanical aptitude.

TRUE or FALSE

3. Lewis Terman helped write the Stanford-Binet intelligence test.

TRUE or FALSE

4. The Stanford-Binet intelligence test measures three intelligence factors: knowledge, quantitative reasoning, and visual-spatial processing.

TRUE or FALSE

5. Mental age refers to average mental ability for a person of a given age.

TRUE or FALSE

6. Mental age can't be higher than chronological age.

TRUE or FALSE

7. An IQ will be greater than 100 when CA is larger than MA.

TRUE or FALSE

8. Average intelligence is defined as an IQ from 90 to 109.

TRUE or FALSE

9. Modern IQ tests give scores as deviation IQs.

TRUE or FALSE

10. Being placed in the 84th percentile means 16 percent of your peers received IQ scores higher than you and 84 percent have IQ scores lower than you.

TRUE or FALSE

11. The WISC is designed to test adult performance intelligence.

TRUE or FALSE

12. The Stanford-Binet, Wechsler's, and the SAT are all group intelligence tests.

TRUE or FALSE

13. In a normal curve, a majority of scores are found near the average.

TRUE or FALSE

14. An IQ above 130 is described as "bright normal."

TRUE or FALSE

15. The correlation between IQ scores and school grades is .50.

TRUE or FALSE

16. Only 12 people out of 100 score above 130 on IQ tests.

TRUE or FALSE

17. AI is frequently based on a set of rules applied to a body of information.

TRUE or FALSE

18. Computer simulations are used to test models of human cognition.

TRUE or FALSE

19. Computers now have the communication skills to fool people into believing they are human, especially via online interactions.

TRUE or FALSE

20. Much human expertise is based on acquired strategies for solving problems.

TRUE or FALSE

Variations in Intelligence—Curved Like a Bell

Survey Question: How does intelligence vary from person to person? Pages 306-309

1. The distribution of IQ scores approximates a bell-shaped curve

TRUE or FALSE

2. Terman discovered that giftedness was an inherited trait; parenting had little to no influence.

TRUE or FALSE

3. Gifted children tend to get average IQ scores by the time they reach adulthood.

TRUE or FALSE

4. IQ is highly and positively correlated with success in art, leadership, and writing.

TRUE or FALSE

5. Gifted persons are more susceptible to mental illness.

TRUE or FALSE

6. Talking in complete sentences at age two is regarded as a sign of giftedness.

TRUE or FALSE

7. Individuals with savant syndrome have exceptional mental ability on one or more narrow areas, such as art or music.

TRUE or FALSE

8. Those with mild intellectual disability can usually learn routine self-help skills.

TRUE or FALSE

9. Genetic abnormalities, fetal damage, birth injuries, and metabolic disorders have little to no influence on intellectual potential

TRUE or FALSE

10. Familial intellectual disability is largely based on an enriched environment.

TRUE or FALSE

Questioning Intelligence—How Intelligent is the Idea of Intelligence?

Survey Question: What are some controversies in the study of intelligence?
Pages 309-314

1. Howard Gardner suggests that each of us has eight different types of intelligence such as being "people smart," "word smart," etc.

TRUE or FALSE

2. The Stanford-Binet, Wechsler's, and the SAT are all culture-fair tests.

TRUE or FALSE

3. The small difference in average IQ scores for African Americans and Anglo Americans is explained by cultural and environmental differences.

TRUE or FALSE

4. IQ scores predict later career success.

TRUE or FALSE

5. Standardized testing is used primarily to select people for school and employment.

TRUE or FALSE

6. Changing intelligence tests would result in a change in the IQ scores of people taking the tests.

TRUE or FALSE

7. The IQs of identical twins are more alike than those of fraternal twins.

TRUE or FALSE

8. Adult intelligence is approximately 50 percent hereditary.

TRUE or FALSE

9. The rapid rise in Western IQ scores has been linked, in part, to video games.

TRUE or FALSE

What Is Thinking?—Brains over Brawn

Survey Question: What is the nature of thought? Pages314-315

1. Cognition refers to the process of encoding, storing, and retrieving information.

TRUE or FALSE

2. Images, concepts, and language may be used to mentally represent problems.

TRUE or FALSE

3. Images are generalized ideas of a class of related objects or events.

TRUE or FALSE

4. Blindfolded chess players mainly use concepts to represent chess problems and solutions.

TRUE or FALSE

Mental Imagery—Does a Frog Have Lips?

Survey Question: In what ways are images related to thinking? Pages 315-317

1. Images are used to make decisions, change feelings, and to improve memory.

TRUE or FALSE

2. Mental images may be used to improve memory and skilled actions.

TRUE or FALSE

3. The visual cortex is activated when a person has a mental image.

TRUE or FALSE

4. The more the image of a shape has to be rotated in space, the longer it takes to tell if it matches another view of the same shape.

TRUE or FALSE

5. People who have good imaging abilities tend to score high on tests of creativity.

TRUE or FALSE

6. The smaller a mental image, the harder it is to identify its details.

TRUE or FALSE

7. People with good kinesthetic imagery tend to learn sports skills faster than average.

TRUE or FALSE

Concepts—I'm Positive, It's a Whatchamacallit

Survey Question: What are concepts? Pages 317–319

1. Concept formation is typically based on examples and rules.

TRUE or FALSE

2. Prototypes are very strong negative instances of a concept.

TRUE or FALSE

3. "Greater than" and "lopsided" are relational concepts.

TRUE or FALSE

4. The semantic differential is used to rate the objective meanings of words and concepts.

TRUE or FALSE

5. The denotative meaning of a concept is its exact definition

TRUE or FALSE

6. Conjunctive concepts are defined by having at least one of several possible features.

TRUE or FALSE

7. Social stereotypes are accurate, oversimplified concepts people use to form mental images of groups of people.

TRUE or FALSE

Language—Don't Leave Home Without It

Survey Question: What is the role of language in thinking? Pages 319–324

1. Bilingualism is the ability to speak three languages.

TRUE or FALSE

2. Two-way bilingual education is widely accepted, and used frequently in U.S. schools.

TRUE or FALSE

3. Children who learn English as a second language often struggle academically because of the added burden of additive bilingualism.

TRUE or FALSE

4. Encoding is the study of the meanings of language.

TRUE or FALSE

5. The Stroop interference test shows that thought is greatly influenced by language.

TRUE or FALSE

6. People can easily name the color of the word without the meaning of the word interfering with their thought processing.

TRUE or FALSE

7. Morphemes are the basic speech sounds of a language.

TRUE or FALSE

8. Syntax is a part of grammar.

TRUE or FALSE

9. Noam Chomsky believes that a child who says, "I drinked my juice," has applied the semantic differential to a simple, core sentence.

TRUE or FALSE

10. American Sign Language (ASL) has 600,000 root signs.

TRUE or FALSE

11. True languages are productive, thus American Sign Language (ASL) is not a true language.

TRUE or FALSE

12. If one is fluent in American Sign Language (ASL), one can sign and understand other gestural languages such as Yiddish Sign.

TRUE or FALSE

13. Animal communication can be described as productive.

TRUE or FALSE

14. Chimpanzees have never learned to speak even a single word.

TRUE or FALSE

15. One of Sarah chimpanzee's outstanding achievements was mastery of sentences involving transformational rules.

TRUE or FALSE

16. Language-trained chimps have been known to hold conversations when no humans were present.

TRUE or FALSE

17. Kanzi's use of grammar is on par with that of a 2-year-old child.

TRUE or FALSE

Problem Solving—Getting an Answer in Sight

Survey Question: What do we know about problem solving? Pages 324-329

1. Except for the simplest problems, mechanical solutions are typically best left to computers.

TRUE or FALSE

2. An algorithm is a learned set of rules (grammar) for language.

TRUE or FALSE

3. Karl Duncker's famous tumor problem could only be solved by trial-and-error.

TRUE or FALSE

4. In solutions by understanding, functional solutions are usually discovered by use of a random search strategy.

TRUE or FALSE

5. Working backward from the desired goal to the starting point can be a useful heuristic.

TRUE or FALSE

6. In problem solving, rapid insights are more likely to be correct than those that develop slowly.

TRUE or FALSE

7. Selective encoding refers to bringing together seemingly unrelated bits of useful information.

TRUE or FALSE

8. Functional fixedness is an inability to see new uses for familiar objects.

TRUE or FALSE

9. Chess experts have an exceptional ability to remember the positions of chess pieces placed at random on a chessboard.

TRUE or FALSE

10. A fixation is a tendency to get "hung up" on wrong solutions.

TRUE or FALSE

11. Fear of making a fool of oneself is a common perceptual barrier to problem solving.

TRUE or FALSE

Creative Thinking—Down Roads Less Traveled

Survey Question: What is creative thinking? Pages 329-332

1. In inductive thinking, a general rule is inferred from specific examples.

TRUE or FALSE

2. Fluency and flexibility are measures of convergent thinking.

TRUE or FALSE

3. In tests of creativity, originality refers to how novel or unusual your idea are compared to others

TRUE or FALSE

4. The Anagrams Test, Unusual Uses Test, and Consequences Test are all tests of creativity.

TRUE or FALSE

5. Creative thinkers typically apply reasoning and critical thinking to novel ideas after they produce them.

TRUE or FALSE

6. Creative ideas combine originality with feasibility.

TRUE or FALSE

7. Creative problem solving temporarily stops during the incubation period.

TRUE or FALSE

8. Creative people have an openness to experience, and they have a wide range of knowledge and interests.

TRUE or FALSE

9. An IQ score of 120 or above means that a person is creative.

TRUE or FALSE

Intuitive Thought—Mental Shortcut? Or Dangerous Detour?

Survey Question: How accurate is intuition? Pages 332-335

1. Intuition is a quick, impulsive insight into the true nature of a problem and its solution.

TRUE or FALSE

2. To form intuitive judgment of teachers, students must observe at least 20 minutes of the teacher's teaching ability.

TRUE or FALSE

3. The probability of two events occurring together is lower than the probability of either one occurring alone.

TRUE or FALSE

4. The representativeness heuristic is the strategy of stating problems in broad terms.

TRUE or FALSE

5. Being logical, most people do not let their emotions interfere when making important decisions.

TRUE or FALSE

6. Framing refers to the way in which a problem is stated or structured.

TRUE or FALSE

7. People often ignore base rates, or the underlying probability of an even occurring, when making decisions.

TRUE or FALSE

8. Wise people possess a mixture of convergent thinking, intelligence, reason, and creativity.

TRUE or FALSE

FINAL SURVEY AND REVIEW

Human Intelligence—The IQ and You

Survey Question: How is human intelligence defined and measured? Pages 302-306

1. The _____ practical intelligence test was assembled in 1904, in Paris, by Alfred _____.

2. Intelligence refers to one's _____ capacity to act _____, think rationally, and deal effectively with the environment.

3. In practice, writing an _____ test provides an _____ definition of intelligence.

4. The core of intelligence consists of general _____ abilities (the _____-factor).

5. A modern version of Binet's test is the _____-Binet Intelligence Scale, 5th Edition. It is composed of age-ranked questions, which get _____ more difficult.

6. The Stanford-Binet measures fluid reasoning, _____ reasoning, visual-spatial processing, working memory, and _____.

7. In the fluid reasoning factor of the Stanford-Binet Intelligence Scale, individuals are asked to fill in the missing shape in a group; the quantitative reasoning scale measures a person's ability to _____ problems involving numbers.

8. A second major intelligence test is the _____ Adult Intelligence Scale, 3rd Edition (WAIS-III). The WAIS-III measures both verbal and performance (nonverbal) intelligence.

9. The original Standford-Binet was better suited for children and _____; the Wechsler Adult _____ Scale was better suited for adults.

10. Intelligence is expressed in terms of an intelligence quotient (IQ). IQ is defined as _____ age (MA) divided by _____ age (CA) and then multiplied by 100.

11. Modern IQ tests no longer calculate IQs directly. Instead, the final score reported by the test is a _____ IQ, which gives a person's relative intellectual standing in his or her age group. An average IQ score of 100 would place a person at the 50th _____.

12. An "average" IQ of 100 occurs when mental age equals _____ age.

13. Intelligence tests have also been produced for use with groups of people. The Scholastic _____ Test (SAT) measures a variety of mental aptitudes, and it can be used to estimate _____.

14. Artificial _____ refers to computer programs capable of doing things that require intelligence when performed by humans.

15. Humans are flexible and can mentally "_____ gears," whereas computers are constrained by an underlying set of _____ rules.

16. Computer _____ are programs that attempt to duplicate human behavior; expert systems respond like a human expert would respond.

17. _____ human problem solving is based on organized knowledge and acquired strategies rather than some general improvement in _____ ability.

Variations in Intelligence – Curved Like a Bell

Survey Question: How much does intelligence vary from person to person?
Pages 306-309

1. When graphed, the _____ (percentage of people receiving each score) of IQ scores approximates a normal (bell-shaped) curve.

2. People with IQs above 140 are considered to be in the gifted or "_____" range.

3. Studies done by Lewis _____ showed that the gifted tend to be successful: They earned _____ degrees, held professional positions, and had written books.

4. IQ reveals potential; it does not guarantee _____.

5. The most successful gifted persons tend to be those who are _____ and motivated to learn and succeed. By criteria other than _____, a large proportion of children might be considered gifted or talented in one way or another.

6. _____ may reveal itself in children in the following: tendency to seek out older children and adults, early fascination with explanations and problem solving, talking in complete sentences around 2-3 years, good memory, early interest in books, showing of _____, understanding, and _____ with others.

7. The terms intellectually disabled and developmentally _____ are applied to those whose IQ falls below 70 or who lack various _____ behaviors.

8. Further classifications of intellectual disability are: _____ (50-55 to 70), moderate (35-40 to 50-55), severe (20-25 to 35-40), and _____ (below 20-25).

9. About 50 percent of the cases of intellectual disability are _____, being caused by birth injuries and fetal damage, _____ disorders, or genetic abnormalities. The remaining cases are of undetermined cause.

10. Many cases of subnormal intelligence are thought to be the result of familial _____ _____ (a low level of intellectual stimulation in the home, poverty, and poor _____).

Questioning Intelligence—How Intelligent is the Idea of Intelligence?

Survey Question: What are some controversies in the study of intelligence?
Pages 309-314

1. One _____ of traditional intelligence testing is its applicability to other cultural groups.

2. Because children from various cultures are taught different _____, cultural-fair intelligence tests have been implemented to accurately assess individuals' _____ abilities and to reduce biases.

3. Culture-_____ tests attempt to measure intelligence without the influence of verbal skills, _____ background, and education level.

4. The Wechsler and Binet scales are designed to measure the IQ of people from middle-class Western cultures. To reduce the influence of _____ skills, cultural background, and educational level when measuring the IQ of people from another culture (e.g., _____) or from a different background (e.g., poor community), culture-fair tests have been implemented.

5. Traditional IQ tests often suffer from a degree of cultural bias that makes them easier for some groups and _____ for others.

6. Culture-fair tests try to measure intelligence in ways that are not strongly affected by cultural background, but no test is _____ culture-free.

7. Differences in the average IQ scores for various _____ groups are based on _____ differences, not genetics (or heredity).

8. IQ is merely an index of intelligence-based tests that offer a _____ definition of intelligence.

9. Howard _____ believes that traditional IQ tests define intelligence too _____.

10. According to Gardner, intelligence consists of abilities in language, logic and math, visual and spatial thinking, music, _____-kinesthetic skills, _____ skills, interpersonal skills, and naturalist skills.

11. Studies of _____ relationships in humans, especially comparisons between fraternal twins and identical twins (who have _____ genes), also suggest that intelligence is partly hereditary.

12. _____ is also important, as revealed by changes in tested intelligence induced by stimulating environments and _____ education.

13. Intelligence therefore reflects the _____ effects of _____ and environment.

14. Differences in the average IQ scores for various racial groups are based on _____ differences, not genetics (or heredity).

15. Improvements in _____, nutrition, and complex technology have most likely contributed to the increase in average IQ over the past 30 years.

16. Practical intelligence ("_____ smarts") may be more highly valued in some minority cultures than analytic intelligence ("_____ smarts").

What Is Thinking?—Brains over Brawn

Survey Question: What is the nature of thought? Pages 314-315

1. Cognition is the mental processing of information involving _____, problem solving, and _____.

2. Thinking is the manipulation of internal representations of _____ problems or situations.

3. Three basic units of thought are _____, concepts, and language or symbols.

Mental Imagery—Does a Frog Have Lips?

Survey Question: In what ways are images related to thinking? Pages 315-317

1. Many of the systems in the brain that are involved in processing visual images work in reverse to create _____ images.

2. Most people have mental images of one kind or another. _____ may be based on _____ stored in memory or they may be created.

3. Mental images may be used to make a decision, solve a problem, change _____, improve a skill, and/or aid memory.

4. The _____ of images used in problem solving may change. Images may be _____-_____ and they may be rotated in space to answer questions.

5. _____ images are created from produced, remembered, or imagined muscular sensations. Kinesthetic sensations and _____ seem to help structure thinking for many people.

Concepts—I'm Positive, It's a Whatchamacallit

Survey Question: What are concepts? Pages 317-319

1. A concept is a _____ idea of a category of objects or events and help us to identify important features of the world.

2. Forming _____ may be based on experiences with positive and _____ instances.

3. Concepts may also be acquired by learning _____ that define the concept.

4. Concepts may be classified as _____ ("and" concepts), disjunctive ("either-or" concepts), or _____ concepts.

5. In practice, we frequently use _____ (general models of the concept class) to identify concepts.

6. _____ concepts lead to social stereotyping and all-or-nothing thinking.

7. The _____ meaning of a word or concept is its exact definition. _____ meaning is personal or emotional.

8. Connotative meaning can be measured with the semantic differential. Most connotative meaning involves the dimensions good-bad, _____-_____, and active-passive.

Language—Don't Leave Home Without It

Survey Question: What is the role of language in thinking? Pages 319-324

1. Thinking in language is influenced by _____. The study of meaning is called _____.

2. The _____ task demonstrates the effectiveness of words influencing our thinking. The meaning of the word interferes with our ability to name the color of the word.

3. Bilingualism is the ability to speak _____ languages.

4. Language allows events to be encoded into symbols for easy mental _____.

5. In _____ bilingualism, learning a second language adds to a child's overall competence. In subtractive bilingualism, children ultimately may lose native language skills and _____ in both languages.

6. Language is built out of _____ (basic speech sounds) and _____ (speech sounds collected into meaningful units).

7. Language carries meaning by combining a set of symbols or _____ according to a set of rules (grammar), which includes rules about word order (_____).

8. Various sentences are created by applying _____ rules to simple statements.

9. A true language is productive and can be used to generate _____ ideas or possibilities. _____ _____ _____ (ASL) and other gestural languages used by the deaf are true languages.

10. Animal communication is relatively limited because it lacks _____ that can be rearranged easily. As a result, it does not have the _____ quality of human language.

11. Studies that make use of _____ (geometric word-symbols) provide the best evidence yet of animal language use.

Problem Solving—Getting an Answer in Sight

Survey Question: What do we know about problem solving? Pages 324-329

1. The solution to a problem may be found _____ (by trial-and-error or by rote application of rules). However, _____-and-_____ solutions are frequently inefficient or ineffective, except where aided by computer.

2. Often a rote solution is achieved through an _____, a learned set of rules that always leads to a _____ solution.

3. Solutions by understanding usually begin with discovery of the general properties of an answer. Next, a number of _____ solutions are proposed.

4. _____ search strategies, like trial-and-error, may work id the number of alternatives is small, but are generally _____.

5. Problem solving is frequently aided by _____. These are strategies that typically narrow the search for _____.

6. When understanding leads to a rapid solution, _____ has occurred. Three elements of insight are selective encoding, selective _____, and selective comparison.

7. The ability to apply selective comparison (comparing _____ solutions to _____ problems) effectively can be influenced by our culture.

8. Insights and other problem-solving attempts can be blocked by _____ (a tendency to repeat wrong solutions).

9. Functional fixedness is a common fixation, but _____ blocks, cultural _____, learned conventions, and perceptual habits are also problems.

Creative Thinking—Down Roads Less Traveled

Survey Question: What is creative thinking? Pages 329-332

1. Thinking may be _____ or inductive, _____ or illogical.

2. _____ thinking involves going from specific facts to general principles; _____ thinking goes from general principles to specific situations.

3. _____ thinking requires divergent thought, characterized by fluency, flexibility, and originality.

4. Tests of creativity, such as the _____ Uses Test, the _____ Test, and the Anagrams Test, measure the capacity for divergent thinking.

5. To be creative, a solution must be practical and _____ as well as original.

6. Five stages often seen in creative problem solving are _____, preparation, incubation, _____, and verification.

7. Studies suggest that creative persons share a combination of thinking skills, _____ characteristics, and a _____ social environment. There is only a _____ correlation between IQ and creativity.

Intuitive Thought—Mental Shortcut? Or Dangerous Detour?

Survey Question: How accurate is intuition? Pages 332-335

1. Intuitive thinking is quick and _____, and often leads to errors. Wrong conclusions may be drawn when an answer seems highly representative of what we already believe is true, that is, when people apply the representativeness heuristic.

2. A second problem is allowing _____ such as fear, hope, anxiety, or _____ to guide thinking in decision making.

3. The third problem is ignoring the _____ rate (or underlying probability) of an event.

4. Clear thinking is usually aided by stating or _____ a problem in broad terms.

5. _____ represents a mixture of convergent thinking, intelligence, reason, creativity, and originality. Wise people approach life with openness and _____.

6. Quickly making sense of _____ _____ of experiences is called "thin-slicing."

Psychology in Action: Enhancing Creativity - Brainstorms

Survey Question: What can be done to improve thinking and promote creativity?
Pages 336-339

1. Some suggestions for enhancing creativity include: breaking _____ _____ and challenging assumptions, defining problems broadly, restating problems in different ways, allowing time for incubation, seeking varied input, looking for _____, and delaying _____.

2. Individuals can become "set" in one way of thinking; this mental set _____ them to possible solutions.

3. One way to restate a problem is to imagine how another person would _____ it.

4. You are _____ likely to think creatively if you feel pressed for time.

5. Worrying about correctness _____ creativity. Therefore, it is important to delay evaluation

6. To live more creatively, try to find something that _____ you every day.

MASTERY TEST

1. The mark of a true language is that it must be
   a. spoken.
   b. productive.
   c. based on spatial grammar and syntax.
   d. capable of encoding conditional relationships.

2. Computer simulations and expert systems are two major applications of
   a. AI.
   b. ASL.
   c. brainstorming.
   d. problem framing.

3. Failure to wear automobile seat belts is an example of which intuitive thinking error?
   a. allowing too much time for incubation
   b. framing a problem broadly
   c. ignoring base rates
   d. recognition that two events occurring together are more likely than either one alone

4. One thing that images, concepts, and symbols all have in common is that they are
a. morphemes.
b. internal representations.
c. based on reverse vision.
d. translated into micromovements.

5. To decide if a container is a cup, bowl, or vase, most people compare it to
a. a prototype.
b. its connotative meaning.
c. a series of negative instances.
d. a series of relevant phonemes.

6. The Anagrams Test measures
a. mental sets.
b. inductive thinking.
c. logical reasoning.
d. divergent thinking.

7. "Either-or" concepts are
a. conjunctive.
b. disjunctive.
c. relational.
d. prototypical.

8. Which term does not belong with the others?
a. selective comparison
b. functional fixedness
c. learned conventions
d. emotional blocks

9. Separate collections of verbal and performance subtests are a feature of the
a. WAIS.
b. Gardner-8.
c. CQT.
d. Stanford-Binet.

10. Intellectual disability is formally defined by deficiencies in
a. aptitudes and kinesthetic skills.
b. intelligence and scholastic aptitudes.
c. language and spatial thinking.
d. IQ and adaptive behaviors.

11. A 12-year-old child with an IQ of 100 must have a mental age of
a. 100.
b. 12.
c. 10.
d. 15.

12. The difference between prime beef and dead cow is primarily a matter of
a. syntax.
b. conjunctive meaning.
c. semantics.
d. the productive nature of language.

13. Culture-fair tests attempt to measure intelligence without being affected by a person's
a. verbal skills.
b. cultural background.
c. educational level.
d. all the preceding

14. Which of the listed terms does NOT correctly complete this sentence: Insight involves selective _____.
a. encoding
b. combination
c. comparison
d. fixation

15. Which of the following is LEAST likely to predict that a person is creative?
a. high IQ
b. a preference for complexity
c. fluency in combining ideas
d. use of mental images

16. "Try working backward from the desired goal to the starting point or current state." This advice describes a
a. syllogism.
b. heuristic.
c. prototype.
d. dimension of the semantic differential.

17. Language allows events to be _____ into _____.
a. translated, concepts
b. fixated, codes
c. rearranged, lexigrams
d. encoded, symbols

18. "A triangle must be a closed shape with three sides made of straight lines." This statement is an example of a
a. prototype.
b. positive instance.
c. conceptual rule.
d. disjunctive concept.

19. Fluency, flexibility, and originality are all measures of
a. inductive thinking.
b. selective comparison.
c. intuitive framing.
d. divergent thinking.

20. The form of imagery that is especially important in music, sports, dance, and martial arts is
a. kinesthetic imagery.
b. semantic imagery.
c. prototypical imagery.
d. conjunctive imagery.

21. Among animals trained to use language, Kanzi has been unusually successful at
a. forming sentences.
b. learning sign language.
c. expressing conditional relationships.
d. forming chains of operant responses.

22. The largest number of people are found in which IQ range?
a. 80-89
b. 90-109
c. 110-119
d. below 70

23. Comparing two three-dimensional shapes to see if they match is easiest if only a small amount of _____ is required.
a. conceptual recoding
b. mental rotation
c. concept formation
d. kinesthetic transformation

24. Questions that involve copying geometric shapes would be found in which ability area of the SB5?
a. fluid reasoning
b. quantitative reasoning
c. visual-spatial processing
d. working memory

25. The good-bad dimension on the semantic differential is closely related to a concept's
a. disjunctive meaning.
b. conjunctive meaning.
c. connotative meaning.
d. denotative meaning.

26. According to Noam Chomsky, surface sentences are created by applying _____ to simple sentences.
    a. encoding grammars
    b. transformation rules
    c. conditional prototypes
    d. selective conjunctions

27. The occurrence of an insight corresponds to which stage of creative thinking?
    a. verification
    b. incubation
    c. illumination
    d. fixation

28. In Peter's classroom, they spend half of the day learning in English and the other half of the day learning in Spanish. This best represents
    a. thin slicing.
    b. heuristics learning.
    c. two-way bilingual education.
    d. syllogistic learning.

29. When one divides a number into another, step-by-step without the aid of a calculator, one is using a(an) _____ to find a solution.
    a. algorithm
    b. conceptual rule
    c. prototype
    d. anagrams Test

30. Winnie took an IQ test and she is ranked in the 97th percentile. Without knowing her actual IQ score, you can assume that
    a. she is smarter than 97 percent of the people who took the test.
    b. she and 97 percent of the others who took the test have the same IQ scores.
    c. she is smarter than 3 percent of the people who took the test.
    d. 97 percent of the people who took the test are smarter than Winnie.

LANGUAGE DEVELOPMENT

Intelligence, Cognition, Language, and Creativity

Word Roots

The Latin word *norma* was the name given to a carpenter's square. This term contributed to several English words that refer to something being standard or typical. Examples used in this text include: norm, normal, normality, abnormal, and abnormality.

The Latin word *vergere* means "to bend or turn." Using the Latin roots *con* (with) and *di* (apart), the English language has evolved to form two terms you will find used in this chapter: *convergent* (to turn with or merge together) and *divergent* (to turn apart or open).

Journey into Psychology: Homo Sapiens (pg. 301)

- (301)   *frenzied cities*: fast-paced cities
- (301)   *placid retreats*: calm, quiet places to go to get away from one's fast-paced life
- (301)   *Lou Gehrig's Disease:* also called amyotrophic lateral sclerosis; marked by progressive degeneration of muscles, beginning in the feet and ending with paralysis of larynx and throat muscles.
- (301)   *short-circuiting:* preventing full communication
- (301)   *synthesizer*: mechanical device for creating artificial sounds
- (301)   *fiercely*: to a high degree

Human Intelligence—The IQ and You (pgs. 302-306)

How is human intelligence defined and measured?

- (302)   *genius*: an exceptionally intelligent person
- (302)   *a flash of brilliance*: an insightful moment
- (302)   *Stanford University*: a highly-respected university in California
- (303)   *spatial*: relating to space
- (303)   *cryptic*: hidden; secret
- (305)   *"shift gears"*: to change, redirect
- (305)   *stymied*: confused
- (306)   *demystified*: uncovered; made clear

Variations in Intelligence—Curved Like a Bell (pgs. 306-309)

How much does intelligence vary from person to person?

- (307)   *persevere*: persist in spite of opposition
- (307)   *blossom*: come forth; develop
- (307)   *precocious*: developed earlier than normal
- (308)   *shortchange*: cheat
- (309)   *PCBs*: polychlorinated biphenyls, industrial chemicals of high toxicity

Questioning Intelligence—How Intelligent is the idea of intelligence? (pgs. 309-314)

What are some controversies in the study of intelligence?

- (309)   *controvery/controversial:* a discussion with decidedly opposing views
- (310)   *tundra*: a level or rolling treeless plain that is characteristic of arctic and subarctic regions, consists of black mucky soil with a permanently frozen subsoil
- (310)   *anecdote*: story, tale
- (310)   *intricate*: complicated
- (310)   *forge*: form; bring into being
- (310)   *real-world success*: success in the world outside of the school environment; practical success
- (311)   *medicine man*: healer and spiritual leader in Native American, Central American, and South American tribal groups; shaman

(311)   ***organic farmer***: farmer who doesn't use chemical pesticides or fertilizers

(310)   ***Einstein***: Albert Einstein (1879-1955), the physicist whose theories of relativity transformed physics and helped to create the atomic age

(310)   ***cultivate***: identify and encourage

(311)   ***siblings***: brothers and sisters

(312)   ***inflate***: artificially increase

(312)   ***orphanage***: a state-operated house where children without parents or relatives to take care of them live until they are adopted

(314)   ***preordain***: to predetermine

What Is Thinking—Brain over Brawn (pgs. 314-315)

What is the nature of thought?

(314)   ***brawn***: muscular strength; suggests that intellectual strength is superior to physical strength

(315)   ***notational system***: a system or process for writing quantities (e.g., the decimal system)

(315)   ***delve***: to dig deep into something

Mental Imagery—Does a Frog Have Lips? (pgs. 315-317)

In what ways are images related to thinking?

(315)   ***"mind's eye"***: hypothetical center of imagination and visual imagery

(316)   ***egg carton***: a box designed to hold one dozen eggs

(315)   ***Thomas Edison***: Thomas Alva Edison (1847-1931), the American inventor who conceived the electric light, phonograph, and microphone

(315)   ***Lewis Carroll***: A pseudonym for Charles Lutwidge Dodgson, the famous English author who wrote *Alice in Wonderland* and *Through the Looking Glass*

Concepts—I'm Positive, It's a Watchamacallit (pgs. 317-319)

How do we learn concepts?

(317)   ***whatchamacallit***: "what you may call it"; used when the exact name for something cannot be remembered

(317)   ***daze***: state of confusion

(317)   ***Pekingese:*** any of a Chinese breed of small short-legged dogs with a broad flat face and a profuse long soft coat

(317)   ***punk***: music marked by extreme and often offensive expressions of social discontent

(317)   ***hip-hop***: a style of music and dance that derives from inner-city street culture; rap music is part of hip-hop

(317)   ***fusion***: a blending of jazz, rock, Latin, and improvisation to form a modern, smooth type of jazz

(317)   ***salsa***: popular music of Latin American origin combining rhythm and blues, jazz, and rock

(317)   ***metal***: energetic and highly amplified rock music with a hard beat

(317)   *rap*: characterized by lyrics that are spoken rather than sung
(318)   *nudist*: person who wears no clothes in groups and special places (nudist camps)
(318)   *movie censor*: person who gives ratings to movies depending on their sexual content and amount of violence
(319)   *boils down*: narrows down; simplifies
(319)   *conscientious*: extremely careful and attentive to details
(319)   *nitpicky*: extremely critical and attentive to details

Language—Don't Leave Home without It (pgs. 319-324)

What is the role of language in thinking?
(319)   *marksmanship*: the art of shooting
(319)   *bartending*: serving drinks at a bar
(319)   *prime beef*: top grade cattle meat ready for consumption
(320)   *"sink or swim"*: one either fails completely or succeeds in an attempt at doing something
(320)   *a rash of*: a huge spreading or increasing of something
(320)   *circumcised*: having the foreskin of the penis removed
(321)   *gestural*: using motions of the hands or body as a means of expression
(321)   *mime*: to imitate actions without using words
(321)   *pantomime*: dramatic presentation that uses no words, only action and gestures
(322)   *remnant*: something that was once used to aid human survival, that is still with us, but is now unnecessary
(322)   *embody*: to represent something
(322)   *sucker* ("That *sucker* I saw yesterday..."): used as a general term to refer to a person or object (slang)
(322)   *gimme*: give me
(322)   *"wet"* (Washoe once *"wet"* on...): urinated
(323)   *plagued*: bothered; caused difficulties

Problem Solving—Getting An Answer in Sight (pgs. 324-329)

What do we know about problem solving?
(324)   *rote*: memorization
(325)   *inoperable*: cannot be operated on; in this case, surgery cannot be performed
(325)   *analogies*: similarities
(325)   *novices*: beginners; amateurs
(327)   *hourglass*: an instrument for measuring time consisting of a glass container having two sections, one above the other; sand, water, or mercury runs from the upper section to the lower in one hour
(327)   *"hung up"*: delayed; detained by
(327)   *preconception*: bias; assumption
(328)   *precariously*: riskily; dangerously
(328)   *ambiguity*: the quality of being understood in two or more possible senses or ways

(328) *frivolous*: not important enough or worthy of receiving attention

(328) *taboos*: restrictions imposed by social custom

Creative Thinking—Down Roads Less Traveled (pgs. 329-332)

What is creative thinking?

(330) *Mozart*: Wolfgang Amadeus Mozart (1756-1791), a famous Austrian composer and pianist

(330) *"harebrained scheme"*: foolish idea

(330) *"stroke of genius"*: clever idea

(330) *saturate*: to fill up as much as possible

(331) *incubation*: period during which ideas are developed

(330) *futile*: useless

(331) *goldsmith*: a craftsman who works with gold

(332) *eccentric*: odd; strange

(332) *inept*: unable; incompetent

(332) *introverted*: being wholly concerned with and interested in one's own mental life

(332) *neurotic:* emotionally unstable or troubled by anxiety

(332) *outlandish*: very out of the ordinary, strange

Intuitive Thought—Mental Shortcut? Or Dangerous Detour? (pgs. 332-335)

How accurate is intuition?

(332) *shortcut*: a method of doing something more directly and more quickly than usual; it usually involves skipping usual steps

(332) *detour*: a longer way than the direct route or usual procedure

(333) *flawed*: containing defects or errors

(333) *pitfall*: a hidden danger or difficulty

(334) *award custody*: when parents divorce, a judge will decide with which parent the child or children shall live

(335) *short-circuit*: an event that reduces the effectiveness of something (thinking) because parts of the process involved were not completed

(335) *feasible*: doable; practical

Solutions

Recite and Review

Human Intelligence—The IQ and You

1. intelligence, test
2. rationally, environment
3. definition
4. intelligence
5. Intelligence, Scale, questions
6. fluid, memory
7. fluid, quantitative
8. Adult, nonverbal
9. children, adults
10. quotient, 100
11. IQs, relative, 50th
12. 100, equals
13. groups, mental
14. computer
15. rules
16. human, expert
17. knowledge

Variations in Intelligence—Curved Like a Bell

1. bell, curve
2. gifted
3. successful
4. potential
5. motivated, IQ
6. older, 2-3
7. *disabled,* 70
8. mild, severe
9. 50, birth
10. intellectual

Questioning Intelligence—How Intelligent is the Idea of Intelligence?

1. applicability, cultural-fair
2. education
3. Western, educational
4. fair
5. bias
6. cultural, culture
7. genetics, heredity
8. IQ
9. traditional
10. math, visual
11. genes, hereditary
12. stimulating
13. Intelligence
14. Improvements, 30
15. Practical, analytic

What Is Thinking?—Brains over Brawn

1. mental, problem
2. internal
3. language

Mental Imagery—Does a Frog Have Lips?

1. visual
2. created
3. images, problem
4. change, space
5. muscular, Kinesthetic

Concepts—I'm Positive, It's a Whatchamacallit

1. category
2. positive
3. concept
4. and, either, or
5. models
6. stereotyping
7. definition, personal
8. good, bad

Language—Don't Leave Home Without It

1. meaning
2. words
3. Bilingualism
4. symbols
5. second, lose
6. sounds, meaningful
7. rules, order
8. rules
9. productive, gestural
10. human
11. geometric

Problem Solving—Getting an Answer in Sight

1. rote, computer
2. rote, learned
3. general, solutions
4. trial, error
5. narrow
6. solution, selective
7. selective
8. wrong
9. fixation, habits

Creative Thinking—Down Roads Less Traveled

1. Thinking
2. specific, general
3. originality
4. creativity
5. practical
6. preparation
7. skills, supportive

Intuitive Thought—Mental Shortcut? Or Dangerous Detour?

1. errors, true
2. fear, anxiety, thinking
3. probability
4. broad
5. convergent, openness
6. thin, slicing

Psychology in Action: Enhancing Creativity - Brainstorms

1. assumptions, varied
2. solutions
3. restate
4. time
5. correctness
6. creatively

CONNECTIONS

Human Intelligence—The IQ and You; Variations in Intelligence—Curved Like a Bell; and Questioning Intelligence—How Intelligent Is the idea of intelligence?

1. D.
2. N.
3. J.
4. H.
5. R.
6. A.
7. O.
8. G.
9. L.
10. B.
11. M.
12. I.
13. K.
14. E.
15. C.
16. P.
17. F.
18. Q.

What is Thinking?—Brains over Brawn; Mental Imagery—Does a Frog Have Lips?; and Concepts—I'm Positive, It's a Whatchamacallit

1. F.	5. K.	9. D.
2. L.	6. C.	10. G.
3. I.	7. B.	11. J.
4. A.	8. E.	12. H.

Language—Don't Leave Home Without It

1. C.	4. E.	7. B.	10. D.
2. J.	5. J.	8. I.	
3. A.	6. G.	9. F.	

Problem Solving—Getting an Answer in Sight

1. F.	4. E.	7. I.	10. G.
2. D.	5. J.	8. H.	
3. A.	6. B.	9. C.	

Creative Thinking—Down Roads Less Traveled; Intuitive Thought—Mental Shortcut? Or Dangerous Detour?; and Psychology in Action: Enhancing Creativity

1. H.	5. D.	9. A.	13. F.
2. B.	6. C.	10. K.	14. N.
3. L.	7. M.	11. E.	15. G.
4. J.	8. I.	12. O.	

Check Your Memory

Human Intelligence—The IQ and You

1. T	6. F	11. F	16. F
2. F	7. F	12. F	17. T
3. T	8. T	13. T	18. T
4. F	9. T	14. F	19. F
5. T	10. T	15. T	20. T

Variations in Intelligence—Curved Like a Bell

1. T	4. F	7. T	10. F
2. F	5. F	8. F	
3. F	6. T	9. F	

Questioning Intelligence—How Intelligent is the Idea of Intelligence?

1. F	4. F	7. T
2. F	5. T	8. T
3. T	6. T	9. T

What Is Thinking?—Brains over Brawn

1. F	2. T	3. F	4. F

Mental Imagery—Does a Frog Have Lips?

1. T	3. T	5. T	7. T
2. T	4. T	6. T	

Concepts—I'm Positive, It's a Whatchamacallit

1. T	3. T	5. T	7. F
2. F	4. F	6. F	

Language—Don't Leave Home Without It

1. F	6. F	11. F	16. T
2. F	7. F	12. F	17. T
3. F	8. T	13. F	
4. F	9. F	14. F	
5. T	10. F	15. F	

Problem Solving—Getting an Answer in Sight

1. T	4. F	7. F	10. T
2. F	5. T	8. T	11. F
3. F	6. T	9. T	

Creative Thinking—Down Roads Less Traveled

1. T	4. T	7. F
2. F	5. T	8. T
3. T	6. T	9. F

Intuitive Thought—Mental Shortcut? Or Dangerous Detour?

1. F	3. T	5. F	7. T
2. F	4. F	6. T	8. T

Final Survey and Review

Human Intelligence—The IQ and You

1. first, Binet
2. general, purposefully
3. intelligence, operational
4. mental, g
5. Stanford, progressively
6. quantitative, knowledge
7. solve
8. Wechsler
9. adolescents, Intelligence
10. mental, chronological
11. deviation, percentile
12. chronological
13. Assessment, intelligence
14. intelligence
15. shift, pre-programmed
16. simulations
17. Expert, thinking

Variations in Intelligence—Curved Like a Bell

1. distribution
2. genius
3. Terman, advanced
4. success
5. persistent, IQ
6. Giftedness
7. kindness, cooperation
8. disabled, adaptive
9. mild, profound
10. organic, metabolic
11. intellectual, disability, nutrition

Questioning Intelligence—How Intelligent is the Idea of Intelligence?

1. limitation
2. skills, intellectual
3. fair, cultural
4. verbal, China
5. harder
6. entirely
7. racial, environmental
8. narrow
9. Gardner, narrowly
10. bodily, intrapersonal
11. family, identical
12. Environment, improved
13. combined, heredity
14. environmental
15. education
16. street, book

What Is Thinking?—Brains over Brawn

1. daydreaming, reasoning
2. external
3. images

Mental Imagery—Does a Frog Have Lips?

1. mental
2. Images, information
3. feelings
4. size, three, dimensional
5. Kinesthetic, micromovements

Concepts—I'm Positive, It's a Whatchamacallit

1. generalized
2. concepts, negative
3. rules
4. conjunctive, relational
5. prototypes
6. Faulty
7. denotative, Connotative
8. strong, weak

Language—Don't Leave Home Without It

1. meaning, semantics
2. Stroop
3. two
4. manipulation
5. added, struggle
6. phonemes, morphemes
7. signs, syntax
8. transformation
9. new, American, Sign, Language
10. symbols, productive
11. lexigrams

Problem Solving—Getting an Answer in Sight

1. mechanically, trial, error
2. algorithm, correct
3. functional
4. Random, ineffective
5. heuristics, solutions
6. insight, combination
7. old, new
8. fixation
9. emotional, values

Creative Thinking—Down Roads Less Traveled

1. deductive, logical
2. Inductive, deductive
3. Creative
4. Unusual, Consequences
5. sensible
6. orientation, illumination
7. personality, supportive, small

Intuitive Thought—Mental Shortcut? Or Dangerous Detour?

1. impulsive
2. emotions, disgust
3. base
4. framing
5. Wisdom, tolerance
6. thin, slivers

Psychology in Action: Enhancing Creativity – Brainstorms

1. mental, sets, analogies, evaluation
2. blinds
3. view
4. less
5. inhibits
6. surprises

Mastery Test

1. b, p. 321
2. a, p. 305
3. c, p. 328
4. b, p. 314
5. a, p. 318
6. d, p. 330
7. b, p. 318
8. a, p. 327-328
9. a, 303-304
10. d, p. 308-309
11. b, p. 304-305
12. c, p. 319
13. d, p. 310
14. d, p. 327
15. a, p. 329
16. b, p. 325-326
17. d, p. 320
18. c, p. 317
19. d, p. 329
20. a, p. 316-317
21. a, p. 323
22. b, p. 305
23. b, p. 315-316
24. c, p. 303
25. c, p. 318-319
26. b, p. 320-321
27. c, p. 331
28. c, p. 320
29. a, p. 324
30. a, p. 304-305

CHAPTER 9

Motivation and Emotion

Chapter Overview

Motivation typically involves needs, drives, goals, and goal attainment. Three types of motives are biological motives, stimulus motives, and learned motives. Most biological motives maintain homeostasis. Motivation can follow cyclic patterns. Circadian rhythms are closely tied to sleep, activity, and energy cycles, which impact our daily performance. Time changes in our schedule can increase errors in our performance as our circadian rhythms adjust to the new time change.

Hunger is influenced by the stomach, blood sugar levels, fat stores in the body, activity in the hypothalamus, diet, external eating cues, emotions, and other factors. Anorexia nervosa and bulimia nervosa are serious and sometimes fatal eating disorders that affect primarily women. Yo-Yo and starvation diets can slow metabolism, making it harder to lose weight, and may lead to other long-term health issues. Behavioral dieting uses self-control techniques to change basic eating patterns and habits.

Thirst takes two forms: extracellular (fluid lost from outside cells) and intracellular (fluid lost from inside cells). This and other basic motives are affected by many factors, but they are primarily controlled by the hypothalamus. Pain avoidance is episodic and partially learned.

The sex drive is non-homeostatic. To some extent, it is influenced by hormone levels in the body. Sexual arousal is related to stimulation of the body's erogenous zones, but arousal is strongly influenced by mental factors. There is little difference in male and female sexual responsiveness. Human sexual response is divided into four phases: (1) excitement, (2) plateau, (3) orgasm, and (4) resolution. Sexual orientation (heterosexuality, homosexuality, and bisexuality) is based on a variety of influences, including biology, heredity, psychology, and sociocultural factors. Sexual dysfunctions involve problems of desire, pain, arousal, or orgasm.

The stimulus motives include drives for information, exploration, manipulation, and sensory input. Drives for stimulation are partially explained by arousal theory. Optimal performance on a task usually occurs at moderate levels of arousal; however, optimal arousal depends on the complexity of the task, which is represented by the Yerkes-Dodson function. Test anxiety is caused by a mixture of excessive worrying and heightened physiological arousal, which can be reduced through preparation, relaxation, rehearsal, and restructuring thoughts.

Social motives, which are learned, account for much of the diversity of human motivation. The need for achievement is a social motive correlated with success in many situations. Self-confidence also affects motivation by influencing the types of challenges that one takes.

Maslow's hierarchy of motives categorizes needs as basic or growth oriented. Self-actualization, the highest and most fragile need, is reflected in meta-needs. In many situations, extrinsic motivation can lower intrinsic motivation, enjoyment, and creativity.

Emotions are linked to basic adaptive behaviors. The major elements of emotion are bodily changes, emotional expressions, and emotional feelings. There are eight basic emotions; all others are combinations of the primary emotions at different intensities. Physiological changes during emotion are caused by adrenaline and the autonomic nervous system (ANS). The sympathetic branch of the ANS arouses the body and the parasympathetic branch quiets it. A polygraph measures a person's general emotional arousal through changes in heart rate, blood pressure, breathing, and galvanic skin response. Its effectiveness has been questioned.

Basic emotional expressions are unlearned. Facial expressions are central to emotion. Body gestures and movements (body language) also express feelings. A variety of theories and hypotheses have been proposed to explain emotion: the James-Lange theory, the Cannon-Bard theory, Schachter's Cognitive Theory of Emotion, attribution and appraisal theory, and the facial feedback hypothesis. Physical arousal can cause us to misattribute or mislabel emotional reactions.

Emotional intelligence involves a combination of skills, such as self-awareness, empathy, self-control, and an understanding of how to use emotions. For success in many situations, emotional intelligence is as important as IQ.

Learning Objectives

1. Describe the condition known as *alexithymia.*
2. Define *motivation* and what factors influence motivation and emotions.
3. Explain the need reduction model and how the incentive value of a goal can affect motivation.
4. Describe and give an example of each of the three types of motives, and define homeostasis.
5. Describe how circadian rhythms affect energy levels, motivation, and performance; explain how and why shift work and jet lag may adversely affect a person, and how to minimize the effects of shifting one's rhythms.
6. Discuss why hunger cannot be fully explained by the contractions of an empty stomach, and describe the relationship of each of the following to hunger:
   a. blood sugar
   b. ghrelin
   c. liver
   d. hypothalamus

    i. feeding system (lateral hypothalamus)
    ii. satiety system (ventromedial hypothalamus)
    iii. blood sugar regulator (paraventricular nucleus)
  e. GLP-1
7. Explain how each of the following is related to overeating and obesity:
  a. a person's set point
  b. the release of leptin
  c. external eating cues
  d. variety and taste
  e. emotions
  f. cultural factors
  g. dietary content
8. Explain the paradox of "yo-yo" dieting.
9. Explain what is meant by behavioral dieting and describe how these techniques can enable you to control your weight.
10. Describe the essential features of the eating disorders anorexia nervosa and bulimia nervosa; explain what causes them and what treatments are available for these eating disorders.
11. Name the brain structure that appears to control thirst, and differentiate extracellular and intracellular thirst.
12. Explain how the drive to avoid pain and the sex drive differ from other primary drives.
13. Describe how the sex drive in humans differs from that of lower animals, and how alcohol and various other drugs affect one's sex drive.
14. Describe the erogenous zones and the similarities and differences in the male and female sexual response cycle, including the four phases of sexual response identified by Masters and Johnson; and define the terms *aphrodisiac* and *sexual script*.
15. Define the term *sexual orientation*; describe the various types of sexual orientation; explain the combination of influences that appears to produce homosexuality.
16. Discuss the four types of sexual dysfunctions and treatments for them, such as drugs and sensate focus.
17. Discuss the importance of the stimulus drives.
18. DescrDescribe the arousal theory, the inverted U function, and the Yerkes-Dodson law; and list the characteristics of high and low sensation-seekers.
19. Explain how one can cope with test anxiety.
20. Describe social motives and explain how they are acquired.
21. Define the need for achievement (nAch) and differentiate it from the need for power; relate this need for achievement to risk taking; and explain the influences of drive and determination in the success of high achievers.
22. Discuss how self-confidence affects motivation; and list seven steps to enhance self-confidence.
23. List (in order) the needs found in Maslow's hierarchy of motives; distinguish between basic needs and growth needs; explain why Maslow's

lower (physiological) needs are considered prepotent; and define and give examples of meta-needs.

24. Distinguish between intrinsic and extrinsic motivation, and explain how each type of motivation may affect a person's interest in work, leisure activities, and creativity.

25. Define the terms *emotions* and *moods*, and explain how emotions aid survival; describe the three major elements of emotions.

26. List the eight primary emotions proposed by Plutchik.

27. Explain the role played by the brain hemispheres when a person experiences two opposite emotions simultaneously.

28. Describe the roles of the sympathetic and parasympathetic branches of the ANS in emotional arousal; explain how the parasympathetic rebound may be involved in cases of sudden death.

29. Discuss the use and limitations of the lie detector (polygraph), and the future techniques to be used for detecting lies.

30. Discuss Darwin's view of human emotion, and which facial expressions appear to be universal and most recognizeable.

31. Describe cultural and gender differences in emotional expression.

32. Discuss kinesics, including the emotional messages conveyed by facial expressions and body language.

33. Describe and give examples of the following theories of emotion:
    a. James-Lange theory
    b. Cannon-Bard theory
    c. Schachter's cognitive theory
    d. the effects of attribution on emotion
    e. the facial feedback hypothesis, including the dangers of suppressing emotions
    f. emotional appraisal
    g. the contemporary model of emotion

34. Describe the concept of emotional intelligence and its five skills, and briefly discuss the benefits of positive emotions.

RECITE AND REVIEW

Motivation—Push Me, Pull Me

Survey Questions: What is motivation? Are there different types of motives? Pages 344-347

1. Motives _____ (begin), sustain (perpetuate), direct, and terminate _____.

2. Motivation typically involves the sequence: _____, drive, _____, and goal attainment (need reduction).

3. Behavior can be activated either by internal needs (_____) or by external stimuli or goals (_____).

4. The attractiveness of a _____ and its ability to initiate action are related to its incentive value (its value above and beyond its capacity to fill a _____).

5. Three principal types of motives are biological motives, stimulus motives, and _____ motives.

6. Most biological motives are necessary for survival, and operate to maintain a _____ state of bodily equilibrium called homeostasis.

7. Stimulus _____ such as curiosity, exploration, and _____ contact are not necessary for survival, but satisfy our needs for stimulation and information.

8. The need for power, affiliation, status, and achievement are _____ motives, and are influenced by _____ and social context.

9. Circadian _____ within the body are closely tied to sleep, activity levels, and energy cycles. Time zone travel and shift work can seriously disrupt _____ and bodily rhythms.

10. If you anticipate a _____ in body rhythms, you can gradually preadapt to your new _____ over a period of days.

Hunger—Pardon Me, My Hypothalamus Is Growling

Survey Questions: What causes hunger? Overeating? Eating disorders? Pages 347-354

1. Hunger is influenced by a complex interplay between distention (fullness) of the _____, hypoglycemia (low _____ sugar), metabolism in the _____, and fat stores in the body.

2. The most direct control of eating is exerted by the hypothalamus, which has areas that act like feeding (_____), and satiety (_____) systems for hunger and eating.

3. The lateral hypothalamus acts as a _____ system; the ventromedial hypothalamus is part of a _____ system; the paraventricular nucleus influences both hunger and satiety.

4. The lining of the stomach produces the _____ ghrelin, which affects the activity of the _____ hypothalamus.

5. When body weight surpasses its set point, _____ is released into the bloodstream; the hypothalamus then tells us to eat less.

6. Radical diets may raise the body's set point, resulting in diet-induced _____.

7. Other factors influencing hunger are the set point for the proportion of _____ in the body, external eating cues, and the attractiveness and variety of _____.

8. Hunger is also influenced by emotions, food availability, and cultural
   _____.

9. Dieting slows the body's rate of _____, making the body more
   efficient at conserving calories and storing them as fat.

10. A successful behavioral dieting approach begins with committing oneself to
    weight loss, _____, counting _____, avoiding snacks,
    developing techniques to control overeating, and charting one's progress.

11. Anorexia nervosa (self-inflicted _____) and bulimia nervosa
    (_____ and purging) are two prominent eating disorders.

12. The majority of individuals with eating disorders are _____; however,
    about 10 percent of anorexics and 25 percent of _____ are male.

13. People with eating disorders usually have _____ views of themselves,
    exaggerated fears of becoming fat, and _____ self-esteem.

14. The media and the popularity of _____, exercise, and sports have
    contributed to the rise of eating disorders.

15. Treatments for anorexia begin with medical diet to restore weight and health,
    and then advance to _____.

16. Both eating disorders tend to involve conflicts about self-image, self-control,
    and _____.

Biological Motives Revisited—Thirst, Pain, and Sex

Survey Questions: Is there more than one type of thirst? In what ways are pain
avoidance and the sex drive unusual? Pages 354-355

1. Like hunger, thirst and other basic motives are affected by a number of
   _____ factors, but are primarily under the central control of the
   hypothalamus in the _____.

2. Thirst may be either intracellular (when _____ is lost from inside
   _____) or extracellular (when _____ is lost from fluids
   surrounding _____).

3. Pain avoidance is unusual because it is episodic (associated with particular
   conditions) as opposed to cyclic (occurring in regular _____).

4. Pain avoidance and pain tolerance are partially _____ (influenced by
   training).

5. Hunger, thirst, and other drives are important for _____ of the
   individual; the _____ drive is important for survival of the group.

6. The sex drive in many lower animals is related to estrus (or "heat") in
   _____.

7. Sex _____ in both males and females may be related to bodily levels
   of androgens.

8. Alcohol and other drugs have been used to increase sexual desire and performance; however these often _____ the sexual response.

9. The sex drive is unusual in that it is non-homeostatic (both its _____ and its reduction are sought).

Sexual Behavior—Mapping the Erogenous Zone

Survey Question: What are the typical patterns of human sexual response?
Pages 355-360

1. Sexual arousal is related to stimulation of the body's erogenous zones (areas that produce erotic _____), but cognitive elements such as _____ and images are equally important.

2. In a series of landmark studies, William _____ and Virginia Johnson directly observed sexual response in a large number of adults.

3. There is little difference in sexual _____ between males and females.

4. Evidence suggests that the sex drive peaks at a _____ age for females than it does for males, although this difference is diminishing.

5. Human sexual response can be divided into four phases: (1) _____, (2) plateau, (3) _____, and (4) resolution.

6. Both males and females may go through all four stages in _____ minutes. But during lovemaking, most females typically take longer than this.

7. Although many _____ are capable of multiple orgasms, an orgasm is not necessary for a satisfying sexual experience.

8. Males experience a refractory period after _____ and ejaculation. Only 5 percent of men are _____-orgasmic.

9. Young Americans seem to be moving from a traditional sexual script to a casual sexual script; this includes "_____ with _____" and "hook-up" scripts.

10. Sexual orientation refers to one's degree of emotional and erotic attraction to members of the same _____, opposite _____, or both _____.

11. A person may be heterosexual, _____, or bisexual.

12. A combination of hereditary, biological, social, and psychological influences combines to produce one's _____ _____.

13. As a group, homosexual men and women do not differ psychologically from _____.

14. _____, counseling, or psychotherapy can alleviate many sexual problems.

Stimulus Motives – Monkey Business

Survey Question: How does arousal relate to motivation? Pages 361-363

1. The stimulus drives reflect needs for information, exploration, manipulation, and _____ input.

2. Drives for stimulation are partially explained by arousal theory, which states that an ideal level of _____ _____ will be maintained if possible.

3. Physical arousal refers to activation of the _____ and nervous system.

4. Sensation seeking scores are based on how your body responds to new, _____, or intense stimulation.

5. Optimal performance on a task usually occurs at _____ levels of arousal. This relationship is described by an inverted U function.

6. The Yerkes-Dodson law further states that for _____ tasks the ideal arousal level is higher, and for _____ tasks it is lower.

7. Test anxiety is caused by a combination of _____ worrying and heightened physiological arousal, which can be reduced with better _____, relaxation, _____, and restructuring thoughts.

Learned Motives—The Pursuit of Excellence

Survey Questions: What are social motives? Why are they important? Pages 363-365

1. _____ motives are learned through socialization and cultural conditioning, and may include the need for success, achievement, _____, money, status, power, love, _____, grades, dominance, power, or belonging.

2. Social motives are not innate; they are learned through _____ and cultural conditioning.

3. One of the most prominent social motives is the _____ for achievement (nAch), which is a need to meet some _____ standard of excellence.

4. High nAch is correlated with _____ in many situations, with occupational choice, and with moderate _____ taking.

5. According to Bloom, intensive practice, _____ coaching, and determination lead to high achievement.

6. Self-confidence affects _____ because it influences the challenges you will undertake, the _____ you will make, and how long you will _____ when things don't go well.

7. To enhance self-confidence, one should do the following: Set goals that are specific, _____, and attainable; advance in _____ steps; find a role model; get expert instructions; and get _____ support.

Motives in Perspective—The View From the Pyramid

Survey Question: Are some motives more basic than others? Pages 365-368

1. Maslow's hierarchy (rank ordering) of motives categorizes needs as _____ and growth oriented.

2. _____ needs in the hierarchy are assumed to be prepotent (dominant) over _____ needs.

3. Basic needs are motivated by _____. If our basic needs are met, we can move on to growth needs and self-actualization.

4. _____-actualization, the highest and most fragile need, is reflected in meta-_____.

5. In many situations, extrinsic motivation (that which is induced by obvious _____ rewards) can reduce intrinsic motivation (engagement for _____ rewards), enjoyment, and creativity.

Inside an Emotion—How Do You Feel?

Survey Questions: What happens during emotion? Pages 368-370

1. Other major elements of emotion are physiological changes in the body, emotional expressions, and emotional _____.

2. Emotions are linked to many basic adaptive _____, such as attacking, retreating, feeding, seeking comfort and reproducing.

3. Emotions aid survival by allowing humans to live in _____, cooperate in raising children, and defend one another.

4. The following are considered to be primary emotions: fear, surprise, _____, disgust, _____, anticipation, joy, and trust (acceptance). Other emotions seem to represent mixtures of the primaries and variations in intensity.

5. Moods are _____-_____ emotional states that often affect day-to-day behavior. Positive moods are more adaptable.

6. The amygdala specializes in producing _____, and is not under the control of higher brain centers.

Physiology and Emotion—Arousal, Sudden Death, and Lying

Survey Questions: What physiological changes underlie emotion? Can "lie detectors" really detect lies? Pages 370-374

1. Physical changes associated with emotion are caused by the action of adrenaline, a _____ released into the bloodstream, and by activity in the autonomic _____ _____ (ANS).

2. The sympathetic _____ of the ANS is primarily responsible for arousing the body, the parasympathetic _____ for quieting it.

3. Sudden death due to prolonged and intense emotion is probably related to parasympathetic _____ (sudden slowing after excess activity). Heart attacks caused by sudden intense emotion are more likely due to sympathetic _____.

4. The polygraph or "lie detector" measures _____ _____ by monitoring heart rate, blood pressure, breathing rate, and galvanic skin response (GSR).

5. The polygraph records general emotional arousal, but cannot tell the difference between _____, fear, anxiety, or excitement.

6. Asking a series of _____ and irrelevant questions may allow the detection of _____, but overall, the accuracy of the lie detector has been challenged by many researchers.

7. Infrared face scans and the use of _____ in analyzing brain activity are possible alternative techniques to polygraph testing.

Expressing Emotions—Making Faces and Talking Bodies

Survey Question: How accurately are emotions expressed by the face and "body language"? Pages 374-376

1. Basic emotional expressions, such as smiling or baring one's teeth when angry, appear to be _____.

2. Facial expressions of _____, anger, disgust, _____, and happiness are recognized by people of all cultures.

3. Asian cultures place high value on group _____, and are less likely to express anger than in Western cultures.

4. In Western culture, women are encouraged to express such emotions as _____, fear, _____, and guilt, and men are expected to express _____ and hostility.

5. Three dimensions of _____ expressions are pleasantness-unpleasantness, attention-rejection, and activation.

6. The study of _____ _____ is known as kinesics.

7. Body gestures and movements (body language) also express _____, mainly by communicating emotional _____.

8. The most general messages conveyed by body language are _____ or tension and liking or diskling.

Theories of Emotion—Several Ways to Fear a Bear

Survey Question: How do psychologists explain emotions? Pages 376-381

1. The James-Lange theory of emotion says that emotional experience _____ an awareness of the bodily reactions of emotion.

2. In contrast, the Cannon-Bard theory says that bodily reactions and emotional experience occur _____ and that emotions are organized in the brain.

3. Schachter's cognitive theory of emotion emphasizes the importance of _____, or interpretations, applied to feelings of bodily arousal.

4. Also important is the process of attribution, in which bodily _____ is attributed to a particular person, object, or situation. Physical arousal can cause us to misattribute or _____ emotional reactions.

5. Emotional appraisal refers to how you think about an event in the _____ place: good/bad, _____/supportive, relevant/irrelevant, etc.

6. The facial feedback hypothesis holds that sensations and information from emotional _____ help define what emotion a person is feeling.

7. Making faces does influence _____ and bodily activities through the _____ nervous system.

8. Restraining emotion can increase activity in the sympathetic _____ system Suppressing emotions can impair _____ and memory.

9. Contemporary views of emotion place greater emphasis on how _____ are appraised. Also, all of the elements of emotion are seen as interrelated and interacting.

Psychology in Action: Emotional Intelligence—The Fine Art of Self-Control

Survey Question: What does it mean to have "emotional intelligence"? Pages 381-382

1. Elements of emotional intelligence are _____-awareness, empathy, an ability to _____ emotions, having a good understanding of emotions, and being able to use emotions to make decisions.

2. Emotionally intelligent people are good at reading facial expressions, tone of voice, and other signs of _____. They also use their _____ (or _____) to enhance thinking and decision making.

3. _____ emotions are not just a luxury. They tend to encourage personal growth and social connection.

CONNECTIONS

Motivation—Forces that Push and Pull

Survey Questions: What is motivation? Are there different types of motives?
Pages 343-348

1. _____ circadian rhythm   A. internal deficiency

2. _____ incentive value   B. goal desirability

3. _____ motivational model   C. learned goals

4. _____ need   D. need reduction

5. _____ changes eating habits   E. steady state

6. _____ homeostasis   F. 24-hour day cycle

7. _____ secondary motives   G. behavioral dieting

Hunger—Pardon Me, My Hypothalamus Is Growling

Survey Questions: What causes hunger? Overeating? Eating disorders? Pages 348-354

1. _____ ventromedial hypothalamus

2. _____ lateral hypothalamus

3. _____ paraventricular nucleus

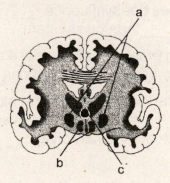

1. _____ satiety system   A. weight/height2 x 703

2. _____ taste aversion   B. classical condition

3. _____ set point   C. thermostat for fat level

4. _____ hunger and satiety   D. lateral hypothalamus

5. _____ body mass index   E. yo-yo dieting

6. _____ weight cycling   F. paraventricular nucleus

7. _____ feeding system   G. ventromedial hypothalamus

Primary Motives Revisited—Thirst, Pain, and Sex

Survey Questions: Is there more than one type of thirst? In what ways are pain avoidance and the sex drive unusual? Pages 354-356

1. _____ episodic drive
2. _____ non-homeostatic
3. _____ intracellular thirst
4. _____ extracellular thirst
5. _____ estrus

A. weight/height^2 x 703
B. result from diarrhea
C. drive to avoid incidences of pain
D. human sex drive
E. result from too much salt intake

Sexual Behavior—Mapping the Erogenous Zone

Survey Question: What are the typical patterns of human sexual response?
Pages 356-359

1. _____ refractory period
2. _____ resolution
3. _____ excitement
4. _____ sexual script
5. _____ erogenous zone
6. _____ orgasm disorder

A. last phase of sexual response
B. delay between orgasms in males
C. sexual "plot"
D. area of the body that produces pleasure
E. inability to have an orgasm
F. first stage of sexual response

Stimulus Drives—Skydiving, Horror Movies, and the Fun Zone, and Social Motives—The Pursuit of Excellence

Survey Questions: How does arousal relate to motivation? What are social motives? Why are they important? Pages 360-364

1. _____ heightened physiological arousal
2. _____ nAch
3. _____ self-confidence
4. _____ moderate risk takers
5. _____ inverted U function

A. standards of excellence
B. impaired test performance
C. high in nAch
D. mixture of arousal and performance
E. believing that one can succeed

Motives in Perspective—A View From the Pyramid, Inside an Emotion—How Do You Feel? and Physiology and Emotion—Arousal, Sudden Death, and Lying

Survey Questions: Are some motives more basic than others? What happens during emotion? Can "lie detectors" really detect lies? Pages 365-373

1. _____ safety and security
2. _____ basic needs
3. _____ love and belonging
4. _____ self-actualization
5. _____ physiological needs
6. _____ esteem and self-esteem
7. _____ growth needs

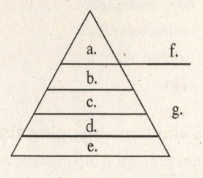

1. _____ meta-needs
2. _____ adrenaline
3. _____ parasympathetic rebound
4. _____ Robert Plutchik
5. _____ irrelevant questions
6. _____ polygraph
7. _____ sympathetic branch
8. _____ relevant questions
9. _____ mood

A. eight primary emotions
B. arousal-producing hormone
C. "Did you murder Hensley?"
D. nonemotional questions
E. prolonged mild emotion
F. fight or flight
G. intense emotional overreaction
H. lie detection
I. self-actualization

Expressing Emotions—Making Faces and Talking Bodies, Theories of Emotion—Several Ways to Fear a Bear, and Psychology in Action: Emotional Intelligence—The Fine Art of Self-control

Survey Questions: How accurately do "body language" and the face express emotions? How do psychologists explain emotions? What does it mean to have "emotional intelligence"? Pages 373-382

1. _____ anxiety
2. _____ sadness
3. _____ authentic happiness
4. _____ James-Lange theory
5. _____ body language
6. _____ facial blend
7. _____ self-awareness
8. _____ Schachter's cognitive theory
9. _____ emotional intelligence

A. arousal + label then emotions
B. bodily arousal then emotions
C. mixing 2+ facial emotions
D. appraisal of loss
E. appraisal of threat
F. kinesics
G. emotional skills
H. in tune with own feelings
I. emphasize natural strengths

CHECK YOUR MEMORY

Motivation—Forces that Push and Pull

Survey Questions: What is motivation? Are there different types of motives? Pages 343-348

1. The terms *need* and *drive* are used interchangeably to describe motivation.

TRUE or FALSE

2. Incentive value refers to the "pull" of valued goals.

TRUE or FALSE

3. Primary motives are based on needs that must be met for survival.

TRUE or FALSE

4. Much of the time, homeostasis is maintained by automatic reactions within the body.

TRUE or FALSE

5. Changes in body temperature are closely related to circadian rhythms.

TRUE or FALSE

6. Adapting to rapid time zone changes is easiest when a person travels east, rather than west.

TRUE or FALSE

Hunger—Pardon Me, My Hypothalamus Is Growling

Survey Questions: What causes hunger? Overeating? Eating disorders? Pages 348-354

1. Cutting the sensory nerves from the stomach abolishes hunger.

TRUE or FALSE

2. Lowered levels of glucose in the blood can cause hunger.

TRUE or FALSE

3. The hypothalamus is involved in the regulation of many motives, including hunger, thirst, and the sex drives.

TRUE or FALSE

4. The paraventricular nucleus is sensitive to neuropeptide Y.

TRUE or FALSE

5. Both glucagon-like peptide 1 (GLP-1) and leptin act as stop signals that inhibit eating.

TRUE or FALSE

6. Dieting speeds up the body's metabolic rate.

TRUE or FALSE

7. People who diet intensely every other day lose as much weight as those who diet moderately every day.

TRUE or FALSE

8. Exercise makes people hungry and tends to disrupt dieting and weight loss.

TRUE or FALSE

9. Radical diets may raise the body's set point, resulting in weight gain.

TRUE or FALSE

10. External cues have little impact on one's tendency to overeat.

TRUE or FALSE

11. The fast-food industry promotes healthy and tasty products that have contributed to the problem of obesity.

TRUE or FALSE

12. "Yo-yo dieting" refers to repeatedly losing and gaining weight through the process of bingeing and purging.

TRUE or FALSE

13. Behavioral dieting changes habits without reducing the number of calories consumed.

TRUE or FALSE

14. Charting daily progress is a basic behavioral dieting technique.

TRUE or FALSE

15. The incentive value of foods is largely determined by cultural values.

TRUE or FALSE

16. Many victims of anorexia nervosa overestimate their body size.

TRUE or FALSE

17. Over time anorexics lose their appetite and do not feel hungry.

TRUE or FALSE

18. Treatment for anorexia begins with counseling.

TRUE or FALSE

Primary Motives Revisited—Thirst, Pain, and Sex

Survey Questions: Is there more than one type of thirst? In what ways are pain avoidance and the sex drive unusual? Pages 354-356

1. Bleeding, vomiting, or sweating can cause extracellular thirst.

TRUE or FALSE

2. Intracellular thirst is best satisfied by a slightly salty liquid.

TRUE or FALSE

3. Tolerance for pain is largely unaffected by learning.

TRUE or FALSE

4. Castration of a male animal typically abolishes the sex drive.

TRUE or FALSE

5. Getting drunk *decreases* sexual desire, arousal, pleasure, and performance.

TRUE or FALSE

Sexual Behavior—Mapping the Erogenous Zone

Survey Question: What are the typical patterns of human sexual response?
Pages 356-359

1. Sexual scripts determine when, where, and with whom we are likely to express sexual feelings.

TRUE or FALSE

2. Male and female patterns of sexual behavior have continued to become less alike in recent years.

TRUE or FALSE

3. Your sexual orientation is revealed, in part, by who you have erotic fantasies about.

TRUE or FALSE

4. Gay males are converted to homosexuality during adolescence by other homosexuals.

TRUE or FALSE

5. Sexual orientation is a very stable personal characteristic.

TRUE or FALSE

6. Sexual orientation is influenced by heredity.

TRUE or FALSE

7. Masters and Johnson's data on human sexuality was restricted to questionnaires and interviews.

TRUE or FALSE

8. During the excitement phase of sexual response, the nipples become erect in both males and females.

TRUE or FALSE

9. In males, orgasm is always accompanied by ejaculation.

TRUE or FALSE

10. Almost all women experience a short refractory period after ejaculation.

TRUE or FALSE

11. Both orgasm and resolution tend to last longer in females than they do in males.

TRUE or FALSE

12. Women tend to go through the phases of sexual response more slowly than men do.

TRUE or FALSE

13. The term *sensate focus* refers to a common sexual pain disorder.

TRUE or FALSE

Stimulus Drives—Skydiving, Horror Movies, and the Fun Zone

Survey Question: How does arousal relate to motivation? Pages 360-363

1. It is uncomfortable to experience both very high and very low levels of arousal.

TRUE or FALSE

2. Disinhibition and boredom susceptibility are characteristics of sensation-seeking persons.

TRUE or FALSE

3. Individuals who score high on the Sensation-Seeking Scales do not engage in high-risk behaviors such as substance abuse.

TRUE or FALSE

4. For nearly all activities, the best performance occurs at high levels of arousal.

TRUE or FALSE

5. Test anxiety is a combination of arousal and excessive worry.

TRUE or FALSE

6. Being over prepared is a common cause of test anxiety.

TRUE or FALSE

Social Motives—The Pursuit of Excellence

Survey Questions: What are social motives? Why are they important? Pages 363-364

1. The need for achievement refers to a desire to have impact on other people.

TRUE or FALSE

2. People high in nAch generally prefer "long shots" or "sure things."

TRUE or FALSE

3. Benjamin Bloom found that high achievement is based as much on hard work as it is on talent.

TRUE or FALSE

4. For many activities, self-confidence is one of the most important sources of motivation.

TRUE or FALSE

Motives in Perspective—A View From the Pyramid

Survey Question: Are some motives more basic than others? Pages 365-367

1. Maslow's hierarchy of needs places self-esteem at the top of the pyramid.

TRUE or FALSE

2. Maslow believed that needs for safety and security are more potent than needs for love and belonging.

TRUE or FALSE

3. Meta-needs are the most basic needs in Maslow's hierarchy.

TRUE or FALSE

4. Maslow believed that most people are motivated to seek esteem, love, and security rather than self-actualization.

TRUE or FALSE

5. Intrinsic motivation occurs when obvious external rewards are provided for engaging in an activity.

TRUE or FALSE

6. People are more likely to be creative when they are intrinsically motivated.

TRUE or FALSE

7. Emotions help people survive by bonding with each other as they socialize and work together.

TRUE or FALSE

8. Happy, positive moods are as equally adaptive as negative moods in influencing creativity, efficiency, and helpfulness to others.

TRUE or FALSE

Inside an Emotion—How Do You Feel?

Survey Questions: What happens during emotion? Can "lie detectors" really detect lies? Pages 368-370

1. Most physiological changes during emotion are related to the release of adrenaline into the brain.

TRUE or FALSE

2. Robert Plutchik's theory lists contempt as a primary emotion.

TRUE or FALSE

3. For most students, elevated moods tend to occur on Saturdays and Tuesdays.

TRUE or FALSE

4. Positive emotions are processed mainly in the left hemisphere of the brain.

TRUE or FALSE

5. The brain area called the amygdala specializes in producing fear.

TRUE or FALSE

Physiology and Emotion—Arousal, Sudden Death, and Lying

Pages 370-373

1. The sympathetic branch of the ANS is under voluntary control and the parasympathetic branch is involuntary.

TRUE or FALSE

2. The parasympathetic branch of the ANS slows the heart and lowers blood pressure.

TRUE or FALSE

3. Most sudden deaths due to strong emotion are associated with the traumatic disruption of a close relationship.

TRUE or FALSE

4. Although not 100 percent accurate, infrared face scans are 50 percent better at detecting lies than polygraph tests.

TRUE or FALSE

5. The polygraph measures the body's unique physical responses to lying.

TRUE or FALSE

6. Only a guilty person should react emotionally to irrelevant questions.

TRUE or FALSE

7. As many as 25 percent of all wrongful convictions include false confessions.

TRUE or FALSE

8. Research suggests that infrared scanning is at least as accurate as polygraph tests for the detection of lies.

TRUE or FALSE

9. The lie detector's most common error is to label innocent persons guilty.

TRUE or FALSE

Expressing Emotions—Making Faces and Talking Bodies

Survey Question: How accurately do "body language" and the face express emotions? Pages 373-375

1. Children born deaf and blind express emotions with their faces in about the same way as other people do.

TRUE or FALSE

2. It is easier to detect angry and scheming facial expressions than happy, sad, or neutral faces.

TRUE or FALSE

3. The "A-okay" hand gesture means "everything is fine" around the world.

TRUE or FALSE

4. Facial blends mix two or more basic expressions.

TRUE or FALSE

5. Liking is expressed in body language by leaning back and relaxing the extremities.

TRUE or FALSE

6. Gestures such as rubbing hands, twisting hair, and biting lips are consistently related to lying.

TRUE or FALSE

7. People from Asian cultures are more likely to express anger in public than people from Western cultures.

TRUE or FALSE

8. In Western cultures, men tend to be more emotionally expressive than women.

TRUE or FALSE

Theories of Emotion—Several Ways to Fear a Bear

Survey Question: How do psychologists explain emotions? Pages 376-380

1. The James-Lange theory of emotion says that we see a bear, feel fear, are aroused, and then run.

TRUE or FALSE

2. The Cannon-Bard theory states that emotion and bodily arousal occur at the same time.

TRUE or FALSE

3. According to Schachter's cognitive theory, arousal must be labeled in order to become an emotion.

TRUE or FALSE

4. Attribution theory predicts that people are most likely to "love" someone who does not agitate, anger, and frustrate them.

TRUE or FALSE

5. Making facial expressions can actually cause emotions to occur and alter physiological activities in the body.

TRUE or FALSE

6. Suppressing emotions takes very little effort.

TRUE or FALSE

7. Emotional appraisal refers to deciding if your own facial expressions are appropriate for the situation you are in.

TRUE or FALSE

8. Suppressing emotions can impair thinking and memory because a lot of energy must be devoted to self-control.

TRUE or FALSE

9. Moving toward a desired goal is associated with the emotion of happiness.

TRUE or FALSE

10. Emotional intelligence refers to the ability to use primarily the right cerebral hemisphere to process emotional events.

TRUE or FALSE

Psychology in Action: Emotional Intelligence—The Fine Art of Self-control

Survey Question: What does it mean to have "emotional intelligence"? Pages 381-382

1. People who excel in life tend to be emotionally intelligent.

TRUE or FALSE

2. People who are empathetic are keenly tuned in to their own feelings.

TRUE or FALSE

3. People who are emotionally intelligent know what causes them to feel various emotions.

TRUE or FALSE

4. Negative emotions can be valuable and constructive because they impart useful information to us.

TRUE or FALSE

5. Positive emotions produce urges to be creative, to explore, and to seek new experiences.

TRUE or FALSE

6. Martin Seligman believes that to be genuinely happy, people must cultivate their own natural strengths.

TRUE or FALSE

7. A first step toward becoming emotionally intelligent is to pay attention to and value your feelings and emotional reactions.

TRUE or FALSE

FINAL SURVEY AND REVIEW

Motivation—Forces that Push and Pull

Survey Questions: What is motivation? Are there different types of motives? Pages 343-348

1. Motives initiate (begin), _____ (perpetuate), and _____ activities.

2. Motivation typically involves the sequence: need, _____, goal, and goal _____ (need reduction).

3. Behavior can be activated either by _____ (push) or by _____ (pull).

4. The attractiveness of a goal and its ability to initiate action are related to its _____ _____.

5. Three principal types of motives are _____ motives, _____ motives, and _____ motives.

6. Most primary motives operate to maintain a steady state of bodily equilibrium called _____.

7. _____ rhythms within the body are closely tied to sleep, activity levels, and energy cycles. Travel across _____ _____ and shift work can seriously disrupt sleep and bodily rhythms.

8. If you anticipate a change in body rhythms, you can gradually _____ to your new schedule over a period of days.

Hunger—Pardon Me, My Hypothalamus Is Growling

Survey Questions: What causes hunger? Overeating? Eating disorders? Pages 348-354

1. Hunger is influenced by a complex interplay between _____ (fullness) of the stomach, _____ (low blood sugar), metabolism in the liver, and fat stores in the body.

2. The most direct control of eating is exerted by the _____, which has areas that act like feeding (start), and _____ (stop) systems for hunger and eating.

3. The _____ hypothalamus acts as a feeding system; the _____ hypothalamus is part of a satiety system; the paraventricular _____ influences both hunger and satiety.

4. Like a thermostat, your brain maintains a _____ _____ in order to control your weight in the long term.

5. Other factors influencing hunger are the _____ _____ for the proportion of fat in the body, external eating _____, and the attractiveness and variety of diet.

6. A successful behavioral dieting approach begins with committing oneself to weight loss, _____, counting _____, developing techniques to control overeating, and charting one's progress.

7. _____ is also influenced by emotions, food availability, and cultural values.

8. _____ nervosa (self-inflicted starvation) and _____ nervosa (gorging and purging) are two prominent eating disorders.

9. Treatments for anorexia begin with _____ diet, and then advance to counseling.

10. Both eating disorders tend to involve conflicts about _____-_____, self-control, and anxiety.

Primary Motives Revisited—Thirst, Pain, and Sex

Survey Questions: Is there more than one type of thirst? In what ways are pain avoidance and the sex drive unusual? Pages 354-356

1. Like hunger, thirst and other basic motives are affected by a number of bodily factors, but are primarily under the central control of the _____ in the brain.

2. Thirst may be either _____ (when fluid is lost from inside cells) or _____ (when fluid is lost from the spaces between cells).

3. Pain avoidance is unusual because it is _____ (associated with particular conditions) as opposed to _____ (occurring in regular cycles).

4. Pain _____ and pain _____ are partially learned.

5. The sex drive in many lower animals is related to _____ (or "heat") in females. The sex drive is unusual in that it is non-_____ (both its arousal and its reduction are sought).

6. Sex drive in both males and females may be related to bodily levels of _____.

Sexual Behavior—Mapping the Erogenous Zone

Survey Question: What are the typical patterns of human sexual response?
Pages 356-359

1. Sexual arousal is related to stimulation of the body's _____ zones (areas that produce erotic pleasure), but _____ elements such as thoughts and images are equally important.

2. There is little _____ in sexual behavior between males and females.

3. Evidence suggests that the sex drive peaks at a later age for _____ than it does for _____, although this difference is diminishing.

4. Sexual _____ refers to one's degree of emotional and erotic attraction to members of the same sex, opposite sex, or both sexes.

5. A person may be _____, homosexual, or _____.

6. A combination of _____, biological, _____, and psychological influences combines to produce one's sexual orientation.

7. As a group, _____ men and women do not differ psychologically from _____.

8. In a series of landmark studies, William Masters and Virginia _____ directly observed sexual response in a large number of adults.

9. Human sexual response can be divided into four phases: (1) excitement, (2) _____, (3) orgasm, and (4) _____.

10. Both males and females may go through all four stages in four minutes. But during lovemaking, most _____ typically take longer than this.

11. Males experience a _____ period after orgasm and ejaculation. Only 5 percent of men are multi-_____.

12. Drugs, counseling, or _____ can help alleviate many sexual problems.

Stimulus Drives—Skydiving, Horror Movies, and the Fun Zone

Survey Question: How does arousal relate to motivation? Pages 360-363

1. The _____ drives reflect needs for information, _____, manipulation, and sensory input.

2. Drives for stimulation are partially explained by _____ _____, which states that an ideal level of physical arousal will be maintained if possible.

3. The desired level of arousal or stimulation varies from person to person, as measured by the _____-_____ *Scale*.

4. Individuals from America, Israel, and Ireland tend to score high on the Sensation-Seeking Scale and they are likely to engage in _____-_____ behaviors.

5. Optimal performance on a task usually occurs at moderate levels of arousal. This relationship is described by an _____ _____ function.

6. The _____-_____ law further states that for simple tasks the ideal arousal level is higher, and for complex tasks it is lower.

7. Test anxiety is caused by a combination of excessive _____ and heightened physiological _____, which can be reduced with better preparation, relaxation, rehearsal, and restructuring thoughts.

Social Motives—The Pursuit of Excellence

Survey Questions: What are social motives? Why are they important? Pages 363-364

1. Social motives are learned through _____ and cultural conditioning.

2. One of the most prominent social motives is the need for _____ (nAch).

3. _____ nAch is correlated with success in many situations, with occupational choice, and with moderate risk taking.

4. _____-_____ affects motivation because it influences the challenges you will undertake, the effort you will make, and how long you will persist when things don't go well.

5. To enhance self-_____, one should do the following: Set goals that are specific, _____, and attainable advance in small steps find a role model get expert instructions and get _____ support.

Motives in Perspective—A View From the Pyramid

Survey Question: Are some motives more basic than others? Pages 365-367

1. Maslow's _____ (rank ordering) of motives categorizes needs as basic and _____ oriented.

2. Lower needs in the hierarchy are assumed to be _____ (dominant) over higher needs.

3. Self-_____, the highest and most fragile need, is reflected in _____ -needs.

4. In many situations, _____ motivation (that which is induced by obvious external rewards) can reduce _____ motivation, enjoyment, and creativity.

Inside an Emotion—How Do You Feel?

Survey Questions: What happens during emotion? Can "lie detectors" really detect lies? Pages 368-370

1. Emotions are linked to many basic _____ behaviors, such as attacking, retreating, feeding, and reproducing.

2. Other major elements of emotion are physiological changes in the body, emotional _____, and emotional feelings.

3. The following are considered to be _____ emotions: fear, surprise, sadness, disgust, anger, anticipation, joy, and trust (acceptance).

Physiology and Emotion—Arousal, Sudden Death, and Lying

Pages 370-373

1. Physical changes associated with emotion are caused by the action of _____, a hormone released into the bloodstream, and by activity in the _____ nervous system (ANS).

2. The _____ branch of the ANS is primarily responsible for arousing the body, the _____ branch for quieting it.

3. Sudden death due to prolonged and intense emotion is probably related to _____ rebound (excess activity). Heart attacks caused by sudden intense emotion are more likely due to _____ arousal.

4. The _____, or "lie detector," measures emotional arousal by monitoring heart rate, blood pressure, breathing rate, and galvanic skin response (GSR).

5. Asking a series of _____ and _____ questions may allow the detection of lying, but overall, the accuracy of the lie detector has been challenged by many researchers.

6. _____ _____ scans and the use of fMRI in analyzing brain activity are possible alternative techniques to the polygraph testing.

Expressing Emotions—Making Faces and Talking Bodies

Survey Question: How accurately do "body language" and the face express emotions? Pages 373-375

1. Basic emotional _____, such as smiling or baring one's teeth when angry, appear to be unlearned.

2. _____ expressions of fear, anger, disgust, sadness, and happiness are recognized by people of all cultures.

3. In Western culture, _____ are encouraged to express such emotions as sadness, fear, shame, and guilt, and _____ are expected to express anger and hostility.

4. Body gestures and movements (body language) also express _____, mainly by communicating emotional tone.

5. Three dimensions of facial expressions are pleasantness-unpleasantness, attention-rejection, and _____.

6. The study of body language is known as _____.

Theories of Emotion—Several Ways to Fear a Bear

Survey Question: How do psychologists explain emotions? Pages 417-421

1. The _____-Lange theory of emotion says that emotional experience follows an awareness of the bodily reactions of emotion.

2. In contrast, the _____-Bard theory says that bodily reactions and emotional experience occur at the same time and that emotions are organized in the brain.

3. Schachter's _____ theory of emotion emphasizes the importance of labels, or interpretations, applied to feelings of bodily _____.

4. Also important is the process of _____, in which bodily arousal is attributed to a particular person, object, or situation.

5. Research on attribution theory has shown that _____ _____ (e.g., increased heart rate from exercise or fear) can be attributed to different sources such as attraction or love for someone.

6. The _____ _____ hypothesis holds that sensations and information from emotional expressions help define what emotion a person is feeling.

7. Making faces does influence _____ and bodily activities through the _____ nervous system.

8. Contemporary views of emotion place greater emphasis on how situations are _____ (evaluated). Also, all of the elements of emotion are seen as interrelated and interacting.

Psychology in Action: Emotional Intelligence—The Fine Art of Self-Control

Survey Question: What does it mean to have "emotional intelligence"? Pages 422-423

1. Emotional _____ involves the following skills: self-awareness, _____, self-control, and an understanding of how to use emotions.

2. Emotionally intelligent people are good at reading _____ expressions, tone of _____, and other signs of emotion.

3. They also use their feelings to enhance _____ and _____ making.

4. Positive emotions are not just a luxury. They tend to encourage personal _____ and _____ connection.

MASTERY TEST

1. Which of the following is NOT one of the signs of emotional arousal recorded by a polygraph?
a. heart rate
b. blood pressure
c. pupil dilation
d. breathing rate

2. Plain water is most satisfying when a person has _____ thirst.
a. intracellular
b. hypothalamic
c. extracellular
d. homeostatic

3. Strong external rewards tend to undermine
a. extrinsic motivation.
b. intrinsic motivation.
c. prepotent motivation.
d. stimulus motivation.

4. Activity in the ANS is directly responsible for which element of emotion?
a. emotional feelings
b. emotional expressions
c. physiological changes
d. misattributions

5. Empathy is a major element of
a. nAch.
b. intrinsic motivation.
c. emotional intelligence.
d. the sensation-seeking personality.

6. The first two phases of the sexual response cycle are
a. excitement, arousal.
b. arousal, orgasm.
c. excitement, plateau.
d. stimulation, arousal.

7. Motivation refers to the ways in which activities are initiated, sustained, and
a. acquired.
b. valued.
c. directed.
d. aroused.

8. The psychological state or feeling we call thirst corresponds to which element of motivation?
a. need
b. drive
c. deprivation
d. incentive value

9. Which facial expression is NOT recognized by people of all cultures?
a. anger
b. disgust
c. optimism
d. fear

10. Learning to weaken eating cues is useful in
a. self-selection feeding.
b. yo-yo dieting.
c. rapid weight cycling.
d. behavioral dieting.

11. Jet lag occurs when a traveler's _____ are out of synchrony with local time.
a. biorhythms
b. circadian rhythms
c. sensation-seeking patterns
d. opponent processes

12. People who score high on tests of the need for achievement tend to be
a. motivated by power and prestige.
b. moderate risk takers.
c. sensation seekers.
d. attracted to longshots.

13. Which theory holds that emotional feelings, arousal, and behavior are generated simultaneously in the brain?
a. James-Lange
b. Cannon-Bard
c. cognitive
d. attribution

14. Compared with people in North America, people in Asian cultures are less likely to express which emotion?
a. anger
b. jealousy
c. curiosity
d. fear

15. Last night, Susan ate almost an entire pizza by herself. She then felt guilty and made herself throw up. If this is not an uncommon series of events, she most likely suffers from
a. bait shyness.
b. low levels of NPY.
c. bulimia nervosa.
d. anorexia nervosa.

16. Goals that are desirable are high in
a. need reduction.
b. incentive value.
c. homeostatic valence.
d. motivational "push."

17. _____ is to pain avoidance as _____ is to the sex drive.
a. Nonhomeostatic; episodic
b. Episodic; nonhomeostatic
c. Nonhomeostatic; cyclic
d. Cyclic; nonhomeostatic

18. A specialist in kinesics could be expected to be most interested in
a. facial blends.
b. circadian rhythms.
c. sensation seeking.
d. primary motives.

19. Coping statements are a way to directly correct which part of test anxiety?
a. overpreparation
b. under-arousal
c. excessive worry
d. compulsive rehearsal

20. Drives for exploration and activity are categorized as
   a. primary motives.
   b. secondary motives.
   c. stimulus motives.
   d. extrinsic motives.

21. Sudden death following a period of intense fear may occur when
   _____ slows the heart to a stop.
   a. a sympathetic overload
   b. adrenaline poisoning
   c. opponent-process feedback
   d. a parasympathetic rebound

22. People who enjoy skydiving and ski jumping are very likely high in
   a. parasympathetic arousal.
   b. extrinsic motivation.
   c. their desires to meet meta-needs.
   d. the trait of sensation seeking.

23. You could induce eating in a laboratory rat by activating the
   a. lateral hypothalamus.
   b. corpus callosum.
   c. rat's set point.
   d. ventromedial hypothalamus.

24. People think cartoons are funnier if they see them while holding a pen
   crosswise in their teeth. This observation supports
   a. the James-Lange theory.
   b. the Cannon-Bard theory.
   c. Schachter's cognitive theory.
   d. the facial feedback hypothesis.

25. Basic biological motives are closely related to
   a. nAch.
   b. homeostasis.
   c. activity in the thalamus.
   d. levels of melatonin in the body.

26. Self-actualization is to _____ needs as safety and security are to
   _____ needs.
   a. growth; basic
   b. basic; meta-
   c. prepotent; basic
   d. meta-; extrinsic

27. Which of the following is NOT a core element of emotion?
   a. physiological changes
   b. emotional expressions
   c. emotional feelings
   d. misattributions

28. The effects of a "supermarket diet" on eating are related to the effects of
_____ on eating.
a. anxiety
b. incentive value
c. metabolic rates
d. stomach distention

29. According to the Yerkes-Dodson law, optimum performance occurs at
_____ levels of arousal for simple tasks and _____ levels
of arousal for complex tasks.
a. higher; lower
b. lower; higher
c. minimum; high
d. average; high

30. Contemporary models of emotion place greater emphasis on
_____, or the way situations are evaluated.
a. appraisal
b. attribution
c. feedback
d. emotional tone

31. Which of the following is NOT a common sexual disorder?
a. sexual pain
b. lack of orgasm
c. sensate focus
d. sexual desire disorder

32. Bart is very sensitive to his emotions and the emotions of others. For
example, when things are tense at work, he is good at staying calm and
helping relax those around him. This best demonstrates
a. emotional avoidance.
b. emotional intelligence.
c. intrinsic motivation.
d. bait shyness.

33. The experience of hunger is based on
a. blood chemistry.
b. the hypothalamus.
c. external eating cues.
d. all of the above

34. Which statement correctly explains why there is an obesity problem in the
United States?
a. The all-you-can-eat dining halls and restaurants tempt people to overeat.
b. Although the food industry has made dinner easier to cook and buy, the food
is high in fat and sugar.
c. Overeating during large meals increases one's body set point.
d. All the preceding

35. Although in some parts of the world, eating monkey eyes is considered a delicacy, to Americans it is not. This difference in preference is largely influenced by
a. cultural values.
b. primary motives.
c. the availability of taste buds.
d. overdeveloped hypothalamus.

36. The causes of anorexia have been attributed to
a. unrealistic comparison of body image to others.
b. seeking control.
c. distorted body image.
d. all the preceding

37. Variables that aid our survival include _____ moods, which help us make better decisions and be more helpful, efficient, and creative. The ability to understand and display _____ expressions such as anger helps us communicate with others.
a. primary; universal
b. negative; natural
c. positive; facial
d. natural; primary

38. According to Martin Seligman, to be genuinely happy one must
a. optimize one's natural strengths.
b. focus on fixing one's weaknesses.
c. strengthen negative emotions to better understand positive emotions.
d. balance both negative and positive emotions.

39. Two possible alternative techniques for detecting lies over polygraph testing are infrared face scans and _____.
a. X-Ray
b. fMRI
c. high score on the SSS
d. low score on the nAch

LANGUAGE DEVELOPMENT

Motivation and Emotion

Word Roots

The Latin verb *movere* means "to move." The English word "move" comes from this root. One form of *movere* is *motivus* (moving). Several psychological and biological terms derive from this root. Examples you will find include motivation and motive.

Motivation—Forces That Push and Pull (pgs. 344-347)

What is motivation? Are there different types of motives?

(345) *incentives*: motivating factors

(345) *in the eye of the beholder*: according to each person; each person will measure the value in their own way

(345) *optimal*: ideal, best

(345) *equilibrium*: balance; stability

(346) *resynchronize*: to return to a state where things co-occur or happen together

(346) *Chernobyl*: city in former U.S.S.R. where a nuclear power plant accident occurred, injuring and killing many people

(346) *Three-Mile Island*: location of a U.S. nuclear power plant accident

(346) *jet lag*: condition characterized by fatigue and irritability that occurs following long flights through several different time zones

(346) *synchronization*: happening at the same time

(346) *"burned the midnight oil"*: stayed up late studying

Hunger—Pardon Me, That's Just My Hypothalamus Growling (pgs. 348-354)

What causes hunger? Overeating? Eating disorders?

(348) *hunger pangs*: extreme feeling of hunger

(348) *inflated conclusion*: an exaggerated and incorrect conclusion

(349) *stigma*: mark or sign of shame

(350) *balloon up*: to gain weight very rapidly

(350) *when your "spare tire" is well inflated*: when you have too much excess weight across your midsection

(350) *radical*: extreme

(350) *obesity*: extreme overweight

(350) *vegans*: those who only eat plant products

(351) *battle of the bulge*: efforts to control overeating and obesity

(352) *debilitating*: weakening; sapping

(352) *bouillon*: a clear broth based on chicken or beef

(352) *threshold*: a set point or amount; a dividing line

(352) *gorge*: eat to excess

(352) *binge*: overdoing it, going on a spree; in this context, the author is referring to excess eating

(352) *purging*: to eject, to get rid of; in this context, vomiting

Primary Motives Revisited—Thirst, Sex, and Pain (pgs. 354-356)

Is there more than one type of thirst? In what ways are pain avoidance and the sex drive unusual?

(354) *perpetuate*: to continue, support

(354) *satiety*: a state of satisfaction

(354) *Gatorade*: a drink that is taken especially after exercise to help restore minerals lost through perspiration

(354) *devotees*: those dedicated to something

Sexual Behavior—Mapping the Erogenous Zone (pgs. 356-359)

What are the typical patterns of human sexual response?

(356) *urological*: involving the urinary tract
(356) *gynecological*: involving the female reproductive system
(356) *revulsion*: disgust
(357) *ebb*: to recede

Stimulus Drives—Skydiving, Horror Movies, and the Fun Zone (pgs. 360-363)

How does arousal relate to motivation?

(360) *skydiving*: the sport of jumping from an airplane with a parachute
(361) *sprinters*: runners who compete in short, fast races
(362) *bungee jumping*: a sport requiring a person to jump off a point of great height with his/her legs tied to a strong elastic rope to prevent him/her from hitting the water or ground below as the rope pulls him/her back a few feet

Social Motives—The Pursuit of Excellence (pgs. 363-365)

What are social motives? Why are they important?

(363) *relish*: enjoy, savor
(363) *exploit*: to use to one's own advantage
(364) *blossom*: to develop
(364) *cultivate*: to develop; grow
(364) *prodigies*: highly talented people, especially children
(364) *eminent*: prominent; famous
(364) *ingredients*: characteristics
(364) *elite*: finest; best
(364) *"talent will surface"*: talent (inborn skill) will eventually become obvious
(364) *emulate*: to model your actions after someone you admire

Motives in Perspective—A View From the Pyramid (pgs. 365-367)

Are some motives more basic than others?

(366) *drudgery*: dull and fatiguing work
(366) *lavishly*: generously
(366) *"bribed"*: paid to act a certain way
(367) *phased out*: to be eliminated over time, with gradual reduction
(367) *"go for broke"*: to move forward, regardless of risk

Inside an Emotion—How Do You Feel? (pgs. 368-370)

What happens during emotion? Can "lie detectors" really detect lies?

(368) *stage fright*: fear of appearing before crowds to perform, give a speech, etc.
(368) *"choking up"*: fail to perform effectively because of fear
(368) *"butterflies"*: feeling of nervousness
(368) *contorts*: twisting of the face into unusual shapes
(369) *"Blue Monday"*: because Monday is the beginning of the work and school week, it is a "blue," or sad day

Physiology and Emotion—Arousal, Sudden Death, and Lying (pgs. 370-373)

(370) *prowler*: a person moving about secretly, as in search of things to steal

(372) *baseline*: a beginning value, often used for comparison purposes

(372) *misgivings*: concerns; doubts

(372) *be thrown off* (the polygraph "may be thrown off"): give inaccurate readings

(373) *inhibit*: to hold back, restrain

Expressing Emotions—Making Faces and Talking Bodies (pgs. 373-375)

How accurately do "body language" and the face express emotion?

(374) *Halloween*: celebrated on October 31; children wear masks and costumes and go to neighbors' houses asking for candy

(375) *"You're an ass!"*: telling someone he or she is a stupid or disagreeable person (usually considered vulgar)

Theories of Emotion—Several Ways to Fear a Bear (pgs. 376-380)

How do psychologists explain emotions?

(377) *slapstick*: type of comedy

(377) *stirred-up*: agitated; aroused

(377) *added an interesting wrinkle*: contributed something new

(377) *"on the sly"*: secretly

(377) *suspension bridge*: a bridge, river, or canyon that has its roadway hanging from cables anchored on each side

(377) *chasm*: deep hole in the earth

(377) *ingenious*: very clever

(378) *billboard*: a large panel displaying outdoor advertising

(379) *demeaned*: lowered a person's pride or self-respect

(380) *snarling*: growling

Emotional Intelligence—The Fine Art of Self Control (pgs. 381-383)

What does it mean to have "emotional intelligence"?

(380) *empathy*: the ability to share in another's thoughts and emotions

(381) *stifle*: to smother; hold back

(381) *sabotage*: ruin future chances of accomplishing something

(381) *amplify*: to make bigger; enlarge

(382) *buffers*: protects; guards

(382) *bereaved*: saddened, often due to loss

(383) *shift work*: working schedule that frequently changes, for example, from day to evening to night, then back to day

Solutions

Recite and Review

Motivation—Push Me, Pull Me

1. initiate, activities
2. need, goal
3. push, pull
4. goal, need
5. learned
6. steady
7. motives, physical
8. learned, culture
9. rhythms, sleep
10. change, schedule

Hunger—Pardon Me, My Hypothalamus Is Growling

1. stomach, blood, liver
2. start, stop
3. feeding, satiety
4. hormone, lateral
5. leptin
6. obesity
7. fat, diet
8. values
9. metabolism
10. exercise, calories
11. starvation, gorging
12. females, bulimics
13. distorted, low
14. fitness
15. counseling
16. anxiety

Biological Motives Revisited—Thirst, Pain, and Sex

1. bodily, brain
2. fluid, cells, water, cells
3. cycles
4. learned
5. survival, sex
6. females
7. drive
8. impair
9. arousal

Sexual Behavior—Mapping the Erogenous Zone

1. pleasure, thoughts
2. Masters
3. responsiveness
4. later
5. excitement, orgasm
6. four
7. women
8. orgasm, multi
9. friends, benefits
10. sex, sex, sexes
11. homosexual
12. sexual, orientation
13. heterosexuals
14. Drugs

Stimulus Motives – Monkey Business

1. sensory
2. physical arousal
3. body
4. unusual
5. moderate
6. simple, complex
7. excessive, preparation, rehearsal

Learned Motives—The Pursuit of Excellence

1. Social, competition, approval
2. socialization
3. need, internal
4. success, risk
5. expert
6. motivation, effort, persist
7. challenging, small, social

Motives in Perspective—The View From the Pyramid

1. basic
2. Lower, higher
3. deficiencies
4. Self, needs
5. external, internal

Inside an Emotion—How Do You Feel?

1. feelings
2. behaviors
3. groups
4. sadness, anger
5. low, intensity
6. fear

Physiology and Emotion—Arousal, Sudden Death, and Lying

1. hormone, nervous, system
2. branch, branch
3. rebound, arousal
4. emotional arousal
5. lying
6. relevant, lying
7. fMRI

Expressing Emotions—Making Faces and Talking Bodies

1. unlearned
2. fear, sadness
3. harmony
4. sadness, shame, anger
5. facial
6. body, language
7. feelings, tone
8. relaxation

Theories of Emotion—Several Ways to Fear a Bear

1. follows
2. at the same time
3. labels
4. arousal, mislabel
5. first
6. threatening
7. expressions
8. emotions, autonomic
9. nervous, thinking
10. situations

Psychology in Action: Emotional Intelligence—The Fine Art of Self-Control

1. self, manage
2. emotion, feelings, emotions
3. Positive

CONNECTIONS

Motivation—Forces that Push and Pull

1. F.   3. D.   5. G.   7. C.
2. B.   4. A.   6. E.

Hunger—Pardon Me, My Hypothalamus Is Growling

1. B.   2. A.   3. C.

1. G.   3. C.   5. A.   7. D.
2. B.   4. F.   6. E.

Primary Motives Revisited—Thirst, Pain, and Sex

1. C.   3. E.   5. B.
2. D.   4. A.

Sexual Behavior—Mapping the Erogenous Zone

1. B.   3. F.   5. D.
2. A.   4. C.   6. E.

Stimulus Drives—Skydiving, Horror Movies, and the Fun Zone, and Social Motives—The Pursuit of Excellence

1. B.   3. E.   5. F.
2. A.   4. C.

Motives in Perspective—A View From the Pyramid, Inside an Emotion—How Do You Feel? and Physiology and Emotion—Arousal, Sudden Death, and Lying

1. D.   3. C.   5. E.   7. F.
2. G.   4. A.   6. B.

1. I.   4. A.   7. F.
2. B.   5. D.   8. C.
3. G.   6. H.   9. E.

Expressing Emotions—Making Faces and Talking Bodies, Theories of Emotion—Several Ways to Fear a Bear, and Psychology in Action: Emotional Intelligence—The Fine Art of Self-control

1. E.   2. D.   3. I.   4. B.

5. F.   7. H.   9. G.
6. C.   8. A.

Check Your Memory

Motivation—Forces that Push and Pull

1. F	3. T	5. T
2. T	4. T	6. F

Hunger—Pardon Me, My Hypothalamus Is Growling

1. F	6. F	11. F	16. T
2. T	7. T	12. F	17. F
3. T	8. F	13. F	18. F
4. T	9. T	14. T	
5. T	10. F	15. T	

Primary Motives Revisited—Thirst, Pain, and Sex

1. T	3. F	5. T
2. F	4. T	

Sexual Behavior—Mapping the Erogenous Zone

1. T	5. T	9. F	13. F
2. F	6. T	10. F	
3. T	7. F	11. T	
4. F	8. T	12. T	

Stimulus Drives—Skydiving, Horror Movies, and the Fun Zone

1. T	3. F	5. T
2. T	4. F	6. F

Social Motives—The Pursuit of Excellence

1. F	2. F	3. T	4. T

Motives in Perspective—A View From the Pyramid

1. F	3. F	5. F	7. T
2. T	4. T	6. T	8. F

Inside an Emotion—How Do You Feel?

1. F   3. F   5. T
2. F   4. T

Physiology and Emotion—Arousal, Sudden Death, and Lying

1. F   4. F   7. T
2. T   5. F   8. T
3. T   6. F   9. T

Expressing Emotions—Making Faces and Talking Bodies

1. T   3. F   5. F   7. F
2. T   4. T   6. F   8. F

Theories of Emotion—Several Ways to Fear a Bear

1. F   4. F   7. F   10. F
2. T   5. T   8. T
3. T   6. F   9. T

Psychology in Action: Emotional Intelligence—The Fine Art of Self-control

1. T   3. T   5. T   7. T
2. F   4. T   6. T

Final Survey and Review

Motivation—Forces that Push and Pull

1. sustain, direct
2. drive, attainment
3. needs, goals
4. incentive, value
5. primary, stimulus, secondary
6. homeostasis
7. Circadian, time, zones
8. preadapt

Hunger—Pardon Me, My Hypothalamus Is Growling

1. distention, hypoglycemia
2. hypothalamus, satiety
3. lateral, ventromedial, nucleus
4. set, point
5. set, point, cues
6. exercise, calories
7. Hunger
8. Anorexia, bulimia
9. medical
10. self, image

Primary Motives Revisited—Thirst, Pain, and Sex

1. hypothalamus
2. intracellular, extracellular
3. episodic, cyclic
4. avoidance, tolerance
5. estrus, homeostatic
6. androgens

Sexual Behavior—Mapping the Erogenous Zone

1. erogenous, cognitive
2. difference
3. females, males
4. orientation
5. heterosexual, bisexual
6. hereditary, social
7. homosexual, heterosexuals
8. Johnson
9. plateau, resolution
10. females
11. refractory, orgasmic
12. psychotherapy

Stimulus Drives—Skydiving, Horror Movies, and the Fun Zone

1. stimulus, exploration
2. arousal, theory
3. Sensation, Seeking
4. high, risk
5. inverted, U
6. Yerkes, Dodson
7. worrying, arousal

Social Motives—The Pursuit of Excellence

1. socialization
2. achievement
3. High
4. Self, confidence
5. confidence, challenging, social

Motives in Perspective—A View From the Pyramid

1. hierarchy, growth
2. prepotent
3. actualization, meta
4. extrinsic, intrinsic

Inside an Emotion—How Do You Feel?

1. adaptive
2. expressions
3. primary

Physiology and Emotion—Arousal, Sudden Death, and Lying

1. adrenaline, autonomic
2. sympathetic, parasympathetic
3. parasympathetic, sympathetic
4. polygraph
5. relevant, irrelevant
6. Infrared, face

Expressing Emotions—Making Faces and Talking Bodies

1. expressions
2. Facial
3. women, men
4. feelings
5. activation.
6. kinesics

Theories of Emotion—Several Ways to Fear a Bear

1. James
2. Cannon
3. cognitive, arousal
4. attribution
5. physical, arousal
6. facial, feedback
7. emotions, autonomic
8. appraised

Psychology in Action: Emotional Intelligence—The Fine Art of Self-Control

1. intelligence, empathy
2. facial, voice
3. thinking, decision
4. growth, social

Mastery Test

1. c, p. 371
2. a, p. 354
3. b, p. 366
4. c, p. 368
5. c, p. 381
6. c, p. 356
7. c, p. 344
8. b, p. 344
9. c, p. 374
10. d, p. 351
11. b, p. 346
12. b, p. 363
13. b, p. 376

14. a, p. 374
15. c, p. 352
16. b, p. 345
17. b, p. 354-355
18. a, p. 375
19. c, p. 361
20. c, p. 345
21. d, p. 370
22. d, p. 362
23. a, p. 348
24. d, p. 378
25. b, p. 345
26. a, p. 365

27. d, p. 368
28. b, p. 351
29. a, p. 360-361
30. a, p. 379
31. c, p. 359
32. b, p. 381
33. d, p. 348-349
34. d, p. 350-351
35. a, p. 350
36. d, p. 353-354
37. c, p. 373-374
38. a, p. 382
39. b, p. 373

CHAPTER 10

Personality

Chapter Overview

Personality refers to unique and enduring behavior patterns. Character is personality evaluated. Personality traits are lasting personal qualities. Personality types are categories defined by groups of shared traits. Behavior is also influenced by self-concept. Personality theories combine various ideas and principles to explain personality. Trait, psychodynamic, behavioristic and social learning, and humanistic theories approach personality from different perspectives.

Allport's trait theory classifies traits as common or individual; he also made the distinction between cardinal, central, or secondary traits. Cattell's trait theory attributes visible surface traits to the existence of 16 underlying source traits. Costa and McCrae's five-factor model further reduces traits to five independent dimensions: Conscientiousness, Agreeableness, Neuroticism, Openness to Experience, and Extraversion. These have been used to predict behavior in certain situations. Most personalities are a mixture of traits, which has costs and benefits depending on lifestyle choices.

Sigmund Freud's psychoanalytic theory emphasizes unconscious forces and conflicts within the personality. Freud proposed that personality had three parts: id, ego, and superego and emphasized that thoughts and emotions could exist as conscious, unconscious, and preconscious levels. Personality developed in psychosexual stages; failure to resolve these stages results in fixations and are associated with certain personality traits. Behavioral theories of personality emphasize learning, conditioning, and the immediate effects of the environment. Social learning theory adds cognitive elements, such as perception, thinking, expectancies, and understanding, to the behavioral view. Many differences between males and females are based on social learning. Certain traits are more "masculine" or "feminine;" androgynous individuals have a mix of both. Humanistic theory emphasizes subjective experiences, personal development, and needs for self-actualization. Carl Rogers emphasizes the self and congruence or incongruence between self-image, possible selves, ideal selves, and behavior. Evaluations of others create internal conditions of worth in children. Organismic valuing develops from unconditional positive regard and contributes to positive self-regard.

Traits appear to interact with situations to determine behavior. Behavioral genetics suggests that heredity influences personality traits. Twin studies suggest that heredity accounts for 25-50 percent of the variability in personality traits. When compared, personality theories can be evaluated in terms of the relative contribution of genetics versus the environment, view of human nature, principle motives, personality structure, personality development, and barriers to growth.

Techniques typically used to assess personality are interviews, direct observation, rating scales, questionnaires, and projective tests.

Shyness is a mixture of social inhibition and social anxiety. It is marked by heightened public self-consciousness and a tendency to regard one's shyness as a lasting trait. Shyness can be lessened by changing self-defeating beliefs and by improving social skills.

Learning Objectives

1. Define the term *personality* and explain how personality differs from character.
2. Define the terms *trait* and *type*; discuss the stability of personality traits; explain the advantages and disadvantages of using type to classify personalities.
3. Describe the characteristics of introverts and extroverts.
4. Explain the terms *self-concept* and *self-esteem* and how they affect behavior and personal adjustment; explain the differences in the basis of self-esteem in Eastern and Western cultures.
5. Define the term *personality theory* and describe the different psychological perspectives regarding personality theory covered in the text.
6. Describe the following trait theories:
    a. Eysenck and the ancient Greeks (Fig. 10.2)
    b. Rentfrow and Gosling's musical personalities
    c. Gordon Allport
    d. Raymond Cattell
    e. the Five-Factor Model of Personality; include a brief discussion of unhealthy perfectionism
7. Discuss Freud's view of personality development, including:
    a. the three parts of the personality
    b. Libido (life insticts) and Thanatos (death instincts)
    c. neurotic and moral anxiety
    d. the three levels of awareness
    e. the psychosexual stages and fixations
    f. the contributions and criticisms of Freud's theory
8. Explain how learning theorists (behaviorists) view the structure of personality, including the terms *situational determinants*, *habit*, *drive*, *cue*, *response*, and *reward*.
9. Explain how learning theory and social learning theory differ.
10. Describe the following social learning concepts: *psychological situation*, *expectancy*, *reinforcement value*, *self-efficacy*, and *self-reinforc*ement.
11. Describe the importance of social reinforcement on personality; explain why feeding, toilet training, sex training, and learning to express anger or aggression are considered critical situations by the behaviorists.

12. Discuss the role of imitation and identification in personality development and how Western cultures encourage boys to engage in instrumental behaviors and girls, in expressive behaviors.

13. Discuss the concept of androgyny and its relationship to masculinity, feminity, and adaptability.

14. Briefly explain how humanism differs from the Freudian and behaviorist viewpoints of personality.

15. Describe Maslow's concept of self-actualization and the characteristics of self-actualizers; and list eight steps to promote self-actualization.

16. Discuss Rogers' views of a fully functioning individual; define his concepts of the *self*, *self-image*, *incongruence*, *being authentic*, *ideal self*, *conditions of worth*, *organismic valuing*, *positive self-regard*, and *unconditional positive regard*.

17. Explain how Markus and Nurius' concept of *possible selves* help to direct our future behavior.

18. Explain trait-situation interaction; define behavioral genetics.

19. Explain how twin studies are used to assess the relative contribution of heredity and environment to a person's personality.

20. Discuss how the similarities in the personalities of twins can be explained, including the fallacy of positive instances.

21. Explain the best way to judge a theory and compare and contrast the trait theories, psychoanalytic theory, behavioristic and social learning theories, and the humanistic theory in terms of:
    a. their views of human nature
    b. whether behavior is seen as free or determined
    c. principal motives
    d. personality structures
    e. the role of the unconscious
    f. the concept of conscience
    g. the developmental emphasis of each
    h. what each sees as barriers to one's personal growth

22. Discuss the following assessment techniques in terms of purpose, method, advantages, and limitations:
    a. structured and unstructured interviews, including the problem of the halo effect
    b. direct observation using rating scales, behavioral assessment, and/or situational testing
    c. personality questionnaires, including the definitions of test *reliability* and *validity* and an overview of the MMPI-2
    d. honesty tests
    e. projective tests, including an overview of the Rorschach and the TAT
    f. a test battery

23. Describe the personality characteristics of sudden murderers, and explain how their characteristics differ from those of habitually violent persons.

24. Describe the characeristics of shyness, its causes, why sand hyness involves public self-consciousness rather than private self-consciousness.

25. Discuss the key difference in shy and not-shy persons, how shyness is maintained by four self-defeating beliefs, and how shyness can be treated by replacing these unproductive beliefs and learning social skills.

RECITE AND REVIEW

The Psychology of Personality—Do You Have Personality?

Survey Questions: How do psychologists use the term *personality*? Pages 388-391

1. Personality is made up of one's unique and relatively stable pattern of thinking, emotions, and _____.

2. Character is personality that has been judged or _____. That is, it is the possession of desirable qualities.

3. Personality traits are stable personal qualities that are inferred from _____; they can be used to predict future behavior.

4. A personality type is a style of personality defined by having a group of related _____ or similar characteristics.

5. Two widely recognized personality _____ are introvert (shy, self-centered person) and extrovert (bold, outgoing person).

6. Behavior and personal adjustment are influenced by self-concept, which is a person's perception of his or her own _____ traits.

7. Culture determines how people go about developing and maintaining _____-_____ (self-evaluation). I in individualistic _____, self-esteem is based on personal success and outstanding performance; in collectivist _____, self-esteem is based on belonging to social groups.

8. People with high self-esteem are confident, _____, and self-respecting, and people with low self-esteem are insecure, _____-_____, and lack confidence.

9. _____ theories combine interrelated concepts, assumptions, ideas, and principles to explain personality.

10. Four major types of personality theories are: _____, psychodynamic, behavior and _____ learning, and humanistic.

The Trait Approach—Describe Yourself in 18,000 Words or Less

Survey Question: Are some personality traits more basic or important than others? Pages 391-395

1. Trait theorists attempt to analyze, _____, and interrelate traits, which are biological predispositions or qualities of personality that are most lasting or characteristic of a person.

2. Research has found a link between personality characteristics and _____. For example, people who value aesthetic experiences, have good _____ skills, and are liberal and tolerant of others tend to prefer jazz, _____, classical, and folk music.

3. Gordon Allport made useful distinctions between common traits (which are shared by most members of a culture) and _____ traits (characteristics of a single person).

4. Allport also identified cardinal traits (a trait that influences nearly all of a person's activities), central traits (core traits of personality), and _____ traits (superficial traits).

5. The theory of Raymond Cattell attributes visible _____ traits to the existence of 16 underlying source traits (which he identified using factor _____).

6. Source traits are measured by the *Sixteen* _____ _____ *Questionnaire* (16 PF).

7. The outcome of the 16 PF and other personality tests may be graphically presented as a _____ profile.

8. The five-factor model of personality reduces traits to five _____ dimensions of personality. The five factors are: extroversion, _____, conscientiousness, neuroticism, and openness to _____.

9. Extroverts tend to earn more during their careers than _____, but are also more likely to take risks and divorce.

10. People who suffer from unhealthy perfectionism set _____ high standards for themselves.

11. People who score _____ in conscientiousness tend to perform well at work and school, have few automobile accidents, and live longer than those who score _____ on this dimension.

Psychoanalytic Theory—Id Came to Me in a Dream

Survey Question: How do psychodynamic theories explain personality? Pages 396-400.

1. Both trait theories and psychodynamic theories believe that personality is based on a set of _____ predispositions.

2. Psychodynamic theories focus on the inner workings of personality, especially hidden or _____ thoughts, needs, and emotions.

3. According to Sigmund Freud's psychoanalytic theory, personality is made up of the id, _____, and superego.

4. The id operates on the pleasure _____; it is irrational and self-serving.

5. The ego is guided by the reality _____; it consciously controls the personality and delays actions until appropriate.

6. The _____ is made up of the conscience and the ego ideal.

7. When the standards of the ego ideal are met, we feel _____; when they are not met, we feel guilt.

8. Libido, derived from the _____ instincts, drives our sexual desires and pleasure seeking. Thanatos is the _____ instinct that fuels aggression and destructive urges.

9. Conflicts within the personality may cause neurotic _____ or moral _____ and motivate use of ego-defense mechanisms.

10. The personality operates on three levels: the _____, preconscious, and unconscious.

11. The id is completely _____; the ego and superego can operate at all three levels of awareness.

12. The Freudian view of personality development is based on a series of psychosexual _____: the _____, anal, phallic, and genital.

13. At each psychosexual stage, a different part of the child's body serves as an _____ zone, or a source of pleasure, frustration, or self-expression.

14. Fixations (unresolved emotional conflicts) at any stage can leave a lasting imprint on _____.

15. Freud's theory pioneered the idea that feeding, toilet training, and early sexual experiences leave an imprint on _____.

16. During the phallic stage of Freud's _____ stages of development, boys must confront and resolve the _____ complex and girls must confront and resolve the Electra complex.

17. At puberty, individuals experience an increase in sexual energies that activate _____ conflicts of earlier stages.

18. Freud's theory has been influential for several reasons: He suggested that adult personality is formed during the _____ _____ years of a person's life; he identified feeding, _____ training, and early sexual experiences as critical events; and he indicated that development proceeds in _____.

19. Freud's theory is difficult to _____ empirically, and has been criticized for overemphasizing _____ in personality development.

Learning Theories of Personality—Habit I Seen You Before?

Survey Question: What do behaviorists and social learning theorists emphasize in their approach to personality? Pages 401-406

1. Behavioral theories of personality emphasize _____, imitation, and immediate effects of the environment.

2. Learning theorists generally stress the effects of prior learning and _____ determinants of behavior.

3. Personality dictates how we respond _____ to certain types of situations.

4. Learning theorists John Dollard and Neal Miller consider _____ the basic core of personality. _____ express the combined effects of drive, cue, response, and _____.

5. _____ learning theory adds cognitive elements, such as perception, thinking, and beliefs, to the behavioral view of personality.

6. Examples of social learning concepts are the _____ situation (the situation as it is perceived), expectancies (expectations about what effects a response will have), and reinforcement _____ (the subjective value of a reinforcer or activity).

7. Albert Bandura believes one's self-efficacy (belief in our _____ to produce a desired outcome) is an important aspect of expectancy. He also believes that self-efficacy beliefs influence the _____ and situations we choose to get into.

8. Self-reinforcement refers to praising, _____, or blaming oneself for making particular responses; it is closely tied to self-_____.

9. Some social learning theorists treat "conscience" as a case of _____-reinforcement.

10. The behavioristic view of personality development holds that social reinforcement in four situations is critical. The critical situations are _____, toilet or cleanliness training, sex training, and _____ or aggression training.

11. Identification (feeling emotionally connected to a person) and _____ (mimicking another person's behavior) are of particular importance in sex (or gender) training.

12. Girls are more likely than boys to engage in _____ aggressive behaviors.

13. In Western culture, _____ are encouraged to engage in instrumental (goal-directed) behaviors; _____ are encouraged to engage in expressive (emotion-oriented) behaviors.

14. Androgynous individuals possess traits considered to be both "_____" and "feminine"; they are typically more flexible in coping with difficult situations and tend to be more satisfied with their lives.

15. Sandra Bem created the Bem _____ _____ Inventory (BSRI) to measure _____, which contains masculine, feminine, and neutral traits.

16. Research conducted by Sandra Bem indicates that roughly one-third of all persons are androgynous (they possess both _____ and _____ traits).

17. Being _____ means that a person is independent and assertive.

18. Being _____ means that a person is nurturant and interpersonally oriented.

Humanistic Theory—Peak Experiences and Personal Growth

Survey Question: How do humanistic theories differ from other perspectives?
Pages 407-411

1. Humanistic theory views human nature as _____, and emphasizes subjective experience, _____ choice, and needs for self-actualization.

2. Abraham Maslow's study of self-actualizers identified characteristics they share, ranging from efficient perceptions of reality to frequent _____ _____ (temporary moments of self-actualization).

3. The process of self-actualization involves multiple steps, some of which include being willing to change, taking _____, examining one's motives, getting involved, and making use of _____ experiences.

4. Carl Rogers' theory views the _____ as an entity that emerges when experiences that match the self-_____ are symbolized (admitted to consciousness), while those that are incongruent are excluded.

5. The incongruent person has a highly unrealistic _____-_____ and/or a mismatch between the _____-_____ and the ideal self.

6. The congruent or _____ functioning person is flexible and open to experiences and feelings.

7. In the development of personality, humanists are primarily interested in the emergence of a _____-_____ and in self-evaluations. It is important to have congruence between one's _____-_____ and ideal self.

8. Possible selves represent our hopes, _____, fears, and goals for who we could be.

9. As parents apply conditions of _____ (standards used to judge thoughts, feelings, and actions) to a child, the child begins to do the same.

10. Internalized conditions of worth contribute to incongruence, they damage _____ self-regard, and they disrupt the organismic _____ process.

11. Unconditional _____ regard (unshakable love and approval from others) contributes to _____ valuing in children and adults.

Traits and Situations – The Great Debate

Survey Question: How do traits and situations affect personality? Page 411-415

1. Temperament refers to the _____ and physiological aspects of one's emotional nature.

2. Personality starts to stabilize around age _____ and continues to "harden" until age _____; personality matures in old age.

3. _____ interact with situations to determine behavior; in a trait-situation interaction, external circumstances influence the expression of a personality trait.

4. Behavioral genetics is the study of _____ behavioral traits.

5. Heredity is responsible for 25 to 50 percent of the variation in personality _____.

6. Studies of separated _____ twins suggest that heredity contributes significantly to adult personality traits. Overall, however, personality is shaped as much, or more, by differences in environment.

7. The trait approach to personality believes that development is driven by both _____ and _____ factors

8. The humanistic perspective has a _____ view of human nature, whereas the psychoanalytic perspective is _____.

9. The role of genetics is emphasized in trait theories, but minimized in _____, social _____, and humanistic theories.

Personality Assessment—Psychological Yardsticks

Survey Question: How do psychologists measure personality? Pages 415-422

1. Techniques typically used for personality assessment are _____, observation, questionnaires, and projective _____.

2. Structured and unstructured _____ provide much information, but they are subject to _____ bias and misperceptions. Intentional deception and the halo effect may also _____ accuracy.

3. Direct observation, sometimes involving situational tests, behavioral assessment, or the use of _____ scales, allows evaluation of a person's actual _____.

4. In situational _____, real-life conditions are simulated and _____ reactions are observed.

5. Personality questionnaires, such as the _____ _____ *Personality Inventory-2* (MMPI-2), are objective and _____, but their validity is open to question.

6. Honesty tests, which are essentially personality _____, are widely used by businesses to make hiring decisions. Their validity is hotly debated.

7. Projective tests ask a subject to project thoughts or feelings onto an ambiguous _____ or unstructured situation.

8. The *Rorschach*, or _____ test, is a well-known projective technique. A second is the _____ *Apperception Test* (TAT).

9. The validity and objectivity of projective tests are quite _____. Nevertheless, projective techniques are considered useful by many clinicians, particularly as part of a _____ battery.

Psychology in Action: Barriers and Bridges—Understanding Shyness

Survey Question: What causes shyness? What can be done about it? Pages 422-425

1. Shyness is a mixture of _____ inhibition and _____ anxiety.

2. Shy persons fail to make _____ contact, retreat when spoken to, speak too _____, and display little interest in conversation.

3. Shy persons tend to lack social skills and they feel social anxiety (because they believe they are being _____ by others).

4. Shy persons also have a self-defeating bias in their _____ (they tend to blame _____ for social failures).

5. Shyness is marked by heightened _____ self-consciousness (awareness of oneself as a _____ object) and a tendency to regard shyness as a lasting trait.

6. Shyness can be lessened by changing self-defeating _____ and by improving _____ skills.

CONNECTIONS

The Psychology of Personality—Do You Have Personality?

Survey Questions: How do psychologists use the term *personality*? Pages 388-391

1. _____ character
2. _____ trait
3. _____ Type A
4. _____ Introverts or extroverts
5. _____ Self-concept
6. _____ melancholic
7. _____ choleric
8. _____ personality
9. _____ phlegmatic
10. _____ sanguine

A. heart attack risk
B. hot-tempered
C. personality evaluated
D. cheerful
E. sluggish
F. sad, gloomy
G. lasting personal quality
H. Carl Jung
I. long-term consistency
J. mental picture of yourself

The Trait Approach—Describe Yourself in 18,000 Words or Less

Survey Question: Are some personality traits more basic or important than others? Pages 391-395

1. _____ Big Five
2. _____ Secondary traits
3. _____ individual traits
4. _____ traits
5. _____ Central traits
6. _____ 16 PF
7. _____ Cardinal trait
8. _____ common traits

A. biological disposition
B. unique qualities
C. source traits
D. culturally typical
E. five universal dimensions
F. dominant core
G. basic building blocks
H. superficial

Psychoanalytic Theory—Id Came to Me in a Dream

Survey Question: How do psychodynamic theories explain personality? Pages 396-400

1. _____ Thanatos	A. mouth
2. _____ Eros	B. pride
3. _____ ego	C. genitals
4. _____ conscience	D. female conflict
5. _____ Latency	E. male conflict
6. _____ ego ideal	F. death instinct
7. _____ Neurotic anxiety	G. elimination
8. _____ oral stage	H. life instinct
9. _____ anal stage	I. guilt
10. _____ phallic stage	J. pleasure principle
11. _____ Moral anxiety	K. reality principle
12. _____ id	L. superego punishment
13. _____ Oedipus complex	M. id impulses
14. _____ Electra complex	N. quiet

Learning Theories of Personality—Habit I Seen You Before?

Survey Question: What do behaviorists and social learning theorists emphasize in their approach to personality? Pages 401-406

1. _____ reward	A. anticipation
2. _____ identification	B. learned behavior pattern
3. _____ Feminine	C. positive reinforcer
4. _____ expectancy	D. external causes
5. _____ situational determinants	E. BSRI
6. _____ imitation	F. belief in one's capability
7. _____ Instrumental	G. signals
8. _____ habits	H. self-praise
9. _____ Masculine	I. attachment to adults
10. _____ cues	J. act like an adult
11. _____ self-efficacy	K. goal-directed
12. _____ Self-reinforcement	L. expressive
13. _____ Emotion-oriented	M. independent
14. _____ androgyny	N. nurturing

Humanistic Theory—Peak Experiences and Personal Growth

Survey Question: How do humanistic theories differ from other perspectives?
Pages 407-411

1. _____ subjective experience   A. self-actualization
2. _____ Incongruence   B. self-image = ideal self
3. _____ unconditional positive regard   C. unshakable love
4. _____ Carl Rogers   D. private perceptions of reality
5. _____ Conditions of worth   E. fully functioning person
6. _____ Abraham Maslow   F. discrepancy
7. _____ Congruence   G. internal evaluation standards

Traits and Situations – The Great Debate

Survey Question: How do traits and situations affect personality? Pages 411-415

1. _____ Sudden murders   A. Hereditary aspects
2. _____ temperament   B. Twin study
3. _____ Interaction   C. trait + situation
4. _____ Minnesota   D. Quiet, overcontrolled

Personality Assessment—Psychological Yardsticks; and Psychology in Action: Barriers and Bridges—Understanding Shyness

Survey Questions: How do psychologists measure personality? What causes shyness? What can be done about it? Pages 415-425

1. _____validity scale
2. _____social anxiety
3. _____Interview
4. _____MMPI
5. _____inkblot
6. _____Behavioral assessment
7. _____private self-consciousness
8. _____situational test
9. _____Direct observation
10. _____public self-consciousness
11. _____honesty test
12. _____self-defeating bias
13. _____halo effect

A. Rorschach
B. integrity at work
C. interview problem
D. personality questionnaire
E. faking good
F. shoot don't shoot
G. view self as social object
H. focus on inner feelings
I. distortion in thinking
J. evaluation fears
K. direct questioning
L. people watching
M. frequency

CHECK YOUR MEMORY

The Psychology of Personality—Do You Have Personality?

Survey Questions: How do psychologists use the term *personality*? Pages 388-391

1. The term *personality* refers to charisma or personal style.

TRUE or FALSE

2. Personality is a person's relatively stable pattern of attitudes.

TRUE or FALSE

3. Character refers to the inherited "raw material" from which personality is formed.

TRUE or FALSE

4. In Asian cultures, self-esteem is strongly tied to personal achievement, rather than group success.

TRUE or FALSE

5. Self-concept refers to your own mental "picture" of your own personality

TRUE or FALSE

6. Traits are stable or lasting qualities of personality, displayed in most situations.

TRUE or FALSE

7. Personality traits typically become quite stable by age 50.

TRUE or FALSE

8. The assumption that with age comes the "grumpy old man" and "cranky old woman" is largely accurate.

TRUE or FALSE

9. Type A individuals have traits that increase their chances of having a heart attack

TRUE or FALSE

10. Paranoid, dependent, and antisocial personalities are regarded as personality types.

TRUE or FALSE

11. Two major dimensions of Eysenck's personality theory are stable-unstable and calm-moody.

TRUE or FALSE

12. Trait theories of personality stress subjective experience and personal growth.

TRUE or FALSE

13. An introvert is bold and outgoing; an extrovert is shy and reserved.

TRUE or FALSE

The Trait Approach—Describe Yourself in 18,000 Words or Less

Survey Question: Are some personality traits more basic or important than others? Pages 391-395

1. Extroverted students tend to study in noisy areas of the library.

TRUE or FALSE

2. Extroverted people find it easier than introverted people to "talk" with people via the Internet.

TRUE or FALSE

3. Peter Rentfrow and Samuel Gosling found that one's preference to music is linked to personality characteristics.

TRUE or FALSE

4. People who are curious about new experiences, enjoy taking risks, and are physically active tend to prefer rock, alternative, and heavy metal music.

TRUE or FALSE

5. Nearly all of a person's activities can be traced to one or two common traits.

TRUE or FALSE

6. Trait theories seek to identify root causes of personality traits

TRUE or FALSE

7. Common traits are characteristics shared by most members of a culture

TRUE or FALSE

8. Roughly seven central traits are needed, on the average, to describe an individual's personality.

TRUE or FALSE

9. Source traits represent the visible features of personality.

TRUE or FALSE

10. Allport used factor analysis to identify central traits.

TRUE or FALSE

11. The 16 PF is designed to measure surface traits.

TRUE or FALSE

12. Judging from scores on the 16 PF, airline pilots have traits that are similar to creative artists.

TRUE or FALSE

13. As one of the Big Five factors, neuroticism refers to having negative, upsetting emotions.

TRUE or FALSE

14. Individuals scoring high in conscientiousness tend to perform well at work and school.

TRUE or FALSE

Psychoanalytic Theory—Id Came to Me in a Dream

Survey Question: How do psychodynamic theories explain personality? Pages 396-400

1. Freud described the id, ego, and superego as "little people" that manage the human psyche.

TRUE or FALSE

2.   The id is totally unconscious.

TRUE or FALSE

3.   The ego is guided by the pleasure principle.

TRUE or FALSE

4.   The superego is the source of feelings of guilt and pride.

TRUE or FALSE

5.   Threats of punishment from the Thanatos cause moral anxiety.

TRUE or FALSE

6.   Oral-dependent persons are gullible.

TRUE or FALSE

7.   Vanity and narcissism are traits of the anal-retentive personality.

TRUE or FALSE

8.   According to Freud, boys experience the Oedipus complex and girls
     experience the Electra complex.

TRUE or FALSE

9.   The genital stage occurs between the ages of three and six, just before
     latency.

TRUE or FALSE

10. Boys are more likely to develop a strong conscience if their fathers are
    affectionate and accepting.

TRUE or FALSE

11. Freud regarded latency as the most important stage of psychosexual
    development.

TRUE or FALSE

12. Erik Erikson's psychosocial stages were derived, in part, from Freud's
    psychosexual stages.

TRUE or FALSE

Learning Theories of Personality—Habit I Seen You Before?

Survey Question: What do behaviorists and social learning theorists emphasize
in their approach to personality? Pages 401-406

1.   Behaviorists view personality as a collection of learned behavior patterns.

TRUE or FALSE

2.   Behaviorists attribute our actions to prior learning and specific situations.

TRUE or FALSE

3. Knowing the consistent ways people respond to certain situations allows us to predict their personality characteristics.

TRUE or FALSE

4. According to Dollard and Miller, habits are acquired through observational learning.

TRUE or FALSE

5. Cues are signals from the environment that guide responses.

TRUE or FALSE

6. An expectancy refers to the anticipation that making a response will lead to reinforcement.

TRUE or FALSE

7. Self-reinforcement is highly related to one's self-esteem.

TRUE or FALSE

8. People who are depressed tend to engage in a high rate of self-reinforcement to make themselves feel better.

TRUE or FALSE

9. Social reinforcement is based on attention and approval from others.

TRUE or FALSE

10. According to Dollard and Miller, early critical situations (such as toilet training) can leave a lasting imprint on personality.

TRUE or FALSE

11. Historically, boys have been encouraged to engage in instrumental behaviors, whereas girls were encouraged to display expressive behaviors.

TRUE or FALSE

12. Androgyny refers to having both masculine and feminine personality traits.

TRUE or FALSE

13. Masculine men and feminine women consistently choose to engage in sex-appropriate activities.

TRUE or FALSE

14. Masculine men find it difficult to accept support from others.

TRUE or FALSE

15. Androgynous persons tend to be more satisfied with their lives than non-androgynous persons.

TRUE or FALSE

Humanistic Theory—Peak Experiences and Personal Growth

Survey Question: How do humanistic theories differ from other perspectives?
Pages 407-411

1. Humanists believe that humans are capable of free choice.

TRUE or FALSE

2. To investigate self-actualization, Maslow studied eminent men and women exclusively.

TRUE or FALSE

3. Self-actualizers usually try to avoid task centering.

TRUE or FALSE

4. Personal autonomy is a characteristic of the self-actualizing person.

TRUE or FALSE

5. Willingness to change, making use of positive experiences, and conforming to the larger society are associated with promoting self-actualization

TRUE or FALSE

6. Information inconsistent with one's self-image is described as incongruent.

TRUE or FALSE

7. Poor self-knowledge is associated with high self-esteem because people do not have to think about their own faults.

TRUE or FALSE

8. Congruence represents a close correspondence between self-image, the ideal self, and the true self.

TRUE or FALSE

9. Images of possible selves typically cause feelings of incongruence.

TRUE or FALSE

10. Rogers believed that organismic valuing is healthier than trying to meet someone else's conditions of worth.

TRUE or FALSE

Traits and Situations – The Great Debate

Survey Question: How do traits and situations personality? Pages 411-415

1. Personality continues to change and evolve throughout the lifespan in response to experience and environmental influences.

TRUE or FALSE

2. The expression of personality traits tends to be influenced by external situations.

TRUE or FALSE

3. Similarities between reunited identical twins show that personality is mostly shaped by genetics.

TRUE or FALSE

4. Intelligence, some mental disorders, temperament, and personality traits are all influenced by heredity.

TRUE or FALSE

5. Studies of identical twins show that personality traits are approximately 70 percent hereditary.

TRUE or FALSE

6. Some of the coincidences shared by identical twins appear to be based on the fallacy of positive instances.

TRUE or FALSE

7. Unrelated people can share amazingly similar personality characteristics due to their age, gender, and living conditions.

TRUE or FALSE

8. Sudden murderers are often quiet, overcontrolled individuals who may become extremely violent when provoked.

TRUE or FALSE

9. Of the personality theories, the psychoanalytic approach is the most positive.

TRUE or FALSE

10. A behaviorist studying personality would be most likely to argue that behavior is governed by free will and rational decision making.

TRUE or FALSE

Personality Assessment—Psychological Yardsticks

Survey Question: How do psychologists measure personality? Pages 415-422

1. Planned questions are used in a structured interview.

TRUE or FALSE

2. The halo effect may involve either a positive or a negative impression.

TRUE or FALSE

3. Rating scales limit the chance that some personality traits will be overlooked or exaggerated.

TRUE or FALSE

4. Personality questionnaires are used to do behavioral assessments.

TRUE or FALSE

5. Judgmental firearms training is a type of honesty test.

TRUE or FALSE

6. Situational testing is of limited use because the participants behave differently, as they know it is not a real-life situation

TRUE or FALSE

7. Items on the MMPI-2 were selected for their ability to identify persons with psychiatric problems.

TRUE or FALSE

8. The validity scale of the MMPI-2 is used to rate Type A behavior.

TRUE or FALSE

9. The psychasthenia scale of the MMPI-2 detects the presence of phobias and compulsive actions.

TRUE or FALSE

10. It is very easy to fake responses to a projective test.

TRUE or FALSE

11. The Thematic Apperception Test is a situational test.

TRUE or FALSE

12. In the Thematic Apperception Test, ink blots are used to find emergent "themes" in someone's personality.

TRUE or FALSE

Psychology in Action: Barriers and Bridges—Understanding Shyness

Survey Question: What causes shyness? What can be done about it? Pages 422-425

1. Shyness is closely related to private self-consciousness.

TRUE or FALSE

2. Not-shy persons believe that external situations cause their occasional feelings of shyness.

TRUE or FALSE

3. The odds of meeting someone interested in socializing are about the same wherever you are.

TRUE or FALSE

4. Open-ended questions help keep conversations going.

TRUE or FALSE

FINAL SURVEY AND REVIEW

The Psychology of Personality—Do You Have Personality?

Survey Questions: How do psychologists use the term *personality*? Pages 388-391

1. Personality is made up of one's unique and relatively _____ pattern of thinking, _____, and behavior.

2. _____ is personality that has been judged or evaluated. That is, it is the possession of _____ qualities.

3. Personality _____ are stable personal qualities that are inferred from behavior; they can be used to _____ future behavior.

4. A personality _____ is a style of personality defined by having a group of related traits or similar characteristics.

5. Two widely recognized personality types are _____ (shy, self-centered person) and _____ (bold, outgoing person).

6. Behavior and personal adjustment are influenced by _____-_____, which is a person's perception of his or her own personality _____.

7. Culture determines how people go about developing and maintaining self-esteem (_____-_____). I in individualistic cultures, _____-_____ is based on personal success and outstanding performance; in collectivist cultures, self-esteem is based on belonging to _____ groups.

8. People with _____ self-esteem are confident, proud, and self-respecting, and people with _____ self-esteem are insecure, self-critical, and lack confidence.

9. Personality theories combine interrelated _____, assumptions, _____, and principles to explain personality.

10. Four major types of personality theories are: trait, _____, behavior and social learning, and _____.

The Trait Approach—Describe Yourself in 18,000 Words or Less

Survey Question: Are some personality traits more basic or important than others? Pages 391-395

1. Trait theorists attempt to _____, classify, and _____ traits, which are _____ predispositions or qualities of personality that are most lasting or characteristic of a person.

2. Research has found a link between personality characteristics and music. For example, people who value _____ experiences, have good verbal skills, and are liberal and tolerant of others tend to prefer _____, blues, classical, and folk music.

3. Gordon Allport made useful distinctions between _____ traits (which are shared by most members of a culture) and _____ traits (characteristics of a single person).

4. Allport also identified _____ traits (a trait that influences nearly all of a person's activities), _____ traits (core traits of personality), and secondary traits (superficial traits).

5. The theory of Raymond Cattell attributes visible surface traits to the existence of _____ underlying _____ traits (which he identified using factor analysis).

6. _____ traits are measured by the _____ *Personality Factor Questionnaire* (16 PF).

7. The _____ of the 16 PF and other personality tests may be graphically presented as a trait profile.

8. The _____-_____ model of personality reduces traits to five universal dimensions of personality. The five factors are: _____, agreeableness, _____, neuroticism, and openness to experience.

9. _____ tend to earn more during their careers than introverts, but are also _____ likely to take risks and divorce.

10. People who suffer from unhealthy _____ set impossibly _____ standards for themselves.

11. People who score high in _____ tend to perform well at work and school, have few automobile accidents, and live longer than those who score low on this dimension.

Psychoanalytic Theory—Id Came to Me in a Dream

Survey Question: How do psychodynamic theories explain personality? Pages 396-400.

1. Both _____ theories and psychodynamic theories believe that personality is based on a set of biological _____.

2. _____ theories focus on the inner workings of personality, especially _____ or unconscious thoughts, _____, and emotions.

3. According to Sigmund Freud's _____ theory, personality is made up of the id, ego, and superego.

4. The id operates on the _____ principle; it is _____ and self-serving

5. The ego is guided by the _____ principle; it _____ controls the personality and delays actions until appropriate.

6. The superego is made up of the _____ and the _____ _____.

7. When the _____ of the ego ideal are met, we feel pride; when they are not met, we feel _____.

8. _____, derived from the life instincts, drives our sexual desires and pleasure seeking. _____ is the death instinct that fuels aggression and destructive urges.

9. Conflicts within the personality may cause _____ anxiety or _____ anxiety and motivate use of ego-defense mechanisms.

10. The personality operates on three levels: the conscious, _____, and _____.

11. The id is completely unconscious; the ego and superego can operate at all _____ levels of awareness.

12. The Freudian view of personality development is based on a series of psychosexual stages: the oral, _____, phallic, and _____.

13. At each _____ stage, a different part of the child's body serves as an erogenous zone, or a source of pleasure, _____, or self-expression.

14. _____ (unresolved emotional conflicts) at any stage can leave a lasting imprint on personality.

15. Freud's theory pioneered the idea that feeding, _____ training, and early sexual experiences leave an imprint on _____.

16. During the _____ stage of Freud's psychosexual stages of development, boys must confront and resolve the Oedipus complex and girls must confront and resolve the _____ complex.

17. At _____, individuals experience an increase in _____ energies that activate unresolved conflicts of earlier stages.

18. Freud's theory has been influential for several reasons: He suggested that adult personality is formed during the first few years of a person's life; he identified _____, toilet _____, and _____ sexual experiences as critical events; and he indicated that development proceeds in stages.

19. Freud's theory is difficult to test _____, and has been criticized for _____ sexuality in personality development.

Learning Theories of Personality—Habit I Seen You Before?

Survey Question: What do behaviorists and social learning theorists emphasize in their approach to personality? Pages 401-406

1. Behavioral theories of personality emphasize learning, _____, and immediate effects of the _____.

2. Learning theorists generally stress the effects of _____ learning and situational _____ of behavior.

3. Personality dictates how we _____ consistently to certain types of situations.

4. Learning theorists John _____ and Neal _____ consider habits the basic core of personality. Habits express the combined effects of _____, cue, _____, and reward.

5. Social learning theory adds _____ elements, such as perception, _____, and beliefs, to the behavioral view of personality.

6. Examples of social learning concepts are the psychological _____ (the situation as it is perceived), _____ (expectations about what effects a response will have), and _____ value (the subjective value of a reinforcer or activity).

7. Albert Bandura believes one's _____-_____ (belief in our ability to produce a desired outcome) is an important aspect of expectancy. He also believes that self-efficacy beliefs influence the activities and _____ we choose to get into.

8. Self-reinforcement refers to _____, rewarding, or _____ oneself for making particular responses; it is closely tied to self-esteem.

9. Some social learning theorists treat "_____" as a case of self-reinforcement.

10. The behavioristic view of personality development holds that social reinforcement in four situations is critical. The critical situations are feeding, _____ or cleanliness training, sex training, and anger or _____ training.

11. _____ (feeling emotionally connected to a person) and imitation (mimicking another person's behavior) are of particular importance in sex (or gender) training.

12. _____ are more likely than _____ to engage in indirectly aggressive behaviors.

13. In _____ culture, boys are encouraged to engage in _____ (goal-directed) behaviors; girls are encouraged to engage in _____ (emotion-oriented) behaviors.

14. Androgynous individuals possess traits considered to be both "masculine" and "_____"; they are typically _____ flexible in coping with difficult situations and tend to be more satisfied with their lives.

15. Sandra _____ created the Bem Sex Role Inventory (BSRI) to measure _____, which contains masculine, feminine, and neutral traits.

16. Research conducted by Sandra _____ indicates that roughly _____-_____ of all persons are androgynous (they possess both masculine and feminine traits).

17. Being masculine means that a person is _____ and assertive.

18. Being feminine means that a person is nurturant and _____ oriented.

Humanistic Theory—Peak Experiences and Personal Growth

Survey Question: How do humanistic theories differ from other perspectives?
Pages 407-411

1. Humanistic theory views human nature as good, and emphasizes _____ experience, free choice, and needs for self-_____.

2. Abraham Maslow's study of self-actualizers identified characteristics they share, ranging from efficient perceptions of _____ to frequent peak experiences (_____ moments of self-actualization).

3. The process of self-actualization involves _____ steps, some of which include being willing to change, taking responsibility, examining one's motives, getting _____, and making use of positive experiences.

4. Carl Rogers' theory views the self as an entity that emerges when experiences that match the self-image are symbolized (admitted to consciousness), while those that are _____ are excluded.

5. The _____ person has a highly unrealistic self-image and/or a mismatch between the self-image and the _____ self.

6. The _____ or fully functioning person is flexible and open to experiences and feelings.

7. In the development of personality, humanists are primarily interested in the emergence of a self-image and in self-_____. It is important to have _____ between one's self-image and ideal self.

8. _____ selves represent our hopes, fantasies, fears, and goals for who we could be.

9. As parents apply conditions of worth (_____ used to judge thoughts, feelings, and actions) to a child, the child begins to do the same.

10. Internalized conditions of worth contribute to incongruence, they damage positive self-regard, and they disrupt the _____ valuing process.

11. Unconditional positive regard (unshakable _____ and _____ from others) contributes to organismic valuing in children and adults.

Traits and Situations – The Great Debate

Survey Question: How do traits and situations affect personality? Page 411-415

1. Temperament refers to the hereditary and _____ aspects of one's emotional nature.

2. Personality starts to _____ around age 3 and continues to "harden" until age 50; personality _____ in old age.

3. Traits interact with _____ to determine behavior; in a trait-situation interaction, external circumstances influence the _____ of a personality trait.

4. Behavioral _____ is the study of inherited behavioral traits.

5. Heredity is responsible for _____ to _____ percent of the variation in personality traits.

6. Studies of separated identical twins suggest that _____ contributes significantly to adult personality traits. Overall, however, personality is shaped as much, or more, by _____ in environment.

7. The _____ approach to personality believes that development is driven by both heredity and environmental factors

8. The _____ perspective has a positive view of human nature, whereas the _____ perspective is negative.

9. The role of genetics is _____ in trait theories, but _____ in behavioristic, social learning, and humanistic theories.

Personality Assessment—Psychological Yardsticks

Survey Question: How do psychologists measure personality? Pages 415-422

1. Techniques typically used for personality assessment are interviews, _____, questionnaires, and _____ tests.

2. Structured and _____ interviews provide much information, but they are subject to interviewer bias and _____. Intentional deception and the halo effect may also lower accuracy.

3. Direct _____, sometimes involving situational tests, behavioral assessment, or the use of rating scales, allows evaluation of a person's actual behavior.

4. In _____ testing, real-life conditions are _____ and spontaneous reactions are observed.

5. Personality _____, such as the *Minnesota Multiphasic Personality Inventory-2* (MMPI-2), are objective and reliable, but their _____ is open to question.

6. _____ tests, which are essentially personality questionnaires, are widely used by businesses to make _____ decisions. Their validity is hotly debated.

7. _____ tests ask a subject to project thoughts or feelings onto an _____ stimulus or unstructured situation.

8. The _____, or inkblot test, is a well-known projective technique. A second is the *Thematic* _____ *Test* (TAT).

9. The validity and _____ of projective tests are quite low. Nevertheless, projective techniques are considered useful by many clinicians, particularly as part of a test battery.

Psychology in Action: Barriers and Bridges—Understanding Shyness

Survey Question: What causes shyness? What can be done about it? Pages 422-425

1. Shyness is a mixture of social _____ and social _____.

2. Shy persons fail to make eye contact, _____ when spoken to, speak too quietly, and display little _____ in conversation.

3. Shy persons tend to lack _____ skills and they feel social anxiety (because they believe they are being evaluated by others).

4. Shy persons also have a self-_____ bias in their thinking (they tend to _____ themselves for social failures).

5. Shyness is marked by _____ public self-consciousness (awareness of oneself as a social object) and a tendency to regard shyness as a _____ trait.

6. Shyness can be lessened by changing self-defeating _____ and by improving _____ skills.

MASTERY TEST

1. The hereditary aspects of a person's emotional nature define his or her
   a. character.
   b. personality.
   c. cardinal traits.
   d. temperament.

2. Two parts of the psyche that operate on all three levels of awareness are the
   a. id and ego.
   b. ego and superego.
   c. id and superego.
   d. id and ego ideal.

3. The four critical situations Miller and Dollard consider important in the development of personality are feeding, toilet training,
   a. sex, and aggression.
   b. cleanliness, and language.
   c. attachment, and imitation.
   d. social learning, and attachment.

4. Scales that rate a person's tendencies for depression, hysteria, paranoia, and mania are found on the
   a. MMPI-2.
   b. Rorschach.
   c. TAT.
   d. 16 PF.

5. In the five-factor model, people who score high on openness to experience are typically
   a. intelligent.
   b. extroverted.
   c. choleric.
   d. a personality type.

6. Maslow used the term _____ to describe the tendency to make full use of personal potentials.
   a. full functionality
   b. self-potentiation
   c. ego-idealization
   d. self-actualization

7. Studies of reunited identical twins support the idea that
   a. personality traits are 70 percent hereditary and 30 percent learned.
   b. childhood fixations influence the expression of personality traits in adulthood.
   c. personality traits are altered by selective mating.
   d. personality is shaped at least as much by environment as by heredity.

8. A person's perception of his or her own personality is the core of
a. temperament.
b. source traits.
c. self-concept.
d. trait-situation interactions.

9. Which of the following concepts is NOT part of Dollard and Miller's behavioral model of personality?
a. drive
b. expectancy
c. cue
d. reward

10. The terms *structured* and *unstructured* apply most to
a. the halo effect.
b. interviews.
c. questionnaires.
d. honesty tests.

11. Behavioral theorists account for the existence of a conscience with the concept of
a. traits of honesty and integrity.
b. the superego.
c. self-reinforcement.
d. conditions of worth.

12. Feelings of pride come from the _____, a part of the
_____.
a. libido, conscience
b. ego ideal, superego
c. reality principle, superego
d. superego, ego

13. Four types of temperament recognized by the early Greeks are: melancholic, choleric, phlegmatic, and
a. sanguine.
b. sardonic.
c. Sagittarian.
d. sagacious.

14. Freud believed that boys identify with their fathers in order to resolve the _____ conflict.
a. Animus
b. Electra
c. Oedipus
d. Persona

15. Maslow regarded peak experiences as temporary moments of
a. task-centering.
b. congruent selfhood.
c. self-actualization.
d. organismic valuing.

16. Ambiguous stimuli are used primarily in the
a. MMPI-2.
b. Shoot-Don't-Shoot Test.
c. Rorschach.
d. 16 PF.

17. A person who is generally extroverted is more outgoing in some situations than in others. This observation supports the concept of
a. trait-situation interactions.
b. behavioral genetic determinants.
c. situational fixations.
d. possible selves.

18. Allport's concept of central traits is most closely related to Cattell's
a. surface traits.
b. source traits.
c. secondary traits.
d. cardinal traits.

19. According to Freud, tendencies to be orderly, obstinate, and stingy are formed during the _____ stage.
a. genital
b. anal
c. oral
d. phallic

20. Which of the following is NOT part of Carl Rogers' view of personality?
a. possible selves
b. organismic valuing
c. conditions of worth
d. congruence

21. Rating scales are primarily used in which approach to personality assessment?
a. projective testing
b. direct observation
c. questionnaires
d. the TAT technique

22. Which theory of personality places the greatest emphasis on the effects of the environment?
a. trait
b. psychodynamic
c. behavioristic
d. humanistic

23. Freudian psychosexual stages occur in the order
   a. oral, anal, genital, phallic.
   b. oral, phallic, anal, genital.
   c. genital, oral, anal, phallic.
   d. oral, anal, phallic, genital.

24. Rogers described mismatches between one's self-image and reality as a state of
   a. moral anxiety.
   b. incongruence.
   c. basic anxiety.
   d. negative symbolization.

25. All but one of the following are major elements of shyness; which does not apply?
   a. private self-consciousness
   b. social anxiety
   c. self-defeating thoughts
   d. evaluation fears

26. People who all grew up in the same culture would be most likely to have the same _____ traits.
   a. cardinal
   b. common
   c. secondary
   d. source

27. A trait profile is used to report the results of
   a. the 16 PF.
   b. situational tests.
   c. the TAT.
   d. the inkblot test.

28. An emphasis on the situational determinants of actions is a key feature of _____ theories of personality.
   a. psychodynamic
   b. projective
   c. behaviorist
   d. humanist

29. Expectancies and the psychological situation are concepts important to
   a. the five-factor model.
   b. development of the superego.
   c. social learning theory.
   d. Maslow.

30. A policeman who accepts emotional support from others, especially from women, would most likely be scored as _____ on the BSRI.
a. androgynous
b. masculine
c. feminine
d. expressive-nurturant

31. The behavioral concept most closely related to the superego is
a. psychological situation.
b. self-reinforcement.
c. reinforcement value.
d. self-concept.

32. Jill was invited to go snowboarding, an activity she has not done before. Jill believes she has the ability to learn snowboarding and keep up with her friends because she is a fast learner. Bandura would say that Jill is high in
a. self-actualizing.
b. organismic valuing.
c. congruence.
d. self-efficacy.

LANGUAGE DEVELOPMENT
Personality

Word Roots

Freud used Latin terms to help define the parts of the personality that he proposed. In Latin, *id* means "it" (the third person singular neuter pronoun) while *ego* means "I" (the first person singular pronoun). He combined *ego* with other words to form other psychoanalytic terms found in this chapter (e.g., *superego* and *ego ideal*).

Journey into Psychology: The Hidden Essence
   (387)   *dilapidated*: falling apart
   (387)   *hooting and whooping*: yelling with pleasure and excitement
   (387)   *radical*: extreme; departure from normal
   (387)   *lumberjack*: logger; one who cuts trees for lumber
   (387)   *decked*: punched
   (387)   *tavern*: place where alcohol is sold and consumed; a bar
   (387)   *zaniest*: silliest; exhibits odd and often comical behavior

The Psychology of Personality—Do You Have Personality (pgs. 388-391)
   How do psychologists use the term *personality*?
   (388)   *charisma*: special magnetic charm or appeal

(388) **keep your bearings:** understand the text; stay on track
(388) **inferred:** resulted from; deduced from observation
(389) **executive type:** a type that derives from the corporate culture; typified by 3-piece suits and briefcases.
(389) **hip-hop type:** a type that derives from inner-city street culture; it includes rap music and a style of dress and dance
(389) **techno geek:** a person who spends much of his or her time with technical things such as computers
(390) **interdependence:** mutually dependent; needing each other

(390) **hotshot:** a person who displays great skills and abilities
(390) **bask in the glow:** enjoy the good feelings
(390) **sketches:** samples of drawings
(390) **pumped up:** made to feel good, strong, and competent
(390) **collectivism:** philosophy that everyone works together for the good of the group; welfare of the group is more important than individual desires
(390) **"think you're hot":** to think overly highly of oneself or one's abilities
(390) **arrogance:** too much pride and sense of self-importance

The Trait Approach—Describe Yourself in 18,000 Words or Less (pgs. 391-395)

Are some personality traits more basic or important than others?
(391) **uninhibited:** not restrained by social norms; informal
(391) **optimistic:** (optimism): the tendency to emphasize the best possible outcome
(391) **pessimistic (pessimism):** the tendency to emphasize the worst possible outcome
(392) **aesthetic:** pleasing and nice to look at
(392) **Hopi of Northern Arizona:** a Native American tribe found primarily in the American southwest
(393) **submissive:** allowing oneself to be governed by another
(394) **loner:** one who avoids social contact with others
(395) **spiteful:** malicious; nasty

Psychoanalytic Theory—Id Came to Me in a Dream (pgs. 396-400)

How do psychodynamic theories explain personality?
(396) **animate:** to give life to
(396) **obstinate:** being stubborn
(396) **executive:** the one in charge
(396) **censor:** one who represses or forbids unacceptable notions or ideas
(397) **chaotic:** confused; totally disorganized
(397) **discharging:** releasing; letting go
(397) **rigidity:** firmness; degree to which something does not change

(397)   *clamors*: the act of demanding
(397)   *"Go for it!"*: go after what you want; do it
(398)   *sublimate*: to redirect an urge toward a more socially accepted activity
(399)   *hang-up*: problem; barrier (399) *exhibitionism*: the act of behaving so that one receives attention
(399)   *they swallow things easily*: this statement has two references: individuals in the oral stage seek pleasure by swallowing things, and these individuals have the tendency to believe anything told to them even if the information is false
(399)   *passive*: inactive and not showing feeling or interest
(399)   *showered with gifts*: being given lots of gifts
(399)   *forte:* originally a musical term meaning loud or strong, it is also used to mean strength or one's specialty
(399)   *Oedipus*: character in a Greek tragedy who unknowingly married his mother and killed his father
(399)   *Electra*: character in a Greek tragedy who killed her mother
(399)   *"on hold"*: postponed; put off until a later time
(400)   *embrace*: believes in; holds to be true
(400)   *offshoot*: development; derivation
(400)   *postulated*: to have claimed without proof

Learning Theories of Personality—Habit I Seen You Before? (pgs. 401-406)

What do behaviorists and social learning theorists emphasize in their approach to personality?
(401)   *mechanistic*: mechanically
(401)   *scrupulous*: having high moral integrity
(402)   *goad*: something that urges or stimulates into action
(404)   *aghast*: horrified
(404)   *with joyful abandon*: in an unrestrained manner; free and careless
(404)   *permissiveness*: tolerance
(404)   *vicariously*: experienced indirectly
(406)   *"shop 'til you drop"*: going shopping until one is exhausted and does not have the energy to move anymore

Humanistic Theory—Peak Experiences and Personal Growth (pgs. 407-411)

How do humanistic theories differ from other perspectives?
(407)   *moldable*: the degree to which something can change
(407)   *inherently*: involved in the framework or essential character of something
(407)   *blossom*: to develop, grow
(407)   *facet*: an area or component
(408)   *"innocence of vision"*: experiencing and seeing the same object like it was seen for the first time

(408) *wry*: ironically humorous
(408) *gleaned from*: gathered information from
(408) *exaltation*: great happiness
(409) *mission*: purpose or goal
(409) *gauge*: measure
(409) *seething*: boiling
(409) *gulf*: a space or an opening
(409) *maladjusted*: disturbed; confused
(410) *entrepreneur*: a capitalist; someone starting a new business
(410) *grossly obese*: extremely overweight
(411) *gut-level response*: arising from one's innermost self; instinctual
(411) *affirmation*: positive assertion
(411) *"prized"*: valued; thought of as important

Traits and Situations – The Great Debate (pgs. 411-415)

(412) *reared apart*: raised in separate homes
(412) *preposterous*: ridiculous; silly
(412) *eerie*: strange
(412) *rival*: be competitive with
(412) *nervous tics*: nervous habits or actions
(412) *excels*: is good at; performs well at
(413) *sizable effect*: to have a considerable effect, or to influence greatly
(413) *"wired in"*: unchangeable
(414) *"someone you could easily push around"*: someone who is easily bullied or influenced by others
(414) *belittlement*: causing to seem little or less
(414) *amnesia*: temporary loss of memory
(414) *off-color jokes*: improper or inappropriate jokes that can be offensive
(414) *boisterous*: being loud, wild, and disorderly in behavior
(414) *fared*: worked out; succeeded

Personality Assessment—Psychological Yardsticks (pgs. 415-422)

How do psychologists measure personality?

(415) *"sized up"*: evaluated; measured
(415) *caught off-guard*: to be surprised by something unexpected
(416) *swayed*: influenced
(416) *punk*: teen or young adult (usually male) that engages in petty crimes
(416) *geek*: expert in some field (usually technology); intellectual, but often lacking in social skills
(416) *"ski bum"*: a person who spends a great deal of time on the ski slopes
(416) *accentuate*: make more obvious
(416) *prelude*: introduction; something that comes before
(416) *withdrawn*: removed from social contact

(417)   *split-second*: very fast
(418)   *satirize*: to make fun of
(419)   *cynicism*: the belief that selfishness motivates human actions
(420)   *fake*: to deliberately answer in a misleading manner

Psychology in Action: Barriers and Bridges—Understanding Shyness (pgs. 422-425)

What causes shyness? What can be done about it?

(422)   *preoccupied*: worried; distracted
(422)   *animation*: movement or activity
(423)   *wrapped up*: too focused on oneself
(423)   *see through*: to understand beyond the surface level
(423)   *"stage fright"*: fear of appearing before crowds to perform, give a speech, etc.
(424)   *broken the ice*: concluded an introduction; became acquainted
(424)   *"Free information":* information that was volunteered; not asked for

Chapter in Review

(426)   *interrelated*: being connected, related together

Solutions

Recite and Review

The Psychology of Personality—Do You Have Personality?

1. behavior
2. evaluated
3. behavior
4. traits
5. types
6. personality
7. self, esteem, cultures, cultures
8. proud, self-critical
9. Personality
10. trait, social

The Trait Approach—Describe Yourself in 18,000 Words or Less

1. classify
2. music, verbal, blues
3. individual
4. secondary
5. surface, analysis
6. Personality, Factor
7. trait
8. universal, agreeableness, experience
9. introverts
10. impossibly
11. high, low

Psychoanalytic Theory—Id Came to Me in a Dream

1. biological
2. unconscious
3. ego
4. principle
5. principle
6. superego
7. pride
8. life, death
9. anxiety, anxiety
10. conscious
11. unconscious
12. stages, oral
13. erogenous
14. personality
15. personality.
16. psychosexual, Oedipus
17. unresolved
18. first, few, toilet, stages
19. test, sexuality

Learning Theories of Personality—Habit I Seen You Before?

1. learning
2. situational
3. consistently
4. habits, Habits, reward
5. Social
6. psychological, value
7. ability, activities
8. rewarding, esteem
9. self
10. feeding, anger
11. imitation
12. indirectly
13. boys, girls
14. masculine
15. Sex, Role, androgyny
16. masculine, feminine
17. masculine
18. feminine

Humanistic Theory—Peak Experiences and Personal Growth

1. good, free
2. peak, experiences
3. responsibility, positive
4. self, image
5. self, image, self, image
6. fully
7. self, image, self, image
8. fantasies
9. worth
10. positive, valuing
11. positive, organismic

Traits and Situations – The Great Debate

1. hereditary
2. 3, 50
3. Traits
4. inherited
5. traits
6. identical
7. heredity, environmental
8. positive, negative
9. behavioristic, learning

Personality Assessment—Psychological Yardsticks

1. interviews, tests
2. interviews, interviewer, lower
3. rating, behavior
4. testing, spontaneous
5. Minnesota, Multiphasic, reliable
6. questionnaires
7. stimulus
8. inkblot, Thematic
9. low, test

Psychology in Action: Barriers and Bridges—Understanding Shyness

1. social, social
2. eye, quietly
3. evaluated
4. thinking, themselves
5. public, social
6. beliefs, social

CONNECTIONS

The Psychology of Personality—Do You Have Personality?

1. C.
2. G.
3. A.
4. H.
5. J.
6. F.
7. B.
8. I.
9. E.
10. D.

The Trait Approach—Describe Yourself in 18,000 Words or Less

1. E.
2. H.
3. B.
4. A.
5. G.
6. C.
7. F.
8. D.

Psychoanalytic Theory—Id Came to Me in a Dream

1. F.
2. H.
3. K.
4. I.
5. N.
6. B.
7. M.
8. A.
9. G.
10. C.
11. L.
12. J.
13. E.
14. D.

Learning Theories of Personality—Habit I Seen You Before?

1. C.
2. I.
3. N.
4. A.
5. D.
6. J.
7. K.
8. B.
9. M.
10. G.
11. F.
12. H.
13. L.
14. E.

Humanistic Theory—Peak Experiences and Personal Growth

1. D.	3. C.	5. G.	7. B.
2. F.	4. E.	6. A.	

Traits and Situations – The Great Debate

1. D.	2. A.	3. C.	4. B.

Personality Assessment—Psychological Yardsticks; and Psychology in Action: Barriers and Bridges—Understanding Shyness

1. E.	5. A.	9. L.	13. C.
2. J.	6. M.	10. G.	
3. K.	7. H.	11. B.	
4. D.	8. F.	12. I.	

Check Your Memory

The Psychology of Personality—Do You Have Personality?

1. F	5. T	9. T	13. F
2. F	6. T	10. T	
3. F	7. T	11. F	
4. F	8. F	12. F	

The Trait Approach—Describe Yourself in 18,000 Words or Less

1. T	5. F	9. F	13. T
2. F	6. F	10. F	14. T
3. T	7. T	11. F	
4. T	8. T	12. F	

Psychoanalytic Theory—Id Came to Me in a Dream

1. F	4. T	7. F	10. T
2. T	5. F	8. T	11. F
3. F	6. T	9. F	12. T

Learning Theories of Personality—Habit I Seen You Before?

1. T	5. T	9. T	13. T
2. T	6. T	10. T	14. T
3. T	7. T	11. T	15. T
4. F	8. F	12. T	

Humanistic Theory—Peak Experiences and Personal Growth

1. T
2. F
3. F
4. T
5. F
6. T
7. F
8. T
9. F
10. T

Traits and Situations – The Great Debate

1. F
2. T
3. F
4. T
5. F
6. T
7. T
8. T
9. F
10. F

Personality Assessment—Psychological Yardsticks

1. T
2. T
3. T
4. F
5. F
6. F
7. T
8. F
9. T
10. F
11. F
12. F

Psychology in Action: Barriers and Bridges—Understanding Shyness

1. F
2. T
3. F
4. T

Final Survey and Review

The Psychology of Personality—Do You Have Personality?

1. stable, emotions
2. Character, desirable
3. traits, predict
4. type
5. introvert, extrovert
6. self, concept, traits
7. self, evaluation, self, esteem, social
8. high, low
9. concepts, ideas
10. psychodynamic, humanistic

The Trait Approach—Describe Yourself in 18,000 Words or Less

1. analyze, interrelate, biological
2. aesthetic, jazz
3. common, individual
4. cardinal, central
5. 16, source
6. Source, Sixteen
7. outcome
8. five, factor, extroversion, conscientiousness
9. Extroverts, more
10. perfectionism, high
11. conscientiousness

Psychoanalytic Theory—Id Came to Me in a Dream

1. trait, predispositions
2. Psychodynamic, hidden, needs
3. psychoanalytic
4. pleasure, irrational
5. reality, consciously
6. conscience, ego, ideal
7. standards, guilt.
8. Libido, Thanatos
9. neurotic, moral
10. preconscious, unconscious
11. three
12. anal, genital
13. psychosexual, frustration
14. Fixations
15. toilet, personality
16. phallic, Electra
17. puberty, sexual
18. feeding, training, early
19. empirically, overemphasizing

Learning Theories of Personality—Habit I Seen You Before?

1. imitation, environment
2. prior, determinants
3. respond
4. Dollard, Miller, drive, response
5. cognitive, thinking
6. situation, expectancies, reinforcement
7. self, efficacy, situations
8. praising, blaming
9. conscience
10. toilet, aggression
11. Identification
12. Girls, boys
13. Western, instrumental, expressive
14. feminine, more
15. Bem, androgyny
16. Bem, one, third
17. independent
18. interpersonally

Humanistic Theory—Peak Experiences and Personal Growth

Survey Question: How do humanistic theories differ from other perspectives?
Pages 407-411

1. subjective, actualization
2. reality, temporary
3. multiple, involved
4. incongruent
5. incongruent, ideal
6. congruent
7. evaluations, congruence
8. Possible
9. standards
10. organismic
11. love, approval

Traits and Situations – The Great Debate

1. physiological
2. stabilize, matures
3. situations, expression
4. genetics
5. 25, 50
6. heredity, differences
7. trait
8. humanistic, psychoanalytic
9. emphasized, minimized

Personality Assessment—Psychological Yardsticks

1. observation, projective
2. unstructured, misperceptions
3. observation
4. situational, simulated
5. questionnaires, validity
6. Honesty, hiring
7. Projective, ambiguous
8. Rorschach, Apperception
9. objectivity

Psychology in Action: Barriers and Bridges—Understanding Shyness

1. inhibition, anxiety
2. retreat, interest
3. social
4. defeating, blame
5. heightened, lasting
6. beliefs, social

Mastery Test

1. d, p. 411
2. b, p. 397
3. a, p. 402
4. a, p. 419–420
5. a, p. 395
6. d, p. 407
7. d, p. 412
8. c, p. 389
9. b, p. 402
10. b, p. 416
11. c, p. 403

12. b, p. 397
13. a, p. 391
14. c, p. 399
15. c, p. 408
16. c, p. 420–421
17. a, p. 414
18. b, p. 393
19. b, p. 399
20. a, p. 409–410
21. b, p. 416
22. c, p. 390–391

23. d, p. 399
24. b, p. 409
25. a, p. 422–424
26. b, p. 392
27. a, p. 393
28. c, p. 401–402
29. c, p. 402–403
30. a, p. 405–406
31. b, p. 403
32. d, p. 403

CHAPTER 11

Health, Stress, and Coping

Chapter Overview

Health psychologists study behavioral risk factors and health-promoting behaviors. Various "lifestyle" diseases are directly related to unhealthy personal habits. To reduce lifestyle diseases, people are encouraged to adopt health-promoting behaviors, such as getting regular exercise, controlling smoking and alcohol use, maintaining a balanced diet, getting good medical care, and managing stress. An understanding of the risks involved in sexual behavior is also important, including knowledge of safer sex practices. In addition to health-promoting behaviors, early prevention programs and community health campaigns have been implemented.

Stress is also a major risk factor. The body reacts to stress in a pattern called the general adaptation syndrome (G.A.S.). In addition, stress may lower the body's immunity to disease. At work, prolonged stress can lead to burnout. Appraisals (both primary and secondary appraisals) greatly affect our stress reactions and coping attempts. Traumatic stressors, such as violence, torture, or natural disasters, tend to produce severe stress reactions.

Frustration and conflict are common sources of stress, and may be caused by external sources (social or nonsocial) that delay or block motivated behavior or by personal characteristics. Frustration increases as the strength, urgency, or importance of a blocked motive increases. Major behavioral reactions to frustration include persistence, more vigorous responding, circumvention, direct aggression, displaced aggression, and escape or withdrawal. Persistence is generally adaptive, but may become stereotyped and inflexible. Ways of coping with frustration include identifying its source, determining if the source is manageable, and deciding if changing the source is worth the effort.

Five major types of conflict are approach-approach, avoidance-avoidance, approach-avoidance, double approach-avoidance, and multiple approach-avoidance. Approach=approach is easiest to resolve; avoidance-avoidance is more difficult, and may lead to inaction or "freezing." Approach-avoidance is characterized by positive and negative aspects that must be weighed. Avoiding hasty decisions, partial trials, compromise, and living with decisions are strategies for coping with conflict.

Anxiety, threat, or feelings of inadequacy frequently lead to the use of defense mechanisms. Common defense mechanisms include compensation, denial, fantasy, intellectualization, isolation, projection, rationalization, reaction formation, regression, repression, and sublimation. Compensation and sublimation are the most positive. Overuse of defense mechanisms may lead to an unrealistic self-image.

Learned helplessness explains some depression and some failures to cope with threat. Mastery training and hope act as an antidote to helplessness. In humans, helplessness may be realized as depression, which is a serious emotional problem, especially in college students. Creating a daily schedule, appreciating even small accomplishments, and challenging negative thoughts are effective coping strategies.

Major life changes can increase susceptibility to illness. The Social Readjustment Rating Scale (SRRS) provides an estimate of health hazards; higher scores are associated with increases in illness. However, immediate health is more closely related to the severity of daily hassles or microstressors. Intense or prolonged stress may cause psychosomatic problems. Many emigrants and refugees experience acculturative stress. The severity of acculturative stress depends, in part, on how one adapts to the new culture.

There are individual differences associated with the experience of stress. People with Type A personalities run a heightened risk of suffering heart disease. People with hardy personality traits are resistant to stress; they tend to experience a sense of commitment (to work family, etc.), perceive control over their lives, and see events as challenges, rather than threats.

The College Life Stress Inventory measures stress in college students. A number of coping skills can be applied to manage stress. Most focus on managing bodily reactions and stress-reducing behaviors. The former includes exercise and relaxation techniques. The latter includes organization, seeking social support, identifying and avoiding upsetting thoughts, and finding the humor in situations.

Learning Objectives

1. Define the terms *health psychology and behavioral medicine*; give examples of lifestyle diseases and behavioral risk factors; describe the disease-prone personality and how an unhealthy lifestyle often creates multiple risks.
2. Explain how health psychologists treat and prevent lifestyle diseases and encourage people to follow nine health-promoting behaviors.
3. Describe the impact of smoking on illness and death and the approaches that have been used to prevent or lessen the risk, such as school-based prevention programs, refusal-skills training, life skills training, community health programs, and role models; define *wellness* and list the characteristics of people who attain optimal wellness.
4. Define *sexually-transmitted disease* (STDs) and list examples, including a discussion of the transmission of HIV/AIDS; describe the behavioral risk factors associated with STDs and safer sex practices to combat the spread of STDs.
5. Define the terms *stress*, *eustress*, and *stress reaction*; discuss the effects of short-term stresses and the impact of long-term stresses by explaining the three stages of the General Adaptation Syndrome; describe how prolonged

stress effects the immune system, including the field of study called psychoneuroimmunology, and how reducing stress can actually boost immune system functioning.

6. List several aspects of stress that make it more intense and damaging; define the terms *stressor*, *pressure*, and *burnout*; and describe the three aspects of burnout, and why it tends to be a problem in helping professions.

7. Give an example of how primary and secondary appraisal are used in coping with a threatening situation; explain how the perception of control of a stressor influences the amount of threat felt.

8. Differentiate problem-focused coping from emotion-focused coping; explain how they may help or hinder each other.

9. Describe the impact of traumatic stress and ways to cope with reactions to severe stress.

10. Define frustration and make a distinction between external and personal sources of frustration, and whether the external obstacles are social or non-social; and list factors that tend to increase frustration.

11. Describe the five common reactions to frustration (Fig. 11.4), including how displaced aggression can result in scapegoating

12. Explain how a stereotyped response to frustration differs from persistence; and discuss three effective ways to avoid frustration.

13. Describe and give examples of each of the following types of conflict:
    a. approach-approach
    b. avoidance-avoidance
    c. approach-avoidance, including the terms *ambivalence* and *partial approach*
    d. double approach-avoidance, including the term *vacillation*
    e. multiple approach-avoidance; and discuss four strategies for coping with conflict

14. Define the term *defense mechanism*; discuss the positive and negative effects of defense mechanisms; and describe the following defense mechanisms and give examples of each (Table 11.3):
    a. compensation
    b. denial
    c. fantasy
    d. identification
    e. intellectualization
    f. isolation
    g. projection
    h. rationalization
    i. reaction formation
    j. regression
    k. repression
    l. sublimation

15. Describe the development of learned helplessness, how attributions affect helplessness, the similarities between learned helplessness and depression, and the effects of hope and mastery training in reducing it.

16. Discuss the problems that contribute to depression among college students, how to recognize depression, and ways to cope with depression effectively.

17. Discuss the relationship between life changes and long-term health; describe the SRRS; and explain how hassles (microstressors) are related to immediate health.

18. Explain how acculturative stress can cause problems and describe four methods for adapting to a new culture and the level of stress associated with each.

19. Distinguish between psychosomatic disorders and hypochondria; list the causes of psychosomatic disorders; and briefly discuss biofeedback in terms of the process involved and its possible applications.

20. Differentiate between Type A and Type B personalities; list ways Type A personalities can reduce their feelings of hostility.

21. Describe the hardy personality, including how this personality views the world and how happiness is related to hardiness.

22. Define the term *stress management*; describe the College Life Stress Inventory; list three responses that are triggered by stress.

23. Discuss the stress management techniques that can be used to diminish or break the cycle of these stress responses.

RECITE AND REVIEW

Health Psychology—Here's to Your Good Health

Survey Questions: What is health psychology? How does behavior affect health?
Pages 429-433

1. Health psychologists are interested in _____ that helps maintain and promote health. The related field of behavioral medicine applies psychology to _____ treatment and problems.

2. Most people today die from lifestyle diseases caused by unhealthy personal _____.

3. Studies have identified a number of behavioral risk factors that increase the chances of _____ (or _____) or injury.

4. A general disease-prone personality pattern also raises the risk of _____ (or _____).

5. _____ diseases can be treated by making specific, minor changes in behavior, such as using less salt or getting more exercise.

6. Health-promoting _____ tend to maintain good health. They include practices such as getting regular exercise, controlling _____ and alcohol use, maintaining a balanced _____, getting good medical care, avoiding _____ deprivation, and managing stress.

7. Attempts to prevent young people from developing unhealthful behaviors, such as smoking and drug use, often make use of refusal _____ training and life skills _____.

8. Health psychologists attempt to promote wellness (a positive state of _____) through community health _____ that educate people about risk factors and healthful behaviors.

9. _____ is a positive state of physical and psychological well-being.

STDs and Safer Sex—Choice, Risk, and Responsibility

Survey Question: How can sexually transmitted diseases be prevented? Pages 434-436

1. A sexually transmitted disease (STD) is an infection passed from one person to another through _____ contact.

2. Individuals who carry STDs may not have any _____, and may not know that their partner is infectious.

3. A recent study found that approximately _____ percent of sexually active teenage _____ reported that they did not believe they would get _____ transmitted diseases (STDs) because their partners _____ _____ show symptoms of STDs.

4. People who are sexually _____, even with only one person, may still be engaging in risky sex from _____ contact with others through their partner's indiscretion.

5. The emergence of _____ _____ deficiency syndrome (AIDS) is caused by the human immunodeficiency _____ (HIV).

6. The first symptoms of AIDS may not appear for up to ten years; during that time, people can unknowingly _____ others.

7. AIDS is spreading more quickly among heterosexuals, _____, African Americans, Hispanics, and children. It is predicted that over the next 15 years, _____ million people will die of AIDS unless preventions are taken.

8. STDs have had a sizable impact on patterns of sexual behavior, including increased awareness of high-_____ behaviors and some curtailment of _____ taking.

9. Safe sex practices include using a _____, selectively choosing only a few sexual partners, and knowing a partner's sexual history before intercourse. Abstinence is the most risk-free policy.

Stress—Thrill or Threat?

Survey Questions: What is stress? What factors determine its severity? Pages 436-440

1. Stress occurs when we are forced to _____ or adapt to external demands.

2. Eustress (_____ stress) is part of a healthy lifestyle; activities that produce good stress are challenging, _____, and energizing.

3. The body reacts to stress in a series of stages called the _____ adaptation syndrome (G.A.S.).

4. The stages of the G.A.S. are alarm, resistance, and exhaustion. The G.A.S. contributes to the development of _____ disorders.

5. Emotional, behavioral, and physical signs of exhaustion emerge when the body's resources are _____. Stress weakens the immune system and lowers the body's resistance to _____ (or _____).

6. Stress is more damaging in situations involving pressure (responding at full capacity for long periods), a lack of _____, unpredictability of the stressor, and _____ or repeated emotional shocks.

7. _____ is intensified when a situation is perceived as a threat and when a person does not feel competent to cope with it.

8. In _____ settings, prolonged stress can lead to burnout, marked by emotional _____, cynicism, depersonalization (detachment from others), and reduced personal accomplishment.

9. The _____ (initial) appraisal of a situation greatly affects our emotional response to it. Stress reactions, in particular, are related to an appraisal of _____.

10. During a _____ appraisal some means of coping with a situation are selected. Coping may be either problem-focused (managing the situation) or emotion-focused (managing one's emotional reactions) or both.

11. A _____ lack of control is just as threatening as an actual lack of control.

12. Problem-focused coping is used to manage or correct a distressing situation (for example, by making a plan of action) and is most effective when facing a _____ stressor.

13. In emotion-focused coping, individuals try to control their emotions; this is best suited to managing your reactions to _____ stressors.

14. Traumatic _____, such as violence, torture, or natural disasters, tend to produce severe _____ reactions.

15. Traumatic _____ leave people feeling threatened, vulnerable, and with the sense that they are losing control over their _____.

16. Severe or _____ traumatic _____ can leave people with lasting emotional handicaps called stress disorders.

Frustration—Blind Alleys and Lead Balloons

Survey Question: What causes frustration and what are typical reactions to it? Pages 440-443

1. Frustration is the negative emotional state that occurs when progress toward a _____ is _____. Sources of frustration may be external or personal.

2. External frustrations are either social or nonsocial, and are based on delay, failure, rejection, loss, and other direct blocking of motives. Personal frustration is related to _____ characteristics over which one has little control.

3. Frustrations of all types become more _____ as the strength, urgency, or importance of the blocked motive increases. Repeated frustrations can accumulate to produce an unexpectedly violent response.

4. Major behavioral reactions to frustration include persistence, more _____ responding, and circumvention of barriers.

5. Other reactions to frustration are _____ aggression, displaced aggression (including scapegoating), and escape, or _____.

6. Psychological _____ or withdrawal may include feigned apathy (pretending not to _____) or the use of drugs.

7. Persistence is normal reaction to _____, but persistence that becomes rigid or inflexible leads to pointless, stereotyped behavior.

8. Ways of _____ with frustration include identifying its source, determining if the source is manageable, and deciding if _____ the source is worth the effort.

Conflict—Yes, No, Yes, No, Yes, No, Well, Maybe

Survey Questions: Are there different types of conflict? How do people react to conflict? Pages 443-446

1. _____ occurs when we must choose between contradictory alternatives.

2. Three basic types of conflict are approach-approach (choice between two _____ alternatives), avoidance-avoidance (both alternatives are _____), and approach-avoidance (a goal or activity has both positive and negative aspects).

3. More complex conflicts are: double approach-avoidance (both alternatives have _____ and _____ qualities) and multiple approach-avoidance (several alternatives each have good and bad qualities).

4. Approach-approach conflicts are usually the _____ to resolve.

5. Avoidance conflicts are _____ to resolve and are characterized by inaction, indecision, freezing, and a desire to escape (called "_____ the field").

6. People usually remain in approach-avoidance conflicts, but fail to fully resolve them. Approach-avoidance conflicts are associated with ambivalence (_____ feelings) and _____ approach.

7. Vacillation (wavering between choices) is the most common reaction to double _____-_____ conflicts.

8. Managing conflicts effectively involves not making hasty decisions, trying out a few _____ at a time, looking for _____, and sticking with the choice.

Psychological Defense—Mental Karate?

Survey Question: What are defense mechanisms? Pages 447-449

1. Anxiety, threat, or feelings of _____ frequently lead to the use of psychological defense mechanisms. These are habitual strategies used to avoid or reduce anxiety.

2. A number of defense mechanisms have been identified, including denial, fantasy, intellectualization, isolation, projection, rationalization, _____ formation, regression, and _____ (motivated forgetting).

3. In denial, individuals _____ refuse to accept or believe an unpleasant reality; in repression, individuals _____ push unpleasant thoughts, impulses or situations from awareness.

4. Using defense mechanisms can _____ us from being overwhelmed by immediate threats, but overuse consumes emotional energy and maintains an _____ self-image.

5. Two defense mechanisms that have some _____ qualities are compensation and sublimation.

Learned Helplessness—Is There Hope?

Survey Question: What do we know about coping with feelings of helplessness and depression? Pages 449-453

1. Learned helplessness is a learned inability to overcome obstacles or to _____ punishment.

2. Helplessness is a psychological state that occurs when _____ appear uncontrollable or due to lasting, _____ factors.

3. Learned helplessness explains the failure to cope with some threatening situations. The symptoms of learned helplessness and depression are nearly _____.

4. Mastery _____ and hope act as antidotes to helplessness.

5. Many college students suffer some symptoms of depression due to being _____ from family, lacking the basic skills necessary for _____ success, abusing alcohol, and feeling they are missing out on life.

6. Symptoms of _____ include having a consistently negative opinion of oneself, engaging in frequent self-blame or criticism, having _____ interpretations of events, and feeling that responsibilities are overwhelming.

7. Depression (a state of deep sadness or despondency) is a serious emotional problem. Actions and thoughts that counter feelings of helplessness tend to _____ depression.

Stress and Health—Unmasking a Hidden Killer

Survey Question: How is stress related to health and disease? Pages 453-460

1. Work with the *Social Readjustment Rating Scale* (SRRS) indicates that a large number of life _____ units (LCUs) can increase susceptibility to _____ or illness.

2. Although useful, the SRRS is appropriate for _____, more established adults; the college _____ _____ Inventory is more appropriate for those in college.

3. Immediate health is more closely related to the intensity and severity of daily annoyances, known as _____ or microstressors.

4. Immigrants and refugees adapting to a new culture often experience a period of _____ _____, or culture shock.

5. _____ involves maintaining your old culture and participating in the new culture.

6. Maintaining your old cultural identity and avoiding contact with members of the new culture is _____.

7. Immigrants who choose to remain _____ from the new culture experience high levels of stress; those who pursue integration in the new culture are minimally stressed, and those who will to _____ are moderately stressed.

8. Intense or prolonged stress may damage the body in the form of psychosomatic disorders (illnesses in which _____ factors play a part).

9. Psychosomatic (mind-body) disorders contribute to actual body damage and changes in functioning, and so have no connection to hypochondria, the tendency to imagine that one has a _____.

10. During biofeedback training, bodily processes are _____ and converted to a signal that indicates what the body is doing.

11. Biofeedback allows alteration of many bodily activities. It shows promise for promoting _____, self-regulation, and for treating some psychosomatic illnesses.

12. People with Type A (_____ attack prone) personalities are competitive, striving, and frequently angry or hostile; and they have a chronic sense of _____ urgency.

13. _____ and hostility are especially likely to increase the chances of heart attack.

14. People who have traits of the hardy personality seem to be unusually resistant to _____, even if they also have Type A traits.

15. Hardy personalities tend to have three traits in common: sense of personal _____ to self, work, and family, feelings of _____ over their lives, and tendency to see life as a series of challenges, rather than threats.

Psychology in Action: Stress Management—Winning the Stress Game

Survey Question: What are the best strategies for managing stress? Pages 460-465

1. Most stress management skills focus on one of three areas: bodily effects, ineffective _____, and upsetting _____.

2. Meditation is a self-control technique that can be used to reduce _____.

3. Benefits of meditation are its ability to _____ anxious thoughts and its ability to promote relaxation.

4. Bodily effects can be managed with exercise, meditation, progressive _____, and guided _____.

5. The impact of ineffective behavior can be remedied by slowing down, getting organized, striking a balance between "good stress" and _____, accepting your limits, and seeking social support

6. Those who _____ down their thoughts and feelings about stressful or positive events are better able to cope with stress, have _____ illnesses, and get better grades than those that do not.

7. A good way to control upsetting thoughts is to replace negative self-statements with _____ coping statements.

8. Humor and the ability to laugh are associated with _____ immunity to disease.

CONNECTIONS

Health Psychology—Here's to Your Good Health, STDs and Safer Sex – Choice, Risk, and Responsibility,and Stress—Thrill or Threat?

Survey Questions: What is health psychology? How does behavior affect health? How can sexually transmitted diseases be prevented? What is stress? What factors determine its severity? Pages 429-440

1. _____ Pressure		A. manage medical problems
2. _____ Behavioral medicine		B. health-damaging habits
3. _____ Lifestyle diseases		C. depressed, anxious, ill
4. _____ community health campaign		D. leading cause of death
5. _____ Burnout		E. education
6. _____ problem-focused coping		F. smoking prevention
7. _____ wellness		G. well-being
8. _____ General Adaptation Syndrome		H. AIDS
9. _____ HIV		I. unprotected sex
10. _____ tobacco		J. using a condom
11. _____ burnout		K. having 2+ sex partners
12. _____ Safer sex practice		L. ANS arousal
13. _____ refusal skills		M. alarm reaction
14. _____ STD		N. urgent demands
15. _____ primary appraisal		O. job stress
16. _____ a behavioral risk factor		P. plans to reduce stress
17. _____ disease-prone personality		Q. "Am I in trouble?"
18. _____ stress reaction		

Frustration—Blind Alleys and Lead Balloons, and Conflict—Yes, No, Yes, No, Yes, No, Well, Maybe

Survey Questions: What causes frustration and what are typical reactions to it? Are there different types of conflict? How do people react to conflict? Pages 440-446

1. _____ frustration
2. _____ displaced aggression
3. _____ Traumatic stress
4. _____ apathy
5. _____ External frustration
6. _____ avoidance-avoidance
7. _____ approach-avoidance
8. _____ approach-approach

A. blocked motive
B. psychological escape
C. scapegoat
D. ambivalence
E. deciding on two negative alternatives
F. deciding on two positive alternatives
G. distress caused by outside sources
H. war

Psychological Defense—Mental Karate? and Learned Helplessness—Is There Hope?

Survey Questions: What are defense mechanisms? What do we know about coping with feelings of helplessness and depression? Pages 447-453

1. _____ compensation
2. _____ denial
3. _____ fantasy
4. _____ intellectualization
5. _____ isolation
6. _____ projection
7. _____ rationalization
8. _____ reaction formation
9. _____ regression
10. _____ repression
11. _____ sublimation

A. fulfilling unmet desires in imagined activities
B. separating contradictory thoughts into "logic-tight" mental compartments
C. preventing actions by exaggerating opposite behavior
D. justifying your behavior by giving reasonable but false reasons for it
E. unconsciously preventing painful thoughts from entering awareness
F. counteracting a real or imagined weakness by seeking to excel
G. retreating to an earlier level of development
H. attributing one's own shortcomings or unacceptable impulses to others
I. protecting oneself from an unpleasant reality by refusing to perceive it
J. working off unacceptable impulses in constructive activities
K. thinking about threatening situations in impersonal terms

1. _____ defense mechanisms
2. _____ feeling despondent
3. _____ learned helplessness
4. _____ mastery training

A. depression
B. Sigmund Freud
C. hope
D. shuttle box

Stress and Health—Unmasking a Hidden Killer, Stress Management—Winning the Stress Game

Survey Questions: How is stress related to health and disease? What are the best strategies for managing stress? Pages 453-465

1. _____ College Life Stress Inventory
2. _____ Social Readjustment Rating Scale
3. _____ hassle
4. _____ hardy personality
5. _____ guided imagery
6. _____ psychosomatic
7. _____ modifying ineffective behavior
8. _____ Type A
9. _____ hypochondriac
10. _____ biofeedback
11. _____ acculturative stress
12. _____ coping statements

A. Life Change Unit
B. mind-body
C. self-regulation
D. cardiac personality
E. stress resistant
F. microstressor
G. stress rating scale
H. Keep It Simple (K.I.S.)
I. stress inoculation
J. emigration
K. imagination
L. visualized relaxation

CHECK YOUR MEMORY

Health Psychology—Here's to Your Good Health

Survey Questions: What is health psychology? How does behavior affect health? Pages 429-433

1. Heart disease, lung cancer, and stroke are typical lifestyle diseases.

TRUE or FALSE

2. A person who is overweight doubles the chance of dying from cancer or heart disease.

TRUE or FALSE

3. One can expect to lose up to 20 years of life expectancy if he/she is overweight by the age of 20.

TRUE or FALSE

4. Illicit use of drugs is the second most common cause of death in the United States, after smoking.

TRUE or FALSE

5. Behavioral risk factors such as smoking, poor diet, or alcohol abuse are linked to infectious diseases.

TRUE or FALSE

6. About 440,000 people die every year from smoking-related diseases.

TRUE or FALSE

7. People with disease-prone personalities are depressed, anxious, and hostile.

TRUE or FALSE

8. Six out of ten smokers enjoy long-term success at quitting smoking.

TRUE or FALSE

9. Consuming one or two drinks a day greatly increases your risk for various health problems.

TRUE or FALSE

10. Unhealthy lifestyles typically involve multiple risks.

TRUE or FALSE

11. Community health campaigns provide refusal skills training to large numbers of people.

TRUE or FALSE

12. Wellness can be described as an absence of disease.

TRUE or FALSE

Psychology in Action: STDs and Safer Sex—Choice, Risk, and Responsibility

Survey Question: How can sexually transmitted diseases be prevented? Pages 434-436

1. Many people suffering from STDs are asymptomatic.

TRUE or FALSE

2. Teenage girls today are well educated about STDs and understand that they may get STDs if they are sexually active.

TRUE or FALSE

3. In terms of STD risk, when you have sex with someone, you are having indirect contact with their previous partners.

TRUE or FALSE

4. About 75 percent of sexually active teens do not know how to use a condom properly.

TRUE or FALSE

5. The first symptoms of AIDS may not appear for up to 10 years.

TRUE or FALSE

6. HIV infections are spread by direct contact with body fluids.

TRUE or FALSE

7. Most women who contract the HIV virus today do so through intravenous drug use.

TRUE or FALSE

8. It is unwise to count on a partner for protection from HIV infection.

TRUE or FALSE

9. HIV infection is the leading cause of death for men and women between the ages of 45 and 64.

TRUE or FALSE

10. Approximately 75 percent of those with HIV were infected through homosexual sex.

TRUE or FALSE

Stress—Thrill or Threat?

Survey Questions: What is stress? What factors determine its severity? Pages 436–440

1. Unpleasant activities produce stress, whereas pleasant activities do not.

TRUE or FALSE

2. In the stage of resistance of the General Adaptation Syndrome, people have symptoms of headache, fever, fatigue, upset stomach, and the like.

TRUE or FALSE

3. Serious health problems tend to occur when a person reaches the stage of exhaustion in the General Adaptation Syndrome,

TRUE or FALSE

4. Stress management training can actually boost immune system functioning.

TRUE or FALSE

5. Initial reactions to stressors are similar to those that occur during strong emotion.

TRUE or FALSE

6. Short-term stresses rarely do any damage to the body.

TRUE or FALSE

7. The perception of control and/or predictability has little effect on stress.

TRUE or FALSE

8. Unpredictable demands increase stress.

TRUE or FALSE

9. Pressure occurs when we are faced with a stressor we can control.

TRUE or FALSE

10. Burnout is especially a problem in helping professions.

TRUE or FALSE

11. Stress is often related to the meaning a person places on events.

TRUE or FALSE

12. Happiness, laughter, and delight all tend to strengthen your immune system

TRUE or FALSE

13. College students cannot experience burnout; this only occurs in health-services fields.

TRUE or FALSE

14. The same situation can be a challenge or a threat, depending on how it is appraised.

TRUE or FALSE

15. In a secondary appraisal, we decide if a situation is relevant or irrelevant, positive or threatening.

TRUE or FALSE

16. When confronted by a stressor, it is best to choose one type of coping—problem focused or emotion focused.

TRUE or FALSE

17. Emotion-focused coping is best suited to managing stressors you cannot control.

TRUE or FALSE

18. A distressed person may distract herself by listening to music, taking a walk to relax, or seeking emotional support from others. Such strategies illustrate problem-focused coping.

TRUE or FALSE

19. Nightmares, grief, flashbacks, nervousness, and depression are common reactions to traumatic stress.

TRUE or FALSE

20. It is possible to have stress symptoms from merely witnessing traumatically stressful events on television.

TRUE or FALSE

21. An excellent way to cope with traumatic stress is to stop all of your daily routines and isolate yourself from others.

TRUE or FALSE

Frustration—Blind Alleys and Lead Balloons

Survey Question: What causes frustration and what are typical reactions to it? Pages 440-443

1. Delays, rejections, and losses are good examples of personal frustrations.

TRUE or FALSE

2. Frustration increases as the strength, urgency, or importance of a blocked motive increases.

TRUE or FALSE

3. The effects of repeated frustrations are less threatening that one major frustration episode.

TRUE or FALSE

4. Scapegoating and apathy are more common responses to frustration than is aggression.

TRUE or FALSE

5. Varied responses and circumvention attempt to directly destroy or remove barriers that cause frustration.

TRUE or FALSE

6. Scapegoating is a good example of escape or withdrawal.

TRUE or FALSE

7. Feigned apathy is an effective form of emotion-focused coping.

TRUE or FALSE

8. Abuse of drugs can be a way of psychologically escaping frustration.

TRUE or FALSE

9. Persistence must be flexible before it is likely to aid a person trying to cope with frustration.

TRUE or FALSE

10. In dealing with frustration, it is important to make the distinction between real and imagined barriers.

TRUE or FALSE

Conflict—Yes, No, Yes, No, Yes, No, Well, Maybe

Survey Questions: Are there different types of conflict? How do people react to conflict? Pages 443-446

1. Approach-approach conflicts are fairly easy to resolve.

TRUE or FALSE

2. Indecision, inaction, and freezing are typical reactions to approach-approach conflicts.

TRUE or FALSE

3. People find it difficult to escape approach-avoidance conflicts.

TRUE or FALSE

4. An avoidance-avoidance conflict is often described as being caught between "the frying pan and the fire."

TRUE or FALSE

5. Wanting to eat, but not wanting to be overweight, creates an approach-approach conflict.

TRUE or FALSE

6. People are very likely to vacillate when faced with a double approach-avoidance conflict.

TRUE or FALSE

7. Trying out important decisions on a part-time basis can help resolve conflicts

TRUE or FALSE

Psychological Defense—Mental Karate?

Survey Question: What are defense mechanisms? Pages 447-449

1. Defense mechanisms are used to avoid or distort sources of threat or anxiety.

TRUE or FALSE

2. Denial is a common reaction to bad news, such as learning that a friend has died.

TRUE or FALSE

3. In reaction formation, a person fulfills unmet desires in imagined achievements.

TRUE or FALSE

4. Repression involves consciously pushing distressing or anxiety-provoking thoughts out of consciousness

TRUE or FALSE

5. A child who becomes homesick while visiting relatives may be experiencing a mild regression.

TRUE or FALSE

6. A man who is unfaithful to his wife, then accuses her of cheating on him, is exhibiting the defense mechanism of rationalization

TRUE or FALSE

7. A person who has inferiority in one aspect of life may go to great lengths to overcome the weakness through compensation.

TRUE or FALSE

8. Both intellectualization and rationalization defend against anxiety by changing or distorting the way one thinks about reality.

TRUE or FALSE

9. Denial and repression are the two most positive of the defense mechanisms.

TRUE or FALSE

Learned Helplessness—Is There Hope?

Survey Question: What do we know about coping with feelings of helplessness and depression? Pages 449-453

1. The deep depression experienced by prisoners of war appears to be related to learned helplessness.

TRUE or FALSE

2. Learned helplessness occurs when events appear to be uncontrollable.

TRUE or FALSE

3. Attributing failure to lasting, general factors, such as personal characteristics, tends to create the most damaging feelings of helplessness.

TRUE or FALSE

4. When compared to other emotions, hope contributes little to individual well-being

TRUE or FALSE

5. Mastery training restores feelings of control over the environment.

TRUE or FALSE

6. Making a daily schedule will only emphasize the goals that a person cannot accomplish and will push him/her deeper into depression.

TRUE or FALSE

7. Depression is more likely when students find it difficult to live up to idealized images of themselves.

TRUE or FALSE

8. Writing rational answers to self-critical thoughts can help counteract feelings of depression.

TRUE or FALSE

Stress and Health—Unmasking a Hidden Killer

Survey Question: How is stress related to health and disease? Pages 453-460

1. Scores on the Social Readjustment Rating Scale are expressed as life control units (LCUs).

TRUE or FALSE

2. A score of 300 LCUs on the Social Readjustment Rating Scale is categorized as a major life crisis.

TRUE or FALSE

3. According to the Social Readjustment Rating Scale, being fired at work involves more LCUs than divorce does.

TRUE or FALSE

4. Microstressors tend to predict changes in health one to two years after the stressful events took place.

TRUE or FALSE

5. Negative stress can negatively impact health, whereas positive stress has positive effects on health

TRUE or FALSE

6. Immigrants who engage in separation divorce themselves from their old culture and adopt the new culture.

TRUE or FALSE

7. Marginalization involves the least amount of stress when compared to the other acculturation patterns.

TRUE or FALSE

8. Psychosomatic disorders involve actual damage to the body or damaging changes in bodily function.

TRUE or FALSE

9. A person undergoing biofeedback can sleep if he or she desires—the machine does all the work.

TRUE or FALSE

10. Type B personalities are more than twice as likely to suffer heart attacks as Type A personalities.

TRUE or FALSE

11. A sense of time urgency, hostility, and chronic anger are strongly related to increased risk for heart attack.

TRUE or FALSE

12. People with the hardy personality type tend to see life as a series of challenges.

TRUE or FALSE

13. People with a hardy personality have had to cope with many adversities and therefore have a negative view of life.

TRUE or FALSE

Psychology in Action: Stress Management—Winning the Stress Game

Survey Question: What are the best strategies for managing stress? Pages 460-465

1. Concern about being pregnant is the most stressful item listed on the College Life Stress Inventory.

TRUE or FALSE

2. The harder you try to meditate the more likely you are to succeed.

TRUE or FALSE

3. Exercising for stress management is most effective when it is done daily.

TRUE or FALSE

4. Guided imagery is used to reduce anxiety and promote relaxation.

TRUE or FALSE

5. Thinking about a supportive person or having a pet present can help lower
    one's stress level.

TRUE or FALSE

6. Merely writing down thoughts and feelings about daily events can provide
    some of the benefits of social support.

TRUE or FALSE

7. To get the maximum benefits, coping statements should be practiced in
    actual stressful situations.

TRUE or FALSE

8. Persistence must be flexible before it is likely to aid a person trying to cope
    with frustration.

TRUE or FALSE

FINAL SURVEY AND REVIEW

Health Psychology—Here's to Your Good Health

Survey Questions: What is health psychology? How does behavior affect health?
Pages 429-433

1. Health psychologists are interested in behavior that helps _____ and
    _____ health. The related field of behavioral medicine applies
    psychology to medical treatment and problems.

2. Most people today die from _____ diseases caused by
    _____ personal habits.

3. Studies have identified a number of _____ risk _____ that
    increase the chances of disease (or illness) or injury.

4. A general _____-prone personality pattern also raises the risk of
    illness (or disease).

5. Lifestyle diseases can be treated by making specific, _____ changes
    in behavior, such as using less salt or getting _____ exercise.

6. _____-_____ _____ tend to maintain
    _____ health. They include practices such as getting regular
    exercise, controlling smoking and alcohol use, maintaining a balanced diet,
    getting good medical care, avoiding sleep deprivation, and managing stress.

7. Attempts to _____ young people from developing unhealthful
    behaviors, such as smoking and drug use, often make use of _____
    skills training and life skills training.

8. Health psychologists attempt to promote _____ (a positive state of health) through community health campaigns that _____ people about risk factors and healthful behaviors.

9. Wellness is a positive state of _____ and _____ well-being.

STDs and Safer Sex—Choice, Risk, and Responsibility

Survey Question: How can sexually transmitted diseases be prevented? Pages 434-436

1. A sexually transmitted _____ (STD) is an _____ passed from one person to another through intimate contact.

2. Individuals who carry STDs may _____ have any symptoms, and may not know that their partner is _____.

3. A recent study found that approximately 90 percent of sexually active teenage girls reported that they did _____ believe they would get sexually transmitted diseases (STDs) because their partners did not show _____ of STDs.

4. People who are sexually active, even with only one person, may still be engaging in risky sex from indirect contact with others through their partner's _____.

5. The emergence of acquired immune _____ syndrome (AIDS) is caused by the human immunodeficiency _____ (HIV).

6. The _____ symptoms of AIDS may not appear for up to _____ years; during that time, people can unknowingly infect others.

7. AIDS is spreading more quickly among _____, women, _____ Americans, Hispanics, and children. It is predicted that over the next _____ years, 65 million people will die of AIDS unless preventions are taken.

8. STDs have had a sizable impact on patterns of sexual behavior, including increased _____ of high-risk behaviors and some curtailment of risk taking.

9. _____ sex practices include using a condom, selectively choosing only a _____ sexual partners, and knowing a partner's sexual history before intercourse. _____ is the most risk-free policy.

Stress—Thrill or Threat?

Survey Questions: What is stress? What factors determine its severity? Pages 436-440

1. Stress occurs when we are forced to adjust or _____ to external demands.

2. _____ (good stress) is part of a healthy lifestyle; activities that produce good stress are challenging, rewarding, and _____.

3. The body reacts to stress in a series of _____ called the general _____ syndrome (G.A.S.).

4. The stages of the G.A.S. are _____, resistance, and _____. The G.A.S. contributes to the development of psychosomatic _____.

5. Emotional, _____, and physical signs of _____ emerge when the body's resources are drained. Stress _____ the immune system and lowers the body's resistance to disease (or illness).

6. Stress is more damaging in situations involving _____ (responding at full capacity for long periods), a lack of control, _____ of the stressor, and intense or repeated emotional shocks.

7. Stress is intensified when a situation is _____ as a threat and when a person does not feel competent to cope with it.

8. In work settings, prolonged stress can lead to _____, marked by emotional exhaustion, cynicism, depersonalization (detachment from others), and reduced _____ accomplishment.

9. The primary (initial) _____ of a situation greatly affects our emotional response to it. Stress reactions, in particular, are related to an _____ of threat.

10. During a secondary _____ some means of coping with a situation are selected. Coping may be either _____-focused (managing the situation) or _____-focused (managing one's emotional reactions) or both.

11. A perceived lack of _____ is just as threatening as an actual lack of _____.

12. _____-focused coping is used to manage or correct a distressing situation (for example, by making a plan of action) and is most effective when facing a _____ stressor.

13. In _____-focused coping, individuals try to control their emotions; this is best suited to managing your reactions to _____ stressors.

14. Traumatic stressors, such as _____, _____, or natural disasters, tend to produce severe stress reactions.

15. Traumatic stresses leave people feeling _____, vulnerable, and with the sense that they are losing _____ over their lives.

16. Severe or _____ traumatic stress can leave people with lasting emotional handicaps called stress _____.

Frustration—Blind Alleys and Lead Balloons

Survey Question: What causes frustration and what are typical reactions to it? Pages 440-443

1. Frustration is the _____ emotional state that occurs when progress toward a goal is blocked. Sources of frustration may be _____ or personal.

2. External frustrations are either _____ or nonsocial, and are based on _____, failure, _____, loss, and other direct blocking of motives. Personal frustration is related to personal characteristics over which one has little control.

3. Frustrations of all types become more intense as the _____, urgency, or _____ of the blocked motive _____. Repeated frustrations can accumulate to produce an unexpectedly _____ response.

4. Major behavioral reactions to frustration include _____, more vigorous responding, and circumvention of barriers.

5. Other reactions to frustration are direct aggression, _____ aggression (including scapegoating), and escape, or withdrawal.

6. Psychological escape or _____ may include feigned apathy (pretending not to care) or the use of drugs.

7. Persistence is normal reaction to frustration, but _____ that becomes rigid or inflexible leads to pointless, _____ behavior.

8. Ways of coping with frustration include _____ its source, determining if the source is _____, and deciding if changing the source is worth the effort.

Conflict—Yes, No, Yes, No, Yes, No, Well, Maybe

Survey Questions: Are there different types of conflict? How do people react to conflict? Pages 443-446

1. Conflict occurs when we must choose between _____ alternatives.

2. Three basic types of conflict are _____-approach (choice between two positive alternatives), avoidance-_____ (both alternatives are negative), and approach-avoidance (a goal or activity has both _____ and negative aspects).

3. More complex conflicts are: double approach-avoidance (_____ alternatives have positive and negative qualities) and multiple approach-avoidance (_____ alternatives each have good and bad qualities).

4. Approach-_____ conflicts are usually the easiest to resolve.

5. Avoidance conflicts are difficult to resolve and are characterized by inaction, _____, freezing, and a desire to _____ (called "leaving the field").

6. People usually remain in approach-avoidance conflicts, but _____ to fully resolve them. Approach-avoidance conflicts are associated with _____ (mixed feelings) and partial approach.

7. Vacillation (_____ between choices) is the most common reaction to double approach-avoidance conflicts.

8. Managing conflicts effectively involves _____ making hasty decisions, trying out a few possibilities at a time, looking for compromises, and _____ with the choice.

Psychological Defense—Mental Karate?

Survey Question: What are defense mechanisms? Pages 447-449

1. Anxiety, _____, or feelings of inadequacy frequently lead to the use of psychological defense mechanisms. These are habitual strategies used to avoid or _____ anxiety.

2. A number of defense mechanisms have been identified, including _____, fantasy, intellectualization, _____, projection, rationalization, reaction formation, _____, and repression (motivated forgetting).

3. In _____, individuals consciously refuse to accept or believe an unpleasant reality; in _____, individuals unconsciously push unpleasant thoughts, impulses or situations from awareness.

4. Using defense mechanisms can protect us from being _____ by immediate threats, but _____ consumes emotional energy and maintains an unrealistic self-image.

5. Two defense mechanisms that have some positive qualities are _____ and sublimation.

Learned Helplessness—Is There Hope?

Survey Question: What do we know about coping with feelings of helplessness and depression? Pages 449-453

1. Learned _____ is a learned inability to overcome _____ or to avoid punishment.

2. Helplessness is a _____ state that occurs when events appear _____ or due to lasting, general factors.

3. Learned helplessness explains the _____ to cope with some threatening situations. The symptoms of learned helplessness and _____ are nearly identical.

4. Mastery training and hope act as _____ to helplessness.

5. Many college students suffer some symptoms of _____ due to being isolated from family, _____ the basic skills necessary for academic success, abusing alcohol, and feeling they are missing out on life.

6. Symptoms of _____ include having a consistently _____ opinion of oneself, engaging in frequent _____-_____ or criticism, having negative interpretations of events, and feeling that responsibilities are overwhelming.

7. Depression (a state of deep sadness or _____) is a serious emotional problem. Actions and thoughts that counter feelings of helplessness tend to reduce depression.

Stress and Health—Unmasking a Hidden Killer

Survey Question: How is stress related to health and disease? Pages 453-460

1. Work with the *Social _____ Rating Scale* (SRRS) indicates that a large number of life change units (LCUs) can increase _____ to accident or illness.

2. Although useful, the SRRS is appropriate for _____, more established adults; the college _____ Stress Inventory is more appropriate for those in college.

3. _____ health is more closely related to the _____ and severity of daily annoyances, known as hassles or microstressors.

4. Immigrants and _____ adapting to a new culture often experience a period of acculturative stress, or culture _____.

5. Integration involves maintaining your _____ culture and participating in the _____ culture.

6. Maintaining your old cultural identity and _____ contact with members of the new culture is separation.

7. Immigrants who choose to remain separate from the new culture experience _____ levels of stress; those who pursue integration in the new culture are _____ stressed, and those who will to assimilate are _____ stressed.

8. Intense or _____ stress may damage the body in the form of _____ disorders (illnesses in which psychological factors play a part).

9. Psychosomatic (mind-body) disorders contribute to _____ body damage and changes in functioning, and so have no connection to _____, the tendency to imagine that one has a disease.

10. During _____ training, bodily processes are monitored and converted to a _____ that indicates what the body is doing.

11. Biofeedback allows alteration of many bodily activities. It shows promise for promoting relaxation, _____-_____, and for treating some psychosomatic illnesses.

12. People with _____ (heart attack prone) personalities are competitive, striving, and frequently angry or hostile; and they have a chronic sense of _____ urgency.

13. Anger and _____ are especially likely to increase the chances of heart attack.

14. People who have traits of the _____ personality seem to be unusually resistant to stress, even if they also have Type A traits.

15. Hardy personalities tend to have three traits in common: sense of _____ commitment to self, _____, and family, feelings of control over their lives, and tendency to see life as a series of challenges, rather than _____.

Psychology in Action: Stress Management—Winning the Stress Game

Survey Question: What are the best strategies for managing stress? Pages 460-465

1. Most stress _____ skills focus on one of three areas: _____ effects, ineffective behavior, and upsetting thoughts.

2. Meditation is a _____-_____ technique that can be used to reduce stress.

3. Benefits of meditation are its ability to interrupt _____ thoughts and its ability to promote _____.

4. Bodily effects can be managed with _____, meditation, _____ relaxation, and guided imagery.

5. The impact of _____ behavior can be remedied by slowing down, getting _____, striking a balance between "good stress" and relaxation, accepting your limits, and seeking social support

6. Those who write down their thoughts and feelings about stressful or positive events are better able to _____ with stress, have fewer _____, and get better _____ than those that do not.

7. A good way to control upsetting thoughts is to replace _____ self-statements with positive _____ statements.

8. Humor and the ability to _____ are associated with better immunity to disease.

MASTERY TEST

1. When stressful events appear to be uncontrollable, two common reactions are
   a. apathy and double-approach conflict.
   b. helplessness and depression.
   c. assimilation and marginalization.
   d. psychosomatic disorders and hypochondria.

2. The *College Life Stress Inventory* is most closely related to the
   a. SRRS.
   b. G.A.S.
   c. K.I.S.
   d. *Disease-Prone Personality Scale.*

3. We answer the question "Am I okay or in trouble?" when making
   a. negative self-statements.
   b. coping statements.
   c. a primary appraisal.
   d. a secondary appraisal.

4. In one study, almost _____ percent of girls thought they had no chance of getting a sexually transmitted disease from a partner.
   a. 25
   b. 40
   c. 75
   d. 90

5. Which of the following is NOT a major symptom of burnout?
   a. emotional exhaustion
   b. depersonalization
   c. reduced accomplishment
   d. dependence on co-workers

6. Persistent but inflexible responses to frustration can become
   a. stereotyped behaviors.
   b. imagined barriers.
   c. negative self-statements.
   d. sublimated and depersonalized.

7. The leading cause of death in the United States is
a. tobacco.
b. diet/inactivity.
c. alcohol.
d. infection.

8. Individuals are most likely to contract the AIDS virus by _____ with an infected person
a. shaking hands
b. having unprotected heterosexual sex
c. sharing drinking glasses
d. sharing towels

9. Both mountain climbing and marital strife
a. are behavioral risk factors.
b. are appraised as secondary threats.
c. cause stress reactions.
d. produce the condition known as pressure.

10. LCUs are used to assess
a. burnout.
b. social readjustments.
c. microstressors.
d. what stage of the G.A.S. a person is in.

11. Sujata is often ridiculed by her boss, who also frequently takes advantage of her. Deep inside, Sujata has come to hate her boss, yet on the surface she acts as if she likes him very much. It is likely that Sujata is using the defense mechanism called
a. reaction formation.
b. Type B appraisal.
c. problem-focused coping.
d. sublimation.

12. Lifestyle diseases are of special interest to _____ psychologists.
a. health
b. community
c. wellness
d. psychosomatic

13. Which of the following is NOT characteristic of the hardy personality?
a. commitment
b. a sense of control
c. accepting challenge
d. repression

14. Unhealthy lifestyles are marked by the presence of a number of
a. health refusal factors.
b. behavioral risk factors.
c. cultural stressors.
d. Type B personality traits.

15. The most effective response to a controllable stressor is
a. problem-focused coping.
b. emotion-focused coping.
c. leaving the field.
d. depersonalization.

16. Delay, rejection, failure, and loss are all major causes of
a. pressure.
b. frustration.
c. conflict.
d. helplessness.

17. There is evidence that the core lethal factor of Type A behavior is
a. time urgency.
b. anger and hostility.
c. competitiveness and ambition.
d. accepting too many responsibilities.

18. A special danger in the transmission of STDs is that many people are
_____ at first.
a. non-infectious
b. androgynous
c. asymptomatic
d. androgenital

19. Which of the following is NOT one of the major health-promoting behaviors listed in the text?
a. do not smoke
b. get adequate sleep
c. get regular exercise
d. avoid eating between meals

20. Ambivalence and partial approach are very common reactions to what type of conflict?
a. approach-approach
b. avoidance-avoidance
c. approach-avoidance
d. multiple avoidance

21. Which of the following terms does not belong with the others?
a. Type A personality
b. stage of exhaustion
c. displaced aggression
d. psychosomatic disorder

22. Coping statements are a key element in
a. stress inoculation.
b. the K.I.S. technique.
c. guided imagery.
d. refusal skills training.

23. Which of the following factors typically minimizes the amount of stress experienced?
a. predictable stressors
b. repeated stressors
c. uncontrollable stressors
d. intense stressors

24. Scapegoating is closely related to which response to frustration?
a. leaving the field
b. displaced aggression
c. circumvention
d. reaction formation

25. The study of the ways in which stress and the immune system affect susceptibility to disease is called
a. neuropsychosymptomology.
b. immunohypochondrology.
c. psychosomatoneurology.
d. psychoneuroimmunology.

26. Refusal skills training is typically used to teach young people how to
a. avoid drug use.
b. cope with burnout.
c. resist stressors at home and at school.
d. avoid forming habits that lead to heart disease.

27. Which combination is most relevant to managing bodily reactions to stress?
a. social support, self pacing
b. exercise, social support
c. exercise, negative self-statements
d. progressive relaxation, guided imagery

28. Stress reactions are most likely to occur when a stressor is viewed as a _____ during the _____.
a. pressure; primary appraisal
b. pressure; secondary appraisal
c. threat; primary appraisal
d. threat; secondary appraisal

29. External symptoms of the body's adjustment to stress are least visible in which stage of the General Adaptation Syndrome (G.A.S.)?
a. alarm
b. regulation
c. resistance
d. exhaustion

30. A perceived lack of control creates a stressful sense of threat when combined with a perceived
a. sense of time urgency.
b. state of sublimation.
c. need to change secondary risk factors.
d. lack of competence.

31. Stress, smoking, and overeating are related to each other in that they are behavioral _____ and they have been linked to
_____.
a. hassles; Type B personality
b. risk factors; infectious diseases
c. sources of burnout; high life expectancy
d. causes of depersonalization; hardy personality

32. Real or imagined social support and encouragement from _____ can reduce one's level of stress.
a. family members
b. friends
c. pets
d. all the preceding

33. Which factor reduces one's stress or emotional distress?
a. humor
b. smoking
c. high blood pressure
d. approach-avoidance

34. When Jimmy's parents bring home his newborn baby brother, he begins to suck his thumb and wet the bed. This reaction best illustrates
a. compensation.
b. reaction formation.
c. regression.
d. sublimation.

35. Jamie is in a tough spot. She recently had a fight with her friends at a party and wants to leave. However, she is past her curfew and will likely get in trouble if she goes home. Her situation best illustrates a(n) _____ conflict.
a. approach-approach
b. avoidance-avoidance
c. avoidance-approach
d. double appraisal

36. Jasmine has recently arrived in the U.S. Although she continues to identify with her old culture, she has eagerly embraced many of the norms associated with the American culture. This best demonstrates
a. marginalization.
b. separation.
c. integration.
d. assimilation.

37. Acculturative stress is associated with
a. anxiety.
b. depression.
c. physical illness.
d. all of the above

LANGUAGE DEVELOPMENT
Health, Stress, and Coping

Word Roots

The Greek word *hypo* means "under" and, when combined with other terms, also means "beneath" or "lowered." For example, the terms *hypochondriac* and *hypochondriasis* come from *hypochondria*, an old anatomical term that once referred to the area under the ribs. (*khondros* in ancient Greek means "cartilage.") Other examples of the use of the root word "hypo" found in this text are: hypothesis, hypothalamus, hypopituitary, hypothyroidism, hypoglycemia, and hypoactive.

Journey into Psychology: Jennifer's amazing Race (p. 428)
(428) *make-or-break:* an event or activity that can determine success or failure in some aspect of one's life
(428) *last leg of the race:* the last portion of a race, right before the finish line; represents point where people direct the last of their resources.
(428) *one-finger salute:* an impolite gesture with the middle finger used to indicate anger or disgust
(428) *swarming:* to hurriedly move as a group in one area
(428) *frantic:* marked by fast and nervous, disordered, or anxiety-driven activity
(428) *darted:* moved suddenly and quickly
(428) *Mini Cooper:* small 2-door car
(428) *colossal:* huge
(428) *cramming:* to prepare hastily for exams (usually for long hours at the expense of sleep and nutritious meals)
(428) *bronchitis:* respiratory illness centered in the lungs

Health Psychology—Here's to Your Good Health (pgs. 429-433)

What is health psychology? Hoes does behavior affect health?

(429) *undertaker:* individual whose job is to prepare the dead for burial

(429) in the long run: eventually

(430) *plaque:* fatty substances deposited in the inner layers of the arteries

(430) *sermonize:* to lecture; to preach

(431) *"silent killer":* a deadly disease with little or no outward warning signs

(431) *burdensome:* oppressive, rigorous

(431) *wheatgrass:* any of the annual grasses (e.g., turf, hay)

(431) *brisk:* quick; fast

(431) *teetotaler:* a person who drinks very little alcohol; an inexperienced drinker who gets drunk very quickly

(431) *cirrhosis:* inflammation of tissue or an organ

(432) *abstain:* to stop; refrain

(432) *curb:* to cut back; to limit oneself

(433) *mass media:* television, radio, newspapers

(433) *labor of love:* a job or activity that one cares about greatly

STDs and Safer Sex—Choice, Risk, and Responsibility (pgs. 434-436)

How can sexually transmitted diseases be prevented?

(434) *lethal:* deadly

(434) *"opportunistic":* taking advantage of any circumstance

(434) *incubation:* the time between infection and noticeable symptoms

(434) **monogamous relationship:** relationship in which an individual only has one "mate" or sexual partner, typical of a marriage or lifetime commitment.

Stress—Threat or Thrill? (pgs. 436-440)

What is stress? What factors determine its severity?

(436) *woes:* troubles; problems

(437) *mobilizes:* gets ready; prepares

(437) *depleted:* used up

(437) *apathy:* lack of concern; indifference

(437) *melodramatic:* exaggerated; overly dramatic

(437) *spleen:* organ that destroys red blood cells, stores blood, and produces white blood cells

(437) *lymph nodes:* rounded masses of lymph tissue (lymph is a fluid that bathes the tissues and contains white blood cells)

(438) *bereavement:* state of grieving after the death of a loved one

(438) *double whammy:* being attacked by two things at once

(438) *takes a toll:* has a negative or harmful effect

(439) *cynicism:* distrust; pessimism

(439) *detachment:* state of being uninvolved, uninterested

(439) *appraisal:* a judgment; evaluation

(439) *appraise:* to judge; evaluate

(439) *the enforcer:* a person who might use physical threat to collect a debt

(440) *shortchanges:* making it less effective

Frustration—Blind Alleys and Lead Balloons (pgs. 440-443)

What causes frustration and what are typical reactions to it?

(440) *blind alleys and lead balloons:* blind alleys lead nowhere; balloons made of lead would not fly; therefore both are symbols of frustration

(440) *impede:* slow; make difficult

(441) *flashbacks:* recurrent vivid visions in one's mind, usually traumatic or distressing

(441) *hypertension:* high blood pressure

(441) *"the straw that broke the camel's back":* a common saying that means the last negative event in a series of negative events

(442) *nomadic:* wandering; having no permanent home

(442) *menacing:* representing a threat

(442) *retaliate:* to get revenge

(442) *hitchhike:* to travel from place to place by getting free rides from motorists

(443) *futile:* useless

Conflict—Yes, No, Yes, No, Yes, No, Well, Maybe (pgs. 443-446)

Are there different types of conflict? How do people react to conflict?

(444) *"the devil and the deep blue sea," "the frying pan and the fire," "A rock and a hard place":* all are common sayings that mean one has to choose between two equally unpleasant choices

(444) *monotonous:* boring; not interesting

(444) *tampered:* interfered

(445) *hasty:* quickly, hurried; often without planning

Psychological Defense—Mental Karate? (pgs. 447-449)

What are defense mechanisms?

(447) *counteracting:* stopping; working against

(447) *compensating:* making up for

(447) *working off:* reducing, eliminating though effort

(447) *tightwad:* someone who is very careful about spending his/her money

(447) *held in check:* kept in place; stopped

(448) *discern:* to notice; perceive

(448) *throws a temper tantrum:* has an emotional display of anger or frustration

(448) *go belly-up:* stop working

(448) *the last straw:* the final event in a series of difficulties

(449) *"pumping iron":* lifting heavy weights in order to build muscle

(449) *Freud would have had a field day:* would have been pleased with all of the possibilities

Learned Helplessness—Is There Hope? (pgs. 449-453)

What do we know about coping with feelings of helplessness and depression?

(450) *concentration camps*: places of imprisonment for soldiers and others during war (e.g., World War II)

(450) *resign*: to give into; to give up to circumstances

(450) *procrastinate:* put off doing

(451) *despondency*: a feeling of hopelessness; sadness

(450) *blunted*: dulled and uninterested

(451) *antidote*: a remedy

(451) *blues*: sadness; despair

(451) *"blue"*: sad

(452) *aspirations*: goals; hopes

(452) *idealized*: made to seem perfect

(452) *"down"*: in a low mood

(452) *"blown it"*: failed

Stress and Health—Unmasking a Hidden Killer (pgs. 453-460)

How is stress related to health and disease?

(454) *foreclosure*: the claim of ownership of a property such as a home when no payment has been made over time

(455) *"To be forewarned is to be forearmed"*: a common saying meaning that if one knows about a danger ahead of time, one can prepare against it

(455) *spawn*: to create; bring forth

(456) *take it easy*: relax

(456) *hives*: an allergic disorder that causes the skin to itch and break out in bumps

(456) *rheumatoid arthritis*: disease characterized by pain, stiffness, and swelling of the joints

(457) *hard driving*: ambitious; being highly motivated

(457) *chafe*: become irritated by

(457) *"bottled up"*: kept inside

(458) *accentuating*: emphasizing; making obvious

(458) *accentuation*: emphasis

(458) *condensation*: a summary

(458) *indignation*: resentment; annoyance

(459) *alienated*: feelings of isolation or withdrawal

Stress Management—The Stress Game (pgs. 460-465)

What are the best strategies for managing stress?

(461) *"uptight"*: tense; nervous

(463) *get blown out of proportion*: become exaggerated in importance

(463) *loafing*: resting; relaxing

(463) *browsing*: looking over casually

(463) *puttering*: moving or acting aimlessly or idly; engaging in trivial tasks

(464) *psyched up*: psychologically ready; prepared

(465) *"Don't sweat the small stuff"*: Expression meaning, "don't spend time worrying about small, insignificant, or trivial things."

Solutions

Recite and Review

Health Psychology—Here's to Your Good Health

1. behavior, medical
2. habits
3. disease, illness
4. illness, disease
5. Lifestyle
6. behaviors, smoking, diet, sleep
7. skills, training.
8. health, campaigns
9. Wellness

STDs and Safer Sex—Choice, Risk, and Responsibility

1. intimate
2. symptoms
3. 90, girls, sexually, did, not
4. active, indirect
5. acquired, immune, virus
6. infect
7. women, 65
8. risk, risk
9. condom

Stress—Thrill or Threat?

1. adjust
2. good, rewarding
3. general
4. psychosomatic
5. drained, disease, illness
6. control, intense
7. Stress
8. work, exhaustion
9. primary, threat
10. secondary
11. perceived
12. controllable
13. uncontrollable
14. stressors, stress
15. stresses, lives
16. repeated, stress

Frustration—Blind Alleys and Lead Balloons

1. goal, blocked
2. personal
3. intense
4. vigorous
5. direct, withdrawal.
6. escape, care
7. frustration
8. coping, changing

Conflict—Yes, No, Yes, No, Yes, No, Well, Maybe

1. Conflict
2. positive, negative
3. positive, negative
4. easiest
5. difficult, leaving
6. mixed, partial
7. approach, avoidance
8. possibilities, compromises

Psychological Defense—Mental Karate?

1. inadequacy
2. reaction, repression
3. consciously, unconsciously
4. protect, unrealistic
5. positive

Learned Helplessness—Is There Hope?

1. avoid
2. events, general
3. identical
4. training
5. isolated, academic
6. depression, negative
7. reduce

Stress and Health—Unmasking a Hidden Killer

1. change, accident
2. older, Life, Stress
3. hassles
4. acculturative, stress
5. Integration
6. separation
7. separate, assimilate
8. psychological
9. disease
10. monitored
11. relaxation
12. heart, time
13. Anger
14. stress
15. commitment, control

Psychology in Action: Stress Management—Winning the Stress Game

1. behavior, thoughts
2. stress
3. interrupt
4. relaxation, imagery
5. relaxation
6. write, fewer
7. positive
8. better

CONNECTIONS

Health Psychology—Here's to Your Good Health, STDs and Safer Sex – Choice, Risk, and Responsibility, and Stress—Thrill or Threat?

1. N.
2. A.
3. B.
4. E.
5. O.
6. P.
7. G.
8. M.
9. H.
10. D.
11. J.
12. J.
13. F.
14. I.
15. Q
16. K.
17. C.
18. L.

Frustration—Blind Alleys and Lead Balloons, and Conflict—Yes, No, Yes, No, Yes, No, Well, Maybe

1. A.
2. C.
3. H.
4. B.
5. G.
6. E.
7. D.
8. F.

Psychological Defense—Mental Karate? and Learned Helplessness—Is There Hope?

1. F.
2. I.
3. A.
4. K.
5. B.
6. H.
7. D.
8. C.
9. G.
10. E.
11. J.

1. B.   2. A.   3. D.   4. C.

Stress and Health—Unmasking a Hidden Killer, Stress Management—Winning the Stress Game

1. G.   4. E.   7. H.   10. C.
2. A.   5. L.   8. D.   11. J.
3. F.   6. B.   9. K.   12. I.

Check Your Memory

Health Psychology—Here's to Your Good Health

1. T   4. F   7. T   10. T
2. T   5. T   8. F   11. F
3. T   6. T   9. F   12. F

Psychology in Action: STDs and Safer Sex—Choice, Risk, and Responsibility

1. T   4. F   7. F   10. F
2. F   5. T   8. T
3. T   6. T   9. F

Stress—Thrill or Threat?

1. F   7. F   13. F   19. T
2. F   8. T   14. T   20. T
3. T   9. F   15. F   21. F
4. T   10. T   16. F
5. T   11. T   17. T
6. T   12. T   18. F

Frustration—Blind Alleys and Lead Balloons

1. F   4. F   7. F   10. T
2. T   5. F   8. T
3. F   6. F   9. T

Conflict—Yes, No, Yes, No, Yes, No, Well, Maybe

1. T   3. T   5. F   7. T
2. F   4. T   6. T

Psychological Defense—Mental Karate?

1. T	4. F	7. T
2. T	5. T	8. T
3. F	6. F	9. F

Learned Helplessness—Is There Hope?

1. T	3. T	5. T	7. T
2. T	4. F	6. F	8. T

Stress and Health—Unmasking a Hidden Killer

1. F	5. F	9. F	13. F
2. T	6. F	10. F	
3. F	7. F	11. T	
4. F	8. T	12. T	

Psychology in Action: Stress Management—Winning the Stress Game

1. F	3. T	5. T	7. T
2. F	4. T	6. T	8. T

Final Survey and Review
Health Psychology—Here's to Your Good Health

1. maintain, promote
2. lifestyle, unhealthy
3. behavioral, factors
4. disease
5. minor, more
6. Health, promoting, behaviors, good
7. prevent, refusal
8. wellness, educate
9. physical, psychological

STDs and Safer Sex—Choice, Risk, and Responsibility

1. disease, infection
2. not, infectious
3. not, symptoms
4. indiscretion.
5. deficiency, virus
6. first, ten
7. heterosexuals, African, 15
8. awareness
9. Safe, few, Abstinence

Stress—Thrill or Threat?

1. adapt
2. Eustress, energizing
3. stages, adaptation
4. alarm, exhaustion, disorders
5. behavioral, exhaustion, weakens
6. pressure, unpredictability
7. perceived
8. burnout, personal
9. appraisal, appraisal
10. appraisal, problem, emotion
11. control, control
12. Problem, controllable
13. emotion, uncontrollable
14. violence, torture
15. threatened, control
16. repeated, disorders

Frustration—Blind Alleys and Lead Balloons

Survey Question: What causes frustration and what are typical reactions to it? Pages 440-443

1. negative, external
2. social, delay, rejection
3. strength, importance, increases, violent
4. persistence
5. displaced
6. withdrawal
7. persistence, stereotyped
8. identifying, manageable

Conflict—Yes, No, Yes, No, Yes, No, Well, Maybe

1. contradictory
2. approach, avoidance, positive
3. both, several
4. approach
5. indecision, escape
6. fail, ambivalence
7. wavering
8. not, sticking

Psychological Defense—Mental Karate?

Survey Question: What are defense mechanisms? Pages 447-449

1. threat, reduce
2. denial, isolation, regression
3. denial, repression
4. overwhelmed, overuse
5. compensation

Learned Helplessness—Is There Hope?

1. helplessness, obstacles
2. psychological, uncontrollable
3. failure, depression
4. antidotes
5. depression, lacking
6. depression, negative, self-blame
7. despondency

Stress and Health—Unmasking a Hidden Killer

1. Readjustment, susceptibility
2. older, Life
3. Immediate, intensity
4. refugees, shock.
5. old, new
6. avoiding
7. high, minimally, moderately
8. prolonged, psychosomatic
9. actual, hypochondria
10. biofeedback, signal
11. self-regulation
12. Type A, time
13. hostility
14. hardy
15. personal, work, threats

Psychology in Action: Stress Management—Winning the Stress Game

1. management, bodily
2. self, control
3. anxious, relaxation
4. exercise, progressive
5. ineffective, organized
6. cope, illnesses, grades
7. negative, coping
8. laugh

Mastery Test

1. b, p. 449-450
2. a, p. 460-461
3. c, p. 439
4. d, p. 434
5. d, p. 439
6. a, p. 442
7. a, p. 429
8. b, p. 434
9. c, p. 436
10. b, p. 453-454
11. a, p. 447-448
12. a, p. 429
13. d, p. 459

14. b, p. 429-431
15. a, p. 440
16. b, p. 440
17. b, p. 457
18. c, p. 434
19. d, p. 431
20. c, p. 444
21. c, p. 437; 442; 457
22. a, p. 464
23. a, p. 438
24. b, p. 442
25. d, p. 438
26. a, p. 432

27. d, p. 462-463
28. c, p. 439-440
29. c, p. 437
30. d, p. 439
31. b, p. 429
32. d, p. 463
33. a, p. 459; 465
34. c, p. 447-448
35. b, p. 444
36. c, p. 455
37. d, p. 455

CHAPTER 12

Psychological Disorders

Chapter Overview

Abnormal behavior is defined by subjective discomfort, deviation from statistical norms, social nonconformity, and cultural or situational contexts. Disordered behavior is maladaptive and marked by loss of control. Insanity is a legal term, not a psychological term, and is established by expert witnesses in court.

Major types of psychopathology are described by DSM-IV-TR, and include: psychotic, organic, mood, anxiety, somatoform, dissociative, personality, sexual and gender, and substance abuse disorders. Risk factors contributing to psychopathology include social, family, psychological, and biological/physical factors. Every culture recognizes the existence of psychological disorders; some are more common to some cultures than others. Revisions to the DSM reflect current research and changes in social attitudes.

Psychosis is a break in contact with reality, and is characterized by delusions and hallucinations. Disturbed emotions, communications, and sensory changes are also present. Organic psychosis results from brain injury (physical or chemical) or disease. Dementia is the most common form of organic psychosis. Alzheimer's Disease is a form of dementia caused by webs and tangles in the brain.

Persons suffering from delusional disorders have delusions of grandeur, persecution, infidelity, romantic attraction, or physical disease. The most common delusional disorder is paranoid psychosis. Schizophrenia is the most common psychosis. Four types of schizophrenia are: disorganized, catatonic, paranoid, and undifferentiated. Explanations of schizophrenia emphasize environmental stress, inherited susceptibility, and biochemical abnormalities.

Mood disorders involve disturbances of emotion. Two moderate mood disorders are dysthymic disorder and cyclothymic disorder. Major mood disorders include bipolar disorders and major depressive disorder. Seasonal affective disorder is another common form of depression. Biological, psychoanalytic, cognitive, and behavioral theories of depression have been proposed. Heredity is clearly a factor in susceptibility to mood disorders.

Anxiety-based disorders are broadly characterized by high levels of anxiety, the use of elaborate defense mechanisms, and reduced life satisfaction. Anxiety disorders include generalized anxiety disorder, panic disorder (with or without agoraphobia), agoraphobia, specific phobias, social phobia, obsessive-compulsive disorders, and posttraumatic or acute stress disorders. Dissociative disorders may take the form of amnesia, fugue, or identity disorder (multiple personality). Somatoform disorders center on physical complaints that mimic disease or disability.

Psychodynamic explanations of anxiety disorders emphasize unconscious conflicts. The humanistic approach emphasizes faulty self-images. The behavioral approach emphasizes the effects of learning, particularly avoidance learning. The cognitive approach stresses maladaptive thinking patterns.

Personality disorders are deeply ingrained maladaptive personality patterns, such as the antisocial personality. In addition to maladaptive patterns of behaviors, personality disorders are diagnosed and differentiated based on the degree of impairment. Ranging from moderate to severe impairment, some personality disorders are narcissistic, histrionic, borderline, schizotypal and antisocial (sociopaths).

Labeling someone with a disorder rather than the problems that people experience can dramatically influence how people with mental disorders are treated and understood. They often are faced with prejudice and discrimination, denied jobs and housing, and accused of crimes they did not commit.

Suicide is statistically related to such factors as age, sex, and marital status. However, in individual cases the potential for suicide is best identified by a desire to escape, unbearable psychological pain, frustrated psychological needs, and a constriction of options. Suicide can sometimes be prevented by the efforts of family, friends, and mental health professionals.

Learning Objectives

1. Indicate the magnitude of mental health problems in this country; define *psychopathology*; and describe the following ways of viewing normality, including the shortcoming(s) of each:
    a. subjective discomfort
    b. statistical abnormality
    c. social nonconformity
    d. situational context
    e. cultural relativity
2. Give examples of how race, gender, and social class continue to affect the diagnosis of various disorders; indicate the two core features of abnormal behavior;
3. Explain how the DSM-IV-TR is used; define *mental disorder*, and briefly describe each of the following categories of mental disorders:
    a. psychotic disorders
    b. organic mental disorders
    c. mood disorders
    d. anxiety disorders
    e. somatoform disorders
    f. dissociative disorders
    g. personality disorders
    h. sexual and gender identity disorders

      i.   substance related disorders

4. Define the term *neurosis* and explain why it was droppped from use.
5. Describe examples of culture-bound syndromes from around the world; list the four general risk factors that contribute to psychopathology.
6. Define *insanity* and explain how it is established in court.
7. List and explain the five major characteristics of psychotic disorders, including a description of the different types of delusions, the most common types of hallucinations, and warning signs of these disorders; and define *organic psychosis* and give examples of this disorder.
8. List the main feature of delusional disorders; and describe the five types of delusional disorders, including details regarding the most common delusional disorder, paranoid psychosis.
9. Discuss schizophrenia, including its frequency, symptoms, and the problems with selective attention.
10. List and describe the four major subtypes of schizophrenia, including how paranoid schizophrenia differs from a paranoid delusional disorder; explain the general relationship between psychosis and violence.
11. Describe the roles of the following as causes of schizophrenia:
    a. the environment, including the prenatal environment, birth complications, early psychological trauma, disturbed family environment, and deviant communication patterns
    b. heredity, including inherited potential and genetic mutations
    c. brain chemistry, including the roles of dopamine and glutamate
    d. brain structure and activity, including information gained through CT, MRI, and PET scans; and explain the stress-vulnerability model
12. Discuss mood disorders, including the following:
    a. the incidence
    b. the two general types
    c. characteristics of the moderate mood disorders of dysthymic and cyclothymic disorders
    d. the characteristics of the three major mood disorders: major depression, bipolar I and bipolar II
    e. how major mood disorders differ from moderate mood disorders, including the term *endogenous*
13. Describe the following explanations for depression:
    a. brain chemicals
    b. psychoanalytic theory
    c. behavioral theories
    d. cognitive theory
    e. social and environmental stresses, including why women experience depression more than men
    f. the role of heredity
    g. the time or season of the year, including the cause, symptoms, and treatment of seasonal affective disorder (SAD)
14. Define *anxiety* and describe the characteristics of anxiety-related disorders.

15. Explain why the term *nervous breakdown* has no formal meaning and how it may be related to adjustment disorders; describe an adjustment disorder, including its characteristics, causes, treatment, and how it differs from anxiety disorders.
16. Describe the following anxiety disorders:
    a. generalized anxiety disorder
    b. panic disorder (without agoraphobia)
    c. panic disorder (with agoraphobia)
    d. agoraphobia (without panic)
    e. specific phobia
    f. social phobia
    g. obsessive-compulsive disorder
    h. acute stress disorder
    i. post-traumatic stress disorder
17. Describe the following dissociative disorders:
    a. dissociative amnesia
    b. dissociative fugue
    c. dissociative identity disorder
18. Describe the following somatoform disorders:
    a. hypochondriasis
    b. somatization disorder
    c. pain disorder
    d. conversion disorder, including "glove anesthesia"
19. Discuss how each of the major perspectives in psychology view the cause of anxiety disorders:
    a. Psychodynamic
    b. humanistic (Rogers)
    c. existential
    d. behavioral, including the terms *avoidance learning* and *anxiety reduction hypothesis*
    e. the cognitive view
20. List and briefly describe the ten different types of personality disorders (see Table 12.3).
21. Provide an in-depth discussion of the distinctive characteristics, causes, and possible treatment of the antisocial personality.
22. Describe Rosenhan's pseudo-patient study and his observations regarding psychiatric labeling; and discuss the dangers of psychiatric labeling, including social stigma.
23. Discuss the following aspects of suicide:
    a. factors that affect suicide rates, including sex, ethnicity, age, and marital status
    b. the immediate causes of suicide
    c. warning signs
    d. common characteristics of suicidal thoughts and feelings
    e. how to help someone who is suicidal
    f. crisis intervention

RECITE AND REVIEW

Normality—What's Normal?

Survey Question: How is abnormality defined? Pages 470-472

1. *Psychopathology* refers to mental _____ themselves or to psychologically _____ behavior.

2. Formal definitions of abnormality usually take into account subjective _____ (private feelings of suffering or unhappiness).

3. Statistical definitions define abnormality as an extremely _____ or _____ score on some dimension or measure.

4. Statistical _____ lines tend to be arbitrary, and statistical definitions tell us little to nothing of the _____ of deviations from the norm.

5. Social nonconformity is a failure to follow societal _____ for acceptable conduct.

6. Frequently, the _____ or situational context within which a behavior takes place affects judgments of normality and abnormality.

7. _____ of the preceding definitions are relative standards.

8. A key element in judgments of disorder is that a person's _____ must be maladaptive (it makes it difficult for the person to _____ to the demands of daily life).

9. People suffering from psychological disorders lose their ability to _____ thoughts, behaviors, or feelings adequately.

10. A _____ disorder is a significant impairment in psychological functioning.

11. Insanity is a _____ term defining whether a person may be held responsible for his or her actions. Sanity is determined in _____ on the basis of testimony by expert witnesses.

Classifying Mental Disorders—Problems by the Book

Survey Question: What are the major psychological disorders? Pages 472-477

1. Major disorders and categories of psychopathology are described in the *Diagnostic and Statistical* _____ *of* _____ *Disorders* (DSM-IV-TR).

2. Psychotic disorders are characterized by a retreat from _____, by hallucinations and delusions, and by _____ withdrawal.

3. Organic mental disorders are problems caused by _____ injuries and _____.

4. Substance related disorders are defined as abuse of or dependence on _____ - or behavior-altering _____.

5. Mood disorders involve disturbances in affect, or _____ that may result in mania (persistent elevated mood), _____ (persistent depressed mood), or a combination of both.

6. Anxiety disorders involve high levels of fear or _____ and distortions in behavior that are _____ related.

7. Somatoform disorders involve physical symptoms that mimic physical _____ or injury for which there is no identifiable _____.

8. Dissociative disorders include cases of sudden amnesia, multiple _____, or episodes of depersonalization.

9. Personality disorders are deeply ingrained, unhealthy _____ patterns that develop in adolescence and persist into adulthood.

10. Sexual and gender disorders include _____ identity disorders, paraphilias, and _____ dysfunctions.

11. In the past, the term *neurosis* was used to describe milder, _____ related disorders. However, the term is fading from use.

12. Psychological disorders are recognized in every _____. For example, Native Americans who are preoccupied with death and the deceased have _____ sickness, and East Asians who experience intense anxiety that their penis, vulva, or nipples are receding into their bodies have _____ disorder.

13. Changes to the DSM-IV-TR reflect current research and social attitudes. For example, _____ identity disorder may be removed, but posttraumatic _____ disorder may be added. Biological, psychological, family, and _____ factors contribute to the development of psychopathology.

Psychotic Disorders—The Dark Side of the Moon

Survey Question: What are the general characteristics of psychotic disorders?
Pages 477-479

1. Psychosis is a _____ in contact with reality.

2. Some common types of delusions are depressive, _____, grandeur, _____, persecution, and reference.

3. Psychosis is marked by delusions, _____ (false sensations), and sensory changes.

4. Other symptoms of psychosis are disturbed emotions, disturbed communication, and _____ disintegration.

5. An organic psychosis is based on known injuries or _____ of the brain.

6. Toxic chemicals, such as _____ or mercury, can cause damage to the brain and cause hallucinations, delusions, and a loss of emotional control.

7. The most common _____ problem is dementia, a serious mental impairment in old age caused by deterioration of the _____.

8. Alzheimer's Disease is the most common form of _____, and appears to be caused by unusual webs and tangles in the brain.

Delusional Disorders—An Enemy Behind Every Tree

Survey Question: What is the nature of a delusional disorder? Page 479-480

1. A diagnosis of delusional disorder is based primarily on the presence of _____, or deeply held false beliefs.

2. Delusions may concern _____ attraction, grandeur, _____ (harassment or threat), infidelity, or physical disease.

3. In delusional disorder, all of the delusions concern experiences that _____ occur in real life.

4. The most common delusional disorder is paranoid psychosis. Because they often have intense and irrational delusions of _____, paranoids may be violent if they believe they are threatened.

Schizophrenia—Shattered Reality

Survey Questions: What forms does schizophrenia take? What causes it? Pages 480-486

1. Schizophrenia is distinguished by a _____ between _____ and emotion, and by delusions, hallucinations, apathy, thinking abnormalities, and communication difficulties.

2. In schizophrenics, emotions may become _____ or very inappropriate.

3. Schizophrenic symptoms are related to problems of "_____ attention," which is an inability to focus on one thing at a time. This may cause an overload of jumbled thoughts, _____, images, and feelings.

4. Disorganized schizophrenia is marked by extreme _____ disintegration and silly, bizarre, or obscene behavior. _____ impairment is usually extreme.

5. Catatonic schizophrenia is associated with stupor, _____ (inability to speak), and odd postures. Sometimes violent and agitated behavior also occurs.

6. In paranoid schizophrenia (the most common type), outlandish delusions of grandeur and _____ are coupled with psychotic symptoms and personality breakdown.

7. In general, only persons who are actively psychotic and currently experiencing psychotic symptoms are at _____ risk for violence; the rest of the time the risk for violence among those who are mentally ill (and do not abuse substances) is _____ different from the non mentally ill.

8. *Undifferentiated schizophrenia* is the term used to indicate a _____ of clear-cut patterns of disturbance.

9. Current explanations of schizophrenia emphasize a combination of environmental _____, inherited susceptibility, and biochemical _____ in the body or brain.

10. A number of environmental factors appear to increase the risk of developing schizophrenia. These include viral _____ during the mother's pregnancy and _____ complications.

11. Early psychological _____ (psychological injury or shock) and a disturbed _____ environment, especially one marked by deviant communication, also increase the risk of schizophrenia.

12. Studies of _____ and other close relatives strongly support heredity as a major factor in schizophrenia.

13. Recent biochemical studies have focused on abnormalities in brain _____ substances, especially glutamate and dopamine and their receptor sites.

14. Additional abnormalities in brain structure or _____ have been detected in schizophrenic brains by the use of CT scans, MRI scans, and PET scans.

15. The dominant explanation of schizophrenia is the _____-vulnerability model; it attributes psychotic disorders to a blend of _____ stress and inherited susceptibility.

Mood Disorders—Peaks and Valleys

Survey Questions: What are mood disorders? What causes them? Pages 487-490

1. Mood disorders primarily involve disturbances of mood or _____.

2. Long-lasting, though relatively moderate, _____ is called a dysthymic disorder.

3. Chronic, though moderate, swings in mood between _____ and _____ are called a cyclothymic disorder.

4. In a bipolar I disorder the person alternates between extreme mania and _____.

5. In a bipolar II disorder the person is mostly _____, but has had at least one episode of hypomania (mild _____).

6. The problem known as major depressive disorder involves extreme sadness and despondency, but no evidence of _____.

7. Major mood disorders more often appear to be endogenous (produced from _____) rather than reactions to _____ events.

8. Biological, psychoanalytic, cognitive, and _____ theories of depression have been proposed. Heredity is clearly a factor in susceptibility to mood disorders.

9. Factors that influence the development of depression include being a woman, being _____, not being married, having limited _____, high levels of _____, and feelings of hopelessness.

10. _____ affective disorder (SAD), which occurs during the _____ months, is another common form of depression.

11. Seasonal depression is more common in the _____ latitudes, where days are very short during the winter. SAD is typically treated with phototherapy.

Anxiety-Based Disorders—When Anxiety Rules

Survey Question: What problems result when a person suffers high levels of anxiety? Pages 490-496

1. Anxiety refers to feelings of apprehension, _____, or uneasiness that is out of proportion to a situation.

2. The term *nervous breakdown* has no formal meaning. However, "breakdowns" do correspond somewhat to adjustment disorders, in which the person is overwhelmed by ongoing _____ stresses beyond their ability to _____.

3. Adjustment disorders _____ when a person's life circumstances improve; anxiety disorders persist.

4. Anxiety disorders include generalized anxiety disorder (chronic _____ and worry) and panic disorder (anxiety attacks, panic, free-_____ anxiety).

5. Panic disorder may occur with or without agoraphobia (fear of _____ places, unfamiliar situations, or leaving the _____).

6. Agoraphobia without panic is the fear that something extremely _____ will happen while away from home.

7. _____ phobias are marked by irrational and unreasonable fears of specific objects or situations, such as insects, birds, animals, and heights.

8. In the anxiety disorder called social phobia, the person fears being _____, evaluated, embarrassed, or humiliated by others in _____ situations.

9. Obsessive-compulsive disorders (obsessions and compulsions), and posttraumatic stress disorder or acute stress disorder (emotional disturbances triggered by severe _____), are also classified as _____ disorders.

10. People with _____-compulsive disorder are plagued with images or thoughts that they cannot force out of _____. To reduce anxiety caused by these constantly occurring images and thoughts, they are compelled to _____ irrational acts.

11. Symptoms of stress disorders include repeated _____ of the traumatic event, avoiding reminders of the event, and _____ emotions. Cognitive impairments and sleep disturbances are also common.

12. Dissociative disorders may take the form of dissociative amnesia (loss of _____ and personal identity) or _____ fugue (confusion about personal identity and flight from familiar surroundings).

13. A more dramatic problem is dissociative identity disorder, in which a person develops _____ personalities.

14. In somatoform disorders, anxieties are expressed through physical complaints that mimic _____ or disability.

15. In hypochondriasis, persons think that they have specific diseases when they are, in fact, _____.

16. In a somatization disorder, the person has numerous _____ complaints. The person repeatedly seeks medical _____ for these complaints, but no organic problems can be found.

17. Somatoform pain refers to discomfort for which there is no identifiable _____ cause.

18. In conversion disorders, actual symptoms of disease or disability develop but their causes are really _____.

19. In Munchausen syndrome, a person may _____ medical problems. In Munchausen syndrome by _____, a person fakes the medical problems of someone in his or her care (usually a mother fabricating a child's illnesses).

20. Anxiety disorders, dissociative disorders, and somatoform disorders all involve high levels of _____, rigid _____ mechanisms, and self-defeating behavior patterns.

Anxiety and Disorder—Four Pathways to Trouble

Survey Question: How do psychologists explain anxiety-based disorders? Pages 496-497

1. The psychodynamic approach emphasizes _____ conflicts within the personality as the cause of disabling anxiety.

2. The humanistic approach emphasizes the effects of a faulty _____-_____.

3. The existential view relates unhealthy anxiety to a loss of _____ in one's life.

4. The behavioral approach emphasizes the effects of previous _____, particularly avoidance _____.

5. Some patterns in anxiety disorders can be explained by the _____ reduction hypothesis, which states that immediate _____ from anxiety rewards self-defeating behaviors.

6. According to the cognitive view, distorted _____ patterns cause anxiety disorders.

Personality Disorders—Blueprints for Maladjustment

Survey Question: What is a personality disorder? Pages 498-499

1. People with borderline _____ disorder tend to react to ordinary criticisms by feeling rejected and _____, which then causes them to respond with anger, self-hatred, and _____.

2. Personality disorders are deeply ingrained _____ personality patterns.

3. The personality disorders are: antisocial, avoidant, _____, dependent, histrionic, narcissistic, obsessive-_____, paranoid, schizoid, and schizotypal.

4. Antisocial persons (sociopaths) seem to lack a _____. They are _____ shallow and manipulative, and tend to be _____ socialized and incapable of felling guilt, shame, fear, loyalty, or love.

5. Psychopaths tend to be "blind" to signs of disgust in _____.

6. Possible causes attributed to people with antisocial _____ disorder include emotional deprivation, _____ abuse as children, and boredom due to receiving little stimulation from the environment.

Disorders in Perspective – Psychiatric Labeling

Pages 499-501

1. People who have _____ disorders are often socially stigmatized, which adds to their problems.

2. David Rosenhan and his colleagues were treated as schizophrenics by _____ _____, even though they did not display any actual symptoms of schizophrenia.

3. David Rosenhan demonstrated the damaging effects of _____ a person with a disorder in our society. They are stigmatized, _____ jobs and housing, and accused of _____ that they did not commit. Treatments for psychological disorders range from hospitalization and _____ to drug therapy. Individuals diagnosed with a major disorder do respond well to drugs and psychotherapy.

Psychology in Action: Suicide—Lives on the Brink

Survey Questions: Why do people commit suicide? Can suicide be prevented?
Pages 501-505

1. There may be as many as _____ attempts for every "successful" suicide.

2. _____ is statistically related to such factors as age, sex, ethnicity, and marital status.

3. Although more _____ attempt suicide, more _____ complete suicide. This is because males use more lethal methods.

4. Among _____ students, suicide is the third leading cause of death. However, more than _____ of suicides are over 45 years old.

5. Major risk factors for suicide include _____ or _____ abuse, a prior attempt, depression, hopelessness, antisocial behavior, suicide by relatives, shame, failure, rejection, and the availability of a _____.

6. In individual cases the potential for suicide is best identified by a desire to _____, unbearable psychological pain, frustrated psychological needs, and a constriction of _____.

7. Suicidal _____ usually precede suicide threats, which progress to suicide attempts. Eight out of every 10 suicides give some _____.

8. Signs of impending suicide include social withdrawal, _____ swings, crisis or emotional shock, personality change, giving away _____ possessions, depression/hopelessness, _____, preoccupations with death, drug use, and suicide threats.

9. In most suicides, the person was _____ about dying or did not want to die.

10. Suicide can often be prevented by the efforts of family, friends, and mental health professionals to establish _____ and rapport with the person, and by gaining day-by-day commitments from her or him.

CONNECTIONS

Normality—What Is Normal?

Survey Questions: How is abnormality defined? Pages 470-472

1. _____ maladaptive
2. _____ subjective discomfort
3. _____ statistical abnormality
4. _____ insanity
5. _____ social nonconformity
6. _____ situational context
7. _____ bell-shaped

A. private feelings of pain
B. too high or too low
C. legal problem
D. eccentric characters
E. abnormal behavior
F. impairs daily life
G. normal

Classifying Mental Disorders—Problems by the Book

Survey Question: What are the major psychological disorders? Pages 472-477

1. _____ DSM-IV-TR
2. _____ post-traumatic embitterment disorder
3. _____ mood disorder
4. _____ Psychosis
5. _____ somatoform disorder
6. _____ Susto
7. _____ organic disorder
8. _____ Communication disorder
9. _____ neurosis
10. _____ paraphilia
11. _____ obsessive-complusive

A. perceived injustice
B. physical symptoms
C. voodoo death
D. outdated term
E. sexual deviation
F. diagnostic manual
G. fear of germs
H. brain pathology
I. mania or depression
J. retreat from reality
K. stuttering

Psychotic Disorders—The Dark Side of the Moon and Delusional Disorders—An Enemy Behind Every Tree

Survey Questions: What are the general characteristics of psychotic disorders? What is the nature of a delusional disorder? Pages 477-480

1. _____ psychosis
2. _____ hallucinations
3. _____ delusion
4. _____ organic psychosis
5. _____ jealous type
6. _____ erotomanic type
7. _____ Dementia
8. _____ persecution type
9. _____ somatic type
10. _____ grandiose type

A. retreat from reality
B. false belief
C. believing a celebrity loves him/her
D. believing one has great talents
E. believing one's body is diseased
F. believing one's partner is unfaithful
G. believing one is being spied on
H. leaded paint
I. imaginary sensations
J. Alzheimer's Disease

Schizophrenia—Shattered Reality

Survey Questions: What forms does schizophrenia take? What causes it? Pages 480-486

1. _____ disorganized type
2. _____ catatonic type
3. _____ undifferentiated type
4. _____ paranoid type
5. _____ psychological trauma
6. _____ Risk factor
7. _____ twin studies
8. _____ dopamine
9. _____ stress-vulnerability

A. displaying rigidity, delusions, and disorganized
B. incoherence, bizarre thinking
C. biological and environmental influences
D. genetics of schizophrenia
E. grandeur or persecution
F. chemical messenger
G. risk factor for schizophrenia
H. stuporous or agitated
I. Viral infection during pregnancy

Mood Disorders—Peaks and Valleys

Survey Questions: What are mood disorders? What causes them? Pages 487-490

1. _____ major depression	A.	produced from within
2. _____ bipolar I	B.	depression and hypomania
3. _____ bipolar II	C.	light treatment
4. _____ endogenous	D.	prolonged sadness and despondency
5. _____ depression risk factors	E.	unmarried Latina woman
6. _____ phototherapy	F.	winter depression
7. _____ SAD	G.	severe mania and depression

Anxiety-Based Disorders—When Anxiety Rules and Anxiety and Disorder—Four Pathways to Trouble

Survey Questions: What problems result when a person suffers high levels of anxiety? How do psychologists explain anxiety-based disorders? Pages 490-497

1. _____ cognitive explanation	A.	afraid to leave the house
2. _____ psychodynamic explanation	B.	fears being observed
3. _____ behavioral explanation	C.	conversion disorder
4. _____ Obsessions	D.	after one month of extreme stress
5. _____ adjustment disorder	E.	caused by unconscious forces
6. _____ generalized anxiety	F.	within weeks after extreme stress
7. _____ Dissociative identity disorder	G.	sudden attacks of fear
8. _____ panic disorder	H.	self-defeating thoughts
9. _____ agoraphobia	I.	chronic free-floating worry
10. _____ Compulsions	J.	fears objects or activities
11. _____ specific phobia	K.	maladaptive pattern of behavior
12. _____ social phobia	L.	dissociation
13. _____ humanistic-existential explanation	M.	faulty self-image and no meaning in life
14. _____ Post-Traumatic Stress Disorder	N.	nervous breakdown
15. _____ acute stress disorder	O.	preoccupations
16. _____ glove anesthesia	P.	irrational acts
17. Munchausen syndomre	Q.	separate identities
18. fugue	R.	fake medical problems

Personality Disorders—Blueprints for Maladjustment

Survey Question: What is a personality disorder? Pages 498-499

1. _____ dependent personality   A. self-importance

2. _____ histrionic personality   B. rigid routines

3. _____ narcissistic personality   C. submissiveness

4. _____ antisocial personality   D. little emotion

5. _____ obsessive-compulsive   E. attention seeking

6. _____ schizoid personality   F. unstable self-image

7. _____ avoidant personality   G. odd, disturbed thinking

8. _____ borderline personality   H. suspiciousness

9. _____ paranoid personality   I. fear of social situations

10. _____ schizotypal personality   J. no conscience

Disorders in Perspective – Psychiatric Labeling; and Psychology in Action: Suicide – Lives on the Brink.

Survey Question: Why do people commit suicide? Can suicide be prevented? Pages 499-505

1. _____ drapetomania   A. culturally disapproved behavior

2. _____ Males   B. psychiatric labeling

3. _____ Warning sign   C. Rosenhan

4. _____ Psuedo-patient study   D. Suicide by firearms

5. _____ Females   E. Suicide by drug overdose

6. _____ Establishing rapport   F. Highest suicide rate

7. _____ social stigma   G. Presence of mental disorder

8. _____ suicide cause   H. Giving away prized possessions

9. _____ Native Americans   I. Suicide prevention

CHECK YOUR MEMORY

Normality—What's Normal?

Survey Question: How is normality defined? Pages 470-472

1. Psychopathology refers to the study of mental disorders and to disorders themselves.

TRUE or FALSE

2. One in eight American adults suffers from a diagnosable mental disorder.

TRUE or FALSE

3. One out of every 10 persons will require mental hospitalization during his or her lifetime.

TRUE or FALSE

4. Subjective discomfort is often a symptom of mental illness, but it is not a necessary criterion for diagnosis.

TRUE or FALSE

5. Statistical abnormality tells us nothing about the meaning of deviations from the norm

TRUE or FALSE

6. Statistical definitions do not automatically tell us where to draw the line between normality and abnormality.

TRUE or FALSE

7. It is often assumed that people who behave in unusual ways suffer from psychological disorders.

TRUE or FALSE

8. In general, abnormal behavior is labeled as psychopathology when it is maladaptive and makes the person lose the ability to control thoughts, behaviors, or feelings

TRUE or FALSE

9. All cultures classify people as abnormal if they fail to communicate with others.

TRUE or FALSE

10. To understand how social norms define normality, a person could perform a mild abnormal behavior in public to observe the public's reaction.

TRUE or FALSE

11. Cultural relativity refers to making personal judgments about another culture's practices.

TRUE or FALSE

12. Being a persistent danger to oneself or others is regarded as a clear sign of disturbed psychological functioning.

TRUE or FALSE

13. Insanity can be established through eyewitness testimony in a court hearing

TRUE or FALSE

Classifying Mental Disorders—Problems by the Book

Survey Question: What are the major psychological disorders? Pages 472-477

1. The Diagnostic and Statistical Manual (DSM) is used by psychologists worldwide, and had existed in its current form since 1952.

TRUE or FALSE

2. Poverty, abusive parents, low intelligence, and head injuries are risk factors for mental disorder.

TRUE or FALSE

3. "Organic mental disorders" is one of the major categories in DSM-IV-TR.

TRUE or FALSE

4. *Koro*, *dhat*, and *zar* are brain diseases that cause psychosis.

TRUE or FALSE

5. Multiple personality is a dissociative disorder.

TRUE or FALSE

6. Neurosis is a legal term, not a type of mental disorder.

TRUE or FALSE

7. Mood disorders are characterized by fear, anxiety, or apprehension.

TRUE or FALSE

8. Personality disorders occur when a person experiences extreme, intense, and long-lasting emotions.

TRUE or FALSE

9. Rage disorder, apathy disorder, and hostile personality disorder may become recognized disorders in the near future.

TRUE or FALSE

Psychotic Disorders—The Dark side of the Moon

Survey Question: What are the general characteristics of psychotic disorders? Pages 477-479

1. The most common psychotic delusion is hearing voices.

TRUE or FALSE

2. Even a person who displays flat affect may continue to privately feel strong emotion.

TRUE or FALSE

3. Extremely psychotic behavior tends to occur in brief episodes.

TRUE or FALSE

4. Severe brain injuries or diseases sometimes cause psychoses.

TRUE or FALSE

5. Children must eat leaded paint flakes before they are at risk for lead poisoning.

TRUE or FALSE

6. Disturbed verbal communication is present only in extreme psychotic episodes.

TRUE or FALSE

7. Alzheimer's Disease is the most common form of dementia, and appears to be caused by unusual webs and tangles in the brain.

TRUE or FALSE

Delusional Disorders—An Enemy Behind Every Tree

Survey Question: What is the nature of a delusional disorder? Page 479-480

1. In delusional disorders, people have auditory hallucinations of grandeur or persecution.

TRUE or FALSE

2. Delusions of persecution are a key symptom of paranoid psychosis.

TRUE or FALSE

3. A person who believes that his body is diseased and rotting has an erotomanic type of delusional disorder.

TRUE or FALSE

4. Delusional disorders are common and are easily treated with drugs.

TRUE or FALSE

5. Many "UFO abductees" may actually be suffering from paranoid psychosis

TRUE or FALSE

Schizophrenia—Shattered Reality

Survey Questions: What forms does schizophrenia take? What causes it? Pages 480-486

1. One person out of 100 will become schizophrenic.

TRUE or FALSE

2. Schizophrenia is the most common dissociative psychosis.

TRUE or FALSE

3. The mentally ill are generally more violent than normal individuals.

TRUE or FALSE

4. Silliness, laughter, and bizarre behavior are common in disorganized schizophrenia.

TRUE or FALSE

5. Periods of immobility and odd posturing are characteristic of paranoid schizophrenia.

TRUE or FALSE

6. At various times, patients may shift from one type of schizophrenia to another.

TRUE or FALSE

7. Exposure to influenza during pregnancy produces children who are more likely to become schizophrenic later in life.

TRUE or FALSE

8. If one identical twin is schizophrenic, the other twin has a 46 percent chance of also becoming schizophrenic.

TRUE or FALSE

9. Excess amounts of the neurotransmitter substance PCP are suspected as a cause of schizophrenia.

TRUE or FALSE

10. The brains of schizophrenics tend to be more responsive to dopamine than the brains of normal persons.

TRUE or FALSE

11. PET scans show that activity in the frontal lobes of schizophrenics tends to be abnormally low.

TRUE or FALSE

12. The stress-vulnerability model suggests that psychotic disorders are caused by a combination of environment and heredity.

TRUE or FALSE

Mood Disorders—Peaks and Valleys

Survey Questions: What are mood disorders? What causes them? Pages 487-490

1. The two most basic types of mood disorder are bipolar I and bipolar II.

TRUE or FALSE

2. It is normal for a person to experience extreme changes in mood or emotion.

TRUE or FALSE

3. In bipolar disorders, people experience both mania and depression.

TRUE or FALSE

4. If a person is moderately depressed for at least two weeks, a dysthymic disorder exists.

TRUE or FALSE

5. A cyclothymic disorder is characterized by moderate levels of depression and manic behavior.

TRUE or FALSE

6. Endogenous depression appears to be generated from within, with little connection to external events.

TRUE or FALSE

7. Behavioral theories of depression emphasize the concept of learned helplessness.

TRUE or FALSE

8. Overall, women are twice as likely as men are to become depressed.

TRUE or FALSE

9. Having limited education, experiencing high levels of stress, not being married, and feeling hopeless are some characteristics that increase a woman's chance of being depressed.

TRUE or FALSE

10. Research indicates that heredity does not play a role in major mood disorder.

TRUE or FALSE

11. SAD is most likely to occur during the winter, in countries lying near the equator.

TRUE or FALSE

12. Phototherapy is used to treat SAD successfully 80 percent of the time.

TRUE or FALSE

Anxiety-Based Disorders—When Anxiety Rules

Survey Question: What problems result when a person suffers high levels of anxiety? Pages 490-496

1. Anxiety is an emotional response to an ambiguous threat.

TRUE or FALSE

2. Adjustment disorders occur when severe stresses outside the normal range of human experience push people to their breaking points.

TRUE or FALSE

3. Sudden, unexpected episodes of intense panic are a key feature of generalized anxiety disorder.

TRUE or FALSE

4. A person who fears he or she will have a panic attack in public places or unfamiliar situations suffers from acrophobia.

TRUE or FALSE

5. Social phobias arise in situations where people can be evaluated, observed, or humiliated in front of others.

TRUE or FALSE

6. Arachnophobia, claustrophobia, and pathophobia are all specific phobias.

TRUE or FALSE

7. Many people who have an obsessive-compulsive disorder are checkers or cleaners.

TRUE or FALSE

8. Post-Traumatic Stress Disorder (PTSD) is a psychological disturbance lasting more than one month after exposure to severe stress.

TRUE or FALSE

9. Multiple personality is the most common form of schizophrenia.

TRUE or FALSE

10. Depersonalization and fusion are the goals of therapy for dissociative identity disorders.

TRUE or FALSE

11. The word somatoform means "body form."

TRUE or FALSE

12. A mother who injects her child with 7-Up in order to solicit medical attention may be suffering from Munchausen syndrome.

TRUE or FALSE

13. An unusual lack of concern about the appearance of a sudden disability is a sign of a conversion reaction.

TRUE or FALSE

Anxiety and Disorder—Four Pathways to Trouble

Survey Question: How do psychologists explain anxiety-based disorders? Pages 496-497

1. Anxiety disorders appear to be partly hereditary.

TRUE or FALSE

2. The psychodynamic approach characterizes anxiety disorders as a product of id impulses that threaten a loss of control.

TRUE or FALSE

3. According to behaviorists, the immediate relief that comes from avoidance behaviors reduced anxiety, which makes it more likely that those behaviors will be repeated.

TRUE or FALSE

4. Carl Rogers interpreted emotional disorders as the result of a loss of meaning in one's life.

TRUE or FALSE

5. Disordered behavior is paradoxical because it makes the person more anxious and unhappy in the long run.

TRUE or FALSE

6. The cognitive view attributes anxiety disorders to distorted thinking that leads to avoidance learning.

TRUE or FALSE

Personality Disorders—Blueprints for Maladjustment

Survey Question: What is a personality disorder? Pages 498-499

1. The "emotional storms" experienced by people with borderline personality disorder is a normal process about which they and their friends have a clear understanding.

TRUE or FALSE

2. Histrionic persons are preoccupied with their own self-importance.

TRUE or FALSE

3. Personality disorders usually appear suddenly in early adulthood.

TRUE or FALSE

4. Having a paranoid personality results in a deep distrust and suspicion of others; however, this rarely impairs daily functioning.

TRUE or FALSE

5. The schizoid person shows little emotion and is uninterested in relationships with others.

TRUE or FALSE

6. *Psychopath* is another term for the borderline personality.

TRUE or FALSE

7. Sociopaths usually have a childhood history of emotional deprivation, neglect, and abuse.

TRUE or FALSE

8. Antisocial behavior typically declines somewhat after age 20.

TRUE or FALSE

9. Antisocial personality disorders are often treated successfully with drugs.

TRUE or FALSE

Disorders in Perspective – Psychiatric Labeling; and Psychology in Action: Suicide—Lives on the Brink

Survey Questions: Why do people commit suicide? Can suicide be prevented? Pages 499-505

1. In Rosenhan's study of psychiatric labeling, hospital staff were worse at distinguishing real from "phony" psychiatric patients than were actual psychiatric patients

TRUE or FALSE

2. Labeling a person with a disorder when they do not have it does not harm them in any way.

TRUE or FALSE

3. People who have been successfully treated for a mental disorder are no longer a threat to society and, therefore, are not stigmatized like criminals.

TRUE or FALSE

4. There is relatively little prejudice or discrimination directed at the mentally ill in American culture.

TRUE or FALSE

5. Drapetomania, childhood masturbation, and nymphomania are considered mental disorders listed in the DSM-IV-TR.

TRUE or FALSE

6. Gender is a common source of bias in judging normality.

TRUE or FALSE

7. More men than women complete suicide.

TRUE or FALSE

8. Suicide rates steadily decline after young adulthood.

TRUE or FALSE

9. The suicide rate for Native Americans is the lowest in the U.S.

TRUE or FALSE

10. Most suicides involve despair, anger, and guilt.

TRUE or FALSE

11. People who threaten suicide rarely actually attempt it—they're just "crying wolf."

TRUE or FALSE

12. Only a minority of people who attempt suicide really want to die.

TRUE or FALSE

13. The risk of attempted suicide is high if a person has a concrete, workable plan for doing it.

TRUE or FALSE

14. Giving away prized possessions is a warning sign that a suicide attempt is imminent

TRUE or FALSE

15. Establishing a rapport with a suicidal person is an important first step to preventing a suicide.

TRUE or FALSE

FINAL SURVEY AND REVIEW

Normality—What's Normal?

Survey Question: How is abnormality defined? Pages 470-472

1. _____ refers to mental disorders themselves or to psychologically unhealthy behavior.

2. Formal definitions of _____ usually take into account subjective discomfort (private feelings of suffering or unhappiness).

3. _____ _____ define abnormality as an extremely high or low score on some dimension or measure.

4. Statistical boundary lines tend to be _____, and statistical definitions tell us little to nothing of the meaning of _____ from the norm.

5. Social _____ is a failure to follow societal standards for _____ conduct.

6. Frequently, the cultural or _____ context within which a behavior takes place affects judgments of _____ and abnormality.

7. All of the preceding definitions are _____ standards.

8. A key element in judgments of disorder is that a person's behavior must be _____ (it makes it difficult for the person to adapt to the demands of daily life).

9. People suffering from psychological disorders lose their _____ to control _____, behaviors, or _____ adequately.

10. A mental disorder is a significant _____ in psychological functioning.

11. Insanity is a legal term defining whether a person may be held _____ for his or her actions. Sanity is determined in court on the basis of testimony by _____ witnesses.

Classifying Mental Disorders—Problems by the Book

Survey Question: What are the major psychological disorders? Pages 472-477

1. Major disorders and categories of psychopathology are described in the _____ and _____ Manual of Mental Disorders (DSM-IV-TR).

2. _____ disorders are characterized by a retreat from reality, by _____ and delusions, and by social withdrawal.

3. _____ mental disorders are problems caused by brain _____ and diseases.

4. _____ related disorders are defined as abuse of or dependence on mood- or _____-altering drugs.

5. _____ disorders involve disturbances in _____, or emotion that may result in _____ (persistent elevated mood), depression (persistent depressed mood), or a combination of both.

6. _____ disorders involve high levels of _____ or anxiety and distortions in behavior that are anxiety related.

7. _____ disorders involve physical symptoms that _____ physical disease or injury for which there is no identifiable cause.

8. _____ disorders include cases of sudden _____, multiple personality, or episodes of depersonalization.

9. _____ disorders are deeply ingrained, unhealthy personality patterns that develop in _____ and persist into adulthood.

10. _____ and gender disorders include gender identity disorders, _____, and sexual dysfunctions.

11. In the past, the term *neurosis* was used to describe milder, anxiety related disorders. However, the term is _____ from use.

12. Psychological _____ are recognized in every culture. For example, Native Americans who are preoccupied with _____ and the deceased have Ghost sickness, and East Asians who experience intense anxiety that their _____, vulva, or _____ are receding into their bodies have Koro disorder.

13. Changes to the DSM-IV-TR reflect current research and _____ attitudes. For example, gender identity disorder may be removed, but _____ embitterment disorder may be added.

14. Biological, _____, family, and social factors contribute to the development of psychopathology.

Psychotic Disorders—The Dark Side of the Moon

Survey Question: What are the general characteristics of psychotic disorders?
Pages 477-479

1. Psychosis is a break in contact with _____.

2. Some common types of _____ are depressive, somatic, _____, influence, persecution, and reference.

3. Psychosis is marked by _____, hallucinations (false sensations), and _____ changes.

4. Other symptoms of psychosis are disturbed _____, disturbed _____, and personality disintegration.

5. An _____ psychosis is based on known injuries or diseases of the brain.

6. Toxic chemicals, such as lead or _____, can cause damage to the brain and cause _____, delusions, and a loss of emotional control.

7. The most common organic problem is _____, a serious mental impairment in old age caused by deterioration of the brain.

8. _____ Disease is the most common form of dementia, and appears to be caused by unusual _____ and _____ in the brain.

Delusional Disorders—An Enemy Behind Every Tree

Survey Question: What is the nature of a delusional disorder? Page 479-480

1. A diagnosis of _____ disorder is based primarily on the presence of delusions, or deeply held false beliefs.

2. Delusions may concern romantic attraction, _____, persecution (harassment or threat), infidelity, or physical disease.

3. In delusional _____, all of the delusions concern experiences that could occur in real life.

4. The most common delusional disorder is _____ psychosis. Because they often have intense and irrational delusions of persecution, paranoids may be violent if they believe they are _____.

Schizophrenia—Shattered Reality

Survey Questions: What forms does schizophrenia take? What causes it? Pages 480-486

1. Schizophrenia is distinguished by a split between thought and _____, and by delusions, hallucinations, _____, thinking abnormalities, and communication difficulties.

2. In schizophrenics, emotions may become blunted or very _____.

3. Schizophrenic symptoms are related to problems of "selective _____," which is an inability to focus on one thing at a time. This may cause an _____ of jumbled thoughts, sensations, images, and feelings.

4. _____ schizophrenia is marked by extreme personality disintegration and silly, bizarre, or obscene behavior. Social _____ is usually extreme.

5. _____ schizophrenia is associated with stupor, mutism (inability to speak), and odd _____. Sometimes violent and agitated behavior also occurs.

6. In _____ schizophrenia (the most common type), outlandish delusions of _____ and persecution are coupled with psychotic symptoms and personality breakdown.

7. In general, only persons who are actively psychotic and currently experiencing psychotic symptoms are at increased risk for _____; the rest of the time the risk for violence among those who are mentally ill (and do not abuse _____) is not different from the non-mentally ill.

8. _____ *schizophrenia* is the term used to indicate a lack of clear-cut patterns of disturbance.

9. Current explanations of schizophrenia emphasize a combination of environmental stress, inherited _____, and biochemical abnormalities in the body or brain.

10. A number of environmental factors appear to _____ the risk of developing schizophrenia. These include viral infection during the mother's _____ and birth complications.

11. Early _____ trauma (psychological injury or shock) and a disturbed family environment, especially one marked by _____ communication, also increase the risk of schizophrenia.

12. Studies of twins and other close relatives strongly support _____ as a major factor in schizophrenia.

13. Recent _____ studies have focused on abnormalities in brain transmitter substances, especially _____ and dopamine and their receptor sites.

14. Additional abnormalities in brain structure or activity have been detected in schizophrenic brains by the use of _____ scans, MRI scans, and _____ scans.

15. The dominant explanation of schizophrenia is the stress-_____ model; it attributes psychotic disorders to a blend of environmental stress and _____ susceptibility.

Mood Disorders—Peaks and Valleys

Survey Questions: What are mood disorders? What causes them? Pages 487-490

1. _____ disorders primarily involve disturbances of mood or emotion.

2. Long-lasting, though relatively moderate, depression is called a _____ disorder.

3. _____, though moderate, swings in mood between depression and elation are called a _____ disorder.

4. In a bipolar _____ disorder the person alternates between extreme mania and depression.

5. In a bipolar _____ disorder the person is mostly depressed, but has had at least one episode of hypomania (mild mania).

6. The problem known as major depressive disorder involves extreme sadness and _____, but no evidence of mania.

7. Major mood disorders more often appear to be _____ (produced from within) rather than reactions to external events.

8. Biological, _____, cognitive, and behavioral theories of depression have been proposed. Heredity is clearly a factor in _____ to mood disorders.

9. Factors that influence the development of depression include being a _____, being Latina, not being married, having limited education, high levels of stress, and feelings of _____.

10. Seasonal _____ disorder (SAD), which occurs during the winter months, is another common form of depression.

11. Seasonal depression is more common in the northern latitudes, where days are very short during the _____. SAD is typically treated with _____.

Anxiety-Based Disorders—When Anxiety Rules

Survey Question: What problems result when a person suffers high levels of anxiety? Pages 490-496

1. Anxiety refers to feelings of apprehension, dread, or _____ that is out of proportion to a situation.

2. The term *nervous* _____ has no formal meaning. However, "_____" do correspond somewhat to adjustment disorders, in which the person is overwhelmed by ongoing life stresses beyond their ability to cope.

3. Adjustment disorders disappear when a person's life circumstances _____; anxiety disorders _____.

4. Anxiety disorders include _____ anxiety disorder (chronic anxiety and worry) and _____ disorder (anxiety attacks, panic, free-floating anxiety).

5. Panic disorder may occur with or without _____ (fear of public places, _____ situations, or leaving the home).

6. Agoraphobia without panic is the fear that something extremely embarrassing will happen while _____ from home.

7. Specific _____ are marked by irrational and unreasonable fears of specific objects or situations, such as _____, birds, animals, and heights.

8. In the anxiety disorder called _____ phobia, the person fears being observed, evaluated, embarrassed, or _____ by others in social situations.

9. Obsessive-compulsive disorders (obsessions and compulsions), and _____ stress disorder or acute _____ disorder (emotional disturbances triggered by severe stress), are also classified as anxiety disorders.

10. People with obsessive-_____ disorder are plagued with images or thoughts that they _____ force out of awareness. To reduce anxiety caused by these constantly occurring images and thoughts, they are compelled to repeat irrational _____.

11. Symptoms of stress disorders include repeated reliving of the _____ event, avoiding reminders of the event, and blunted emotions. Cognitive impairments and sleep _____ are also common.

12. _____ disorders may take the form of dissociative amnesia (loss of memory and personal identity) or dissociative _____ (confusion about personal identity and flight from familiar surroundings).

13. A more dramatic problem is dissociative identity disorder, in which a person develops multiple _____.

14. In _____ disorders, anxieties are expressed through _____ complaints that mimic disease or disability.

15. In _____, persons think that they have specific diseases when they are, in fact, healthy.

16. In a _____ disorder, the person has numerous physical complaints. The person repeatedly seeks medical treatment for these complaints, but no _____ problems can be found.

17. Somatoform _____ refers to discomfort for which there is no identifiable physical cause.

18. In _____ disorders, actual symptoms of disease or disability develop but their causes are really psychological.

19. In _____ syndrome, a person may fake medical problems. In Munchausen syndrome by proxy, a person fakes the medical problems of _____ in his or her care (usually a mother fabricating a child's illnesses).

20. Anxiety disorders, dissociative disorders, _____ somatoform disorders all involve high levels of anxiety, rigid defense mechanisms, and _____-_____ behavior patterns.

Anxiety and Disorder—Four Pathways to Trouble

Survey Question: How do psychologists explain anxiety-based disorders? Pages 496-497

1. The _____ approach emphasizes unconscious conflicts within the personality as the cause of disabling anxiety.

2. The _____ approach emphasizes the effects of a faulty self-image.

3. The _____ view relates unhealthy anxiety to a loss of meaning in one's life.

4. The _____ approach emphasizes the effects of previous learning, particularly avoidance learning.

5. Some patterns in anxiety disorders can be explained by the anxiety _____ hypothesis, which states that immediate relief from anxiety _____ self-defeating behaviors.

6. According to the _____ view, distorted thinking patterns cause anxiety disorders.

Personality Disorders—Blueprints for Maladjustment

Survey Question: What is a personality disorder? Pages 498-499

1. People with _____ personality disorder tend to react to ordinary criticisms by feeling rejected and abandoned, which then causes them to respond with _____, self-hatred, and impulsiveness.

2. _____ disorders are deeply ingrained maladaptive personality patterns.

3. The personality disorders are: _____, avoidant, borderline, _____, histrionic, narcissistic, obsessive-compulsive, _____, schizoid, and schizotypal.

4. Antisocial persons (_____) seem to lack a conscience. They are emotionally shallow and _____, and tend to be poorly socialized and incapable of felling guilt, shame, fear, loyalty, or love.

5. Psychopaths tend to be "blind" to signs of _____ in others.

6. Possible causes attributed to people with antisocial personality disorder include emotional _____, physical abuse as children, and _____ due to receiving little stimulation from the environment.

Disorders in Perspective – Psychiatric Labeling

Pages 499-501

1. People who have mental disorders are often socially _____, which adds to their problems.

2. David Rosenhan and his colleagues were treated as _____ by hospital staff, even though they did not display any _____ symptoms of schizophrenia.

3. David Rosenhan demonstrated the damaging effects of labeling a person with a disorder in our society. They are stigmatized, denied jobs and _____, and accused of crimes that they did _____ commit.

4. Treatments for psychological disorders range from _____ and psychotherapy to _____ therapy. Individuals diagnosed with a major disorder do respond _____ to drugs and psychotherapy.

Psychology in Action: Suicide—Lives on the Brink

Survey Questions: Why do people commit suicide? Can suicide be prevented?
Pages 501-505

1. There may be as many as 25 attempts for every "_____" suicide.

2. Suicide is statistically related to such factors as _____, sex, ethnicity, and _____ status.

3. Although more women _____ suicide, more men _____ suicide. This is because males use more lethal methods.

4. Among college students, suicide is the _____ leading cause of death. However, more than half of suicides are over _____ years old.

5. Major risk factors for suicide include alcohol or drug abuse, a prior attempt, _____, hopelessness, _____ behavior, suicide by relatives, shame, failure, rejection, and the _____ of a firearm.

6. In individual cases the potential for suicide is best identified by a desire to escape, unbearable psychological _____, frustrated psychological needs, and a _____ of options.

7. Suicidal thoughts usually precede suicide _____, which progress to suicide attempts. _____ out of every 10 suicides give some warning.

8. Signs of impending suicide include social withdrawal, mood swings, crisis or emotional shock, _____ change, giving away prized _____, depression/hopelessness, aggression, preoccupations with death, drug use, and suicide threats.

9. In most suicides, the person was ambivalent about dying or did _____ want to die.

10. Suicide can often be _____ by the efforts of family, friends, and mental health professionals to establish communication and rapport with the person, and by gaining day-by-day _____ from her or him.

MASTERY TEST

1. The difference between an acute stress disorder and PTSD is
a. how long the disturbance lasts.
b. the severity of the stress.
c. whether the anxiety is free-floating.
d. whether dissociative behavior is observed.

2. A person is at greatest risk of becoming schizophrenic if he or she has
a. schizophrenic parents.
b. a schizophrenic fraternal twin.
c. a schizophrenic mother.
d. a schizophrenic sibling.

3. A core feature of all abnormal behavior is that it is
   a. statistically extreme.
   b. associated with subjective discomfort.
   c. ultimately maladaptive.
   d. marked by a loss of contact with reality.

4. Excess amounts of dopamine in the brain, or high sensitivity to dopamine,
   provides one major explanation for the problem known as
   a. PTSD.
   b. schizophrenia.
   c. major depression.
   d. SAD.

5. The descriptions "acro," "claustro," and "pyro" refer to
   a. common obsessions.
   b. specific phobias.
   c. free-floating anxieties.
   d. hypochondriasis.

6. Glove anesthesia strongly implies the existence of a _____ disorder.
   a. organic
   b. depersonalization
   c. somatization
   d. conversion

7. In the stress-vulnerability model of psychosis, vulnerability is primarily
   attributed to
   a. heredity.
   b. exposure to influenza.
   c. psychological trauma.
   d. disturbed family life.

8. A patient believes that she has a mysterious disease that is causing her body
   to "rot away." What type of symptom is she suffering from?
   a. bipolar
   b. delusion
   c. neurosis
   d. cyclothymic

9. Phototherapy is used primarily to treat
   a. postseasonal depression.
   b. SAD.
   c. catatonic depression.
   d. affective psychoses.

10. Psychopathology is defined as an inability to behave in ways that
    a. foster personal growth and happiness.
    b. match social norms.
    c. lead to personal achievement.
    d. do not cause anxiety.

11. Which of the following is NOT characteristic of suicidal thinking?
a. desires to escape
b. psychological pain
c. frustrated needs
d. too many options

12. Fear of using the rest room in public is
a. a social phobia.
b. an acute stress disorder.
c. a panic disorder.
d. an adjustment disorder.

13. A person who displays personality disintegration and delusions of persecution suffers from _____ schizophrenia.
a. disorganized
b. catatonic
c. paranoid
d. undifferentiated

14. You find yourself in an unfamiliar town and you can't remember your name or address. It is likely that you are suffering from
a. paraphilia.
b. Alzheimer's disease.
c. a borderline personality disorder.
d. a dissociative disorder.

15. A major problem with statistical definitions of abnormality is
a. calculating the normal curve.
b. choosing dividing lines.
c. that they do not apply to groups of people.
d. that they do not take norms into account.

16. Repeatedly seeking help from medical professionals for fake medical conditions, and/or craving the attention that being sick attracts are characteristics of
a. Conversion disorder
b. Munchausen syndrome
c. Psychosomatic disorder
d. Hypochondriasis

17. DSM-IV-TR primarily describes and classifies _____ disorders.
a. mental
b. organic
c. psychotic
d. cognitive

18. The most direct explanation for the anxiety-reducing properties of self-defeating behavior is found in
   a. an overwhelmed ego.
   b. avoidance learning.
   c. the loss of meaning in one's life.
   d. the concept of existential anxiety.

19. A person with a(an) _____ personality disorder might be described as "charming" by people who don't know the person well.
   a. avoidant
   b. schizoid
   c. antisocial
   d. dependent

20. Schizophrenia may be linked to an imbalance of _____ in the brain
   a. serotonin and epinephrine
   b. serotonin and glutamate
   c. glutamate and dopamine
   d. dopamine and serotonin

21. One of the most powerful situational contexts for judging the normality of behavior is
   a. culture.
   b. gender.
   c. statistical norms.
   d. private discomfort.

22. A person who is manic most likely suffers from a(an) _____ disorder.
   a. anxiety
   b. somatoform
   c. organic
   d. mood

23. The principal problem in paranoid psychosis is
   a. delusions.
   b. hallucinations.
   c. disturbed emotions.
   d. personality disintegration.

24. The most at-risk population for suicide is
   a. Caucasian women under the age of 30
   b. African Americans under the age of 30
   c. Caucasian males over the age of 65
   d. Latina females over the age of 75

25. A problem that may occur with or without agoraphobia is
   a. dissociative disorder.
   b. somatoform disorder.
   c. panic disorder.
   d. obsessive-compulsive disorder.

26. Hearing voices that don't exist is an almost sure sign of a _____ disorder.
   a. psychotic
   b. dissociative
   c. personality
   d. delusional

27. A conversion reaction is a type of _____ disorder.
   a. somatoform
   b. dissociative
   c. obsessive-compulsive
   d. postpartum

28. The existence, in the past, of "disorders" such as "drapetomania" and "nymphomania" suggests that judging normality is greatly affected by
   a. gender.
   b. cultural disapproval.
   c. levels of functioning.
   d. subjective discomfort.

29. Which of the following terms does NOT belong with the others?
   a. neurosis
   b. somatoform disorder
   c. personality disorder
   d. dissociative disorder

30. Threats to one's self-image are a key element in the _____ approach to understanding anxiety and disordered functioning.
   a. Freudian
   b. humanistic
   c. existential
   d. behavioral

31. Which of the following is NOT classified as an anxiety disorder?
   a. adjustment disorder
   b. panic disorder
   c. agoraphobia
   d. obsessive-compulsive disorder

32. Cyclothymic disorder is most closely related to
   a. neurotic depression.
   b. major depressive disorder.
   c. bipolar disorder.
   d. SAD.

33. Age-related disturbances in memory, reasoning, judgment, impulse control, and personality may be characteristic of
   a. borderline personality disorder
   b. koro
   c. dementia
   d. schizophrenia

34. Pretending to possess a delusional disorder by walking around campus on a sunny day with a raincoat on and holding an open umbrella over one's head and, when inside, continuing to hold the open umbrella over one's head is a way to
a. understand how social norms define normality.
b. determine how normality is defined.
c. test cultural relativism.
d. all the preceding

35. A person who sometimes is friendly, charming, impulsive, moody, extremely sensitive to ordinary criticisms, and suicidal has the _____ personality disorder.
a. dependent
b. borderline
c. dissociative
d. narcissistic

36. Koro, Amok, and bulimia nervosa are typically found in certain regions among particular groups of people, making these disorders
a. Culture-bound
b. Age-related
c. Geographically trapped
d. Transmitted via television

37. Individuals who believe that a musical performance or song was created by the artist just for them might be suffering from _____ delusions
a. grandiose
b. erotomanic
c. jealous
d. somatic

38. A person who is "blind" to signs that would disgust others, charming, lacks a conscience, and feels no guilt, shame, fear, loyalty, or love has the _____ personality disorder.
a. histrionic
b. schizoid
c. avoidant
d. antisocial

39. Knowing that Lloyd is suffering from bipolar disorder and currently is undergoing treatment, Joan assumes that he will relapse sooner or later and, therefore, refuses to hire him as a delivery person. Joan's reaction and response to Lloyd's application reflects the impact of
a. labeling a person with a disorder rather than the problem.
b. prejudice and discrimination.
c. stigmatism.
d. all the preceding

40. Charles has difficulty leaving his home for vacation. He has to check the locks on all of the windows and doors repeatedly; this sometimes takes three hours. Charles most likely suffers from
   a. obsessive-compulsive disorder.
   b. agoraphobia.
   c. somatization.
   d. a free-floating fugue.

41. Fred is convinced that he will be famous. In fact, he is not shy about telling people what a great musician he is. Fred most likely suffers from which personality disorder?
   a. antisocial
   b. dependent
   c. narcissistic
   d. histrionic

42. George was recently arrested for walking into the bank without pants on; as this is the third time he has done this in a month, he was recently referred to a psychologist for a _____ disorder.
   a. Mood
   b. Sexual
   c. Narcissistic
   d. antisocial

LANGUAGE DEVELOPMENT
Psychological Disorders

Word Roots

Skhizein in Greek means "split." In addition to such English words as "schism," the names for several mental disorders discussed in this chapter derive from this root: schizoid, schizotypal, and schizophrenia. The term *schizophrenia* evolved from two Greek words, *skhizein* (split) and *phren* (mind). (*Phren,* itself, gave rise to the term *phrenology,* which was found in an earlier chapter.)

Journey into Psychology: Beware the Helicopters (p. 469)
   (469) *incapacitated*: incapable of functioning normally
   (469) *maze*: confusing, intricate network of passages
   (469) *magnitude*: great size or extent

Normality—What's Normal? (pgs. 470-472)
   How is normality defined?
   (470) **"That guy is really wacko. His porch lights are dimming."**
   "Yeah, the butter's sliding off his waffle. I think he's ready to go postal.": slang expressions for "crazy" and "insane" (which are themselves slang words for mental illness)

(470) *snap judgments*: hurried decisions

(470) *churchgoing*: one who attends church regularly; also indicates someone who is moral and virtuous

(470) *flagrantly*: obviously offensive

(470) *reclusive*: secluded; to prefer being away from others

(470) *eccentric*: deviating from conventional or accepted behavior or conduct, especially in odd or whimsical ways

(470) *anguish*: distress; suffering; sorrow

(470) **on top of the world**: great; wonderful

(470) **where to draw the line**: where to find the dividing point between two positions

(471) *facet*: an area or component

(471) *defecate*: to empty the bowels

(472) *commitment*: the sending of someone to a mental institution; it may be involuntary

Classifying Mental Disorders—Problems by the Book (pgs. 472-477)

(473) *delirium*: extreme confusion

(473) *hyperactive*: excess activity

(474) *ingrained*: innate; firmly fixed

(474) *exhibitionism*: sexual stimulation through the exposure of one's genitalia to others to obtain shock

(474) *fetishism*: erotic fixation on an object or bodily part

(474) *voyeurism*: obtaining sexual gratification from observing unsuspecting individuals who are partly undressed, naked, or engaged in sexual acts

(474) *amok*: a confused state; in a violent state

(474) *maladies*: illnesses

(474) *apathetic*: showing little or no feeling or concern

(478) *empirical*: based on careful observation or experience

Psychotic Disorders—The Dark side of the Moon (pgs. 477-479)

What are the general characteristics of psychotic disorders?

(478) *emitting*: giving off

(478) *grandeur*: importance, magnificence

(478) *"I can't handle it"*: inability to cope with life's difficulties

(478) *chaotic*: confused; totally disorganized

(478) *"word salad"*: the result of not following the proper use of grammar when speaking English; when one constructs sentences in a seemingly random manner; words are thrown together in a sentence much like vegetables are tossed in together in a salad.

(478) *disintegration*: breaking apart

(478) *fragmented*: state of being broken apart; in fragments, or pieces

Delusional Disorders—An Enemy Behind Every Tree (pgs. 479-480)

What is the nature of a delusional disorder?

(479) *imposter*: someone posing as someone else; a fake
(480) *maligned*: to be criticized, smeared
(480) *crank letter*: irrational, eccentric letter
(480) *conspiracy*: secret plan

Schizophrenia—Shattered Reality (pgs. 480-486)

What forms does schizophrenia take? What causes it?

(481) *stupor*: a state of mental apathy and dullness
(481) *mutism*: inability to speak
(481) *preoccupation*: excessive concern
(482) *enigma*: something hard to understand or explain; puzzle
(483) *laden*: full of
(483) *prying*: looking for information; being nosy
(483) *PCP ("angel dust")*: a psychedelic drug that causes vivid mental imagery (see chapter 5)
(485) *fissuring*: divisions among the lobes of the brain
(486) *vulnerability*: open to influence; easily hurt
(486) *"recipe" for psychosis*: a description for generating psychosis
(486) *"ingredients" (for psychosis)*: list of factors that contribute to psychosis

Mood Disorders—Peaks and Valleys (pgs. 487-490)

What are mood disorders? What causes them?

(487) *bout*: spell; attack
(487) *down:* weakened or incapable; depressed
(487) *bleak*: lacking warm or cheerful qualities
(487) *despondency*: depression
(487) *subdued*: quiet; passive
(488) *strife*: biter or sometimes violent conflict
(488) *"cabin fever"*: extreme irritability and restlessness resulting from living in isolation or within a confined indoor area for a long period
(489) *foreboding*: feeling that something harmful or bad is going to happen
(489) *latitudes*: distance from the Earth's equator
(489) *New England:* area of the United States comprising the states of Maine, New Hampshire, Vermont, Massachusetts, Rhode Island, & Connecticut

Anxiety-Based Disorders—When Anxiety Rules (pgs. 490-496)

What problems result when a person suffers high levels of anxiety?

(490) *apprehension:* suspicion or fear especially of future evil
(491) *clammy*: damp
(493) *jingle*: short verse or song used repetitively with commercials to fix them in your memory

(493) *recluse*: hermit; one who prefers to be alone
(493) *gruesome:* inspiring horror or repulsion
(494) *perversely:* turned away from what is right or good
(494) *flamboyant:* marked by or given to strikingly elaborate or colorful display or behavior

Anxiety and Disorder—Four Pathways to Trouble (pgs. 496-497)

How do psychologists explain anxiety-based disorders?
(497) *crushing need*: a severe need, desire

Personality Disorders—Blueprints for Maladjustment (pgs. 498-499)

What is a personality disorder?
(498) *gouging*: forcing out with the thumb
(498) *turbulent*: rough; unstable
(498) *hypersensitive*: touchy; highly sensitive
(498) *wary*: cautious
(498) *flamboyant*: elaborate or colorful behavior; showy
(499) *"bat an eyelash"*: show a response

Disorder in Perspective—Psychiatric Labeling (pgs.499-501)

(499) *pseudo*: false; pretended
(500) *phony*: fake; false
(500) *checking up on*: investigating
(500) *grappling*: struggling and trying to cope
(500) *stigma*: mark or sign of shame

Psychology in Action: Suicide—Lives on the Brink (pgs. 501-505)

Why do people commit suicide? Can suicide be prevented?
(503) *fallacy*: false belief
(504) *rapport*: a good relationship or closeness
(504) *tip the scales*: have a deciding influence
(504) *harmonious*: having the parts agreeably related
(505) *imminent*: about to happen; coming up

Chapter in Review (pgs. 506-508)

(506) *outlandish*: very unusual; strange

Solutions

Recite and Review

Normality—What's Normal?

1. disorders, unhealthy
2. discomfort
3. high, low
4. boundary, meaning
5. standards
6. cultural
7. All
8. behavior, adapt
9. control
10. mental
11. legal, court

Classifying Mental Disorders—Problems by the Book

1. Manual, Mental
2. reality, social
3. brain, diseases
4. mood, drugs
5. emotion, depression
6. anxiety, anxiety
7. disease, cause
8. personality
9. personality
10. gender, sexual
11. anxiety
12. culture, Ghost, Koro
13. gender, embitterment, social

Psychotic Disorders—The Dark Side of the Moon

1. break
2. somatic, influence
3. hallucinations
4. personality
5. diseases
6. lead
7. organic, brain
8. dementia

Delusional Disorders—An Enemy Behind Every Tree

1. delusions
2. romantic, persecution
3. could
4. persecution

Schizophrenia—Shattered Reality

1. split, thought
2. blunted
3. selective, sensations
4. personality, Social
5. mutism
6. persecution
7. increased, not
8. lack
9. stress, abnormalities
10. infection, birth
11. trauma, family
12. twins
13. transmitter
14. activity
15. stress, environmental

Mood Disorders—Peaks and Valleys

1. emotion
2. depression
3. depression, elation
4. depression
5. depressed, mania
6. mania
7. within, external
8. behavioral
9. Latina, education, stress
10. Seasonal, winter
11. northern

Anxiety-Based Disorders—When Anxiety Rules

1. dread
2. life, cope
3. disappear
4. anxiety, floating
5. public, home
6. embarrassing
7. Specific
8. observed, social
9. stress, anxiety
10. obsessive, awareness, repeat
11. reliving, blunted
12. memory, dissociative
13. multiple
14. disease
15. healthy
16. physical, treatment
17. physical
18. psychological
19. fake, proxy
20. anxiety, defense

Anxiety and Disorder—Four Pathways to Trouble

1. unconscious
2. self, image
3. meaning
4. learning, learning.
5. anxiety, relief
6. thinking

Personality Disorders—Blueprints for Maladjustment

1. personality, abandoned, impulsiveness
2. maladaptive
3. borderline, compulsive
4. conscience, emotionally, poorly
5. others
6. personality, physical

Disorders in Perspective – Psychiatric Labeling

1. mental
2. hospital, staff
3. labeling, denied, crimes, psychotherapy

Psychology in Action: Suicide—Lives on the Brink

1. 25
2. Suicide
3. women, men
4. college, half
5. alcohol, drug, firearm
6. escape, options
7. thoughts, warning
8. mood, prized, aggression
9. ambivalent
10. communication

CONNECTIONS

Normality—What Is Normal?

1. F.
2. A.
3. B.
4. C.
5. D.
6. E.
7. G.

Classifying Mental Disorders—Problems by the Book

1. F.
2. A.
3. I.
4. J.
5. B.
6. C.
7. H.
8. K.
9. D.
10. E.
11. G.

Psychotic Disorders—The Dark Side of the Moon; and Delusional Disorders—An Enemy Behind Every Tree

1. A.	4. H.	7. J.	10. D.
2. I.	5. F.	8. G.	
3. B.	6. C.	9. E.	

Schizophrenia—Shattered Reality

1. B.	4. E.	7. D.
2. H.	5. G.	8. F.
3. A.	6. I.	9. C.

Mood Disorders—Peaks and Valleys

1. D.	3. B.	5. E.	7. F.
2. G.	4. A.	6. C.	

Anxiety-Based Disorders—When Anxiety Rules; and Anxiety and Disorder—Four Pathways to Trouble

1. H.	6. I.	11. J.	16. C.
2. E.	7. Q.	12. B.	17. R.
3. K.	8. G.	13. M.	18. L.
4. O.	9. A.	14. D.	
5. N.	10. P.	15. F.	

Personality Disorders—Blueprints for Maladjustment

1. C.	4. J.	7. I.	10. G.
2. E.	5. B.	8. F.	
3. A.	6. D.	9. H.	

Disorders in Perspective – Psychiatric Labeling; and Psychology in Action: Suicide – Lives on the Brink.

1. A.	4. C.	7. B.
2. D.	5. E.	8. G.
3. H.	6. I.	9. F.

Check Your Memory

Normality—What's Normal?

1. T	5. T	9. T	13. F
2. F	6. T	10. T	
3. F	7. T	11. F	
4. T	8. T	12. T	

Classifying Mental Disorders—Problems by the Book

1. F	4. F	7. F
2. T	5. T	8. F
3. F	6. F	9. T

Psychotic Disorders—The Dark side of the Moon

1. F	3. T	5. F	7. T
2. T	4. T	6. F	

Delusional Disorders—An Enemy Behind Every Tree

1. F	3. F	5. T
2. T	4. F	

Schizophrenia—Shattered Reality

1. T	4. T	7. T	10. T
2. F	5. F	8. T	11. T
3. F	6. T	9. F	12. T

Mood Disorders—Peaks and Valleys

1. F	4. F	7. T	10. F
2. F	5. T	8. T	11. F
3. T	6. T	9. T	12. T

Anxiety-Based Disorders—When Anxiety Rules

1. T	5. T	9. F	13. T
2. F	6. T	10. F	
3. F	7. T	11. T	
4. F	8. T	12. F	

Anxiety and Disorder—Four Pathways to Trouble

1. T	3. T	5. T
2. T	4. F	6. F

Personality Disorders—Blueprints for Maladjustment

1. F	4. F	7. T
2. F	5. T	8. F
3. F	6. F	9. F

Disorders in Perspective – Psychiatric Labeling and Psychology in Action: Suicide—Lives on the Brink

1. T
2. F
3. F
4. F
5. F
6. T
7. T
8. F
9. F
10. T
11. F
12. T
13. T
14. T
15. T

Final Survey and Review

Normality—What's Normal?

1. Psychopathology
2. abnormality
3. Statistical, definitions
4. arbitrary, deviations
5. nonconformity, acceptable
6. situational, normality
7. relative
8. maladaptive
9. ability, thoughts, feelings
10. impairment
11. responsible, expert

Classifying Mental Disorders—Problems by the Book

Survey Question: What are the major psychological disorders? Pages 472-477

1. Diagnostic, Statistical
2. Psychotic, hallucinations
3. Organic, injuries
4. Substance, behavior
5. Mood, affect, mania
6. Anxiety, fear
7. Somatoform, mimic
8. Dissociative, amnesia
9. Personality, adolescence
10. Sexual, paraphilias
11. fading
12. disorders, death, penis, nipples
13. social, posttraumatic
14. psychological

Psychotic Disorders—The Dark Side of the Moon

1. reality
2. delusions, grandeur
3. delusions, sensory
4. emotions, communication
5. organic
6. mercury, hallucinations
7. dementia
8. Alzheimer's, webs, tangles

Delusional Disorders—An Enemy Behind Every Tree

1. delusional
2. grandeur
3. disorders
4. paranoid, threatened

Schizophrenia—Shattered Reality

1. emotion, apathy
2. inappropriate
3. attention, overload
4. Disorganized, impairment
5. Catatonic, postures
6. paranoid, grandeur
7. violence, substances
8. Undifferentiated
9. susceptibility
10. increase, pregnancy
11. psychological, deviant
12. heredity
13. biochemical, glutamate
14. CT, PET
15. vulnerability, inherited

Mood Disorders—Peaks and Valleys

1. Mood
2. dysthymic
3. Chronic, cyclothymic
4. I
5. II
6. despondency
7. endogenous
8. psychoanalytic, susceptibility
9. woman, hopelessness
10. affective
11. winter, phototherapy

Anxiety-Based Disorders—When Anxiety Rules

1. uneasiness
2. breakdown, breakdowns
3. improve, persist
4. generalized, panic
5. agoraphobia, unfamiliar
6. away
7. phobias, insects
8. social, humiliated
9. posttraumatic, stress
10. compulsive, cannot, acts
11. traumatic, disturbances
12. Dissociative, fugue
13. personalities.
14. somatoform, physical
15. hypochondriasis
16. somatization, organic
17. pain
18. conversion
19. Munchausen, someone
20. and, self, defeating

Anxiety and Disorder—Four Pathways to Trouble

1. psychodynamic
2. humanistic
3. existential
4. behavioral
5. reduction, rewards
6. cognitive

Personality Disorders—Blueprints for Maladjustment

1. borderline, anger
2. Personality
3. antisocial, dependent, paranoid
4. sociopaths, manipulative
5. disgust
6. deprivation, boredom

Disorders in Perspective – Psychiatric Labeling

1. stigmatized
2. schizophrenics, actual
3. housing, not
4. hospitalization, drug, well

Psychology in Action: Suicide—Lives on the Brink

1. successful
2. age, marital
3. attempt, complete
4. third, 45
5. depression, antisocial, availability
6. pain, constriction
7. threats, Eight
8. personality, possessions
9. not
10. prevented, commitments

Mastery Test

1. a, p. 493
2. a, p. 483
3. c, p. 471
4. b, p. 483-485
5. b, p. 492
6. d, p. 494-495
7. a, p. 486
8. b, p. 480
9. b, p. 489
10. a, p. 470
11. d, p. 504
12. a, p. 492-493
13. d, p. 481
14. d, p. 494

15. b, p. 470
16. b, p. 495
17. a, p. 472
18. b, p. 497
19. c, p. 498-499
20. c, p. 483-484
21. a, p. 471
22. d, p. 487
23. a, p. 480
24. c, p. 502
25. c, p. 491
26. a, p. 477-478
27. a, p. 494-495
28. b, p. 500

29. a, p. 474-475
30. b, p. 496
31. a, p. 491
32. c, p. 487
33. c, p. 478
34. d, p. 471
35. b, p. 498
36. a, p. 474
37. b, p. 479-480
38. d, p. 498-499
39. d, p. 499-500
40. a, p. 493
41. c, p. 498
42. b, p. 474

CHAPTER 13

Therapies

Chapter Overview

Psychotherapies may be classified as individual, group, insight, action, directive, nondirective, time-limited, positive, supportive, and combinations of these. Primitive and superstitious approaches to treating mental illness have included trepanning and demonology. More humane treatment began in 1793 with the work of Philippe Pinel in Paris.

Freudian psychoanalysis seeks to release repressed thoughts and emotions from the unconscious through dream analysis, free association, and analysis of transference and resistance. Brief psychodynamic therapy has largely replaced traditional psychoanalysis, which can take years to complete. Psychotherapy can produce improvement in many patients, especially those with depression, eating disorders, substance abuse, social phobias, and personality disorders.

Client-centered (or person-centered) therapy is a nondirective humanistic technique dedicated to creating an atmosphere of growth. Existential therapies focus on the meaning of life choices. Gestalt therapy attempts to rebuild thinking, feeling, and acting into connected wholes.

Psychological services are now available through radio, telephone, and other media. Media psychologists are encouraged to offer advice, not therapy. Distance therapy raises ethical questions but also offers anonymity, services to rural areas, and services at reduced cost. Video therapy may become a major source of mental health care in the future.

Behavior therapists use behavior modification techniques such as aversion therapy, systematic desensitization, operant shaping, extinction, and token economies. Of the various behavioral techniques, desensitization has been the most successful form of treatment to reduce fears, anxiety, and psychological pain. New trends include the use of virtual reality exposure and eye-movement desensitization and reprocessing.

Cognitive therapists attempt to change troublesome thought patterns. Major distortions in thinking include selective perception, overgeneralization, and all-or-nothing thinking. In rational-emotive behavior therapy, clients learn to recognize and challenge their own irrational beliefs. Unrealistic beliefs (B) cause individuals to misinterpret the links between an activating event (A) and an emotional consequence (C). Problem gamblers typically hold a number of cognitive distortions and mistaken beliefs, all of which contribute to an illusion of control.

Group therapies may be based on individual therapy methods or special group techniques. Psychodrama often involves role reversal and the mirror technique. Family therapy is typically focused on specific problems. Group awareness training includes encounter groups and sensitivity groups.

All psychotherapies offer a caring relationship, emotional rapport, a protected setting, catharsis, explanations for one's problems, a new perspective, and a chance to practice new behaviors. Many basic counseling skills underlie the success of therapies. Culturally-skilled therapists also include clients' cultural beliefs and traditions. Because of the high cost of mental health services, future therapy may include: short-term therapy, solution-focused, problem-solving approaches, masters-level practitioners, Internet services, telephone counseling, and self-help groups.

Three medical approaches to the treatment of psychological disorders are pharmacotherapy, electroconvulsive therapy, and psychosurgery. When using drugs as a form of treatment, patients must be aware of the trade-offs between the benefits and risks of drug use. Most professionals recommend using limited amounts of electoconvulsive therapy (ECT) with drug therapy to treat depression. When other therapeutic techniques are not effective at reducing mental illness symptoms, deep lesioning is considered. However, psychosurgery cannot be reversed.

Mental hospitalization can serve as a treatment for psychological disorders. Prolonged hospitalization has been discouraged by deinstitutionalization and by partial-hospitalization policies. Unfortunately, many discharged from hospitals end up in jail or homeless. Community mental health centers attempt to prevent mental health problems before they become serious.

Cognitive and behavioral techniques such as covert sensitization, thought stopping, covert reinforcement, and desensitization can aid self-management. In most communities, competent therapists can be located through public sources or by referrals.

Learning Objectives

1. Define *psychotherapy* and describe the following aspects of various therapies:
   - a. individual therapy
   - b. group therapy
   - c. insight therapy
   - d. action therapy
   - e. directive therapy
   - f. non-directive therapy
   - g. time-limited therapy
   - h. supportive therapy
   - i. positive therapy
2. Discuss what a person can expect the outcomes of therapy to be, and list the elements of positive mental health.
3. Briefly describe the history of the treatment of psychological problems, including trepanning, demonology, exorcism, ergotism, and the work of Philippe Pinel.

4. Discuss the development of psychoanalysis and its four basic techniques:
   a. free association
   b. dream analysis, including the terms *latent content, manifest content*, and *dream symbols*
   c. analysis of resistance
   d. transference
5. Dcuss the brief psychodyanamic therapy used today and why it took the place of traditional psychoanalysis.
6. Explain how the insight therapy of humanistic approaches differs from insight gained through traditional psychoanalysis.
7. Describe the core features of the following humanistic approaches and compare them to each other:
   a. Rogers' client-centered therapy
   b. Existential therapy
   c. Perls' Gestalt therapy
8. Discuss the advantages and disadvantages of media (TV and talk-radio) psychologists, telephone therapists, and internet therapy; describe the APA recommendation regarding these therapies; explain how videoconferencing can solve some of the problems of these long-distance therapies.
9. Describe behavior therapy and contrast the goal of behavior therapy with the goal of insight therapies.
10. Define *behavior modification*; explain how classical conditioning affects behavior and how it is used in aversion therapy, including the procedure known as rapid smoking, the response-contingent shocks used in Vogler's treatment of alcoholism, and the justification of aversion therapy based on its long-term benefits.
11. Discuss the behavioral approach of desensitization, including:
   a. the hierarchy
   b. reciprocal inhibition
   c. the problems desensitization is used to treat
   d. how systematic desensitization is performed
   e. how to achieve relaxation using the tension-release method
   f. the techniques of vicarious desensitization, virtual reality expsoure, and eye movement desensitixation and reprocessing (EMDR)
12. List and briefly describe the seven operant principles most frequently used by behavior therapists; explain how nonreinforcement and time-out can be used to bring about extinction of a maladaptive behavior; describe a token economy.
13. Explain how cognitive therapies differ from behavioral therapies.
14. Describe the three thinking errors Beck said underlie depression and what can be done to correct such thinking.
15. Discuss Ellis' rational-emotive behavior therapy (REBT), including the A-B-C of the therapy, the ten most common irrational beliefs, and the three core ideas that Ellis' said served as the basis for most of these irrational beliefs.
16. Identify common cogntive distortions or mistaken beleifs that contribute to problem gambling.

17. List the advantages of group therapy, and briefly describe each of the following group therapies:
    a. psychodrama, including role-playing, role reversal, and the mirror technique
    b. family therapy
    c. large group awareness training, including sensitivity groups, encounter groups, large group awareness training, and the concept of the *therapy placebo effect*
18. Discuss the effectiveness of therapy, in general; the four core features and goals of all psychotherapies; and the strengths of each type of psychotherapy (see Table 13.2).
19. Describe how psychotherapy will likely look in the future.
20. Discuss the skills necessary to be a culturally skilled therapist; and the nine basic counseling skills and list of helping behaviors that can be used by anyone to comfort a person in distress.
21. Discuss the three types of somatic therapy:
    a. pharmacotherapy, including the three major types of drugs, examples of each type (see Table 13.4), and the benefits and limitations of drug therapy, such as the risk-benefit ratio
    b. electoconvulsive therapy (ECT), including how it is performed and what most experts believe regarding this therapy
    c. psychosurgery, including the prefrontal lobotomy and deep lesioning techniques
22. Describe the role of hospitalization and partial hospitalization in the treatment of psychological disorders; explain what deinstitutionalization is and how halfway houses have attempted to help in easing the patient's return to the community; and discuss the roles of the community mental health centers and the work of paraprofessionals within these centers.
23. Describe how persons can apply behavioral principles to themselves in order to solve everyday problems by using each of the following:
    a. covert sensitzation
    b. thought stopping
    c. covert reinforcement
    d. self-directed desensitization, including the procedure for constructing a hierarchy and using the hierarchy
24. Explain how a person can find professional help by discussing each of the following topics:
    a. indicators that signal the need for professional help
    b. sources for locating a therapist (see Table 13.5)
    c. deciding on the type of therapist, such as a psychiatrist, psychologist, counselor, social worker, peer counselor, or self-help group
    d. finding out about the therapist's qualifications
    e. how to evaluate a therapist, including danger signals to watch for in therapy

RECITE AND REVIEW

Psychotherapy—The Talking Cure

Survey Questions: How do psychotherapies differ? Page 510

1. Psychotherapy is any psychological technique used to facilitate _____ changes in a person's personality, _____, or adjustment.

2. _____ therapies seek to produce personal understanding. Action therapies try to directly change troublesome thoughts, feelings, or behaviors without seeking insight into their origins.

3. Directive therapists provide strong _____. Nondirective therapists assist, but clients are expected to solve their own problems.

4. Positive therapy seeks to nurture _____ _____ and actively solve problems; it does not attempt to fix what is "wrong" with a person.

5. Therapies may be conducted either individually or in groups, and they may be open-ended or _____ limited (restricted to a set number of sessions).

Origins of Therapy—Bored Out of Your Skull

Survey Question: How did psychotherapy originate? Page 511

1. Primitive approaches to mental illness were often based on _____ beliefs in demons, witchcraft, and magic.

2. Trepanning, or trephining, involved boring a hole in the _____.

3. Demonology attributed mental disturbance to supernatural forces, such as possession by the devil or on curses, and prescribed _____ as the cure.

4. In some instances, the actual cause of bizarre behavior may have been ergotism, or _____ fungus _____.

5. More humane treatment began in 1793 with the work of Philippe Pinel, who created the first _____ _____ in Paris.

6. Sigmund Freud is credited with creating _____ while working with cases of hysteria.

Psychoanalysis—Expedition into the Unconscious

Survey Question: Is Freudian psychoanalysis still used? Pages 512-514

1. Sigmund Freud's psychoanalysis was the first formal _____.

2. Psychoanalysis was designed to treat cases of hysteria (physical symptoms without known _____ causes).

3. Psychoanalysis seeks to release repressed thoughts, memories, and emotions from the _____ and resolve _____ conflicts.

4. The psychoanalyst uses _____ association, _____ analysis, and analysis of resistance and transference to reveal health-producing insights.

5. In free association, individuals say whatever comes to mind without worrying whether the ideas are painful, _____, or illogical.

6. Freud believed that in order to uncover the individual's unconscious _____ and feelings, a psychoanalyst must conduct _____ analysis to discover the _____ content that is expressed through the manifest content of a person's dream.

7. Resistances, or blockages in the flow of ideas, may reveal _____ conflicts

8. Transference is the tendency to transfer feelings from an important person in one's past to the _____.

9. _____ psychodynamic therapy (which relies on psychoanalytic theory but is brief and focused) is as effective as other major therapies.

10. Some critics have argued that traditional psychoanalysis may frequently receive credit for _____ remissions of symptoms. However, psychoanalysis has been shown to be better than no treatment at all.

Humanistic Therapies—Restoring Human Potential

Survey Question: What are the major humanistic therapies? Pages 514-516

1. _____ therapies try to help people live up to their potential and live rich, rewarding lives. While Sigmund Freud studied the unconscious, Carl Rogers explored conscious thoughts and feelings.

2. Carl Rogers' client-centered (or _____-centered) therapy is nondirective and is dedicated to creating a safe atmosphere of _____.

3. In client-centered therapy, unconditional _____ regard (unshakable personal acceptance), _____ (feeling what another is feeling), authenticity (genuine honesty), and reflection (rephrasing, repeating, and summarizing) are combined to give the client a chance to solve his or her own problems.

4. Existential therapies focus on the problems of existence, such as meaning, choice, and responsibility, and on the end result of the _____ one makes in life.

5. Clients in _____ therapy are encouraged to discover self-imposed limitations in personal identity through confrontation.

6. The goal of Gestalt therapy is to rebuild thinking, feeling, and acting into connected _____ and to help clients break through _____ in experience.

7. The Gestalt approach is more _____ than client-centered therapy or existential therapy, and encourages clients to become fully aware of their feelings.

8. Frederick Perls' Gestalt therapy emphasizes immediate _____ of thoughts and feelings and discourages people from dwelling on what they ought to do or should do.

Therapy at a Distance—Psych Jockeys and Cybertherapy

Survey Question: Can therapy be conducted at a distance? Pages 520-521

1. Media psychologists, such as those found on the radio, are supposed to restrict themselves to _____ listeners, rather than actually doing _____.

2. Media psychologists may cross the line between _____ and therapy.

3. Distance therapies are marked by a lack of _____ cues, such as facial expressions, body language, and tone of voice that may aid a therapist in making a diagnosis

4. Advantages of distance therapy include anonymity, _____ cost, and _____ availability to rural areas.

5. Telephone therapists and cybertherapists working on the _____ may or may not be competent. Even if they are, their effectiveness may be severely limited.

6. In an emerging approach, _____ is being done at a distance, through the use of videoconferencing (two-way _____-_____ links).

Behavior Therapy—Healing by Learning

Survey Question: What is behavior therapy? Pages 522-526

1. Behavior therapists use various behavior modification techniques that apply _____ principles to change human behavior.

2. In behavior modification, classical and _____ conditioning are used to alter behavior.

3. Classical conditioning is a basic form of _____ in which existing reflex responses are _____ with new conditioned stimuli.

4. In aversion therapy, classical conditioning is used to associate maladaptive behavior with _____ or other unpleasant events in order to inhibit undesirable responses.

5. To be most effective, aversive _____ must be response-contingent (closely connected with responses).

6. In desensitization, gradual _____ and reciprocal inhibition break the link between fear and particular situations.

7. Classical conditioning also underlies _____ desensitization, a technique used to reduce fears, phobias, and anxieties.

8. Typical steps in desensitization are: Construct a fear hierarchy, learn to produce total _____, and perform items on the hierarchy (from least to most disturbing).

9. Desensitization may be carried out in real settings or it may be done by vividly _____ scenes from the fear hierarchy.

10. The tension-release method allows individuals, through practice, to _____ their bodies' tensed muscles and to learn to _____ them on command.

11. Desensitization is most effective when it is directly experienced, but it is also effective when it is administered vicariously, that is, when clients watch _____ perform the feared responses.

12. In a newly developed technique, virtual _____ exposure is used to present _____ stimuli to patients undergoing desensitization.

13. Another new technique called eye-movement desensitization and reprocessing (EMDR) shows promise as a treatment for traumatic _____ and _____ disorders.

Operant Therapies—All the World Is a Skinner Box?

Survey Question: What roles do operant principles play in behavior therapy?
Pages 523-526

1. Behavior modification also makes use of operant principles, such as positive reinforcement, nonreinforcement, extinction, punishment, shaping, stimulus _____, and _____ out.

2. Nonreward can extinguish troublesome behaviors. Often this is done by simply identifying and eliminating _____.

3. Time out is an extinction technique in which attention and approval are withheld following undesirable _____.

4. Time out can also be done by _____ a person from the setting in which misbehavior occurs, so that it will not be reinforced.

5. Attention, approval, and concern are subtle _____ that are effective at _____ human behaviors.

6. To apply positive reinforcement and operant shaping, symbolic rewards known as tokens are often used. Tokens allow _____ reinforcement of selected target _____.

7. Full-scale use of _____ in an institutional setting produces a token economy.

8. Toward the end of a token economy program, patients are shifted to social rewards such as recognition and _____.

Cognitive Therapy—Think Positive!

Survey Question: Can therapy change thoughts and emotions? Pages 526-529

1. Cognitive therapy emphasizes changing _____ patterns that underlie emotional or behavioral problems.

2. Aaron Beck's cognitive therapy for depression corrects major distortions in thinking, including _____ perception, overgeneralization, and all-or-nothing _____.

3. The goals of cognitive therapy are to correct distorted thinking and/or teach improved coping _____.

4. In a variation of cognitive therapy called rational-emotive behavior therapy (REBT), clients learn to recognize and challenge their own irrational _____, which lead to upsetting consequences.

5. Some _____ beliefs that lead to conflicts are: I am worthless if I am not loved, I should be _____ competent, I should _____ on others who are stronger than I am, and it is easier for me to avoid difficulties than to face them.

6. Albert Ellis showed clients how their beliefs (B) about an _____ experience (A) ability to cause an emotional consequence (C) led to _____ suffering.

7. Ellis says that most irrational beliefs come from three core ideas: "I _____ perform well and be approved of by significant others," "you _____ treat me fairly," and "conditions _____ be the way I want them to be."

8. The Gambler's Fallacy leads us to believe that a sting of _____ must be soon followed by _____.

9. Individuals who are problem gamblers hold several irrational beliefs, including belief in a _____ gambling skill, errors of _____, the Gambler's Fallacy, selective memory, over _____ of cues, having luck as a trait, and erroneous probability biases.

Group Therapy—People Who Need People

Survey Question: Can psychotherapy be done with groups of people? Pages 529-531

1. Group therapy is _____ done with more than one person.

2. Group therapies have the advantages of allowing individuals to _____ _____ or directly experience their problems and gathering support and input from those who have _____ problems.

3. Group therapy may be a simple extension of _____ methods or it may be based on techniques developed specifically for groups.

4. In psychodrama, individuals use _____ playing, _____ reversals, and the mirror technique to gain insight into incidents resembling their real-life problems.

5. In family therapy, the family group is treated as a _____ so that the entire _____ system is changed for the better.

6. Although they are not literally _____, sensitivity groups and encounter groups attempt to encourage positive personality change.

7. In recent years, commercially offered large-group awareness _____ have become popular.

8. The therapeutic benefits of large-group techniques are questionable and may reflect nothing more than a _____ placebo effect.

Psychotherapy—An Overview

Survey Question: What do various therapies have in common? Pages 534-538

1. After 13 to 18 weekly one-hour therapy sessions, _____ percent of all patients showed an improvement. However, the average patient receives only _____ therapy sessions and only 20 percent of patients reported feeling better.

2. Almost all psychotherapies have the _____ of restoring hope, courage and optimism; gaining insight; resolving conflicts; and changing _____ patterns of behavior.

3. To alleviate personal problems, all psychotherapies offer a caring relationship and _____ rapport in a protected _____.

4. All therapies encourage catharsis, and they provide explanations for the client's _____.

5. In addition, psychotherapy provides a new perspective and a chance to practice new _____.

6. Psychotherapy in the future may include short-term therapy, _____-focused approaches, _____-help groups, Internet services, _____ counseling, paraprofessional, and master-level practitioners.

7. Many basic _____ skills are used in therapy. These include listening actively and helping to clarify the problem.

8. Effective therapists also focus on feelings and avoid giving unwanted _____.

9. It helps to accept the person's perspective, to reflect thoughts and feelings, and to be patient during _____.

10. In counseling it is important to use _____ questions when possible and to maintain confidentiality.

11. Many _____ barriers to effective counseling and therapy exist.

12. Culturally skilled _____ have the knowledge and skills needed to intervene successfully in the lives of clients from diverse cultural backgrounds.

13. Culturally skilled therapists must be able to establish rapport with a person from a _____ cultural background and adapt traditional theories and techniques to meet the needs of clients from non-European ethnic or racial groups.

Medical Therapies—Psychiatric Care

Survey Question: How do psychiatrists treat psychological disorders? Pages 535-539

1. Three _____ (bodily) approaches to treatment of psychosis are pharmacotherapy (use of _____), electroconvulsive therapy (ECT) (brain shock for the treatment of depression), and psychosurgery (surgical alteration of the _____).

2. Pharmacotherapy is done with _____ (minor tranquilizers to reduce anxiety), antipsychotics (which reduce delusions and _____), and antidepressants (_____ elevators).

3. All psychiatric drugs involve a trade-off between _____ and benefits. Many have unpleasant or harmful _____ effects.

4. In electroconvulsive therapy (ECT), electrical current is passed through the brain to produce a seizure that is thought to "reset" the _____ and hormonal balance.

5. Implanted electrodes may allow for _____ brain stimulation.

6. If psychosurgery is necessary, deep _____, where a small targeted area in the brain is _____, is the preferred alternative to a lobotomy.

7. _____ or _____ hospitalization is considered a form of treatment for mental disorders.

8. Prolonged hospitalization has been discouraged by deinstitutionalization (reduced use of commitment to treat mental disorders) and by _____-hospitalization policies.

9. Halfway _____ within the community can help people make the transition from a hospital or institution to _____ living.

10. Community mental health centers were created to help avoid or minimize _____.

11. Community mental health centers also have as their goal the prevention of mental health problems through education, consultation, and _____ intervention.

Psychology in Action: Self-Management and Seeking Professional Help

Survey Questions: How are behavioral principles applied to everyday problems? How could a person find professional help? Pages 539-545

1. In covert sensitization, aversive _____ are used to discourage unwanted behavior.

2. Thought stopping uses mild _____ to prevent upsetting thoughts.

3. Covert reinforcement is a way to encourage desired _____ by mental rehearsal.

4. Desensitization pairs _____ with a hierarchy of upsetting images in order to lessen fears.

5. In most communities, a competent and reputable therapist can usually be located through public sources of information or by a _____.

6. Practical considerations such as _____ (or _____) and qualifications enter into choosing a therapist. However, the therapist's personal characteristics are of equal importance.

7. Self-help _____, made up of people who share similar problems, can sometimes add valuable support to professional treatment.

CONNECTIONS

Psychotherapy—The Talking Cure; Origins of Therapy—Bored Out of Your Skull; and Psychoanalysis—Expedition into the Unconscious

Survey Questions: How do psychotherapies differ? How did psychotherapy originate? Is Freudian psychoanalysis still used? Pages 510-514

1. _____ positive therapy
2. _____ trepanning
3. _____ exorcism
4. _____ Brief psychodynamic therapy
5. _____ ergotism
6. _____ Phillipe Pinel
7. _____ free association
8. _____ Sigmud Freud
9. _____ dream analysis
10. _____ transference

A. tainted rye
B. old relationships
C. hysteria
D. Bicêtre Asylum
E. latent content
F. possession
G. enhanced personal strength
G. release of evil spirits
I. saying anything on mind
J. direct questioning

Humanistic Therapies—Restoring Human Potential;Can and Therapy at a Distance—Psych Jockeys and Cybertherapy

Survey Question: What are the major humanistic therapies? Can therapy be conducted at a distance? Pages 514-518

1. _____ telephone therapy
2. _____ authenticity
3. _____ unconditional positive regards
4. _____ Empathy
5. _____ rephrasing
6. _____ Atmosphere of growth
7. _____ distance therapy
8. _____ existentialist
9. _____ Media psychologist
10. _____ Carl Rogers
11. _____ Gestalt therapy

A. reflection
B. client centered
C. no facades
D. being in the world
E. lacking visual cues
F. video counseling
G. whole experiences
H. unshakable personal acceptance
I. client centered therapy
J. through client's eyes
K. public education

Behavior Therapy—Healing by Learning

Survey Question: What is behavior therapy? Pages 518-523

1. _____ behavior modification
2. _____ unconditioned response
3. _____ Reciprocal inhibition
4. _____ virtual reality exposure
5. _____ Tension-release
6. _____ vicarious desensitization
7. _____ Immediate discomfort
8. _____ Systematic desensitization
9. _____ Eye Movement Desensitization and Reprocessing (EMDR)
10. _____ rapid smoking

A. unlearned reaction
B. easing post-traumatic stress
C. secondhand learning
D. applied behavior analysis
E. aversion therapy
F. fear hierarchy
G. computer-generated fear images
H. response-contingent shocks
I. one emotion blocks another
J. deep muscle relaxation

Operant Therapies—All the World Is a Skinner Box? and Cognitive Therapy—Think Positive!

Survey Questions: What role do operant principles play in behavior therapy? Can therapy change thoughts and emotions? Pages 523-529

1. _____ overgeneralization
2. _____ Aaron Beck
3. _____ Gambler's Fallace
4. _____ time-out
5. _____ All-or-nothing thinking
6. _____ Exchange behaviors for goods/services
7. _____ Rational Emotive Behavioral Therapy (REBT)
8. _____ Albert Ellis
9. _____ symbolic rewards

A. removing reinforcement
B. tokens
C. cognitive therapy
D. thinking error
E. irrational beliefs
F. token economy
G. right or wrong
H. ABC
I. Losses then wins

Group Therapy—People Who Need People; Psychotherapy—An Overview; and Medical Therapies—Psychiatric Care

Survey Questions: Can psychotherapy be done with groups of people? What do various therapies have in common? How do psychiatrists treat psychological disorders? Pages 529-539

1. _____ psychodrama
2. _____ family therapy
3. _____ Valium
4. _____ sensitivity group
5. _____ Group therapy
6. _____ encounter group
7. _____ Clozaril
8. _____ basic counseling skills
9. _____ Community facility
10. _____ therapeutic alliance
11. _____ Zoloft
12. _____ catharsis
13. _____ pharmacotherapy
14. _____ Electro-Convulsive Therapy (ECT)
15. _____ psychosurgery

A. avoid giving advice
B. enhanced self-awareness
C. emotional release
D. cause of memory loss
E. prefrontal lobotomy
F. systems approach
G. drug therapy
H. role reversals
I. caring relationship
J. intense interactions
K. Alcoholics Anonymous
L. Anxiolytic
M. Antidepressant
N. Antipsychotic
O. halfway house

Psychology in Action: Self-Management and Seeking Professional Help

Survey Questions: How are behavioral principles applied to everyday problems? How could a person find professional help? Pages 539-545

1. _____ covert reinforcement
2. _____ unethical practices
3. _____ Crisis hotline
4. _____ qualified therapist
5. _____ Thought-stopping
6. _____ covert sensitization
7. _____ Peer counselors
8. _____ self-help group

A. positive imagery
B. shared problems
C. aversive imagery
D. therapist encourages dependency
E. American Psychiatrist Association
F. prevent upsetting thoughts
G. telephone service
H. nonprofessional helpers

CHECK YOUR MEMORY

Psychotherapy—The Talking Cure

Survey Questions: How do psychotherapies differ? Pages 510

1. A goal of positive therapy is to "fix" a person's weaknesses to enhance their personal strength.

TRUE or FALSE

2. A particular psychotherapy could be both insight- and action-oriented.

TRUE or FALSE

3. With the help of psychotherapy, chances of improvement are fairly good for phobias and low self-esteem.

TRUE or FALSE

4. Psychotherapy is sometimes used to encourage personal growth for people who are already functioning well.

TRUE or FALSE

5. Personal autonomy, a sense of identity, and feelings of personal worth are elements of mental health.

TRUE or FALSE

6. Psychotherapy usually involves personal transformation – a major "overhaul" of the psyche

TRUE or FALSE

Origins of Therapy—Bored Out of Your Skull

Survey Question: How did psychotherapy originate? Pages 511

1. Trepanning was really an excuse to kill people since none of the patients survived.

TRUE or FALSE

2. Exorcism sometimes took the form of physical torture.

TRUE or FALSE

3. Trepanning was the most common treatment for ergotism.

TRUE or FALSE

4. Modern evidence suggests that those treated in the past for demon possession likely suffered from psychological disorders, such as depression and schizophrenia.

TRUE or FALSE

5. Phillipe Pinel was the first person to successfully treat ergotism.

TRUE or FALSE

6. The problem Freud called hysteria is now called a somatoform disorder.

TRUE or FALSE

7. The first psychotherapy was created by Phillipe Pinel in Paris in 1793

TRUE or FALSE

Psychoanalysis—Expedition into the Unconscious

Survey Question: Is Freudian psychoanalysis still used? Pages 512-514

1. During free association, patients try to remember the earliest events in their lives.

TRUE or FALSE

2. Freud called transference "the royal road to the unconscious."

TRUE or FALSE

3. Using dream analysis, a therapist seeks to uncover the latent content or symbolic meaning of a person's dreams.

TRUE or FALSE

4. The manifest content of a dream is its surface or visible meaning.

TRUE or FALSE

5. In an analysis of resistance, the psychoanalyst tries to understand a client's resistance to forming satisfying relationships.

TRUE or FALSE

6. Therapists use direct interviewing as part of brief psychodynamic therapy.

TRUE or FALSE

7. If members of a waiting list control group improve at the same rate as people in therapy, it demonstrates that the therapy is effective.

TRUE or FALSE

8. The goal of brief psychodynamic therapy explores unconscious conflicts using direct questioning.

TRUE or FALSE

Humanistic Therapies—Restoring Human Potential

Survey Question: What are the major humanistic therapies? Pages 514-516

1. Through client-centered therapy, Carl Rogers sought to explore unconscious thoughts and feelings.

TRUE or FALSE

2. The client-centered therapist does not hesitate to react with shock, dismay, or disapproval to a client's inappropriate thoughts or feelings.

TRUE or FALSE

3. In a sense, the person-centered therapist acts as a psychological mirror for clients.

TRUE or FALSE

4. Existential therapy emphasizes our ability to freely make choices.

TRUE or FALSE

5. According to the existentialists, our choices must be courageous.

TRUE or FALSE

6. Existential therapy emphasizes the integration of fragmented experiences into connected wholes.

TRUE or FALSE

7. Gestalt therapy may be done individually or in a group.

TRUE or FALSE

8. Gestalt therapists urge clients to intellectualize their feelings.

TRUE or FALSE

Therapy at a Distance—Psych Jockeys and Cybertherapy

Survey Question: Can therapy be conducted at a distance? Pages 516-518

1. The APA suggests that media psychologists should discuss only problems of a general nature.

TRUE or FALSE

2. Under certain conditions, telephone therapy can be as successful as face-to-face therapy.

TRUE or FALSE

3. Telephone counseling is positively related to the success rate for smokers trying to quit.

TRUE or FALSE

4. The problem with doing therapy by videoconferencing is that facial expressions are not available to the therapist or the client.

TRUE or FALSE

5. Anonymity and reduced cost are two advantages of distance counseling and therapy services

TRUE or FALSE

Behavior Therapy—Healing by Learning

Survey Question: What is behavior therapy? Pages 518-523

1. Behavior modification, or applied behavior analysis, uses classical and operant conditioning to directly alter human behavior.

TRUE or FALSE

2. Aversion therapy is based primarily on operant conditioning.

TRUE or FALSE

3. For many children, the sight of a hypodermic needle becomes a conditioned stimulus for fear because it is often followed by pain.

TRUE or FALSE

4. Rapid smoking creates an aversion because people must hyperventilate to smoke at the prescribed rate.

TRUE or FALSE

5. In aversion therapy for alcohol abuse, the delivery of shock must appear to be response-contingent to be most effective.

TRUE or FALSE

6. Poor generalization of conditioned aversions to situations outside of therapy can be a problem.

TRUE or FALSE

7. During desensitization, the steps of a hierarchy are used to produce deep relaxation.

TRUE or FALSE

8. Relaxation is the key ingredient of reciprocal inhibition.

TRUE or FALSE

9. Clients typically begin with the most disturbing item in a desensitization hierarchy.

TRUE or FALSE

10. Desensitization is most effective when people are directly exposed to feared stimuli.

TRUE or FALSE

11. The tension-release method is used to produce deep relaxation.

TRUE or FALSE

12. Live or filmed models are used in vicarious desensitization.

TRUE or FALSE

13. During eye-movement desensitization and reprocessing (EMDR), clients concentrate on pleasant, calming images.

TRUE or FALSE

Operant Therapies—All the World Is a Skinner Box?

Survey Question: What role do operant principles play in behavior therapy?
Pages 523-526

1. Operant punishment is basically the same thing as nonreinforcement.

TRUE or FALSE

2. Shaping involves reinforcing ever closer approximations to a desired response.

TRUE or FALSE

3. An undesirable response can be extinguished by reversing stimulus control.

TRUE or FALSE

4. Misbehavior tends to decrease when others ignore it.

TRUE or FALSE

5. To be effective, tokens must be tangible rewards, such as slips of paper or poker chips.

TRUE or FALSE

6. The value of tokens is based on the fact that they can be exchanged for other reinforcers.

TRUE or FALSE

7. A time-out involves removing an individual from a situation in which reinforcement occurs

TRUE or FALSE

8. A goal of token economies is to eventually switch patients to social reinforcers.

TRUE or FALSE

Cognitive Therapy—Think Positive!

Survey Question: Can therapy change thoughts and emotions? Pages 526-529

1. Cognitive therapy is especially successful in treating depression.

TRUE or FALSE

2. In overgeneralization, there is a tendency to think that one upsetting event applies to other unrelated situations

TRUE or FALSE

3. Depressed persons tend to magnify the importance of events.

TRUE or FALSE

4. Cognitive therapy is as effective as drugs for treating many cases of depression.

TRUE or FALSE

5. Stress inoculation is a form of rational-emotive behavior therapy (REBT).

TRUE or FALSE

6. The A in the ABC analysis of REBT stands for "anticipation."

TRUE or FALSE

7. The C in the ABC analysis of REBT stands for "consequence."

TRUE or FALSE

8. According to Rational Emotive Behavioral Therapy (REBT), you would hold an irrational belief if you believe that you should depend on others who are stronger than you.

TRUE or FALSE

9. Individuals who are problem gamblers often have cognitive distortions related to gambling

TRUE or FALSE

10. Problem gamblers often attribute wins to good luck, but losses to poor skill.

TRUE or FALSE

Group Therapy—People Who Need People

Survey Question: Can psychotherapy be done with groups of people? Pages 529-531

1. Group therapy was first conducted to take advantage of input from individuals suffering the same problems

TRUE or FALSE

2. In both psychodrama and role-reversal, problems are re-enacted to encourage individuals to consider other perspectives

TRUE or FALSE

3. The mirror technique is the principal method used in family therapy.

TRUE or FALSE

4. Family therapists try to meet with the entire family unit during each session of therapy.

TRUE or FALSE

5. The therapy placebo effect occurs when individuals attribute improvements to the medication they receive during group therapy.

TRUE or FALSE

6. A "trust walk" is a typical sensitivity group exercise.

TRUE or FALSE

7. Sensitivity groups attempt to tear down defenses and false fronts.

TRUE or FALSE

8. Large-group awareness training has been known to create emotional crises where none existed before.

TRUE or FALSE

Psychotherapy—An Overview

Survey Question: What do various therapies have in common? Pages 531-535

1. In all psychotherapies, a therapeutic alliance must be created in a protected setting.

TRUE or FALSE

2. Half of all people who begin psychotherapy feel better after 13-18 sessions.

TRUE or FALSE

3. Emotional rapport is a key feature of the therapeutic alliance.

TRUE or FALSE

4. Therapy gives clients a chance to practice new behaviors.

TRUE or FALSE

5. An increase in short-term therapy, telephone counseling, and self-help groups in the future is likely the result of the high cost of mental health services.

TRUE or FALSE

6. Regarding the future of psychotherapy, experts predict that the use of psychoanalysis will increase.

TRUE or FALSE

7. Competent counselors do not hesitate to criticize clients, place blame when it is deserved, and probe painful topics.

TRUE or FALSE

8. Closed questions tend to be most helpful in counseling another person.

TRUE or FALSE

9. Cultural barriers to effective counseling include differences in language, social class, and non-verbal communication.

TRUE or FALSE

10. A necessary step toward becoming a culturally skilled therapist is to adopt the culture of your clients as your own.

TRUE or FALSE

Medical Therapies—Psychiatric Care

Survey Question: How do psychiatrists treat psychological disorders? Pages 535-539

1. Major mental disorders are primarily treated with psychotherapy.

TRUE or FALSE

2. When used for long periods of time, major tranquilizers can cause a neurological disorder.

TRUE or FALSE

3. Two percent of all patients taking clozaril suffer from a serious blood disease.

TRUE or FALSE

4. The use of drugs in the treatment of major psychological disorders has allowed people to return to the community, where they can be treated on an outpatient basis

TRUE or FALSE

5. Major tranquilizers, produce relaxation or reduce anxiety.

TRUE or FALSE

6. Electro-Convulsive Therapy (ECT) treatments are usually given in a series of 20 to 30 sessions, occurring once a day.

TRUE or FALSE

7. ECT is most effective when used to treat depression.

TRUE or FALSE

8. To reduce a relapse, antidepressant drugs are recommended for patients with depression following ECT treatment.

TRUE or FALSE

9. The prefrontal lobotomy is the most commonly performed type of psychosurgery today.

TRUE or FALSE

10. Psychosurgeries performed by deep lesioning can be reversed if necessary.

TRUE or FALSE

11. In the approach known as partial hospitalization, patients live at home.

TRUE or FALSE

12. Admitting a person to a mental institution is the first step to treating the disorder.

TRUE or FALSE

13. Deinstitutionalization increased the number of homeless persons living in many communities.

TRUE or FALSE

14. Most halfway houses are located on the grounds of mental hospitals.

TRUE or FALSE

15. Crisis intervention is typically one of the services provided by community mental health centers.

TRUE or FALSE

16. Most people prefer to seek help from a professional doctor over a paraprofessional because of their approachability.

TRUE or FALSE

Psychology in Action: Self-Management and Seeking Professional Help

Survey Questions: How are behavioral principles applied to everyday problems? How could a person find professional help? Pages 539-545

1. To do covert sensitization, you must first learn relaxation exercises.

TRUE or FALSE

2. Disgusting images are used in thought stopping.

TRUE or FALSE

3. Covert reinforcement should be visualized before performing steps in a fear hierarchy.

TRUE or FALSE

4. Approximately one-third of all American households have someone who has received mental health treatment in the last year.

TRUE or FALSE

5. Significant changes in your work, relationships, or use of drugs or alcohol can be signs that you should seek professional help.

TRUE or FALSE

6. Marital problems are the most common reason for seeing a mental health professional.

TRUE or FALSE

7. For some problems, paraprofessional counselors and self-help groups are as effective as professional psychotherapy.

TRUE or FALSE

8. All major types of psychotherapy are about equally successful.

TRUE or FALSE

9. If your level of psychological discomfort is comparable to a level of physical discomfort for which you would ordinarily go to see a doctor or a dentist, then that is a sign you may want to consider seeing a psychologist

TRUE or FALSE

10. Research suggests that the type of therapy used is more important that the characteristics of the therapist.

TRUE or FALSE

11. All therapists are equally qualified and successful at treating mental disorders.

TRUE or FALSE

12. Therapists who make sexual advances, repeated verbal threats, and encourage prolonged dependence are danger signals to watch for in psychotherapy

TRUE or FALSE

FINAL SURVEY AND REVIEW

Psychotherapy—The Talking Cure

Survey Questions: How do psychotherapies differ? Page 510

1. _____ is any psychological technique used to facilitate positive changes in a person's personality, behavior, or adjustment.

2. Insight therapies seek to produce personal _____. _____ therapies try to directly change troublesome thoughts, feelings, or behaviors without seeking insight into their origins.

3. Directive therapists provide _____ guidance. Nondirective therapists _____, but clients are expected to solve their own problems.

4. Positive therapy seeks to _____ positive traits and actively solve problems; it does not attempt to _____ what is "wrong" with a person.

5. Therapies may be conducted either _____ or in groups, and they may be _____-_____ or time limited (restricted to a set number of sessions).

Origins of Therapy—Bored Out of Your Skull

Survey Question: How did psychotherapy originate? Page 511

1. Primitive approaches to mental illness were often based on superstitious beliefs in _____, witchcraft, and _____.

2. Trepanning, or _____, involved boring a _____ into the skull.

3. Demonology attributed mental disturbance to _____ forces, such as possession by the devil or on _____, and prescribed exorcism as the cure.

4. In some instances, the actual cause of _____ behavior may have been ergotism, or ergot _____ poisoning.

5. More humane treatment began in _____ with the work of Philippe _____, who created the first mental hospital in Paris.

6. _____ _____ is credited with creating psychotherapy while working with cases of hysteria.

Psychoanalysis—Expedition into the Unconscious

Survey Question: Is Freudian psychoanalysis still used? Pages 512-514

1. Sigmund Freud's psychoanalysis was the _____ formal psychotherapy.

2. _____ was designed to treat cases of hysteria (_____ symptoms without known physical causes).

3. Psychoanalysis seeks to release _____ thoughts, memories, and emotions from the unconscious and resolve unconscious _____.

4. The _____ uses free association, dream analysis, and analysis of _____ and transference to reveal health-producing insights.

5. In _____ association, individuals say whatever comes to mind without worrying whether the ideas are painful, embarrassing, or _____.

6. Freud believed that in order to uncover the individual's unconscious desires and feelings, a _____ must conduct dream analysis to discover the latent content that is expressed through the manifest content of a person's dream.

7. Resistances, or _____ in the flow of ideas, may reveal unconscious conflicts

8. _____ is the tendency to transfer feelings from an important person in one's past to the therapist.

9. Brief psychodynamic therapy (which relies on psychoanalytic theory but is brief and focused) is _____ effective as other major therapies.

10. Some critics have argued that traditional psychoanalysis may frequently receive credit for spontaneous _____ of symptoms. However, psychoanalysis has been shown to be better than _____ treatment at all.

Humanistic Therapies—Restoring Human Potential

Survey Question: What are the major humanistic therapies? Pages 514-516

1. Humanistic therapies try to help people live up to their _____ and live rich, rewarding lives. While Sigmund Freud studied the _____, Carl Rogers explored _____ thoughts and feelings.

2. Carl Rogers' _____-_____ (or person-centered) therapy is nondirective and is dedicated to creating a _____ atmosphere of growth.

3. In client-centered therapy, _____ positive regard (unshakable personal acceptance), empathy (feeling what another is feeling), _____ (genuine honesty), and reflection (rephrasing, repeating, and summarizing) are combined to give the client a chance to solve his or her own problems.

4. _____ therapies focus on the problems of existence, such as _____, choice, and responsibility, and on the end result of the choices one makes in life.

5. Clients in existential therapy are encouraged to discover self-imposed _____ in personal identity through confrontation.

6. The goal of _____ therapy is to rebuild thinking, feeling, and acting into connected wholes and to help clients break through gaps in _____.

7. The _____ approach is more directive than client-centered therapy or existential therapy, and encourages clients to become fully _____ of their feelings.

8. Frederick _____' Gestalt therapy emphasizes immediate awareness of thoughts and feelings and _____ people from dwelling on what they ought to do or should do.

Therapy at a Distance—Psych Jockeys and Cybertherapy

Survey Question: Can therapy be conducted at a distance? Pages 520-521

1. _____ psychologists, such as those found on the _____, are supposed to restrict themselves to educating listeners, rather than actually doing therapy.

2. Media psychologists may cross the line between advice and _____.

3. Distance therapies are marked by a lack of interpersonal cues, such as facial _____, body language, and tone of voice that may aid a therapist in making a _____.

4. Advantages of _____ therapy include _____, reduced cost, and increased availability to rural areas.

5. Telephone therapists and _____ working on the Internet may or may not be competent. Even if they are, their effectiveness may be severely _____.

6. In an emerging approach, therapy is being done at a distance, through the use of _____ (two-way audio-video links).

Behavior Therapy—Healing by Learning

Survey Question: What is behavior therapy? Pages 522-526

1. Behavior therapists use various behavior _____ techniques that apply learning principles to _____ human behavior.

2. In behavior modification, _____ and operant conditioning are used to alter behavior.

3. Classical conditioning is a basic form of learning in which existing _____ responses are associated with new _____ stimuli.

4. In _____ therapy, classical conditioning is used to associate _____ behavior with pain or other unpleasant events in order to inhibit undesirable responses.

5. To be most effective, _____ stimuli must be response- _____ (closely connected with responses).

6. In _____, gradual adaptation and reciprocal inhibition break the link between fear and particular situations.

7. Classical conditioning also underlies systematic desensitization, a technique used to reduce fears, _____, and anxieties.

8. Typical steps in desensitization are: Construct a fear _____, learn to produce total relaxation, and perform items on the hierarchy (from _____ to _____ disturbing).

9. Desensitization may be carried out in _____ settings or it may be done by vividly imagining scenes from the fear hierarchy.

10. The _____-release method allows individuals, through practice, to recognize their bodies' _____ muscles and to learn to relax them on command.

11. Desensitization is most effective when it is directly experienced, but it is also effective when it is administered _____, that is, when clients _____ models perform the feared responses.

12. In a newly developed technique, _____ reality exposure is used to present fear stimuli to patients undergoing _____.

13. Another new technique called eye-movement desensitization and _____ (EMDR) shows promise as a treatment for _____ memories and stress disorders.

Operant Therapies—All the World Is a Skinner Box?

Survey Question: What roles do operant principles play in behavior therapy? Pages 523-526

1. Behavior _____ also makes use of operant principles, such as positive reinforcement, _____, extinction, punishment, shaping, stimulus control, and time out.

2. Nonreward can extinguish _____ behaviors. Often this is done by simply identifying and _____ reinforcers.

3. Time out is an _____ technique in which attention and approval are withheld following undesirable responses.

4. Time out can also be done by removing a person from the _____ in which misbehavior occurs, so that it will not be _____.

5. Attention, _____, and concern are subtle reinforcers that are effective at maintaining human _____.

6. To apply _____ reinforcement and operant shaping, symbolic rewards known as _____ are often used. Tokens allow immediate reinforcement of selected target behaviors.

7. Full-scale use of tokens in an institutional setting produces a token _____.

8. Toward the end of a token economy program, patients are shifted to _____ rewards such as recognition and approval.

Cognitive Therapy—Think Positive!

Survey Question: Can therapy change thoughts and emotions? Pages 526-529

1. _____ therapy emphasizes changing thinking patterns that underlie _____ or behavioral problems.

2. Aaron _____ cognitive therapy for depression corrects major _____ in thinking, including selective perception, overgeneralization, and all-or-nothing thinking.

3. The goals of _____ therapy are to correct distorted _____ and/or teach improved coping skills.

4. In a variation of cognitive therapy called _____-emotive behavior therapy (REBT), clients learn to recognize and challenge their own irrational beliefs, which lead to upsetting _____.

5. Some irrational beliefs that lead to conflicts are: I am worthless if I am not loved, I _____ be completely competent, I _____ depend on others who are stronger than I am, and it is easier for me to _____ difficulties than to face them.

6. Albert Ellis showed clients how their _____ (B) about an activating experience (A) ability to cause an emotional _____ (C) led to unnecessary suffering.

7. Ellis says that most _____ beliefs come from three core ideas: "I must perform well and be approved of by significant others," "you must treat me fairly," and "_____ must be the way I want them to be."

8. The Gambler's _____ leads us to believe that a sting of losses must be soon followed by wins.

9. Individuals who are problem gamblers hold several irrational beliefs, including belief in a magnified gambling _____, errors of attribution, the Gambler's Fallacy, _____ memory, over interpretation of cues, having luck as a trait, and erroneous probability biases.

Group Therapy—People Who Need People

Survey Question: Can psychotherapy be done with groups of people? Pages 529-531

1. _____ therapy is psychotherapy done with more than one person.

2. Group therapies have the _____ of allowing individuals to act out or directly experience their _____ and gathering support and input from those who have similar problems.

3. _____ therapy may be a simple extension of individual methods or it may be based on techniques developed specifically for groups.

4. In _____, individuals use role playing, role reversals, and the mirror technique to gain insight into incidents resembling their real-life problems.

5. In _____ therapy, the family group is treated as a unit so that the entire family system is changed for the better.

6. Although they are not literally psychotherapies, _____ groups and encounter groups attempt to encourage _____ personality change.

7. In recent years, commercially offered large-group _____ trainings have become popular.

8. The therapeutic benefits of _____-_____ techniques are questionable and may reflect nothing more than a therapy _____ effect.

Psychotherapy—An Overview

Survey Question: What do various therapies have in common? Pages 534-538

1. After 13 to 18 weekly _____-_____ therapy sessions, 50 percent of all patients showed an improvement. However, the average patient receives only five therapy sessions and only _____ percent of patients reported feeling better.

2. Almost all psychotherapies have the goals of restoring hope, _____ and optimism; gaining insight; _____ conflicts; and changing unacceptable patterns of behavior.

3. To alleviate personal problems, all _____ offer a caring relationship and emotional rapport in a protected setting.

4. All therapies encourage _____, and they provide explanations for the client's problems.

5. In addition, psychotherapy provides a new _____ and a chance to practice new behaviors.

6. Psychotherapy in the future may include short-term therapy, solution-focused approaches, self-help groups, _____ services, telephone _____, _____, and master-level practitioners.

7. Many basic counseling skills are used in therapy. These include listening _____ and helping to _____ the problem.

8. Effective therapists also focus on _____ and avoid giving unwanted advice.

9. It helps to accept the person's _____, to reflect thoughts and feelings, and to be patient during silences.

10. In counseling it is important to use open questions when possible and to maintain _____.

11. Many cultural _____ to effective counseling and therapy exist.

12. _____ skilled therapists have the knowledge and skills needed to intervene successfully in the lives of clients from _____ cultural backgrounds.

13. Culturally skilled therapists must be able to establish _____ with a person from a different _____ background and adapt traditional theories and techniques to meet the needs of clients from non-European _____ or racial groups.

Medical Therapies—Psychiatric Care

Survey Question: How do psychiatrists treat psychological disorders? Pages 535-539

1. Three somatic (bodily) approaches to treatment of psychosis are _____ (use of drugs), electroconvulsive therapy (ECT) (brain shock for the treatment of depression), and _____ (surgical alteration of the brain).

2. Pharmacotherapy is done with anxiolytics (minor tranquilizers to reduce _____), antipsychotics (which reduce _____ and hallucinations), and antidepressants (mood _____).

3. All psychiatric _____ involve a trade-off between risks and benefits. Many have unpleasant or _____ side effects.

4. In _____ therapy (ECT), electrical current is passed through the brain to produce a _____ that is thought to "reset" the biochemical and hormonal balance.

5. Implanted _____ may allow for precise brain stimulation.

6. If _____ is necessary, deep lesioning, where a small targeted area in the brain is destroyed, is the preferred alternative to a lobotomy.

7. Mental or Psychiatric _____ is considered a form of treatment for mental disorders.

8. Prolonged hospitalization has been discouraged by _____ (reduced use of commitment to treat mental disorders) and by partial-hospitalization policies.

9. _____ houses within the community can help people make the _____ from a hospital or institution to independent living.

10. _____ mental health centers were created to help avoid or minimize hospitalization.

11. Community mental health centers also have as their goal the prevention of mental health problems through _____, consultation, and crisis intervention.

Psychology in Action: Self-Management and Seeking Professional Help

Survey Questions: How are behavioral principles applied to everyday problems? How could a person find professional help? Pages 539-545

1. In _____ sensitization, aversive images are used to discourage unwanted behavior.

2. Thought _____ uses mild punishment to prevent upsetting thoughts.

3. Covert _____ is a way to encourage desired responses by mental rehearsal.

4. Desensitization pairs relaxation with a _____ of upsetting images in order to lessen fears.

5. In most communities, a competent and _____ therapist can usually be located through _____ sources of information or by a referral.

6. _____ considerations such as cost (or fees) and qualifications enter into choosing a therapist. However, the therapist's _____ characteristics are of equal importance.

7. _____-_____ groups, made up of people who share similar problems, can sometimes add valuable support to _____ treatment.

MASTERY TEST

1. In desensitization, relaxation is induced to block fear, a process known as
a. systematic adaptation.
b. vicarious opposition.
c. stimulus control.
d. reciprocal inhibition.

2. Role reversals and the mirror technique are methods of
a. psychodrama.
b. person-centered therapy.
c. family therapy.
d. brief psychodynamic therapy.

3. One thing that both trepanning and exorcism have in common is that both were used
a. to treat ergotism.
b. by Pinel in the Bicêtre Asylum.
c. to remove spirits.
d. to treat cases of hysteria.

4. Many of the claimed benefits of large-group awareness trainings appear to represent a therapy _____ effect.
a. remission
b. education
c. placebo
d. transference

5. Inducing seizures is a standard part of using
a. Gestalt therapy.
b. antidepressants.
c. Electro-convulsive Therapy (ECT).
d. cybertherapy.

6. Which counseling behavior does not belong with the others listed here?
a. paraphrasing
b. judging
c. reflecting
d. active listening

7. Identification of target behaviors is an important step in designing
a. a desensitization hierarchy.
b. activating stimuli.
c. token economies.
d. encounter groups.

8. A person who wants to lose weight looks at a dessert and visualizes maggots crawling all over it. The person is obviously using
a. systematic adaptation.
b. covert sensitization.
c. stress inoculation.
d. systematic desensitization.

9. Which of the following is NOT a humanistic therapy?
a. client-centered
b. Gestalt
c. existential
d. cognitive

10. Not many emergency room doctors drive without using their seatbelts. This observation helps explain the effectiveness of
a. systematic desensitization.
b. aversion therapy.
c. covert reinforcement.
d. the mirror technique.

11. Telephone counselors have little chance of using which element of effective psychotherapy?
a. empathy
b. nondirective reflection
c. the therapeutic alliance
d. accepting the person's frame of reference

12. Which of the following is a self-management technique?
a. thought stopping
b. vicarious reality exposure
c. REBT
d. EMDR

13. A good example of a nondirective insight therapy is _____ therapy.
a. client-centered
b. Gestalt
c. psychoanalytic
d. brief psychodynamic

14. Which statement about psychotherapy is true?
a. Most therapists are equally successful.
b. Most techniques are equally successful.
c. Therapists and clients need not agree about the goals of therapy.
d. Effective therapists instruct their clients not to discuss their therapy with anyone else.

15. Analysis of resistances and transferences is a standard feature of
a. client-centered therapy.
b. Gestalt therapy.
c. REBT.
d. psychoanalysis.

16. Both classical and operant conditioning are the basis for
a. desensitization.
b. token economies.
c. behavior therapy.
d. aversion therapy.

17. Rational-emotive behavior therapy is best described as
a. insight, nondirective, individual.
b. insight, supportive, individual.
c. action, supportive, group.
d. action, directive, individual.

18. Deep lesioning is a form of
a. ECT.
b. psychosurgery.
c. pharmacotherapy.
d. PET.

19. Identifying and removing rewards is a behavioral technique designed to bring about
a. operant shaping.
b. extinction.
c. respondent aversion.
d. token inhibition.

20. Culturally skilled therapists must be aware of their own cultural backgrounds, as well as
a. the percentage of ethnic populations in the community.
b. that of their clients.
c. the importance of maintaining confidentiality.
d. the life goals of minorities.

21. A behavioral therapist would treat acrophobia with
a. desensitization.
b. aversion therapy.
c. covert sensitization.
d. cybertherapy.

22. Which technique most closely relates to the idea of nondirective therapy?
a. confrontation
b. dream analysis
c. role reversal
d. reflection

23. Overgeneralization is a thinking error that contributes to
a. depression.
b. somatization.
c. phobias.
d. emotional reprocessing.

24. An intense awareness of present experience and breaking through emotional impasses is the heart of
a. action therapy.
b. Gestalt therapy.
c. time-limited therapy.
d. REBT.

25. Which of the following in NOT a "distance therapy"?
a. REBT
b. telephone therapy
c. cybertherapy
d. telehealth

26. Virtual reality exposure is a type of
a. psychodrama.
b. ECT therapy.
c. cognitive therapy.
d. desensitization.

27. Electro-convulsive Therapy (ECT) is most often used to treat
a. psychosis.
b. anxiety.
c. hysteria.
d. depression.

28. Which of the following is most often associated with community mental health programs?
a. pharmacotherapy
b. covert reinforcement
c. crisis intervention
d. REBT

29. An element of positive mental health that therapists seek to promote is
a. dependency on therapist.
b. a sense of identity.
c. personal autonomy and independence.
d. both B and C

30. Which theory relies on dream analysis to uncover the unconscious roots of neurosis?
a. existential
b. psychoanalytic
c. client-centered
d. telehealth

31. Experts predict that, in the near future, traditional forms of psychotherapy will be replaced by short-term, solution-focused, telephone, and self-help group therapy; this is a reflection of
a. the lack of time available in people's busy lives to seek mental health services.
b. fewer people needing mental health services.
c. societal pressures to reduce costs of mental health services.
d. people being afraid to reveal their mental illness .

32. A therapist shows a patient complete acceptance, regardless of what the patient says during therapy; the therapist is showing the patient
a. desensitization.
b. remission.
c. unconditional positive regard.
d. conditional positive regard.

33. Whenever Dr. Thorp asks his patient, Judy, about her mother, she changes the subject or refuses to talk until Dr. Thorp moves on to something else. This best represents
a. resistance.
b. transference.
c. symbolization.
d. free association.

34. During therapy, Timothy is encouraged to examine the assumption that he must be successful in every domain of life in order to be a person of any worth. This best fits which form of therapy?
a. psychoanalytic
b. Gestalt therapy
c. rational-emotive behavior therapy
d. telephone therapy

LANGUAGE DEVELOPMENT
Therapies

Word Roots

Therapeia in Greek means "treatment" and is derived from another Greek word, *therapeuein* (to attend, nurse, or administer treatment to). Two important terms in this chapter derive from this root: *therapy* and *psychotherapy*.

Journey into Psychology: The Duck Syndrome (pg. 509)
- (509) *"I feel like I'm losing my mind":* the stress in my life is more than I can handle
- (509) *absenteeism:* frequent absences

Psychotherapy—The Talking Cure (pgs. 510)
How do psychotherapies ?
- (510) *"major overhaul":* complete repair

Origins of Therapy—Bored Out of Your Skull(pgs. 511)
How did psychotherapy originate?
- (511) *Archeological:* the scientific study of material remains
- (511) *Stone Age:* the first known period of prehistoric human culture characterized by the use of stone tools
- (511) *witchcraft:* use of sorcery or magic by a person (a witch) believed to have such power
- (511) *inhospitable:* harsh, hostile
- (511) *wizards:* persons believed to be skilled in magic
- (511) *squalid:* dirty; filthy
- (511) *psychoanalysis is the "granddaddy" of more modern psychotherapies:* psychoanalysis is the first and oldest form of psychotherapy from which others are descended

Psychoanalysis—Expedition Into the Unconscious (pgs. 512-514)
Is Freudian psychoanalysis still used?
- (512) *stemming from:* coming from or arising from
- (512) *self-defeating:* in opposition to oneself
- (512) *impotence:* inability to perform sexually
- (512) *roadblocks:* large barriers placed on a road to prohibit the passing of vehicles; here used as a metaphor to indicate a barrier to progress

Humanistic Therapies—Restoring Human Potential (pgs. 514-516)

What are the major humanistic therapies?

(514)   *"atmosphere of growth":* conditions that will allow the patient to improve

(515)   *phony fronts:* fake images of ourselves; facades

(515)   *brush with death:* a dangerous situation that could have been fatal

(515)   *maladjusted:* disturbed; confused

(516)   *stop intellectualizing:* stop analyzing the situation

Therapy at a Distance—Psych Jockeys and Cybertherapy (pgs. 516-518)

Can therapy be conducted at a distance?

(516)   *psych jockeys:* radio psychologists; because music announcers on the radio are called "disc jockeys," Coon calls radio psychologists "psych jockeys"

(516)   *cybertherapy:* psychology via computer

(516)   *videoconferencing:* communication through a two-way setup that involves video (through the use of television or computer monitors), audio (through speakerphones or computer speakers), and microphones

(517)   *online:* accessing and using the Internet

(517)   *anonymous:* unidentified

(517)   *intercepted:* read or found out by others

(517)   *Skype:* program that allows individuals to use the internet and camera to both talk to and see each other

Behavior Therapy—Healing by Learning (pgs. 518-523)

What is behavior therapy?

(518)   *covert:* hidden

(518)   *aversion:* intense dislike

(519)   *hypodermic needle:* needle used to inject medication under the skin

(520)   *interminable:* never ending or continuous

(521)   *vicarious:* to experience something through another person

(521)   *claustrophobia:* fear of small, closed-in spaces, such as closets

(522)   *flashbacks:* remembered images of events from the past

(523)   *berserk:* crazy; derives from "berserker," a particularly fierce type of early Norse warrior

Operant Therapies—All the World's Skinner Box? (pgs. 523-526)

What role do operant principles play in behavior therapy?

(523)   *slot machine:* a device in a gambling casino into which a patron puts money and hopes to win a larger amount of money

(524)   *industrial settings:* factories

(524)   *subsided:* lessened

(524) *sheepishly*: in an embarrassed or timid manner

(525) *delinquent*: one who violates or ignores conventional rules and laws.

(525) *mute*: not speaking

(526) *incentive*: motivating factors

Cognitive Therapy—Think Positive! (pgs. 526-529)

Can therapy change thoughts and emotions?

(526) *distortions/distorted*: unclear; misinterpreted

(527) *easy as A-B-C*: easy as learning the alphabet

(527) *"I must be a total zero"*: I must be worthless

(527) *dumped*: abruptly ended a relationship with

(528) *self-talk*: what people tell themselves

Group Therapy—People Who Need People (pgs. 529-531)

Can psychotherapy be done with groups of people?

(530) *role-play*: pretend to be another

(530) *human potential*: belief that humans have the potential to be fully alive and functioning at the highest level possible

(530) *encounter group "casualties"*: refers to people who either quit the group or who were asked to leave.

(531) *versatility*: flexibility; adaptability

Psychotherapy—An Overview (pgs. 531-535)

What do various therapies have in common?

531) *tricky*: difficult

(532) *rapport*: a good relationship

(532) *sanctuary*: a safe place

(533) *distilled*: extracted or taken from

(533) *paraphrasing*: summarizing; rewording

(534) *catharsis*: getting rid of one's problems through the process of purging by releasing emotions

(533) *down about school*: unmotivated or depressed about school

(533) *hassling*: annoying; bothering

(535) *gossip*: to share personal information with someone about other people

Medical Therapies—Psychiatric Care (pgs. 535-539)

How do psychiatrists treat psychological disorders?

(535) *Slant*: bias

(536) *rhythmic*: reoccurring with regularity

(536) *bad spot*: difficult situation

(537) *"vegetables"*: people whose brains only function to the degree of keeping the body alive; they are not conscious and no longer have higher brain functions

(537) *stupor*: a state of limited consciousness

(538) **joined the ranks of the homeless**: become homeless

(538)   ***bright spot:*** something to look forward to; something to be enjoyed

(538)   ***wavering:*** unreliable

(538)   ***"been there":*** have had similar experiences

Psychology in Action: Self-Management and Seeking Professional Help (pgs. 539-545)

How are behavioral principles applied to everyday problems? How could a person find professional help?

(540)   ***curb:*** to control or restrain

(540)   ***"grossed out":*** disgusted

(540)   ***maggots:*** fly larvae; symbol of disgust, as they are usually found around decaying organic matter (e.g., garbage)

(540)   ***"put yourself down":*** criticize yourself harshly

(541)   ***with conviction:*** with force

(542)   ***dismayed:*** upset; alarmed

(544)   ***reputable:*** having a good reputation; honest

(544)   ***integrity:*** honesty

(548)   ***terminate:*** end; stop

Solutions

Recite and Review

Psychotherapy—The Talking Cure

1. positive, behavior
2. Insight
3. guidance
4. positive, traits
5. time

Origins of Therapy—Bored Out of Your Skull

1. superstitious
2. skull
3. exorcism
4. ergot, poisoning
5. mental, hospital
6. psychotherapy

Psychoanalysis—Expedition into the Unconscious

1. psychotherapy
2. physical
3. unconscious, unconscious
4. free, dream
5. embarrassing
6. desires, dream, latent
7. unconscious
8. therapist
9. Brief
10. spontaneous

Humanistic Therapies—Restoring Human Potential

1. Humanistic
2. person, growth
3. positive, empathy
4. choices
5. existential
6. wholes, gaps
7. directive
8. awareness

Therapy at a Distance—Psych Jockeys and Cybertherapy

1. educating, therapy
2. advice
3. interpersonal
4. reduced, increased
5. Internet
6. therapy, audio, video

Behavior Therapy—Healing by Learning

1. learning
2. operant
3. learning, associated
4. pain
5. stimuli
6. adaptation
7. systematic
8. relaxation
9. imagining
10. recognize, relax
11. models
12. reality, fear
13. memories, stress

Operant Therapies—All the World Is a Skinner Box?

1. control, time
2. reinforcers
3. responses
4. removing
5. reinforcers, maintaining
6. immediate, behaviors
7. tokens
8. approval

Cognitive Therapy—Think Positive!

1. thinking
2. selective, thinking
3. skills
4. beliefs
5. irrational, completely, depend
6. activating, unnecessary
7. must, must, must
8. losses, wins
9. magnified, attribution, interpretation

Group Therapy—People Who Need People

1. psychotherapy
2. act, out, similar
3. individual
4. role, role
5. unit, family
6. psychotherapies
7. trainings
8. therapy

Psychotherapy—An Overview

1. 50, five
2. goals, unacceptable
3. emotional, setting
4. problems
5. behaviors
6. solution, self, telephone
7. counseling
8. advice
9. silences
10. open
11. cultural
12. therapists
13. different

Medical Therapies—Psychiatric Care

1. somatic, drugs, brain
2. anxiolytics, hallucinations, mood
3. risks, side
4. biochemical
5. precise
6. lesioning, destroyed
7. Mental, Psychiatric
8. partial
9. houses, independent
10. hospitalization
11. crisis

Psychology in Action: Self-Management and Seeking Professional Help

1. images
2. punishment
3. responses
4. relaxation
5. referral
6. cost
7. groups

CONNECTIONS

Psychotherapy—The Talking Cure; Origins of Therapy—Bored Out of Your Skull; and Psychoanalysis—Expedition into the Unconscious

1. G.	4. J.	7. I.	10. B.
2. H.	5. A.	8. C.	
3. F.	6. D.	9. E.	

Humanistic Therapies—Restoring Human Potential; Can and Therapy at a Distance—Psych Jockeys and Cybertherapy

1. E.	4. J.	7. F.	10. B.
2. C.	5. A.	8. D.	11. G.
3. H.	6. I.	9. K.	

Behavior Therapy—Healing by Learning

1. D.	4. G.	7. H.	10. E.
2. A.	5. J.	8. F.	
3. I.	6. C.	9. B.	

Operant Therapies—All the World Is a Skinner Box? and Cognitive Therapy—Think Positive!

1. D.	4. A.	7. E.
2. C.	5. G.	8. H.
3. I.	6. F.	9. B.

Group Therapy—People Who Need People; Psychotherapy—An Overview; and Medical Therapies—Psychiatric Care

1. H.	5. K.	9. O.	13. G.
2. F.	6. J.	10. I.	14. D.
3. L.	7. N.	11. M.	15. E.
4. B.	8. A.	12. C.	

Psychology in Action: Self-Management and Seeking Professional Help

1. A.	3. G.	5. F.	7. H.
2. D.	4. E.	6. C.	8. B.

Check Your Memory

Psychotherapy—The Talking Cure

1. F		3. T		5. T	
2. T		4. T		6. F	

Origins of Therapy—Bored Out of Your Skull

1. F		3. F		5. F		7. F
2. T		4. T		6. T		

Psychoanalysis—Expedition into the Unconscious

1. F		3. T		5. F		7. F
2. F		4. T		6. T		8. T

Humanistic Therapies—Restoring Human Potential

1. F		4. T		7. F
2. F		5. T		8. T
3. T		6. F		9. F

Therapy at a Distance—Psych Jockeys and Cybertherapy

1. T		3. T		5. T
2. T		4. F		

Behavior Therapy—Healing by Learning

1. T		5. T		9. F		13. F
2. F		6. T		10. T		
3. T		7. F		11. T		
4. F		8. T		12. T		

Operant Therapies—All the World Is a Skinner Box?

1. F		3. F		5. F		7. T
2. T		4. T		6. T		8. T

Cognitive Therapy—Think Positive!

1. T		4. T		7. T		10. F
2. T		5. F		8. T		
3. T		6. F		9. T		

Group Therapy—People Who Need People

1. F	3. F	5. F	7. F
2. T	4. F	6. T	8. T

Psychotherapy—An Overview

1. T	4. T	7. F	10. F
2. T	5. T	8. F	
3. T	6. F	9. T	

Medical Therapies—Psychiatric Care

1. F	5. F	9. F	13. T
2. T	6. F	10. F	14. F
3. T	7. T	11. T	15. T
4. T	8. T	12. F	16. F

Psychology in Action: Self-Management and Seeking Professional Help

1. F	4. F	7. T	10. F
2. F	5. T	8. T	11. F
3. F	6. F	9. T	12. T

Final Survey and Review

Psychotherapy—The Talking Cure

1. Psychotherapy
2. understanding, Action
3. assist
4. nurture; fix
5. individually, open, ended

Origins of Therapy—Bored Out of Your Skull

1. demons, magic
2. trephining, hole
3. supernatural, curses
4. bizarre, fungus
5. 1793, Pinel
6. Sigmund, Freud

Psychoanalysis—Expedition into the Unconscious

1. first
2. Psychoanalysis, physical
3. repressed, conflicts.
4. psychoanalyst, resistance
5. free, illogical.
6. psychoanalyst
7. blockages
8. Transference
9. as
10. remissions, no

Humanistic Therapies—Restoring Human Potential

1. potential, unconscious, conscious
2. client, centered, safe
3. unconditional, authenticity
4. Existential, meaning
5. limitations
6. Gestalt, experience
7. Gestalt, aware
8. Perls, discourages

Therapy at a Distance—Psych Jockeys and Cybertherapy

1. Media, radio
2. therapy
3. expressions, diagnosis.
4. distance, anonymity
5. cybertherapists, limited
6. videoconferencing

Behavior Therapy—Healing by Learning

1. modification, change
2. classical
3. reflex, conditioned
4. aversion, maladaptive
5. aversive, contingent
6. desensitization
7. phobias
8. hierarchy, least, most
9. real
10. tension, tensed
11. vicariously, watch
12. virtual, desensitization
13. reprocessing, traumatic

Operant Therapies—All the World Is a Skinner Box?

1. modification, nonreinforcement
2. troublesome, eliminating
3. extinction
4. setting, reinforced
5. approval, behaviors
6. positive, tokens
7. economy
8. social

Cognitive Therapy—Think Positive!

1. Cognitive, emotional
2. Beck's, distortions
3. cognitive, thinking
4. rational, consequences
5. should, should, avoid
6. beliefs, consequence
7. irrational, conditions
8. Fallacy
9. skill, selective

Group Therapy—People Who Need People

1. Group
2. advantages, problems
3. Group
4. psychodrama
5. family
6. sensitivity, positive
7. awareness
8. large, group, placebo

Psychotherapy—An Overview

1. one, hour, 20
2. courage, resolving
3. psychotherapies
4. catharsis
5. perspective
6. Internet, counseling, paraprofessional
7. actively, clarify
8. feelings
9. perspective
10. confidentiality
11. barriers
12. Culturally, diverse
13. rapport, cultural, ethnic

Medical Therapies—Psychiatric Care

1. pharmacotherapy, psychosurgery
2. anxiety, delusions, elevators
3. drugs, harmful
4. electroconvulsive, seizure
5. electrodes
6. psychosurgery
7. hospitalization
8. deinstitutionalization
9. Halfway, transition
10. Community
11. education

Psychology in Action: Self-Management and Seeking Professional Help

1. covert
2. stopping
3. reinforcement
4. hierarchy
5. reputable, public
6. Practical, personal
7. Self, help, professional

Mastery Test

1. d, p. 520
2. a, p. 530
3. c, p. 511
4. c, p. 530-531
5. c, p. 536
6. b, p. 533-534
7. c, p. 525
8. b, p. 540
9. d, p. 514-516
10. b, p. 519
11. c, p. 516-518; 532
12. a, 540-541

13. a, p. 514
14. b, p. 531-532
15. d, p. 512-513
16. c, p. 518
17. d, p. 527-528; 532
18. b, p. 537
19. b, p. 523
20. b, p. 534
21. a, p. 520
22. d, p. 510; 515
23. a, p. 526
24. b, p. 515-516

25. a, p. 515-518
26. d, p. 521-522
27. d, p. 536
28. c, p. 543
29. d, p. 510
30. b, p. 512
31. c, p. 532-533
32. c, p. 515
33. a, p. 512
34. c, p. 527-528

CHAPTER 14

Social Behavior

Chapter Overview

Social psychology is the study of behavior in social situations. Affiliating with others is related to needs for approval, support, friendship, information, and reassurance. Social comparison theory holds that we affiliate to evaluate our actions, feelings, and abilities.

Interpersonal attraction is increased by physical proximity, frequent contact, physical attractiveness, competence, similarity, and self-disclosure. Romantic love is marked by mutual absorption between lovers who also like one another. Sternberg's Triangular Theory of Love proposes that different kinds of love evolve from different combinations of intimacy, passion, and commitment. Evolutionary psychology attributes human mating patterns to the reproductive challenges faced by men and women since the dawn of time.

Social groups that we belong to and the roles we take on greatly influence our behaviors. The dimensions of any group include group structure, cohesion, and norms. Group cohesiveness is strong for in-group members who tend to attribute positive traits to members of the group. Negative qualities tend to be attributed to out-group members.

Attribution theory summarizes how we make inferences about behavior. The fundamental attributional error is to think that the actions of others are the result of internal causes. Because of an actor-observer bias, we tend to attribute our own behavior to external causes.

Social influence refers to how our behavior is changed by the behavior of others, and can range form mild (mere presence of others) to strong (coercion). The mere presence of others can improve or impair performance. Group sanctions, importance of belonging to a group, group size, and unanimity affect conformity. In groupthink, the need to maintain group approval overrides critical thinking, but can be prevented. Foot-in-the-door, Door-in-the-face, and the Low-Ball are all techniques for soliciting compliance, which is bending to the wishes of a non-authority. Milgram's shock studies on obedience found that individuals will obey a legitimate authority long after demands have become unreasonable, although decreased proximity to authority reduced obedience

Coercion is used to force someone to change his or her beliefs or behavior against their will. Brainwashing is a type of coercion that forces change through unfreezing, change, and refreezing. Cults often use high-pressure techniques similar to brainwashing to recruit new members.

Self-assertion is one method to reduce the pressure to conform, obey, and comply with others' suggestions. Self-assertion involves clearly stating your wants and needs to others without hurting others. Learning to be assertive can be aided by rehearsal and role-playing.

Attitudes have belief, emotional, and action components. Attitudes are formed through direct contact, interacting with others, childrearing, group membership, the mass media, and chance conditioning. Attitude change is related to reference group membership, to deliberate persuasion, and to personal experiences. Effective persuasion occurs when characteristics of the communicator, the message, and the audience are well matched. Cognitive dissonance theory explains how attitudes are maintained and changed.

Prejudice is a negative attitude held toward out-group members. Prejudice can be attributed to scapegoating, personal prejudice, group prejudice, and authoritarian personality traits. Intergroup conflict leads to hostility and stereotyping. Status inequalities tend to build prejudices. Equal-status contact and superordinate goals tend to reduce these problems.

Ethologists blame aggression on instincts. Biological explanations emphasize brain mechanisms and physical factors. Aggression tends to follow frustration, especially when aggression cues are present. Social learning theory relates aggressive behavior to the influence of aggressive models, including those found in the media. Parents can effectively reduce the impact the media has on their children by doing things such as monitoring what is watched, showing disapproval of the behavior exhibited by TV or video game heroes, and contrasting the violent solutions found in the media with realistic, real-world examples.

Bystander apathy occurs when bystanders are unwilling to help during an emergency due to diffusion of responsibility. Four decision points that must be passed before we give help to others are: noticing, defining an emergency, taking responsibility, and selecting a course of action. Helping is less likely at each point when other potential helpers are present. Giving help tends to encourage others to help too.

Multiculturalism is an attempt to give equal status to different ethnic, racial, and cultural groups. Actions that can be taken to reduce conflict and misunderstanding between members of different ethnic groups include being aware of stereotyping, seeking individuating information, and understanding that race is a social construction. Cultural awareness is a key element in promoting greater social harmony.

Learning Objectives

1. Define *social psychology*; discuss our need to afflilate, and describe the social comparison theory, including how meaningful evaluations take place.
2. Define *interpersonal attraction*, and describe the following factors that influence interpersonal attraction:
     a. physical proximity
     b. physical attractiveness, including the halo effect

    c. competence

    d. similarity, including homogamy; and discuss the effects of varying degrees of self-disclosure on interpersonal relationships

3. Discuss the concept of *mutual absorption*.

4. Describe Sternberg's Triangular Theory of Love; define the following components and describe how they can be combined to form different types of love:

    a. Intimacy

    b. Passion

    c. Commitment

5. Describe the field of evolutionary psychology and how this field of study explains the different mate selection preferences of males and females.

6. Discuss the following dimensions of being in a social group:

    a. social roles, including ascribed roles, achieved roles, and role conflict

    b. group structure

    c. group cohesivenss

    d. in-groups and out-groups

    e. status

    f. group norms

7. Discuss the process of attribution, including the difference between external and internal causes; explain the fundamental attibution error and the actor-observer bias; and describe gender differences in attributing success.

8. Define social influence and explain the different kinds of social influence.

9. Describe Asch's experiment on conformity.

10. Explain how groupthink may contribute to poor decision-making and list ways to prevent it.

11. Describe how the following factors affect conformity:

    a. group sanctions

    b. the importance of the group

    c. the number of group members

    d. the unanimity of the group

    e. the power of an ally

12. Explain how compliance differs from conformity, and describe the following methods of gaining compliance: a. foot-in-the-door; b. door-in-the-face; and c. low-ball technique.

13. Describe Milgram's study of obedience, and discuss how each of the following factors affected the degree of obedience in Milgram's follow-up experiments:

    a. prestige of the authority

    b. distance between the teacher and the learner

    c. distance from the authority

    d. group support; and give examples of "crimes of obedience" in world events and everyday life

14. Differentiate between brainwashing (i.e., coercion) and other persuasive techniques; describe the techniques used in brainwashing; discuss the relative permanence of attitude changes brought about by brainwashing.

15. Describe how cults are able to recruit, convert, and retain their members, and how cult leaders differ from true spiritual leaders.

16. Discuss the following aspects of assertiveness training:
    a. your three basic rights, including the concept of self-assertion
    b. a comparison of assertive, non-assertive, and aggressive behaviors (see Table 14.2)
    c. the importance of practice, using rehearsal and role-playing, so that one can be assertive even under stress

17. Define *attitude*; describe the belief, emotional, and action components of an attitude; list and give examples of six ways in which attitudes are acquired; explain three reasons why people may exhibit discrepancies between attitudes and behavior, and how conviction affects attitudes.

18. Explain the difference between membership groups and reference groups, including how one's point of reference affects attitude change; define *persuasion* and explain how the characteristics of the communicator, audience, and message affect attitude change.

19. Explain cognitive dissonance theory; list five strategies for reducing dissonance (see Table 14.3); describe how the amount of justification affects the amount of dissonance felt, and why we are especially likely to experience dissonance after causing an event that we wish hadn't happened.

20. Differentiate between the concepts of prejudice and discrimination; describe how prejudice may be a form of scapegoating; distinguish between the two sources of prejudice, personal and group prejudices; explain how prejudice can be considered a general personality characteristic by discussing the following:
    a. the authoritarian personality
    b. ethnocentrism
    c. the use of the F scale to measure authoritarian beliefs
    d. how authoritarian beliefs are learned as children

21. Describe the shared beliefs that tend to trigger intergroup conflict; explain the characterisitics of social stereotypes and how they can amplify the conflict between groups; describe symbolic prejudice; and explain how some elements of prejudice appear to be unconscious.

22. Describe Jane Elliot's experiment in which prejudice was caused by status inequalities; explain how reducing the complex American society into two oversimplified stereotypes, "red and blue states," has lead to an increase in between-group prejudice; and describe how more frequent equal-status contact between groups in conflict could reduce prejudice and stereotyping.

23. Describe the summer camp experiment in which superordinate goals were used to help reduce the conflict between the two groups; explain how superordinate goals can be applied to reduce global conflict and to reduce prejudices within ordinary classrooms through the jigsaw classrooms and their goal of mutual interdependence.

24. Define *aggression*, and discuss the role of each of the following in aggressive behavior:
   a. instincts and why psychologists question this theory
   b. biology, including physical factors and the effects of drugs and alcohol
   c. the frustration-aggression hypothesis
   d. aversive stimuli, including the activation of aggressive cues and the weapons effect
   e. social learning theory

25. Explain how television can teach new antisocial actions, serve as a disinhibiting factor, cause desensitization to violence, increase aggressive thoughts, and make one more prone to aggress when faced with frustrating situations or cues; list seven ways by which parents can buffer the impact of television on children's behavior.

26. Define prosocial behavior; describe the Kitty Genovese case in terms of bystander apathy;

27. Explain how the presence of other people can influence bystanders' willingness to help.

28. Describe four conditions that need to exist before bystanders are likely to give help.

29. Discuss factors, such as heightened and emotional arousal and the empathy-helping relationship, that make one more likely to help; describe how one can "de-victimize" oneself and be more likely to receive help.

30. Define the term *multiculturalism*; discuss eight ways in which a person can become more tolerant; explain how a person can develop cultural awareness.

RECITE AND REVIEW

Affiliation and Attraction—Come Together

Survey Questions: Why do people affiliate? What factors influence interpersonal attraction? Pages 550-552

1. _____ psychology studies how individuals behave, think, and feel in social situations.

2. The need to affiliate is tied to needs for _____, support, friendship, and _____.

3. Social comparison theory holds that we affiliate to _____ our actions, feelings, and abilities.

4. Interpersonal attraction is increased by physical proximity (_____) and frequency of _____.

5. The halo effect causes individuals to rate attractive people as _____ appealing on other _____ dimensions, such as intelligence and social skill.

6. Friends tend to be _____ in terms of _____, gender, and ethnicity.

7. Initial acquaintance and _____ are influenced by physical attractiveness (beauty), competence (high ability), and similarity (being alike).

8. A large degree of _____ on many dimensions is characteristic of _____ selection, a pattern called homogamy.

9. Self-disclosure (_____ oneself to others) occurs to a greater degree if two people like one another.

10. Self-disclosure follows a reciprocity _____: Low levels of self-disclosure are met with low levels in return, moderate self-disclosure elicits personal replies, and overdisclosure tends to inhibit _____-_____ by others.

Liking and Loving—Dating, Rating, Mating

Pages 552-555

1. Sternberg's _____ Theory of Love states that different forms of love arise from different combinations of three basic components: Intimacy, _____, and commitment.

2. In Sternberg's Triangular Theory of Love, intimacy refers to feelings of _____ and affection, passion refers to deep emotional and/or sexual feelings, and commitment involves the determination to stay _____ in a long-term relationship

3. Consummate love is considered the most _____ form of love, as passion, intimacy, and commitment contribute relatively equal amounts.

4. Romantic love is associated with mutual _____ between people.

5. Empty love exists when two people have made a long-term _____ to one another, but the relationship lacks _____ and intimacy.

6. Evolutionary psychology attributes human _____ patterns to the differing reproductive challenges faced by men and women since the dawn of time.

7. David Buss has found that men are more interested in _____ sex than are women.

8. Men tend to prefer _____, more physically attractive partners; women tend to prefer _____ partners who appear to be industrious, have _____ status, and are economically successful.

9. Men tend to become jealous over real or imagined _____ infidelity; women tend to become jealous over _____ infidelity.

Humans in a Social Context—People, People, Everywhere

Survey Question: How does group membership affect our behavior? Pages 555-557

1. One's position in _____ defines a variety of roles to be played.

2. _____ _____, which may be achieved or ascribed, are particular behavior patterns associated with social positions.

3. Some roles in social groups are ascribed (_____ and not under personal control), while others are achieved (_____ _____ through special effort).

4. When two or more _____ roles are held, role conflict may occur.

5. Two dimensions of a group are group structure (network of _____, communication pathways, and power) and group cohesiveness (members' desire to _____ in the group). Group cohesion is strong for _____-_____ members.

6. Members of the _____-_____ identify themselves based on a combination of dimensions such as nationality, _____, age, _____, income, etc. People tend to attribute _____ traits to members of their in-group and negative traits to members of the _____-_____.

7. Positions within _____ typically carry higher or lower levels of status. High status is associated with special privileges and respect.

8. Norms are _____ of conduct enforced (formally or informally) by _____.

9. Attribution theory is concerned with how we make inferences about the _____ of behavior.

10. Behavior can be attributed to internal _____ or external _____.

11. The fundamental attributional _____ is to ascribe the actions of others to _____ causes. This is part of the actor-observer bias in which we ascribe the behavior of others to _____ causes and our own behavior to _____ causes.

Social Influence—Follow the Leader

Survey Question: What have psychologists learned about social influence? Pages 558-560

1. Social influence refers to alterations in _____ brought about by the behavior of _____.

2. The _____ form of social influence is mere presence, which refers to changing behavior just because other people are _____.

3. Compliance occurs when we change our behavior in response to a request from someone who has _____ to _____ social power or authority; obedience occurs when we change our behavior in response to direct demands from someone with _____.

4. If you are confident in your abilities, having other people nearby will facilitate (_____) your performance; if you are not confident, then performance will be _____.

5. Social loafers tend to _____ (work less hard) when they are part of a _____ than when they are individually responsible for work.

6. Conformity to group pressure is a familiar example of social influence. Virtually everyone _____ to a variety of broad social and cultural _____.

7. Conformity pressures also exist within small _____. The famous Asch experiments demonstrated that various _____ sanctions encourage conformity.

8. People who live in cultures that emphasize group _____ are _____ likely to conform than those that do not.

9. Group _____, the importance of belonging to a group, group _____, and unanimity influence degree of conformity.

10. Groupthink refers to compulsive conformity in group _____ _____. Victims of groupthink seek to maintain each other's approval, even at the cost of critical thinking.

11. To _____ groupthink, group leaders should designate each group member as a "_____ evaluator," avoid revealing personal preferences at the beginning, state the problems without _____, invite an outside member to play "Devil's Advocate," hold group members accountable, and encourage open inquiry.

12. The presence of too many alternatives can lead to _____ in group decision making.

Compliance—A Foot in the Door

Pages 561-562

1. Compliance with direct _____ by a person who has little or no social _____ is another means by which behavior is influenced.

2. Three strategies for inducing compliance are the _____-in-the-door technique, the door-in-the-_____ approach, and the low-ball technique.

3. In the foot-in-the-door technique, individuals comply with _____ demands if they have agreed to a _____ request first; in the door-in-the-face technique, people will generally agree to a _____ request after refusing a _____ request.

4. People succumb to "low-balling" when they _____ to a request, but then the terms of acting are made _____ desirable.

Obedience—Would You Electrocute a Stranger?

Pages 562-564

1. Obedience to _____ has been investigated in a variety of experiments, particularly those by Stanley Milgram.

2. Psychiatrists predicted that only 1 percent of the individuals who participated in Milgram's study would go to the _____ volt level; in actuality, 65% of participants administered _____ levels of shock.

3. _____ in Milgram's studies decreased when distance between the learner and the victim decreased, when the authority figure was absent, and when others refused to obey.

4. Recent research suggests that in addition to excessive obedience to _____, many people show a surprising passive compliance to unreasonable _____.

Forced Attitude Change—Brainwashing and Cults

Pages 564-566

1. Coercion occurs when you are forced to change your beliefs or your behavior _____ your will.

2. Brainwashing is a form of _____ attitude change. It depends on control of the target person's total environment.

3. Three steps in brainwashing are unfreezing (loosening) old attitudes and beliefs, _____, and refreezing (rewarding and strengthening) new attitudes and beliefs.

4. In a cult, members give their allegiance to a leader, whose _____ is more important than the beliefs he or she preaches. They follow the dictates of the leader without question.

5. Many cults recruit new members with high-pressure indoctrination techniques resembling _____.

6. Cults attempt to catch people when they are vulnerable. Then they combine isolation, displays of _____, discipline and rituals, intimidation, and escalating commitment to bring about _____.

Assertiveness Training—Standing Up For Your Rights

Survey Question: How does self-assertion differ from aggression? Pages 566

1. People are _____ to assert themselves, perhaps because they have been rewarded for compliant behavior in the past, they have anxiety about "making a scene," or they do not want to feel disliked by others.

2. Assertiveness _____ provides instruction in how to be self-assertive.

3. Assertiveness training teaches people that they have three basic rights: you have the right to _____, to request, and to right a _____.

4. _____ expresses one's feelings and desires at the expense of others.

5. Learning to be _____ is accomplished by role-playing and rehearsing assertive actions.

Attitudes—Belief + Emotion + Action

Survey Question: How are attitudes acquired and changed? Pages 568-570

1. Attitudes are learned tendencies to respond in a _____ or _____ way to other people, objects, or groups.

2. Attitudes are made up of a belief component, an emotional component, and an _____ component.

3. Attitudes summarize your _____ of objects, and predict or direct future actions.

4. Attitudes may be formed by _____ contact, interaction with others, the effects of _____-rearing practices, and social pressures from group membership.

5. Peer group influences, the mass _____, and _____ conditioning (accidental learning) also appear to be important in attitude formation.

6. The _____ consequences of actions, how we think others will _____ our actions, and habits all influence whether attitudes are converted to actions.

7. Attitudes held with conviction are most likely to be _____ in behavior.

Attitude Change—Meet the "Seekers"

Pages 570-572

1. People tend to change their attitudes to match those of their reference group (a group the person _____ with and refers to for guidance).

2. Persuasion is any deliberate attempt to _____ attitudes or beliefs through information and _____.

3. Effective persuasion occurs when characteristics of the communicator, the _____, and the audience are well matched.

4. In general, a likable and believable communicator who repeats a credible message that arouses _____ in the audience and states clear-cut _____ will be persuasive.

5. Repeating a message that is backed up by _____ and facts as frequently as possible will be persuasive.

6. Maintaining and changing attitudes is closely related to needs for _____ in thoughts and actions. Cognitive dissonance theory explains the dynamics of such needs.

7. Cognitive dissonance occurs when there is a _____ between thoughts or between thoughts and actions.

8. The amount of reward or justification (reasons) for one's actions influences whether _____ occurs.

9. We are motivated to _____ dissonance when it occurs, often by changing beliefs or attitudes.

Prejudice—Attitudes that Injure

Survey Question: What causes prejudice and intergroup conflict? Pages 573-574

1. Prejudice is a _____ attitude held toward members of various social groups.

2. Racism, ageism, and sexism are specific types of prejudice based on race, age, and _____ (or _____).

3. Discrimination is a combination of _____ and racism, and leads to the unequal treatment of people who should have the same _____ as others.

4. One theory attributes prejudice to scapegoating, which is a type of displaced _____.

5. A second account says that prejudices may be held for personal reasons such as direct threats to a person's wellbeing (personal prejudice) or simply through adherence to group _____ (group prejudice).

6. Prejudiced individuals tend to have an authoritarian _____, characterized by rigidity, inhibition, intolerance, and _____-simplification.

7. Authoritarians tend to be very ethnocentric (they use their own _____ as a basis for judging all others).

8. Ethnocentrism refers to placing one's own racial group "at the center," usually by _____ all other groups

9. The _____ scale, or F scale, measures authoritarianism.

Intergroup Conflict—The Roots of Prejudice

Pages 574-578

1. Intergroup _____ gives rise to hostility and the formation of social stereotypes (oversimplified images of members of various groups).

2. Symbolic prejudice, or prejudice expressed in _____ ways, is common today.

3. _____ inequalities (differences in power, prestige, or privileges) tend to build prejudices.

4. Equal-status contact (social interaction on an equal footing) tends to _____ prejudice.

5. Superordinate _____ (those that rise above all others) usually reduce intergroup conflict.

6. Jane Elliot demonstrated that prejudice could easily be created in the classroom when she separated children based on _____ color.

7. On a small scale, jigsaw _____ (which encourage cooperation through _____ interdependence) have been shown to be an effective way of combating prejudice.

8. Stereotype _____ occurs when individuals think they are being judged in terms of a stereotype.

Aggression—The World's Most Dangerous Animal

Survey Question: How do psychologists explain human aggression? Pages 579-583

1. Aggression refers to any action carried out with the _____ of harming another person.

2. Ethologists explain aggression as a natural expression of inherited _____.

3. Biological explanations emphasize brain mechanisms and physical factors that _____ the threshold (trigger point) for aggression.

4. Physical factors such as low _____ sugar, allergy, specific brain diseases, and hormones do not cause aggression, but may make aggression _____ likely.

5. According to the frustration-_____ hypothesis, frustration and _____ are closely linked.

6. Frustration is only one of many aversive _____ that can arouse a person and make aggression more likely. Aggression is especially likely to occur when _____ cues (stimuli associated with aggression) are present.

7. Social learning theory has focused attention on the role of aggressive _____ in the development of aggressive behavior.

8. Aggressive _____ on television encourage aggression because they desensitize (lower the sensitivity of) _____ to violence and disinhibit (remove restraints against) aggressive impulses.

9. By the end of elementary school, children will have seen about 8,000 _____ and 100,000 other violent acts on TV. Reducing exposure to violent _____ is one way to lower aggression.

10. Parents can help to reduce the media's negative effects on children by creating a warm, _____ environment at home, modeling positive ways of coping, limiting media time, and closely _____ what the child experiences.

Prosocial Behavior—Helping Others

Survey Question: Why are bystanders so often unwilling to help in an emergency? Pages 583-586

1. Prosocial behavior is _____, constructive, or altruistic toward others.

2. In 1964, Kitty Genovese was _____ on a sidewalk in Queens, New York. Even though 38 people heard the attack, no one called the _____ or tried to get involved. This incident was instrumental in launching research into _____ apathy.

3. Bystander apathy is the unwillingness of bystanders to offer _____ to others during emergencies.

4. Four decision points that must be passed before a person gives help are: _____, defining an emergency, taking responsibility, and selecting a course of action.

5. Helping is _____ likely at each point when other potential helpers are present, as everyone believes that someone _____ will help.

6. In real emergencies, the need for action is _____ because each person attempts to appear calm.

7. Diffusion of responsibility spreads the _____ for helping among several people; this actually limits who will help.

8. Helping is encouraged by general arousal, empathic _____, being in a good mood, low effort or _____, and perceived similarity between the victim and the helper.

9. To ensure you receive help when needed, it is better to directly _____ responsibility, such as pointing to someone and saying, "I'm injured, I need _____ to call an ambulance."

Psychology in Action: Multiculturalism—Living with Diversity

Survey Question: How can we promote multiculturalism and social harmony?
Pages 591-594

1. Multiculturalism is an attempt to give _____ status to different ethnic, racial, and cultural groups.

2. To _____ prejudice, one can do the following: Be _____ of stereotyping, seek individuating information, beware of _____-world beliefs, avoid unnecessary social competition, understand that race is a _____ construction, and look for commonalities.

3. By accepting the value of _____ to the _____, people can become less prejudiced.

4. _____ awareness is a key element in promoting greater social harmony.

5. Greater tolerance can be encouraged by neutralizing stereotypes with individuating information (which helps see others as _____).

6. Tolerance comes from looking for commonalties with others and by avoiding the effects of just-world _____, self-fulfilling prophecies, and _____ competition.

CONNECTIONS

Affiliation and Attraction—Come Together and Liking and Loving—Dating, Rating, Mating

Survey Questions: Why do people affiliate? What factors influence interpersonal attraction? Pages 550-555

1. _____ competency	A.	comparing ourselves to others
2. _____ Jealously	B.	return in kind
3. _____ Self-disclosure	C.	a person's proficiency
4. _____ reciprocity	D.	affinity to others
5. _____ Commitment	E.	desire to associate
6. _____ proximity	F.	nearness
7. _____ Halo effect	G.	generalized favorable impressions
8. _____ interpersonal attraction	H.	similar in age, sex, and ethnicity
9. _____ Companionate love	I.	sharing
10. _____ social comparison	J.	intimacy + passion + commitment
11. _____ Friends	K.	long-term
12. _____ need to affiliate	L.	sexual infidelity
13. _____ Evolutionary psychology	M.	origins of behavior
14. _____ Consummate love	N.	long-term couples

Humans in a Social Context—People, People, Everywhere

Survey Question: How does group membership affect our behavior? Pages 555-557

1. _____ achieved role	A.	privilege and importance
2. _____ Out-group	B.	rule or standard
3. _____ ascribed role	C.	assigned role
4. _____ In-group	D.	relating self to others
5. _____ attribution	E.	voluntary role
6. _____ Role conflict	F.	social inference
7. _____ norm	G.	two different roles
8. _____ Group cohesiveness	H.	degree of attraction
9. _____ social comparison	I.	"us"
10. _____ Attribution	J.	"them"
11. _____ status	K.	inference

Social Influence—Follow the Leader; Compliance—A Foot in the Door; and Obedience—Would You Electrocute a Stranger?

Survey Question: What have psychologists learned about social influence? Pages 558-564

1. _____ conformity
2. _____ Social loafing
3. _____ assertiveness
4. _____ Solomon Asch
5. _____ broken record
6. _____ Groupthink
7. _____ obedience
8. _____ Mere presence
9. _____ group sanctions
10. _____ Stanley Milgram
11. _____ compliance
12. _____ Low-ball technique
13. _____ foot-in-the-door

A. self-assertion technique
B. salesperson's tactic
C. honest expression
D. following authority
E. yielding to requests
F. matching behavior
G. rewards and punishments
H. other people
I. less effort in a group
J. misguided loyalty
K. conformity
L. change in terms
M. obedience

Forced Attitude Change —Brainwashing and Cults; and Assertiveness Training – Standing up for Your Rights

Survey Questions: How does self-assertion differ from aggression? Pages 564-568

1. _____ brainwashing
2. _____ cult recruitment
3. _____ self-assertion
4. _____ cult
5. _____ unwilling change
6. _____ Aggression
7. _____ conversion

A. coercion
B. authoritarian group
C. high-pressure techniques
D. love bombing
E. achieving goals with self-respect
F. thought reform
G. achieving goals while hurting others

Attitudes—Belief + Emotion + Action and Attitude change—Meet the "Seekers"

Survey Question: How are attitudes acquired and changed? Pages 568-572

1. _____ Mean world view
2. _____ dissonance
3. _____ attitude
4. _____ Parental influence
5. _____ reference group
6. _____ persuasion
7. _____ Habits
8. _____ chance conditioning

A. belief + emotion + action
B. coincidence
C. child-rearing
D. dangerous and threatening
E. standard for social comparison
F. long standing behaviors
G. change attitude with arguments
H. uncomfortable clash

Prejudice—Attitudes that Injure and Intergroup Conflict—The Roots of Prejudice

Survey Questions: What causes prejudice and intergroup conflict? Pages 573-578

1. _____ scapegoat
2. _____ Jigsaw classroom
3. _____ stereotype
4. _____ Personal prejudice
5. _____ superordinate
6. _____ Stereotype threat
7. _____ symbolic prejudice
8. _____ Status inequality
9. _____ discrimination
10. _____ Group prejudice
11. _____ authoritarianism
12. _____ Equal-status contract
13. _____ ethnocentric

A. aggression target
B. above all others
C. group centered
D. unequal treatment
E. oversimplified image
F. F Scale
G. modern bias
H. threat to one's own interests
I. conform to group norms
J. judgment in a situation
K. difference in power and prestige
L. equal footing
M. mutual interdependence

Aggression—The World's Most Dangerous Animal; Prosocial Behavior—Helping Others; and Multiculturalism—Living with Diversity

Survey Questions: How do psychologists explain human aggression? Why are bystanders so often unwilling to help in an emergency? How can we promote multiculturalism and social harmony? Pages 579-589

1. _____ bystander apathy   A. "tossed salad"
2. _____ desensitization   B. reduced emotional sensitivity
3. _____ Social competition   C. remove inhibition
4. _____ prosocial   D. feeling someone's anguish
5. _____ Ethologist   E. aggression cue
6. _____ disinhibition   F. Kitty Genovese
7. _____ Self-fulfilling prophecy   G. intent to harm
8. _____ weapons effect   H. altruistic behavior
9. _____ Media violence   I. people get what they deserve
10. _____ empathic arousal   J. animal behavior
11. _____ aggression   K. mainstream media
12. _____ multiculturalism   L. rivalry
13. _____ just-world beliefs   M. expectations for behavior

CHECK YOUR MEMORY

Affiliation and Attraction—Come Together

Survey Questions: Why do people affiliate? What factors influence interpersonal attraction? Pages 550-552

1. The need to affiliate is a basic human characteristic.

TRUE or FALSE

2. Interpersonal attraction to someone takes weeks to develop.

TRUE or FALSE

3. Social comparisons are used to confirm objective evaluations and measurements.

TRUE or FALSE

4. Useful social comparisons are usually made with persons similar to ourselves.

TRUE or FALSE

5. Nearness has a powerful impact on forming friendships.

TRUE or FALSE

6. Physical proximity leads us to think of people as competent and therefore worth knowing.

TRUE or FALSE

7. The halo effect is the tendency to generalize a positive or negative first impression to other personal characteristics.

TRUE or FALSE

8. Physical attractiveness is closely associated with intelligence, talents, and abilities.

TRUE or FALSE

9. Homogamy, marrying someone who is like oneself, does not apply to unmarried couples.

TRUE or FALSE

10. The risk of divorce is higher than average for couples who have large differences in age and education.

TRUE or FALSE

11. In choosing mates, women rank physical attractiveness as the most important feature.

TRUE or FALSE

12. In general, we tend to be attracted to people who demonstrate competence or talent.

TRUE or FALSE

13. Self-disclosure is a major step toward friendship.

TRUE or FALSE

14. Overdisclosure tends to elicit maximum self-disclosure from others.

TRUE or FALSE

15. People often feel freer to express their true feelings when interacting on the Internet.

TRUE or FALSE

Liking and Loving—Dating, Rating, Mating

Pages 552-555

1. According to Sternberg, different forms of love arise from different combinations of four basic components.

TRUE or FALSE

2. Intimacy refers to feelings of connectedness and affection between two people

TRUE or FALSE

3. Consummate love occurs when there is a relatively equal contribution of intimacy, commitment, and passion

TRUE or FALSE

4. Compared to women, men are generally more interested in causal sex, as it increases their fertility rate

TRUE or FALSE

5. In general, women tend to invest fewer resources in raising offspring than do men

TRUE or FALSE

6. Where their mates are concerned, men tend to be more jealous over a loss of emotional commitment than they are over sexual infidelities.

TRUE or FALSE

Humans in a Social Context—People, People, Everywhere

Survey Question: How does group membership affect our behavior? Pages 555-557

1. Son, husband, and teacher are achieved roles.

TRUE or FALSE

2. Persons of higher status tend to receive special treatment and privileges.

TRUE or FALSE

3. A group could have a high degree of structure but low cohesiveness.

TRUE or FALSE

4. "Us and them" refers to members of the in-group perceiving themselves as one unit and everyone else as the out-group.

TRUE or FALSE

5. The more trash that is visible in public places, the more likely people will be to litter.

TRUE or FALSE

6. If someone always salts her food before eating, it implies that her behavior has an external cause.

TRUE or FALSE

7. Attributing the actions of others to external causes is the most common attributional error.

TRUE or FALSE

8. Lower group status tends to bestow special privileges and respect

TRUE or FALSE

9. Norms tend to be widely accepted, but unspoken, standards for behavior that is considered appropriate by a group

TRUE or FALSE

10. According to the fundamental attribution error, we are more likely to attribute external causes to other's behavior and internal causes to our own behavior.

TRUE or FALSE

Social Influence—Follow the Leader

Survey Question: What have psychologists learned about social influence? Pages 562-564

1. Conformity situations occur when a person becomes aware of differences between his or her own behavior and that of a group.

TRUE or FALSE

2. The mere presence of others can cause us to change behavior.

TRUE or FALSE

3. Most subjects in the Asch conformity experiments suspected that they were being deceived in some way.

TRUE or FALSE

4. Seventy-five percent of Asch's subjects yielded to the group at least once.

TRUE or FALSE

5. People who are anxious are more likely to conform to group pressure.

TRUE or FALSE

6. Groupthink is more likely to occur when people emphasize the task at hand rather than the bonds between group members.

TRUE or FALSE

7. Rejection, ridicule, and disapproval are group norms that tend to enforce conformity.

TRUE or FALSE

8. A unanimous majority of three is more powerful than a majority of eight with one person dissenting.

TRUE or FALSE

9. People tend to work harder when they are part of a group due to social sanctions.

TRUE or FALSE

Compliance—A Foot in the Door

Pages 561-562

1. The foot-in-the-door effect is a way to gain compliance from another person.

TRUE or FALSE

2. The low-ball technique involves changing the terms that a person has agreed to so that they are less desirable from the person's point of view.

TRUE or FALSE

3. If you agreed to allow a big sign to be put in your yard after agreeing to display a small sign in your window, your compliance was won over through the use of the door-in-the-face technique.

TRUE or FALSE

4. Compliance refers to situations in which one person alters his or her behavior to a legitimate authority figure.

TRUE or FALSE

Obedience—Would You Electrocute a Stranger?

Pages 562-564

1. Milgram's famous shock experiment was done to study compliance and conformity.

TRUE or FALSE

2. Over half of Milgram's "teachers" went all the way to the maximum shock level.

TRUE or FALSE

3. Being face-to-face with the learner had no effect on the number of subjects who obeyed in the Milgram experiments.

TRUE or FALSE

4. People are less likely to obey an unjust authority if they have seen others disobey.

TRUE or FALSE

5. People often obey a legitimate authority long after that person's demands have become unreasonable.

TRUE or FALSE

6. Milgram's subjects caused the "learner" in the experiment to experience a heart attack; this was a source of stress for many participants.

TRUE or FALSE

7. Milgram's studies demonstrated that people who obey an authority figure often rationalize that they are not responsible for their actions.

TRUE or FALSE

Coercion—Brainwashing and Cults

Pages 564-566

1. Some American POWs in the Korean War signed false confessions.

TRUE or FALSE

2. True brainwashing requires a captive audience.

TRUE or FALSE

3. In brainwashing, the target person is housed with other people who hold the same attitudes and beliefs that he or she does.

TRUE or FALSE

4. In most cases, the effects of brainwashing are very resistant to further change.

TRUE or FALSE

5. Cult leaders, like David Koresh, use brainwashing as a technique to persuade people to conform.

TRUE or FALSE

6. A cult is a group in which the belief system is more important than the leader who espouses it.

TRUE or FALSE

7. Adolescents are less likely to be recruited into cults because of parental influence.

TRUE or FALSE

8. Cults play on emotions and discourage critical thinking.

TRUE or FALSE

9. Cult members are typically isolated from former reference groups.

TRUE or FALSE

Assertiveness Training – Standing Up for Your Rights

Survey Question: How does self-assertion differ from aggression? Pages 566-568

1. Many people have difficulty asserting themselves because they have learned to be obedient and good.

TRUE or FALSE

2. Self-assertion involves the rights to request, reject, and retaliate.

TRUE or FALSE

3. In order to be assertive, you should never admit that you were wrong.

TRUE or FALSE

4. In contrast to assertive behavior, aggression involves engaging in self-denying and inhibited behaviors that involve giving up one's goals for the good of the group.

TRUE or FALSE

5. In assertiveness training, assertive actions are practiced through role-playing and rehearsal until they can be repeated at will, even under stress.

TRUE or FALSE

Attitudes—Belief + Emotion + Action

Survey Question: How are attitudes acquired and changed? Pages 568-570

1. Attitudes predict and direct future actions.

TRUE or FALSE

2. What you think about the object of an attitude makes up its belief component.

TRUE or FALSE

3. Attitudes are only composed of our positive or negative opinions of others. They do not include a behavioral component.

TRUE or FALSE

4. If both parents belong to the same political party, their child probably will too.

TRUE or FALSE

5. A person who deviates from the majority opinion in a group tends to be excluded from conversation.

TRUE or FALSE

6. Attitudes can be formed through coincidence, or chance conditioning in which random repeated experiences influence how we evaluate a particular person or object.

TRUE or FALSE

7. Direct contact is the least influential way of forming an attitude.

TRUE or FALSE

8. Heavy TV viewers feel safer than average because they spend so much time in security at home.

TRUE or FALSE

9. An attitude held with conviction is more likely to be acted upon.

TRUE or FALSE

10. Our attitudes are more likely to match those held by members of our reference groups than our membership groups.

TRUE or FALSE

Attitude Change—Meet the "Seekers"

Pages 570-572

1. Persuasion refers to a deliberate attempt to change a person's reference groups.

TRUE or FALSE

2. Persuasion is less effective if the message appeals to the emotions.

TRUE or FALSE

3. For a poorly informed audience, persuasion is more effective if only one side of the argument is presented.

TRUE or FALSE

4. Persuasion refers to any deliberate attempt to change attitudes or beliefs through force or brainwashing

TRUE or FALSE

5. Effective persuasion generally has three components: the communicator, the message, and the audience.

TRUE or FALSE

6. A persuasive message should not be repeated; doing so just weakens its impact.

TRUE or FALSE

7. You are more likely to be persuaded by someone who appears to have nothing to gain if the audience accepts the message

TRUE or FALSE

8. Acting contrary to one's attitudes or self-image causes cognitive dissonance.

TRUE or FALSE

9. Public commitment to an attitude or belief makes it more difficult to change.

TRUE or FALSE

10. The greater the reward or justification for acting contrary to one's beliefs, the greater the cognitive dissonance felt.

TRUE or FALSE

11. Dissonance is especially likely to be felt when a person causes an undesired event to occur.

TRUE or FALSE

Prejudice—Attitudes that Injure

Survey Question: What causes prejudice and intergroup conflict? Pages 573-574

1. Sexism is a type of prejudice.

TRUE or FALSE

2. The term *racial profiling* refers to giving preferential treatment to some students seeking admission to college.

TRUE or FALSE

3. Scapegoating is a prime example of discrimination.

TRUE or FALSE

4. Many children show signs of race bias as early as three years of age.

TRUE or FALSE

5. A person who views members of another group as competitors for jobs displays group prejudice.

TRUE or FALSE

6. Authoritarian persons tend to be prejudiced against all out-groups.

TRUE or FALSE

7. The *F* in F Scale stands for fanatic.

TRUE or FALSE

8. An authoritarian would agree that people can be divided into the weak and the strong.

TRUE or FALSE

Intergroup Conflict—The Roots of Prejudice

Pages 574-578

1. Social stereotypes can be positive as well as negative.

TRUE or FALSE

2. Symbolic prejudice is the most obvious and socially unacceptable form of bigotry.

TRUE or FALSE

3. Symbolic prejudice occurs when people understand the causes of prejudice and do not discriminate against minorities.

TRUE or FALSE

4. The key to creating prejudice in Jane Elliot's experiment was her use of scapegoating to cause group conflict.

TRUE or FALSE

5. Equal-status contact tends to reduce prejudice and stereotypes.

TRUE or FALSE

6. Superordinate groups help people of opposing groups to see themselves as members of a single larger group.

TRUE or FALSE

7. Both racial prejudice and racism can lead to discrimination.

TRUE or FALSE

8. Group prejudice occurs when members of another ethnic group are perceived as a threat to one's own interests.

TRUE or FALSE

9. Social stereotypes tend to be oversimplified images of various groups, which tend to divide people into "us" and "them" categories.

TRUE or FALSE

10. Opinions on affirmative action, busing, and immigration may reveal symbolic prejudices.

TRUE or FALSE

11. Elementary school teacher Jane Elliot sought to teach her students about prejudice and discrimination by separating the class into two groups based on hair color.

TRUE or FALSE

12. Subordinate goals will often help to restore peace between two groups experiencing conflict.

TRUE or FALSE

13. In jigsaw classrooms, mutual interdependence is created by requiring that children rely on each other in order to learn a lesson completely.

TRUE or FALSE

Aggression—The World's Most Dangerous Animal

Survey Question: How do psychologists explain human aggression? Pages 579-583

1. Ethologists argue that humans learn to be aggressive by observing aggressive behavior in lower animals.

TRUE or FALSE

2. Specific areas of the brain are capable of initiating or ending aggression.

TRUE or FALSE

3. Intoxication tends to raise the threshold for aggression, making it more likely.

TRUE or FALSE

4. Higher levels of the hormone testosterone are associated with more aggressive behavior by both men and women.

TRUE or FALSE

5. The frustration-aggression hypothesis says that being aggressive is frustrating.

TRUE or FALSE

6. People exposed to aversive stimuli tend to become less sensitive to aggression cues.

TRUE or FALSE

7. Murders are less likely to occur in homes where guns are kept.

TRUE or FALSE

8. Social learning theorists assume that instinctive patterns of human aggression are modified by learning.

TRUE or FALSE

9. Aggressive crimes in TV dramas occur at a much higher rate than they do in real life.

TRUE or FALSE

10. Only about 30 percent of popular video games contain violent content.

TRUE or FALSE

11. Children who see violence in the community tend to be less likely to engage in violence themselves.

TRUE or FALSE

Prosocial Behavior—Helping Others

Survey Question: Why are bystanders so often unwilling to help in an emergency? Pages 583-586

1. In the Kitty Genovese murder, no one called the police until after the attack was over.

TRUE or FALSE

2. Researchers have attempted to explain the bystander effect in terms of diffusion of responsibility.

TRUE or FALSE

3. In an emergency, the more potential helpers present, the more likely a person is to get help.

TRUE or FALSE

4. The first step in giving help is to define the situation as an emergency.

TRUE or FALSE

5. Emotional arousal, especially empathic arousal, lowers the likelihood that one person will help another.

TRUE or FALSE

6. You are more likely to help a person who seems similar to yourself.

TRUE or FALSE

7. In many emergency situations it can be more effective to shout "Fire!" rather than "Help!"

TRUE or FALSE

Psychology in Action: Multiculturalism—Living with Diversity

Survey Question: How can we promote multiculturalism and social harmony?
Pages 586-589

1. Multiculturalism is an attempt to blend multiple ethnic backgrounds into one universal culture.

TRUE or FALSE

2. The emotional component of prejudicial attitudes may remain even after a person intellectually renounces prejudice.

TRUE or FALSE

3. Both prejudiced and unprejudiced people are equally aware of social stereotypes.

TRUE or FALSE

4. Individuating information forces us to focus mainly on the labels attached to a person.

TRUE or FALSE

5. From a scientific point of view, "race" is a matter of social labeling, not a biological reality.

TRUE or FALSE

6. People who hold just-world beliefs assume that people generally get what they deserve.

TRUE or FALSE

7. Each ethnic group has strengths that members of other groups could benefit from emulating.

TRUE or FALSE

8. Individuals who wish to become more tolerant should beware of stereotyping, seek individuating information, and become aware of any self-fulfilling prophecies.

TRUE or FALSE

9. In social conflict theory, rivalry occurs between groups, with one group regarding itself as superior to other groups.

TRUE or FALSE

FINAL SURVEY AND REVIEW

Affiliation and Attraction—Come Together

Survey Questions: Why do people affiliate? What factors influence interpersonal attraction? Pages 550-552

1. Social psychology studies how individuals _____, think, and feel in _____ situations.

2. The need to _____ is tied to needs for approval, support, _____, and information.

3. Social _____ theory holds that we affiliate to evaluate our actions, _____, and abilities.

4. Interpersonal attraction is increased by physical _____ (nearness) and _____ of contact.

5. The _____ effect causes individuals to rate attractive people as more appealing on other unrelated dimensions, such as _____ and social skill.

6. _____ tend to be similar in terms of age, gender, and _____.

7. Initial acquaintance and attraction are influenced by _____ attractiveness (beauty), _____ (high ability), and _____ (being alike).

8. A large degree of similarity on many dimensions is characteristic of mate selection, a pattern called _____.

9. Self-_____ (revealing oneself to others) occurs to a _____ degree if two people like one another.

10. Self-disclosure follows a reciprocity norm: _____ levels of self-disclosure are met with low levels in return, _____ self-disclosure elicits personal replies, and _____ tends to inhibit self-disclosure by others.

Liking and Loving—Dating, Rating, Mating

Pages 552-555

1. Sternberg's Triangular Theory of Love states that different forms of love arise from different combinations of _____ basic components: _____, passion, and _____.

2. In Sternberg's Triangular Theory of Love, _____ refers to feelings of connectedness and affection, _____ refers to deep emotional and/or sexual feelings, and _____ involves the determination to stay together in a long-term relationship

3. _____ love is considered the most complete form of love, as passion, intimacy, and commitment contribute relatively equal amounts.

4. _____ love is associated with mutual absorption between people.

5. _____ love exists when two people have made a long-term commitment to one another, but the relationship lacks passion and intimacy.

6. Evolutionary psychology attributes human mating patterns to the differing _____ challenges faced by men and women since the dawn of time.

7. David Buss has found that _____ are more interested in casual sex than are _____ .

8. _____ tend to prefer younger, more physically attractive partners; _____ tend to prefer older partners who appear to be industrious, have high status, and are economically successful.

9. _____ tend to become jealous over real or imagined sexual infidelity; _____ tend to become jealous over emotional infidelity.

Humans in a Social Context—People, People, Everywhere

Survey Question: How does group membership affect our behavior? Pages 555-557

1. One's position in groups defines a variety of _____ to be played.

2. Social _____, which may be achieved or _____, are particular behavior patterns associated with social positions.

3. Some roles in social groups are _____ (assigned and not under personal control), while others are _____ (voluntarily attained through special effort).

4. When two or more contradictory roles are held, _____ _____ may occur.

5. Two dimensions of a group are group _____ (network of roles, communication pathways, and power) and group _____ (members' desire to remain in the group). Group cohesion is strong for in-group members.

6. Members of the in-group identify themselves based on a combination of dimensions such as _____, ethnicity, age, religion, income, etc. People tend to attribute positive traits to members of their _____ - _____ and _____ traits to members of the out-group.

7. Positions within groups typically carry _____ or lower levels of status. _____ status is associated with special privileges and respect.

8. _____ are standards of conduct enforced (formally or informally) by groups.

9. Attribution theory is concerned with how we make _____ about the causes of behavior.

10. Behavior can be attributed to _____ causes or _____ causes.

11. The fundamental _____ error is to ascribe the actions of others to internal causes. This is part of the actor-_____ bias in which we ascribe the behavior of others to internal causes and our own behavior to external causes.

Social Influence—Follow the Leader

Survey Question: What have psychologists learned about social influence? Pages 558-560

1. Social _____ refers to alterations in behavior brought about by the _____ of others.

2. The gentlest form of social influence is _____ _____, which refers to changing behavior just because other people are nearby.

3. _____ occurs when we change our behavior in response to a request from someone who has little to no social power or _____; _____ occurs when we change our behavior in response to direct demands from someone with authority.

4. If you are _____ in your abilities, having other people nearby will _____ (improve) your performance; if you are not confident, then performance will be impaired.

5. Social _____ tend to loaf (work less hard) when they are part of a group than when they are _____ responsible for work.

6. _____ to group pressure is a familiar example of social influence. Virtually everyone conforms to a variety of broad social and _____ norms.

7. _____ pressures also exist within small groups. The famous Asch experiments demonstrated that various group _____ encourage conformity.

8. People who live in cultures that _____ group cooperation are more likely to _____ than those that do not.

9. _____ sanctions, the importance of _____ to a group, group size, and unanimity influence degree of conformity.

10. _____ refers to compulsive conformity in group decision making. Victims of groupthink seek to maintain each other's approval, even at the cost of _____ thinking.

11. To avoid groupthink, group _____ should designate each group member as a "critical _____," avoid revealing personal _____ at the beginning, state the problems without bias, invite an outside member to play "Devil's Advocate," hold group members _____, and encourage open inquiry.

12. The presence of too many _____ can lead to deadlock in group decision making.

Compliance—A Foot in the Door

Pages 561-562

1. _____ with direct requests by a person who has little or no social power is another means by which behavior is influenced.

2. Three strategies for inducing compliance are the foot-in-the-_____ technique, the _____-in-the-face approach, and the _____-ball technique.

3. In the _____-in-the-_____ technique, individuals comply with large demands if they have agreed to a small request first; in the _____-in-the-_____ technique, people will generally agree to a smaller request after refusing a major request.

4. People succumb to "low-_____" when they agree to a request, but then the terms of acting are made less desirable.

Obedience—Would You Electrocute a Stranger?

Pages 562-564

1. _____ to authority has been investigated in a variety of experiments, particularly those by Stanley _____.

2. Psychiatrists predicted that only _____ percent of the individuals who participated in Milgram's study would go to the 450 volt level; in actuality, _____ percent of participants administered all levels of shock.

3. Obedience in Milgram's studies _____ when distance between the learner and the victim _____, when the authority figure was absent, and when others refused to obey.

4. Recent research suggests that in addition to excessive obedience to authority, many people show a surprising passive compliance to _____ requests.

Forced Attitude Change—Brainwashing and Cults

Pages 564-566

1. _____ occurs when you are forced to change your beliefs or your behavior against your will.

2. _____ is a form of forced attitude change. It depends on control of the target person's _____ environment.

3. Three steps in brainwashing are _____ (loosening) old attitudes and beliefs, changing, and _____ (rewarding and strengthening) new attitudes and beliefs.

4. In a _____, members give their allegiance to a leader, whose personality is more important than the _____ he or she preaches. They follow the dictates of the leader without question.

5. Many cults recruit new members with _____-_____ indoctrination techniques resembling brainwashing.

6. Cults attempt to catch people when they are _____. Then they combine isolation, displays of affection, discipline and rituals, _____, and escalating commitment to bring about conversion.

Assertiveness Training – Standing Up For Your Rights.

Survey Question: How does self-assertion differ from aggression? Pages 566-

1. People are reluctant to assert themselves, perhaps because they have been _____ for compliant behavior in the past, they have anxiety about "making a _____," or they do not want to feel disliked by others.

2. _____ training provides instruction in how to be self-_____.

3. Assertiveness training teaches people that they have three basic rights: you have the right to refuse, to _____, and to _____ a wrong.

4. Aggression expresses one's feelings and desires at the _____ of others.

5. Learning to be assertive is accomplished by _____-playing and _____ assertive actions.

Attitudes—Belief + Emotion + Action

Survey Question: How are attitudes acquired and changed? Pages 568-570

1. _____ are learned tendencies to respond in a positive or negative way to other people, _____, or groups.

2. Attitudes are made up of a _____ component, an emotional component, and an action component.

3. Attitudes summarize your evaluation of objects, and _____ or direct future actions.

4. Attitudes may be formed by direct _____, interaction with others, the effects of child-_____ practices, and social pressures from _____ membership.

5. _____ group influences, the mass media, and chance _____ (accidental learning) also appear to be important in attitude formation.

6. The immediate _____ of actions, how we think others will evaluate our actions, and _____ all influence whether attitudes are converted to actions.

7. Attitudes held with _____ are most likely to be expressed in behavior.

Attitude Change—Meet the "Seekers"

Pages 570-572

1. People tend to change their attitudes to match those of their _____ group (a group the person identifies with and refers to for _____).

2. _____ is any _____ attempt to change attitudes or beliefs through information and arguments.

3. Effective _____ occurs when characteristics of the _____, the message, and the _____ are well matched.

4. In general, a _____ and believable communicator who repeats a _____ message that arouses emotion in the audience and states clear-cut conclusions will be persuasive.

5. Repeating a message that is backed up by _____ and facts as frequently as possible will be persuasive.

6. Maintaining and _____ attitudes is closely related to needs for consistency in thoughts and actions. Cognitive _____ theory explains the dynamics of such needs.

7. Cognitive _____ occurs when there is a clash between thoughts or between _____ and actions.

8. The amount of reward or _____ (reasons) for one's actions influences whether dissonance occurs.

9. We are motivated to reduce dissonance when it occurs, often by _____ beliefs or attitudes.

Prejudice—Attitudes that Injure

Survey Question: What causes prejudice and intergroup conflict? Pages 573-574

1. _____ is a negative attitude held toward members of various social groups.

2. Racism, _____, and sexism are specific types of prejudice based on _____, age, and gender (or sex).

3. _____ is a combination of prejudice and racism, and leads to the unequal treatment of people who should have the same rights as others.

4. One theory attributes prejudice to _____, which is a type of displaced aggression.

5. A second account says that prejudices may be held for personal reasons such as direct threats to a person's wellbeing (_____ prejudice) or simply through adherence to group norms (_____ prejudice).

6. Prejudiced individuals tend to have an _____ personality, characterized by rigidity, inhibition, _____, and over-simplification.

7. Authoritarians tend to be very _____ (they use their own group as a basis for judging all others).

8. Ethnocentrism refers to placing one's own racial group "at the _____," usually by rejecting all other groups

9. The Fascism scale, or F scale, measures _____.

Intergroup Conflict—The Roots of Prejudice

Pages 574-578

1. Intergroup conflict gives rise to _____ and the formation of social stereotypes (oversimplified images of members of various groups).

2. _____ prejudice, or prejudice expressed in disguised ways, is common today.

3. Status _____ (differences in power, _____, or privileges) tend to build prejudices.

4. _____-status contact (social interaction on an _____ footing) tends to reduce prejudice.

5. _____ goals (those that rise above all others) usually _____ intergroup conflict.

6. _____ Elliot demonstrated that prejudice could easily be created in the _____ when she separated children based on eye color.

7. On a small scale, _____ classrooms (which encourage cooperation through mutual _____) have been shown to be an effective way of combating prejudice.

8. _____ threat occurs when individuals think they are being judged in terms of a stereotype.

Aggression—The World's Most Dangerous Animal

Survey Question: How do psychologists explain human aggression? Pages 579-583

1. _____ refers to any action carried out with the intention of _____ another person.

2. _____ explain aggression as a natural expression of _____ instincts.

3. Biological explanations emphasize _____ mechanisms and physical factors that lower the threshold (_____ point) for aggression.

4. Physical factors such as low blood sugar, _____, specific brain diseases, and _____ do not cause aggression, but may make aggression more likely.

5. According to the _____-aggression hypothesis, frustration and aggression are closely _____.

6. Frustration is only one of many _____ stimuli that can arouse a person and make aggression more likely. Aggression is especially likely to occur when aggression cues (stimuli associated with _____) are present.

7. Social _____ theory has focused attention on the role of aggressive models in the development of _____ behavior.

8. Aggressive models on television _____ aggression because they desensitize (lower the sensitivity of) viewers to violence and _____ (remove restraints against) aggressive impulses.

9. By the end of elementary school, children will have seen about _____ murders and _____ other violent acts on TV. Reducing exposure to violent media is one way to lower aggression.

10. Parents can help to reduce the media's _____ effects on children by creating a warm, safe environment at home, _____ positive ways of coping, limiting media time, and closely monitoring what the child experiences.

Prosocial Behavior—Helping Others

Survey Question: Why are bystanders so often unwilling to help in an emergency?
Pages 583-586

1. _____ behavior is helpful, constructive, or altruistic toward others.

2. In 1964, Kitty _____ was murdered on a sidewalk in Queens, New York. Even though 38 people heard the attack, no one called the police or tried to get involved. This incident was instrumental in launching research into bystander _____.

3. Bystander _____ is the unwillingness of bystanders to offer help to others during _____.

4. _____ decision points that must be passed before a person gives help are: noticing, defining an _____, taking responsibility, and selecting a course of _____.

5. _____ is less likely at each point when other _____ helpers are present, as everyone believes that someone else will help.

6. In real _____, the need for action is underestimated because each person attempts to appear _____.

7. _____ of responsibility spreads the responsibility for helping among several people; this actually _____ who will help.

8. Helping is _____ by general arousal, empathic arousal, being in a good mood, _____ effort or risk, and perceived similarity between the _____ and the helper.

9. To ensure you receive help when needed, it is better to directly assign _____, such as pointing to someone and saying, "I'm injured, I need you to call an _____."

Psychology in Action: Multiculturalism—Living with Diversity

Survey Question: How can we promote multiculturalism and social harmony?
Pages 591-594

1. _____ is an attempt to give equal status to different ethnic, racial, and cultural groups.

2. To reduce _____, one can do the following: Be aware of _____, seek individuating information, beware of just-_____ beliefs, avoid unnecessary social competition, understand that race is a social construction, and look for _____.

3. By accepting the value of openness to the other, people can become _____ prejudiced.

4. Cultural awareness is a key element in promoting greater social _____.

5. Greater _____ can be encouraged by neutralizing stereotypes with _____ information (which helps see others as individuals).

6. _____ comes from looking for commonalties with others and by avoiding the effects of just-world beliefs, self-fulfilling prophecies, and social competition.

MASTERY TEST

1. Homogamy is directly related to which element of interpersonal attraction?
a. competence
b. similarity
c. beauty
d. proximity

2. The weapons effect refers to the fact that weapons can serve as aggression
a. thresholds.
b. cues.
c. models.
d. inhibitors.

3. Suspicion and reduced attraction are associated with
a. reciprocity.
b. self-disclosure.
c. competence and proximity.
d. overdisclosure.

4. The Seekers' renewed conviction and interest in persuading others after the world failed to end can be explained by the
a. social competition hypothesis.
b. frustration-persuasion hypothesis.
c. group's just-world beliefs.
d. theory of cognitive dissonance.

5. One thing that REDUCES the chances that a bystander will give help in an emergency is
a. heightened arousal.
b. empathic arousal.
c. others who could help.
d. similarity to the victim.

6. One consequence of seeing aggression portrayed on TV is a loss of emotional response, called
a. disinhibition.
b. disassociation.
c. deconditioning.
d. desensitization.

7. If you are speaking to a well-informed audience, it is important to
   _____ if you want to persuade them.
   a. repeat your message
   b. give both sides of the argument
   c. be likable
   d. appeal to their emotions

8. "President of the United States" is
   a. an ascribed role.
   b. an achieved role.
   c. a structural norm.
   d. a cohesive role.

9. Where attribution is concerned, wants, needs, motives, or personal
   characteristics are perceived as
   a. external causes.
   b. situational attributions.
   c. discounted causes.
   d. internal causes.

10. Asch is to _____ experiments as Milgram is to _____
    experiments.
    a. compliance; assertion
    b. conformity; obedience
    c. autokinetic; social power
    d. groupthink; authority

11. Social psychology is the scientific study of how people
    a. behave in the presence of others.
    b. form into groups and organizations.
    c. form and maintain interpersonal relationships.
    d. make inferences about the behavior of others.

12. Which view of human aggression is most directly opposed to that of the
    ethologists?
    a. social learning
    b. brain mechanisms
    c. attributional
    d. innate releaser

13. Creating superordinate goals is an important way to
    a. reduce group conflict.
    b. break the frustration-aggression link.
    c. promote bystander intervention.
    d. reverse self-fulfilling prophecies.

14. A key element in the effectiveness of jigsaw classrooms is
a. deindividuation.
b. the promotion of self-fulfilling prophecies.
c. mutual interdependence.
d. selecting competent student leaders.

15. Group structure involves all but one of the following elements. Which does NOT belong?
a. roles
b. communication pathways
c. allocation of power
d. social comparison

16. Groupthink is a type of _____ that applies to decision making in groups.
a. conformity
b. social comparison
c. social power
d. obedience

17. A good antidote for social stereotyping is
a. adopting just-world beliefs.
b. creating self-fulfilling prophecies.
c. accepting status inequalities.
d. seeking individuating information.

18. An important difference between brainwashing and other types of persuasion is that brainwashing
a. requires a captive audience.
b. is almost always permanent.
c. changes actions, not attitudes and beliefs.
d. is reversed during the refreezing phase.

19. In Milgram's studies, the smallest percentage of subjects followed orders when
a. the teacher and learner were in the same room.
b. the teacher received orders by phone.
c. the teacher and learner were face-to-face.
d. the experiment was conducted off campus.

20. The most basic attributional error is to attribute the behavior of others to _____ causes, even when they are caused by _____ causes.
a. inconsistent, consistent
b. internal, external
c. random, distinctive
d. situational, personal

21. Evolutionary theories attribute mate selection, in part, to the _____ of past generations.
a. food-gathering habits
b. tribal customs
c. maternal instincts
d. reproductive success

22. People tend to act like what is beautiful is good. However, beauty has little connection to
a. talents.
b. intelligence.
c. ability.
d. all the preceding traits

23. Which of the following gives special privileges to a member of a group?
a. convergent norms
b. high cohesiveness
c. actor-observer bias
d. high status

24. Your actions are most likely to agree with one of your attitudes when
a. the actions reverse an old habit.
b. the attitude is held with conviction.
c. you know that others disagree with your position.
d. you score high on an attitude scale.

25. When we are subjected to conformity pressures, the _____ of a majority is more important than the number of people in it.
a. unanimity
b. cohesion
c. proximity
d. comparison level

26. If it is easier for Anglo-Americans to get automobile insurance than it is for African Americans, then African Americans have experienced
a. discrimination.
b. scapegoating.
c. ethnocentrism.
d. personal prejudice.

27. The Bennington College study showed that attitudes are not affected very much by
a. membership groups.
b. childrearing.
c. reference groups.
d. chance conditioning.

28. Members of the _____ are people who share similar values, goals, interest, and identify themselves as belonging to a same group.
   a. in-group
   b. out-group
   c. pepgroup
   d. essential group

29. In April 1993 in Waco, Texas, David Koresh used a mixture of manipulation, isolation, deception, and fear to gain absolute loyalty and obedience from a group of followers who ultimately committed suicide at his request. This is an example of
   a. brainwashing.
   b. scapegoating.
   c. desensitization.
   d. discrimination.

30. Which theory combines learning principles with cognitive processes, socialization, and modeling to explain human behavior?
   a. social learning
   b. individuating information
   c. existential
   d. multiculturalism

31. Billy's new neighbor is from Pakistan. Because Billy wants to avoid misunderstandings and conflict when he meets and talks to his neighbor, he attends a cultural event sponsored by the Pakistani student club at his university. Billy is attempting to
   a. see how much they are alike.
   b. increase his cultural awareness of other's culture.
   c. reduce stereotypes and prejudicial views of others.
   d. all the preceding.

32. You ask your friend to review a few pages of your term paper and she agrees. Later, you ask her to read the whole paper, the goal you wanted all along. This process best describes the
   a. low-ball technique.
   b. set-and-hook technique.
   c. door-in-the-face technique.
   d. foot-in-the-door technique.

33. If a group's decision-making is frozen because the group considers too many alternative actions, it faces
   a. deadlock.
   b. groupthink.
   c. conformity.
   d. compliance.

34. If Jennifer wants Art to like her, which of the following is LEAST LIKEY to be effective?

a. Showing her independence by disagreeing with Art
b. Sitting next to Art in his classes
c. Engaging on moderate self-disclosure
d. Making herself physically attractive (e.g., makeup)

LANGUAGE DEVELOPMENT
Social Behavior

Word Roots

As an adjective, the word *social* is taken from the Latin, *sociālis*. This refers to companionship or a connection between people. You will find the term *social* throughout this chapter: social psychology, social comparison, social influence, and social learning.

Journey into Psychology: Love and Hate (p. 549)
(549)   *wryly*: clever and ironically humorous
(549)   *naïve:* ignorantly innocent
(549)   *harassed*: annoyed repeatedly and persistently
(549)   *shunned*: deliberately avoided or cast aside
(549)   *reviled*: subject to abusive language
(549)   *"Romeo and Juliet" stories*: reference to a play by
Shakespeare in which two lovers came from feuding families; they met
            with tragic ends in their quest to be together.
(549)   *tapestry*: heavy, reversible textile that has designs or
            pictures
woven into it
(549)   *"sampler"*: brief introduction

Affiliation and Attraction—Come Together (pgs. 550-552)
Why do people affiliate? What factors influence interpersonal attraction?
(550)   *rampant*: widespread
(550)   *"birds of a feather flock together"*: just as birds of one type
            tend to stay together, so do people or things with similar
            characteristics group together
(550)   *"familiarity breeds contempt"*: a common saying meaning
            that the more one knows about a person, the less one likes that
            person
(550)   *"opposites attract"*: the belief that persons with opposite
            personalities, interests, values, etc. will be attracted to one
            another

(550)   ***"absence makes the heart grow fonder"*:** a common saying meaning that if friends or lovers are separated they will grow fonder of each other

(550)   ***folklore*:** traditional customs, stories, or sayings of a people

(551)   ***halo effect*:** the tendency to rate a person too high or too low on the basis of a single trait

(552)   ***governed*:** controlled

Liking and Loving—Dating, Rating, Mating (pgs. 552-555)

(553)   ***imprint*:** a mark

(554)   ***infidelity*:** unfaithfulness

(554)   ***"trophy wives"*:** wives chosen primarily for their physical attractiveness so men can "show them off"

(554)   ***sire*:** to be the father of

(554)   ***allies*:** friends

Humans in a Social Context—People, People, Everywhere (pgs. 555557)

How does group membership affect our behavior?

(555)   ***streamline*:** simplify

(555)   ***flunk*:** fail

(566)   ***exert*:** apply

(557)   ***lax*:** not strict

(557)   ***inferences*:** guesses

(557)   ***tuba*:** large brass musical instrument that makes a deep sound

(557)   ***Sousa march*:** reference to the music of John Philip Sousa; marches are pieces of music with a strong beat suitable for marching

(557)   ***cheapskates*:** stingy, miserly people

Social Influence—Follow the Leader (pgs. 558-560)

What have social psychologists learned about social influence?

(558)   ***shooting pool:*** playing a game of billiards; one "shoots" a cue ball with a cue stick.

(559)   ***lethal*:** deadly

(559)   ***yielded*:** gave in; conformed

(559)   ***erred*:** made a mistake

(559)   ***"rock the boat"*:** disturb the situation; make changes

(559)   ***Columbia space shuttle disaster*:** reference to the space shuttle accident that killed all the astronauts on board in February, 2003

(559)   ***Mars Climate Orbiter*:** signals from the orbiter probe were lost as it entered orbit around Mars; no signal has been detected since

(559)   ***devil's advocate*:** one who argues in support of the less accepted or approved alternative

(559)　***deadlock***: a situation where no one is willing to change his/her decision; therefore, the situation has come to a complete stop and is not moving forward

(560)　***ridicule***: teasing someone or making them the object of laughter

(560)　***sanctions***: rules or laws

(560)　***in your corner***: on your side; supportive of you

Compliance—A Foot in the Door (pgs. 561-562)

(561)　***cappuccino:*** a hot beverage consisting of espresso coffee and steamed milk, often served with powdered cinnamon and topped with whipped cream.

(562)　***bump the price up***: increase the price

Obedience—Would You Electrocute a Stranger? (pgs. 562-564)

(562)　***electrocute***: to deliver electric shock

(562)　***concentration camps***: places were enemy prisoners and political prisoners are held

(562)　***provocative***: tending to stimulate or excite interest

(564)　***shabby***: run down; poorly kept

(564)　*knuckle under*: submit

(564)　***"simulated"***: pretend; faked

(564)　***"sanctioned massacres"***: authorized slaying of large masses of people at one time

(564)　***fortitude***: courage; strength

Coercion—Brainwashing and Cults (pgs. 564-566)

(564)　***POW camps:*** Prisoner of War camps; place where captured enemies were held and tortured.

(555)　***allegiance***: loyalty; commitment

(565)　***infallible***: perfect; without fault

(565)　***errant***: misbehaving

(565)　***indoctrination***: training; teaching

(565)　***succumbed:*** given in to

Assertiveness Training – Standing Up for Your Rights (pgs. 566-568)

How does self-assertion differ from aggression?

(566)　***making a scene***: exhibiting anger or improper behavior

(567)　***poise***: dignity; good posture

(567)　***pent-up***: held in; unexpressed

Attitudes—Belief + Emotion + Action (pgs. 568-570)

How are attitudes acquired and changed?

(568)　***euthanasia***: the ending of one's life to end suffering

Attitude change – Meet the "Seekers" (pgs. 570-572)

(570)　***blitz***: any swift, vigorous attack, barrage, or defeat

(572)　***antiquated***: very old; out of date

Prejudice—Attitudes that Injure (pgs. 573-574)

What causes prejudice and intergroup conflict?

(573)   *infractions*: rule violations
(574)   *anti-Semitism*: prejudice against Jewish individuals
(574)   *fascism*: a strict, dictator-controlled system of government
(574)   *bigotry*: prejudice; bias

Intergroup Conflict—The Roots of Prejudice (pgs. 574-578)

(574)   *jarring*: harsh
(574)   *strife*: conflict; trouble
(575)   *demeaning*: degrading
(575)   *busing*: a policy whereby students are sent to schools outside of their district; it is designed, in part, to get inner-city children into better schools
(575)   *"the benefit of the doubt"*: to believe something good about someone, rather than something bad, when you have the possibility of doing either

Aggression—The World's Most Dangerous Animal (pgs. 579-583)

How do psychologists explain human aggression?

(581)   *"bean balls"*: a baseball pitch thrown with the intention to hit the batter
(582)   *begets*: produces; causes

Prosocial Behavior—Helping Others (pgs. 583-586)

Why are bystanders so often unwilling to help in an emergency?

(583)   *alienation*: emotional isolation or dissociation
(584)   *sidelong*: indirect; sideways
(584)   *"fake each other out"*: to pretend to be other than genuine
(585)   *intercom system:* electronic intercommunication system, often between two rooms.

Psychology in Action: Multiculturalism—Living with Diversity (Pgs. 586-589)

How can we promote multiculturalism and social harmony?

(586)   *"tossed salad":* in a salad, all vegetables retain their individual properties, but are part of a larger whole.
(586)   *"melting pot"*: older expression used to describe the US population: implies that individual characteristics were melted together to create a new product.

Solutions

Recite and Review

Affiliation and Attraction—Come Together

1. Social
2. approval, information.
3. evaluate
4. nearness, contact
5. more, unrelated
6. similar, age
7. attraction
8. similarity, mate
9. revealing
10. norm, self-disclosure

Liking and Loving—Dating, Rating, Mating

1. Triangular, passion
2. connectedness, together
3. complete
4. absorption
5. commitment, passion
6. mating
7. casual
8. younger, older, high
9. sexual, emotional

Humans in a Social Context—People, People, Everywhere

1. groups
2. Social, roles
3. assigned, voluntarily, attained
4. contradictory
5. roles, remain, in, group
6. in, group, ethnicity, religion, positive, out, group
7. groups
8. standards, groups
9. causes
10. causes, causes
11. error, internal, internal, external

Social Influence—Follow the Leader

1. behavior, others
2. gentlest, nearby
3. little, no, authority
4. improve, impaired
5. loaf, group
6. conforms, norms
7. groups, group
8. cooperation, more
9. sanctions, size
10. decision, making
11. avoid, critical, bias
12. deadlock

Compliance—A Foot in the Door

1. requests, power
2. foot, face
3. large, small, smaller, major
4. agree, less

Obedience—Would You Electrocute a Stranger?

1. authority
2. 450, all
3. Obedience
4. authority, requests

Forced Attitude Change—Brainwashing and Cults

1. against
2. forced
3. changing
4. personality
5. brainwashing
6. affection, conversion

Assertiveness Training—Standing Up For Your Rights.

1. reluctant
2. training
3. refuse, wrong
4. Aggression
5. assertive

Attitudes—Belief + Emotion + Action

1. positive, negative
2. action
3. evaluation
4. direct, child
5. media, chance
6. immediate, evaluate
7. expressed

Attitude Change—Meet the "Seekers"

1. identifies
2. change, arguments
3. message
4. emotion, conclusions
5. statistics
6. consistency
7. clash
8. dissonance
9. reduce

Prejudice—Attitudes that Injure

1. negative
2. gender, sex
3. prejudice, rights
4. aggression
5. norms
6. personality, over
7. group
8. rejecting
9. Fascism

Intergroup Conflict—The Roots of Prejudice

1. conflict
2. disguised
3. Status
4. reduce
5. goals
6. eye
7. classrooms, mutual
8. threat

Aggression—The World's Most Dangerous Animal

1. intention
2. instincts
3. lower
4. blood, more
5. aggression, aggression
6. stimuli, aggression
7. models
8. models, viewers
9. murders, media
10. safe, monitoring

Prosocial Behavior—Helping Others

1. helpful
2. murdered, police, bystander
3. help
4. noticing
5. less, else
6. underestimated
7. responsibility
8. arousal, risk
9. assign, you

Psychology in Action: Multiculturalism—Living with Diversity

1. equal
2. reduce, aware, just, social
3. openness, other
4. Cultural
5. individuals
6. beliefs, social

CONNECTIONS

Affiliation and Attraction—Come Together and Liking and Loving—Dating, Rating, Mating

1. C.
2. L.
3. I.
4. B.
5. K
6. F.
7. G.
8. D.
9. N.
10. A.
11. H.
12. E.
13. M.
14. J.

Humans in a Social Context—People, People, Everywhere

1. E.
2. J.
3. C.
4. I.
5. F.
6. G.
7. B.
8. H.
9. D.
10. K.
11. A.

Social Influence—Follow the Leader; Compliance—A Foot in the Door; and Obedience—Would You Electrocute a Stranger?

1. F.
2. I.
3. C.
4. K.
5. A.
6. J.
7. D.
8. H.
9. G.
10. M.
11. E.
12. L.
13. B.

Forced Attitude Change—Brainwashing and Cults and Assertiveness Training—Standing up for Your Rights

1. F.
2. C.
3. E.
4. B.
5. A.
6. G.
7. D.

Attitudes – Belief + Emotion + Action; Attitude change – Meet the "Seekers"

1. D.
2. H.
3. A.
4. C.
5. E.
6. G.
7. F.
8. B.

Prejudice—Attitudes that Injure and Intergroup Conflict—The Roots of Prejudice

1. A.	5. B.	9. D.	13. C.
2. M.	6. J.	10. I.	
3. E.	7. G.	11. F.	
4. H.	8. K.	12. L.	

Aggression—The World's Most Dangerous Animal; Prosocial Behavior—Helping Others; and Multiculturalism—Living with Diversity

1. F.	5. J.	9. K.	13. I.
2. B.	6. C.	10. D.	
3. L.	7. M.	11. G.	
4. H.	8. E.	12. A.	

Check Your Memory

Affiliation and Attraction—Come Together

1. T	5. T	9. F	13. T
2. F	6. F	10. T	14. F
3. F	7. T	11. F	15. T
4. T	8. F	12. T	

Liking and Loving—Dating, Rating, Mating

1. F	3. T	5. F
2. T	4. T	6. F

Humans in a Social Context—People, People, Everywhere

1. F	4. T	7. F	10. F
2. T	5. T	8. F	
3. T	6. F	9. T	

Social Influence—Follow the Leader

1. T	4. T	7. F
2. T	5. T	8. T
3. F	6. F	9. F

Compliance—A Foot in the Door

1. T	2. T	3. F	4. F

Obedience—Would You Electrocute a Stranger?

1. F	3. F	5. T
2. T	4. T	6. T

Coercion—Brainwashing and Cults

1. T	4. F	7. F
2. T	5. T	8. T
3. F	6. F	9. T

Assertiveness Training – Standing Up for Your Rights

1. T	3. F	5. T
2. F	4. F	

Attitudes—Belief + Emotion + Action

1. T	4. T	7. F	10. T
2. T	5. T	8. F	
3. F	6. T	9. T	

Attitude Change—Meet the "Seekers"

1. F	4. F	7. T	10. F
2. F	5. T	8. T	11. T
3. T	6. F	9. T	

Prejudice—Attitudes that Injure

1. T	3. F	5. F	7. F
2. F	4. T	6. T	8. T

Intergroup Conflict—The Roots of Prejudice

1. T	5. T	9. T	13. T
2. F	6. T	10. T	
3. F	7. T	11. F	
4. F	8. F	12. F	

Aggression—The World's Most Dangerous Animal

1. F	4. T	7. F	10. F
2. T	5. F	8. F	11. F
3. F	6. F	9. T	

Prosocial Behavior—Helping Others

1. T	3. F	5. F	7. T
2. T	4. F	6. T	

Psychology in Action: Multiculturalism—Living with Diversity

1. F	4. F	7. T
2. T	5. T	8. T
3. T	6. T	9. F

Final Survey and Review

Affiliation and Attraction—Come Together

1. behave, social
2. affiliate, friendship
3. comparison, feelings
4. proximity, frequency
5. halo, intelligence
6. Friends, ethnicity
7. physical, competence, similarity
8. homogamy
9. disclosure, greater
10. Low, moderate, overdisclosure

Liking and Loving—Dating, Rating, Mating

1. three, Intimacy, commitment
2. intimacy, passion, commitment
3. Consummate
4. Romantic
5. Empty
6. reproductive
7. men, women
8. Men, women
9. Men, women

Humans in a Social Context—People, People, Everywhere

1. roles
2. roles, ascribed
3. ascribed, achieved
4. role, conflict
5. structure, cohesiveness
6. nationality, in, group, negative
7. higher, High
8. Norms
9. inferences
10. internal, external
11. attributional, observer

Social Influence—Follow the Leader

1. influence, behavior
2. mere, presence
3. Compliance, authority, obedience
4. confident, facilitate
5. loafers, individually
6. Conformity, cultural
7. Conformity, sanctions
8. emphasize, conform
9. Group, belonging
10. Groupthink, critical
11. leaders, evaluator, preferences, accountable
12. alternatives

Compliance—A Foot in the Door

1. Compliance
2. door, door, low
3. foot, door, door, face
4. balling

Obedience—Would You Electrocute a Stranger?

1. Obedience, Milgram.
2. 1, 65
3. decreased, decreased
4. unreasonable

Forced Attitude Change—Brainwashing and Cults

1. Coercion
2. Brainwashing, total
3. unfreezing, refreezing
4. cult, beliefs
5. high, pressure
6. vulnerable, intimidation

Assertiveness Training – Standing Up For Your Rights.

1. rewarded, scene
2. Assertiveness, assertive.
3. request, right
4. expense
5. role, rehearsing

Attitudes—Belief + Emotion + Action

1. Attitudes, objects
2. belief
3. predict
4. contact, rearing, group
5. Peer, conditioning
6. consequences, habits
7. conviction

Attitude Change—Meet the "Seekers"

1. reference, guidance
2. Persuasion, deliberate
3. persuasion, communicator, audience
4. likable, credible
5. statistics
6. changing, dissonance
7. dissonance, thoughts
8. justification
9. changing

Prejudice—Attitudes that Injure

1. Prejudice
2. ageism, race
3. Discrimination
4. scapegoating,
5. personal, group
6. authoritarian, intolerance
7. ethnocentric
8. center
9. authoritarianism.

Intergroup Conflict—The Roots of Prejudice

1. hostility
2. Symbolic
3. inequalities, prestige
4. Equal, equal
5. Superordinate, reduce
6. Jane, classroom
7. jigsaw, interdependence
8. Stereotype

Aggression—The World's Most Dangerous Animal

1. Aggression, harming
2. Ethologists, inherited
3. brain, trigger
4. allergy, hormones
5. frustration, linked
6. aversive, aggression
7. learning, aggressive
8. encourage, disinhibit
9. 8,000, 100,000
10. negative, modeling

Prosocial Behavior—Helping Others

1. Prosocial
2. Genovese, apathy
3. apathy, emergencies
4. Four, emergency, action
5. Helping, potential
6. emergencies, calm
7. Diffusion, limits
8. encouraged, low, victim
9. responsibility, ambulance

Psychology in Action: Multiculturalism—Living with Diversity

1. Multiculturalism
2. prejudice, stereotyping,
   world, commonalities
3. less
4. harmony
5. tolerance, individuating
6. Tolerance

Mastery Test

1. b, p. 552
2. b, p. 581
3. d, p. 552
4. d, p. 571
5. c, p. 583
6. d, p. 582
7. b, p. 571
8. b, p. 555
9. d, p. 557
10. b, p. 559-560; 562-563
11. a, p. 550
12. a, p. 579-580
13. a, p. 576-577
14. c, p. 578
15. d, p. 555-556
16. a, p. 559
17. d, p. 574-575; 587
18. a, p. 565
19. b, p. 564
20. b, p. 557
21. d, p. 553-554
22. d, p. 551
23. d, p. 556
24. b, p. 570
25. a, p. 560
26. a, p. 575
27. c, p. 570
28. a, p. 556
29. a, p. 565
30. a, p. 581
31. d, p. 586-589
32. d, p. 561
33. a, p. 559
34. a, p. 551

Behavioral Statistics

Chapter Overview

Descriptive statistics are used to summarize data. Inferential statistics are used to make decisions and generalizations or to draw conclusions. Graphical statistics, such as histograms and frequency polygons, provide pictures (graphs) of groups of numbers. Measures of central tendency, such as the mean, median, and mode, supply a number describing an "average" or "typical" score in a group of scores. The range and standard deviation are measures of variability, or the spread of scores. Standard scores (z-scores) combine the mean and standard deviation in a way that tells how far above or below the mean a particular score lies. The normal curve is a bell-shaped distribution of scores that has useful and well-known properties.

Although psychologists are ultimately interested in entire populations, they must usually observe only a representative sample. Nevertheless, it is possible to tell if the results of an experiment are statistically significant (unlikely to be due to chance alone).

When measurements, scores, or observations come in pairs, it is possible to determine if they are correlated. The correlation coefficient tells if the relationship between two measures is positive or negative and how strong it is. While correlations are quite useful, correlation does not demonstrate causation.

Learning Objectives

1. Define and distinguish between the two major types of statistics, descriptive and inferential statistics; and list the three types of descriptive statistics.
2. Describe graphical statistics, including the terms *frequency distribution*, *histogram*, and *frequency polygon*.
3. Define measures of central tendency, including the mean, median, and mode.
4. Define measures of variability, including the range, standard deviation, and standard scores (z-scores).
5. Describe the normal curve and include its relationship to the standard deviation and z-scores.
6. Define and give examples of the use of inferential statistics; and distinguish between a population and a sample, including the concepts of representative sample and random sample.
7. Explain the concept of statistical significance.

8.   Describe the concept of correlation and how scatter diagrams are used; distinguish among positive relationships, negative relationships, and zero correlations; define the coefficient of correlation; and state the meaning of a perfect positive and perfect negative correlation.

9.   Briefly discuss the value of correlations for making predictions; explain the concept of percent of variance; and discuss the relationship between correlation and cause-and-effect determination.

RECITE AND REVIEW

Descriptive Statistics—Psychology by the Numbers

Survey Question: What are descriptive statistics? Pages 594-599

1.   Descriptive statistics are used to _____ data. Inferential statistics are used to make decisions and generalizations or to draw _____.

2.   Three basic types of _____ statistics are graphical statistics, measures of central tendency, and measures of variability.

3.   A frequency distribution organizes data by breaking an entire range of scores into _____ of equal size. Then, the number of scores falling in each _____ is recorded.

4.   Graphical statistics provide _____ (graphs) of collections of numbers.

5.   A histogram is drawn by placing _____ intervals on the abscissa (_____ line) and frequencies on the ordinate (_____ line) of a graph.

6.   Next, vertical bars are drawn for each class interval, with the _____ of the bars being determined by the number of scores in each class.

7.   A frequency polygon (line graph) results when points are plotted at the _____ of each class interval and connected by lines.

8.   Measures of central tendency are numbers describing an "_____" or "typical" score in a group of scores.

9.   The mean is calculated by _____ all the scores for a group and then dividing by the total number of scores.

10. The mean is sensitive to extremely _____ or extremely _____ scores in a given distribution.

11. The median is found by arranging scores from the highest to the lowest and then selecting the _____ score.

12. The mode is the _____ _____ occurring score in a group of scores.

13. Measures of variability tell how varied or widely _____ scores are.

14. The range is the _____ score minus the _____ score.

15. The standard deviation is calculated by finding the difference between each score and the _____. These differences are then _____. Then the squared deviations are totaled and their mean is found.

16. Standard scores (_____-scores) are found by subtracting the _____ from a score. The resulting number is then divided by the standard deviation.

17. Standard scores tell how far above or below the _____ a particular score lies.

18. When they are collected from large groups of people, many psychological measures form a normal _____.

19. In a normal curve, 68 percent of all scores fall between plus and minus 1 standard deviations from the _____.

20. Ninety-five percent of all cases fall between plus and minus _____ standard deviations from the mean.

21. Ninety-nine percent of all cases fall between plus and minus _____ standard deviations from the mean.

Correlation—Rating Relationships

Survey Question: How are correlations used in psychology? Pages 599-602

1. When measurements, scores, variables, or observations come in pairs, it is possible to determine if they are correlated (varying together in an _____ fashion).

2. The simplest way to visualize a correlation is by using a _____ diagram, in which the intersection of data from two measures is plotted as a _____ point.

3. In a positive relationship, increases in the X measure (or score) are matched by _____ on the Y measure (or score).

4. In a negative relationship, increases in the X measure (or score) are matched by _____ on the Y measure (or score).

5. The coefficient of correlation tells if the relationship between two measures is _____ or _____, and how strong it is.

6. The most commonly used correlation coefficient is called the _____ r.

7. A _____ positive relationship is indicated by +1.00; a _____ negative relationship is indicated by -1.00. Stronger relationships fall closer to these extremes.

8. The percent of variance (amount of _____ in scores) is accounted for by the correlation and can be derived by multiplying the _____ by itself.

9. While correlations are quite useful, correlation does not _____ causation.

Inferential Statistics—Significant Numbers

Survey Question: What are inferential statistics? Pages 602-603

1. The _____ _____ of subjects, objects, or events of interest in a scientific investigation is called a population.

2. When an entire population cannot be observed, a sample (smaller cross section) of the _____ is selected.

3. Samples must be representative (they must truly reflect the characteristics of the _____).

4. _____ drawn from representative samples are assumed to apply to the entire population.

5. Tests of statistical significance tell how often the results of an experiment could have occurred by _____ alone.

6. An experimental result that could have occurred only 5 times out of 100 (or less) by chance alone is considered _____.

CONNECTIONS

Descriptive Statistics—Psychology by the Numbers

Survey Question: What are descriptive statistics? Pages 594-599

1. _____ histogram
2. _____ standard deviation
3. _____ frequency distribution
4. _____ normal curve
5. _____ range
6. _____ standard score
7. _____ mean

A. grouped scores
B. picture of frequencies
C. central tendency
D. spread of scores
E. average squared difference
F. z-score
G. model distribution

Correlation—Rating Relationships and Inferential Statistics—Significant Numbers

Survey Questions: How are correlations used in psychology? What are inferential statistics? Pages 599-603

1. _____ population
2. _____ sample
3. _____ Positive relationship
4. _____ representative
5. _____ zero correlation
6. _____ scatter diagram
7. _____ Pearson *r*
8. _____ Negative relationship
9. _____ *r* squared

A. subset
B. graphed correlation
C. randomly selected
D. correlation coefficient
E. no relationship
F. entire set
G. percent of variance
H. increase in X corresponds to increase in Y
I. increase in X corresponds to decrease in Y

CHECK YOUR MEMORY

Descriptive Statistics—Psychology by the Numbers

Survey Question: What are descriptive statistics? Pages 594-599

1. Descriptive statistics extract and summarize information.

TRUE or FALSE

2. Inferential statistics are used to make pictures (graphs) out of data.

TRUE or FALSE

3. Measures of variability are descriptive statistics.

TRUE or FALSE

4. A frequency distribution is made by recording the most frequently occurring score.

TRUE or FALSE

5. A frequency polygon is a graphical representation of a frequency distribution.

TRUE or FALSE

6. On a graph, the ordinate is the line that shows the frequency of scores at the center of each class interval.

TRUE or FALSE

7. The mean, median, and mode are all averages.

TRUE or FALSE

8. The median is the most frequently occurring score in a group of scores.

TRUE or FALSE

9. To find the mode, you would have to know how many people obtained each possible score.

TRUE or FALSE

10. The standard deviations can be different in two groups of scores even if their means are the same.

TRUE or FALSE

11. To find the range, you would have to know what the highest and lowest scores are.

TRUE or FALSE

12. To find a z-score you must know the median and the standard deviation.

TRUE or FALSE

13. A z-score of one means that a person scored exactly at the mean.

TRUE or FALSE

14. The majority of scores are found near the middle of a normal curve.

TRUE or FALSE

15. Fifty percent of all scores are found below the mean in a normal curve.

TRUE or FALSE

Correlation—Rating Relationships

Survey Question: How are correlations used in psychology? Pages 599-602

1. A scatter diagram is a plot of two sets of unrelated measurements on the same graph.

TRUE or FALSE

2. In a positive relationship, increases in measure X are matched by increases in measure Y.

TRUE or FALSE

3. A correlation coefficient of .100 indicates a perfect positive relationship.

TRUE or FALSE

4. The Pearson r ranges from −.100 to +.100.

TRUE or FALSE

5. Correlations allow psychologists to make predictions.

TRUE or FALSE

6. Two correlated measures may be related through the influence of a third variable.

TRUE or FALSE

7. Correlation proves that one variable causes another if the correlation coefficient is significant.

TRUE or FALSE

Inferential Statistics—Significant Numbers

Survey Question: What are inferential statistics? Pages 602-603

1. Psychologists prefer to study entire populations whenever it is practical to do so.

TRUE or FALSE

2. Random selection of subjects usually makes a sample representative.

TRUE or FALSE

3. A result that could have occurred by chance alone 25 times out of 100 is considered statistically significant.

TRUE or FALSE

4. A probability of .05 or less is statistically significant.

TRUE or FALSE

FINAL SURVEY AND REVIEW

Descriptive Statistics—Psychology by the Numbers

Survey Question: What are descriptive statistics? Pages 594-599

1. _____ statistics are used to summarize data. _____ statistics are used to make decisions and generalizations or to draw conclusions.

2. Three basic types of descriptive statistics are _____ statistics, measures of _____ tendency, and measures of variability.

3. A _____ distribution organizes data by breaking an entire range of scores into classes of equal size. Then, the number of _____ falling in each class is recorded.

4. _____ statistics provide pictures (_____) of collections of numbers.

5. A _____ is drawn by placing class intervals on the _____ (horizontal line) and frequencies on the _____ (vertical line) of a graph.

6. Next, vertical _____ are drawn for each class interval, with the height of the bars being determined by the _____ of scores in each class.

7. A frequency _____ (line graph) results when points are plotted at the center of each class interval and _____ by lines.

8. Measures of central _____ are numbers describing an "average" or "typical" score in a _____ of scores.

9. The _____ is calculated by adding all the scores for a group and then dividing by the total number of scores.

10. The mean is sensitive to _____ high or _____ low scores in a given distribution.

11. The _____ is found by arranging scores from the highest to the lowest and then selecting the middle score.

12. The _____ is the most frequently occurring score in a group of scores.

13. Measures of variability tell how _____ or widely spread scores are.

14. The _____ is the highest score minus the lowest score.

15. The _____ deviation is calculated by finding the difference between each score and the mean. These _____ are then squared. Then the squared deviations are totaled and their mean is found.

16. _____ scores (z-scores) are found by subtracting the mean from a score. The resulting number is then divided by the standard deviation.

17. Standard scores tell how far _____ or _____ the mean a particular score lies.

18. When they are collected from large groups of people, many psychological measures form a _____ curve.

19. In a normal curve, _____ percent of all scores fall between plus and minus 1 standard deviations from the mean.

20. _____-_____ percent of all cases fall between plus and minus 2 standard deviations from the mean.

21. _____-_____ percent of all cases fall between plus and minus 3 standard deviations from the mean.

Correlation—Rating Relationships

Survey Question: How are correlations used in psychology? Pages 599-602

1. When measurements, scores, variables, or observations come in _____, it is possible to determine if they are _____ (varying together in an orderly fashion).

2. The simplest way to visualize a correlation is by using a scatter _____, in which the _____ of data from two measures is plotted as a single point.

3. In a _____ relationship, increases in the X measure (or score) are matched by increases on the Y measure (or score).

4. In a _____ relationship, increases in the X measure (or score) are matched by decreases on the Y measure (or score).

5. The _____ of correlation tells if the relationship between two measures is positive or negative, and how _____ it is.

6. The most commonly used correlation _____ is called the Pearson *r*.

7. A perfect _____ relationship is indicated by +1.00; a perfect _____ relationship is indicated by -1.00. Stronger relationships fall closer to these extremes.

8. The percent of _____ (amount of variation in scores) is accounted for by the correlation and can be derived by multiplying the *r* by itself.

9. While correlations are quite useful, correlation does not demonstrate _____.

Inferential Statistics—Significant Numbers

Survey Question: What are inferential statistics? Pages 602-603

1. The entire set of _____, objects, or events of interest in a scientific investigation is called a _____.

2. When an entire population cannot be _____, a sample (smaller cross section) of the population is selected.

3. _____ must be representative (they must truly reflect the characteristics of the population).

4. Conclusions drawn from _____ samples are assumed to apply to the entire population.

5. Tests of _____ significance tell how often the results of an experiment could have occurred by chance alone.

6. An experimental result that could have occurred only _____ times out of 100 (or less) by _____ alone is considered significant.

MASTERY TEST

1. _____ statistics are especially valuable for decision making and drawing conclusions.
   a. Graphical
   b. Descriptive
   c. Inferential
   d. Significant

2. Measures of central tendency are _____ statistics.
   a. graphical
   b. descriptive
   c. inferential
   d. significant

3. Sorting scores into classes is a necessary step in creating a
   a. frequency distribution.
   b. correlation.
   c. scatter diagram.
   d. variability plot.

4. Vertical bars are used to indicate frequencies in a
   a. frequency polygon.
   b. scatter diagram.
   c. normal distribution.
   d. histogram.

5. Which is NOT a measure of central tendency?
   a. mean.
   b. range.
   c. mode.
   d. median.

6. A group of scores must be arranged from lowest to highest in order to find the
   a. mean.
   b. midst.
   c. mode.
   d. median.

7. The _____ is sensitive to extremely high or low scores in a distribution.
   a. mean
   b. midst
   c. mode
   d. median

8. Which is a measure of variability?
   a. Pearson r.
   b. z-score.
   c. midst.
   d. range.

9. What two statistics are needed to calculate a standard score?
a. range and midst.
b. mean and standard deviation.
c. range and mode.
d. standard deviation and z-score.

10. If the mean on a test is 90, and the standard deviation is 10, a person with a z-score of –1 scored _____ on the test.
a. 70
b. 597-598
c. 100
d. 110

11. The largest percentage of scores falls between _____ SD in a normal curve.
a. 0 and +1
b. +1 and –1
c. +2 and +3
d. –3 and –2

12. What percent of all cases are found between +3 SD and –3 SD in a normal curve?
a. 50
b. 86
c. 95
d. 99

13. An effective way to make sure that a sample is representative is to
a. use random selection.
b. calculate the correlation coefficient.
c. make sure that the standard deviation is low.
d. use a scatter diagram.

14. Results of an experiment that have a chance probability of _____ are usually regarded as statistically significant.
a. .5
b. .05
c. 1.5
d. 1.05

15. A good way to visualize a correlation is to plot a
a. frequency histogram.
b. polygon coefficient.
c. scatter diagram.
d. normal ordinate.

16. When measure X gets larger, measure Y gets smaller in a
a. zero correlation.
b. positive relationship.
c. variable relationship.
d. negative relationship.

17. When plotted as a graph, a zero correlation forms a cluster of points in the shape of a
a. diagonal oval to the right.
b. diagonal oval to the left.
c. horizontal line.
d. circle.

18. The largest possible correlation coefficient is
a. 1.
b. .001.
c. 100.
d. 10.

19. To find the percent of variance in one measure accounted for by knowing another measure, you should square the
a. mean.
b. z-score.
c. Pearson r.
d. standard deviation.

20. Correlations do not demonstrate whether
a. a relationship is positive or negative.
b. a cause-and-effect connection exists.
c. knowing one measure allows prediction of another.
d. two events are really co-relating.

LANGUAGE DEVELOPMENT
APPENDIX
Behavioral Statistics

Word Roots

Statisticus is a Latin term that means "state of affairs" and comes from an earlier Latin word *status* that means "condition" or "position." An 18th century German political scientist first used the German term *statistisch* to refer to the evaluation of data. This eventually became the English word "statistics."

Journey into Psychology: Statistics from "Heads" to "Tails" (p. 593)

- (593) **heads**: the side of a coin with the face on it
- (593) **tails**: the side of a coin opposite the face
- (593) *"game of chance"*: gambling
- (593) **recoup**: get an amount back equivalent to your losses
- (593) *"skinned"*: lose all your money
- (593) **unbiased**: not leaning one way or the other
- (593) **hypothetical**: fictional; imaginary

Descriptive Statistics—Psychology by the Numbers (pgs. 594-599)

- (594) **simulated**: made up data
- (594) **hypnotic susceptibility**: one's ability to be hypnotized
- (595) **raw data**: original set of data from a survey, experiment, sample, etc.
- (595) **placebo**: a substance having no effect but given to a patient or subject of an experiment who supposes it to be a medicine
- (595) **multimillionaire**: a person who has two or more millions of dollars
- (596) **agitated**: excited and upset
- (597) **psychological variables**: concepts in psychology, such as attitude, aggression, intelligence, etc., that can be measured according to some scale

Correlation—Rating Relationships (pgs. 599-602)

- (599) **IQ**: a measure of intelligence; intelligence quotient; mental age divided by chronological age

Inferential Statistics—Significant Numbers (pgs. 602-603)

- (603) **loaded coin**: a coin that has the tendency to land only on one side (e.g., always landing on heads-up)
- (603) **inferred**: to have come to a conclusion

Solutions

Recite and Review

Descriptive Statistics—Psychology by the Numbers

1. summarize, conclusions
2. descriptive
3. classes, class
4. pictures
5. class, horizontal, vertical
6. height
7. center
8. average
9. adding
10. high, low
11. middle
12. most, frequently
13. spread
14. highest, lowest
15. mean, squared
16. z, mean
17. mean
18. curve
19. mean
20. 2
21. 3

Correlation—Rating Relationships

Survey Question: How are correlations used in psychology? Pages 599-602

1. orderly
2. scatter, single
3. increases
4. decreases
5. positive, negative
6. Pearson
7. perfect, perfect
8. variation, r
9. demonstrate

Inferential Statistics—Significant Numbers

1. entire, set
2. population
3. population
4. Conclusions
5. chance
6. significant.

CONNECTIONS

Descriptive Statistics—Psychology by the Numbers

1. B.
2. E.
3. A.
4. G.
5. D.
6. F.
7. C.

Correlation—Rating Relationships and Inferential Statistics—Significant Numbers

1. F.
2. A.
3. H.
4. C.
5. E.
6. B.
7. D.
8. I.
9. G.

Check Your Memory

Descriptive Statistics—Psychology by the Numbers

1. T
2. F
3. T
4. F
5. T
6. F
7. T
8. F
9. T
10. T
11. T
12. F
13. F
14. T
15. T

Correlation—Rating Relationships

1. F
2. T
3. F
4. F
5. T
6. T
7. F

Inferential Statistics—Significant Numbers

1. T
2. T
3. F
4. T

Final Survey and Review

Descriptive Statistics—Psychology by the Numbers

1. Descriptive, Inferential
2. graphical, central
3. frequency, scores
4. Graphical, graphs
5. histogram, abscissa, ordinate
6. bars, number
7. polygon, connected
8. tendency, group
9. mean
10. extremely, extremely
11. median
12. mode
13. varied
14. range
15. standard, differences
16. Standard
17. above, below
18. normal
19. 68
20. Ninety, five
21. Ninety, nine

Correlation—Rating Relationships

1. pairs, correlated
2. diagram, intersection
3. positive
4. negative
5. coefficient, strong
6. coefficient
7. positive, negative
8. variance
9. causation

Inferential Statistics—Significant Numbers

1. subjects, population
2. observed
3. Samples
4. representative
5. statistical
6. 5, chance

Mastery Test

1. c, p. 602-603
2. b, p. 594-595
3. a, p. 594
4. d, p. 594
5. b, p. 595
6. d, p. 595-596
7. a, p. 595
8. d, p. 596
9. b, p. 597
10. b, p. 597-598
11. b, p. 597
12. d, p. 597
13. a, p. 602
14. b, p. 603
15. c, p. 599
16. d, p. 600
17. d, p. 600
18. a, p. 600
19. c, p. 600-601
20. b, p. 602